K

Evolving Explanations of Development

Evolving Explanations of Development

Ecological Approaches to Organism–Environment Systems

Edited by

Cathy Dent-Read
Patricia Zukow-Goldring

AMERICAN PSYCHOLOGICAL ASSOCIATION
WASHINGTON, DC

Published by
American Psychological Association
750 First Street, NE
Washington, DC 20002

Copies may be ordered from
APA Order Department
P.O. Box 92984
Washington, DC 20090-2984

In the UK and Europe, copies may be ordered from
American Psychological Association
3 Henrietta Street
Covent Garden, London
WC2E 8LU England

Typeset in Minion by University Graphics, Inc., York, PA
Printer: United Book Press, Inc., Baltimore, MD
Cover Designer: Minker Design, Bethesda, MD.
Technical/Production Editor: Tanya Y. Alexander

Library of Congress Cataloging-in-Publication Data

Evolving explanations of development: ecological approaches to organism-environment
   systems / Cathy Dent-Read, Patricia Zukow-Goldring, editors.
      p.   cm.
   Includes bibliographical references and indexes.
   ISBN 1-55798-382-8 (casebinding   :   alk. paper)
      1. Developmental psychology.   2. Environmental psychology.
   I. Dent-Read, Cathy.   II. Zukow, Patricia Goldring.
   BF713.5E96   1997
   155.9—DC21   96-46275
                                                                              CIP

British Library Cataloguing-in-Publication Data
A CIP record is available from the British Library

Printed in the United States of America
First edition

APA Science Volumes

APA expects to publish volumes on the following conference topics:

Psychology Beyond the Threshold: Conference on General and Applied
    Experimental Psychology and a Festschrift for William N. Dember
Psychophysiological Study of Attention
Structure and Context in Language Processing

As part of its continuing and expanding commitment to enhance the dissemination of scientific psychological knowledge, the Science Directorate of the APA established a Scientific Conferences Program. A series of volumes resulting from these conferences is produced jointly by the Science Directorate and the Office of Communications. A call for proposals is issued twice annually by the Scientific Directorate, which, collaboratively with the APA Board of Scientific Affairs, evaluates the proposals and selects several conferences for funding. This important effort has resulted in an exceptional series of meetings and scholarly volumes, each of which has contributed to the dissemination of research and dialogue in these topical areas.

The APA Science Directorate's conferences funding program has supported 45 conferences since its inception in 1988. To date, 30 volumes resulting from conferences have been published.

WILLIAM C. HOWELL, PHD
Executive Director

VIRGINIA E. HOLT
Assistant Executive Director

Contents

Contributors

Reuben M. Baron, Department of Psychology, University of Connecticut
Jane E. Clark, Department of Kinesiology, University of Maryland at College Park
Robin Panneton Cooper, Department of Psychology, Virginia PolyTechnic Institute and State University
Cathy Dent-Read, Center for the Study of Women, University of California, Los Angeles
Paula Fitzpatrick, Department of Psychology, University of Connecticut
Alan Fogel, Department of Psychology, University of Utah
Eleanor J. Gibson, Department of Psychology, Cornell University
James A. Green, Department of Psychology, University of Connecticut
Gwen E. Gustafson, Department of Psychology, University of Connecticut
Claes von Hofsten, Umea Universitet, Sweden
Timothy D. Johnston, College of Arts and Sciences, University of North Carolina
Endre Kadar, Department of Psychology, University of Portsmouth, England
Katherine A. Loveland, University of Texas Mental Sciences Institute, Developmental Neuropsychology, Houston
David B. Miller, Department of Psychology, University of Connecticut
Karl M. Newell, Department of Kinesiology, Pennsylvania State University
Anne D. Pick, Institute of Child Development, University of Minnesota
Nancy de Villiers Rader, Department of Psychology, Ithaca College
Edward S. Reed, Department of Psychology, Franklin & Marshall College

Philippe Rochat, Department of Psychology, Emory University

A. W. Smitsman, Faculteit der Sociale, Katholieke Universiteit Nijmegen, The Netherlands

Patricia Zukow-Goldring, Center for the Study of Women, University of California, Los Angeles

Preface

In editing and contributing to this book, we enlarged our views of development, incorporating evolutionary biology, practice theories, and sociohistorical views, to examine emergent perceiving, acting, and knowing. Our focus is consistent with a growing movement among scholars around the world toward theories of lived development that encompass nested levels of complexity reflexively affecting the developing organism and its environment. The strength of a growing paradigm shift can be seen in postmodern critiques of science across many disciplines, including biology, anthropology, psychology, and sociology. In harmony with this change, the scholars represented in this book express in their work a dissatisfaction with reductionistic cognitive approaches to development. Their unrest derives in part from the restrictions of mechanistic theories concentrating on narrow intra-individual structures or frozen snapshots of organisms and events that do not account for the multiplicity of dynamic processes organizing both organism and environment. We seek to restore biology, culture, and history to psychology, the study of behaving organisms.

Scholars participating in this paradigm shift engage in research that ranges from studying the dynamic set of processes emerging within the individual to exploring the larger unfolding panorama of culture constituting itself in and through daily activities (expressed by its members, artifacts, and environment). In searching for a more encompassing and coherent approach, scholars studying development must make explicit core assumptions informing their own perspectives, determine the limitations as well as the advantages of those perspectives, compare their view with other approaches that take organism–environment mutuality as a given, and assess the changes this approach may engender by opening up some fields of research and eliminating others. We have asked the contributors to this book to engage in this task, so that a set of shared practices or methods might be found. This shared foundation may serve as a basis for broader lines of research and for exposing further inadequacies inherent in traditional mechanistic theory.

When we invited this group of scholars to participate, we had several immediate goals: getting like-minded people together who do not ordinarily attend the same conferences or publish in the same journals, disseminating these approaches to a larger audience by compiling in one book a wide range of studies, providing an overview to undergraduate textbook authors so that this approach will be as easily accessible to college students in the United States as it is in Europe, and making available a book that might serve as a graduate seminar text. Gathering in one publication the work by researchers who use different ecological approaches demonstrates how the different approaches can strengthen the field and how they can work together to lead to a more complete theory of development than is currently available.

At a more personal level, each of us has been asked many times why we choose to work from a nontraditional paradigm. Avante garde rebels? Mavericks? Hardly. We received rigorous training in theory and experimental research in developmental psychology that has served us well. Later we found that this approach to research could not explain the growth and development of the children we observed. As graduate students with purple-tinged fingers from the latest circulating dittoed manuscript provided by Nancy Rader, we discussed this or that paragraph or chapter from

James Gibson's last book. The heady excitement of seeing dead ends vanish and solutions appear attracted both of us to his theory of direct perception (ecological realism). Whereas both of us studied linguistics, one focused more on perception and metaphor and the other on ethnomethodology and anthropology. We have enriched each other's vision, propagating change sometimes in the face of resistance. This book resulted from the equal efforts of both of us. In the past 20 years, many others with similar beginnings have found the work of both James and Eleanor Gibson a rich resource for exploring development. We wanted others to see what the theory and research has to offer.

We are grateful to those who have supported our efforts in bringing this book to a broad audience of informed professionals. We thank the American Psychological Association Science Directorate, the University of Connecticut (Research Foundation and College of Letters and Sciences), the National Science Foundation, the Society for Research in Child Development, and the University of California, Irvine Research Foundation for funding an APA Scientific Conference held in the fall of 1994 at the University of Connecticut. An anonymous reviewer provided insightful comments and suggestions. Finally, we wish to recognize the excellent APA editorial staff, especially Mary Lynn Skutley and Beth Beisel.

1

Introduction: Ecological Realism, Dynamic Systems, and Epigenetic Systems Approaches to Development

Cathy Dent-Read and Patricia Zukow-Goldring

The body repeats the landscape. They are the source of each other and create each other.

M. LeSueur, *The Ancient People and the Newly Come*

Explanations of development are themselves developing and evolving. Prevailing theories change as research reveals new applications and unforeseen nuances, and their limitations appear as well. Calls for a paradigm shift arise when a theory fails to account for "normal" or "legitimate" observed phenomena and excludes anomalous events whose investigation may undermine mainstream scientific practice (Kuhn, 1970). Scholars currently proposing changes in theory actively advocate some radical breaks with the mainstream theories that have informed developmental research during a substantial part of the 20th century. In particular, three relatively new and quickly emerging areas of research in psychology may contribute to a more complete and coherent ecological theory of development. In this book, we have collected for the first time reports of work on these ecological approaches to development.

Unlike traditional views, ecological realism,[1] dynamic systems, and epigenetic systems consider the ecology of whole organism–environment systems as the theoretical bedrock of their perspectives. All three of these ecological approaches have developed since the 1950s but somewhat independently. They draw on different theoretical sources, empirical findings, and methods. By bringing together in one volume work by researchers in these three fields, we hope to delineate the advantages and limitations of each approach and to work toward a more complete understanding of development.

Scholars in each of these three fields explore more than unidirectional or bidirectional effects of organism–environment relations. They examine various ways in which organism and environment mutually determine each other throughout development. In this introduction, we provide a brief, schematic overview of the manner in which prevailing developmental theories treat the relation between animal and environment. Next, we discuss some drawbacks derived from neo-Darwinian presuppositions underlying these positions, especially organism–environment dualism, molecular gene theory, and animal–machine analogies. To highlight these limitations, we place these problems in a broader context by discussing relevant theories in biology and exploring parallels between these theories and related ideas in psychology. This reframing allows an evaluation of the degree to which these three new views offer more coherent answers to central questions in ecology and development than have previous theo-

---

[1]At about the time ecological realism was beginning in visual perception studies (J. Gibson, 1950) and epigenetic systems work was continuing to emerge in comparative psychology (Kuo, 1976; Schneirla, 1960) another ecological approach was developing. These ecological psychologists (Barker, 1968; Bronfenbrenner, 1979, 1989, 1993; Bronfenbrenner & Crouter, 1983; Brunswick, 1947; K. Lewin, 1943; Schoggen, 1989; Stokols & Altman, 1987) focused on the effect of the "natural or customary habitat of a species, culture, or individual" (Brunswick, 1947, p. 3) on behavior. Important research arising from this approach that has affected the entire field of psychology includes consideration of the ecological validity of settings selected for research, the generalizability of results to similar ecological landscapes, and the degree to which nested levels of social and physical environments affect behavior. Many people would agree with Bronfenbrenner's definition (1993) of *development* as the interaction of person and environmental factors that promote "continuity and change" within the person over time. Within these formulations, however, are unexamined assumptions. These assumptions often involve the source of organization in development, that is, what develops, that mental events are mediated, and the appropriate unit of behavior to analyze. The term *ecological realism* was first used in an article summarizing J. Gibson's (1966, 1979) theory of direct perception and pointing out how such a view characterizes cognition (Turvey & Carello, 1981).

ries. The chapter ends with a summary of the contributions made by eco-logical realism, dynamic systems, and epigenetic systems to overcoming these difficulties.

TRADITIONAL THEORIES OF DEVELOPMENT

Prevailing theories generally attempt to explain the changes in form, func-tion, and complexity observed during development by seeking causes in the child, in the environment, or in some combination of the two. Even a cursory reviewing of developmental textbooks demonstrates that re-search inspired by theory falls loosely into four clusters of organism–environment relations. A two-by-two matrix summarizes the possible re-lations between the active or passive child and an active or passive envi-ronment. Assuming that both child and environment were relatively pas-sive, studies of motor development in the 1930s and 1940s by Gesell and McGraw documented a predictable maturation of abilities along a devel-opmental time line for normal children (Gesell, 1939; McGraw, 1932, 1945). This natural unfolding required little of the pliable child or of a relatively invisible environment. A passive child and an active environment are assumed by both behaviorism and psychodynamic theory, both of which characterize the environment as actively heavy-handed, relentlessly pulling and pushing along the re-active child with carrot and stick or love and its loss (Freud 1923/1974, 1938/1973; Skinner, 1953; Watson, 1930). Cognitive theories such as Piagetian and information-processing models conceptualize the child as actively testing the passive environment to con-struct or confirm progressively more complex models in the mind (Atkin-son & Schifrin, 1968; Klahr & Wallace, 1976; Piaget, 1936/1952, 1937/1954). Vygotsky (1978) adopts a sociohistorical position and posits the interplay of an active child in a dynamic environment to explain de-velopment. Despite these variations, a consistent theme holds these per-spectives together: Some sequence of forces from child or environment (or both) impel development forward.

These four types of theories share certain assumptions about organ-ism and environment that derive from neo-Darwinist work in biology.

The modern mainstream biological theory of the relation between organism and environment comes from neo-Darwinist molecular theory. Two maxims summarize this stance: (a) genes control physiology and behavior over the course of development, and (b) organisms survive by adapting to a pre-existing environment. In summary, the neo-Darwinist position on evolution states that species arise and populations endure through natural selection and adaptation to an existing environment. Genes are the mechanism of inheritance and, thus, the mechanism of evolution. Currently, most biologists claim that molecular gene processes control and explain form and function in living organisms (Barlow, 1995; Olson, 1995). Environmental variations affect evolution and individual development, but it is always the organism that evolves, rather than the organism–environment system (cf. Lotka, 1925). In this view, the environment is both distinct from organisms and autonomous in relation to them (Ho, 1991).

The following quote from T. H. Huxley (1867, cited in Sheldrake, 1980, p. 125) aptly summarizes the neo-Darwinist conception of behavior. His statements reduce the complexity of a living organism to that of a machine. The telling use of the animal–machine metaphor confirms that the position has not changed noticeably in the past 130 years:

> Zoological physiology is the doctrine of the functions or actions of animals. It regards animal bodies as machines impelled by various forces and performing a certain amount of work which can be expressed in terms of the ordinary forces of nature. The final object of physiology is to deduce the facts of morphology on the one hand, and those of ecology on the other, from the laws of the molecular forces of matter.

Striking parallels to this stream in biology occur in psychology. A reading of any current textbook on cognition confirms that modern mechanistic theories of brain and mind are highly similar to Huxley's account. The mechanistic theory of mind includes computer science models of information processing, storage, and so forth in which the anatomy of the brain and physiology are used to explain human mental functioning. Informed by neo-Darwinism, modern mainstream psychology responds to questions relating organism and environment by asserting that genes carry the blueprints for the mechanisms that somehow eventually interact with the environment to cause behavior and the development of behavior. In this view, the infant's brain comes equipped with hypothesized ideal knowledge or innate operations (or both). These mechanisms, thus, gradually construct abstract plans or schemas that guide future behavior (e.g., Carey & Gelman, 1991; Spelke, 1988).

In the mechanistic account, child and environment are separated whether the child matures autonomously, learns incrementally on the basis of a simple set of principles, or makes qualitative leaps in functioning triggered by or sampled from environmental events. Mind is believed to function in isolation from the environment, supplementing incomplete samplings of environmental events with innate plans or acquired schemas. The theory requires that mechanisms inside the child mediate between mind and body, controlling behavior and development. Individuals, thus, experience the world indirectly "as through a glass darkly," assisted by inference, recall, and symbols. As a result, much theorizing and research activity concentrates on simulating the endogenous mechanisms that cause behavior and development.

CRITIQUES OF NEO-DARWINISM

The presuppositions and solutions proposed by contemporary psychological theories consistently display a "metaphysical urge to contain ontogenetic variety within genetic boundaries" (Oyama, 1989, p. 11). At a minimum, the theories outlined above explicitly or implicitly assume that the basic developmental building blocks arise from a one-way flow of information—from genetic code to mature creature. In these models, child and environment, mind and body, and so on successively may affect each other, but this dualism or separation of one from the other precludes adequately explaining behavior or development. Critics of traditional theories maintain that physiology and behavior constitute different levels of development; physiology cannot completely explain behavior (Costall,

1989; Gottlieb, 1991a; Michaels & Carello, 1981). In other words, physiology supports behavior but does not cause it.

A growing dissatisfaction with the theories outlined above has led to new answers to questions about development. Such answers have arisen in biology, especially in the fields of embryogenesis and morphogenesis, and in psychology among those working on ecological realist, epigenetic systems, and dynamic systems approaches to development. Proponents of these approaches to development have critiqued the mechanistic theory of living organisms on at least two grounds. First, genetic expression alone cannot account for the growing complexity observed in developing organisms. Genes do not become more complex with development, but organisms do. The theory, thus, does not account for observations. Second, organism and environment form a system; the environment does not exist independently of organisms and force them to adapt. Traditional theory, thus, limits what phenomena are noticed and studied. Critiques from biology, comparative psychology, and developmental psychology illustrate limitations and overextensions of the neo-Darwinian position, which (a) cannot explain embryogenesis, epigenesis, and ontogeny of form and function; and (b) includes unwarranted extensions of gene theory to explanations of brain function.

The first criticism, that genes cannot cause development, applies both to mechanistic theories in biology and to mechanistic theories in psychology, especially in developmental psychology—the field that focuses on the development of ordered patterns of behavior. This criticism is expressed in a number of ways. First, biological and behavioral development are both epigenetic in that they involve increasing complexity of form. Therefore, forms and patterns cannot be explained indefinitely in terms of preceding forms or patterns. (For a statement of this argument in relation to cognitive development, see Turvey & Fitzpatrick, 1993.) Second, developing organisms, tissues, and behaviors show remarkable powers of regulation and adjustment to perturbation (e.g., Ho, 1991). (In psychology this phenomenon has been dubbed *plasticity*, and a large literature covers the topic.) Third, intense investigation in biology has provided no evidence of physical or chemical processes that control morphogenesis in animal embryos (Sheldrake, 1980, 1981; R. Lewin, 1984). Although no one understands tissue differentiation, statements that assume that this process is understood obscure the gap between molecular biology and behavioral development. For example, some assert that the vertebrate brain encodes stimulus information according to genetic instruction (Kovach & Wilson, 1988; see Gottlieb, 1991a, for this critique).

The second criticism, that organism and environment form a system rather than existing as separate interacting entities, is a topic that has been worked on extensively in developmental psychology (e.g., Dent, 1990; Gottlieb, 1991a, 1991b, 1993; Johnston, 1987; Oyama, 1985). Research confirms that the differentiation of all organ systems, including the nervous system, takes place through influences above the cell level (e.g., Edelman, 1987). For example, the position of a cell in undifferentiated tissue determines the type of cell it becomes in differentiated organ tissue. Furthermore, researchers have demonstrated that individual experience alters gene expression during ontogenetic development; thus, genes do not by themselves produce differentiated phenotypic traits (e.g., Kollar & Fisher, 1980).

At a more global level, cell biologists have found extensive evidence that cells evolved by symbiosis with bacteria and that microbial interactions have had profound effects on the surface sediments and the atmosphere of the Earth (Margulis, 1981; Margulis & Olendzenski, 1992). This latter stream in biological thinking meshes with the work done in psychology on the mutuality and reciprocity of organism and environment (J. Gibson, 1979; Lombardo, 1987; Swenson & Turvey, 1991) and leads to the understanding that organisms and their environments do not "interact" or cause each other. Certainly the environment does not cause organisms. Rather, organisms and environments form reciprocal wholes, in which each plays a complementary role: Organisms act and adapt, environments support and surround.

MECHANISTIC VERSUS SYSTEMS APPROACHES

For psychology, the problems found in mainstream theories arise from claims that schemes, neural connections, or mental models internal to the organism constitute the source of organization in development. Other key assumptions include the notion that interaction with the environment works indirectly by triggering or affecting the construction of the internal mechanisms that actually guide behavioral development. Such theories assume pre-existing plans for behavior in both the organism and the environment (such as genes, brain organization, and social settings). The problem, however, with assuming pre-existing plans as the source of organization in the organism or in the development of the organism is one of infinite regression. The result is a futile search for the "head" decision maker. Such plans never actually explain the source of behavior's organization. Finite physiological mechanisms and anatomical architecture cannot contain the infinite possibilities available in emerging behavior (Reed, 1985; Shaw & Bransford, 1977). Notwithstanding these objections, researchers who assume that traits or behaviors come with the creature will be less inclined to be curious about how behavior evolves in real time in a real place in a real creature.

Biological anthropology research makes a similar point: Biology must not be conflated with genetics. The biological process of becoming an organism continues through the life course; it *is* life (Ingold, 1991a). This view holds that organisms are not some undifferentiated, inchoate mass given form from preordained plans pushed by genes and pulled by environment (Ingold, 1986, 1991a, 1991b). In the same vein, neither culture nor a predisposition to acquire it find their source in genetic material or environmental forces. That is, members do not manipulate inherited tendencies to cooperate, communicate, and interact as a means to engrave new members with culture. Members do not socialize novices as a person might shape a tool from a piece of flint or slowly add layers of veneer or varnish to attain a predetermined form. Persons are not made—they grow through active participation with others. The social process of becoming a person is part of the biological process. As people take in, enfold, differentiate physiologically in and through social relationships, they bring out, unfold, enact such changes. Emerging developmental theories in psychology posit that development entails incorporating ways of perceiving that reveal the affordances of social relationships. People continuously constitute themselves and their "culture" as they engage in ongoing daily activities (Cole, 1989; Lave & Wenger, 1991).

In summary, a mechanistic approach posits that development is predetermined by genetic codes and controlled by the brain. However, systems approaches to development posit that the genotype alone can never predict the form a phenotype takes (Oyama, 1989)—that is, there is no phenotype without an environment (Johnston & Gottlieb, 1990). Animals inherit environments as much as genes (e.g., West & King, 1987). The supposed autonomy and separation of individual creatures arising from the mechanistic view blinds scholars to many necessary, but nonobvious, conditions for life and development. For instance, the pervasive effects of gravity itself on the form a phenotype takes are never accounted for in a neo-Darwinist explanation. The universal aspects of the environment that support all life, and that life causes, are necessarily left out of such an account.

CHANGING DEVELOPMENTAL THEORIES: ECOLOGICAL REALISM, DYNAMIC SYSTEMS, AND EPIGENETIC SYSTEMS

The ecological realist, dynamic systems, and epigenetic systems approaches to development avoid the problems of theories informed by neo-Darwinism by asserting that the effect of organism and environment are inseparably linked: They do not make separate contributions to development. That is, the contribution of one cannot be measured without the other; organisms and environments form reciprocal wholes, in which each plays a complementary role. Researchers who adopt this approach ask what genes are inside of instead of what is inside of genes (see West & King, 1987). In other words, these scientists ask: How do organisms adapt and environments surround? These new approaches agree that organization in behavior emerges out of the coordinated action of animals in their natural surround. For instance, the V formation in migratory bird flight results not from innate motor programs, but from the fact that the easiest place to fly (i.e., the place with the least resistance) is just off and slightly behind the wing tip of the bird in front (Gould & Heppner, 1974). In this case, it is clear that a distinctive behavior emerges from the organism's relationship with the environment (in this case the bird's position within the airflow). Similarly, the question–answer form of conversation emerges out of two people coordinating what they know to bring themselves into shared understanding (Ochs, Schieffelin, & Platt, 1979). Each of the three ecological approaches brings certain strengths and limitations to the task of explaining development.

Ecological Realism

Ecological realism is the only theory that provides a good account of how organisms continuously stay in contact with their environment. Ecological realism draws from work on the fit between organism and environment, focusing on the dynamic pickup of perceptual structure that specifies the particular physical layout and guides action in that setting. Cycles of perceiving and acting continuously direct what people do and inform the differentiation of the their perceptual systems (J. Gibson, 1966, 1979). One limitation of this view, however, concerns the mutuality of organism and environment. Mutuality is assumed, but rarely studied. Furthermore, few researchers conduct their investigations in ecologically valid settings relevant to the lives of the organisms they study. Fewer still conduct longitudinal studies sampling behavior often enough to reveal the crucial configuration of events consistently leading to change.

Dynamic Systems

Dynamic systems theory has the important strength of providing a coherent explanation and method for actually studying the mutuality of organism and environment. This approach elegantly describes how aspects of the organism and the environment "self-organize" to produce behavior in the service of a task. Dynamic systems uses work from chaos theory in physics and mathematics as well as pattern formation. Research in this area explores the self-organizing of multiple levels of functioning within an individual over time in typical environments that result in species-typical behaviors such as locomoting and reaching (Thelen, 1989; Thelen & Ulrich, 1991). Dynamic systems approaches have been applied most often to topics in motor development (Thelen & Smith, 1994). For example, aspects of the organism such as frequency and amplitude of kicking and aspects of the environment such as stiffness and dampness coefficients of a spring form one system that self-organizes into coherent behavior to perform a task, such as sustained bouncing in a Jolly Jumper (Goldfield, Kay, & Warren, 1993). A major limitation of this theory is that it does not include a more than cursory account of how the organism makes contact with the environment (von Hofsten, 1989). How organisms perceive in an adaptive way in the natural world remains rarely studied. A group of researchers combine studies of perceiving and acting with dynamic systems models and methods (see recent issues of *Ecological Psychology* for examples), but this approach generally has not been used to study development. Some studies are beginning that constitute more than a reworking of topics in light of dynamic systems ideas (e.g., Goldfield et al., 1993). The degree to which models and methods of dynamic systems, rather than just the guiding ideas, are used in developmental research is a topic of debate (see Beek & Hopkins, 1992).

Epigenetic Systems

Among those who use the three ecological approaches, only adherents of epigenetic systems theory actually study organisms in their natural environment, develop descriptions and methods of study that apply to the natural environment, and make use of work on evolution in explaining development. By studying species-typical behavior in laboratory and natural habitats, they have shown that nonobvious experiences provided by the (social) environment, rather than some sort of inborn priming, crucially informs development (Johnston & Gottlieb, 1981; Schneirla, 1960). Epigenetic systems work has been influenced by evolutionary theory and morphogenesis. Investigators from this approach look at the co-actions of organism and environment that contribute to development. These researchers more explicitly study the role of the environment in bringing about species-typical behavior and change usually attributed to innate mechanisms. Epigenetic theory, however, gives no explicit explanation of how organisms maintain contact with their environment.

Mutuality in the Three Ecological Approaches

Although all three approaches described above can, in some sense, be labeled *ecological*, they differ in the way they view and research the mutuality of organism and environment. This volume presents different authors' views from within these three perspectives and explores the differences among the three approaches.

The ecological realist approach takes the mutuality of organism and environment as a given. Although mutuality is a basic assumption (see Eleanor J. Gibson's chapter "An Ecological Psychologist's Prolegomena for Perceptual Development: A Functional Approach" in this volume), most of the research conducted within this approach uses the traditional method of controlling something about the environment and observing the organism's response in the laboratory. Studies that examine interaction or natural settings are more likely to discover how organisms change their environment and how changes in the environment can constitute development. Studies on these topics constitute the first part of this book.

From the epigenetic and dynamic systems points of view, the organism and its environment are the system. The organism is the self-organizing part, and its environment is the guiding or structuring part. The research deriving from these two approaches, however, stresses the development of the *organism*, with little discussion of related changes in the environment. Whereas epigenetic research is sometimes conducted in natural settings, epigeneticists generally do not study how an organism's behavior affects the environment. For example, although the environment's effects on the development of ducklings' calls has been investigated, no investigations have been conducted on the effect of ducklings' behavior on the maternal call. An exception is the work on human social development showing that an infant's ability to locomote changes the social behavior of the adults around them (Gustafson, 1984). The dynamic systems approach comes closest to using the idea of mutuality in its research methods—aspects of the organism and of the environment are both measured and used to explain how the organism behaves and develops. For example, conversation has been studied as waveforms of behavior on the part of partners in which change in body position and amplitude of speech are measured and used to characterize conversation as a two-person system carrying out a task (Newtson, 1993). Even using this method, however, researchers do not study how the organism changes its environment, but rather how the system changes when the task changes.

One area of debate between ecological realism and the two other systems concerns the manner in which organisms maintain contact with their environments at the level of acting on and knowing what the environment affords. The theory of direct perception constitutes the ecological realist approach and can account for species-specific perception as well as for how even young infants attend and move in coordinated ways. Whereas systems approaches have not articulated in as much detail how organisms perceive and know the environments that surround them, they have developed methods to study and describe organism–environment mutualities. Therefore, a melding of these three approaches would greatly benefit developmental research. The strengths and limitations of each approach are made more explicit throughout the book.

The ecological realism perspective predominates in this book for two reasons. First, ecological realism takes a unique stance in psychology as the only theoretical approach that studies direct perception. In this view, the central problem of study concerns how organisms perceive and act adaptively by resonating to the perceptual structure in ambient energy around them. Second, the theory of ecological realism has generated research on a wide variety of topics in psychology. A great deal of work has gone into describing the structure that organisms use as they perceive and act, including a large literature on infant perceptual development. For more than 50 years Eleanor J. Gibson has pioneered developmental studies of direct perception in a broad range of situations including visual cliffs, surfaces of support, and object exploration. For the most part, these studies investigated how direct perception contributes to an individual coming to know the world through exploratory activities. Her intellectual descendants have taken her work gradually into other areas of infancy:

perceiving amodal invariants (e.g., Bahrick, 1983, 1994; Bahrick & Pickens, 1994; Walker-Andrews & Lennon, 1985), emotions (e.g., Walker, 1982; Walker-Andrews, 1986), reaching (e.g., Rader & Stern, 1982), and special populations (Loveland, 1991, 1993). The range of topics is now being extended to social interaction, language, and topics typically considered cognitive, such as categorizing and remembering. Some of the most recent work in all areas of developmental psychology informed by ecological realism is represented in this book. The chapter by Eleanor J. Gibson covers many of these topics and provides an overview of how perceptual development forms the foundation of cognitive and social development.

Conversely, fewer chapters are included on dynamic systems and epigenetic systems work than ecological realism for several reasons. Several recent books cover the latest applications of dynamic systems methods (e.g., Smith & Thelen, 1993; Thelen & Smith, 1994). Furthermore, the shorter history of dynamic systems in developmental psychology results in a smaller range of topics and studies available. We chose one article on a prototypical topic in dynamic systems research (Jane Clark on the development of the motor skill of walking) and one on a topic that is a relatively new extension for this theory (Alan Fogel on creativity). As with dynamic systems, epigenetic systems work is well represented in other volumes (e.g., special section of *Developmental Psychology* titled "Canalization of Behavioral Development," 1991). Epigenetic systems has a long history in developmental psychology and has generated a large body of research, much of it focusing on animal behavior and comparative psychology. We chose one chapter on a prototypical topic (David B. Miller's article on the development of responses to calls in ducklings) and one on a topic less frequently studied from this perspective (James A. Green and Gwen E. Gustafson's article on the early ontogenesis of social interaction in human infants).

ORGANIZATION OF THE BOOK

Ecological realist, dynamic systems, and epigenetic systems approaches all posit principles of integration by which individuals develop as whole organisms, and the chapters in this volume are divided into three parts, reflecting each approach. We hope that those working in any of these three approaches will benefit from the work done in the other areas.

Each part begins with an introduction that fully describes the theoretical approach. It also discusses how the ideas central to the approach are similar or different across the various chapters in the part. In addition, each chapter in the volume is followed by a short commentary on the strengths, weaknesses, and implications of that contributor's approach as well as avenues for integrating the perspectives. We hope these commentaries encourage the development of a dialogue across the multiple perspectives on development.

Each chapter in the volume presents the chapter author(s)' research of interest. To clarify the relations among these different ecological approaches to development and to broaden each chapter's discussion, we asked researchers to keep the following four questions in mind when presenting their research results:

1. What is your definition of development, that is, what is developing and how?
2. What issues does your approach confront that other ecologically oriented theories do not?
3. What are the limitations of your approach to development; what does the approach *not* account for?
4. When your ecological approach is used, what questions about development are no longer relevant, what questions are revised, and what new questions emerge?

Although the chapters are not explicitly organized around these four questions, these questions emerge as the central themes in the book, and we hope readers also keep these questions in mind as they review this material.

FUTURE DIRECTIONS

In 1830, Goethe commented on the two opposite processes of understanding used by natural scientists: differentiating details and perceiving wholes. He understood that separating and connecting are two functions of the mind that are related as are inhaling and exhaling. The separating function, when taken alone, leads to atomistic theories such as the mechanistic theories outlined above, which also hold that nature functions by fixed laws.

> If we see only what is fixed, the same, we come to think it must be so. . . . But if we see the anomalies, misformations, gigantic deformities, then we recognize that the rule is indeed firm and eternal but is at the same time alive, that creatures do not grow from the rule but can within it transform themselves into the misshapen, but at any time, as if held back by reins, must acknowledge the unavoidable majesty of the law. (Goethe, 1830/1985, p. 321)

How far beyond atomistic mechanistic theories have we gone in explaining the development of individuals and of behavior? The theories represented in this book—the ecological realist, epigenetic systems, and dynamic systems approaches—all attempt to study organism–environment systems or mutualities. Such an attempt represents a major step beyond traditional mechanistic theories. As the reports herein reveal, work on ecological approaches to development has not yet perfected methods of studying organism–environment systems truly as systems, rather than as organisms responding to environments. The work also has yet to explain the origin of new forms of behavior in ways consistent with the assumption that the organism in its environment is the basic unit of study.

In this book, we have collected for the first time reports of work from various ecological approaches to development with the goal of challenging, provoking, and perhaps inspiring others to take a similar path. We hope that the dialogue inspired by bringing together work from ecological realism, dynamic systems, and epigenetic systems approaches to development will spark some creativity in us all.

REFERENCES

Atkinson, R. C., & Schifrin, R. M. (1968). Human memory: A proposed system and its control processes. In K. W. Spence & J. T. Spence (Eds.), *Advances in the psy-*

chology of learning and motivation (Vol. 2, pp. 90–195). San Diego, CA: Academic Press.

Bahrick. L. E. (1983). Infants' perception of substance and temporal synchrony in multimodal events. *Infant Behavior and Development, 6,* 429–451.

Bahrick, L. E. (1994). The development of infants' sensitivity to arbitrary intermodal relations. *Ecological Psychology, 6,* 111–123.

Bahrick, L. E., & Pickens, J. N. (1994). Amodal relations: The basis for intermodal perception and learning in infancy. In D. J. Lewkowicz & R. Lickliter (Eds.), *Development of intersensory perception in human infants* (pp. 205–233). Hillsdale, NJ: Erlbaum.

Barker, R. G. (1968). *Ecological psychology: Concepts and methods for studying the environment of human behavior.* Stanford, CA: Stanford University Press.

Barlow, D. (1995). Gametic imprinting in mammals. *Science, 270,* 1610–1613.

Beek, P., & Hopkins, B. (1992). Four requirements for a dynamical systems approach to the development of social coordination. *Human Movement Science, 11,* 425–442.

Bronfenbrenner, U. (1979). *The ecology of human development.* Cambridge, MA: Harvard University Press.

Bronfenbrenner, U. (1989, April). *The developing ecology of human development: Paradigm lost or paradigm regained.* Paper presented at the biannual meeting of the Society for Research in Child Development, Kansas City, Missouri.

Bronfenbrenner, U. (1993). The ecology of cognitive development: Research models and fugitive findings. In R. Wozniak and K. Fisher (Eds.), *Development in context: Acting and thinking in specific environments* (pp. 3–44). Hillsdale, NJ: Erlbaum.

Bronfenbrenner, U., & Crouter, A. C. (1983). The evolution of environmental models in developmental research. In P. H. Mussen (Series Ed.) & W. Kessen (Vol. Ed.), *Handbook of child psychology: Vol. I. History, theory, and method* (pp. 357–414). New York: Wiley.

Brunswick, E. (1947). *Systematic and representative design of psychological experiments.* Berkeley: University of California Press.

Carey, S., & Gelman, R. (Eds.). (1991). *The epigenesis of the mind: Essays on biology and cognition.* Hillsdale, NJ: Erlbaum.

Cole, M. (1989). Cultural psychology: A once and future discipline? In J. J. Berman (Ed.), *Cross-cultural psychology: Current theory and research: Nebraska Symposium on Motivation* (Vol. 37, pp. 279–335). Lincoln: University of Nebraska Press.

Costall, A. (1989). A closer look at "direct perception." In A. Gellatly, D. Rogers, & J. A. Sloboda (Eds.), *Cognition and social worlds* (pp. 10–21). Oxford, England: Clarendon Press.

Dent, C. (1990). An ecological approach to language development: An alternative functionalism [Special issue]. *Developmental Psychology, 23*, 679–703.

Edelman, G. (1987). *Neural Darwinism: The theory of neuronal group selection.* New York: Basic Books.

Freud, S. (1973). *An outline of psychoanalysis.* London: Hogarth. (Original work published 1938)

Freud, S. (1974). *The ego and the id.* London: Hogarth. (Original work published 1923)

Gesell, A. (1939). Reciprocal interweaving in neuromotor development. *Journal of Comparative Neurology, 70*, 161–180.

Gibson, J. (1950). *The perception of the visual world.* Boston: Houghton-Mifflin.

Gibson, J. (1961). Ecological optics. *Vision Research, 1*, 253–262.

Gibson, J. (1966). *The senses considered as perceptual systems.* Boston: Houghton Mifflin.

Gibson, J. (1979). *An ecological approach to visual perception.* New York: Houghton Mifflin.

Goethe, J. (1985). Principles of zoological philosophy. In P. Antonelli (Ed., B. Taylor, Trans.), *Mathematical essays on growth and the emergence of form* (pp. 311–332). Edmonton, Canada: University of Alberta Press. (Original work published 1830)

Goldfield, E., Kay, B., & Warren, W. (1993). Infant bouncing: The assembly and tuning of action systems. *Child Development, 64*, 1128–1142.

Gottlieb, G. (1991a). Experiential canalization of behavioral development: Theory. *Developmental Psychology, 27*, 4–13.

Gottlieb, G. (1991b). Experiential canalization of behavioral development: Results. *Developmental Psychology, 27*, 35–39.

Gottlieb, G. (1993). Foreword. In G. Turkewitz and D. Devenny (Eds.), *Developmental time and timing* (pp. IX–X). Hillsdale, NJ: Erlbaum.

Gould, L., & Heppner, F. (1974). The vee formation of Canada geese. *The AUK, 91*, 494–506.

Gustafson, G. (1984). Effects of the ability to locomote on infants' social and exploratory behaviors: An experimental study. *Developmental Psychology, 20*, 397–405.

Ho, M.-W. (1991). The role of action in evolution: Evolution by process and the ecological approach to perception. *Cultural Dynamics, 4,* 336–354.

Huxley, T. H. (1867). *Science gossip* (p. 74). London: Robert Hardwicke.

Ingold, T. (1986). Introduction. In T. Ingold (Ed.), *What is an animal?* (pp. 1–15). London: Unwin Hyman.

Ingold, T. (1991a). Becoming persons: Consciousness and sociality in human evolution. *Cultural Dynamics, 4,* 355–378.

Ingold, T. (1991b). Evolutionary models in the social sciences: Introduction. *Cultural Dynamics, 4,* 239–250.

Johnston, T. (1987). The persistence of dichotomies in the study of behavioral development. *Developmental Review, 7,* 149–182.

Johnston, T., & Gottlieb, G. (1981). Development of species identification in ducklings: What is the role of imprinting? *Animal Behavior, 29,* 1082–1099.

Johnston, T., & Gottlieb, G. (1990). Neophenogenesis: A developmental theory of phenotypic evolution. *Journal of Theoretical Biology, 147,* 471–495.

Klahr, D., & Wallace, J. G. (1976). *Cognitive development: An information-processing view.* Hillsdale, NJ: Erlbaum.

Kollar, E., & Fisher, C. (1980). Tooth induction in chick epithelium: Expression of quiescent genes for enamel synthesis. *Science, 207,* 993–995.

Kovach, J., & Wilson, G. (1988). Genetics of color preferences in quail chicks: Major genes and variable buffering by background genotype. *Behavioral Genetics, 18,* 645–661.

Kuhn, T. (1970). *The structure of scientific revolutions* (rev. ed.). Chicago: University of Chicago Press.

Kuo, Z-Y. (1976). *The dynamics of behavioral development.* New York: Plenum Press.

Lave, J., & Wenger, E. (1991). *Situated learning: Legitimate peripheral participation.* New York: Cambridge University Press.

Lewin, K. (1943). Defining the 'field at a given time'. *Psychological Review, 50,* 292–310.

Lewin, R. (1984). Why is development so illogical? *Science, 224,* 1327–1329.

Lombardo, T. (1987). *The reciprocity of perceiver and environment.* Hillsdale, NJ: Erlbaum.

Lotka, A. J. (1925). *Elements of physical biology.* Baltimore: Williams & Wilkins.

Loveland, K. A. (1991). Social affordances and interaction. II: Autism and the affordances of the human environment. *Ecological Psychology, 3,* 99–119.

Loveland, K. A. (1993). Autism, affordances, and the self. In U. Neisser (Ed.), The perceived self: Ecological and interpersonal sources of self-knowledge (pp. 237–253). Cambridge, MA: Cambridge University Press.

Margulis, L. (1981). *Symbiosis in cell evolution.* San Francisco: W. H. Freeman.

Margulis, L., & Olendzenski, L. (Eds.). (1992). *Environmental evolution: Effects of the origin and evolution of life on planet earth.* Boston: Massachusetts Institute of Technology.

McGraw, M. B. (1932). From reflex to muscular control in the assumption of an erect posture and ambulation in the human infant. *Child Development, 3,* 291–297.

McGraw, M. B. (1945). *The neuromuscular maturation of the human infant.* New York: Columbia University Press.

Michaels, C., & Carello, C. (1981). *Direct perception.* Englewood Cliffs, NJ: Prentice Hall.

Newtson, D. (1993). The dynamics of action and interaction. In L. Smith & E. Thelen (Eds.), *A dynamic systems approach to development: Applications* (pp. 241–264). Cambridge, MA: MIT Press.

Ochs, E., Schieffelin, B., & Platt, M. (1979). Propositions across utterances and speakers. In E. Ochs & B. Schieffelin (Eds.), *Developmental pragmatics.* San Diego, CA: Academic Press

Olson, M. (1995). A time to sequence. *Science, 270,* 394–396.

Oyama, S. (1985). *The ontogeny of information: Developmental systems and evolution.* Cambridge, England: Cambridge University Press.

Oyama, S. (1989). Ontogeny and the central dogma: Do we need the concept of genetic programming in order to have an evolutionary perspective? In M. Gunnar & E. Thelen (Eds.) *Systems and development. Minnesota Symposium on Child Development, Vol. 22* (pp. 1–34). Hillsdale, NJ: Erlbaum.

Piaget, J. (1952). *The origins of intelligence in children.* New York: Harcourt Brace. (Original work published 1936)

Piaget, J. (1954). *The construction of reality in the child.* New York: Basic Books. (Original work published 1937)

Rader, N., & Stern, J. (1982). Visually elicited reaching in neonates. *Child Development, 53,* 1004–1007.

Reed, E. (1985). An ecological approach to the evolution of behavior. In T. Johnston & A. Pietrewicz (Eds.), *Issues in the ecological study of learning* (pp. 357–385). Hillsdale, NJ: Erlbaum.

Schneirla, T. (1960). Instinctive behavior, maturation: Experience and development. In B. Kaplan & S. Wapner (Eds.), *Perspectives in psychological theory: Essays in honor of Heinz Werner* (pp. 303–334). New York: International Universities Press.

Schoggen, P. (1989). *Behavior settings: A revision and extension of Roger G. Barker's Ecological Psychology.* Stanford, CA: Stanford University Press.

Shaw, R., & Bransford, J. (1977). Introduction: Psychological approaches to the problem of knowledge. In R. Shaw & J. Bransford (Eds.), *Perceiving, acting, and knowing* (pp. 1–39). Hillsdale, NJ: Erlbaum.

Sheldrake, R. (1980). Three approaches to biology: Part I. The mechanistic theory of life. *Theoria to Theory, 14,* 125–144.

Sheldrake, R. (1981). Three approaches to biology: Part III. Organicism. *Theoria to Theory, 14,* 301–311.

Skinner, B. F. (1953). *Science and human behavior.* New York: Appleton-Century-Crofts.

Smith, L., & Thelen, E. (1993). *A dynamic systems approach to development: Applications.* Cambridge, MA: MIT Press.

Stokols, D., & Altman, I. (1987). Conceptual strategies of environmental psychology. In D. Stokols & I. Altman (Eds.), *Handbook of environmental psychology* (pp. 41–70). New York: Wiley.

Swenson, R., & Turvey, M. (1991). Thermodynamic reasons for perception–action cycles. *Ecological Psychology, 3,* 317–348.

Thelen, E. (1989). Self-organization in developmental processes: Can systems approaches work? In M. Gunnar & E. Thelen (Eds.), *Systems in development: The Minnesota Symposia in Child Psychology* (Vol. 22, pp. 77–117). Hillsdale, NJ: Erlbaum.

Thelen, E., & Smith, L. B. (1994). *A dynamic systems approach to the development of cognition and action.* Cambridge, MA: MIT Press.

Thelen, E., & Ulrich, B. D. (1991). Hidden skills. *Monographs of the Society for Research in Child Development, 56*(1, Serial No. 223).

Turvey, M., & Carello, C. (1981). Cognition: The view from ecological realism. *Cognition, 10,* 313–321.

Turvey, M., & Fitzpatrick, P. (1993). Commentary: Development of perception–action systems and general principles of pattern formation. *Child Development, 64,* 1175–1190.

von Hofsten, C. (1989). Motor development as the development of systems: Comments on the special section. *Developmental Psychology, 25,* 950–953.

Vygotsky, L. (1978). *Mind in society* [Translated and edited by M. Cole, V. John-Steiner, S. Scribner, & E. Souberman]. Cambridge, MA: Harvard University Press.

Walker, A. S. (1982). Intermodal perception of expressive behaviors by human infants. *Journal of Experimental Child Psychology, 33,* 514–535.

Walker-Andrews, A. S. (1986). Intermodal perception of expressive behaviors: Relation of eye and voice? *Developmental Psychology, 22,* 373–377.

Walker-Andrews, A. S., & Lennon, E. (1985). Auditory–visual perception of changing distance by human infants. *Child Development, 22,* 373–377.

Watson, J. B. (1930). *Behaviorism.* Chicago: Chicago University Press.

West, M. J., & King, A. P. (1987). Settling nature and nurture into an ontogenetic niche. *Developmental Psychobiology, 20,* 549–562.

2

An Ecological Psychologist's Prolegomena for Perceptual Development: A Functional Approach

Eleanor J. Gibson

*P*rolegomena refers to a prefatory essay for a field of study.[1] I intend it to include a framework for my field expressed in a set of propositions, some of them assumptions, some definitions, and some testable hypotheses. I aim to explain these and when necessary provide evidence to support their reasonableness. My field is the way perception develops in humans, but I think the propositions I suggest have a wider application to cognition in general. There is a need, I think, for a consistent story of perceptual and cognitive development as an alternative to a Piagetian or information-processing view. I particularly want to provide an alternative to the received view of perceptual development provided by information processors that rests on construction of a static representation of an object or a scene (Julesz, 1984; Treisman, 1988). The process begins with discrimination of individual features, which are at a later stage assembled by some mysterious attentive process. Plenty of developmental psychologists support this view. Here is one description of the process:

---

[1]See, for example, E. B. Titchener's (1929) *Systematic Psychology: Prolegomena*. New York: MacMillan.

Whereas individual features are detected automatically and in parallel (a *preattentive* process), relations among features must be reconstructed by an item-for-item serial search involving focused attention (an *attentive* process). The object percept that is generated by the attentive process is then identified by comparing it with representations in long-term memory. (Bhatt & Rovee-Collier, 1994, p. 142)

Another author (Cohen, 1991, p. 5) also embraced an orthodox information processing perspective as follows:

From this perspective, the central assumption is that infants process visual information sequentially by attending to a series of self-contained, relatively independent, information processing units. The nature of these units must be determined empirically. In general, for infants under about 4 months of age, the units are assumed to be simple features or characteristics of patterns, objects, and events, such as size, shape, orientation, color, direction of movement, and perhaps certain amodal properties, such as intensity or irregularity.

How these features are to be assembled is not obvious. "As infants develop" (said Cohen), "they begin to be able to process the relations among lower-order units and in so doing are able to form a simple more abstract or complex, higher-order unit" (p. 7).

I want an account of perceptual development that is without jargon, that accords with what we have now learned from years of research with infants, and that deals with functioning in the world: making contact with other people, using things, finding our way to places, like human beings with all the rights and privileges pertaining thereto. In trying to provide a step-by-step account, I find (to my surprise) that it bears a certain resemblance to the introduction to my dissertation (E. Gibson, 1940), when I attempted to set forth a "miniature system" for verbal learning and retention on the basis of principles of differentiation and generalization. For that occasion, the propositions had to be very formal, with axioms and proofs, a sort of Hullian and Pythagorean mix. The method was ponderous and pretentious, but there is nevertheless an advantage in setting down basic assumptions and arguments for an explicit view of a field of study.

I am going to borrow ideas from all my friends, bending their brain-children to the effort to give a proper theoretical account of perceptual development, with some of its implications for cognitive development in a broad sense. I begin with propositions that are fundamental to the ecological approach as a whole and proceed to those that apply more particularly to my field and to cognitive development. The propositions are divided into three sets: general propositions with wide application for psychology, propositions that are related more particularly to perceptual and behavioral change, and propositions that advance into "cognition proper," as some might say. I think their roots are in perception and that they show development along functional paths like the earlier propositions. I believe they could be carried farther.

GENERAL PROPOSITIONS

1. *Animal–environment reciprocity.* The proper unit for study is an organism in the environment in which it evolved, functioning in a reciprocal relationship. The environment affords opportunities for an animal to act by way of its evolved perception and action systems. These opportunities include events, objects, and places of all kinds, both physical and social. The affordance relationship is basic to all later propositions. *Affordance* (J. J. Gibson, 1979) refers to an animal–environment fit, a relationship in which the animal possesses the equipment and the abilities to take advantage of what the environment offers. This is an objective relationship, which the animal may or may not perceive or act upon.

2. *Perception–action reciprocity.* Perception and action are interdependent: Perception obtains information for action, and action has consequences that inform perception about both the organism itself and the events that it perpetrates. Perception, which has the function of obtaining information, is active and exploratory. Action is both exploratory and performatory: exploratory in the sense of foraging for information and performatory in the sense of controlling environmental consequences. Infor-

mation about the organism's own power and propensities can only be obtained through action.

3. *Tasks.* Behavior, both cognitive and outwardly observable actions, goes on over time and is organized in eventlike functional segments called *tasks.* Tasks may be instigated and constrained by both organismic and environmental factors. In other words, behavior is not a chain of reflexes, nor is it random. It can be parsed into segments that are ordered by functions that the behavior serves. Spontaneous activity in the service of supporting a dynamic organism–environmental relationship is the natural condition of an organism. Breathing is such an activity, and so is making contact with the world. Obtaining information requires making contact with the world through perceptual and action systems.

Task is a familiar concept in theories of behavior dynamics and the ecological approach. Describing the development of reaching, for example, Thelen, Corbetta, Kamm, Spencer, and Schneider (1993, p. 1084) said, "the reacher temporarily marshals the dynamic properties of the body in the environment to create a device that is specific to the task"; and again, "what must be 'within' the infant is the desire to obtain the seen toy and some ability to adjust arm forces and stiffness to get the hand in the ball park of the object" (p. 1087). The dynamics of the body are "successively adapted" to the requirements of the task (p. 1058). Actions may be specific to a task, which imposes its own particular constraints (Bingham, 1988), but task requirements are not always perfectly specific. They may become more so in the course of learning about perception–action relationships, but flexibility within tasks may exist along with task constraints (Bernstein, 1967; Lashley, 1942).

As an example of increasing specificity of a task, consider an experiment by Goldfield, Kay, and Warren (1993). Six-month-old infants were placed in swinging seats that bounced ("Jolly Jumpers"), their feet just touching the floor, in a harness hung from a spring. Babies were not instructed, of course, but they spontaneously made contact with the floor and pushed against it. After several sessions the infants were bouncing, having discovered the spring in the course of exploring their own action properties in relation to the unaccustomed situation. A more specific task emerged as the infants discovered movement patterns that optimized the dynamics of the spring in relation to their own physical exertions. They developed oscillatory, sustained patterns, clearly evaluating their exploratory activities and opting for a state that minimized exertion and maximized a stable frequency of motion. In this task, the "strategy" adopted may be specific to the constraints the task imposes, but one could expect flexibility too, in the sense that changed conditions (resetting the spring or putting heavy shoes on the baby) would bring about new exploratory activity and adaptive shifts in the pattern. In this example, the task is in a sense given the infant, but tasks in early infancy more often arise spontaneously from the baby's natural environment and his or her normal needs.

Despite the ubiquity of the term, few of its users have given us a definition of *task* or commented on the term's meaning and use. An exception is K. M. Newell (1986), who proposed three task constraints on performance: (a) the goal of the task, (b) rules specifying or constraining task dynamics (possibly ontogenetic limitations), and (c) implements or machines specifying or constraining task dynamics. I am interested particularly in the first.

> All tasks have goals that relate to the product and outcome of the action. In the majority of tasks the way in which the performer may satisfy the outcome of the act is not specified. That is, most tasks do not specify the pattern of coordination to be used by the performer. (Newell, 1986, p. 352)

I take from Newell the notions that tasks have goals that relate to outcomes and that units of behavior embedded within the larger task unit may be variable, depending on many factors, a point that is considered under *Flexibility*. Reed (1990) coined the term *task space*, which appears to imply potential variability of internal organization and subordinate units. I borrow it to emphasize the modifiability of the internal organization of tasks.

4. *Nested units*. Tasks, themselves embedded in an ongoing stream of behavior, in turn contain subordinate, embedded, nested units, percep-

tion–action cycles of varied length. Subordinate (nested) units may change as tasks are practiced or change themselves with development (see *Flexibility*).

5. *Hallmarks of behavior.* Behavior is marked uniquely by properties (hallmarks) that are inherent in it and that develop with growth and learning. Three properties that are of special concern to the ecological approach to development are control, prospectivity, and flexibility. The first two are implied within the affordance relationship, they both characterize and drive development, and thus both are basic for studying developmental change.

Control and prospectivity are implied within the affordance relationship because perceiving and acting on an affordance requires selection of the appropriate action from the organism's repertoire (control) and expectation of some consequences if the selection is to be guided by what is perceived (prospectivity). Flexibility of selection depends on the constraints of the task (which may or may not coincide with a particular affordance). To observe these properties in behavior, we choose segments of behavior long enough to be deemed "tasks" incorporating subordinate units (perception–action cycles).

6. *Control.* Control (or agency) indicates selection of potential units of behavior with respect to affordances available to the organism. Control is obtained and operates within a task setting. Controlled behavior is also referred to as intentional. Controlled behavior has been observed soon after birth, and it shows marked changes with development (see Propositions Involving Change in the Course of Perceptual Development).

7. *Prospectivity.* Prospectivity refers to the forward-looking character of behavior. For example, nested (embedded) units within a task are organized so that units such as postural change, change of location, and other preparatory actions may precede units involved in attaining a goal or end of a task.

The term *prospectivity* is borrowed from D. Lee (1993) and is also used extensively by C. von Hofsten (1993). Lee (1993) wrote that "control has to be prospective" (p. 43). He used the example of collision with objects or persons. "The where, when and how of the collision must be perceived ahead in time and the body prepared for it. Therefore, a crucial aspect of body–environment coupling is predictive perceptual information" (p. 43).

Von Hofsten (1993) pointed out that actions must be prepared, because the whole skeletal and musculature system (the total postural background) is involved. He provided an excellent example of an infant reaching for an object. Recorded responses showed that the trunk muscles and the abdominal muscles are involved in the total act before the reaching arm is itself extended. Changes in the organization of the action are required as the child grows and acquires new action systems, and of course as the affordances change with different environmental opportunities. Prospectivity increases vastly in complexity and temporal foresight as development proceeds (see the next section). Von Hofsten (1993, p. 255) stated that "motor learning from the present perspective is a question of getting to know what may be called the 'task space', so that different paths can be taken through the space toward the goal, and the smoothest and most economical path can be sought."

8. *Flexibility.* Flexibility refers to the potential interchange of units within a task, as required by constraints imposed by structural changes of the organism or shifting environmental conditions. Flexibility increases as greater range of selectivity is made possible by developing action systems, by differentiation of tasks, and by encountering new environmental conditions.

The quotation above from Hofsten referring to paths that can be taken through the "task space" is a reminder that behavior is not inflexible and that there are usually alternate paths to a goal. Bernstein (1967) emphasized the number of degrees of freedom in the coordination of behavior. Lashley often spoke of the flexibility of behavior and the power of an organism to substitute an alternate means or strategy to complete a task or reach a goal (Lashley, 1933, 1942). Lashley had an often reprinted demonstration of the writing of two blindfolded individuals with the right hand, the left hand, both hands mirror reversed, and with the teeth (Lashley, 1942). I discovered this principle by good fortune in my first published research (J. J. Gibson, Jack, & Raffel, 1932). Subjects (college students were conditioned to withdraw the index finger of the right (or left) hand from an electrode, the shock signalled by the sound of a buzzer. Following conditioning, the subject was asked to place the finger of the other hand on the electrode. It was withdrawn as briskly as the supposedly conditioned one.

The necessity of providing for some flexibility in behavior was recognized by Hull (1934a, 1934b), who, despite his allegiance to conditioning principles and the device of chaining reflexes, published two papers on the "habit-family hierarchy" in which he tried to account for flexibility in the sense of transfer of means within tasks. Although I do not consider his solution acceptable, it underlines the importance of flexibility and behavior change. I return to the problem in the next section.

PROPOSITIONS INVOLVING CHANGE IN THE COURSE OF PERCEPTUAL DEVELOPMENT

9. *Perceptual learning in development.* Changes with development include both growth of perception and action systems and learning. Learning must be studied in the species-typical environment, in the context of development.

Earlier investigations often attempted to study "pure" learning, that is, learning in highly artificial situations that eliminated natural, contextual factors. However, learning is inextricably intertwined with all the factors that affect development and is not truly isolable as a process. Present-day cognitive scientists tend to study learning (when they do it at all) entirely within a verbal context that has little or no relevance for perceptual development (e.g., learning about dinosaurs or solving math problems). Far from studying perceptual development in isolation or in made-up tasks, we must study it as perceptual and action systems (including ones related to speech) are emerging and changing.

10. *What is learned.* What is learned is the perception of *affordances:* that is, to perceive what the layout, the objects, and the events in the environment afford for action in relation to oneself (this particular organism).

Infancy is an ideal time to study perceptual learning, for two reasons: (a) infants *must* learn this way, because they have as yet no access to language; and (b) because they have so much to learn—everything there is to know about the world outside the womb and also how the equipment and dynamics of their own bodies may or may not be able to cope with the events and situations that surround them. The question is, what does the world afford, and how can this individual act to use effectively the information provided by perception?

Newborns discriminate many features of the world, such as sounds, light and darkness, touches, pressure, energy generated by their own movements, gratings of varied coarseness, dot arrangements, movements of surfaces, and three-dimensional objects (Slater & Morison, 1991). Much accumulated research attests to the rather impressive discriminatory abilities of even the youngest of infants. However, perceiving the affordance of objects, places, and happenings—how they can be acted upon—requires learning. When and how these affordances are learned is our challenge.

11. *When learning occurs.* When learning occurs depends, in part, on maturing perceptual and action systems, as rate-determining or limiting factors. Other organismic, environmental, and task factors interact with these.

Learning to use both hands for reaching and manipulating an object, for example, depends on developing posture, among other things. Sitting must be stable for the hands to be freed, and visual acuity must have reached a level adequate for manipulative visual examination of a portable object to produce new information.

12. *How learning occurs.* How learning occurs includes three principles, all dependent on perception itself: One is spontaneous exploratory activity; the second is observation of the consequences of exploratory activity; and the third is selection of one of the variable means of exploration. I consider each of the three in turn.

a. *Exploratory activity.* Exploration is a natural function of a developing organism, as much as breathing. An animal spontaneously exercises the developing systems, foraging for information about itself (its powers) and about the surrounding environment. Perception is an active process (J. J. Gibson, 1966). An active visual system, for example, includes adjustments of the pupils, fixation, adjustments of posture to optimize viewing, and use of manipulative and locomotor systems as they become viable, to optimize the visual information (e.g., bringing an object closer or rotating it in the hands). As new systems become available, they are "tried out" for use in the service of searching. Practice with exploratory activities may result in minimizing and optimizing the search, or elaborating it with more complex coordinations (e.g., asymmetric use of the hands in manipulation).

b. *Consequences of exploration.* When exploratory activity results in any kind of contact with the environment (e.g., seeing, hearing, or feeling something or changing location of objects or oneself in relation to them), the consequences of the contact yield further information about environmental supports in relation to the activity of the organism. This is an outcome that gives rise to perceptual learning and the eventual realization of an affordance.

For example, contact with an object that brings it into view or into the mouth yields consequences of several kinds, including new information about the object or perhaps the accomplishment of a task in hand (e.g., eating or chewing something). The consequence may also be undesirable in relation to the task, such as awkward movements that yield delay, or injury, or loss of an object toward which the activity was directed.

c. *Selection.* Generally speaking, learning happens through a process of variation and selection. Variation is accomplished by way of exploratory activity, which in turn yields consequences that provide further information. One more step in the process, selection, is crucial. How is it that one organization of perceiving–acting or one strategy wins out, so to speak, among the alternatives? This is the question that has traditionally spawned arguments, rhetoric, and disagreement. *Reinforcement* has traditionally been the most popular term; *insight* had its day.

I believe that selection is determined by more than one factor. We can identify some of these factors. In my earlier theory I identified reduction of uncertainty (E. J. Gibson, 1969) as the determining factor. I still favor this factor; it certainly works for perpetual learning. Consider the example of an adult examining stereograms made up of dot figures (so-called Julesz figures) that, when looked at properly, yield some clear and interesting figure, such as a cornucopia, but when improperly fixated yield nothing but a hash. The visual system searches, wandering over the dual field, but suddenly it reaches the correct adjustment and the unified figure pops out. The heterogeneous mass has been resolved into order. Curiously enough, the system can retrieve the search strategy and another time can repeat the process. We cannot call this insight (whatever that is), because we could not describe in words what the process of search was, but it yielded something clear, orderly, and economical. I believe that order and economy are key factors in selection, not just for adults performing a trick task, but even more for developing organisms faced with serious tasks, ones that contribute to their knowledge of the world and how to get along in it.

Studies of infants given learning tasks that can yield an orderly and economical solution, such as choosing the unifying information (e.g., synchrony or common motion) are easily accomplished by quite young infants. Although we certainly need to know more about the selection process, we can be pretty sure of the importance of perception–action cycles that are relevant to the task, economical (eliminating unnecessary activity), and orderly. It is a good rule to minimize and optimize for the most economical process that is relevant to the goal of the task. Discerning order that yields predictability is also a way of advancing the prospectivity of behavior.

13. *Development of control.* Learning to perceive and realize an affordance means gaining control of that behavior. It can henceforth be used intentionally, in either a performatory or exploratory fashion. Achieving control of a behavior allows it to be selected for embedding within a task (if it is not the end of the task itself), as a potential means or as an exploratory device.

An example of achieving control through learning an affordance is the situation used in many experiments by Rovee-Collier (Rovee & Rovee, 1969; Rovee-Collier & Gekoski, 1979). Infants (2 to 6 months of age) are provided with a ribbon attached to an ankle at one end and to a mobile placed above their crib at the other. Lying on their back so as to command a view of the mobile, the infants kick their legs spontaneously, making the mobile turn synchronously with their kicks (a consequence known to Skinnerians as *conjugate reinforcement*). Infants in this situation quickly discover that thrusts of their own legs drive the mobile, as both rate and intensity of kicking affect its visible spinning. As McKirdy and Rovee (1978, p. 81) put it:

> The major advantage of the procedure is the control which it permits the infant over his own reinforcing consequences. By being able to continuously alter the values of his response-produced stimulation along a continuum of 0 to 100% with respect to the appropriate units of a given quality and modality of stimulus, the infant can *optimize* his response consequences by adjusting their values to meet his moment-to-moment preferences.

Controls given noncontingent reinforcement did not increase or optimize kicks with experience in the situation. Withdrawal of conjugate reinforcement, leaving the infant without control of the mobile's movement, at first intensified kicking and sometimes resulted in crying and fussing (Rovee-Collier & Gekoski, 1979). Facial expressions have been found to alter as the infants discover their powers of control, evoking smiles, and on the other hand when the possibility of control has been withdrawn by the experimenter, evoking distress or puzzlement (Lewis, Sullivan, & Brooks-Gunn, 1985). The latter findings suggest that discovery and exercise of control are motivating.

Other experimental arrangements that permit infant control (e.g., by head turning or high-amplitude sucking) attest to the same point, that young infants learn through their own spontaneous exploratory movements that they can effect changes in the world. This discovery is the foundation for *agency,* a sense of a self separate from the world that can perform intentionally, on its own power, and act on the world. Indeed, infants are capable of learning quite early that they can control an act of another person (Mosier & Rogoff, 1994) and do so.

14. *Development of prospectivity.* Achieving control increases the potential prospectivity of behavior, its anticipatory aspect, by making possible reorganization of preparatory acts within the task and increasing or decreasing complexity of nested subordinate units.

Because control permits intentional selection of affordance relationships, once they are learned they may be selected for their task relationships and organized into more economical or more complex episodes of task performance. Anticipation of consequences increases in specificity, resulting in differentiation of affordances.

15. *Changes in task organization with development.* Tasks are originally perceptually undifferentiated internally, as long as their function is sufficiently fulfilled. Tasks become perceptually differentiated and can be reorganized internally by selection of subunits nested within the whole (a) as affordances are learned, (b) as control of action is achieved, and (c) as prospectivity is extended.

Knowledge of affordances expands as the exploratory range offered by development of action systems and a widening environment present new opportunities for learning. Tasks expand in complexity as perceptual differentiation occurs, by discovery of subunits in an affordance relationship to a final goal of a task. Perception–action units that have previously realized an affordance can often serve as exploratory means toward accomplishing a new task, creating a "higher order" affordance relationship.

Locomotion provides an example. Learning to walk upright realizes an affordance relationship of its own (using the two legs to support oneself and move upright over the ground), an activity that is highly motivating and is exercised and practiced spontaneously. Once this activity is performed smoothly and economically, however, the hands and arms are no longer needed for maintaining balance, and an infant discovers that an object can be transported while walking. The activity becomes a means for transporting an object to a new location. At first, the portage is motivating, a task in itself. We used such a task (carrying a colored golf ball down a corridor, exchanging it, and carrying another one back) in an experiment (Schmuckler & Gibson, 1989) as a way of keeping a young walker walking. Just as walking is subordinated to carrying, so carrying is eventually subordinated to relocating an object for a further goal. Means–end selection becomes a new mechanism of exploring, learning, and achieving control. The span of prospectivity of behavior is potentially lengthened in this way and a new hierarchy of control in internal structural organization of tasks becomes possible.

16. *Differentiation of ends and means.* The description above is essentially one of differentiation of ends and means. This achievement was referred to by Piaget (1952, p. 229) as the coordination of "two hitherto independent schemata":

> These means are henceforth entirely differentiated from the end itself, the child's behavior consequently consisting in a coordination of two independent schemata—the one, final (the schema assigning an end to the action), the other transitional (the schema utilized as means)—and no longer in the application of a more or less complex schema.

I am uneasy talking about "independent schemata" and I think it more likely that a process of differentiation within a task results in the perceptual discovery of a useful relationship of one affordance to another, serving the function of completing a task—as well as carrying out the infant's intention. Means are already achievable affordances; they must be perceived as relevant and nested with respect to further task goals.

Willats (1989) and Koslowski and Bruner (1972) have provided experimental examples of infants discovering the means relationship. The process entails the discovery of the affordances of the subordinate units first and then the recognition that these are containable within the primary task. Consider the case of an infant attempting to reach an object just out of arm's length, placed on a movable surface such as a cloth or a turntable. To discover the means, the infant must first perceive the object as not quite reachable. Pulling the cloth or fiddling with the turntable is an attractive alternative in itself, however, and is always explored thoroughly before its consequence of bringing the object within reach is discovered. Koslowski and Bruner (1972) found that when an object was placed on the end of a rotating surface, a direct approach to both the object and to the end of the rotating arm preceded the strategy of turning the arm before reaching. The child had to differentiate the action of the rotating arm and its consequence from the total task before discovering the relationship of the subordinate action to the goal of seizing the toy at the end.

A fair number of research methods probe infants' success at differentiating means from ends, such as the A not B task, detour tasks, and use of simple tools. In the course of daily activities, babies naturally encounter many such tasks. It is important to ask whether such a task, once solved, provides a generalizable means that transfers to a different task.

17. *Development of flexibility.* Perceiving means (subordinate affordance units) as possible selections for carrying out new tasks is one route to flexibility. Increasing flexibility by transfer of means from task to task is characteristic of development and becomes a major feature of successful problem solving. Multiplication of perceived means–end relations and within-task differentiation underlies the likelihood of transfer.

Our understanding of transfer and flexibility of behavior is at present poor and full of contradictions. We hear a lot about "domain specificity," especially in infants, and references to the importance of a particular context in development. Context may refer to features of just one particular task (e.g., Rovee-Collier's kicking to move a mobile) or much more generally, to comparison of one culture with another (Rogoff, 1990). Rovee-Collier and her colleagues have investigated the effect of small changes in situational features of the mobile-moving task (e.g., changes in the crib lining or changes in the decorative features of the mobile). Such changes in context are apt to prevent generalization (Rovee-Collier & Sullivan, 1980), but infants have been found to generalize to a change of context when they have had prior practice with varying contexts (Fagan, Morrongiello, Rovee-Collier, & Gekoski, 1984). Transfer of another kind (bilateral) does appear to occur within this task. When 3-month-old infants were trained to kick one leg in order to activate a mobile, the rate of kicking the other leg decreased. When the ribbon was moved to the other leg, the rate for the newly attached leg increased (Rovee-Collier, Morrongiello, Aron, & Kuperschmidt, 1978). In this situation, behavior at first becomes more specific with practice as kicking is restricted to a single leg, differentiated from kicking with both legs. When the ribbon is attached to the other leg, however, control is flexibly transferred to that leg. It would be interesting to know whether the control of the mobile would generalize to an arm.

In considering how flexibility supported by transfer of a means or strategy of control to a new task develops, there seem to be three underlying factors. One is the acquisition of a repertoire of learned, well-practiced, controllable affordance achievements, such as controlled reaching, some sort of locomotion, pulling a string, or pulling a supportive cloth. A second is the development of differentiated subordinate task relations. It is not clear whether this discovery of nested relations is always specific to a task at first. Third, there must be perception of the relation between a practiced subordinate act as a means to new goals.

The second point (the necessity of distinguishing separate units within a task) is illustrated by the turntable task (Koslowski & Bruner, 1972). The infant must perceive that there are two parts or separate steps to reaching the toy: pushing the turntable or lever and reaching for the toy. In this case, both are attractive as affordances. A quite different example would be perceiving the causal relation in a Michotte presentation, such as one object rolling along a path, striking another, and sending the second object off (launching). Showing this scene to infants of 7 months or so has been tried with uncertain success (Leslie, 1982, 1984). Older children understand the dynamic relationship of the two objects (Olum, 1956).

The third factor, detecting the usefulness of a means in a new task, is especially interesting. Adolph (in press) conducted a longitudinal study of infants traversing an inclined slope. She started the infants on the downward path, so to speak, as soon as they could crawl on all fours. Slopes varied from 10° to 40°. In the beginning, most infants attempted to crawl down slopes that were too steep and had to be rescued. A few weeks later, in the same situation, they had learned new means of coping with the steep slope (e.g., backing down, calling for help, simply refusing). Eventually, these same children began to walk upright. However, when they first encountered the steep slope as walkers, they did not make use of the strategies they had mastered and again had to be rescued.

Another example is Kaye's (1979) study of pretraining an infant with a means for solving a detour task in which a toy was placed behind a screen.

One group received no pretraining, whereas a second group was taught to reach around a screen. When an object was placed behind the screen, the strategy of reaching around was not used by the pretrained group.

One area that should be studied is how children obtain a goal object by several steps, and especially, how they transfer a means as a subordinate step to a new task. Certainly the development of new abilities and getting them under firm control is an essential factor. Incorporating them in an exploratory search for access to a goal is another. Search for information to support action goes on from birth. Perhaps the development of new modes of exploration is the key to flexibility in novel task situations.

PROPOSITIONS ABOUT HIGHER ORDER COGNITION

The following propositions are beyond the province of my area of perceptual development, as such, but they are included to demonstrate the continuity with cognition and the basic role of perception, as here conceived, in other cognitive activities.

18. *Flexibility and problem solving.* Increasing flexibility by transfer of means from task to task is a major feature of successful problem solving.

Generalization of information occurs at many levels. Perceiving similarities between situations and between tasks permits transfer of means to accomplish new (different) goals. Objects frequently have multiple affordances and so can provide means to different ends. Children naturally learn different affordances for objects and events, given the opportunity and the appropriate cultural surroundings. Familiar tools such as spoons are first used by infants to afford sucking, biting on, and banging. With a little assistance and example by caretakers they are used, sloppily at first and then skillfully, for transporting food to the mouth. They may serve later as levers or even as musical instruments. Using a spoon to feed another person (or a doll) is an example of transfer of means. The affordance of spoons is even used metaphorically at some later age (note such terms as *spoon fed* and *born with a silver spoon in the mouth*). All these variations are flexible uses of an originally simple object, carried to another situation as a tool or a means of problem solving or communication—that is, as a route to the goal of another task.

19. *Discovery of roles through transfer of means.* Perceiving subordinate affordance units as means within varied tasks leads to perception of different relationships or roles for objects and the self. The first to be discovered (I would expect) would be the roles of agent versus patient–object (the mover vs. the moved). The role of agent, the controller or cause of change, can be perceived in oneself moving an object and is eventually extended, by transfer, to embedded control units, such as using a stick to strike another object or to move the object within reach. The stick now affords moving something else and is a subordinate controlling or causal agent.

One's own hand can be viewed as acting to control an event, serving as a causal agent. By extension (transfer of the same relationship) an external agent–object event (someone else's hand moving an object) may be perceived as a causal event. An experiment by Leslie (1984) provided evidence for this achievement in 28-week-old infants. Using the habituation method, infants were presented until habituation occurred with a film of a hand reaching out, grasping, and carrying off a doll. After an interval, the film was presented in mirror reversal, so the event itself was essentially identical. A second group was tested on a film presented in the original orientation, but the hand did not make contact with the doll, which was moved off by an invisible wire. The first change was unnoticed, but the second induced recovery of looking. In other words, a change in the pick-up event in which the hand did not fulfill the role of agent was noticed and observed at length, whereas a noncausal change in the filmed event was not. When an inanimate object was substituted (in a control experiment) for the hand, there was no apparent dishabituation. Leslie suggested that "hands are seen from an early age as agents of change" (p. 32). This may be important in development of abstract concepts of agency that can be transferred flexibly from one task to another.

20. *Perceiving another person as a causal agent.* It is a corollary of the last proposition that the agent–object relationship, once observed in an external event, can be perceived and generalized to other events in which another person is the agent or mover. Infants do appear rather early to use other per-

sons as a tool or means to an end (Mosier & Rogoff, 1994), but this proposition goes further in stating that another person will, after sufficient opportunity for generalization, be perceived as an agent. In other words, they perceive another person as a potential controller of an event, as having intentions.

Tomasello (1993) proposed that infants observe intention in others sometime between 9 and 18 months—that they are aware of another person "having concrete goals or purposes." He pointed out that this knowledge depends on "the clear differentiation between means and ends in the infant's instrumental acts. This is, in a sense, the 'raw material' for understanding that others act intentionally." Tomasello went on to relate this discovery to perspective taking and then to "interpersonal attention," a foundation for social cognition.

21. *Agency as an abstract concept.* Perceiving embedded events in which agent and object are distinguished, when experience is sufficiently varied, provides information for general attribution of agency. That is, perceiving the role of controller in oneself and also in others leads to a superordinate, inclusive concept of agency. The behavior of oneself and other persons is viewed as potentially intentional and autonomous. To answer William James's (1879) question, we are not automata!

22. *The concept of animacy.* Perception of agency permits observation of spontaneous action in others and thus gives information for differentiating between live and inanimate objects. Objects may be potential tools and a means to achieve an affordance, but their function is not spontaneous and must be controlled.

Contrived (trick) spontaneity of action in objects is apparently noted fairly early by infants and is surprising (Baillargeon, 1994), but it seems likely (though not well substantiated) that a sophisticated concept of animacy includes agency and that the concept of animacy is at first overgeneralized, as Piaget (1933) argued long ago.

CONCLUSION

Having beaten my way to at least a mention of concepts and social cognition, I rest my case for the moment, realizing that there is a long way to go but feeling pretty confident that we are off to a good start. I say we, because I do not want this view to be just perceptual development as I see it.

I am not worried that we do not have all of the answers. Nobody does. The important thing now is to ask the right questions. That is the root of the trouble with the stance of the present establishment. The information processors, I grant, have some facts, but they aren't necessarily answers to the important questions, such as how people perceive what is going on around them so as to make good use of what the world offers. We have to begin with appropriate concepts and the right questions. I doubt that hypotheses about elaborate mechanisms are as likely to help as revising and refining our questions, our concepts, and our functional framework.

REFERENCES

Adolph, K. E. (in press). Learning in the development of infant locomotion. *Monographs of the Society for Research in Child Development.*

Baillargeon, R. C. (1994). Physical reasoning in young infants: Seeking explanations for unexpected events. *British Journal of Developmental Psychology, 12,* 9–33.

Baillargeon, R., & Graber, M. (1987). Where's the rabbit? 5.5-month-old infants' representation of the height of a hidden object. *Cognitive Development, 2,* 375–392.

Bernstein, N. (1967). *The coordination and regulation of movements.* Oxford, England: Pergamon.

Bhatt, R. S., & Rovee-Collier, C. (1994). Perception and 24-hour retention of feature relations in infancy. *Developmental Psychology, 30,* 142–150.

Bingham, G. P. (1988). Task-specific devices and the perceptual bottleneck. *Human Movement Science, 7,* 225–264.

Cohen, L. B. (1991). *Infant attention: An information processing approach.* Norwood, NJ: Ablex.

Fagan, J. W., Morrongiello, B. A., Rovee-Collier, C. K., & Gekoski, M. J. (1984). Expectancies and memory retrieval in three-month-old infants. *Child Development, 55,* 936–943.

Gibson, E. J. (1940). A systematic application of the concepts of generalization and differentiation to verbal learning. *Psychological Review, 47,* 196–229.

Gibson, E. J. (1969). *Principles of perceptual learning and development.* New York: Appleton–Century–Crofts.

Gibson, J. J. (1966). *The senses considered as perceptual systems.* Boston: Houghton-Mifflin.

Gibson, J. J. (1979). *The ecological approach to visual perception.* Boston: Houghton-Mifflin.

Gibson, J. J., Jack, E. J., & Raffel, G. (1932). Bilateral transfer of the conditioned response in the human subject. *Journal of Experimental Psychology, 15,* 416–421.

Goldfield, E. C., Kay, B. A., & Warren, W. H., Jr. (1993). Infant bouncing: The assembly and tuning of action systems. *Child Development, 64,* 1128–1142.

Hull, C. (1934a). The concept of the habit-family hierarchy and maze learning: Part I. *Psychological Review, 41,* 33–52.

Hull, C. (1943b). The concept of the habit-family hierarchy and maze learning: Part II. *Psychological Review, 41,* 134–152.

James, W. (1879). Are we automata? *Mind, 4,* 1–22.

Julesz, B. (1984). *Toward an axiomatic theory of preattentive vision.* New York: Wiley.

Kaye, K. (1979). *The development of skills.* New York: Academic Press.

Koslowski, B., & Bruner, J.S. (1972). Learning to use a lever. *Child Development, 43,* 790–799.

Lashley, K. S. (1933). Integrative function of the cerebral cortex. *Physiological Reviews, 13,* 1–42.

Lashley, K. S. (1942). The problem of cerebral organization in man. *Biological Symposia, 7,* 301–322.

Lee, D. N. (1993). Body-environment coupling. In U. Neisser (Ed.), *The perceived self* (pp. 43–67). New York: Cambridge University Press.

Leslie, A. M. (1982). The perception of causality in infants. *Perception, 11,* 173–186.

Leslie, A. M. (1984). Infant perception of a manual pick-up event. *British Journal of Developmental Psychology, 2,* 19–32.

Lewis, M., Sullivan, M. W., & Brooks-Gunn, J. (1985). Emotional behavior during the learning of a contingency in early infancy. *British Journal of Developmental Psychology, 3,* 307–316.

McKirdy, L. W., & Rovee, C. K. (1978). The efficacy of auditory and visual conjugate reinforcers in infant conditioning. *Journal of Experimental Child Psychology, 25,* 80–89.

Mosier, C. E., & Rogoff, B. (1994). Infants' instrumental use of their mothers to achieve their goals. *Child Development, 65,* 70–79.

Newell, K. M. (1986). Constraints on development of coordination. In M. G. Wade

& H. T. A. Whiting (Eds.), *Motor development in children: Aspects of coordination and control* (pp. 341–360). Dordrecht, The Netherlands: Martinus Nijhoff.

Olum, V. (1956). Developmental differences in the perception of causality. *American Journal of Psychology, 69*, 417–423.

Piaget, J. (1933). *Children's philosophies.* Worcester, MA: Clark University Press.

Piaget, J. (1963). *The origins of intelligence in children.* New York: Norton. (Original work published 1952)

Reed, E. S. (1990). Changing theories of postural development. In M. Woollacott & A. Shumway-Cook (Eds.), *Development of posture and gait across the life span* (pp. 3–24). Columbia: University of South Carolina Press.

Rogoff, B. (1990). *Apprenticeship in thinking: Cognitive development in social context.* New York: Oxford University Press.

Rovee, C. K., & Rovee, D. T. (1969). Conjugate reinforcement of infant exploratory behavior. *Journal of Experimental Child Psychology, 8*, 33–39.

Rovee-Collier, C. K., & Gekoski, M. J. (1979). The economics of infancy: A review of conjugate reinforcement. In H. W. Reese & L. P. Lipsitt (Eds.), *Advances in Child Development and Behavior* (Vol. 13, pp. 195–255). New York: Academic Press.

Rovee-Collier, C. K., Morrongiello, B. A., Aron, M., & Kuperschmidt, J. (1978). Topographical response differentiation and reversal in 3-month-old infants. *Infant Behavior and Development, 1*, 323–333.

Rovee-Collier, C., & Sullivan, M. W. (1980). Organization of infant memory. *Journal of Experimental Psychology: Human Learning and Memory, 6*, 798–807.

Schmuckler, M. A., & Gibson, E. J. (1989). The effect of imposed optical flow on guided locomotion in young walkers. *Bristish Journal of Developmental Psychology, 7*, 193–206.

Slater, A., & Morison, V. (1991). *Visual attention and memory at birth.* Norwood, NJ: Ablex.

Thelen, E., Corbetta, D., Kamm, K., Spencer, J. P., & Schneider, K. (1993). The transition to reaching: Mapping intention and intrinsic dynamics. *Child Development, 64*, 1058–1098.

Titchener, E. B. (1929). *Systematic psychology: Prolegomena.* New York: MacMillan.

Tomasello, M. (1993). Joint attention as social cognition (No. 25, pp. 1–36). Emory Cognition Project. Emory University, Atlanta GA.

Treisman, A. (1988). Features and objects. The Fourteenth Bartlett Memorial Lecture. *The Quarterly Journal of Experimental Psychology, 40A*, 201–237.

Von Hofsten, C. (1993). Prospective control: A basic aspect of action development. *Human Development, 36,* 253–270.

Willats, P. C. (1985, July). *Development and rapid adjustment of means–end behavior in infants aged six to eight months.* Paper presented at the bienniel meeting of the International Society for the Study of Behavioral Development, Tours, France.

Willatts, P. (1989). *Development of problem-solving in infancy.* Hillsdale, NJ: Erlbaum.

Younger, B. A., & Cohen, L. B. (1986). Developmental change in infants' perception of correlations among attributes. *Child Development, 57,* 803–815.

Ecological Realism

Ecological Realism

Cathy Dent-Read and Patricia Zukow-Goldring

The ecological realist approach to visual perception focuses on the adaptation or fit between organism and environment (Gibson, 1966, 1979). In this view, the organism and its environment exist only in relation to each other and mutually define and determine each other. The idea of mutuality in psychology originated in this work on perception, which soundly rejects the dualist separation of mind and body and of organism and environment (Still & Good, 1992). Succinctly stated: There is no organism without an environment, and there can be no environment without an organism (see also Lewontin, 1982, p. 160).

According to the theory of direct perception (Gibson, 1966, 1979), all knowing originates in the mutuality of organism and environment. Later work has distinguished between the concepts of reciprocity and mutuality (e.g., Lombardo, 1987; Shaw & Turvey, 1981). This important distinction requires some elaboration. *Reciprocity* is a relation between aspects of a system that function in distinct but complementary ways; *mutuality* describes the functional unity of the subsystems in which one aspect requires the other (Shaw & Turvey, 1981; Turvey & Fitzpatrick, 1993). Thus, as an example of reciprocity, perceiving and acting form a system in which they share a common basis, the environment. That is, the perceptual structure that specifies the world also specifies how the organism acts in the world. Specifically, the visual flow pattern generated when a person walks specifies edges, surfaces of support, and (at the still point in the flow) the point the person is approaching. As with perceiving and acting, organism and environment are reciprocal elements that require each other's existence. An organism requires a certain kind of surround in order to live, and the environment must surround an organism to be an environment. Otherwise it is just a physical location.

According to biological perspectives grounded in ecological realism, the action of an organism in its environment ceaselessly and mutually transforms all elements of the system from genes to the cultural–historical context, which precipitates new configurations of organism–environment relations (Ho, 1991). Thus, the development of organisms is also the development of environments for organisms (Costall, 1995; Ingold, 1991).

The ecological realist approach adds an essential ingredient to this relationship in its focus on direct perception. Direct perceiving keeps the organism in contact with the environment, and, therefore, the organism and environment complete each other, forming the system that they do. When researchers define *perceiving* as maintaining contact with the environment without mental mediation (Gibson, 1979), they find evidence of the dynamic perceptual richness continuously detected by creatures on the move. For instance, humans perceive reflected ambient light that specifies its source in the environment, including surfaces, their textures, and occlusions of one by the other. As people move about they perceive what persists (structural invariants) and what changes (transformational invariants). The process of development, then, is one of differentiation in which the organism becomes a more skilled perceiver, in contact with a more and more differentiated world.

This theory of direct perception emphasizes emergent knowing, the continuous perceptual updating of the person acting in a dynamic environment, rather than foreknowledge in the form of innate ideas or prior representation. Perceiving does not occur within the organism but is a continual process of coordinating with the environment (Michaels &

Carello, 1981). That is, a creature with particular bodily capabilities (effectivities) detects particular opportunities for action (affordances) during ongoing activities. We see the world the way we do because of the way we are (Sanders, in press). Similarly, guiding action does not occur in the organism (e.g., by means of programs or plans) but arises in and through acting in the local details of a particular environment (Shaw & Turvey, 1981). For instance, direct perception theory rejects priming the child with *a priori* knowledge of space, opting instead to study the conditions under which people perceive themselves as situated in space (Still & Good, 1992). That is, knowing is embodied, not parceled out to the brain. Knowing is "part and parcel" of what the self perceives and does, inextricably linked with knowing what the environment offers the self for action.

Robin Cooper's studies of infant perceptual learning focus on qualities of infant-directed versus adult-directed speech. She studies how aspects of the early developmental context (e.g., infant–caregiver interactions) provide important structure for infant speech perception and how as active listeners the nature of information pickup in infants changes during the first months after birth. Philippe Rochat views the origins of self-knowledge as the discovery of the ecological self (Neisser, 1993). This aspect of the self emerges from the action potentials of the infant's own body. Rochat maintains that detecting amodal invariants in self-produced movement forms the basis of early self-knowledge. Nancy Rader investigates how motivation, maturation, and expectations affect perceptual differentiation and development. Rader studies infants' perception of what objects afford that have in the past been positive or negative, the relation of brain maturation to performance on a search task, and the reactions of infants with Down's syndrome to separation from their mothers. Claes von Hofsten investigates reaching as a means to understand object perception, and posits that knowing that objects are entities depends on intuitive theories of the physical world. Infants learn to guide action by moving and thereby perceiving variants and invariants in accomplishing a task. Children also learn about problems that arise when coordinating with the external world, and about information that makes it possible to guide action prospectively. Patricia Zukow-Goldring presents a social ecological realism that integrates aspects of the theory of direct perception, eco-cultural approaches, and ethnomethodology/linguistic anthropology. Her findings document that caregivers make amodal invariant relations (tim-ing, tempo, intensity, and rhythmicity) prominent as they gather and di-rect attention to animate beings, objects, and actions, and that infants pick up these regularities in their mothers' speech and action. Cathy Dent-Read reports on a naturalistic study of the emergence of metaphor and pretend. Consonant with the ecological realist approach to language, metaphor is conceptualized as a way of seeing one thing in terms of another kind of thing that it resembles. Dent-Read shows that metaphor can emerge early in the ontogenesis of language and that it is distinct from pretend. Smits-man asserts that organism and environment form a unified system. Smits-man studies how any hand-held tool changes the prehensile system as a whole and "becomes" part of the organism. For instance, grasping a rod changes the length of the arm, which reflexively permits novel action pos-sibilities, while restricting others. Anne Pick's chapter directly deals with the question of how cognition relates to perceiving: She reports on inves-tigations of the perceptual activities used by preschool children in group-ing objects. She shows that when children perceive affordances they can act on them and use them to group objects.

Three questions are important to keep in mind when comparing the studies included in this section of the book: To what extent do the authors use ideas from the theory of direct perception? How are the authors ex-tending the behavior to be studied? How are the authors extending or elab-orating the theory of direct perception?

The authors use the ideas of direct perception to varying degrees. Whereas some posit direct perceiving as the main source of knowing (Zukow-Goldring, Dent-Read, Smitsman), one places perceiving and cog-nizing on a continuum (Pick), and others bring in concepts of innate ideas and mental representation to explain certain aspects of knowing (von Hof-sten, Rader, Cooper, Rochat).

Some authors study classic situations of acting in relation to a dy-namic environment, and some study situations new to direct perception theory, such as object sorting or natural social interaction. Classically studied behaviors such as speech perception (Cooper), reaching (Rader, von Hofsten), locomotion across a surface (Rader), and limb perception (Rochat) are examined, but results are applied to new topics of investigation such as verbal meaning (Cooper), remembering (Rader), and knowledge of self (Rochat). Other researchers are extending the behaviors to be studied into new areas such as lexical development arising from infant–caregiver interaction (Zukow-Goldring), the emergence of metaphor (Dent-Read), tool use (Smitsman), and object sorting (Pick).

Finally, the authors vary in the extent to which they endeavor to extend the theory of direct perception. Rader, Zukow-Goldring, and Dent-Read extend the core ideas of ecological realism further than the other authors. These extensions move into the area of memory, social relationships, and early language use, but the authors all endeavor to work with a realist epistemology. Some researchers in the ecological realist group focus on the development of various kinds of organism–environment systems: infant–caregiver (Zukow-Goldring), speaker–listener (Dent-Read), organism–tool (Smitsman), and child–object (Pick). These systems are, again, seen to develop through processes of differentiation. Specifically, as an organism differentiates its action, the relevant aspect of the environment (caregiver, listener, tool, object) becomes a more differentiated environment supporting or acting with the organism.

Given this broad range of topics studied and problems posed, several new questions for developmental study have emerged from work in the ecological realist tradition. Is perceiving always linked to acting? Where does perceiving stop and cognizing begin—or is there no sharp boundary? What are the boundaries of the organism, both as perceived by self and by others? Is the process of differentiation sufficient to account for developmental changes, especially those that are nonlinear? Are the methods used currently adequate for studying mutualities, as opposed to organisms? The work in this section represents the beginning of answers to these questions; we hope it motivates others to take up the challenge of solving these core problems in developmental psychology.

REFERENCES

Costall, A. (1995). Socializing affordances. *Theory and Psychology, 5*, 1–27.

Gibson, J. (1966). *The senses considered as perceptual systems.* Boston: Houghton Mifflin.

Gibson, J. (1979). *An ecological approach to visual perception.* New York: Houghton Mifflin.

Ho, M.-W. (1991). The role of action in evolution: Evolution by process and the ecological approach to perception. *Cultural Dynamics, 4*, 336–354.

Ingold, T. (1991). Becoming persons: Consciousness and sociality in human evolution. *Cultural Dynamics, 4*, 355–378.

Lewontin, R. C. (1982). Organism and environment. In H. C. Plotkin (Ed.), *Learning, development, and culture* (pp. 151–172). Chichester, England: Wiley.

Lombardo, T. (1987). *The reciprocity of perceiver and environment.* Hillsdale, NJ: Erlbaum.

Michaels, C., & Carello, C. (1981). *Direct perception.* Englewood Cliffs, NJ: Prentice Hall.

Sanders, J. (in press). Affordances: An ecological approach to first philosophy. In H. Haber & G. Weiss (Eds.), *Perspectives on embodiment: The intersection of nature and culture.* New York: Routledge.

Shaw, R., & Turvey, M. (1981). Coalitions as models for ecosystems: A realist perspective on perceptual organization. In R. Kubovy & K. Pomerantz (Eds.), *Perceptual organization* (pp. 343–415). Hillsdale, NJ: Erlbaum.

Still, A., & Good, J. (1992). Mutualism in the human sciences: Toward the implementation of a theory. *Journal for the Theory of Social Behavior, 22*(2), 105–128.

Turvey, M., & Fitzpatrick, P. (1993). Commentary: Development of perception–action systems and general principles of pattern formation. *Child Development, 64*, 1175–1190.

3

An Ecological Approach to Infants' Perception of Intonation Contours as Meaningful Aspects of Speech

Robin Panneton Cooper

The goal of this chapter is to facilitate the integration of an ecological view into the study of perceptual development in infants. Ecological views assume that all levels of functioning are embedded within a system that is constantly in flux. Influences on behavior at any level are always dependent on the state of the system at a given point in time. Although ecological views are relevant for many aspects of organismic functioning, they may be particularly germane for those interested in the development of behavior because by definition, *development* is the study of change over time. Perspectives that are inherently dynamic (e.g., ecological views) are advantageous because the primary task of developmentalists is to explain how phenomena transform from one time to another. I maintain that the ecological perspective espoused by J. J. Gibson (1966, 1979) and E. J. Gibson (1991) provides a new and refreshing framework for current findings and also opens the door to future inquiry by posing questions for researchers that otherwise might remain unasked. More specifically, I recast some of the research on infants' processing of intonation contours in caretakers' speech from an ecological perspective to illuminate what appears to be an interesting, dynamic change in perception. Before beginning this analysis, it is necessary to clarify what is meant here by an ecological view of perceptual development.

AN ECOLOGICAL VIEW OF
PERCEPTUAL DEVELOPMENT

According to J. J. Gibson (1979), *perception* can be defined as a process by which organisms acquire information about their worlds and as a "registering of certain definite dimensions of invariance in the stimulus flux together with definite parameters of disturbance" (p. 249). Although what is perceived and how perception informs reality is a matter of historical controversy (Reed, 1988), no psychologist would disagree that perception is fundamental to an understanding of behavioral functioning because it is the primary avenue through which animals "know" their worlds. Disagreement does arise, however, in discussions of what is perceived and how perception takes place. What distinguishes an ecological view of perception from nonecological views is the former's emphasis on the mutuality of the organism–environment relationship, in that neither can be specified without reference to the other. In this view, both organism and environment are structured in ways that must be understood in order to explain perceptual functioning (Garner, 1974; J. J. Gibson, 1979). Rather than having to construct information about their worlds, organisms must extract information from objects and events with which they coexist. In other words, information is neither *in* an object nor *in* the mind of the observer of the object; rather, it is available in the *relationship* between observers and objects. J. J. Gibson (1979) created the concept of *affordance* to capture the essence of this process, referring to the active pickup of information about objects and events that are meaningful. Gibson used the term *meaning* in a nontraditional way in that it is not something that observers bestow on objects. Rather, perception involves the pickup of information about "value-rich ecological objects" (Gibson, 1979, p. 140), with such value or meaning arising from the organism–object mutuality.

The goal of an ecologically oriented view of perceptual development is not only to identify meaningful sources of information that afford action across the life span, but to explain how such meaning arises out of the changing organism–environment mutuality. According to one model of perceptual development proposed by Aslin and Smith (1988), changes in perceptual functioning most likely arise out of the coaction of several concurrent processes: (a) changes in sensory system functioning (called *sensory primitives*), (b) improvements in perception with practice (perceptual learning), and (c) the incorporation of aids to comprehension into perceptual activity (e.g., words and pictures). Aslin and Smith agreed with J. J. Gibson that sensory input is not primary to perception, in that the stimulation of receptor sites is not conceptually equivalent to the activation of perceptual systems. When awake, organisms are constantly in the business of actively exploring and experiencing events and being aware of structure in their environments (J. J. Gibson, 1979, p. 240, called perception a "psychosomatic act"). However, perceptual system activity is clearly influenced by sensory input, and this is important to emphasize when taking a developmental view of perception because the nature of sensory system functioning changes markedly throughout the life span, particularly during infancy. Thus, the concept of sensory primitives is a necessary feature of any theory of perceptual development.

Similarly, Aslin and Smith also agreed with J. J. Gibson in his contention that perception does not need to be mediated through cognition (e.g., mental representations of objects) but rather that perception is direct. In this view, perception is one mode of cognition, an awareness of existing objects, events, places, persons, and so on. However, awareness can also be nonperceptual as in one's memories of objects, events, places, and persons that no longer exist (Reed, 1988). As with sensory primitives, the inclusion of nonperceptual (indirect) awareness, which Aslin and Smith (1988) referred to as "higher-order representation" (p. 439) is also important for theories of perceptual development because changes in activities such as language, memory, and anticipation certainly affect (and are affected by) perceptual functioning.

Extending the ecological perspective to the study of perceptual development, E. J. Gibson (1987) has articulated a framework from within which much of the current literature on infant perception can be viewed. The following are her main propositions: perception (a) is active in that infants seek out information by exploring their worlds, (b) depends on motion in that all meaningful information is time dependent (e.g., changes in the flux of available energy), (c) relies on the infant's ability to perceive constancies in the flow of information (the perception of structural invariance), and (d) is intermodally coordinated throughout development. According to E. J. Gibson's (1991) ecological view of development, one of the driving forces behind perceptual activity is the reduction of uncertainty in that organisms seek out invariance in their seas of informational flux. What develops is not the ability to perceive, but rather the act of perceiving itself (Adolph, Eppler, & Gibson, 1993; E. J. Gibson, 1991). Called *perceptual learning*, this process involves the progressive specification of information in the world through experience. When, then, does perception begin? Most recent reviews of the perceptual literature concentrate on the abilities and capacities of infants within the first postnatal year, including the earliest days after birth (Aslin, 1987; Aslin & Smith, 1988; Gibson, 1987; von Hofsten, 1983). However, there is a growing literature on the importance of experience in affecting perceptual functioning in fetuses, although most of this work involves species other than humans (e.g., Lickliter & Banker, 1994; Smotherman & Robinson, 1987). Suffice it to say that perception begins when sensory system functioning allows for the pickup of information and that such functioning begins prenatally in a large number of mammalian and avian species, including humans (Fifer & Moon, 1995; Gottlieb, 1971).

One important implication of the ecological view for development is that the extraction of information that specifies the world is ever-changing and that our understanding of this change demands attention to the structure of the organism doing the perceiving as well as the structure of the information to be perceived, with changes in either structure resulting in perceptual reorganizations. This kind of dynamic view of perception renders such concepts as biological predisposition, unconditioned stimulus, innate idea, or genetic template valueless because they bypass the actual process of perceptual learning (J. J. Gibson, 1979, p. 253). That is, such terms assume that information is meaningful without the benefit of any prior perceptual functioning. Because such notions are common in the developmental literature (see Johnston, 1987, and Lickliter & Berry, 1990, for discussions), it is a challenge to those more sympathetic to an ecological perspective to offer alternative explanations regarding how and why information becomes meaningful.

By way of meeting this challenge, I focus on a specific finding in the area of infant speech perception: infants' perception of intonation contours. By definition, intonation contours in speech are patterns of pitch (i.e., fundamental frequency or F_0) changes over time. Although present to various degrees in all languages, these patterns are particularly enhanced in adults' speech to infants (infant-directed or ID speech), not only in American English but in languages throughout the world (Fernald et al., 1989; Grieser & Kuhl, 1987; H. Papousek & Papousek, 1991; Shute & Wheldall, 1989). Intonation contours are of primary interest to developmentalists because of the meaning that they potentially afford the infant (Fernald, 1984). For example, exaggerated contours in maternal speech may act to increase arousal, facilitate localization of speakers, maintain attention, and differentially control affective state. At issue here are the conditions under which such meaning becomes available for infant perception. One view holds that infants are predisposed (presumably through an innately endowed sensitivity) to attend and respond differentially to exaggerated intonation contours (Ferland & Mendelson, 1989; Fernald, 1992; Jusczyk & Bertoncini, 1988). Contrary to this position, I maintain that infants are not predisposed to attend selectively to exaggerated intonation contours in speech. Rather, they learn through experience to differentiate and extract intonation contours from the ongoing speech stream, and do so within the infant–caretaker relationship. These perceived structures come to have meaning through their function in the infant–caretaker exchange. To construct this argument, I discuss the effect that ID speech has on infant attention, the context-specific use of contours in mothers' speech to infants, and infant perception of contours. In conclusion, I present a model for how intonation contours become meaningful aspects of speech for infants in the first months after birth.

THE EFFECTS OF ID SPEECH ON INFANT ATTENTION AND AFFECT

It is well established that adults exaggerate several characteristics of their speech to infants. Generally, ID speech is higher pitched, more variable in pitch, contains wider pitch excursions, consists of relatively brief utterances, and is more rhythmic than adult-directed (AD) speech (Fernald & Simon, 1984; Fernald et al., 1989; Grieser & Kuhl, 1988; Jacobson, Boersma, Fields, & Olson, 1983; M. Papousek, Papousek, & Haekel, 1987; Shute & Wheldall, 1989; Stern, Spieker, Barnett, & MacKain, 1983). Fernald (1985) was the first to demonstrate that 4-month-olds preferred ID to AD female speech. Using a conditioned head-turn procedure, she found that infants turned more often in the direction necessary to produce ID speech. Subsequently, several studies have shown infant preferences for female ID speech across the first postnatal year. For example, during a fixed-trial procedure, both 4- to 5-month-olds and 7- to 9-month-olds looked longer at a monitor when female or male ID speakers were broadcast compared with female or male AD speakers (Werker & McLeod, 1989). Testing considerably younger infants, Cooper and Aslin (1990) showed that newborns and 1-month-olds attended to a visual display longer when looking produced female ID speech compared to AD speech. Pegg, Werker, and McLeod (1992) extended this finding to 2-month-olds and found that infants preferred male as well as female ID speech over AD speech.

In all of the studies just mentioned, preference was defined as more attention directed toward some visual display as a function of hearing ID speech. The term *preference*, however, suggests that some event not only differentially sustains attention but is positively valenced as well. In this regard, a few studies have also found that ID speech increases both positive facial affect and arousal in infants. Werker and McLeod (1989) videotaped infants as they watched displays of female and male ID and AD speech. The tapes of the infants were then judged for their interest, interactiveness, and positive facial emotion. Using composite scores,

Werker and McLeod found that infants were rated more positively when viewing female (but not male) ID speech. This result suggests that infant reactivity to ID speech may play an important role in regulating interchanges between infants and caretakers. More recently, Kaplan, Goldstein, Huckeby, and Cooper (1995) showed that after they had habituated 4-month-olds to a visual display (a black-and-white checkerboard pattern), ID speech successfully dishabituated visual attention to the familiarized display whereas AD speech did not. In this paradigm, dishabituation to the checkerboard is conceptualized as evidence for sustained arousal.

Taken together, the experimental findings show that ID speech increases infant attention, positive affect, and arousal throughout the first year after birth. Although ID speech is composed of several features, its most prominent characteristic seems to be expanded intonation contours. The phrase *expanded intonation contour* refers to the fact that the fundamental frequency (pitch) of the adult's voice is generally higher but also more variable, elongated, and continuous when directed toward an infant. Experimental interest in intonation contours in ID speech has arisen out of their potential role in regulating attention, emotion, and language learning during early development (Fernald, 1984, 1992). Fernald (1992) has recently proposed an interesting model for how intonation patterns in speech change functionally across the first year of life. According to this four-stage model, intonation contours (a) are initially biologically relevant signals in that infants are predisposed to differentially respond to them; (b) become better regulators of infant attention, arousal, and affect through experience; (c) evolve into true communicative signals, conveying intention and emotion in others; and (d) eventually act as perceptual attractors to important linguistic units in speech (e.g., object labels). Fundamental to this view is the notion that intonation contours in ID speech are good acoustic candidates (i.e., functional invariants) for communicative meaning. That is, their simplicity, redundancy, and context dependency may enhance their perceptual saliency.

INTONATION CONTOURS AS POTENTIAL COMMUNICATIVE SIGNALS

The literature on speech to infants now contains several descriptively rich and parametrically quantified analyses of adults' contextual use of intonation contours. Stern, Spieker, and MacKain (1982) recorded mothers' speech to their 2-, 4-, and 6-month-old infants and found that the mothers used various contours depending on the nature of their interactions. For example, mothers frequently emitted rising contours when their infants were gazing away from their faces and sinusoidal contours when the infants were gazing at their faces.

Such differential use of contours as a function of caregiving context has been replicated and expanded in several studies by Mechtild Papousek and her colleagues (M. Papousek & Papousek, 1989; M. Papousek et al., 1987; M. Papousek, Papousek, & Symmes, 1991). Generally these authors have found that caretakers (primarily mothers) modulate the prosodic form of their utterances to both accommodate and regulate young infants' attention and arousal. These studies have established the contour-in-context phenomenon cross-culturally (e.g., American, German, Mandarin Chinese; H. Papousek & Papousek, 1991), complementing the previously discussed work on cross-cultural use of ID speech (e.g., Fernald et al., 1989).

Although it is interesting that intonation contours appear to be used selectively in caretakers' speech to infants, it is not clear from these descriptive studies whether intonation contours actually impart meaning. In other words, does a particular contour type convey intention to the listener? To address this issue, Fernald (1989) recorded adults speaking to other adults and also to infants in five different interactional contexts: comfort, approval, prohibition, attention, and play. Although the utterances that were chosen to reflect these various intentional categories differed on several dimensions (average pitch, duration, numbers of syllables), they also differed in their general prosodic "shape." For example, utterances from the approval category were generally "falling" in that they went from high to low pitch values, whereas attention-bid utterances showed a general rise–fall pattern. Selected exemplars from each category were low-pass filtered so as to remove their lexical content. Thus, the adult listeners could not use word information to guide them in their categorization of utterances. Fernald then assessed the accuracy with which adults could classify the intonation contours according to communicative intent. She found that although adults were fairly accurate in their general classification performance, it was easier for them to correctly categorize the ID compared to AD contours.

Clearly, these studies establish that intonation contours are commonly available in adults' speech to infants and that they potentially afford meaning for the infant. Whether infants perceive intonation contours as communicative signals, however, remains unclear. To establish that intonation contours are meaningful to infants, it is necessary to examine whether and to what extent infants respond to them differentially.

INFANTS' PERCEPTION OF INTONATION CONTOURS

An important study by Fernald and Kuhl (1987) investigated which of three prosodic features were most influential in controlling infants' attention to ID speech: intonation contour, amplitude, or temporal features. Using an operant head-turning procedure, they tested 4-month-olds with the following acoustic contrasts: (a) sine wave analogs of ID versus AD speech, (b) tones of constant frequency that followed the amplitude envelopes of ID versus AD speech, and (c) tones of constant frequency and amplitude that followed the temporal patterning of ID versus AD speech. The only preference found was for the sine wave analogs of ID speech. This suggests that intonation contours occurring in natural speech to infants have greater perceptual salience than amplitude or temporal features. Fernald and Kuhl (1987) suggested that infants are predisposed to attend to exaggerated contours, possibly because of their greater physiological arousal of the auditory system (see Juscyzk & Bertoncini, 1988, for a similar argument). This view is consistent with Haith's (1981) explanation of patterns of visual exploration in young infants. Haith argued that infants scan areas of high visual contrast and medium spatial frequency because such input maximizes cortical firing in the visual system. If 4-month-old infants are biologically predisposed to differentially attend to exaggerated speech contours (possibly because such sounds are inherently more arousing and maximize cortical firing in the auditory system), it is typically assumed that younger infants would respond in a similar fashion. In other words, explanations that involve concepts such as "predispositions" are often generalized backwards in developmental time (i.e., to younger ages as well).

Cooper and Aslin (1994) explored the development of infants' perception of intonational contours in a series of experiments with 1-month-olds. The purpose of the first experiment was to examine whether fundamental frequency characteristics were sufficient to account for 1-month-olds' preferences for ID speech. ID and AD recordings of a female speaker were low-pass filtered at 400 Hz in order to remove lexical content but preserve most of the fundamental frequency contours (along with lower harmonic, amplitude, and durational information). Although these filtered recordings were difficult to comprehend linguistically (i.e., adults could correctly identify only 65% and 63% of the ID and AD utterances, respectively), they clearly maintained a speechlike quality and were easily classified according to their intended receivers (i.e., adults correctly classified 93% of all of the utterances as being either ID or AD).

Infants were tested using a preference procedure in which their attention to a visual display resulted in their hearing one of the filtered recordings. Trials were infant controlled in that trial length was determined by the onset and offset of each infant's fixation of the visual display. The recordings alternated across trials with order of presentation counterbalanced across infants (see Cooper, 1993, for a more detailed discussion of this procedure). For this and all subsequent analyses reported in this chapter, we conducted mixed analyses of variance (ANOVAs) on average looking times to test for between-subject effects (order of presentation), within-subject effects (speech type), and their interaction. In this first experiment, no significant effects were found as a function of hearing ID-filtered ($M = 30.4$ s) and AD-filtered ($M = 31.0$ s) speech. This finding is fairly representative of individual performance, because only 5 of the 12 infants showed longer average looking times to the ID-filtered speech ($p <$ .39, binomial).

This lack of preference for the low-frequency prosodic features of ID speech stands in contrast to Fernald and Kuhl's (1987) finding that 4-month-old infants preferred simulated intonation contours of ID speech over those of AD speech. This difference could possibly stem from the inability of younger infants to discriminate speech types on the basis of lower frequency information alone. Several studies suggest that this was not the case. Spence and DeCasper (1987) found that newborns preferred an unfiltered female voice to a low-pass filtered version, which implies that the infants could discriminate these recordings. However, because these authors used a filter cutoff frequency of 1000 Hz (considerably higher than the 400 Hz cutoff in the Cooper and Aslin, 1994, study), it is possible that they captured the necessary frequencies required for discrimination. In a study more comparable to the one by Cooper and Aslin (1994), Mehler et al. (1988) found that newborns were able to discriminate native from nonnative speech recordings, even when they were low-pass filtered at 400 Hz. Similarly, Fifer and Moon (1995) tested newborns with a recording of the maternal voice that was either unfiltered or low-pass filtered at 500 Hz and found that newborns preferred the low-pass version. Moreover, a study on prenatal auditory functioning in humans found that healthy late-term fetuses could discriminate a female from a male voice when both were reciting the same sentence (Lecanuet, Granier-Deferre, Jacquet, Capponi, & Ledru, 1993). Because the voice recordings were transmitted to the fetus through the maternal abdomen, tissue, and fluid, the fetuses most likely relied on the lower (less attenuated) frequencies for discrimination.

Although it appears from the literature that younger infants should be able to discriminate low-pass filtered speech recordings, we (Cooper and Aslin, 1994, Experiment 2) decided to assess discrimination directly in a second experiment. Using a slightly different procedure, we presented 1-month-olds with the same filtered recording (either ID or AD) on each trial until their looking times habituated (with two groups of infants receiving reversed orders). After habituation, half of the infants in each group heard a novel filtered recording, whereas the other half heard the familiar recording for an additional two trials and then heard the novel recording. These extra trials were designed to control for spontaneous recovery of looking during habituation (see Bertenthal, Haith, & Campos, 1983). In addition to order, this analysis also included extra trials as an additional between-subjects factor. Results of the ANOVA showed that regardless of order of presentation or extra trials, infants increased their looking on the two test trials that produced the novel recording ($M = 20.4$ s) compared to the two trials preceding the change in speech type independent of whether they were "extra" trials or not ($M = 13.9$ s), indicating that they discriminated ID-filtered from AD-filtered speech.

In most habituation procedures, the dependent measure of primary interest is response recovery on novel test trials as an indication of discrimination. In addition to discrimination, however, other aspects of performance in such procedures have been interpreted as indicators of behavioral preference. For example, in their habituation study, Pegg et al. (1992) found that 7-week-olds looked significantly longer across the first three trials of the procedure when looking produced ID compared to AD speech. We also analyzed average looking times across the first three trials of the habituation phase but found no significant difference (t test) as a function of ID-filtered ($M = 38.6$ s) or AD-filtered ($M = 33.4$ s) speech. Because the length of the habituation phase was infant controlled, it is possible that infants would take longer to habituate to a more interesting (compared to less interesting) event. However, there was no significant difference in average time to habituation as a function of speech type.

The lack of 1-month-olds' preference for the lower frequency features of ID speech was not due to their inability to discriminate it from AD speech. Moreover, additional measures of preference showed no differential responding to the two kinds of filtered speech. Although exaggerations in the fundamental frequency characteristics of speech are certainly important to understanding young infants' interest in ID speech (Cooper & Aslin, 1990), they are apparently not sufficient to account for this preference. Other studies have shown that young infants are more responsive to complex as opposed to simple (e.g., pure tones) auditory stimuli (Clarkson & Berg, 1979; Hutt, Hutt, Lenard, Bernuth, & Muntjewerff, 1968; Trehub & Curran, 1979; Turkewitz, Birch, & Cooper, 1972). Because ID speech not only contains exaggerated intonation features but a richer harmonic structure as well, it may be that the preference for ID speech in younger infants is a function of both. We (Cooper & Aslin, 1994, Experiment 4) tested this possibility in a subsequent experiment by presenting 1-month-olds with two ID speech recordings that were similar in their lower frequency, amplitude, and durational characteristics but different in spectral complexity. Using the preference procedure discussed earlier, we tested 1-month-olds with unfiltered and filtered ID speech recordings. Because the filtered ID speech recording sounded quieter than the unfiltered ID speech when played at the same intensity level, we constructed two pairs of recordings for this experiment. In one pair, the unfiltered recording was judged by adults to be louder, and in the second pair the filtered speech was judged by adults to be as loud or louder. Within each order condition, half of the infants heard one of these two tapes. In addition to order, this analysis also included the tape version as a between-subjects factor. The results of the ANOVA showed that independent of order and perceived loudness, the infants looked longer when listening to unfiltered ID ($M = 32.8$ s) compared to filtered ID ($M = 23.1$ s) speech.

When listening to two speech recordings that were similar in lower frequency, amplitude, and durational information but different in spectral complexity, 1-month-olds preferred the latter. If intonation contours have perceptual precedence over other characteristics, then the infants should have shown no preference. In a related study, Colombo (1985) measured looking times of 2- and 4-month-olds when looking produced tone sequences of different rates and spectral complexities. Colombo found that looking times increased with the number of harmonics and were generally unaffected by rate. However, although this result can be interpreted as a preference for greater spectral complexity, the number of harmonics in the tone sequences was confounded with highest absolute frequency. Thus, the infants may have simply preferred the tones with the highest frequencies. This interpretation can also explain the results of our last experiment, in that 1-month-olds preferred natural ID to low-pass filtered ID speech.

In contrast, preference for highest absolute frequency cannot explain the results obtained by Colombo and Horowitz (1986). In this study, 4-month-olds showed no preference for a tone that was modulated to simulate the typical fundamental frequency range of ID speech over either a less modulated tone or a monotone. It is important to note that the most modulated tone in the Colombo and Horowitz study was not as representative of naturally occurring intonation contours as those used by Fernald and Kuhl (1987), even though it contained a frequency sweep typical of ID speech. The sine wave analogs used by Fernald and Kuhl also contained naturally occurring temporal patterns and frequency excursions, possibly enhancing their salience because of their closer fit with natural ID speech. To test this possibility, our next experiment (Cooper & Aslin, 1994, Experiment 3) was conducted to see whether 1-month-olds would prefer the isolated intonation contours of ID speech over those of AD speech.

Fernald and Kuhl (1987) generated the intonation contours by analyzing the fundamental frequency characteristics of natural ID and AD speech recordings and then using these values to generate ID and AD sine-wave analogs. We used a similar method to extract the intonation contours from our original ID and AD speech recordings that we had used previously in a study showing that one-month-olds and newborns prefer ID speech (see Cooper & Aslin, 1990). As in our other preference experiments, infants could listen to both ID and AD contours (on alternate trials) by looking at a visual display. As before, the order of presentation of these contours was counterbalanced across infants. The results of the ANOVA showed a significant interaction between order of presentation and type of contour, with those infants who heard the ID contours first showing longer average looking times on ID trials than infants who heard the AD contours first. In other words, preference for the ID contours was found only for those infants who heard these contours on the first trial. This interaction appeared to be carried by long looking times on the first trial of the session depending on which contour was heard (for ID, $M = 63.5$ s; for AD, $M = 25.7$ s). To evaluate the effect of the first trial on these results, we conducted a subsequent analysis on mean looking times minus the first trials. This second ANOVA showed no significant main effects or interactions. Thus, although there appeared to be no systematic preferences for either contour type in this experiment, the infants did look considerably longer on first trials when looking produced the ID contours, suggesting that they had an initial arousing affect. This effect, however, was not strong enough to sustain differential attention across the rest of the trials.

Collectively, these experiments from our laboratory have shown that ID speech differentially maintains the attention of young infants but that one of the most prominent features of ID speech, the intonation contour, is not as perceptually salient as it appears to be for older infants. However, the last experiment discussed above suggests that ID contours are initially more arousing. Because the preference procedure that we used is not designed to assess arousal, a better behavioral index is needed. Such a study was recently conducted by Kaplan, Goldstein, Huckeby, Owren, and Cooper (1995). In this study, 4-month-olds were tested in a habituation–dishabituation paradigm that is specifically designed to look at the ability of a novel stimulus event to produce and sustain arousal (termed *Thompson–Spencer dishabituation*). Generally, infants were given 12 consecutive trials of a checkerboard display. On the first 8 trials, there was no accompanying soundtrack. On Trial 9, however, a soundtrack was played concomitant with the display. Of primary interest was the amount of attention to the checkerboard on Trial 10, when the checkerboard was again projected silently. Using different sets of ID and AD recordings in the first two experiments, Kaplan et al. found that infants looked longer on Trial 10 if they heard natural ID speech (but not AD speech) on Trial 9. In other words, the presentation of ID speech on Trial 9 appeared to increase the infants' arousal, enhancing their tendency to look at the display on Trial 10. However, no such dishabituation was found in a third experiment when infants heard synthetic ID or AD contours on Trial 9. In a final experiment, infants were tested with four additional synthetic versions of ID and AD speech: (a) F_0 only that contained no harmonics, (b) $F_0 + 1$ harmonic, (c) $F_0 +$ five harmonics, and (d) harmonics only that lacked F_0. The results showed that only the recording with $F_0 + 5$ harmonics resulted in significant increases in looking on Trial 10. Moreover, the harmonics only recording resulted in a significant decrease in looking on Trial 10, suggesting that the lack of F_0 made this stimulus particularly uninteresting.

Taken together, these studies demonstrate that the properties or features of ID speech that govern infants' attention do not seem to be constant in magnitude or kind across the first months of postnatal life. Whereas older infants respond differentially to the pitch characteristics (i.e., absolute pitch, pitch range, and pitch excursion) of ID speech, younger infants are less likely to respond to these features in isolation. This is problematic for the view that older infants are biologically predisposed to attend differentially to the intonation contours found in ID speech if one assumes that biological predispositions should operate similarly at earlier points in developmental time. An alternative hypothesis is that infants come to perceive intonation contours as meaningful through their perceptual learning about such events in the speech stream. This ecological view is expanded in the last section of this chapter.

CONTEXTUAL EFFECTS ON INFANTS' SPEECH PREFERENCES

As discussed at the beginning of this chapter, the Gibsons's ecological perspective strongly emphasizes the integral relationship between organisms and the environments in which they live. To put it more forcefully, this view posits that it is impossible to conduct any analysis of one without reference to the other, because the structure of each has been forged over both evolutionary and ontogenic time. According to the ecological stance, it is important that this organism–environment mutuality be integrated into the way in which researchers design their studies of perceptual development. Too often, the predominant research emphasis is on the organism doing the perceiving and not on the information to be perceived (Johnston, 1985). The literature on infant preference for ID speech exemplifies this bias in that few studies have framed the phenomenon within the context in which speech preferences develop, namely the infant–caretaker (particularly mother) interaction.

Notably, Glenn and Cunningham (1983) found that both nonhandi-capped and handicapped (Down's syndrome) 9-month-olds would ma-nipulate a device in such a way as to produce a recording of their own mother's ID speech more frequently than her AD speech. No other stud-ies of infant preference for ID speech have used the maternal voice. This may be due in part to the early discontinuation of the term *motherese* when it was found that adults with or without parental status, across many cul-tures and of both genders, exaggerated their speech to infants. Nonethe-less, it is important at some point to study the development of infants' at-tention to the speech of their own caretakers, because it is primarily in this context that early perceptual, social, and cognitive development takes place. We recently conducted a series of experiments on infant preference for motherese (Cooper, Abraham, Berman, & Staska, 1996).

Using the preference procedure discussed earlier, 1-month-old infants were tested with natural recordings of their own mothers speaking to their infants and also to an adult interviewer (Cooper et al., 1996, Experiment 1). We reasoned that because infants at this age prefer their mother's voice (DeCasper & Fifer, 1980; Fifer & Moon, 1995; Mehler et al., 1978) and also prefer female ID speech (Cooper & Aslin, 1990; Pegg et al., 1992), mater-nal ID speech would be particularly attractive to young infants. Surpris-ingly, we found no significant preference for maternal ID ($M = 30.6$ s) over AD ($M = 36.3$ s) speech at this age. Because we had previously found a tendency for infants to look longer on the first trial for some types of speech sounds over others, we also analyzed the average looking times on the first trial in this experiment. There was a significant difference in av-erage looking times on the first trial, with infants looking longer when hearing maternal AD ($M = 69.6$ s) compared to maternal ID ($M = 31.5$ s) speech. We then reanalyzed the mean looking times apart from the first trial to determine whether longer initial looks to AD speech were mask-ing an ID speech preference. The results of this second ANOVA were sim-ilar to the first in that no significant effects were found.

Contrary to our expectations, 1-month-olds did not prefer maternal ID to maternal AD speech. This is surprising given that other studies with same-aged infants demonstrated a preference for unfamiliar female ID speech (Cooper & Aslin, 1990; Pegg et al., 1992). To verify that our ID and AD speech recordings differed from each other in their typical character-istics, we conducted acoustic analyses on their average F_0, minimum and maximum F_0, F_0 range, and utterance duration. Statistical tests revealed that all of these measures were significantly exaggerated in the maternal ID speech. Thus, the 1-month-olds' lack of preference for motherese seems to be related to the presence of the maternal voice per se. To test this fur-ther, we (Cooper et al., 1996, Experiment 2) conducted a second experi-ment with an additional group of 1-month-olds who were not related to the female voices on the tapes. In this experiment, each infant was tested with one of the tapes from the previous experiment, so that he or she heard an unfamiliar female ID and AD speech. The results of the ANOVA from this experiment revealed a significant effect of speech type, with longer average looking times for ID ($M = 34.3$ s) over AD ($M = 24.8$ s) speech.

One-month-olds prefer ID over AD speech, provided that the speaker is not their own mother. When listening to their own mother's voice, in-fants at this age showed no preference. Because Glenn and Cunningham (1983) found a preference for maternal ID speech in 9-month-olds, in-fants' interest in the nature of their mothers' speech must change over the first postnatal year, although there is little available evidence to suggest when this change takes place. In a longitudinal study, Stern, Spieker, Bar-nett, and MacKain (1983) recorded different prosodic and linguistic as-pects of maternal speech to infants during the newborn period, and at 4, 12, and 24 months of age. Their results showed that mothers exaggerated the pitch characteristics of their ID speech most when the infants were ap-proximately 4 months old. These authors hypothesized that this contex-tual change occurs because of the face-to-face play situation that is emerg-ing at this time; the mother's motivation toward her infant changes from one of maintaining calm and quietness to eliciting and maintaining in-terest and happiness. It is possible that infants learn to prefer maternal ID speech in this context.

To test the possibility that preference for maternal ID speech devel-ops within the first months after birth, we (Cooper et al., 1996, Experiment 3) conducted a third experiment using natural maternal ID and AD recordings with 4-month-old infants. As in our study with 1-month-olds, these infants could listen to recordings of maternal ID and AD speech on alternating trials, with the order of initial presentation counterbalanced across infants. The results of the ANOVA showed a significant preference for maternal ID ($M = 23.4$ s) over maternal AD ($M = 19.9$ s) speech. Thus, although infants in previous investigations have shown preferences for ID speech, they have done so under conditions in which they were unfamiliar with the speaker. When placed in a more ecologically valid context (e.g., the mother–infant interaction), differential attention to maternal ID speech seems to emerge as the experiential history and context of the infant changes.

A MODEL FOR THE DEVELOPMENT OF MEANING IN INTONATION CONTOURS

The goal of this chapter was to reveal how the development of infants' perception of intonation contours, particularly in the context of maternal speech, follows an interesting and somewhat surprising path. Although there is evidence that even from the first days after birth, infants attend more to speech when its prosodic features are highly exaggerated (Cooper & Aslin, 1990; Pegg et al., 1992), younger infants are different from infants around 4 months of age in that they do not prefer isolated intonation contours extracted from ID speech. Given what is known about auditory functioning in the young infant, this lack of preference does not seem to be the result of an inability to resolve such signals. In this sense, younger infants' lack of preference for intonation contours is not the result of an immature "sensory primitive" (e.g., inability to discriminate pitch changes). Rather, it is possible that the perceptual representation of intonational contours emerges within the first months after birth (Aslin & Smith, 1988). *Perceptual representation* refers to neural activity that occurs in the process of information pickup and is accessible in real time. In other words, *representation* does not refer to some mental model or schema that exists independently of the perceptual process that gives rise to it. Moreover, the nature of how such representations form over the first months after birth takes place within the context of the infant–caretaker relationship. As the experiments presented above demonstrate, infants' attentiveness to ID speech must be qualified by the relationship between the infant and the speaker. By 1 month of age, most infants have had a considerable amount of experience with the maternal voice in different contexts. Presumably, late-term fetuses experience the maternal voice in utero (Querleu, Renard, Boutteville, & Crepin, 1989; Richards, Frentzen, Gerhardt, McCann, & Abrams, 1992). Moreover, several studies have shown that prenatal experience with specific auditory events presented by the mother (e.g., her reading a story or singing a melody out loud) can affect postnatal perception in newborns (DeCasper & Spence, 1986; Panneton, 1985). Therefore, by the time most full-term infants are born, they have experienced the maternal voice, particularly as she speaks to others around her (i.e., AD speech).

After birth, infants continue to experience the maternal voice, with the addition of the new infant–mother context. Generally, mothers engage in typical ID speech as they interact with their young infants (Fernald & Simon, 1984; Stern et al., 1983). This multicontextual experience with the features of mothers' speech may account for our finding that 1-month-olds do not prefer maternal ID over AD speech. That is, the infant's recognition of mother occurs in either context and overrides any differential responding to ID speech. Thus, when recognition of the speaker is removed (i.e., the speaker is an unfamiliar female), the ID speech preference emerges. With experience, infants apparently integrate their recognition of the maternal voice into the infant–mother context and come to prefer her voice when she is speaking to them.

How do intonation contours come to be meaningful for infants? Fernald's (1992) proposal is helpful in answering this question, in that her model implicitly assumes that perception of contours becomes progressively differentiated across the first months after birth. Eventually, infants come to extract important invariant properties from the occurrence of intonation contours in specific communicative contexts (e.g., rising contours signify attention-eliciting conditions whereas rising–falling contours signify attention-holding conditions). It is at this point that intonation contours can be considered communicative signals, in that they relay information about intent to the infant. Thus, Fernald's (1992) model is generally compatible with an ecological perspective with the exception of its proposal for initial biological predispositions to differentially attend to intonation contours. Given that there is contradictory evidence regarding this last claim (Cooper & Aslin, 1994; Kaplan et al., 1995), a reformulation of this model seems warranted.

An alternative model developed to account for infants' perception of the emotional expressions of others may be instructive here. One study (Klinnert, Campos, Sorce, Emde, & Svejda, 1983) proposed a four-stage developmental sequence during which infants come to use facial expressions of others (particularly caretakers) to guide their behavior in an adaptive manner. The first three stages of this model are discussed in relation to their relevance for understanding developmental changes in auditory perception. In the first stage, newborns and young infants (up to approximately 2 months of age) are unable to use facial information in a meaningful way, largely because of the deficient nature of their visual experiences. Of course, infants at this age can see, but because of visual immaturities (Aslin & Smith, 1988) and the apparent control of visual activity by contrast sensitivity and spatial frequency characteristics (Banks & Salapatek, 1981; Haith, Bergman, & Moore, 1977; Kleiner, 1987), it is doubtful that they perceive facial expressions. Analogously, the argument here is that a similar initial stage exists for infants' auditory perception. Although newborns and young infants prefer ID speech (at least when spoken by unfamiliar females and males), they do so because such speech is high in stimulus contrast relative to the ambient array in which it occurs. Exaggerated intonation contours certainly add to this contrast but not necessarily in a dominant way. ID speech is perceptually bundled in that it also contains higher amplitude, a richer harmonic structure, and greater temporal coherence than AD speech. However, intonation contours as patterns have no meaning for infants at this age.

In the second stage of Klinnert et al.'s (1983) model (from approximately 2 to 5 months of age), infants begin to discriminate features of faces that are correlated with specific emotion expressions. Also during this period, infants begin to perceive visual patterns independently of their stimulus contrast features. For example, Dannemiller and Stephens (1988) showed that 4-month-olds (but not 1-month-olds) preferred a black-on-white facial display over its phase reversed counterpart, presumably because the former appeared more "facelike." However, according to Klinnert et al., infants at this stage still do not perceive affective meaning in the visual patterns that they attend to. A similar process seems to take place in infants' perception of intonation contours. That is, during this stage, infants begin to discriminate the typical intonation contours of ID speech from other types of speech, even when the contours are presented in a nonspeech context (e.g., Fernald & Kuhl, 1987). It is important to note, however, that in two other studies also studying 4-month-olds, no differential responding to ID speechlike contours were found (Colombo & Horowitz, 1986; Kaplan et al., 1995). It is possible that infants are just beginning to perceptually differentiate intonation contours at about 4 months of age.

In the third stage of Klinnert et al.'s model (from approximately 5 to 8 months of age), infants begin to pick up meaningful information from affective expressions. This emerging perceptual representation is evidenced by infants' abilities to match the concomitant visual and vocal components of emotional expressions, to detect invariant information across similar expressions when they are portrayed by different individuals, and to produce selective emotional responses to certain expressions in others (Walker-Andrews, 1984). Similar indices of infants' perception of meaning in intonation contours have been found during this stage. In a study by Fernald (1993), 5-month-olds were rated as significantly more positive in their facial affect when listening to ID approval utterances than ID prohibition utterances (infants were also watching a video of a female face). As stated previously, Werker and McLeod (1989) also found increased positive affect in 5- and 8-month-old infants when they were viewing a female ID speech display (i.e., face + voice). Four-month-olds have also shown a preference for recordings of approval over disapproving ID utterances (M. Papousek, Bornstein, Nuzzo, Papousek, & Symmes, 1990). Recently, Spence and Moore

(1994) tested 6-month-olds with low-pass filtered ID utterances produced in different interactional contexts (i.e., approving or comforting). In a fixed-trial habituation procedure, infants heard exemplars from one of these categories every time the infant fixated a geometric figure in the visual display. During the test period, infants heard either a novel exemplar from a novel category or a novel exemplar from the familiar category. Spence and Moore found that infants looked significantly longer on test trials that presented the novel category. A similar finding was reported by Ferland and Mendelson (1989). In this study, 10-month-olds responded categorically to changes in the contours of synthetic tones, while ignoring changes in fundamental frequency and harmonic structure.

Thus, across several studies, older infants show increasing tendencies to respond selectively to intonation contours, be it through their categorization of contours, their facial reactions to contours, or in their willingness to pay attention to some contours over others. It is interesting that most of these studies have involved the use of a display that included both visual and auditory components. Although not all of the studies mentioned have used faces (e.g., Spence & Moore, 1994), it may be that the human face is an important facet of infants' perceptual learning about contours as meaningful units of speech. That is, the movement in the face that co-occurs with movement in the voice may help to disambiguate the function that certain contours convey to the infant (Sullivan & Horowitz, 1983; Walker-Andrews, 1984). Of interest here would be studies on infants who are limited in their abilities to pick up intermodal information during caretaking interactions, such as blind or deaf infants. Such infants may come to rely on (i.e., be perceptually sensitive to) unimodal information (e.g., the pitch contour alone) sooner than infants who are responsive to multimodal information. On the other hand, deaf and blind infants may take longer to extract meaning from faces and voices compared to their hearing and seeing counterparts.

The ability of infants to process contour information while ignoring changes in more local features has also been investigated in studies of music perception by Trehub and her colleagues (see Trehub, 1987, and Trehub & Trainor, 1990, for general discussions). In several studies with infants around 7 months old, Trehub has found that infants tend to perceive the global, relational properties of melodies (i.e., the melodic contours) rather than their specific note frequencies or internote intervals. Thus, during the middle of their first postnatal year, infants' perceptual representations of both speech and some nonspeech events often center on directional changes in pitch patterns (i.e., contours).

CONCLUSION

In summary, the general position that has been advanced in this chapter is that infants' perception of intonation contours as meaningful aspects of speech emerges during the first year after birth, through the progressive differentiation–specification of intonation contours in the ID speech context. I have argued that infants (a) initially attend more to speech that is highly contrastive in its acoustic properties (e.g., louder, more rhythmic, and exaggerated in its pitch patterning), that leads them to (b) differentiate and extract intonation contours as perceptual invariants from the speech stream, and (c) eventually learn that such patterns have meaning in that they are used in specific contexts by caretakers with specific intentions. In this way, intonation contours come to afford action for infants. For example, certain contours (rising) may increase the probability that infants stop what they are currently doing and focus attention elsewhere, whereas others (rising, falling) may increase the likelihood that they continue to focus their attention on some ongoing event. Of course, the progressive perceptual differentiation for intonation contours that I have just summarized could be attributed to a maturational mechanism that simply endows infants with better perceptual skills as they age. To complete the argument for perceptual learning, we must conduct studies with infants who vary in such things as their overall exposure to intonation contours in caretakers' speech as well as the dependability or reliability of such contours depending on their contextual usage. According to the model advanced in this chapter, we would expect a positive relationship between the amount and context boundedness of intonation contours in caretakers' speech and infants' abilities to perceive the affordances of such contours, ruling out maturation as a main mechanism for perceptual improvement.

Although we have little direct evidence for the action-based perception of intonation contours in speech, we do know that infants perceive affordances during interactions. For example, Murray and Trevarthen (1987) found that young infants showed increased distress and active attempts to terminate exchanges with their caretakers when the contingency of the exchange was disrupted through video manipulation. Similarly, Cohn and Tronick (1983) found that young infants actively averted their gazes when their mothers became unresponsive during face-to-face interactions. Thus, even young infants directly perceive the invariant structure that uniquely specifies dyadic exchange (e.g., temporal synchrony). Likewise, infants' perceptual activity becomes guided through the invariant structure of intonation contours in the speech of caretakers.

The ecological view of development is particularly well-adapted as a framework for this model because this perspective emphasizes progressive changes in infants' abilities to differentiate information in their worlds. Specifically, infants are better able to extract invariant information about events over time as they actively orient their sensory systems toward sources of stimulation. Rather than saying that infants are predisposed to attend to intonation contours in speech (functionally locating the cause in the infant), the ecological view posits that the cause for perceptual activity lies in the organism–environment fit. This reorientation encourages a search for explanations in the changing dynamic between the sensory capabilities of infants and the context in which development is taking place (e.g., the mother–infant interaction).

REFERENCES

Adolph, K. E., Eppler, M. A., & Gibson, E. J. (1993). Development of perception of affordances. In C. Rovee-Collier & L. P. Lipsitt (Eds.), *Advances in infancy research* (Vol. 8, pp. 51–98). Norwood, NJ: Ablex.

Aslin, R. N. (1987). Visual and auditory development in infancy. In J. D. Osofsky (Ed.), *Handbook of infant development* (2nd ed., pp. 5–97). New York: Wiley.

Aslin, R. N., & Smith, L. B. (1988). Perceptual development. *Annual Review of Psychology, 39,* 435–473.

Banks, M. S., & Salapatek, P. (1981). Infant pattern vision: A new approach based on the contrast sensitivity function. *Journal of Experimental Child Psychology, 31,* 1–45.

Bertenthal, B. I., Haith, M. M., & Campos, J. J. (1983). The partial-lag design: A method for controlling spontaneous regression in the infant-control habituation paradigm. *Infant Behavior and Development, 6,* 331–338.

Clarkson, M. G., & Berg, W. K. (1979). Cardiac deceleration in neonates is influenced by temporal pattern and spectral complexity of auditory stimuli. *Psychophysiology, 7,* 122–135.

Cohn, J. F., & Tronick, E. Z. (1983). Three-month-old infants' reactions to simulated maternal depression. *Child Development, 54,* 185–193.

Colombo, J. (1985). Spectral complexity and infant attention. *Journal of Genetic Psychology, 146,* 519–526.

Colombo, J., & Horowitz, F. D. (1986). Infants' attentional responses to frequency modulated sweeps. *Child Development, 57,* 287–291.

Cooper, R. P. (1993). The effect of prosody on young infants' speech perception. In C. Rovee-Collier & L. P. Lipsitt (Eds.), *Advances in infancy research* (Vol. 8, pp. 137–167). Norwood, NJ: Ablex.

Cooper, R. P., Abraham, J., Berman, S., & Staska, M. (1996). *The development of infant preference for motherese.* Manuscript submitted for publication.

Cooper, R. P., & Aslin, R. N. (1990). Preference for infant-directed speech in the first month after birth. *Child Development, 61,* 1584–1595.

Cooper, R. P., & Aslin, R. N. (1994). Developmental differences in infant attention to the spectral properties of infant-directed speech. *Child Development, 65,* 1663–1677.

Dannemiller, J. L., & Stephens, B. R. (1988). A critical test of infant pattern preference models. *Child Development, 59,* 210–216.

DeCasper, A. J., & Fifer, W. P. (1980). Of human bonding: Newborns prefer their mothers' voices. *Science, 208,* 1174–1176.

DeCasper, A. J., & Spence, M. J. (1986). Newborns prefer a familiar story over an unfamiliar one. *Infant Behavior and Development, 9,* 133–150.

Ferland, M. B., & Mendelson, M. J. (1989). Infants' categorization of melodic contour. *Infant Behavior and Development, 12,* 341–355.

Fernald, A. (1984). The perceptual and affective salience of mothers' speech to infants. In L. Feagans, C. Garvey, & R. Golinkoff (Eds.), *The origins and growth of communication* (pp. 5–29). Norwood, NJ: Ablex.

Fernald, A. (1985). Four-month-old infants prefer to listen to motherese. *Infant Behavior and Development, 8,* 181–195.

Fernald, A. (1989). Intonation and communicative intent in mothers' speech to infants: Is the melody the message? *Child Development, 60,* 1497–1510.

Fernald, A. (1992). Human maternal vocalizations to infants as biologically relevant signals: An evolutionary perspective. In J. H. Barkow, L. Cosmides, & J. Tooby (Eds.), *The adapted mind: Evolutionary psychology and the generation of culture* (pp. 391–428). New York: Oxford University Press.

Fernald, A. (1993). Approval and disapproval: Infant responsiveness to vocal affect in familiar and unfamiliar languages. *Child Development, 64,* 657–674.

Fernald, A., & Kuhl, P. (1987). Acoustic determinants of infant perception for motherese speech. *Infant Behavior and Development, 10,* 279–293.

Fernald, A., & Simon, T. (1984). Expanded intonation contours in mothers' speech to newborns. *Developmental Psychology, 20,* 104–113.

Fernald, A., Taeshcher, T., Dunn, J., Papousek, M., de Boysson-Bardies, B., & Fukui, I. (1989). A cross-language study of prosodic modifications in mothers' and fathers' speech to preverbal infants. *Journal of Child Language, 16,* 477–501.

Fifer, W. P., & Moon, C. (1995). The effects of fetal experience with sound. In J. P. Lecanuet, N. A. Krasnegor, W. P. Fifer, & W. P. Smotherman (Eds.), *Fetal behavior: A psychobiological perspective* (pp. 351–366). Hillsdale, NJ: Erlbaum.

Garner, W. R. (1974). *The processing of information and structure.* Hillsdale, NJ: Erlbaum.

Gibson, E. J. (1987). Introductory essay: What does infant perception tell us about theories of perception? *Journal of Experimental Psychology: Human Perception and Performance, 13,* 515–523.

Gibson, E. J. (1991). *An odyssey in learning and perception.* Cambridge, MA: MIT Press.

Gibson, J. J. (1966). *The senses considered as perceptual systems.* Boston: Houghton-Mifflin.

Gibson, J. J. (1979). *The ecological approach to visual perception.* Hillsdale, NJ: Erlbaum.

Glenn, S. M., & Cunningham, C. C. (1983). What do babies listen to most? A developmental study of auditory preferences in nonhandicapped infants and infants with Down's syndrome. *Developmental Psychology, 19,* 332–337.

Gottlieb, G. (1971). *Development of species identification in birds.* Chicago: University of Chicago Press.

Grieser, D. L., & Kuhl, P. K. (1988). Maternal speech to infants in a tonal language: Support for universal prosodic features in motherese. *Developmental Psychology, 24,* 14–20.

Haith, M. M. (1981). *Rules that babies look by.* Hillsdale, NJ: Erlbaum.

Haith, M. M., Bregman, T., & Moore, M. J. (1977). Eye contact and face scanning in early infancy. *Science, 198,* 853–855.

Hutt, S. J., Hutt, C., Lenard, H. G., von Bernuth, H., & Muntjewerff, W. J. (1968). Auditory responsivity in the human neonate. *Nature, 218,* 888–890.

Jacobson, J. L., Boersma, D. C., Fields, R. B., & Olson, K. L. (1983). Paralinguistic features of adult speech to infants and small children. *Child Development, 54,* 436–442.

Johnston, T. D. (1985). Environmental constraints and the natural context of behavior: Grounds for an ecological approach to the study of infant perception. In G. Gottlieb & N. A. Krasnegor (Eds.), *Measurement of audition and vision in the first year of postnatal life* (pp. 91–108). Norwood, NJ: Ablex.

Johnston, T. D. (1987). The persistence of dichotomies in the study of behavioral development. *Developmental Review, 7,* 149–182.

Jusczyk, P. W., & Bertoncini, J. (1988). Viewing the development of speech perception as an innately guided learning process. *Language and Speech, 31,* 217–238.

Kaplan, P. S., Goldstein, M., Huckeby, E. R., & Cooper, R. P. (1995). Habituation, sensitization, and infants' responses to motherese speech. *Developmental Psychobiology, 28,* 45–57.

Kaplan, P. S., Goldstein, M., Huckeby, E. R., Owren, M. J., & Cooper, R. P. (1995). Dishabituation of visual attention by infant- versus adult-directed speech: Effects of frequency modulation and spectral composition. *Infant Behavior and Development, 18,* 209–223.

Kleiner, K. A. (1987). Amplitude and phase spectra as indices of infants' pattern preferences. *Infant Behavior and Development, 10,* 49–60.

Klinnert, M. D., Campos, J. J., Sorce, J. F., Emde, R. N., & Svejda, M. (1983). Emotions as behavior regulators: Social referencing in infancy. In R. Plutchik & H. Kellerman (Eds.), *Emotion: Theory, research, and experience* (pp. 57–86). New York: Academic Press.

Lecanuet, J.-P., Granier-Deferre, C., Jacquet, A.-Y., Capponi, I., & Ledru, L. (1993).

Prenatal discrimination of a male and a female voice uttering the same sentence. *Early Development and Parenting, 2,* 217–228.

Lickliter, R., & Banker, H. (1994). Prenatal components of intersensory development in precocial birds. In D. Lewkowicz & R. Lickliter (Eds.), *The development of intersensory perception: Comparative perspective* (pp. 59–80). Hillsdale, NJ: Erlbaum.

Lickliter, R., & Berry, T. (1990). The phylogeny fallacy: Developmental psychology's misapplication of evolutionary theory. *Developmental Review, 10,* 348–364.

Mehler, J., Bertonicini, J., Barriere, M., & Jassik-Gerschenfeld, D. (1978). Infant recognition of the mother's voice. *Nature, 7,* 491–497.

Mehler, J., Jusczyk, P., Lambertz, G., Halsted, N., Bertoncini, J., & Amiel-Tison, C. (1988). A precursor of language acquisition in young infants. *Cognition, 29,* 143–178.

Murray, L., & Trevarthen, C. (1987). Emotional regulation of interactions between two-month-olds and their mothers. In T. M. Field & N. A. Fox (Eds.), *Social perception in infants* (pp. 177–197). Norwood, NJ: Ablex.

Panneton, R. K. (1985). *Prenatal experience with melodies: Effect on postnatal auditory preference in human newborns.* Unpublished doctoral dissertation, University of North Carolina at Greensboro.

Papousek, H., & Papousek, M. (1991). Innate and cultural guidance of infants' integrative competencies: China, the United States, and Germany. In M. Bornstein (Ed.), *Cultural approaches to parenting* (pp. 23–44). Hillsdale, NJ: Erlbaum.

Papousek, M., Bornstein, M. H., Nuzzo, C., Papousek, H., & Symmes, D. (1990). Infant responses to prototypical melodic contours in parental speech. *Infant Behavior and Development, 13,* 539–545.

Papousek, M., & Papousek, H. (1989). Forms and functions of vocal matching in interactions between mothers and their precanonical infants. *First Language, 9,* 137–158.

Papousek, M., Papousek, H., & Haekel, M. (1987). Didactic adjustments in fathers' and mothers' speech to their three-month-old infants. *Journal of Psycholinguistic Research, 16,* 491–516.

Papousek, M., Papousek, H., & Symmes, D. (1991). The meaning of melodies in motherese in tone and stress languages. *Infant Behavior and Development, 14,* 415–440.

Pegg, J. E., Werker, J. F., & McLeod, P. J. (1992). Preference for infant-directed over adult-directed speech: Evidence from 7-week old infants. *Infant Behavior and Development, 15,* 325–345.

Querleu, D., Renard, X., Boutteville, C., & Crepin, G. (1989). Hearing by the human fetus. *Seminars in Perinatology, 13,* 409–420.

Reed, E. S. (1988). *James J. Gibson and the psychology of perception.* New Haven, CT: Yale University Press.

Richards, D. S., Frentzen, B., Gerhardt, K. J., McCann, M. E., & Abrams, R. M. (1992). Sound levels in the human uterus. *Obstetrics and Gynecology, 80,* 186–190.

Shute, B., & Wheldall, K. (1989). Pitch alterations in British motherese: Some preliminary acoustic data. *Journal of Child Language, 16,* 503–512.

Smotherman, W. P., & Robinson, S. R. (1987). Psychobiology of fetal experience in the rat. In N. A. Krasnegor, E. M. Blass, M. A. Hofer, & W. P. Smotherman (Eds.), *Perinatal development: A psychobiological perspective* (pp. 39–60). New York: Academic Press.

Spence, M. J., & DeCasper, A. J. (1987). Prenatal experience with low-frequency maternal-voice sounds influence neonatal perception of maternal voice samples. *Infant Behavior and Development, 10,* 133–142.

Spence, M. J., & Moore, D. (1994, June). *Six-month-olds' categorization of infant-directed prosody.* Poster presented at the International Conference for Infant Studies, Paris, France.

Stern, D. N., Spieker, S., Barnett, R. K., & MacKain, K. (1983). The prosody of maternal speech: Infant age and context related changes. *Journal of Child Language, 10,* 1–15.

Stern, D. N., Spieker, S., & MacKain, K. (1982). Intonation contours as signals in maternal speech to prelinguistic infants. *Developmental Psychology, 18,* 727–735.

Sullivan, J. W., & Horowitz, F. D. (1983). Infant intermodal perception and maternal multimodal stimulation: Implications for language development. In L. P. Lipsitt & C. Rovee-Collier (Eds.), *Advances in infancy research* (Vol. 2, pp. 183–239). Norwood, NJ: Ablex.

Trehub, S. E. (1987). Infants' perception of musical patterns. *Perception and Psychophysics, 41,* 635–641.

Trehub, S. E., & Curran, S. (1979). Habituation of infants' cardiac response to speech stimuli. *Child Development, 50,* 1247–1250.

Trehub, S. E., & Trainor, L. J. (1990). Rules for listening in infancy. In J. T. Enns (Ed.), *The development of attention: Research and theory* (pp. 87–119). Amsterdam: Elsevier.

Turkewitz, G., Birch, H. G., & Cooper, K. K. (1972). Responsiveness to simple and complex auditory stimuli in the human newborn. *Developmental Psychobiology*, *5*, 7–19.

von Hofsten, C. (1983). Foundations for perceptual development. In C. Rovee-Collier & L. P. Lipsitt (Eds.), *Advances in infancy research* (Vol. 2, pp. 241–264). Norwood, NJ: Ablex.

Walker-Andrews, A. S. (1984). Infants' perception of the affordances of expressive behaviors. In C. Rovee-Collier & L. P. Lipsitt (Eds.), *Advances in infancy research* (Vol. 5, pp. 174–221). Norwood, NJ: Ablex.

Werker, J. F., & McLeod, P. J. (1989). Infant preference for both male and female infant-directed talk: A developmental study of attentional and affective responsiveness. *Canadian Journal of Psychology*, *43*, 230–246.

Comment on Cooper

Timothy D. Johnston

Fernald and Simon's (1984) finding that very young infants respond preferentially to a pattern of intonation contours that adults spontaneously use in talking to them (*motherese* or *infant-directed* [ID] *speech*) was compatible with a trend that by 1984 had become general in developmental psychology. Far from being the "blooming, buzzing confusion" proposed by William James (1890), the perceptual world of the infant was being revealed to be richly structured by a variety of "biological predispostions" to attend to salient features of the environment. The research that Robin Cooper describes in this chapter reveals some problems with the story about biological dispositions that seems so thoroughly compatible with Fernald's finding. From Cooper's research, it turns out that attributing the infant's response to intonation contours to a set of biological predispositions is at best a serious oversimplification; in fact, there is a complex and interesting story to be told about the very early development of infants' preferences for ID speech. I do not attempt to identify the specific implications of Cooper's research for theories of the develop-

---

Johnston comments on Cooper from an epigenetic systems perspective.

ment of language comprehension. Instead, I point out that her research provides a very clear example of something that I suggest is a general feature of developmental explanations—namely, that invoking predispositions, in any guise, does not make any explanatory headway at all. In fact, I suggest that invoking predispositions in order to explain the emergence of some behavior tends to ensure that whatever explanation is eventually constructed will have solidly nondevelopmental elements embedded in it that will prove very difficult to eradicate. These elements may take any of several forms: instincts, innate categories, predispositions, constraints, blueprints, plans, programs, and so forth.

Why do I say these are all nondevelopmental? Because they all presume what they are supposed to explain, namely the origin of order and organization. A predisposition *is* an ordering and so we must ask, as part of our developmental analysis, where *that* ordering comes from. We may be told that it comes from the genes, which simply presumes that the genes (a genetic blueprint perhaps) have the ordering and doesn't explain where *that* ordering comes from. When we do this, we are engaged in a kind of explanatory shell game, borrowing order from one place to pay it off somewhere else without realizing that we never seem to get around to discharging any of these loans. Ultimately, of course, we borrow from the Federal Reserve Bank of explanatory order, namely the genes—the genes are, at least in relation to complicated cognitive things like speech perception, so impenetrably mysterious that one is pretty safe attributing anything to them. We can say of the genes what William James (1890) said about the soul: "Whatever you are totally ignorant of, assert it to be the explanation of everything" (p. 347).

Of course, this is not a new criticism. It is just what Zing-Yang Kuo (1922) said about instinct in the 1920s, and what Daniel Lehrman (1953) said about instinct in the 1950s, and what Susan Oyama (1985) has argued more recently in her book *The Ontogeny of Information*. Information, or order, Oyama argued, is something that emerges in the course of development, not something that exists beforehand and guides development. (A very similar point has been made by Michael Turvey, Scott Kelso, Esther Thelen, and others about the order in movement—order emerges in the course of the assembly of the movements, it does not exist before-hand in a motor program.)

The problem, as most clearly suggested by Oyama, is in the way we think about information. Information has been an important concept in psychology, but it is also quite problematic. We often talk as if it were some influential substance located in specific parts of a system, so we ask whether information is *in* the organism or *in* the environment; we speak of infor-mation being *in* the genes and being *read out* of the genes during devel-opment; we ask what information is in the mother's voice and are thus led to ask how the infant extracts that information. In fact, information defines a kind of relationship, not a kind of substance. An informational relationship exists between two systems (such as a developing organism and its environment or between an infant and its mother) if one of them can influence the other in some systematic way. Just as ecological psy-chologists have warned against thinking of affordance relationships as properties, we must be careful not to think as information in the nonre-lational way I have been describing.

Cooper's analysis is very much in line with this view of information. Rather than asking where the information in the mother's voice comes from and how the infant is able to extract it, she asks how the informa-tional relationship between the infant and the mother's voice develops over the course of early life. This is both a more developmental and a more ecological formulation of the problem than the predominant approach that she criticizes.

REFERENCES

Fernald, A., & Simon, T. (1984). Expanded intonation contours in mothers' speech to newborns. *Developmental Psychology, 20*, 104–113.

James, W. (1890). *Principles of psychology.* New York: Holt.

Kuo, Z.-Y. (1922). How are our instincts acquired? *Psychological Review, 29,* 344–365.

Lehrman, D. S. (1953). A critique of Konrad Lorenz's theory of instinctive behavior. *Quarterly Review of Biology, 28,* 337–363.

Oyama, S. (1985). *The ontogeny of information: Developmental systems and evolution.* Cambridge, England: Cambridge University Press.

4

Early Development of the Ecological Self

Philippe Rochat

By the time they are 3 months old, infants commonly grab their feet and bring them into their field of view for long bouts of exploration. These long episodes of focused visual and haptic exploration of intertwined toes and fingers raise questions regarding the origins of knowledge about the self, a fundamental issue for developmental psychology. To what extent do infants understand that they are exploring their own bodies? When and how do they develop a sense of self as an entity, situated in the environment and differentiated from other objects (including people)? What is the nature of self-knowledge at the origins of development, and does it emerge prior to mirror self-recognition? These questions have been traditionally addressed within the context of emerging self-recognition (i.e., mirror self-recognition). In light of recent progress in infancy research, the self-recognition or mirror-based view on the origins of self-knowledge is inadequate. The ecological approach to perception and action, and in particular the principle of coperception and the theory of

[1]The writing of this chapter was supported by National Institute of Mental Health Grant No. MH50385-01 and a 1994 Summer Research Grant Award from Emory University. I thank Susan Hespos, Rachel Morgan, and Michael Tomasello for their comments.

affordances formulated by J. J. Gibson (1979), provide a new, compelling way to look at the problem of the origins of self-knowledge.

In this chapter, I attempt to illustrate an ecological approach to the early development of perception and action in general and to the problem of the origins of self-knowledge in particular. First, I discuss the theoretical assumptions and principles of an ecological approach to early development and contrast them with traditional views. Then I review theoretical issues regarding the origins of self-knowledge in particular and compare the proposed ecological approach with the traditional view that postulates an original state of fusion and undifferentiation of the infant with the environment and that suggests that self-knowledge emerges with the expression of a conceptual self (i.e., self-recognition in front of a mirror). I review evidence demonstrating that infants from the onset of development are capable of directed action, expressing a sense of self as differentiated, organized, and situated agent in the environment. The growth of the ecological self is viewed as a main feature of early development.

OUTLINE OF AN ECOLOGICAL APPROACH TO BEHAVIOR AT BIRTH AND EARLY DEVELOPMENT

The proposed ecological approach to early behavior is grounded in the basic assumption that development originates from a mutual relationship between the neonate and the environment. Although no developmental theories deliberately overlook the organism–environment interaction as a source of behavioral changes and transformations, traditional views often account for this interaction in antagonistic terms, in particular in terms of a fundamental conflict between forces originating from the individual and pressures originating from the environment. Classic examples of such views are the tripartite model of psychosexual (personality) development proposed by Freud (1961) and the model of equilibration advanced by Piaget (1961) to account for cognitive development. Both models regard development as a vector resulting from the integration of conflictual forces from the organism and the environment.

In contrast to such theories, which emphasize conflict and contradiction as the source of developmental changes, another (ecological) way to look at development is to view it as the expansion of fundamental fits or functional links between organism and environment, expressed from birth. According to this view, children do not become sudden communicators as they start to use conventional language in their second year of life; rather, communication is a precocious behavioral propensity linking infants to their human environment (Stern, 1985; Trevarthen, 1974). Language simply adds new means for effecting the communicative function. The view of early development as the growth and expansion of basic behavioral propensities linking the young organism to its environment emphasizes functional continuity in development, rather than conflict and structural discontinuity.

Recent progress in infancy research prompts a radical revision of traditional conceptions of young infants' behavior as "random, unstructured, and . . . inconsistent" (Spitz, 1965, p. 54). It is now well established that the world of the newborn is not the buzzing confusion depicted by William James (1890). Much of the new findings provided by the recent surge of infant studies support the basic assumption of the ecological view, which assumes that organism–environment mutualities are expressed and expand from birth. Evidence demonstrates the existence of basic behavioral propensities, or functional fits, linking young infants to their environment. Instead of viewing infant behavior as random and disorganized, I propose that it is best described as a complex network of functional organizations that are operational from birth. The expression of these organizations correspond to behavioral propensities that guide the early transactions of the infant with the environment. Because of the existence of these propensities, early behavior can be viewed as functional "acts" rather than mechanistic "responses" or "reflexes," best described as a collection of action systems that are defined by the hypothetical function they serve (Reed, 1982). Sucking, for example, is a complex act expressed from birth and should be viewed as part of the nutritional or feeding system. This perspective, validated by recent research, is one that calls for a further understanding of the functional specificity of infant behavior (Rochat & Senders, 1991).

In his outline of a theory of action systems, Reed (1982) identified basic action systems expressed from birth that form the functional axes of early development. Aside from nutrition, these basic action systems include the orientation, communication, locomotion, and exploration systems. This categorization is based on what appear, to an observer, to be differential orientations and attunements of an active organism toward particular aspects of the environment. This functional taxonomy has great heuristic value, offering a molar view of infant behavior inclusive of its mutuality to the environment. It is an alternative to a mechanistic view that conceives of infant behavior as a collection of sensorimotor loops or reflexes, triggered by nonspecific stimulations. Rather than occurring in a vacuum, infant action is seen as inextricably tied to the environment and its resources or affordances for action (E. J. Gibson, 1982; J. J. Gibson, 1979; Rochat & Reed, 1987). Newborns are viewed as actively oriented toward the discovery of possibilities for action provided by the environment, including objects, people, goals, obstacles, and dangers. Again, in development, action systems define important axes or avenues of change. Considered as functional constraints, they scaffold early behavioral evolution.

As mentioned above, young infants appear remarkably selective and attuned to particular environmental features and resources. From the origins of development, infant behavior manifests a practical knowledge or "knowhow" regarding particular features and objects of the environment that have basic survival values. Newborns display a functional predisposition to engage in complex and optimal transactions with certain aspects of the environment. Systematic head orientation toward a sound source (Clifton, Morrongiello, Kulig, & Dowd, 1981), mouth orientation toward a familiar odor (Macfarlane, 1975), and rooting and mouth opening toward a perioral stimulation as an apparent preparation for sucking (Koupernik & Dailly, 1968; Rochat, 1993a) are examples of such functional predisposition expressed by neonates immediately after birth.

The expression from birth of a functional link between behavior and vital resources in the environment suggest the existence of a pure form of procedural knowledge: a sort of functional protocognition that is integral to the newborn's behavioral propensities. In relation to the rooting and sucking of the neonate, the attainment of the functional goal of feeding that ultimately guides these behavioral patterns depends on the a priori existence of a specific object in the environment: the nipple. This dependence is functional and ecological in the sense that the optimum functioning of sucking behavior is linked to a particular object that pre-exists in the environment. The nipple is an object that can be viewed as a mediator between the infant and the nutritional resource of the environment. As an a priori object of the environment, the nipple must be defined from a functional point of view, in relation to specific characteristics framed by the codesign or mutual compatibility (Turvey & Shaw, 1987) between the infant's mouth and the maternal breast or any of its substitutes (e.g., rubber nipple, pacifier, thumb). From an ecological perspective, there is a functional reciprocity between the two, as they evolved to fit one another (codesign), existing for each other a priori. When the newborn is hungry and his or her behavior is guided by the functional goal of ingesting food through rooting, sucking, and swallowing, such behavior is oriented toward the oral capture of a particular physical entity, corresponding minimally to a "suckable" object and optimally to a nutritional nipple. The behavioral orientation expressed by the infant from birth is based on the functional mutuality existing between particular features of the organism (e.g., the mouth and its functioning) and particular objects furnishing the environment (e.g., suckable objects).

WHAT DEVELOPS IN THE COURSE OF THE FIRST WEEKS, AND HOW?

Behavioral propensities, action systems, and the functional goals attached to these systems define important axes or avenues of change, providing basic directions to early behavioral development. They form functional constraints, canalizing and supporting early ontogeny. New skills rapidly develop within each of the particular action systems, the functioning of these systems overlapping and becoming increasingly integrated. A good example is the early development of oral action in the course of the first 6 months. When presented with rubber nipples that are more or less eccentric in relation to the shape and material of the biological nipple, infants within weeks become increasingly sensitive to eccentric nipples, engaging in significantly less sucking activity and more oral exploration (Rochat, 1983). Such development points to the progressive differentiation and integration of a double functional orientation of infants' oral activity: feeding and exploration. At the onset of development, newborns' oral activity is essentially oriented toward feeding through the well-organized and biologically determined sucking behavior (Crook, 1979). Within weeks, the mouth develops as the primary instrument of exploration, serving the double function of feeding and investigating objects in the environment (Rochat & Senders, 1991). By 6 months, the hands appear to take over the status of the mouth as a privileged instrument of haptic exploration. From 5 months on, infants tend to bring less novel objects to the mouth, developing new manipulatory skills such as fingering behavior, which allows fine haptic exploration of larger, graspable objects in coordination with vision (Rochat, 1989, 1993a).

Within the context of action systems and their complex interactions, there is an important process, viewed as an essential factor of early development, which might explain how early behavioral growth occurs. This process is the precocious ability as well as propensity to detect regularities in the environment, to pick up invariant information. It underlies rapid progress in detecting the affordances of the environment and in attaining the functional goals attached to the various action systems expressed at birth. Note that the propensity to detect invariant information is not exclusive to the infancy period, but represents an important factor underlying perception, action, and cognitive development at all stages (E. J. Gibson, 1969; J. J. Gibson, 1979; Piaget & Inhelder, 1974). However, infancy research demonstrates that this propensity is pervasive early in life, probably driving perceptual and action development from birth. For example, studies demonstrate that 1- to 2-month-olds have the ability to transfer information from one perceptual system (oral) to another (vision). After exploring various shaped and textured objects with their mouth, infants show signs of visual recognition of these objects, transferring amodal information from the oral to the visual system (Gibson & Walker, 1984; Meltzoff & Borton, 1979). These findings indicate that young infants detect invariant properties and regularities beyond the immediate diversity of perceptual experiences. Evidence of neonatal imitation also demonstrates the early ability of infants to pick up visual information specifying another person's behavior (e.g., tongue protrusion) and to match this information through another modality (i.e., proprioception) in order to reproduce this behavior motorically (Meltzoff, 1990). Note that this interpretation is valid to the extent that early imitation cannot be merely reduced to fixed action patterns or automatically triggered responses (e.g., see Anisfeld, 1991, and the empirical counterevidence advanced by Meltzoff, 1989). Again, the early propensity to detect invariant features of perceived objects, events, and people allows infants to gain increased control over the resources of their environment and to detect new affordances in the context of the various action systems and the functional goals they serve.

Among all objects explored by infants, the body is invariably present. From birth it is always felt, no matter what they are doing. The same mouth is involved in any feeding activity, the same legs are moving when kicking, the same face is expressing emotion when interacting with others. The repetition of the same actions allows the fine tuning of the body in relation to what the environment affords for action. In learning about affordances, infants learn equally about their own bodies and about their bodies' potential for action. Self-knowledge is indeed an important aspect of early development, often overlooked by developmentalists.

THE BODY AS A PRIMARY OBJECT OF KNOWLEDGE IN INFANCY

More than a century ago, William James (1890) distinguished two kinds of selves, the "I" and the "Me." The "I" corresponds to the self as agent and experimenter in the environment. It is the existential or situated self. The "Me," on the other hand, corresponds to the empirical or identified self: "what he [the individual] considers his, not only his body ... but his clothes and his house" (James, 1890, p. 291). James's distinction is important because it accounts for two distinct levels associated with the problem of self-knowledge. It underscores the difference between the self that is identified, hence conceptualized, and the self as it is experienced at a phenomenal level in the transactions with the environment. The identified self ("me") entails recognition and recall, hence conceptual and declarative knowledge (an explicit sense of self according to Case, 1991). By contrast, the situated self ("I") does not entail recognition and recall; rather, it is based on the perception of the self as a differentiated and organized entity, situated as an agent in the environment. The recent discovery of remarkable abilities in young infants suggest that in development, expression of a situated self precedes and announces recognition and understanding of the self as an identified entity or explicit object of reflection.

The acquisition of novel knowledge about the world by young infants implies that they know basic things about themselves. If they search for a nipple, they possess the implicit knowledge that they own a mouth. When learning about the invariance of objects, they also learn about the permanence of their own bodies among other objects (Neisser, 1993). At a basic level, object knowledge and self-knowledge are inseparable. As J. J. Gibson (1979) proposed, perception implies coperception of the object and of the perceiver itself. This principle is true for young infants as well. For example, when perceiving an object as reachable, infants as well as adults perceive the relative distance of this object in reference to their own situation in the environment. By definition, the detection of any affordances for action implies some kind of self-knowledge: knowledge about the body, its effectivities, and its situation in the environment. By extension, knowing about objects is knowing about oneself. When infants start to plan manual action in order to retrieve an object hidden behind an occluder, this planning entails an understanding of some kind of object permanence (out of sight does not mean out of mind), as well as self permanence in terms of the enduring situation of the body in relation to the hidden object. Lewis and Brooks-Gunn (1979, p. 10) suggested that "The early differentiation of self and other should take place at the same time the child is differentiating its mother from others and is acquiring object permanence." At least at the origins of development and prior to the emergence of more reflective, explicit knowledge by the second year, there is a basic reciprocity between object knowledge, the knowledge of what objects afford for action, and knowledge about the body, its effectivities, and situation in the environment. Note that this type of implicit or preconceptual knowledge about the self is not specifically human, probably an emergent property of any biological system that perceives and acts in relation to functional goals (see Rochat, 1995, for various comparative and noncomparative approaches to this basic question).

Theories of development, and in particular theories on the origins of self-knowledge, often overlook that the body is a primary object of discovery for the young infant, an object of knowledge prior to the emergence of the conceptual self typically measured by tests of self-recognition in front of a mirror or other medias (see below). The discovery of the body's effectivities in relation to the resources (affordances) of the environment is indeed a major achievement of early development. This discovery proceeds according to the same propensity or natural ability expressed from birth to detect invariant features of objects and events, except that it is oriented toward the body and the specification of what Neisser (1991) labeled the *ecological self.* The ecological self corresponds to a sense of self as a differentiated entity, a situated agent in the environment. It develops as part of the increased control of infants over the resources of their environment and the emergence of new skills to achieve functional goals. This sense of an ecological self, of the body as agent situated in the environment, is a major product of development from birth and in the course of the first few months. Before moving on to discuss research supporting this model, I describe traditional ways in which the early development of self-knowledge has been approached.

The vast majority of experimental studies dealing with the development of self-knowledge have reduced this problem to the emergence of the identified or conceptual self. In these studies, children of different ages are typically presented with their own image, whereas the experimenter records the behavioral expression of self-recognition. The most common experimental paradigm includes self-recognition in front of a mirror and sometimes self-recognition in photographs or audiovisual recordings. The traditional mirror technique (Gallup, 1970; Guillaume, 1926; Preyer, 1887; Zazzo, 1981) continues to generate important studies, such as using mirrors to deform the image of the self (Mounoud & Vinter, 1981; Orbach, Traub, & Olson, 1980). Using the procedure elaborated by Gallup (1970) in his study of self-recognition in chimpanzees, Lewis and Brooks-Gunn (1979) reported that 15- to18-month-old toddlers looking at themselves in a mirror showed embarrassment on noticing that rouge has been applied to their nose by the experimenter (the "rouge" task). While staring at themselves in the mirror, they typically bring one of their hands to their nose. This behavior is interpreted as a sign of self-recognition. Zazzo (1981) showed that although 18-month-olds manifest self-recognition in the rouge task, it is only 3 to 6 months later that toddlers placed in front a mirror will turn around to look directly at a light they see blinking in the mirror. When presented with photographs or video recordings, children start spontaneously naming and pointing at themselves at about age 18 months (Lewis & Brooks-Gunn, 1979). Zazzo (1981) reported that by 3 years of age, children recognize themselves with no hesitation on a video recording and resist the experimenter's countersuggestion that images projected on the screen might not actually be of them.

Researchers have expressed reservations regarding the use of self-recognition in a mirror as an experimental paradigm to capture the developmental origin of self-knowledge. These reservations are based on considerations regarding the complexity of the mirror situation and the difficulty of determining the relevant information picked up by the infant when looking at the mirror. For instance, Loveland (1986) observed that self-recognition in a mirror requires the child to have mastered the perceptual and conceptual problem associated with the mirror as a reflecting object in the environment. Furthermore, she noted that self-recognition in a mirror is by definition indirect, because it is based on the perception of a bidimensional projection of the body that is inverted around its axis of symmetry. It affords visual perception pertaining to regions of the infant's own body that are not otherwise directly accessible to this modality (e.g., the face). For all these reasons, self-recognition in a mirror might imply a particular perceptual learning that adds up to the expression of an implicit sense of self. Mirror self-recognition probably consists of more than what is required for a knowledge of an "implicit" sense of self (see Case, 1991).

Many studies confirm that at around 18 months of age children manifest unequivocal self-recognition and self-identification in front of a mirror. Nevertheless, this fact should not be understood as the developmental origin of the sense of self. Prior to self-recognition, or explicit self-identification of any kind, infants manifest an early (implicit) sense of self (Butterworth, 1990; Rochat, 1993c). The early capacity to detect amodal information and to extract perceptual information that corresponds to spatiotemporal invariants of the stimulation allows young infants not only to perceive objects and events, but also to situate themselves as perceivers and actors in the environment (the process of coperception emphasized by J. J. Gibson, 1979). This early capacity underlies the infant's ability to perceive a situated self.

EVIDENCE FOR AN EARLY SENSE OF SELF: THE ECOLOGICAL SELF

Evidence suggests that from the onset of development infants differentiate between themselves and the environment. This differentiation forms the basis for the development of self-knowledge in infancy (Butterworth, 1991; Donaldson, 1992; E. J. Gibson, 1993; Rochat, 1993c). In early theories of development, newborn infants were traditionally described as being in a state of fusion or undifferentiation with the environment (Piaget, 1952; Preyer, 1887; Wallon, 1942/1970). Contemporary research in infancy challenges the idea of an initial fusion, shedding a new light on the developmental origins of self-knowledge. In addition to neonatal imitation, evidence of an early sense of self as a differentiated entity in the environment is provided by the fact that infants within the first weeks of life adjust their posture differentially on the basis of vestibular–proprioceptive information or visual information specifying either ego motion or motion of the surroundings (Bertenthal & Bai, 1989; Butterworth & Hicks, 1977; Jouen, 1984). Facts demonstrating precocious sensitivity and attunement to ongoing social interaction (Murray & Trevarthen, 1985; Tronick, 1980) and the ability displayed from birth to effect sensorimotor responses such as sucking to control auditory events (De Casper & Fifer, 1980; Eimas, 1982; Juscyk, 1985) or visual events (Kalnins & Bruner, 1973; Siqueland & DeLucia, 1969) further suggest that young infants express an early sense of self as agentive entities (Rochat, 1993c). The idea of an initial state of fusion with the environment is inconsistent with the empirical data assembled by recent research. From the onset of development self-knowledge is expressed in the form of a differentiation between interoceptive and exteroceptive stimulations and the ability to control features of the environment (Butterworth, 1990; Rochat, 1993c). However, questions remain regarding what kind of perceptual information determined the young infant's expression of a differentiated self.

From birth, infants experience contrasted perceptual and sensorimotor events that uniquely specify the self. When infants cry, the sound they hear is combined with kinesthetic and proprioceptive feedback. This intermodal combination is uniquely specifying the perceived self. Sounds originating from another person or any other objects in the environment will never share the same intermodal invariants. By the second month, when infants start to vocalize and to babble, they appear to explore systematically the specificities of their own voice and the potentials (or affordances) of their own vocal track.

Newborns show a robust propensity to bring their hands in contact with their face and mouth (Rochat, Blass, & Hoffmeyer, 1988). Some authors have observed that newborn infants spend up to 20% of their waking hours with hands contacting the facial region (Korner & Kraemer, 1972). This simple observation has implications for the perceptual basis of self-knowledge at the origins of development. As in the case of self-produced sound, when manually touching their own faces, newborns are experiencing a sensorimotor and perceptual event that uniquely specifies the self. This intermodal event is the *double touch* of the cutaneous surface of the hand contacting the cutaneous surface of the facial region, which could be any other region of the body surface (von Glasersfeld, 1988). Contacts of the baby with any other physical objects, surfaces, or persons in the environment never correspond to a double touch intermodal event.

When do young infants start to show discrimination of unique perceptual events that specify themselves? In an ongoing experiment conducted at the Emory Infant Laboratory, my colleagues and I are assessing whether newborns discriminate between double touch stimulations and various external cutaneous (tactile) stimulations. Preliminary results indicate that such discrimination might occur very early in development. In this project, newborns' rooting responses are systematically analyzed (i.e., head turn and oral orienting toward a perioral tactile stimulation) in four different conditions. In one condition, the perioral stimulation originates from the index finger of the experimenter who is placed behind the infant and rubs intermittently the infant's left or right cheek for 20 seconds. At the beginning of stimulation, the infant's head is oriented at the center. In a second condition, the infant is stimulated by a pacifier held by the experimenter. In a third condition, infants are stimulated by their own hand, either left or right, gently held by the experimenter and rubbing their cheek. In contrast to the other conditions, this condition provides the infant with a double touch experience. Finally, in a fourth control condition, the hand of the infant is brought close to the cheek by the experimenter, without touching it. In this last condition, infants are stimulated only with the movement component of the arm passively moved toward the cheek by the experimenter.

Preliminary results obtained with six 3- to 4-week-old infants, each stimulated in each condition once to the right and once to the left side ($N = 12$ instances), suggest that the proportion of observed rooting in the direction of the stimulation depends on the condition. Infants tend to root more toward either the experimenter's finger and the pacifier, compared to their own hands. No rooting is observed in the fourth condition where the tactile component is absent. These preliminary observations indicate that early on, young infants might express differential responding to self versus external tactile stimulations (in other words, between "double" touch, specifying the self, and "single" touch, specifying external stimulations). Again, it is important to emphasize the importance of haptic stimulations early in life, these stimulations being potentially a source for the perceptual specification of the self, hence part of the perceptual basis of an early sense of self.

EARLY PERCEPTION OF BODY EFFECTIVITIES

Considering the infant's predisposition to process amodal information and the active engagement of the neonate in interacting with the environment, Stern (1985) suggested that from birth through the first 2 months, infants start forming a sense of an emergent self. According to Stern, infants experience the organizing process of the self from the moment they are born. This organizing process starts with the first interaction of the infant with the environment, and in particular with the first social interaction. Sroufe (1990) proposed that during the first 6 months, regularities in the dyadic organization of the infant–mother interaction provide sufficient information for infants to form rudiments of an inner organization, or "preintentional" self (Sroufe, 1990). According to Sroufe, the preintentional self precedes the "intentional" self in development, emerging by 6 months when infants start to demonstrate purposeful acts to control their human environment (Sroufe, 1990). According to Case (1991, p. 218), 4-month-old infants manifest a clear sense of self stemming from the experience of personal agency in the environment. From this stage, infants begin to build a model of their own capabilities and a sense of self as an "object" in the environment. Our own research also demonstrates that progress in the control of posture during the first 6 months of life changes the way infants interact with the environment. In particular, the ability to sit independently by age 4–5 months is linked to the emergence of fine haptic exploration (fingering) and trunk involvement in reaching (Rochat, 1989, 1992; Rochat & Goubet, 1995). Progress in postural control is viewed as an important determinant of the emerging sense of self in early development (Rochat & Bullinger, 1994). It is now well established that 6-month-old infants discriminate with great accuracy whether an object is within reach or out of reach (Clifton, Perris, & Bullinger, 1991; Yonas & Hartman, 1993). As mentioned previously, this ability implies that infants have a sense of their situation as agents in the environment and in particular a sense of their situation as reachers in relation to the object they plan to capture.

Infants are accurate in perceiving the effectivities of their own body for reaching (Rochat & Goubet, 1993). In two studies, we presented infants with an object for reaching, presented successively at four different distances. Infants were placed in an upright infant seat with the object centered at their shoulders' height. The nearest distance placed the object about 30 cm from the infant's torso, in alignment with the toes. The other three distances expanded from this referential distance by 5 inches. At Distances 1 and 2, the object was within reach of the infant. At Distance 3, it was at the limit of prehensile space; the infant could eventually touch it, but with intense stretching forward of the trunk and upper limbs. At Distance 4, the object was out of reach for the infant. During 30-s presentations, we scored frequency and duration of gazing at the object, latency to reach, and reach attempts. In the first study, we compared three groups of 10 infants aged 5–6 months on the basis of their relative ability to control independent sitting (i.e., their ability to coordinate reaching of hands and leaning of the trunk).

Results show that at Distances 3 and 4, gazing activities and the frequency of reach attempts increased depending on the infant's relative sitting ability. With increased control over self-sitting, infants demonstrated an expansion of the perceived limits of prehensile space. In the second study, 60 5- to 7-month-olds were analyzed with either light (2 g) or heavy (200 g) bracelets attached to their wrists. Reaching with heavy bracelets moved forward the infant's center of mass when reaching and reduced the limits of maximum reachability without losing balance. The rationale was that if infants were sensitive to this change, they should reach less with the heavy bracelets. Results indicate that at Distances 3 and 4 only, frequency of reach attempts decrease when infants are wearing the heavy bracelets compared to when they are wearing the light ones. These results suggest that infants as young as 5 months are sensitive to what their body affords for action, detecting and adjusting with remarkable accuracy the perception of their own body's effectivities. They adjust the planning of their activity (reaching) by perceiving sudden experimental changes in their bodily characteristics (i.e., weighted limbs causing forward displacement of their body's center of mass). These results indicate that when starting to reach, infants appear to plan their reach on the basis of their perception of their situation in the environment and particular postural constraints. They detect visual and proprioceptive information specifying their relation as actors to the object and the points of maximum extension of the body without losing balance (i.e., points of postural reversibility). Note that the detection of points of postural reversibility determine the perceived limits of prehensile space by the infant and by adults (Rochat & Wraga, 1993). This detection is the direct expression of the ecological self, implying a sense of the body's effectivities in the planning of a reach act. However, what is the process underlying the early sense of self, and in particular the early development of the ecological self? I propose that self-exploration (i.e., the exploration of one's own body) is an important determinant of such development.

SELF-EXPLORATION BY YOUNG INFANTS

The few developmental studies describing infant behavior in front of a mirror in the course of the first year (i.e., prior to the first signs of self-recognition) suggest that before they are 6 months old, infants are actively involved in discovering their own reflection and show signs of perceptual discrimination between themselves and others. Although this discrimination does not imply self-recognition, it forms the basis of an early sense of self as a differentiated entity. Dixon (1957) described a first stage at around 4 months of age in which infants look briefly and soberly at themselves in the mirror but show immediate recognition and sustained attention to their mothers' reflection. Field (1979) demonstrated that 3-month-olds respond differentially to a mirror image of the self versus viewing an infant peer. In this study, the infant's facial expression, manual behavior, visual activity, and cardiac response were recorded systematically, and the results suggested a precocious discrimination between self-perception in the mirror and perception of others. Amsterdam (1972)

reported that between the ages of 3 and 5 months, infants show little social behavior in front of the mirror (i.e., they do not smile, laugh, and vocalize); such behavior becomes prominent by 6 months. In her study, Amsterdam showed that between the ages of 3 and 12 months, the majority
of infants spend time observing their own movement in the mirror, exploring the particular visual–proprioceptive correspondence offered by the
mirror's reflection. By age 14 months, infants become less interested in
their own movement, and by 20 months they begin to withdraw and to
show embarrassment in front of the mirror (Amsterdam, 1972; Lewis &
Brooks-Gunn, 1979). It thus appears that in the context of the mirror situation, self-exploration is particularly prominent during the first year.
Aside from the mirror situation, self-exploration is evident starting at 3
months of age, when infants display long episodes of self-examination, in
particular exploration of their hands in motion (Piaget, 1952). Such self-
exploration of the hands has been recently documented in newborn infants (van der Meer, 1993).

Some studies have attempted to isolate the information (visual, proprioceptive, haptic) young infants might be sensitive to when engaged in
self-exploration. Papousek and Papousek (1974) placed 5-month-olds in
front of two different video images of either themselves or of others. This
method allowed the assessment of the discriminant variables between the
two video images on the basis of the preferential looking of the infant. Re-
porting only pilot observations with 11 infants, Papousek and Papousek
found that infants prefer to look at images of the self or of others allowing for eye contact. Using a similar procedure but placing 1- to 24-month-
old infants in front of two mirrors that were either flat, blurred, or distorted, Schulman and Kaplowitz (1976) showed that prior to 6 months,
infants tend to look more often at the clear rather than the blurred image
of themselves and showed less interest in the distorted image compared
to the flat nondistorted mirror image. Schulman and Karplowitz noted
that compared with older infants, 1- to 6-month-olds spend more time
looking at a particular mirror although they do not yet show complex behavior such as looking at a particular body part, followed by an immediate inspection of its reflection in the mirror. Lewis and Brooks-Gunn

(1979), like most early infancy researchers (Guillaume, 1926; Wallon, 1942/1970), have suggested that the origins of self-perception correspond to the discovery by the young infant of the contingency between visual and proprioceptive feedback from body movements.

Using the principle of the choice method introduced by Papousek and Papousek (1974) but presenting infants with nonfacial images of the self, in particular their legs, Bahrick and Watson (1985) demonstrated the early detection of proprioceptive–visual contingency. On one of the TV monitors the infants had access to a contingent view of their legs and on another was simultaneously presented a noncontingent, prerecorded, view of the baby's own legs or the view of another baby's leg movements wearing identical booties (yoked-control design). The 5-month-olds look preferentially to the noncontingent view. Bahrick and Watson also observed this phenomenon in a situation where an occluder prevented the infants from seeing their legs directly. Three-month-olds show split preferences, looking either much longer at the contingent or much longer at the noncontingent view. Overall, Bahrick and Watson demonstrated that early perceptual discrimination of the self does not correspond only to facial images of the self but includes other parts of the body. This is important, because it shows that infants are sensitive to visual and proprioceptive contingency in general and not only to the contingency of eye contact as suggested by previous researchers who emphasized the social rather than perceptual context in which first discrimination between self and others takes place (Dixon, 1957; Papousek & Papousek, 1974).

SELF-EXPLORATION AND THE DETECTION OF INTERMODAL INVARIANTS BY YOUNG INFANTS: NEW EVIDENCE

As mentioned at the beginning of this chapter, 3-month-old infants spend a great deal of time exploring their own bodies moving and acting in the environment. They appear to be attracted and actively involved in investigating the rich intermodal redundancies, temporal contingencies, and spatial congruence of self-perception. If they appear fascinated by the simultaneous experience of seeing and feeling the limbs of their own body moving in space at such a young age, the question is whether they are actually detecting the intermodal invariants specifically attached to self-produced movements.

Recently, we collected evidence of such detection in 3- to 5-month-olds (Rochat & Morgan, 1993, 1995). We demonstrated that by age 3 months, when infants start to show systematic visual and proprioceptive self-exploration, they become sensitive to spatial invariants specifying the self: that, for example, when feeling their own legs moving in a particular direction in space, they expect to see their legs moving in a similar direction. The demonstration of such calibrated intermodal space by young infants is based on five experiments recently conducted at the Emory Infant Laboratory. As a general paradigm, we used infants' preferential looking to different on-line views of their legs from the waist down. This paradigm is a modified version of the one used by Bahrick and Watson (1985). Infants were placed in front of a large television monitor with a split screen. On either side of the split screen was displayed a particular on-line view of the infant's legs, from different cameras placed at different angles or with optical characteristics such as a left–right reversal. To entice the infant to visually attend to the TV display, attractive striped socks were put on the infant and a small microphone was placed under the infant's feet that picked up a rustling–scratching sound each time the infant produced a leg movement. The sound of the leg movements was amplified and was heard by the infant from a speaker placed centrally on top of the TV. A camera placed under the TV provided a close-up of the infant's face for later preferential looking analysis, synchronized with the audio recording of the infant's leg activities. Blind coders entered in real time on two channels the infant's gazing at either the right or left side of the split screen, while the synchronized spectrogram of the audio recording of the infant's leg activity was entered in another channel and digitized into one second bouts of leg activity. In short, this technique allowed the co-analysis of preferential looking for either views of the legs and the amount of self-produced leg activity.

The rationale for these experiments was that if infants showed discrimination between the two views of their legs, they should look preferentially at one of the views and produce a differential amount of leg activity while looking at the preferred view. In all experiments, infants were presented with two different on-line views of their own legs on the split screen. In the first experiment, infants were presented with an ego and an observer's view of their own legs (see Figure 1A). Each view was provided by a camera placed either above and behind the infant, or above and in front of the infant. There were two basic spatial differences between the two views: orientation and relative movement directionality of the legs.

Regarding the experimental design, in all experiments infants were recorded 5 minutes in front of the display. The side of the view was counterbalanced among infants of each age group ($n = 10$). Overall, in the first experiment, infants at both ages and starting from 3 months of age expressed a differentiation between the two views of their legs: (a) They tended to look significantly longer at the observer's view (i.e., the noncongruent view); (b) after multiple comparisons between the two views, they tended to settle their gaze toward the preferred view as a function of the 5 min of testing time; and (c) they generated significantly more leg activity while looking at the observer's view (noncongruent) compared to the ego (congruent) view, expressing an increase in self-exploration in the context of the nonfamiliar view.

To untangle the confound between differences in spatial orientation and spatial directionality of the two on-line views presented in the first experiment, we conducted a second experiment where both views of the legs portrayed a similar orientation (two ego views), the two views being only different in relation to leg movements' directionality (see Figure 1B). Inversion of movement directionality was obtained by using a camera with a left–right inverted tube. Again, infants were recorded 5 min in front of the display. The side of the view was counterbalanced among infants of each age group ($n = 10$). Overall, in the second experiment, infants continued to express a differentiation between the two views of their legs: (a) They tended to look significantly longer at the reversed view (i.e., the incongruent view); (b) following frequent comparisons between the views, they tended to settle their gaze toward the preferred view as a function of the 5 min of testing time; and (c) they generated significantly more leg activity while looking at the

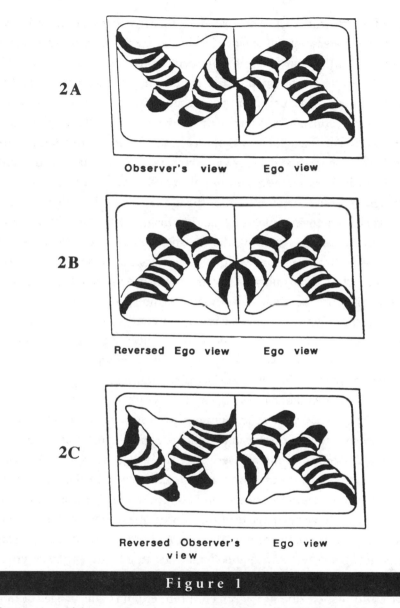

Figure 1

The two views of their own legs as seen by the infants on the TV display in the first experiment (2A), the second experiment (2B), and the third experiment (2C). From "Spatial Determinants in the Perception of Self-produced Leg Movements by 3- to 5-Month-Old Infants" by P. Rochat and R. Morgan, 1995, *Developmental Psychology, 31*, p. 629. Copyright 1995 by the American Psychological Association.

reversed ego (incongruent) compared to the ego (congruent) view, expressing an increase of self-exploration in the context of the incongruent view that varied only in terms of movement's directionality.

In Experiment 1 orientation and movement directionality were confounded. To assess further movement directionality as a spatial determinant of the infants' apparent differentiation of the two views, we conducted a third experiment where the two views presented to the infant varied in orientation, as in Experiment 1, but with movement directionality congruent with the infant's own movements in both views (see Figure 1C). Again, infants were recorded 5 min in front of the display. The side of the view was counterbalanced among infants of each age group ($n = 10$). In contrast to the first two experiments, infants did not show any preference for the view that was spatially incongruent with their own legs, any settling of their gazing as a function of testing time, or any significant increase in leg activity while looking at either view. Taken together, the results of these three experiments indicate that infants as young as 3 months show some discrimination between congruent and incongruent views of self-produced leg movements, the spatial determinant of this early discrimination being movement directionality rather than spatial orientation.

We (Morgan & Rochat, 1994) conducted two novel experiments to address the question of whether young infants are sensitive to changes in the relative position of their own legs they see moving on a screen. Again, 3- and 4–5-month-old infants were tested in a slightly modified procedure, presented with a composite, on-line (ego) view of their own legs, which kept constant both orientation and movement directionality of either leg, but altered their relative position on the screen. In the normal condition, infants saw their legs in their normal relative positions: the right leg to the right of the screen and the left leg to the left. In the reversed condition, the legs positions were reversed: the left leg to the right and the right leg to the left side of the screen. Both left and right images of one leg originated from two separate cameras placed behind and above the infant. Infants were shown the normal and reversed conditions in four alternating sequences of 2 minutes. Order of presentation was counterbalanced among infants of each age group.

The rationale of this experiment was the following: it was predicted that if infants perceive the contrast between the normal and reversed conditions, they would tend to look and kick differentially across these two conditions. Results of this experiment showed that infants from 3 months of age manifest differential looking and kicking behavior across the two conditions. For both groups, infants tended to reduce their looking and leg activity when presented with a reversed relative location of their legs on the screen. These results suggest that young infants are sensitive to differences in the relative movements or the featural characteristics of the legs (i.e., the relative bending of the legs at the knees and ankles) across the two conditions.

To control for the potential determinant of the relative featural characteristics of the infant's legs (the legs' bending), which changed between normal and reversed conditions, we conducted another study where features of the legs were maintained constant while relative leg position was varied across conditions (normal and reversed). Again, we tested infants successively in the two conditions, wearing bulky socks to cover the bending of the legs. In contrast to the preceding experiments, the results indicated for both age groups ($n = 10$ infants in each), there was no significant difference in looking, gaze switching, and leg activity between the normal and the reversed conditions. These results and those of the preceding experiment indicate that featural characteristics of the legs combined with relative movement directionality form important spatial determinants in the perception of self-produced leg movements by infants as young as 3 months of age. Results of the second experiment suggest that relative movement directionality alone is not a significant spatial determinant in the perception of self-produced movements. In our view, these results can be interpreted as the early expression of a calibrated intermodal space of the body or, in other words, the early expression of a perceptually based body schema.

Overall, the reported observations demonstrate that long before mirror self-recognition, and probably from birth, infants develop an early sense of self that is perceptual and action based. Self-exploration by young infants and the detection of intermodal invariants specifying the self as agent are early facts of life. They are the source of a preconceptual self that develops rapidly in the course of the first months, announcing and preparing for later self-recognition.

CONCLUSION: REINTERPRETING THE ORIGINS OF SELF-KNOWLEDGE WITHIN AN ECOLOGICAL APPROACH

On the basis of the empirical evidence presented above, it is possible to renew the interpretation of the developmental origins of self-knowledge in the following way.

At the onset of development, infants have a sense of self based on intermodal perception and on the calibration of the different sensorimotor systems (e.g., visual, tactile, proprioceptive, auditory), which are typically co-engaged or working together within the repertoire of the newborn's action systems (e.g., sucking, rooting, grasping, orienting, imitating). Self-knowledge is primitively based on invariant information linked to the co-engagement of different modalities in self-produced movements. On the basis of their propensity to detect regularities, infants pick up intermodal invariants linked to self-produced movements. These invariants specify directly their own body as a differentiated and agentive entity in the environment.

In the course of the first weeks, as action systems expand and get further integrated, the perceived self is enriched by the infant's discovery of new intermodal invariants that accompany the development of new action patterns (e.g., reaching) and the detection of novel affordances (e.g., reachable objects). In general, from birth and long before the behavioral evidence of self-recognition in front of a mirror, infants manifest an early sense of self as a differentiated, coordinated, and agentive entity in the environment (Rochat, 1993c). This early sense of self corresponds to what authors have labeled the "I" (James, 1890); the "implicit self" (Case, 1991); the "existential self" (Lewis & Brooks-Gunn, 1979); or the "ecological self" (Neisser, 1991, 1993).

In an ecological perspective, the origins of self-knowledge are perception and action based. Active proprioception plays a central role in the determination of an early sense of self. It provides infants from birth with information about the self as an invariant entity. Early behavior such as orienting, exploring, or imitating are by definition self-produced and directed, as opposed to triggered or passive as in the case of passive transports and postural adjustment caused by actions of caretakers or automatic responses such as the Moro response. Because from birth there are self-produced actions oriented toward functional goals, there may be rudiments of means–ends differentiation and coordination, a basic expression of the ecological self. Progress in infancy research suggests strongly the existence of an early dissociation and coordination between actions of the body and particular environmental resources, as in the case of oral–haptic exploration by neonates (Rochat, 1983) or neonatal imitation (Meltzoff & Moore, 1977). It is in this context that an implicit sense of self emerges, forming the origins of self-knowledge.

As proposed by Meltzoff (1990, p. 142), self-knowledge might be primarily mediated by pure spatiotemporal movement patterns: "there are good theoretical reasons for thinking that the first psychologically primary notion of self concerns not one's featural peculiarities but rather one's movements, body postures, and powers." Aside from the evidence of early imitation, recent research demonstrates that young infants are attuned to proprioceptive information in order to control complex actions such as reaching for a sound emitting or glowing object in the dark (Clifton, Rochat, Robin, & Berthier, 1994). Active proprioception combined with vestibular information is a self-referential system operating from birth, an integral part of any self-produced action and exploration that involve multiple modalities. This system provides basic information about the self as actor, whether it is in the context of an interaction with physical or biological resources (i.e., objects or people). This means that at least early on, the ecological self would develop equally within the social and physical realm. By the second month, when infants become markedly more people oriented and socially aware with the emergence of social expressions such as oriented smiling, the social context probably gains in importance over the world of physical objects in determining new forms of self-knowledge.

In conclusion, considering the inseparability of perception and action from birth, together with the basic principle of coperception emphasized by Gibson, it is reasonable to postulate that from the onset of development, information specifying the self as a differentiated, agentive, and situated entity in the environment does exist and is actively used by young infants. This information is at the origins of self-knowledge, announcing and preparing for the emergence of the conceptual self that has been extensively studied by developmental psychologists using mirror self-recognition tests. The enormous challenge for developmentalists is to understand and account for the functional link between the early sense of an ecological self, and the later sense of a conceptual–explicit self expressed by children capable of identifying themselves in specular as well as mental reflections. This question has not been addressed within the ecological approach presented in this chapter.

REFERENCES

Amsterdam, B. (1972). Mirror self-image reactions before age two. *Developmental Psychobiology, 5,* 297–305.

Anisfeld, M. (1991). Neonatal imitation. *Developmental Review, 11,* 60–97.

Bahrick, L. E., & Watson, J. S. (1985). Detection of intermodal proprioceptive-visual contingency as a potential basis of self-perception in infancy. *Developmental Psychology, 21,* 963–973.

Bertenthal, B. I., & Bai, D. L. (1989). Infants' sensitivity to optical flow for controlling posture. *Developmental Psychology, 25,* 936–945.

Butterworth, G. (1990). Self-perception in infancy. In Cicchetti & K. M. Beeghly (Eds.), The self in transition: Infancy to childhood (pp. 119–137). Chicago: The University of Chicago Press.

Butterworth, G., & Hicks, L. (1977). Visual proprioception and postural stability in infancy: A developmental study. *Perception, 6,* 255–262.

Case, R. (1991). Stages in the development of the young child's first sense of self. *Developmental Review, 11,* 210–230.

Clifton, R. K., Morrongiello, B. A., Kulig, J. W., & Dowd, J. M. (1981). Newborns' orientation toward sound: Possible implications for cortical development. *Child Development, 52,* 833–838.

Clifton, R. K., Perris, E. E., & Bullinger, A. (1991). Infants' perception of auditory space. *Developmental Psychology, 27,* 187–197.

Clifton, R. K., Rochat, P., Robin, D. J., & Berthier, N. E. (1994). Multimodal perception in the control of infant reaching. *Journal of Experimental Psychology: Human Perception and Performance, 20,* 876–886.

Crook, C. K. (1979). The organization and control of infant sucking. In H. W. Reese & L. P. Lipsitt (Eds.), *Advances in child development and behavior* (Vol. 14, pp. 209–246). San Diego, CA: Academic Press.

De Casper, A. J., & Fifer, W. P. (1980). Of human bonding: Newborns prefer their mother's voice. *Science, 208,* 1174–1176.

Dixon, J. C. (1957). Development of self recognition. *Journal of Genetic Psychology, 91,* 251–256.

Donaldson, M. (1992). *Human minds: An exploration.* New York: Penguin Books.

Eimas, P. D. (1982). Speech perception: A view of the initial state and perceptual mechanisms. In J. Mehler, M. Garrett, & E. Walker (Eds.), *Perspectives on mental representation: Experimental and theoretical studies of cognitive processes and capacities* (pp. 339–360). Hillsdale, NJ: Erlbaum.

Field, T. M. (1979). Differential behavioral and cardiac responses of 3-month-old infants to a mirror and peer. *Infant Behavior and Development, 2,* 179–184.

Freud, S. (1961). The ego and the id. In J. Strachey (Ed. & Trans.), *The standard edition of the complete psychological works of Sigmund Freud* (Vol.19, pp. 3–66). London: Hogarth.

Gallup, G. G., Jr. (1970). Chimpanzees: Self-recognition. *Science, 167,* 86–87.

Gibson, E. J. (1969). *Principles of perceptual learning and development.* New York: Appleton-Century-Crofts.

Gibson, E. J. (1982). The concept of affordances in development: The renascence of functionalism. In W. Andrew Collins (Ed.), *The concept of development, the Minnesota Symposia on Child Psychology* (Vol. 3, pp. 55–81). New York: Wiley.

Gibson, E. J. (1993). Ontogenesis of the perceived self. In U. Neisser (Ed.), *The perceived Self: Ecological and interpersonal sources of self-knowledge* (pp. 25–42). New York: Cambridge University Press.

Gibson, E. J., & Walker, A. S. (1984). Development of knowledge of visual-tactual affordances of substance. *Child Development, 55,* 453–460.

Gibson, J. J. (1979). *The ecological approach to visual perception.* Boston: Houghton-Mifflin.

Glasersfeld, E. von. (1988). *The construction of knowledge: Contributions to conceptual semantics.* Salinas, CA: Intersystems Publications.

Guillaume, P. (1926). *L'imitation chez l'enfant* [Child imitation]. Paris: Alcan.

James, W. (1890). *The principles of psychology.* New York: Henry Holt & Co.

Jouen, F. (1984). Visual-vestibular interactions in infancy. *Infant Behavior and Development, 7,* 135–145.

Juczyck, P. W. (1985). The high-amplitude sucking technique as a methodological tool in speech perception research. In G. Gottlieb & N. A. Krasnegor (Eds.), *Measurement of audition and vision in the first year of postnatal life* (pp. 195–222). Norwood, NJ: Ablex.

Kalnins, I. V., & Bruner, J. S. (1973). The coordination of visual observation and instrumental behavior in early infancy. *Peception, 2,* 307–314.

Korner, A. F., & Kraemer, H. C. (1972). Individual differences in spontaneous oral behavior in neonates. In J. F. Bosma (Ed.), *Third Symposium on Oral Sensation an Perception* (pp. 335–346). Bethesda, MD: U.S. Department of Health, Education and Welfare Publication.

Koupernik, C., & Dailly, R. (1968). *Developpement neuro-psychique du nourrisson: sémiologie normale et pathologique* [Infant neuropsychological development]. Paris: Presses Universitaires de France.

Lewis, M., & Brooks-Gunn, J. (1979). *Social cognition and the acquisition of self.* New York: Plenum Press.

Loveland, K. A. (1986). Discovering the affordances of a reflecting surface. *Developmental Review, 6,* 1–24.

Macfarlane, A. (1975). Olfaction and the development of social preferences in the human neonate. In R. Porter & M. O'Connor (Eds.), *Parent-infant interation, CIBA Fundation Symposium 33* (pp. 103–117). Amsterdam: Elsevier-North Holland.

Meltzoff, A. N. (1990). Foundations for developing a concept of self: The role of imitation in relating self to other and the value of social mirroring, social modeling, and self practice in infancy. In K. Cicchetti & M. Beeghly (Eds.), *The self in transition: Infancy to childhood* (pp. 139–164). Chicago: The University of Chicago Press.

Meltzoff, A. N., & Borton, R. W. (1979). Intermodal matching in human neonates. *Nature, 282,* 403–404.

Meltzoff, A. N., & Moore, M. K. (1977). Imitation of facial and manual gestures by human neonates. *Science, 198,* 75–78.

Morgan, R., & Rochat, P. (1994, June). *Perception of self-produced leg movements by 3–5-month-old infants in conditions of conflicting visual-proprioceptive feedback.* Poster presented at the International Conference on Infant Studies, Paris, France.

Mounoud, P., & Vinter, A. (1981). Le développement de l'image de soi chez l'enfant de 3 à 11 ans. Reconnaissance du visage dans un miroir déformant. *La reconnaissance de son image chez l'enfant et l'animal* [Face recognition in a deforming mirror]. Paris: Delachaux et Niestlé.

Murray, L., & Trevarthen, C. (1985). Emotional regulation of interaction between two-month-olds and their mothers. In T. M. Field & N. A. Fox (Eds.), *Social perception in infants* (pp. 177–197). Norwood, NJ: Ablex.

Neisser, U. (1991). Two perceptually given aspects of the self and their development. *Developmental Review, 11,* 197–209.

Neisser, U. (1993). The self perceived. In U. Neisser (Ed.), *The perceived self: Ecological and interpersonal sources of self-knowledge* (pp. 3–24). Cambridge, England: Cambridge University Press.

Orbach, J., Traub, A. L., & Olson, R. (1980). Etudes psychophysiques sur l'image du corps. Image spéculaire du corps ouvrage èditè par J. Corraze [Psychophysiological studies of self-image: Specular image of the body]. Paris: Collection Rhadamanthc.

Papousek, H., & Papousek, M. (1974). Mirror-image and self recognition in young infants: A new method of experimental analysis. *Developmental Psychobiology, 7,* 149–157.

Piaget, J. (1952). *The origin of intelligence in children.* New York: International Universities Press.

Piaget, J. (1961). *The psychology of intelligence.* Totowa, NJ: Littlefield, Adams & Co.

Piaget, J., & Inhelder, B. (1974). *The child's construction of quantities: Conservation and atomism.* London: Routledge & Kegan Paul.

Preyer, W. (1887). *L'âme de l'enfant* [The soul of the child]. Paris: Alcan.

Reed, E. S. (1982). An outline of a theory of action systems. *Journal of Motor Behavior, 14,* 98–134.

Rochat, P. (1983). Oral touch in young infants: Responses to variations of nipple characteristics in the first months of life. *International Journal of Behavioral Development, 6,* 123–133.

Rochat, P. (1989). Object manipulation and exploration in 2- to 5-month-old infants. *Developmental Psychology, 25,* 871–884.

Rochat, P. (1992). Self-sitting and reaching in 5–8-month-old infants: The impact of posture and its development on early eye–hand coordination. *Journal of Motor Behavior, 24,* 210–220.

Rochat, P. (1993a). Hand–mouth coordination in the newborn: Morphology, determinants, and early development of a basic act. In G. J. P. Savelsbergh (Ed.), *The development of coordination in infancy* (pp. 265–288). Advances in Psychology Series. Amsterdam: Elsevier Publisher.

Rochat, P. (1993b). L'objet des actions du bébé (The object young infants' action). In V. Pouthas & F. Jouen (Eds.), *Les comportements du bébé: Expression de son savoir?* [Infant behavior: Expression of knowledge?] (pp. 209–232). Brussels, Belgium: Mardaga Publisher.

Rochat, P. (1993c) Connaissance de soi chez le bébé [Self-knowledge in infancy]. *Psychologie Française, 38*(1), 41–51.

Rochat, P. (Ed.). (1995). *The self in infancy: Theory and research.* Amsterdam: Elsevier/North-Holland.

Rochat, P., Blass, E. M., & Hoffmeyer, L. B. (1988). Oropharyngeal control of hand–mouth coordination in newborn infants. *Developmental Psychology, 24,* 459–463.

Rochat, P., & Bullinger, A. (1994). Posture and functional action in infancy. In A. Vyt, H. Bloch, & M. Bornstein (Eds.), *Francophone perspectives on structure and process in mental development* (pp. 15–34). Hillsdale, NJ: Erlbaum.

Rochat, P., & Goubet, N. (1993, March). *Determinants of infants' perceived reachability.* Poster presented at the 60th Meeting of the Society for Research in Child Development, New Orleans, Lousiana.

Rochat, P., & Goubet, N. (1995). Development of sitting and reaching in 5–6 month-old infants. *Infant Behavior and Development, 18*(1), 53–68.

Rochat, P., & Morgan, R. (1993). Self-perception by 3 month-old infants. In S. Valenti & J. B. Pittenger (Eds.), *Studies in perception and action* (Vol. 2, pp. 14–18). Hillsdale, NJ: Erlbaum.

Rochat, P., & Morgan, R. (1995). Spatial determinants in the perception of self-produced leg movements by 3- to 5-month-old infants. *Developmental Psychology, 31,* 626–636.

Rochat, P., & Reed, E. S. (1987). Le concept d'affordance et les connaissances du nourrisson. *Psychologie Francaise, 32*(1–2), 97–104.

Rochat, P., & Senders, S. J. (1991). Active touch in infancy: Action systems in development. In M. J. Weiss & P. R. Zelazo (Eds.), *Newborn attention: Biological constraints and the influence of experience* (pp. 412–442). NJ: Ablex.

Rochat, P., & Wraga, M. J. (1993). Postural determinants of perceived reachability. In S. Valenti & J. B. Pittenger (Eds.), *Studies in perception and action* (Vol. 2, pp. 30–35). Hillsdale, NJ: Erlbaum.

Schulman, A. H., & Karplowitz, C. (1976). Mirror-image response during the first two years of life. *Developmental Psychobiology, 10*(3), 133–142.

Siqueland, E. R., & DeLucia, C. A. (1969). Visual reinforcement of non-nutritive sucking in human infants. *Science, 165,* 1144–1146.

Spitz, R. A. (1965). *The first year of life: A psychoanalytic study of normal and deviant development of object relations.* New York: International Universities Press.

Sroufe, A. (1990). An organizational perspective on the self. In D. Cicchetti & M. Beeghly (Eds.), *The self in transition: Infancy to childhood* (pp. 281–307). Chicago: University of Chicago Press.

Stern, D. (1985). *The interpersonal world of the infant.* New York: Basic Books.

Trevarthen, C. (1974). The psychobiology of speech development. In E. H. Lenneberg (Ed.), *Language and brain: Developmental aspects.* Neurosciences Research Program Bulletin, *12,* 570–585.

Tronick, E. (1980). On the primacy of social skills. In D. B. Sawin, L. O. Walder, & J. H. Penticuff (Eds.), *The exceptional infant: Psychosocial risks in infant environment transactions* (pp. 227–254). New York: Bruner & Mazel.

Turvey, M.T., & Shaw, R. (1987). The primacy of perceiving: An ecological reformulation of perception as a point of departure for understanding memory. In L. G. Nilsson (Ed.), *Perspectives on memory research: Essays in honor of Uppsala University's 500th Anniversary* (pp. 94–118). Hillsdale, NJ:Erlbaum.

Van der Meer, A. L. H. (1993, August). *Arm movements in the neonate: Establishing a frame of reference for reaching.* Paper presented at the 7th International Conference on Event Perception and Action, Vancouver, British Columbia, Canada.

Wallon, H. (1970). *De l'acte à la pensée: Essai de psychologie comparée* [From action to thought: Essay in compared psychology]. Collection Champs. Paris: Flammarion. (Original work published 1942)

Yonas, A., & Hartman, B. (1993). Perceiving the affordance of contact in 4- and 5-month-old infants. *Child Development, 64,* 298–308.

Zazzo, R. (1981). Miroir, images, espaces. In P. Mounoud & A. Vinter (Eds.), *La reconnaissance de son image chez l'enfant et l'animal* [Children's and animals' recognition of their own image]. Collection Textes de Base en Psychologie (pp. 77–110). Neuchatel, Paris: Delachaux et Niestlé.

Comment on Rochat

Paula Fitzpatrick

The main challenge for developmental theory is to account for the emergence of complex and stable behavioral patterns from rather primitive initial forms. In his chapter, Rochat outlines an ecological approach that takes the assumption that infants are born with basic behavioral propensities that guide interactions with the environment as its starting point. These basic predispositions to engage in functional activities are the source or axes of developmental change. The propensities expand and grow through the ability to detect regularities in the environment (i.e., invariants). The expansion and integration of these propensities allow the detection of new invariants, which, in turn, support new actions, and so on. I focus my discussion on one of the major themes of the chapter, namely, the importance of the coupling of perception and action.

Rochat points out that the ability to detect invariants is intimately tied to one's ability to move and act on one's environment and vice versa. Infants learn about their bodies and its potential for action through their constant investigation of, predominantly, intermodal invariants: They see

Fitzpatrick comments on Rochat from an ecological realist perspective.

and feel their limbs moving in space and hence become attuned to the correspondence between visual and proprioceptive feedback resulting from body movements. The interdependence between perception and action is an important theme that is also emphasized in more dynamic treatments of development. The dynamical perspective uses a framework for understanding development in terms of self-organizing principles of stability, instability, and behavioral transitions. Characterizing how behavioral patterns emerge from the interaction of many components is the concern. In broad strokes, behavioral patterns can be thought of as collectives or attractive states of the very many component parts of the system, including perceptual variables. Under certain circumstances, particular patterns are preferred and act as attractors in the sense that they are stable states and are chosen more often. Other patterns are possible but more difficult to maintain and hence are unstable. Changes in circumstances (e.g., task, environmental, intentional), however, can alter the stability characteristics of the coordinative modes and result in the discovery of more optimal solutions, previously stable patterns becoming unstable, or new stable configurations appearing. Hence, changes in behavior can be conceptualized as a series of changes in stability characteristics of coordinative modes: the various components cooperate to produce stability or change. These changes are tied to sensitivity to relevant perceptual information. For example, increasing attunement to relevant perceptual information, perceiving consequences of actions and adjusting behavior appropriately, attending more closely to task constraints, all potentially engender changes in the stability of behavioral patterns.

Often, research is characterized as an investigation of either perception or action. Indeed, the dependent measures and theoretical language of the two perspectives tend to emphasize either perceiving or acting. The conceptual tools of an ecological approach such as Rochat's stress, for example, perceptual invariants, whereas more dynamical approaches use the language of stability, instability, and transitions. In one case the focus is on perceptual abilities with a recognition of the importance of movements, and in the other case the focus is on movements themselves with an acknowledgment of the importance of perceptual components. My aim here is to highlight the continuity between work such as Rochat's and more dynamically focused treatments of development. This is accomplished by discussing two research programs that investigate the development of reaching: Rochat's and Thelen's.

Infants tend to begin reaching for objects at around four months of age and by six months are adept at perceiving whether an object is within reach (Clifton, Perris, & Bullinger, 1991; Yonas & Hartman, 1993). As discussed in his chapter, Rochat (1992; Rochat & Goubet, in press) has demonstrated that independent sitting competence is linked to an infant's reaching ability. His research has shown that infants not capable of independent sitting, when provided with sufficient postural support, will reach for an object. Without postural support, these same infants will not reach, suggesting that the development of postural control alters the way infants interact with their environment. Furthermore, these changes in behavior implicate perception of relevant information, namely, perception of object "reachability" and points of postural reversibility. To further test these perceptual abilities Rochat and Goubert (1993) studied how accurate infants are at perceiving whether an object is within reach. Objects were presented at one of four distance: two within reach, one at the limit of prehensile space, and one out of reach. Infants with good control of independent sitting were more likely to reach for objects presented at the limits of "reachability," demonstrating an expanded perception of prehensile space. In another study, infants' arms were weighted in perturb postural stability. Results show that infants reach less with weighted limbs, indicating they are able to perceive when reaching for an object will result in loss of balance. Taken together, this research suggests that relatively young infants have a sense of their body's effectivities and are able to adjust their behavior on the basis of detecting concurrent perceptual information.

To reiterate, the continuous interplay between perception and action guiding and shaping reaching behavior is implicated. Thelen's research (e.g., Thelen et al., 1993) focuses on the movement solutions involved in learning to reach more than the perceptual underpinnings. She has shown that infants modulate their preferred movements or intrinsic dynamics to achieve the task goal of contracting a (desired) object. In brief, this entails adjusting and controlling limb stiffness and energy: stiffening the limbs (in the case of high-activity infants), increasing movement velocity (in the case of low-activity infants). Whereas this research emphasizes the forms of the reaching movements and how these change developmentally, Thelen points to the fact that the sculpting and modulating of forces is dependent on perception, perceiving the consequences of movements, for example. The continual process of perceptual–motor exploration and discovery is essential for fine tuning the intrinsic dynamics to achieve well-controlled and accurate reaches. A major concern of developmental research from a dynamical perspective is to isolate and manipulate critical factors that move a system through points of stability or from one behavioral form to another. As Thelen (1995) points out, "simulating developmental change" is an important way to understand the process of how a system moves into new configurations, from one performance level to another. Although Rochat does not discuss his findings in these terms, his reaching experiments can be seen as simulating developmental change. Increasing the postural support of infants not capable of independent sitting allowed them to perform (i.e., reach for objects) at a higher level; adding weights to the limbs of independent sitters forced them to perform at a lower level. In conclusion, this account of the development of reaching nicely demonstrates the need to study both the movements that allow for the detection of invariants and achievement of task goals and the perceptual capabilities necessary to perceive those invariants. To have a complete and coherent account of development, the commonalities and links between action research and perception research must be articulated.

REFERENCES

Clifton, R. K., Perris, E. E., & Bullinger, A. (1991). Infant's perception of auditory space. *Developmental Psychology, 27*, 187–197.

Rochat, P. (1992). Self-sitting and reaching in 5–8 month-old infants: The impact of posture and its development on early eye–hand coordination. *Journal of Motor Behavior, 24*(2), 210–212.

Rochat, P., & Goubet, N. (1993). *Determinants of infants' perceived reachability.* Poster presented at the 60th Meeting of the Society for Research in Child Development, New Orleans, LA.

Rochat, P., & Goubet, N. (in press). Development of sitting and reaching in 5–6 month-old infants. *Infant Behavior and Development, 18.*

Thelen, E. (1995). Motor development: A new synthesis. *American Psychologist, 50,* 79–95.

Thelen, E., Corbetta, D., Kamm, K., Spencer, J. P., Schneider, K., & Zernicke, R. F. (1993). The transition to reaching: Mapping intention and intrinsic dynamics. *Child Development, 64,* 1058–1098.

Yonas, A., & Hartman, B. (1993). Perceiving the affordance of contact in four- and five-month-old infants. *Child Development, 64,* 298–308.

5

Change and Variation in Responses to Perceptual Information

Nancy de Villiers Rader

M y goal in this chapter is to set forth my current conceptualization of the organism–environment relationship, introducing developmentally significant issues that this particular approach creates, describing the relationship of these issues to contrasting views, and illustrating how my infant research addresses them. The view of the developing organism put forth here has its roots in Gibsonian theory, epistemology, evolutionary biology, and developmental disabilities. The core from which this conceptualization builds is a consideration of changes in the response of an individual over time to the same environmental event. This consideration leads to an attempt to articulate the processes that participate in effecting this change and that also create individual variability. The concept of development inherent in this presentation is one in which the organism–environment relationship is continually changing as the organism's nervous system and form emerge out of basic biological processes and environmental interactions. These changes result in an organism with

The author acknowledges the assistance of undergraduate students who were part of her Research Team at Ithaca College. Support for the preparation of this chapter was provided through a Faculty Research Grant from Ithaca College.

new values for the likelihood of motoric, perceptual, or cognitive responses to the environment.

DIRECT PERCEPTION AND DEVELOPMENT

My work stems from a set of fundamentals inherent to a direct theory of perception (see, e.g., J. J. Gibson, 1961, 1966, 1979). A primary tenet is that sensory information is sufficient to specify the environment at the level of the organism. In other words, given an appropriately complex analysis of sensory arrays over time, there is a corresponding invariant for any given event, object, or layout. Therefore, there is no need for cognitively based inferences, interpretations, and guesses to make sense of meaningless sensory stimulation. This tenet is in evident contrast with a constructive approach that posits that meaningful perception relies on learning to interpret sensory data through cognition (Gregory, 1972). A corollary of the direct perception tenet of sufficient information is that cognitive constructs such as mental representations are unnecessary and misleading in explaining perception. In contrast, a constructivist approach requires mental representations as the memory mechanisms that provide the knowledge required for the sensory interpretations to occur. A second tenet is that information pickup results in the perception of affordances. That is, what the environment offers an organism (i.e., what it affords that organism) is apprehended on the pickup of the specifying information. Finally, information pickup and the perception of affordances are constrained by evolutionary history. That is, the type of information picked up and the nature of what is afforded varies with the nature of the organism, a nature that has been shaped by evolutionary pressures.

There is certainly much in a direct theory of perception still to be fleshed out, such as identifying the information that specifies particular "objects" of perception and demonstrating that organisms can and do pick up and use this information to respond adaptively to the environment. A common approach that has been taken in the study of direct perception is a psychophysical one, where the relationship between the physical input and a psychological response is sought. While acknowledging that the analysis of the information from a Gibsonian perspective is much more complex than that of traditional psychophysics, there are nonetheless important questions for development that go beyond such a descriptive approach.

One question that arises from a developmental perspective within a direct theory of perception is how an organism comes to the point of using or being able to use information in the sensory array. Young organisms, like mature ones, can be seen to respond not at all to information present, or they may respond in one way to information present at one point in time and in another way to the same information at another point in time. For those working within a theory of direct perception, this consideration makes it necessary to analyze the origins of an organism's ability to pick up and respond to information in a particular way. It also requires an analysis of the organism's motivational and emotional states. Such analyses should also contribute to an understanding of individual differences, including the identification of differences that might derive initially from biological factors at the genetic level. The remainder of this chapter offers a theoretical structure for such an analysis and a description of three research projects with infants in terms of this theoretical structure.

HIDDEN AFFORDANCES

A consideration of the problem of development has led me to consider the case of what I have termed *hidden affordances* (Rader, 1993) as a means to analyze one type of change over time to perceptual information. When J. J. Gibson discussed affordances, he did so as one who was sensitive to the complexities of the sensory array over time and to the richness of the organism–environment relationship, but, also, primarily, as a psychophysicist. He argued that, given that the composition and layout of surfaces determine what they afford, and given that the sensory array specifies the nature of those surfaces, then pickup of information in the sensory array in perceiving those surfaces results in perception of the affordances they provide (J. J. Gibson, 1979, p. 127). For example, the size of an object relative to an organism determines whether it is graspable, and that size is specified by aspects of the optic array. We might also add that the chemical nature of that object is what makes it edible and that this is specified by gustatory information. Yet, what of the situation where a child has tasted an object, found it attractive, and then sees it again? At the point of this second viewing, there is a discontinuity in time as to the sensory specification of its edibility. The affordance of a pleasant taste is not specified by the information available while only viewing the object. In this sense, the affordance of the pleasant taste sensation is "hidden"; it is not in the light. Someone who had not tasted the object in the past could not perceive its taste by vision alone. The taste is revealed to the unknowing through gustatory exploration as keys hidden in a coat pocket can be revealed by jingling. In the future, the taste will be known from appearance alone on the basis of *past* exploration. A psychologist working from a direct theory of perception yet interested in development must answer the question of how the optic array *itself* comes to produce desire for the object on the basis of past exploration. In this case there is no amodal invariant across the two modalities; information from one modality alone creates a response based on previous experience with a second modality that does not share structured information.

A traditional learning theorist would say that the organism must associate the sight of the object and the taste and then describe the conditions under which such an association occurs. A classic cognitive psychologist would make reference to an internal representation of the object and might talk about the representation of the object acquiring the property of taste; a reference would surely be made about the organism *remembering* how good the object tasted. In contrast, Gibson referred to the organism's perception of a compound invariant or an invariant of an invariant (J. J. Gibson, 1979, p. 140). That is, an invariant relationship exists between the information for the gustatory system and the information for the visual system, and the organism perceives this higher order invariance. The case of what I refer to as a hidden affordance is, then, one type of compound invariant. It should be pointed out, however, that creating the construct of a hidden affordance has led me into territory Gibson clearly avoided. Nevertheless, I believe that this territory must be explored if development is to be more fully explained from the perspective of direct perception.

I believe that focusing on hidden affordances in particular is important in that they seem to lie at the heart of what learning theorists and cognitive psychologists call learning and memory (but well within the realm of perception given the formulation presented here). They are certainly an important aspect of the development of knowledge. I also think it important to highlight hidden affordances because they are key to understanding much of what many think of as heavily dependent on internal representations. For example, in Neisser's (1991) most recent view of cognition, he separates out a system of direct perception from a knowledge system based on representation. According to this account, the child perceives the object as a graspable object in a particular location on the basis of direct perception, but as that object that tasted good yesterday on the basis of internal representations. Implications of a hidden affordance analysis spread readily to such areas as early word acquisition, surely considered dependent on mental representations and solidly in the realm of cognition. Yet, the situation of a child learning what a word means is perhaps not that different from the example given above using sight and taste. When a child initially hears a linguistic sound stream, the auditory experience does not in and of itself lead to meaningful perception (i.e., the affordance of the sound stream is hidden). Clearly, the affordance is not specified by the sensory information in the way that structured light from a chair specifies "sit-on-ability." The infant must learn the affordance over a period of experience by detecting the invariant relationship between the referent and its sign. By the account presented here, hearing the sign brings with it the perception of the affordances of the referent in the same way that seeing the object brings with it the perception of its taste.

NEEDS, EMOTIONS, AND ATTENTION

In considering the organism–environment relation, one must consider needs as related to the goals of the organism. Organisms change their goals over time. These goals may change from minute to minute or across years. The particular needs of the organism at a particular time determine what information is searched for and the type of response made, if any. An apple says "eat me" when someone who likes apples is hungry but not when two youngsters are having an apple fight or an artist is arranging a still life. It is not that the affordance of eating is not there, but that this is not the affordance related to the goal of the organism at that time. And, while it may be not only perceivable but perceived, it will not be acted upon. Such goal setting may often be linked to biologically timed events. For example, hormonal changes combined with cultural expectations may increase the likelihood that a goal becomes finding a mate.

Furthermore, the particular emotional state of an organism has a profound influence on the pickup of information and on the response made. A highly aroused individual does not select the same information or make the same responses as a relaxed individual. The crying infant does not show the same responses to an object or event as an infant in a quiet alert state. This aspect of the organism's state is fluctuating in time and not a developmental issue per se; however, the relative time spent in different emotional states clearly is.

Some changes in responses to information over time can be characterized as attentional. In a chapter I wrote with E. J. Gibson (E. J. Gibson & Rader, 1979), we defined *attention* as bringing perception in line with the task at hand. With practice, as one develops expertise, the pickup of information becomes more economical and control over the response systems becomes more precise. When a task is defined, by the self or by another, attention is "good" if the perceptual systems efficiently select out the information needed to perform that task. For example, processing the information needed to hurl a projectile across a room may be considered good attention if the task at hand is to sink a basketball in a hoop. It would not be considered good attention by a classroom teacher if the teacher had defined the task as comprehending a page in a textbook. Of course, from the viewpoint of the child interested in sending an airborne eraser to her friend, such perceptual processes would constitute attention for this self-defined task. The child's problem has to do not with an absence of something internal called *attention*, but with the choice of task. This role of task setting leads to a consideration of the organism's motivation and goals.

THE "RE-CREATION" OF PERCEPTUAL INFORMATION

Many aspects of what is generally considered to be important in the development of an individual involve speech, writing, or drawing. In the perspective presented here, these abilities are viewed as resulting from the re-creation of perceptual information, that is, creating the information original to the initial perceiving. Not only do human organisms pick up information and perceive affordances, but they are, to some extent, able to produce that information. A simple form of re-creation is imitation. Humans, perhaps uniquely, are also able to produce information in the form of speech, writing, drawing, and even mental imagery. Speech, for example, produces information that specifies meaning for the listener. Drawing produces for the viewer information that specifies objects or layouts. This way of characterizing these behaviors is radically different not only from a representional account but from other ecologically oriented accounts as well. What is being proposed here is not that there are internal representations that are necessary to give meaning to perceptual data, but that the perceptual systems can recreate information that was picked up at points distant in time from the initial experience. This information re-creation allows humans to respond and communicate in many ways that otherwise would not be possible. Given this analysis, one would wish to determine what makes such re-creation possible and how this activity contributes further to exploration and discovery.

PROCESSES OF CHANGE

The problem of responses that vary across time is not unique to an ontogenetic perspective; however, it tends to be ignored by those who study adult performance. (An exception to this is research studying improvements in motor control with practice or the acquisition of expertise for some task.) Perceptual learning refers broadly to changes in the organism–environment relationship over time and brought about by experience. As such, it is a type of learning at any age. Perceptual learning has been characterized by E. J. Gibson (1967, 1988) as a discovery process leading to differentiation of the environment. The organism perceives more of the world with experience—discovering patterns, synchronicities, invariants in the perceptual flow, and higher order invariants. Many excellent studies have shown that infants are capable of perceptual learning, as shown by their ability to discover a host of environmental relationships (see, e.g., Adolph, Eppler, & Gibson, 1993; E. J. Gibson, 1988). With discovery of the regular relationships between events over time, expectations develop. The infant who perceives the movement of a mobile with a leg kick comes to expect the mobile to move when the same leg movement is made again. The infant is attuned to relationships that occur together over time and builds a set of expectations that allow prediction and planning (Rader, 1989).

However, while we can often describe what is discovered, how are we to characterize the organismic changes that occur as these discoveries are made? Is it possible to detail the state of the organism at different points in time? What allows the discovery process to occur and what constrains it? Is *what* can be discovered limited at different stages in development? For example, can infants respond to hidden affordances as defined above? This particular question is addressed in a later section of the chapter that describes infant research. Obviously, there are limits on the type of response that can be made. For example, some ontogenetic changes in response come about because of somatic growth. At one point in development a child is only able to swipe at an object; later, the child is able to contact an object, at another point crawl to an object, and at another time walk to it. It follows that some types of discovery dependent on the ability to locomote or manipulate are not available at all ages. However, other changes in response are not so easily accounted for. For example, why does stranger distress typically appear so long after the ability to discriminate faces occurs?

Are there instances where responses change as the result of "maturation," defined here as a change in the nervous system that creates new potential for response? This concept of maturation is far from the idea of an "unfolding" of a response that has been preprogrammed. The idea of maturation as a change in response potential is, I believe, quite compatible with a dynamic analysis of developmental changes (see Fogel & Thelen, 1987). Activity within the environment results in the coordination of response components that allow a more advanced response. However, ontogenetic time may still be important for determining when and how that coordination occurs. The "initial state" of the organism should not be taken for granted in a developmental approach; it itself must be accounted for. A toddler may understand the game of "catch" but be unable to bring the arms and hands into position with the necessary timing so that the ball is caught. Changes in the ability to reach accurately, catch a ball, climb steps, or perform a cartwheel do not come about strictly as the result of perceptual learning. The organism undergoes physical changes that result in a change in the potential to respond, as well as changes in the ability to respond brought about through a discovery process, often in the context of assistance from caregivers in the environment (e.g., see Zukow, 1986, 1989).

Certainly, changes do occur in the organism that are genetically programmed to occur over time. Examples of these time-tagged changes are those involving hormone production. Other related changes, such as myelinization, tissue differentiation, and somatic growth occur at different rates throughout development. Changes in the architecture of the nervous system, the speed of neural transmissions, or body strength and shape affect the potential to pick up and respond to information (see Caplan, 1980; K. R. Gibson & Peterson, 1991). Just as phylogenetic differences exist for information pickup and response, so do ontogenetic differences. These species differences have their origins fundamentally at the level of the nature and structure of the nervous system. So too must ontogenetic differences.

Related to the view of maturation as important in ontogenetic change is the notion of a critical period (Schneirla & Rosenblatt, 1963; Scott, Stewart, & de Ghett, 1974). For example, humans are particularly sensitive to certain aspects of language information during specific periods of time

(Lenneberg, 1967; Long, 1990; Werker & Tees, 1984). Are there periods of time when the organism is "tuned" to search out other kinds of information? For those observing children 3 to 6 years old, it is obvious that they are particularly tuned to perceptual information related to gender identity. The smallest sampling appears to be sufficient to create new responses concerning what to wear and what kinds of games to play. Again, the suggestion is not that there is an all-encompassing control of behavior through neural preprogramming, but that the system is in a different state at different periods of ontogenetic time, stemming, at least in part, from the biologically controlled timing of events.

Table 1 summarizes the relations between these sources of change in the developing organism and the kinds of changes that have been described.

ONTOGENETIC VARIABILITY

In addition to focusing on a changing organism, an ontogenetic perspective brings up issues of variation across individuals. Are individual differences to be accounted for solely by differences in the environment with which the organism interacts? Or are there differences in the ways organisms are initially tuned or become so through particular patterns of growth or rates of maturation? (See Rader, 1985.) In considering the

Table 1

Changes in the Organism–Environment Relationship With Development

Types and Sources of Change

- Change in knowledge on the basis of discovery
- Change in potential on the basis of physical growth
- Change in goals on the basis of internally and externally derived needs
- Change in efficiency on the basis of practice
- Change in re-creativity on the basis of discovery, potential, and practice

organism–environment relationship, we should consider differences across individuals as much as differences across species.

An epigenetic approach was described by Aristotle in the fourth century B.C. to account for organ development, on the basis of interaction among simple parts or constituents of the egg (see Waddington, 1953). In the case of ontogenetic specialization, constituent parts include components of action and perception in the context of a particular nervous system in a given state.

An extreme case of variation based primarily in the organism rather than the environment occurs when a child has a named disorder, such as Down syndrome. Here we must look at differences in response to the same information that are engendered by the disorder. We must search for group invariance across organismic variation.

THREE STUDIES OF INFANTS

In this section of the chapter, I present three infant research projects carried out in my laboratory with student collaborators. This research both has derived from and contributed to the conceptualization of the organism–environment relationship described above. One issue that is addressed concerns the ability of young infants to perceive "hidden affordances" as indicated by their reaching behavior both before and after tasting an object. A second issue covered is the contribution of maturation to the visual cliff avoidance response, as an example of a change in the potential to respond. Finally, variability between Down syndrome and normally developing infants in responding to mother and stranger approaches is examined as an example of inherent differences.

Reaching

Bower's early research on reaching was concerned with the visual abilities of infants. For example, he and his colleagues sought to determine whether infants perceive size and distance veridically, despite the "problem" of size constancy, and to see whether neonatal infants discriminate visually between two- and three-dimensional stimuli (Bower, 1972; Bower,

Broughton, & Moore, 1970; Bower, Dunkeld, & Wishart, 1979). The focus of this research was not on ontogenetic change but on establishing how early perceptual abilities were present. Whereas other researchers did not replicate his claim that infants less than 2 weeks old differentially reach for two- and three-dimensional stimuli (DiFranco, Muir, & Dodwell, 1978; Dodwell, Muir, & DiFranco, 1976), further research has shown the infant to be very much tuned to information specifying a graspable object. For example, Rader and Stern (1982) found that arm extensions in infants 8–16 days old were more likely to occur in the presence of either a ball or picture of a ball than in the absence of patterned stimulation. Bower et al. (1970) and von Hofsten (1982) reported that, although unable to make contact with an object, neonates aimed their reaches in its direction.

During the first year of life, infants develop the ability to take into account characteristics of the object and make hand–finger adjustments in preparation for reaching a goal. Bruner and Koslowski (1972) found that grasplike hand shapes occurred more often in infants 8–22 weeks old when the object was of a graspable size. Yonas and Hartman (1993) observed that 5-month-olds were less likely to reach for an object if it was beyond reach. Newell, Scully, McDonald, and Baillargeon (1989) showed that infants as young as 4 months used grip configurations appropriate to the object properties of size and shape. Von Hofsten and Ronnqvist (1988) found that 5-month-old infants showed adaptive changes in grasping relative to the target size only when they were close to contact with the object, whereas 9-month-old infants adjusted their grasping actions during the reach. Lockman, Ashmead, and Bushnell (1984) and Morrongiello and Rocca (1989) reported similar results. Ashmead and his associates (Ashmead, McCarty, Lucas, & Belvedere, 1993) have found that 9-month-olds are better able than 5-month-olds to change the path of their reaches with changes in visual information.

Von Hofsten (1980) has suggested that what develops is mainly the mobility aspects of reaching, which make for more economical and flexible reaching. He described (1979, 1991) the nature of change in the structuring of the reach from about 15 weeks through 31 weeks of age. The reaching response during this time is changing more and more toward the two-phase structure (see Jeannerod, 1981, 1984) used by adults. Matthew and Cook (1990) reported a similar change in the nature of the motor response between the ages of 4.5 and 7 months, and they detailed the corrections that occur throughout the reach. Thelan and her associates (Thelan et al., 1993) have examined the changes in motor control in infants from 12 to 22 weeks of age by recording the activity of individual muscles. They found that infants during this age period can adjust the force and compliance of the arm while reaching.

The overall picture created by this body of research is that adaptive functioning is increasing throughout infancy. The infant begins with some responsiveness in the arm and hand systems on presentation of appropriate stimulation and builds on this action to achieve a more expert level of responding. Yet, neither an infant nor an adult reaches whenever perceptual information specifying a graspable object is available. A goal of the conceptualization presented here is to understand this variability in response through taking into account the state of the organism at the time the object is presented. This state would consist of the organism's motivational and emotional settings, as well as its atunement and response capacity.

An adult organism is more likely to reach for something if what it affords matches current needs. Can this level of coordination between motivation, perception, and action be seen in the young infant? To test this, Rader and Vaughn (1991) conducted a study to determine whether a young infant's arm and hand responses to a graspable object are affected by past experiences of taste. In terms of the ontogenetic conceptualization presented earlier, this study concerned both an infant's response to information as influenced by goals and the ability to discover and use a hidden affordance. Infants were presented visually with a pretzel-shaped teething ring both before and after experiencing its taste as either sweet or bitter. The question was whether infants would vary their responses due to hidden affordance of taste.

Fifty-seven infants 2.0 to 6.6 months were tested and videotaped as they sat in a contoured infant seat with a foam neck support. During the pretasting and posttasting trials, the object was suspended at fingertip distance for a period of 2 minutes. Following the pretasting trials, the infant was removed from the infant seat and placed on the parent's lap. The parent then showed the infant an identical teething ring that had been flavored with either a sugar solution or a quinine-alum solution and placed the teething ring in the infant's mouth over a 3-minute period. Following this tasting procedure, the infant was returned to the infant seat for the posttasting trials.

The infant's reaches, thumb flexions, and leg kicks were coded by assistants blind to the taste condition. A *reach* was defined as any extension of the arm away from the body that occurs while the infant is attending to the object. *Thumb flexion* was defined as a thumb bent toward the palm during attending. *Leg movements* included extension or moving apart of the legs in any direction. Leg kicks were included as an indication of overall activity level.

Infants were divided into the following three age groups for analysis of the data: 2–3.4, 3.5–5, and 5.1–6.6 months. Figure 1 shows the group means by age for the reaching measure, and Figure 2 shows the group means across all ages for the thumb flexion measure. Analyses of the data revealed that the two older age groups showed the effect of taste on reaching, whereas the youngest group did not. However, infants across age groups showed an increase in thumb flexion when the object had tasted sweet and a decrease when the object had tasted bitter. Taste conditions did not affect leg kicks. The absence of an effect of taste conditions on leg kicks allowed us to interpret the arm and hand responses in terms of a specialized response, as opposed to a generalized increase in activity level caused by the taste experience. Infants as young as 2 months of age responded to the hidden taste experience by adjusting the thumb relative to the palm, an action necessary in later grasping. Beginning at age 3.5 months, infants responded to the taste experience by adapting the reaching response.

The results of this study show that infants as young as 2 months of age are capable of a very sophisticated discovery process that involves hidden affordances. They are capable of perceiving the relationship between taste and appearance and then using that relationship in perceiving the af-

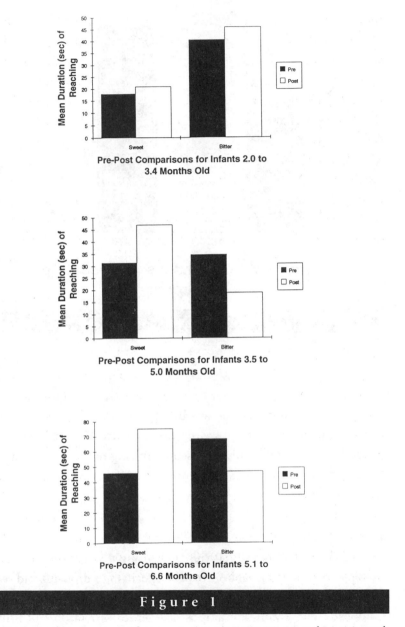

Figure 1

Changes in the reaching response with taste experience in 2–3.4, 3.5–5.0, and 5.1–6.6 month old infants.

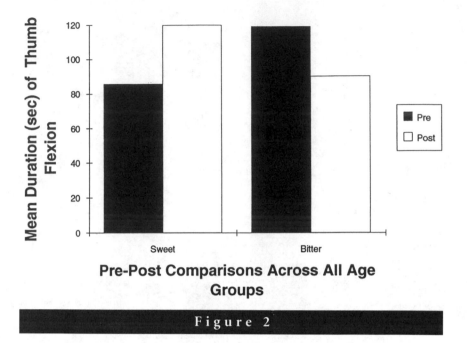

Pre-Post Comparisons Across All Age Groups

Figure 2

Changes in thumb flexion with taste experience across all age groups.

fordance of the object at a later time, on the basis of its appearance alone. In this study, response change was brought about as the result of experience and the discovery process. To ensure that the infants' reaching was the result of tasting the object presented during reaching trials, a follow-up study had infants taste a different object. In this case infants' reaching was not affected by taste.

Visual Cliff Avoidance

E. J. Gibson and Walk's (1960) research using a visual cliff showed that most infants pick up visual information specifying a drop-off and respond adaptively by avoiding it. Later research by Campos and his associates (Campos & Langer, 1971; Campos, Langer, & Krowitz, 1970; Schwartz, Campos, & Baisel, 1973) found that cardiac acceleration, taken to indicate a fear response, was correlated with an infant's age. Older infants showed heart rate acceleration when placed on the glass over the cliff, whereas younger infants did not. On the basis of this and subsequent research using days of crawling experience as a variable (e.g., Bertenthal & Campos, 1984; Bertenthal, Campos, & Barrett, 1984; Campos, Hiatt, Ramsey, Henderson, & Svejda, 1978), Campos and his associates have suggested that an infant's response to depth at an edge is developed through experience locomoting in the environment. Other studies document developmental changes in responses to varying surfaces of support or nonsupport but do not support crawling experience per se as the factor inducing change (e.g., Adolph et al., 1993; E. J. Gibson et al., 1987).

Studies done in my laboratory have investigated differences between infants who cross and those who avoid the visual cliff in an attempt to understand processes that lead to avoidance. Rader, Bausano, and Richards (1980) tested infants as soon as they were able both to crawl and to use a walker. Experience crawling and using the walker varied considerably. Babies were tested on a cliff in a walker and when crawling. One finding was that even babies who avoided the cliff when crawling crossed readily in a walker. This suggests that the adaptive use or pickup of information is dependent on the particular locomotor program or on the posture of the infant. We also found a strong negative relationship between the amount of crawling experience and avoidance of the visual cliff. Those babies who crossed the visual cliff had more days of crawling experience than those who avoided it. A follow-up study (Richards & Rader, 1981, 1983) confirmed this negative relationship. Moreover, crawling experience did not affect the heart rate response. Heart rate was primarily related to age at testing, particularly for the avoiding infants. Infants who crossed the visual cliff spent more time looking down toward the glass on the deep side, indicating that their crossing was not the result of a failure to orient in the direction of the specifying information.

A study by Rader, Spiro, and Richards (1981) looked at infant behavior when a "visual plank" was used on the deep side of the visual cliff. Infants were tested both with the plank and without it. Those infants who crossed the visual cliff made some use of the plank. They spent more time in the plank area when it was there (79%) compared to when it was not (33%). However, hands and knees often were off the plank, and the locomotor behavior would have led to a fall in the case of an actual plank. One interpretation of this result is that the locomotion of these infants was not tightly controlled by the information specifying the plank.

A study by Rader and Ashley (1983) used an actual cliff to see what role tactile information plays in determining the crossing of the visual cliff. Babies were tested on both a visual and an actual cliff. Safety was provided in the case of the actual cliff through a harness connected to an overhead arm that moved as the infant moved. In this study, we also gathered information from parents on the number of falls infants had at home. Latencies for the deep side and the actual cliff did not differ. Infants were as likely to venture out off the actual cliff as they were the visual cliff. Thus, even in the absence of either tactile or visual information specifying a surface of support, some infants continue to locomote. Parents of the infants who fell off the actual cliff reported more falls at home than parents of avoiding infants; virtually no falls were reported for the avoiding infants.

Rader and Topinka (1988) reported the results of a longitudinal study designed to look at changes in visual cliff avoidance in infants during the period of 7.0–11.5 months of age. Initial testing occurred when the infant could locomote at least 4 feet. Three groups were identified: (a) infants who avoided on the initial testing, (b) infants who crossed on the initial testing but avoided subsequently, and (c) infants who did not avoid throughout the study. For those infants who avoid the visual cliff at some point, the infants who avoid the visual cliff at the first testing had an average of 0.5 months of crawling experience, whereas those who crossed at the first testing but later avoided had an average of 3.4 months of crawling experience when they avoided. Infants who never avoided had an average of 3.8 months of crawling experience at the last testing at 11.5 months of age. Thus, crawling experience per se is not the process that results in perception of the affordance of a nontraversable surface. Moreverover, of the 13 infants who crossed on their first testing, 7 of them avoided by 11.5 months of age, and the other 6 had longer latencies than at their initial testing. Again, falls at home were related to crossing behavior—those infants who crossed the visual cliff had the most falls at home. Eventually, those infants who cross the visual cliff become avoiders. But what accounts for their slow development in this regard?

Because this set of studies indicated that discovery through experience was not the critical process in inducing an avoidance response, a study was carried out by Rader (1991) to look at the possibility of a difference in the pattern of neural maturation between infants who cross and infants who avoid. To investigate maturational differences, a task was used that was derived from the delayed response task used to study frontal lobe function. The frontal system is considered to be very critical in impulse control and important in predicting the consequences of action (Teuber, 1964, 1972). Work by Goldman-Rakic (for a review, see Goldman-Rakic, 1987) has detailed the relationship between maturation of the prefrontal lobe and monkeys' performance on a delayed response task. She and Diamond (Diamond & Goldman-Rakic, 1989) have shown that this relationship holds when the delayed response task is converted to a Piagetian AB task (Stage V object permanence task) with a brief delay. Diamond (1988, 1991) suggested that the perseveration errors made by young infants on the AB task result, at least in part, from the lack of inhibitory control mediated by frontal lobe function. Moreover, Bell and Fox (1989) reported that increases in frontal lobe alpha in infants between 7 and 12 months of age are related to the ability to tolerate long delays on the AB task. Thus, there is considerable evidence to support using a Piagetian AB task with a delay as an index of frontal lobe maturation.

To investigate differences between crossing and avoiding infants in terms of prefrontal lobe development, infants who were tested at 10 months of age on a visual cliff apparatus were also tested for their ability to solve a modified Piagetian AB task with a 3-second delay. This was tested at the time the infants were seen for the visual cliff task and every 6 weeks afterwards until successful solution. The results were striking. Infants who avoided for at least 4 minutes were compared with infants who crossed within 2 minutes. The ages at which these two groups achieved successful avoidance on the AB task differed significantly. The avoiding infants reached criterion at 13.0 months, whereas the crossing infants did not reach criterion until 17.1 months. This finding suggests that infants' avoidance of a surface of nonsupport depends on their ability to inhibit loco-motor activity. In other words, the perceptual–motor links involving the ability to inhibit motor behavior may not be available for some infants at the time they start to crawl.

The results of this group of studies using varying surfaces of support suggest a very different kind of ontogenetic change than that involved in reaching for an object after the taste has been discovered. In that case, dis-covery of the relationship between the object's taste and its appearance underlies the change in response. The infant perceives the hidden affor-dance of taste on subsequent presentation of the object as the result of a discovery process based in experience. In the case of avoiding a drop-off, however, the ontogenetic processes of change appear to be quite different. Some infants with little or no experience avoid the visual cliff. Those who do cross the cliff do so despite considerable crawling experience until they are nearing the end of the first year. These infants' inappropriate responses to the visual cliff appear to be related to a slower pattern of frontal lobe maturation. As this maturation occurs, the potential for them to pro-duce an inhibitory motor response—to avoid a surface of nonsupport—changes.

Responses to Mother and Stranger Approaches in Down Syndrome Infants

Researchers studying Down syndrome infants have concluded that their emotional response is restricted as compared with infants who have not been diagnosed with a developmental disability. However, this work is lim-ited in helping us understand the organism–environment relationship, in part because it has ignored the function of the response in the environ-ment. The purpose of the third study to be described here was to analyze the interpersonal responses of Down syndrome and normal infants to both the mother and a stranger (Croniser, Rader, & Giles, 1993). A 7-point "Be-havioral Relations Scale" (ranging from negative to positive) was created to measure the infant's response in terms of how it would be received by the person approaching. The scale takes into account facial expressions, attention, and whole body responses. Heart rate was also recorded.

The Down syndrome and normally developing infants were matched for level of cognitive development using scores on the Adaptive scale of the Revised Gesell Developmental Schedule (Knobloch & Pasamanick, 1974). The mean adaptive age for both groups was 38.1 weeks. Performance on both the Language and Personal–Social scales was very similar for the two groups. Moreover, the two groups did not differ on a Stage IV object permanence test or in level of visual acuity. The mean chronological age for the Down syndrome group was 56 weeks; for the normally developing group it was 38 weeks.

The infant sat alone at a table in a Sassy Seat, as the mother or stranger approached. The approach was choreographed by having the approacher follow instructions on a tape recording. Infants were divided into those with Adaptive Scale scores below 40 weeks and with scores above 40 weeks. For both the Down syndrome and the normally developing infants with Adaptive Scale scores less than 40 weeks, the approach of the stranger and the mother produced positive responses. Moreover, for both groups of infants with Adaptive Scale scores greater than 40 weeks, the responses to the approach of the stranger were similar and positive. However, striking differences appeared between these two groups of infants when the mother approached. Whereas the Down syndrome group started out with a somewhat negative response to the mother at a distance, the response became more positive as she began to interact and approach the infant. For the normally developing infants, on the other hand, the response to the mother's approach was clearly negative. Infants became more upset as the mother came closer. The heart rate data complemented the behavioral data. All infants showed a decrease in heart rate as the stranger approached until the stranger actually touched the infant. A similar pattern was also shown by the Down syndrome infants to the approach of the mother. However, the normally developing infants with Adaptive Scale scores over 40 weeks showed an elevation in heart rate during the approach of the mother. An analysis of the range of expressive responses made showed that this was the same for both groups of infants, although Down syndrome babies tended to show more "attentive" responses and fewer "cry-face or fussy" responses.

This study found that Down syndrome infants did not respond in the same way as normal infants to the approach of the mother when their adaptive ages were 40 weeks or higher. Infants with Down syndrome attended to and smiled at the approaching mother, whereas the normal infants showed increasing signs of distress. The pattern of response by the Down syndrome infants is consistent with parents' descriptions of them as "easy going, affectionate, and loving." What might account for the variability in response between the two sets of infants? Perhaps the normal infant was upset over the mother's approach because the infant had expectations that were violated. Yet, if so, why would a Down syndrome baby, matched for level of cognitive development, not have these expectations too? Perhaps the Down syndrome baby had them but reacted differently to their violation. Or, possibly, the normally developing infant may have anticipated being picked up sooner in the course of the approach, and so arousal and distress occurred during the approach, instead of only at the touch segment. In other words, perhaps the normally developing baby's response to the mother's approach was a proactive, future-oriented response that typically leads to being picked up more quickly by the mother or even to being picked up at times she was not planning to do so. This active approach to effecting change in the environment appears more typical of the normally developing child than of a Down syndrome child. Whatever its cause, such an approach is likely to lead to more interaction with the caregiver, thereby affecting experience and, in turn, development.

The results of this study highlight the claim that the response an individual infant makes to a particular event is determined, at least in part, by the initial nature of that organism's nervous system. By looking at variability in responses across two such different groups, we may learn more about the processes underlying development.

EPILOGUE

I have argued here that a description of ontogenetic development requires a close look at the particular behavioral change involved. In some cases the young infant appears capable of rather sophisticated discovery of

higher order relationships, with changes in responses deriving from experience in a way similar to what would occur in a mature organism. For
example, the reaching study described shows that very young infants are
able to adapt their responses to information that they have discovered
through experience and that is not immediately present. They are also able
to respond to information in relation to their motivational state. Yet, many
questions are raised for ecological psychologists by these findings. When
infants respond to a taste experienced at a prior time on being presented
with a graspable object, can it be said that they perceive the affordance of
taste at that time? The infant perceived the relationship between taste and
appearance in the past and is now responding to the appearance in terms
of that previously perceived relationship. I suggested earlier that this situation is similar to that of early word acquisition. The infant's caregiver
uses gesture and inflection to create a relationship between the word's
sound and its referent. (See Schmidt, 1991; Zukow, 1990; Zukow-Goldring,
1993.) Later, the infant perceives the meaning of the sound in terms of
that referent. If we can understand this process, I believe that we can address more issues typically considered to be in the realm of cognition from
the perspective of direct perception. Moreover, language production,
melody production, imagery, and explicit memory should be addressed by
considering these acts as the re-creation of information. Humans seem almost unique in this capacity, and it is one that can be lost independent of
perception. Yet, I do not think it necessary to create a "representation" system separate from a "direct perception" system to account for this
capacity.

The research linking avoidance of the visual cliff with frontal lobe
function suggests that some types of ontogenetic change in the response
to information seem to depend on reaching a particular level of maturation. An infant may not respond with avoidance to information specifying a drop-off because the inhibitory system is not yet sufficiently mature.
As direct perception theorists, how are we to describe what happens when
that infant crawls off an edge? Clearly, the affordance a drop-off offers—
falling—is not responded to in an adaptive way. Would we say that the infant picks up the information specifying a drop-off but does not perceive

the affordance? Does the infant perceive the affordance but not respond appropriately? What would that imply about the meaning of perceiving an affordance? These are questions that a theory of direct perception must address.

Finally, the research comparing normally developing infants with Down syndrome infants illustrates differences in response to the same information when infants are matched according to adaptive age. An important goal of direct perception should be to explain how the original nature of the organism interacts with experience to create such response differences. I hope this becomes a new direction for future research by those who take an ecological stance.

REFERENCES

Adolph, K. E., Eppler, M. A., & Gibson, E. J. (1993). Crawling versus walking infants' perception of affordances for locomotion over sloping surfaces. *Child Development, 64*, 1158–1174.

Ashmead, D. H., McCarty, M. E., Lucas, L. S., & Belvedere, M. C. (1993). Visual guidance in infants' reaching toward suddenly displaced targets. *Child Development, 64*, 1111–1127.

Bell, M. A., & Fox, N. A. (1989, June). *EEG correlates of the development of motor inhibition.* Paper presented at the 97th meeting of the American Psychological Society, Arlington, VA.

Bertenthal, B. I., & Campos, J. J. (1984). A reexamination of fear and its determinants on the visual cliff. *Psychophysiology, 21*, 413–417.

Bertenthal, B. I., Campos, J. J., & Barrett, K. C. (1984). Self-produced locomotion: An organizer of emotional, cognitive, and social development in infancy. In R. N. Emde & R. J. Harmon (Eds.), *Continuities and discontinuities in development* (pp. 175–209). New York: Plenum.

Bower, T. G. R. (1972). Object perception in infants. *Perception, 1*, 15–30.

Bower, T. G. R., Broughton, J. M., & Moore, M. K. (1970). Demonstration of intention in the reaching behavior of neonate humans. *Nature, 228*, 679–681.

Bower, T. G. R., Dunkeld, J., & Wishart, J. G. (1979). Infant perception of visually presented objects. *Science, 208*, 1137–1138.

Bruner, J. S., & Koslowski, B. (1972). Visually preadapted constituents of manipulatory action. *Perception, 1*, 3–14.

Campos, J. J., Hiatt, S., Ramsay, D., Henderson, C., & Svejda, M. (1978). The emergence of fear on the visual cliff. In M. Lewis & L. Rosenblum (Eds.), *The development of affect* (pp. 149–182). New York: Plenum.

Campos, J. J., & Langer, A. (1971). The visual cliff: Discriminative cardiac orienting responses with retinal size held constant. *Psychophysiology, 8*, 264–265.

Campos, J. J., Langer, A., & Krowitz, A. (1970, October). Cardiac response on the visual cliff in prelocomotor human infants. *Science, 170*, 196–197.

Caplan, D. (Ed.). (1980). *Biological studies of mental processes.* Cambridge, MA: The MIT Press.

Croniser, M., Rader, N., & Giles, C. (1993, March). *Responses to mother and stranger approaches in normal and Down Syndrome infants.* Paper presented at the meeting of the Society for Research in Child Development, New Orleans, LA.

Diamond, A. (1988). Abilities and neural mechanisms underlying AB performance. *Child Development, 59*, 523–527.

Diamond, A. (1991). Neuropsychological insights into the meaning of object concept development. In S. Carey & R. Gelman (Eds.), *The epigenesis of mind: Essays on biology and cognition* (pp. 67–110). Hillsdale, NJ: Erlbaum.

Diamond, A., & Goldman-Rakic, P. (1989). Comparison of human infants and rhesus monkeys on Piaget's AB task: Evidence for dependence on dorsolateral prefrontal lobe cortex. *Experimental Brain Research, 74*, 24–40.

DiFranco, D., Muir, D. W., & Dodwell, P. C. (1978). Reaching in very young infants. *Perception, 7*, 385–392.

Dodwell, P. C., Muir, D. W., & DiFranco, D. (1976, October). Responses of infants to visually presented objects. *Science, 194*, 209–211.

Fogel, A., & Thelen, E. (1987). Development of early expressive and communicative action: Reinterpreting the evidence from a dynamic systems perspective. *Developmental Psychology, 23*, 747–761.

Gibson, E. J. (1967). *Principles of perceptual learning and development.* New York: Appleton-Century-Crofts.

Gibson, E. J. (1988). Exploratory behavior in the development of perceiving, acting, and the acquiring of knowledge. *Annual Review of Psychology, 39*, 1–41.

Gibson, E. J., & Rader, N. (1979). Attention: The perceiver as performer. In G. Hale & M. Lewis (Eds.), *Attention and cognitive development* (pp. 1–21). New York: Plenum.

Gibson, E. J., Riccio, G., Schmuckler, M. A., Stoffregen, T. A., Rosenberg, D., & Taormina, J. (1987). Detection of the traversability of surfaces by crawling and walking infants. *Journal of Experimental Psychology: Human Perception and Performance, 13*, 533–544.

Gibson, E. J., & Walk, R. (1960). The "visual cliff." *Scientific American, 202*, 64–71.

Gibson, J. J. (1961). Ecological optics. *Vision Research, 1*, 253–262.

Gibson, J. J. (1966). *The senses considered as perceptual systems.* New York: Houghton Mifflin.

Gibson, J. J. (1979). *The ecological approach to visual perception.* Boston: Houghton Mifflin.

Gibson, K. R., & Peterson, A. (Eds.). (1991). *Brain maturation and cognitive development: Comparative and cross-cultural perspectives.* New York: Aldine de Gruyter.

Goldman-Rakic, P. (1987). Development of cortical circuitry and cognitive function. *Child Development, 58*, 601–622.

Gregory, R. L. (1972, June 23). Seeing as thinking. *Times Literary Supplement*, pp. 707–708.

Hofsten, C. von. (1979). Development of visually guided reaching: The approach phase. *Journal of Human Movement Studies, 5*, 160–178.

Hofsten, C. von. (1980). Predictive reaching for moving objects by human infants. *Journal of Experimental Child Psychology, 30*, 369–382.

Jeannerod, M. (1981). Intersegmental coordination during reaching at natural visual objects. In J. Long & A. Baddeley (Eds.), *Attention and performance ix* (Vol. 9, pp.153–168). Hillsdale, NJ: Erlbaum.

Jeannerod, M. (1984). The timing of natural prehension movements. *Journal of Motor Behavior, 16*, 235–254.

Knobloch, H., & Pasamanick, B. (Eds.). (1974). *Gesell and Amatruda's developmental diagnosis.* New York: Harper & Row.

Lenneberg, E. (1967). *Biological foundations of language.* New York: Wiley.

Lockman, J. J., Ashmead, D. H., & Bushnell, E. W. (1984). The development of anticipatory hand orientation during infancy. *Journal of Experimental Child Psychology, 37*, 176–186.

Long, M. H. (1990). Maturational constraints on language development. *Studies in Second Language Acquisition, 12*, 251–285.

Matthew, A., & Cook, M. (1990). The control of reaching movements by young infants. *Child Development, 61*, 1238–1258.

Morrongiello, B. A., & Rocca, P. T. (1989). Visual feedback and anticipatory hand orientation during infants' reaching. *Perceptual and Motor Skills, 69*, 787–802.

Neisser, U. (1991, August). *The ecological and social roots of cognition.* Paper presented at the 99th Annual Convention of the American Psychological Association, San Francisco, CA.

Newell, K. M., Scully, D. M., McDonald, P. V., & Baillargeon, R. (1989). Task constraints and infant grip configurations. *Developmental Psychobiology, 22,* 817–832.

Rader, N. (1985). Change and variation: A proposal concerning the importance of heterochrony in development. In G. Butterworth, J. Rutkowska, & M. Scaife (Eds.), *Evolution and developmental psychology* (pp. 22–29). Sussex, England: The Harvester Press.

Rader, N. (1989, July). *Anticipation in infant event perception: Looking into the future.* Paper presented at the Fifth International Conference on Event Perception and Action, Oxford, OH.

Rader, N. (1991, April). *Maturational differences between avoiding and crossing infants on a "visual cliff."* Paper presented at the 62nd meeting of the Eastern Psychological Association, New York, NY.

Rader, N. (1993, August). Responses to invisible affordances: Intentionality in infancy. In P. Zukow-Goldring (Chair), *An ecological approach to development.* Symposium conducted at the Seventh International Conference on Event Perception and Action, Vancouver, Canada.

Rader, N., & Ashley, S. (1983, April). *Avoidance behavior on an "actual cliff."* Paper presented at the biennial meeting of the Society for Research in Child Development, Detroit, MI.

Rader, N., Bausano, M., & Richards, J. E. (1980). On the nature of the visual-cliff avoidance response in human infants. *Child Development, 51,* 61–68.

Rader, N., Spiro, D. J., & Richards, J. E. (1981, April). *Surface perception in infants who fail to avoid a visual cliff.* Paper presented at the annual meeting of the Western Psychological Association, Los Angeles, CA.

Rader, N., & Stern, J. D. (1982). Visually elicited reaching in neonates. *Child Development, 53,* 1004–1007.

Rader, N., & Topinka, C. W. (1988, August). *A longitudinal study of visual cliff avoidance.* Paper presented at the 96th Annual Convention of the American Psychological Association, Atlanta, GA.

Rader, N., & Vaughn, L. A. (1991, July). *The intentionality of reaching behavior in infants 2–4 months of age.* Paper presented at the 11th biennial meeting of the International Society for the Study of Behavioural Development, Minneapolis, MN.

155

Richards, J. E., & Rader, N. (1981). Crawling-onset age predicts visual cliff avoidance in infants. *Journal of Experimental Psychology: Human Perception and Performance, 7*, 382–387.

Richards, J. E., & Rader, N. (1983). Affective, behavioral, and avoidance responses on the visual cliff: Effects of crawling onset age, crawling experience, and testing age. *Psychophysiology, 20*, 633–641.

Schmidt, C. L. (1991, July). *Temporal coordination of name and gesture: An exploratory study*. Paper presented at the meeting of the International Society for the Study of Behavioural development, Minneapolis, MN.

Schneirla, T. C., & Rosenblatt, J. S. (1963). "Critical periods" in the development of behavior. *Science, 139*, 1110–1116.

Schwartz, A. N., Campos, J. J., & Baisel, E. J. (1973). The visual cliff: Cardiac and behavioral responses on the deep and shallow sides at five and nine months of age. *Journal of Experimental Child Psychology, 15*, 86–99.

Scott, J. P., Stewart, J. M., & de Ghett, V. J. (1974). Critical periods in the organization of systems. *Developmental Psychobiology, 7*, 489–513.

Teuber, H. L. (1964). The riddle of frontal lobe function in man. In J. M. Warren & K. Akert (Eds.), *The frontal granular cortex and behavior* (pp. 410–444). New York: McGraw-Hill.

Teuber, H. L. (1972). Unity and diversity of frontal lobe functions. *Acta Neurobiological Experimentalis, 32*, 615–656.

Thelan, E., Corbetta, D., Kamm, K., Spencer, J. P., Schneider, K., & Zernicke, R. F. (1993). The transition to reaching: Mapping intention and intrinsic dynamics. *Child Development, 64*, 1058–1098.

von Hofsten, C. (1982). Eye-hand coordination in the newborn. *Developmental Psychology, 18*, 450–461.

von Hofsten, C. (1991). Structuring of early reaching movements: A longitudinal study. *Journal of Motor Behavior, 23*, 280–292.

von Hofsten, C., & Ronnqvist, L. (1988). Preparation for grasping an object: A developmental study. *Journal of Experimental Psychology: Human Perception and Performance, 14*, 610–621.

Waddington, C. H. (1953, September). How do cells differentiate? *Scientific American, 189*, 1008–1016.

Werker, J. F. & Tees, R. C. (1984). Cross language speech perception: Evidence for perceptual reorganization during the first year of life. *Infant Behavior and Development, 7*, 49–63.

Yonas, A., & Hartman, B. (1993). Perceiving the affordance of contact in four- and five-month-old infants. *Child Development, 64,* 298–308.

Zukow, P. G. (1986). The relationship between interaction with the caregiver and the emergence of play activities during the one-word period. *British Journal of Developmental Psychology, 4,* 223–234.

Zukow, P. G. (1989). Siblings as effective socializing agents: Evidence from Central Mexico. In P. G. Zukow (Ed.), *Sibling interactions across cultures: Theoretical and methodological issues* (pp. 79–105). New York: Springer-Verlag.

Zukow, P. G. (1990). Socio-perceptual bases for the emergence of language: An alternative to innatist approaches. *Developmental Psychobiology, 23,* 705–726.

Zukow-Goldring, P. (1993, August). When gestures speak louder than words: Educating attention to the relation between words and world. In P. Zukow-Goldring (Chair), *An ecological approach to development.* Symposium conducted at the Seventh International Conference on Event Perception and Action, Vancouver, Canada.

Comment on Rader

Edward S. Reed

R ader's studies are provocative from a number of points of view. She
has chosen to stress the possibility that neural maturation plays a significant role in the developmental changes that she documents. The argument for this is necessarily inferential and subject to debate. In this
comment I suggest what I see as a stronger case that one might make with
these very same data: that perception, from its earliest functional appearance in infancy, is a source of *knowledge*, as well as (or sometimes even instead of) a guide for action.

Rader's concept of "hidden affordances" is a reminder to us that the
environment is rich in stimulation and that optical information is not always the best or the only source of information about objects or events.
In particular, and like Smitsman (this volume), Rader is interested in how
children learn about *relations* among environmental features. Some of
these relations might be called cross-modal ones: What is it about the looks
of the flame that tells the child the flame is hot? Others of these relations

---

Reed comments on Rader from an ecological realist perspective.

might be called *response produced*: What is it about the look of the rubber ducky that tells the child that it will squeak when pushed?

James Gibson (1966) considered these issues conceptually, but he did not develop experimental procedures for testing these questions as Rader has done. Nevertheless, what he had to say is useful in interpreting Rader's results:

> Psychologists have become accustomed to thinking of an association as something that is formed between two sensory impressions. . . . They realized, of course, that there had to be a conjunction of events— fire and smoke, for example—before the psychological association could be formed, but this was not what they were interested in. Let us consider, however, the *fact* of ecological associations, as distinguished from the *formation* of associations. . . . To the extent that a fire *always* conjoins an optical flame with an acoustic sound, a cutaneous warmth, an a volatile odor, the combination is invariant and constitutes a stimulus of higher order. . . . The act of perceiving a fire . . . might just as well be considered the pickup of the associated variables of information as the associating of sensory data. Two things are necessary: the dimensions of quality must have been differentiated, and the invariant combinations of quality must be detected. (Gibson, 1966, pp. 271–272)

Rader's study with the differentially tasting teething rings seems to me to fit in with an obvious developmental interpretation of Gibson's analysis. Children do not have to *learn* to associate separate sensory qualities; on the contrary, even 2-month-olds gave behavioral evidence of *knowing* that a teething ring tasted good or bad after a single perceptual encounter with it. On this view, infants need to learn to *dis*associate the various properties of objects. For example, exposure to a sequence of teethers with a variety of tastes might be needed for infants to learn that taste is *not* necessarily associated with the looks of the teethers. Rader's claim that infants have to "recreate" the gustatory information when they see the teether only makes sense if one *assumes* that taste and looks are *separable*. Given the processed nature of food in our modern human environment, children probably do come to realize that separation—but there is no evidence that they start their perceptual life with this idea.

The group of infants who cross a visual cliff also seem to show a certain kind of knowledge separated from their activities. Taken together, Rader's studies suggest that these children know what a cliff is but cannot control their actions appropriately yet. In particular, Rader speculates that these children cannot inhibit the urge to cross the cliff. This is a very useful reminder of the complexity of real world perception: A baby who sees her mother across a visual cliff perceives both a desirable goal and—possibly—an undesirable outcome if she crawls out to try to achieve the goal. If the goal has a high enough valence, this expectancy of falling might not outweigh the desirability of trying to get the goal. (Of course, once one locomotes onto a visual cliff one discovers haptic information for the support of locomotion.)

Finally, Rader's studies of infants with Down syndrome also seem to reveal a lack of an expectancy (of the mother coming to pick them up) of at least a stronger perception of current positives in this situation, which make acting on the expectancy less likely.

It seems to me that in all these cases, perception supports the knowledge and expectancies about the baby's circumstances, and this knowledge may conflict with other aspects of the child's perception of that situation. This is the normal way of the world, and we are indebted to Nancy Rader for showing us how such complexities can be teased apart experimentally.

REFERENCE

Gibson, J. J. (1966). *The senses considered as perceptual systems.* Boston: Houghton-Mifflin.

6

On the Early Development of Predictive Abilities

Claes von Hofsten

Cognition and action are intimately interlinked. All actions are geared to the future, and controlling them requires knowledge of upcoming events. We continuously need to know what is going to happen in both the near and the distant future in order to plan our activities and to coordinate our movements. To be able to predict what is going to happen next, we have to rely on the regularities or invariances of the events in the world like physical laws, mobility constraints, rules of social relations and communication, and the specific opportunities and constraints of the task. I posit that cognitive activities like perceiving, attending, remembering, feeling, and thinking originally evolved to enable organisms to use these rules in order to prepare and organize their behavior for future events and activities.

The linkage between action and cognition is especially apparent in development. Recent research indicates that newborns are prepared for action but must develop their predictive abilities in order to coordinate their movements, plan their activities, and attain their goals (von Hofsten, 1993). I suggest that the quality and the accuracy of the predictions changes with age and that the desire to be in control of the future drives cognitive development. In the following I argue for this theoretical position and present some data that supports it.

WAYS OF PREDICTING THE FUTURE

One way to grasp the future is to learn about the rules that govern events in the world and in one's own body and use them to predict what is going to happen next. Some of the rules, like Newton's classical laws of physics, are very general and invariant over many tasks, whereas other rules, indeed most of them, are much more heuristic and task dependent. The important rule in downhill skiing to "always keep the weight on the valley ski" is such an example. In social skills most rules are task specific. For instance, in dancing it helps to know the rules of the specific dance one is trying to perform to be able to coordinate one's movements with the partner. Through experience we gain knowledge of such rules and contingencies. They act as constraints on our future actions.

Rarely, however, are the rules explicit (as in dancing), nor can they always be made explicit (as in the case of the valley ski). Action knowledge is tacit in most cases. It is more a question of being familiar with the different dimensions of the task and how they are related to each other because they define its constraints and possibilities. The different parameters of a task may be said to define a "task space." I suggest that a geographical environment with different types of terrain may serve as a metaphor of this task space. One is easily lost in a new geographical environment, just as one is lost in a new task. However, through systematic exploration one gets to know the positions of landmarks, where paths lead, and eventually one forms a mental map of its layout. Furthermore, one learns about its affordances: which parts are easy to negotiate, which parts are difficult, and which parts should be avoided altogether. Finally, one learns what to look for in each specific part of the environment and in each specific situation, in order to make transportation efficient and safe. When the environment is known, it is always possible to find the smoothest and most economical route through it independently of the previous ones taken. If unexpected problems or obstacles are encountered, a different route may be found that leads to the same goal. This is also true for a task space. The knowledge gathered through systematic exploration of a task is structured into a frame of reference for action that makes planning possible. This is the basis of skill. The importance of practice and repetition is not to stamp in patterns of movement or achieve an immutable program, but rather to encourage the functional organization of action systems (Reed, 1990).

No task space, however, can ever be completely known to us because every new encounter reveals new aspects of it. It is a bad idea to drive from home to work with one's eyes closed, even after driving the same route for 20 years. A simple limb movement is so complex that it is virtually impossible totally to predict all aspects of it in advance (Bernstein, 1967). In other words, no movements can be entirely guided by ideas and thought. Our ability to represent the world does not liberate us from reality. Knowing the task space is, to a large degree, a question of knowing what to look for. Perception is needed throughout the execution of any action in order to steer it, adaptively. Its task is always prospective. It informs the actor about upcoming problems so they can be dealt with ahead of time or at an early stage when they are harmless.

To perceive what has not yet happened may sound paradoxical, but events obeying the classical laws of physics clearly not only tell us what has already happened but, more importantly, how they are going to evolve in the near future. For instance, Lee (1993) has shown that the relative expansion of elements in the optic array supplies information about upcoming encounters with external objects and surfaces and time-to-contact with them and whether the encounter is going to be rough or smooth. Our perceptual system seems tuned to that kind of information. Lee and associates have shown that hummingbirds use it for homing in on a flower (Lee, Reddish, & Rand, 1991), pigeons for guiding their landing (Lee, Davies, Green, & van der Weel, 1993), gannets for guiding their diving into the sea (Lee & Reddish, 1981), and long jumpers for determining their takeoff (Lee, Lishman, & Thompson, 1982).

Representations serve as frames of reference for perception, which in turn can unfold the detailed information necessary for guiding our movements in their finest details. The purpose of our ability to represent the world is not to make us independent of perception, but rather to make perception more effective. This is not done by adding detail and clarity, as has often been thought in the past (Helmholtz, 1925). Rather, the advantage of being able to expand perception and action in space and time beyond what is immediately perceivable is that it provides an overview. In an overview, new global structures of the world become distinguishable, providing frames of reference for the more detailed structures embedded within them. I believe that perceiving and representing are just different sides of the same coin. Both are necessary for dealing with what is going to happen next.

Using the visual field as a metaphor may be instructive. Foveal vision gives fine details whereas peripheral vision provides only a very degraded view of the world with no details distinguishable. Lack of foveal vision is therefore a severe handicap. However, the task of peripheral vision is not to give details, but to provide a frame of reference for foveal vision and to guide it quickly and efficiently to points of interest in the visual field, which then can be inspected for detail and clarity. On the other hand, foveal vision alone is not very useful. Poor peripheral vision or "tunnel vision" is also a severe handicap. The strength of our visual system is that it combines overview and details in an optimal fashion. Another important property of the visual field is that there is a trade-off between detailed and overview vision, not a dichotomy. The same trade-off, I believe, holds true for the relationship between perception and representation. Representations of the world have fewer details but provide more overview than direct perception. The larger the time–space window used to view the world, the fewer details it provides but the broader the overview.

DEVELOPMENT OF PROSPECTIVE CONTROL

From the moment they are born, infants are deeply engaged in exploring the external world and their ability to act in it. This is clearly reflected in their cognitive development. It has even been suggested that cognitive development should be divided into phases characterized by the emergence of new means for exploring the world: looking, reaching, and locomotion (Gibson, 1988). Whereas the infant is engaged in mastering a certain action, perception and other cognitive activities related to that action show rapid development. Berthenthal and Campos (1991) have pointed out that the onset of locomotion has a number of dramatic effects on perception and cognition including changes in the perception of the visual cliff and in the ability to conceive of space in allocentric terms.

Exploratory actions were traditionally thought of as being focused on the external world and on objects and events in it, but they may just as well be focused on one's own actions. It seems quite clear that the way to learn about one's own movement capabilities is to move. This is how infants learn about the properties that change and those that remain invariant during the execution of an action, depending on the posture of the body and how the movements are performed, and this is how they learn about problems that arise when coordinating with the external world (von Hofsten, 1993). During the early months of life, infants devote much of their daily activity to exploring their action possibilities. Movements are performed over and over again with slight alternations. Piaget (1953) was so impressed by this fact that he labeled several of the early developmental stages *stages of circular reactions.*

Even though experience is necessary for developing actions, biology has also prepared the child for acquiring such skills. Strong selective forces have favored the evolution of means for extracting prospective information and represent them in a form suitable for action. It has made the visual system sensitive to motion and change and made animals able to extract optical information about upcoming encounters with external objects and surfaces (Lee, 1993). It has also favored the evolution of brain structures suitable for constructing predictive mental models. For example, the cerebellum seems to be a good structure for modelling the motor system predictively (see, e.g., Kawato & Gomi, 1992) and the prefrontal cortex for representing upcoming events in the world and providing overviews for action (see, e.g., Knight & Grabowecky, 1995).

An important part of the biological preparation for acquiring action skills has to do with the motives of infants. They stubbornly persist in their attempts to perform actions that they obviously have not yet mastered; why they do so is puzzling. They can hardly get much reward from the repeated failures. However, from a biological point of view the stubbornness makes sense. It ensures that an activity-based structuring process begins that is self-organizing.

By studying the development of action, we may learn about the ways in which infants are prepared for prospective control and how they develop their ability to look into the future. Insights into these evolving skills have important implications for our understanding of development of action control, perceptual development, and the development of the child's ability to represent the world. I elucidate these points by discussing five problems encountered in the course of producing an action. Three of them—producing an intended movement, coordinating movement and posture, and coordinating different body parts involved in the action—concern internal problems. The two remaining problems—controlling approach and coordinating actions with external events—concern fitting actions to the environment.

PRODUCING AN INTENDED MOVEMENT

A basic problem for all actions is the lag in the sensorimotor system. It takes time to process information, it takes time to get the appropriate commands to the efferents, and it takes time to activate the muscles that shape the movement. In addition, the inertia of the system introduces a mechanical lag; that is, it takes time before the contraction of a muscle has an effect. All these lags may amount to several hundred milliseconds; if adjustments were prepared only after problems arose, movements would be discontinuous and jerky. In other words, the motor system could not function on an ad hoc basis. According to Kawato and Gomi (1992) the cerebellar symptoms of hypotonia, hypermetria, and intentional tremor can be understood as a degraded performance when motor control is forced to rely solely on negative feedback after the internal models are destroyed or cannot be updated (or both).

At the same time, the possibilities of predicting how a movement evolves are severely limited (Bernstein, 1967). Many muscles are involved in producing a controlled movement, and the muscles are not related to each other or to the movement in any simple way. Gravity affects the production of the movement differently for different orientations of the limb in space. The viscoelastic properties of muscles, joints, and tendons also affect the final form of movement. Therefore, active muscular contractions are needed both for producing a goal-directed movement and for keeping the induced and passive forces under control. The individual must continuously monitor the limb movement and adjust muscle forces to meet the upcoming force field ahead of time; otherwise the movement goes astray.

Despite all these problems, infants are able to control their arm movements at an early age. Neonates perform reaching movements toward a seen object, implying some visual control of arm movements (von Hofsten, 1982). They have also opposed pulling forces on the hand in order to maintain it in the visual field (Van der Meer, van der Weel, & Lee, 1995). This was true for the hand toward which the neonate turned and for the opposite hand when it was seen in a video monitor. However, neonates seem unable to construct multistep reaching movements in which each step is a further approximation of object position. Between 2 and 3 months of age the movement sequences become longer and more vigorous as the child systematically works at getting to the target (Thelen et al., 1993; von Hofsten, 1986). From the onset of functional reaching infants are focused on this activity, and their skill at it improves rapidly (von Hofsten 1979, 1991). At 30 weeks of age, a majority of reaches were found to consist of no more than two units, just like adult reaching movements. The first of these, the transport unit, became larger with age and covered a greater proportion of the approach, indicating better ability to plan the movement.

COORDINATING MOVEMENT AND POSTURE

Coordination and regulation of purposeful movements are only possible in relation to a stable context—that is, the posture of the body. The problem is that the movements themselves affect the equilibrium of the body.

When a body part is moved, the point of gravity of the whole body is displaced, which pushes it out of equilibrium if nothing is done about it. Gravity is a strong force and when body equilibrium is disturbed, posture becomes quickly uncontrollable. Therefore, disturbances have to be foreseen or detected at an early stage if balance is to be maintained without interruption of ongoing activity.

To stand on their own, children must learn how limb movements affect the point of gravity and the nature of the reactive forces that arise during movement. They must learn to perceive their body sway and how to prospectively control it. The task is even more difficult for the small child than for the adult. When standing up, the body acts as a standing pendulum. The natural sway frequency of a pendulum is inversely proportional to the square root of its length. A child who is only half the size of an adult therefore sways with a frequency that is 40% higher than that of the adult and has 40% less time to react to balance disturbances. In other words, when infants start to stand on their own by the end of the first year of life, they have mastered the most difficult balance problem they will ever face.

Postural control is definitely a limiting factor in manual development. If the infant is given active postural support, goal-directed reaching can be observed at an earlier age than otherwise possible. For instance, the neonatal reaching observed by von Hofsten (1982) was performed by properly supported infants. When infants at about 9 months of age become able to control balance while sitting without support, they also seem to have some ability to prepare the reach through postural adjustments ahead of time. Von Hofsten and Woollacott (1990) studied postural adjustments of 9-month-old infants reaching for an object in front of them while balancing the trunk. Each infant was seated astride on one of the knees of an accompanying parent who supported the child by the hips. Muscle responses were recorded from the abdominal and trunk extensor muscles as well as from the deltoid muscle of the reaching arm. The results showed that trunk muscles were used in the reaching actions of these 9-month-old infants. Trunk extensors and sometimes abdominal muscles were activated prospectively before the arm extended forward.

Postural preparations are not something separate and independent of the goal-directed movement but are an integrated part of the reaching action. Reaching for an object does not only involve the upper limb. The whole body is engaged in accomplishing the reaching act, and trunk adjustments both before the arm is extended and after it has arrived at its goal are important parts of that process. Figure 1 shows that reaching in 9-month-olds is embedded in an envelope of trunk adjustments.

COORDINATING DIFFERENT BODY PARTS

An action generally involves movements of more than one body part. In manual actions, the two hands generally collaborate in achieving a goal. In looking, the movements of the head and the eyes collaborate in controlling gaze, and in talking, the vocal tract and the lungs collaborate in producing the speech sounds. Actions involving more than one body part can only be accomplished if the movements of the different parts are timed and scaled to each other. This is only possible if each body part "knows" what the other body parts are going to do ahead of time, which in turn requires the movements of the different body parts to be subordinate to one common system or mechanism. Precise timing also requires monitoring the movements of each body part prospectively.

Stabilizing gaze is a good example of these principles. It is so crucial for vision that it has even been suggested that the most important reason for evolving movable eyes is for the purpose of stabilizing gaze rather than scanning the surrounding (Walls, 1962). Stabilizing gaze is important for at least three reasons. First, if detailed information is needed about an external object, it is of crucial importance to keep it within the foveal region of the visual field. Second, it is crucial to minimize slippage of its retinal projection. Even the slightest retinal motion causes gross deteriorations in acuity. Finally, although linear visual flow is informative of the spatial layout of the environment (motional parallax), rotational flow is not; in fact, rotational flow masks the information conveyed by the linear flow (Warren & Hannon, 1990). Therefore, rotational flow must be minimized.

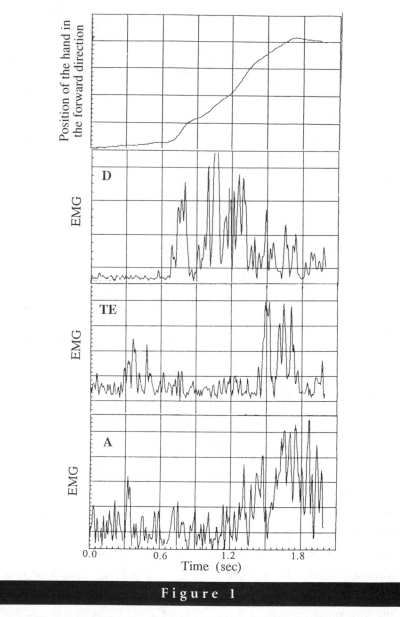

Figure 1

Example of one infant's responses from the deltoid (D) of the reaching arm, the abdominal (A) muscles, and the trunk extensor (TE) muscles plus records of the relative displacements of the reaching hand. In this specific example, the reach was performed with the left hand. It can be seen that the TE muscles start increasing firing well before the D muscle. The A muscles have some activation before the D muscle too, but the major activation occurs toward the end of the reach (see von Hofsten & Woollacott, 1990, for unpublished raw data used to create figure).

The eyes have dual functions in stabilizing gaze. First, they should collaborate with the head in tracking an object while the individual, the object, or both are moving. The relative amount of head and eye movements that make up visual tracking is quite variable, but they must add up to the target motion in order to stabilize gaze on it. To avoid lagging the target, the observer must predict how it moves in relation to his or her body. Visual as well as proprioceptive and vestibular information are important in this respect. Visual tracking is confined to rather slow changing motions. The ability rapidly deteriorates for changes above 0.6 Hz gaze (see Barnes, 1993).

Second, eye movements should compensate for head movements unrelated to the fixation task. Such head movements may arise as a result of more gross body movements like locomotion, from external perturbations of the head or body, or from the internal regulations of the head movements themselves. Such head movements are generally changing much faster than the head movements participating in the tracking. The vestibular system is best designed to deal with these higher frequency changes of head position. Some studies (Benson, 1970; Hyden, Istl, & Schwartz, 1982; Jell, Stockwell, Turnipseed, & Guedry 1988; Tomlinson, Saunders, & Schwartz, 1980) reported that the eyes compensate more or less perfectly with no phase lag for head oscillations between 1 Hz and 6 Hz. This is possible because the vestibular system senses head acceleration and computes velocity. If head acceleration and velocity are known, compensatory eye movements can be monitored prospectively.

Newborn infants seems to have some ability to track a moving target smoothly. This ability, however, seems crucially dependent on the size of the stimulus. Dayton and Jones (1964) found that neonates pursued a large moving visual field with smooth eye movements, but when a small target was used the movements were saccadic. Furthermore, such eye movements underwent rapid postnatal development toward smooth following during the first few months of life. Later studies have generally supported these findings (Aslin, 1981; Bloch & Carchon, 1992; Kremenitzer, Vaughan, Kurtzberg, & Dowling, 1979; Roucoux, Culee, & Roucoux, 1983). Aslin (1981) used a black bar 2° wide and 8° high moving sinusoidally in a horizontal path. He found only saccadic following of the target up to 6 weeks of age after which smooth pursuit began to be observed. The improved ability to track smaller targets smoothly is probably a function of a number of factors, including sensory and attentional development.

From an early age, infants use both head and eyes when tracking an object. The head is used more and more actively as control over it increases. Bloch and Carchon (1992) found that 30-day-old infants used the head more than newborns in the tracking of a target. Von Hofsten and Rosander (1996) found the same trend in the tracking of 1- to 3-month-old infants. However, even in the 1-month-olds head movements contributed significantly to stabilizing gaze on the target. A tracking record where the head contributed significantly is shown in Figure 2. The head and eye records in Figure 2 add almost perfectly to the target motion, which is an indication of a functioning central gaze mechanism governing head and eye movements. The importance of head movements in tracking continues to increase with age. Daniel and Lee (1990) studied tracking in 11- to 28-week-old infants and found that some of the oldest infants used predominantly head movements in tracking.

Von Hofsten and Rosander (1996) found that modulations of head velocity at frequencies 1–6 Hz were consistently accompanied by reciprocal modulations of eye velocity in very young infants without systematic lag. This can be seen in Figure 3. Even at 1 month of age, the phase lag between eye velocity and head slip (target velocity minus head velocity) was found to be approximately 0 ms. Eye and head movements were poorly scaled to each other at that age, but the fit had improved considerably at 3 months of age.

In summary, the vestibular–ocular loop seems to be present at birth but it becomes functional and adjusted to its task over time. Compensatory eye movements without a lag require prediction. If there is no lag, then the amplitude of the tracked motion must also be predicted in order to have full compensation. During continuous head movements, vestibular information could, in principle, be used prospectively in both these respects for stabilizing gaze on the target. The timing problem is, however, relatively simpler than the scaling problem because the factors

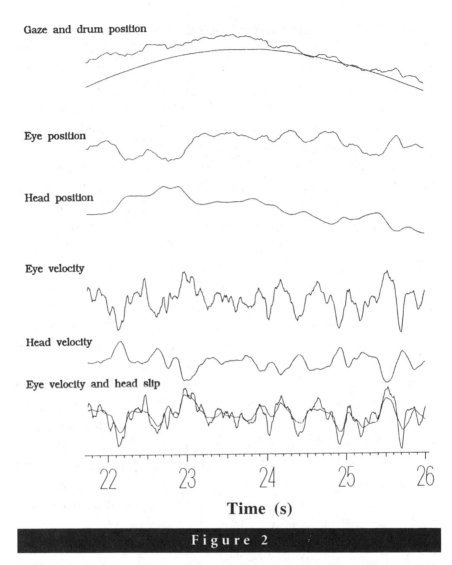

Gaze and drum position

Eye position

Head position

Eye velocity

Head velocity

Eye velocity and head slip

22   23   24   25   26

Time (s)

Figure 2

A 3-month-old infant inspecting a 0.1 Hz oscillation of a wide angle visual grating of 0.14 c/deg. Head slip is here defined as target velocity minus head velocity. Peak cross-correlation between eye velocity and head slip was 0.84 at a lead of the eyes of 0.008 s.

determining the various kinds of delays (receptor delays, processing delays, and mechanical delays) are relatively constant. When determining the amplitude of the compensatory eye movements the distance to the fixa-

175

3-month-old infant

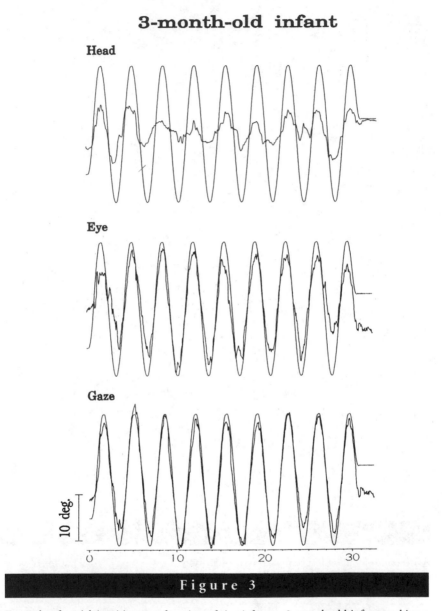

Figure 3

Example of a trial (position as a function of time) from a 3-month-old infant tracking a wide angle visual grating of 0.14 c/deg. The gain for head, eye, and gaze were 0.17, 0.72, and 0.89.

tion target must be taken into account. It has recently been shown that such adjustments of the vestibular–ocular response are performed prospectively during vergence eye movements in monkeys by adjusting the gain of the compensatory eye movement to the distance of the target to be moved to (Snyder, Lawrence, & King, 1992).

The result of von Hofsten and Rosander (1996) also showed that the compensatory eye movements overlaid the tracking eye movements. In other words, young infants seem simultaneously to be able to perform tracking eye movements and to compensate for head movements unrelated to the tracking. These two abilities develop in parallel.

FITTING ACTIONS TO THE EXTERNAL WORLD

Actions must negotiate properties of the environment. Obstacles have to be avoided and encounters anticipated. When walking in a cluttered terrain, a suitable ground support has to be found for each step and the encounter with the support has to be precisely timed. When reaching for an object, the individual must prepare for the encounter by opening the hand, orienting it appropriately, and closing it relative to the encounter with the object. Some events are irreversible and simply must be dealt with ahead of time. As the foot is lowered toward the ground in a stepping movement, the quality of the ground must be foreseen (whether it is hard, soft, or slippery), or else the smoothness of walking is disrupted.

In the act of reaching for a stationary object there are several problems that must be dealt with in advance, if the encounter with the object is to be smooth and efficient. The reaching hand must adjust to the orientation, form, and size of the object. Securing the target must be timed in such a way that the hand starts to close around it in anticipation and not as a reaction. Such timing has to be planned and can only occur under visual control. Tactually controlled grasping is only initiated after contact, and by necessity it induces an interruption in the reach-and-grasp act. Thus, the emergence of visual control of grasping is crucial for the development of manual skill.

Already at the onset of purposeful reaching, infants crudely adjust the orientation of the hand to the orientation of the object before it is encountered (Lockman, Ashmead, & Bushnell, 1984; Morrongiello & Rocca, 1986; von Hofsten & Fazel-Zandy, 1984). Such adjustments are necessary for getting an enlongated object into the hand in the right way. Adjusting the hand to the size of a target is less crucial. Instead of doing that, it is also possible to open the hand fully during the approach, a strategy used by adults when reaching for an object under time stress (Wing, Turton, & Fraser, 1986). Von Hofsten and Rönnqvist (1988) monitored the distance between thumb and index fingers in reaches performed by 5- and 6-month-olds, 9-month-olds, and 13-month-olds. Spherical targets of 15, 25, and 35 mm in diameter were used. They found that the infants in the two older age groups adjusted the opening of the hand to the size of the target reached for, but not the youngest ones. Von Hofsten and Rönnqvist (1988) also determined when the distance between thumb and index finger started to diminish during the approach. At all three age levels, the hand started to close in anticipation of the encounter with the object. However, there were differences between the age groups. For the two younger groups, the hand first moved to the neighborhood of the target and then started to close around it (see Figure 4). For the 13-month-olds, the grasping action typically started during the approach, well before touch, indicating that, at this age, the grasping movement was becoming integrated with the approach movement (see Figure 4).

Figure 4

Examples from a 5-month-old infant and a 13-month-old infant of how the hand opens and closes during the reach. The upper diagrams show the thumb-indexfinger separation and the lower ones the distance from hand to target. The dotted lines in the figures indicate when the hand starts to close and the dashed lines when the encounter with the object occur. Adapted from "Preparation for Grasping an Object: A Developmental Study," by C. von Hofsten and L. Ronnqvist, 1988, *Journal of Experimental Psychology: Human Perception and Performance, 14*, p. 615. Copyright 1988 by the American Psychological Association.

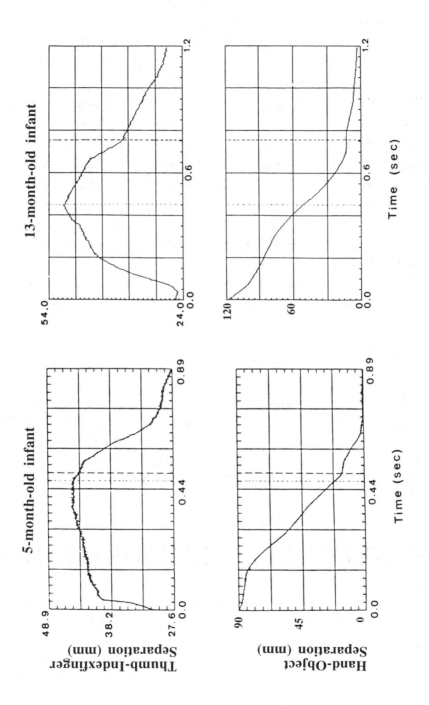

COORDINATING ACTIONS WITH EXTERNAL EVENTS

External events can only be negotiated if one can predict how they evolve over time and space. Perception is designed to provide detailed predictions of what is imminently going to happen. At larger time scales it is of increasing importance to base predictions on ideas of what is going to happen on the basis of rules and regularities of the events. Representation and perception play complementary roles in prospective control as pointed out above. For instance, the catching of a ball must be initiated long before it arrives, and the hand must be aimed toward a future location of the ball. If this location is outside reach, the body must be moved toward this point before the ball arrives there. To prepare the catch it helps to know something about the characteristics of the motion and how it depends on different kinds of throws and different winds, but the imminent catching has to rely on prospective perception. When dancing with a partner, the future movements of the partner must be anticipated if coordination is going to be maintained. Even though it helps to know the rules of dancing, there are many degrees of freedom within those rules and direct perception is necessary for anticipating the partner's next step. Finally, when engaging in social communication, passes and facial gestures must be appropriately timed. We must know when information is sent by the partner so that we can be prepared to perceive it and respond to it. We must know when it is appropriate to start sending our messages and when it is appropriate to stop. This requires that we plan and perceive what is going to happen next. Only then can communication flow smoothly.

We have studied how the actions of infants are predictively coordinated with object motion in both looking (von Hofsten & Rosander, 1996) and reaching (von Hofsten, 1980, 1983; von Hofsten, Vishton, Spelke, Feng, & Rosander, 1994). The prediction of a moving object's future position is possible because object motion is subject to physical constraints, including *continuity* (objects move only on connected paths), *solidity* (objects move only on unobstructed paths, such that two objects never occupy the same place at the same time), *gravity* (objects accelerate downward in the absence of support), and *inertia* (objects undergo motion in the absence of forces and change their motion smoothly when forces are present; Spelke, Breinlinger, Macomber, & Jacobson 1992).

Two kinds of prediction of target motion may be distinguished. Predictions could be extrapolations of the seen motion. By inspecting how the object moves during a short time frame it is generally possible to extrapolate a continuous motion into the next time window. Such predictions are fundamental to the ability of biological organisms to overcome the processing lags of their systems. However, perceptually based extrapolations can only predict smoothly changing motions, and they only work over short time frame (Pavel, 1990). The second kind of prediction might be called *logical prediction* because it is based on rules. The individual who wants to reach out and grasp a moving object must initiate the reach far ahead and must therefore be able to make a more long-term prediction of when the object will be within reach. Furthermore, the prediction of an abrupt turn of the motion, such as when the target hits a surface and bounces back, cannot be based on simple linear extrapolation. It has to be predicted from a set of rules or principles. When are infants able to master these different prediction problems?

Looking

In von Hofsten and Rosander (1996), 1-, 2-, and 3-month-olds tracked a wide-angle, sinusoidally moving, target. The results showed that the tracking accomplished by the 1-month-old infants was associated with a substantial lag of around 200 ms (see Figure 5). However, lags diminished quickly over age. The results indicated that predictive strategies were used by at least some of the 2- and 3-month-olds.

What kind of information might drive the smooth tracking in young infants? If the tracking was a steplike updating of target velocity, the average lag would be equal to half the updating time. However, gaze position would not lag target position systematically. Within each cycle of motion, gaze would lag the target as it speeds up and be ahead of it as it slows down. Such tracking could account for the performance of the 1-month-olds and some of the 2- and 3-month-olds reported in von Hofsten and Rosander

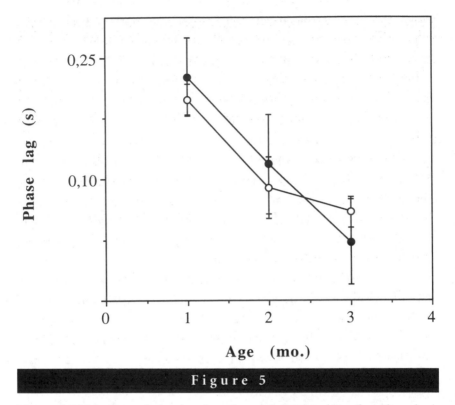

Figure 5

Mean and S.E.M. of eye velocity phase lags of young infants' tracking of a wide angle visual grating of 0.14 c/deg. The results from two target velocities are shown, 0.2 Hz (filled circles) and 0.3 Hz (unfilled circles). From "The Development of Gaze Control and Predictive Tracking in Young Infants," by C. von Hofsten and K. Rosander, 1996, *Vision Research*, 36, p. 87. Copyright 1996 by Elsevier Science. Adapted with permission.

(1996). However, for those cases where little or no systematic lag was found between the tracking and gaze velocities, the individual must have taken the velocity changes of the target stimulus into account. This could be realized by forming a predictive model of the regular sinusoidal target motion, but it is clearly not the only possibility. A more local process is also conceivable.

Reaching

Research by von Hofsten (1980, 1983) provides evidence that infants' object-directed reaching is predictive. As soon as infants begin reaching for stationary objects and grasping them successfully (at about 18 weeks), they also begin to catch moving objects. Infants caught an object that approached them by initiating their arm and hand motions before the object was within reaching distance, aiming ahead of the object's current position toward a place where the paths of the object and the hand would intersect. Aiming was accurate on the first attempted reach for an object.

The objects always traveled on the same circular path (albeit at variable speeds and distances and from variable starting positions), and infants tended to watch the object moving in its circular path before attempting their first reach. As their reaches were well timed even the first time that they viewed an object moving at a given distance and velocity, infants evidently predicted that an object moving at a certain speed maintains that rate of motion. From these studies, we do not know, however, whether predictive reaching is guided by other spatiotemporal constraints on object motion.

By manipulating the temporal properties of the motion, we may learn about some of these constraints. The simplest case is to stop the motion. Figure 6 shows an infant reaching for an object moving in a circular path that stops in "midflight." Clearly, she continues to reach toward a point where she would capture the object had it continued.

Head Movements and Reaching

Systematic study of the principles guiding predictive reaching requires manipulation of the spatial as well as the temporal properties of object motion. We have initiated such a line of studies (von Hofsten et al., 1993). Infants were presented with an object moving on a screen at a predetermined velocity on a predesigned path. The object motions were produced by a large computer-controlled plane plotter, the pen of which had been replaced with a small magnet. The plotting area was topped with a sheet of aluminum that served as the background for an object, which was supported by a 12-cm wooden dowel rod attached to a second magnet. When the magnet on the object's supporting rod was placed on the aluminum sheet directly over the plotter magnet, the combined attraction held the

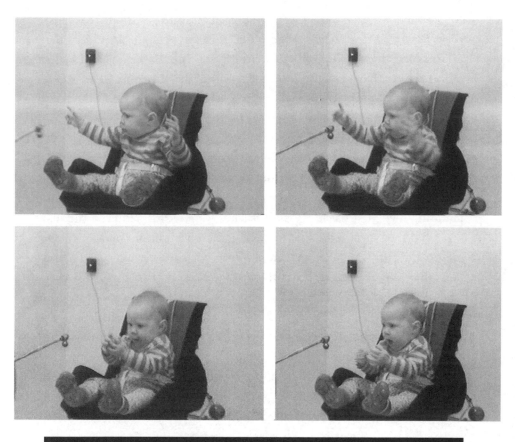

Figure 6

An 8-month-old infant reaching for an object that moves at 60 cm/s and stops 200 ms before the end of the reach. Top left: 300 ms into the reach. Top right: 500 ms into the reach; the object stops. Bottom left: the end of the reach; the infant grasps at the position the object would have occupied if it had continued to move. Bottom right: 300 ms later; the infant redirects attention toward the object's true position.

object in place and caused it to undergo whatever motion the plotter produced. By using the commands originally intended to direct the motion of the plotter pen, this apparatus enabled us to direct the motion of any small object very precisely, anywhere along the surface of the plotter, and at any velocity up to 60 cm/s.

In a first series of experiments (von Hofsten et al., 1993), 6-month-old infants were presented with objects that moved on four different paths along the diagonals of the screen (see Figure 7). The object either continued straight on along the whole diagonal (paths A and C) or made a sudden turn at the midpoint of the screen and continued along the other diagonal (paths B and D). The two types of motion were equally frequent, and they were either presented in a randomized order or in blocks. When presented in blocks, it was possible to predict which kind of motion would be presented next.

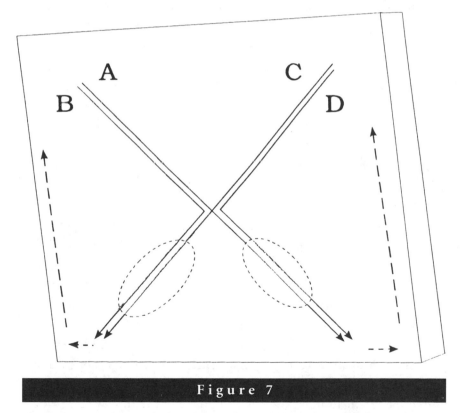

Figure 7

The display screen showing the four different motion paths used in von Hofsten et al. (1994). Paths A and C are straight. The upper part of B and D follow one of the diagonals whereas the lower part follows the other. The dashed areas indicate where the object is within reach of the centrally positioned infant.

To keep the object centered in the visual field and to catch it, infants' head and arm movements had to be prospectively guided. To catch the objects continuing along the same diagonal, extrapolations of the object motion is sufficient. For the objects making a sudden turn, however, a rule-based prediction would be necessary, which could only be learned during the course of the experiment.

The head tracking and reaching observed provided evidence that the infants had a strong tendency to extrapolate the object motion on a straight path past the point of intersection of the four paths. Both on trials with linear motion and on trials with nonlinear motion, infants' heads moved smoothly in the direction of the object's initial motion even after the object reached the midpoint where, on half the trials, it turned. Head tracking continued undisturbed more than 150 ms after the object had stopped and changed direction before it began to slow down. Reaching appeared to accommodate more slowly to a change in object motion. On linear trials as well as on trials where the object made a sudden turn, the hand contralateral to the origin of the object motion moved toward a point which the object would have reached had it continued on its original path. The hand was moved up to 300 ms after the object had changed direction. The infants showed no tendency to predict the sudden jump, not even after 12 such trials.

Mechanical effects of inertia could not account for the reaching patterns obtained in this experiment. The infants did not simply track the linear motion of the object by moving their hand in the same direction as the object's motion. Rather, their reaching motions with the contralateral hand converged on points at which the object would enter the infant's reaching space had it continued in linear motion. Depending on the initial position of the hand, this convergence could be accomplished either by moving in the same direction as the object or by moving in the opposite direction. In the latter case, effective reaching required the infant to move the hand opposite to the direction in which its own head was turning, in order to intercept the object (see also von Hofsten, 1980).

The present findings therefore provide evidence that 6-month-old infants reach predictively by extrapolating the linear motion of target objects. In a world consisting of freely moving objects with mass, subject to inertia, linear extrapolations of object motion provide a reasonable heuristic guide to reaching and visual tracking. Changes in object motion are generally smooth and gradual. A short-range process for extrapolating linear motion therefore will support effective tracking and aiming for objects under many conditions. The results suggest, however, that more rule-based predictions were involved as well, because the hand contralateral to the direction of object motion often started to prepare for catching the object already when the object was at the beginning of its motion.

These studies raise questions regarding the kind of motions infants are able to extrapolate. Although not straight, constant-speed motions were used in the reported experiment, the results by von Hofsten (1983) suggested that 8-month-old infants are able to extrapolate circular motions in catching tasks, and Aslin (1981) and von Hofsten and Rosander (1996) reported that 3-month-olds are able to extrapolate sinusoidal movements in a looking task. Do these extrapolations depend on continuously available visual information, or can object motion be predicted over occlusions? Predicting object motion over occlusion either requires extrapolation over longer time–space intervals or more rule-based predictions. Rule-based predictions could be based on such constraints on object motion as continuity, solidity, no action at a distance, and gravity. It is expected that over the period of infancy, infants improve their ability to extract invariances defining complex motions, expand their predictions further into the future, and become increasingly able to base their predictions on logical rules. Another question evoked by the results is whether mastery in predicting external events relies on one single process or separate processes for separate actions. Our preliminary results (von Hofsten, Feng, Spelke, & Vishton, 1994) indicated that object occlusion disrupts predictive reaching but not predictive looking in 6-month-old infants. Further research with different displays and motion paths are currently being performed to shed light on these questions.

A FUNCTIONAL APPROACH

I have argued that action control requires information about the future and that this is one of the greatest challenges facing cognitive development. I proposed that cognition originally evolved to enable humans to prepare and organize behavior for future events and activities. Furthermore, I argued that the emergence of skill is task related: It comes about through the systematic exploration of the task. Skill has to do with getting to know the task space defined by the different parameters of the task.

The present functional approach provides a means for explaining the relationship between conception, representation, and perception and how they relate to action. From an action perspective, the functions of these processes are not different. The function of all of them is to help us predict what is going to happen next, but the means by which they help to fulfill this function are different. Focusing on action also implies focusing on the tasks to be solved. Different tasks may require different kinds of knowledge of the future. The metaphor of task space highlights this fact.

At the sensorimotor level, control seems more continuous, whereas more global aspects of actions appear to be controlled in a more steplike fashion (now and then we stop, think, and reconsider). In line with this, Miller, Galanter, and Pribram (1960) used an analogue computer metaphor for describing the lower levels of control and a digital computer metaphor for describing the higher levels. This distinction may not be real. Fine-grain analysis of goal-directed movements demonstrate that they are also constructed in steps or pulses (von Hofsten, 1979, 1991).

Another difference between sensorimotor control and the planning of everyday activities concerns the involvement of deliberate thinking. Deliberate thinking is an important part of tasks such as organizing a picnic but is often insignificant in tasks such as organizing a reaching movement. Deliberate thinking takes time, which puts certain limitations on the tasks in which it could be involved. The closer one gets to the implementation of the action the more important timing becomes and the more crucial it is to have direct access to information about the future without the involvement of consiousness. Recent research on neurologically impaired human patients (Goodale & Milner, 1992) and from electrophysiological and behavioral studies in monkeys (Ungenleider & Mishkin, 1982) even suggest that there are different systems for representing visual information used in gearing the motor system to the external world and in evaluating and thinking about it.

The advantage of deliberate thinking is the flexibility in evaluating different action alternatives and unforeseen events it provides. This is needed at the macro level. Closer to the implementation, flexibility is also needed but the problems are different. At this level it is not so much a question of being flexible in setting the goals when facing changing conditions as it is to flexibly organize the movements to get there.

This functional approach may not only help us to understand the development of perception, action, and cognition, but also to relate those developments to biology. There have been strong selective forces favoring the evolution of means for extracting prospective information, representing the future in our minds, and gaining control over future events. Prospective control and predictive abilities is not something that suddenly emerges at some point in development. Perception is always linked to action, and through that link they are both related to meaning. We must understand in what ways biology has facilitated the solution of the prediction problem.

This perspective may finally help us to better understand developmental problems from movement pathologies to behavioral problems. Coordination dysfunctions and clumsiness are, at least, partly due to deficient prospective control (Lee, Daniel, Turnball, & Cook, 1990; Van der Weel, van der Meer, & Lee, 1991). Moreover, insight into such pathologies like schizophrenia could be gained from this perspective. Among other things, it expresses itself as an inability to predict the future (Weinberger, Berman, Gold, & Goldberg, 1994).

THE IMPORTANCE OF MULTIPLE APPROACHES TO DEVELOPMENT

Although the present approach focuses on what develops, it does not specifically address the questions related to developmental transitions and the emergence of new form. Development is determined by genotypic, phenotypic, environmental, and other factors, and it is always active and dynamic. It therefore seems necessary to approach the problem of developmental change from some kind of systems theory. Enlightening attempts in that direction have been made by Piaget (1971), Gesell (1945), and Thelen (1989), among others. Thelen used a mathematical model, called the *dynamic systems model*, as a metaphor for development. Even though this model is not able to predict development, it seems to be a good frame of reference for thinking about development, transitions, and the emergence of new form. The problem with a mathematical model is that it is not in itself a theory of development, and therefore it does not concern itself with the content or the schedule of development. For instance, what determines the emergence of reaching? Why does functional reaching only emerge at about 3 to 4 months of age when even neonates have been shown to perform visually directed arm movements (von Hofsten, 1982)? Why does it emerge at all?

Development is a complex process. To understand it we must address questions of motives, functions, and the different problems facing an acting developing organism. We also must address questions regarding the emergence of new forms by which problems may be solved better and easier. One single approach cannot deal equally well with all these various aspects. Functional approaches, like the one presented here, are designed to address questions of the motives and problems facing an acting organism and the development of specific competence. Systems approaches are designed to address questions regarding the process of change and emergence of new means by which problems may be solved. Only together do they begin to give us an understanding of how development comes about.

REFERENCES

Aslin, R. N. (1981). Development of smooth pursuit in human infants. In D. F. Fisher, R. A. Monty, & J. W. Senders (Eds.), *Eye movements: Cognition and visual perception.* Hillsdale, NJ: Erlbaum.

Barnes, G. R. (1993). Visual–vestibular interaction in the control of head and eye movement: The role of visual feedback and predictive mechanisms. *Progress in Neurobiology, 41,* 435–472.

Benson, A. J. (1970). Interactions between semicircular canals and gravireceptors. In D. Dusbey & D. Reidel (Eds.), *Recent advances in aerospace medicine* (pp. 249–261). Dordrecht, The Netherlands: Reidel.

Bernstein, N. (1967). *The coordination and regulation of movements.* Oxford, England: Pergamon.

Bertenthal, B. I., & Campos, J. J. (1991). A systems approach to the organizing effects of self-produced locomotion during infancy. In C. Rovee-Collier & L. P. Lipsitt (Eds.), *Advances in infant research* (Vol 6, pp. 1–60). Norwood, NJ: Ablex.

Bloch, H., & Carchon, I. (1992). On the onset of eye-head co-ordination in infants. *Behavioural Brain Research, 49,* 85–90.

Daniel, B. M., & Lee, D. (1990). Development of looking with head and eyes. *Journal of Experimental Child Psychology, 50,* 200–216.

Dayton, G. O., & Jones, M. H. (1964). Analysis of characteristics of fixation reflex in infants by use of direct current electrooculography. *Neurology, 14,* 1152–1156.

Gesell, A. (1945). *The embryology of behavior.* New York: Harper.

Gibson, E. J. (1988). Exploratory behavior in the development of perceiving, acting, and the acquiring of knowledge. *Annual Review of Psychology, 39,* 1–41.

Goodale, M. A., & Milner, D. A. (1992). Separate visual pathways for perception and action. *Trends in Neuroscience, 15,* 20–25.

Helmholtz, J. von. (1925). *Physiological optics,* Vol. 3 (J. P. C. Southhall, Ed.). Rochester, NY: Optical Society of America.

Hydén, D., Istl, Y. E., & Schwartz, D. W. F. (1982). Human visuo–vestibular interaction as a basis for quantitative clinical diagnosis. *Acta Otolaryngology, 94,* 53–60.

Jell, R. M., Stockwell, C. W., Turnipseed, G. T., & Guedry, F. E. (1988). The influence of active versus passive head oscillation, and mental set on the human vestibulo–ocular reflex. *Aviation, Space, and Environmental Medicine, 59,* 1061–1065.

Kawato, M., & Gomi, H. (1992). The cerebellum and VOR/OKR learning models. *Trends in Neuroscience, 15,* 445–453.

Knight, R. T., & Grabowecky, M. (1995). Escape from linear time: Prefrontal cortex and consious experience. In M. Gazzaniga (Ed.), *The cognitive neurosciences* (pp. 1357–1371). Cambridge, MA: MIT Press.

Kremenitzer, J. P., Vaughan, H. G., Kurtzberg, D., & Dowling, K. (1979). Smooth-pursuit eye movements in the newborn infant. *Child Development, 50,* 442–448.

Lee, D. N. (1993). Body–environment coupling. In U. Neisser (Ed.), *The perceived self: Ecological and interpersonal sources of self-knowledge* (pp. 43–67). New York: Cambridge University Press.

Lee, D. N., Daniel, B. M., Turnball, J., & Cook, M. L. (1990). Basic perceptuo-motor dysfunctions in cerebral palsy. In M. Jeannerod (Ed.), *Attention and performance: Vol. 13. Motor representation and control* (pp. 583–603). Hillsdale, NJ: Erlbaum.

Lee, D. N., Davies, M. N. O., Green, P. R., & van der Weel, F. R. (1993). Visual control of velocity of approach by pigeons when landing. *Journal of Experimental Biology, 180*, 85–104.

Lee, D. N., Lishman, J. R., & Thompson, J. A. (1982). Visual regulation of gait in long jumping. *Journal of Experimental Psychology: Human Perception and Performance, 8*, 448–459.

Lee, D. N., & Reddish, P. E. (1981). Plummeting gannets: A paradigm of ecological optics. *Nature, 293*, 293–294.

Lee, D. N., Reddish, P. E., & Rand, D. T. (1991). Areal docking by hummingbirds. *Naturwissenschaften, 78*, 526–527.

Lockman, J. J., Ashmead, D. H., & Bushnell, E. W. (1984). The development of anticipatory hand orientation during infancy. *Journal of Experimental Child Psychology, 37*, 176–186.

Miller, G. A., Galanter, E., & Pribram, K. (1960). *Plans and the structure of behavior.* New York: Holt, Rinehart & Winston.

Morrongiello, B., & Rocca, P. (1986, April). *Age-related changes in reaching behavior.* Paper presented at the International Conference on Infant Studies. Los Angeles, CA.

Pavel, M. (1990). Predictive control of eye movement. In E. Kowler (Ed.), *Eye movements and their role in visual and cognitive processes. Reviews of oculomotor research,* (Vol. 4, pp. 71–114). Amsterdam: Elsevier.

Piaget, J. (1953). *The origins of intelligence in the child.* New York: Routledge.

Piaget, J. (1971). *Biology and knowledge.* Chicago: University of Chicago Press.

Reed, E. S. (1990). Changing theories of postural development. In M. Woollacott & A. Shumway-Cook (Eds.), *Development of posture and gait across the life span.* Columbia: University of South Carolina Press.

Roucoux, A., Culee, C., & Roucoux, M. (1983). Development of fixation and pursuit eye movements in human infants. *Behavioural Brain Research, 10*, 133–139.

Snyder, L. H., Lawrence, D. M., & King, W. M. (1992). Changes in vestibulo–ocular reflex (VOR) anticipate changes in vergence angle in monkey. *Vision Research, 32,* 569–575.

Spelke, E. S., Breinlinger, K., Macomber, J., & Jacobson, K. (1992). Origins of knowledge. *Psychological Review, 99,* 605–632.

Thelen, E. (1989). Self-organization in developmental processes: Can systems approaches work? In M. Gunnar & E. Thelen (Eds.), *Systems and development: The Minnesota Symposia on Child Development* (Vol. 22, pp. 77–117). Hillsdale, NJ: Erlbaum.

Thelen, E., Corbett, D., Kamm, K., Spencer, I. P., Schneider, K., & Zernicker, R. F. (1993). The transition to reaching: Mapping intention and intrinsic dynamics. *Child Development, 64,* 1058–1099.

Tomlinson, R. D., Saunders, G. E., & Schwartz, D. W. F. (1980). Analysis of human vestibulo–ocular reflex during active head movements. *Acta Otolaryngology, 90,* 184–190.

Ungenleider, L. G., & Mishkin, M. (1982). Two cortical systems. In D. J. Ingle, M. A. Goodale, & R. J. W. Mansfield (Eds.), *The analysis of visual behavior* (pp. 549–586). Cambridge, MA: MIT Press.

Van der Meer, A. L. H., van der Weel, F. R., & Lee, D. N. (1995). The functional significance of arm movements in neonates. *Science, 267,* 693–695.

Van der Weel, F. R., van der Meer, A. H. L., & Lee, D. N. (1991). Effect of task on movement control in cerebral palsy: Implications for assessment and therapy. *Developmental Medicine and Child Neurology, 33,* 419–426.

von Hofsten, C. (1979). Development of visually guided reaching: The approach phase. *Journal of Human Movement Studies, 5,* 160–178.

von Hofsten, C. (1980). Predictive reaching for moving objects by human infants. *Journal of Experimental Child Psychology, 30,* 369–382.

von Hofsten, C. (1982). Eye–hand coordination in newborns. *Developmental Psychology, 18,* 450–461.

von Hofsten, C. (1983). Catching skills in infancy. *Journal of Experimental Psychology: Human Perception and Performance, 9,* 75–85.

von Hofsten, C. (1986). The early development of the manual system. In B. Lindblom & R. Zetterström (Eds.), *Precursors of early speech* (pp. 175–188). Basingstoke, New Hampshire: Macmillan.

von Hofsten, C. (1991). Structuring of early reaching movements: A longitudinal study. *Journal of Motor Behavior, 23,* 280–292.

von Hofsten, C. (1993). Prospective control: A basic aspect of action development. *Human Development, 36,* 253–270.

von Hofsten, C., & Fazel-Zandy, S. (1984). Development of visually guided hand orientation in reaching. *Journal of Experimental Child Psychology, 38,* 208–219.

von Hofsten, C., Feng, Q., Spelke, E. S., & Vishton, P. (1994, June). *Infants predictive head turning and reaching for fully visible and occluded objects* [abstract]. Paper presented at the International Conference on Infant Studies. Paris, France.

von Hofsten, C., & Rönnqvist, L. (1988). Preparation for grasping an object: A developmental study. *Journal of Experimental Psychology: Human Perception and Performance, 14,* 610–621.

von Hofsten, C., & Rosander, K. (1996). The development of gaze control and predictive tracking in young infants. *Vision Research, 36,* 81–96.

von Hofsten, C., Vishton, P., Spelke, E. S., & Feng, Q. (1993, Nov. 3). Principles of predictive action in 6-month-old infants [abstract]. Psychonomics, Washington, DC. Manuscript submitted for publication.

von Hofsten, C., & Woollacott, M. (1990). [Postural preparations for reaching in 9-month-old infants]. Unpublished raw data.

Walls, L. L. (1962). The evolutionary history of eye movements. *Vision Research, 8,* 34–42.

Warren, W. H., & Hannon, D. J. (1990). Eye movements and optical flow. *Journal of the Optical Society of America, A7,* 160–169.

Weinberger, D. R., Berman, K. F., Gold, J., & Goldberg, T. (1994). Neural mechanisms of future-oriented processes: In vivo physiological studies of humans. In M. M. Haith, J. B. Benson, R. J. Roberts Jr., & B. Pennington (Eds.), *The development of future oriented processes* (pp. 221–242). Chicago: Chicago University Press.

Wing, A. M., Turton, A., & Fraser, C. (1986). Grasp size and accuracy of approach in reaching. *Journal of Motor Behavior, 18,* 245–261.

Comment on von Hofsten

Karl M. Newell

Claes von Hofsten's chapter outlines a functional perspective to the early development of predictive abilities. Prospective control in action is a problem that has consumed von Hofsten's research career, and the chapter is liberally illustrated with empirical examples of infant predictive capacities over a wide range of experimental protocols. One of the hallmarks of von Hofsten's empirical work has been the many innovative demonstrations of precocious infant prospective control in action. The theoretical issue emphasized in the chapter is the functional relation of perception and representation in predicting the future control of action. I wish to address three issues in my commentary: the problems of prospective control, the coordination of posture and movement, and the role of theory in perception and representation in studying the development of infants' predictive abilities.

PROBLEMS OF PROSPECTIVE CONTROL

Von Hofsten identifies and reviews five problems of prospective control that are encountered by infants in action. These problems are not unique

Newell comments on von Hofsten from an ecological realist perspective.

to infants, however; a number of elements are also evident in normal healthy adults performing a wide variety of actions, particularly in the early stages of learning to accommodate to a particular task constraint. For example, it is well established that adults learning a reaching or pointing task tend to increase the duration of the initial phase of the movement and decrease the number of discrete units with practice. Adults also learn how to coordinate movement and posture and the different body parts involved in action when engaged in the practice and performance of a given task. Fitting actions to external contexts and environmental constraints is also integral to adult action. An interesting issue is to identify the confluence of constraints to action that produce the same limitations across the life span in prospective control.

The age-related contrasts in these problems of prospective control have nearly all involved cross-sectional experimental designs in the studies quoted by von Hofsten. The persistence of these age-related differences in prospective control would be tested more severely in longitudinal designs. It would also be useful to examine the influence of relatively intense practice sessions with infants on the respective tasks to obtain more veridical estimates of the age-related limitations in prospective control. Von Hofsten has pushed the lower age boundaries as hard as anyone in providing demonstrations of the early predictive abilities of infants, but there may still be room for advances in this area under different experimental conditions.

Longitudinal designs and practice effects also would be useful to assess the nature of the qualitative changes in the development of prospective control in the different problem areas identified by von Hofsten. The transitions in the qualitative components of prospective control were not addressed in this chapter. Recent work from my laboratory on the development of coordination suggests that individuals of all ages tend to follow similar preferred pathways to the changing patterns of coordination that accompany practice to a given task constraint. What differs the most across children and adults learning the same new action pattern is the degree of freezing on the initial coordination solution to the task goal. Younger children tend to freeze a greater number of biomechanical degrees of freedom than adults even when practice and general experiential effects are considered. The observation of preferred pathways of transitions in the other areas of prospective control would provide further evidence of common principles to the acquisition of coordination in action that are independent of the task and age of the individual.

The principles of the acquisition of coordination are related to the issue of exploration, a topic that is central to von Hofsten's perspective on the development of prospective control. That is, some patterns of exploration (search strategies) may consistently appear in the transitions associated with the acquisition of the elements of prospective control. Our work on the acquisition of coordination suggests that there are preferred pathways to these transitions, just as there appear to be preferred coordination mode solutions to a given set of constraints to action. The determination of the systematic and unsystematic components to exploration in the development of action would be a useful empirical venture in all of the areas of prospective control identified by von Hofsten.

POSTURE AND MOVEMENT

One of the problems of prospective control highlighted by von Hofsten is what he calls the fitting together of posture and movement. In essence he argues that postural control has to be both reactive and prospective in accommodating to ongoing instrumental limb movement in purposeful action. Through the years von Hofsten has provided a number of empirical examples to support the notion that postural control is a significant limiting factor in action development of the infant. One example is the demonstration that given the appropriate postural support young infants engage in goal-directed reaching actions at an earlier age than is otherwise possible.

The general principle driving this relation of posture and movement could be more general than merely applying to the control of the torso and arms in posture and reaching. That is, there may be systematic relations to be observed in the coordination of all functional units of the system including the control of the eyes, head, torso, arms, and legs. The developmental progressions observed in infancy and early childhood in the prospective control of these systems again may follow general rules of the change in coordination in the fitting of actions to either external or internal goals. This view also suggests that the five areas of prospective control identified by von Hofsten may not be as independent as is implied in the chapter.

PERCEPTION AND REPRESENTATION

Von Hofsten clearly proposes that perception and representation are necessary and provide complementary processes to predict the future elements of action. For von Hofsten representation provides the global structures of the world, and perception provides the immediate details that may be embedded in these global structures to guide action. The functional approach to predictive abilities outlined by von Hofsten does not, however, endorse or examine any particular theoretical positions or propositions in regard to perception and representation in prospective control of action. Furthermore, the view outlined here does not make any explicit links to extant theories of development.

The functional approach outlined by von Hofsten appears by design to be atheoretical, although his work over the years seems to be sympathetic to the ideas of Gibson (1966, 1979) on perception. Von Hofsten believes that the high complexity of development warrants a multidimensional operational approach to the functional problems of development. In certain circumstances theory undoubtedly can be constraining to empirical work, but it also acts as a goal and guide to systematic empirical activity. The history of science also suggests that new theoretical perspectives in any domain are rarely constructed in a bottom–up inductive fashion from data. There is no question, however, that the important empirical observations reported here by von Hofsten on the functional development of prospective control in action have to be considered in any related theoretical perspective to the development of action.

REFERENCES

Gibson, J. J. (1966). *The senses considered as perceptual systems.* Boston, MA: Houghton-Mifflin.

Gibson, J. J. (1979). *The ecological approach to visual perception.* Boston, MA: Houghton-Mifflin.

7

A Social Ecological Realist Approach to the Emergence of the Lexicon: Educating Attention to Amodal Invariants in Gesture and Speech

Patricia Zukow-Goldring

Knowing is both direct and culturally directed.[1] The clay artifacts in Figure 1 illustrate this point and its import for development. These discs are plain or incised, grayish white or adobe colored, ranging in size from 3/8 inches in diameter to somewhat less than 2 inches, solid or hollow, less than 1/4 inch in width, and often slightly concave on the edge. Note that it is nearly impossible to identify these objects. (Guesses by colleagues have ranged from divination artifacts to pre-Columbian hockey pucks.) What to do with them presents another challenge, with the exception, perhaps, of the most stereotyped, rudimentary, or self-directed actions typical of infants, such as grasping and sucking. The futility of attempting to detect the affordances (action potentials) of things detached

[1]See also, Costall, 1995; Heft, 1989; Ingold, 1991a; Loveland, 1991; Rader, personal communication, June 1995; Still & Costall, 1991. My special thanks to Nancy Rader for suggesting a more gracefully turned phrasing.

The National Institute of Mental Health, the Spencer Foundation, and the Michelle F. Elkind Foundation provided funds for this research. I thank Anne Macdonald, Doug Macbeth, Nancy Rader, Cathy Dent-Read, Kelly Ferko, Tim Johnston, Alan Costall, Chuck Goodwin, Jim Good, Diane Poulin-Dubois, Kate Loveland, David Messer, Ted Wachs, and an anonymous reviewer for their comments on previous versions of this chapter. Mike Owens merits special mention for his technical expertise in generating the digital images illustrating the vignettes. My gratitude extends as well to Leonard Konopelski for photography and drawing and to Jeff Holtzman for the video grabs.

Figure 1

Clay artifacts.

from the effectivities (capabilities) of the body, culture, and physical setting of those who formed them strongly suggests that these discs cannot "tell us" what they afford. Affordances emerge, instead, from the lived relation of persons, place, and culture.

My claim emerges from investigating how infants come to know what everyone already knows. No single existing theory, however, provides an adequate basis for examining this issue. Determining the methods or practices by which infants become adept members of their culture is a challenge that requires investigating how they come to perceive—notice, engage in, and talk about ongoing events in the company of other people. I examine what perceiving and acting with caregivers in a particular time and place offer the developing infant. My research focuses on the period from 6 months of age through the emergence of the early lexicon during the one-word level. This time frame provides a window through which to observe the infant's rapid transition from quite restricted participation in everyday life to a much fuller contribution during ongoing events. The social ecological realist approach that I introduce provides a means to investigate educating attention, the practice that may precipitate lexical development.

The puzzle for me has been to see how infants learn the relation between world and word: between what is going on and what is said. Given infants are immersed in a continuous perceptual flow, how do these cultural novices begin to detect and participate in assembling the structure and organization of everyday events? In particular, how do infants come to perceive the relation between the auditory structure in speech and a specific subsegment of the whole spectrum of perceptual structure (visual, tactile, olfactory, auditory, proprioceptive) available at any one moment during some daily activity?

In this chapter, I first provide an overview of ecological realism. I next discuss the limitations that these questions pose to other developmental theories. Then I present social ecological realism and sketch some problems and prospects for this approach to (lexical) development. In the following section, I propose a reinterpretation of some early infant studies in terms of attention and discuss the link between studies of early perceptual learning and the emergence of the lexicon. I subsequently illustrate theory and method with empirical studies of educating attention. Finally, I consider the strengths and weaknesses of a social ecological realism, its implications, and avenues for future developmental research and theory.

ECOLOGICAL REALISM

For J. J. Gibson (1966, 1979), knowing is a direct noticing of what the world affords for action. According to ecological realism, the perceptual structure detectable in ambient light uniquely specifies its source. In harmony with the natural laws of ecological optics (and by extension to ecological acoustics and so on), detectable mathematical relations specify what creatures see, hear, touch, and smell (J. J. Gibson, 1966; Lee, 1980; Lombardo, 1987). For instance, creatures that evolved to detect functionally significant opportunities for action perceive higher order patterns of light, not the stimuli of physics, such as wave length. Individuals detect perceptual structure that specifies surfaces, edges that occlude one another, texture, rigidity, and so on. Creatures detect the perceptual structure that specifies the unchanging invariant aspects of ongoing events (the something that something is happening to) as well as the structure specifying transformation and change (the something that is happening) during cycles of perceiving and acting (Michaels & Carello, 1981, p. 26).[2]

Acting–perceiving cycles emerge in daily life. Creatures whose bodies have particular effectivities or capabilities detect perceptual structures in their environments' physical layout that specify affordances or opportunities for action (J. J. Gibson, 1979; Mace, 1977; Michaels & Carello, 1981; Shaw & Turvey, 1981; Turvey et al., 1981). Effectivities of the body and affordances of the creature's environment are dual complements like foot and shoe; the one is made "of" the other. A foot that arches, twists, and flexes slips into a thonged shoe whose partitioning invites smaller toes to one side and big toe to the other; the thong slips on its mirror-imaged foot. Once shod, the intelligibility or meaningfulness of the perceptual structure arises as a person with such shoes perceives what persists and what changes as he or she moves in and through the environment (Ingold, 1991b). Perceiving the physical layout of a room permits a person to detect whether a surface supports locomotion, provides traction for such a shoe, and more. Simultaneously, the person negotiates moving through a setting filled with things that move and things that do not. As a person moves, affordances of the physical layout flow in and out of the perceptual field, some becoming prominent and others receding from view. However, as people do what they can see and concomitantly see what to do next, can they count on novices seeing the same options? Probably not.

---

[2]In contrast, according to cognitive and information processing positions, people perceive and know the world indirectly. In that view, mental mechanisms assemble an interface between the dualisms of mind–body, person–environment and so on by constructing meaning from flawed perceptual input or enhancing the output of faulty perceptual systems (or both). For comparisons of Gibson's ecological realism and theories based on indirect perception and dualism, see Costall, 1995; E. J. Gibson and Rader, 1979; E. C. Goldfield, 1983; Reed, 1986; Shaw and Bransford, 1977; Still and Costall, 1991; and Turvey, Shaw, Reed and Mace, 1981.

OTHER VIEWS OF CHILD DEVELOPMENT

How do infants come to know? Explanations of this achievement vary. Metaphors describing the degree to which infants arrive preattuned to their environment range from easily inscribed, clean slates (Locke, 1699/1938) to complexly preprogrammed entities (Carey & Gelman, 1991; Wexler, 1990). Few scholars today would agree with Watson (1930), who proposed that infants arrive in this world with early propensities that caregivers can easily overwrite. By placing them in the proper controlled environment, infants can be shaped at will as "doctor, lawyer, artist, . . . and, yes, even beggar-man and thief" (Watson, 1930, p. 104). Many others reject the notion that (children's) behavior unfolds over time from genetic programs (Dent-Read & Zukow-Goldring, this volume; Johnston & Gottlieb, 1990; Oyama, 1985). Debates over this topic continue unabated, but most would concur that infants at birth are *cultural* blank slates. A world of the most mundane activities of daily life, communication, and permissible conduct must be learned and taught (Vygotsky, 1978; Zukow, 1989, 1990). These achievements do not occur in a social vacuum but in the midst of daily life. The inadequacies of those abandoned by society or lacking some crucial abilities to detect what the social world affords, such as "wild" children and the autistic, display the primacy of culture for development (Itard, 1801/1982; Loveland, 1991; MacLean, 1977).

Cognitive theories concentrate on autonomous mental mechanisms untouched by direct contact with ongoing events to explain the growing abilities of children, whereas ecological approaches emphasize that the social world guides development. Neither tells us the particulars of *how* children make sense, and thus learn, from the details of actual events. Cognitive theories examine "what" children put in their own heads (Piaget, 1962), and information-processing models assume a great portion of the "what" comes with the head (Carey & Gelman, 1991; Markman, 1989). Behaviorist accounts of learning diverge as well by ignoring all sources of knowing found in heads and by attributing learning to unidirectional forces originating in the environment (Skinner, 1953). In contrast, many scholars argue that culture is performed, not preformed (Garfinkel, 1967; Ingold, 1991a; Kendon, 1990; Moerman, 1988). That is, cultures manifest and reproduce themselves continuously as novice and expert members practice them in daily life (Cole, 1989; Lave & Wenger, 1991; Weisner, 1996; Whiting & Edwards, 1988). These approaches, variously called *ecological, ecocultural,* or *cultural–historical,* move away from focusing on the static *what* of learning and elaborate the active *where* instead. Bronfenbrenner's (1979) nested sets of activities within a culture, elaborated further by Cole (1989) and Wachs (1992), have alerted researchers to the necessity of considering the interplay of macro- and micro-environments on development.[3] However, although these views maintain *that* children learn during interaction, they usually attribute the *how* to cognitive models without explaining the particulars. If knowing is not transmitted, how do novices come to know what the physical and social world affords? To focus on how people know, an epigram from ecological realism suggests that psychologists "ask not what's inside your head, but what your head's inside of" (Mace, 1977, p. 43).

Many researchers who look outside the person stress the importance of culture for development. These scholars carefully document accounts of people's daily activities and physical surround by adhering to ecologically valid methods that render members' interpretations, rather than impose those of the researcher (Bronfenbrenner, 1979; Cole, Hood, & McDermott, 1978; Malpass, 1977). However, they do not directly deal with how the reciprocal relation of individuals and their environments informs knowing. In contrast, the mutuality or reflexive relation of individuals and their environments grounds studies of direct perception (J. J. Gibson, 1966, 1979; Shaw & Turvey, 1981), epigenetic systems (Gottlieb, 1991a, 1991b; Green & Gustafson, this volume; Miller, this volume), and dynamical systems (Clark, this volume; Fogel, this volume; Thelen & Smith, 1994). Most of these researchers engage in laboratory research that is rather far removed from the ordinary occasions in which behavior emerges. Of these, only researchers informed by the ecological realism of Gibson investigate the detecting of perceptual structure that guides what people do as they

---

[3]Dent-Read (this volume) discusses the advantages of a more dynamic approach informed by J. J. Gibson's ecological realism (1966, 1979) entailing nested levels of organism–environment mutualities.

go about their daily lives (J. J. Gibson, 1966, 1979; for collections–reviews, see Kubovy & Pomerantz, 1981; Reed, 1986; Shaw & Bransford, 1977; Turvey et al., 1981; Warren & Shaw, 1985). The next section addresses some of these differences in view and adds the *social* to the notion that knowing is direct by discussing how children come to know as they interact with others.

A SOCIAL ECOLOGICAL REALISM

This chapter introduces a *social* ecological realism informed by J. J. Gibson and E. J. Gibson, cultural–historical approaches, and ethnomethodology–linguistic anthropology to explain how infants gradually become adept members of their cultures. My approach integrates analyses designed to investigate how caregivers and infants reciprocally select and detect the perceptual structure that informs action with a concern for how cultures reproduce themselves through the development of new members.[4]

Some provocative findings from research addressing the relation between the saying-and-showing of a speaker and the seeing-and-hearing of a recipient provide a fresh outlook for addressing these issues. Studies of everyday life by ethnomethodologists and linguistic anthropologists (Garfinkel, 1967; C. Goodwin, 1994, in press; M. H. Goodwin & C. Goodwin, 1986; Kendon, 1990; Macbeth, 1994; Moerman, 1988) document that as people engage in daily life they continuously embody their verbal messages by making them visible to one another in a seamless ensemble of spectacle and talk. Macbeth (1994) discussed the "irreducible indexicality" of speech, arguing persuasively that members produce talk to be "seen and heard." Participants rely on the audio–*visible* character of talk to find out what it affords in local settings. Thus, rather than perceptual structure flowing by infants like some uncut home movie, perhaps someone is

---

[4]For perspectives addressing social affordances, the opportunities that people offer each other for action and interaction, see Costall, 1995; Ginsburg and Harrington, 1993; Good and Still, 1989; McArthur and Baron, 1983; and Smith and Ginsburg, 1989. For other discussions of development, see E. C. Goldfield, 1983; Loveland, 1991, 1993; Ingold, 1991a; Reed, 1993; Still and Costall, 1991; and Valenti and Good, 1991.

editing the flow. Marking the relation between what people say and what they do may make the connection between word and world prominent, perceptually available, tangible. This chapter explores the methods or practices that caregivers use to nurture infants' perceptual learning, specifically in the "educating of attention" that contributes significantly to the emergence of the lexicon (J. J. Gibson, 1979; Ingold, 1991a; Zukow, 1989; Zukow-Goldring, 1997; Zukow-Goldring & Ferko, 1994).

Problems Facing a Social Ecological Realism

In this section, I address some apparent theoretical differences between ecological realist, cultural–historical, and ethnomethodological or linguistic anthropological approaches. None of the three alone provides a basis for seeing how members assemble (shared) meaning, whereas integrating facets of these three positions makes it possible to observe the "lived orderliness" of what people say and do day in and day out. From my perspective, people have methods or practices to reduce ambiguity[5] so daily activities can unfold. These methods appear to entail sharing the perceptual structure that guides action. Coordinating differences in view depends on educating one another to perceive a common ground for action or to notice the other's point of view. These same methods may assist caregivers in giving infants a boost that lets them perceive how to participate in an unfamiliar cultural world. Caregivers make evident culturally relevant methods of perceiving and ways of acting.

Perceiving a Consensus

Findings and implications from sociocultural perspectives, J. J. Gibson's ecological realism, and ethnomethodology or linguistic anthropology must be edited and then integrated to reach a vantage point robust enough to inform an inquiry into the emergence of the lexicon. First, an incompatibility, a seeming paradox, must be addressed. Sociocultural approaches emphasize that people share cultural practices and have a common understanding of the organization of everyday life (Bronfenbrenner, 1979;

---

[5]See Ginsburg and Harrington (1993) for the "objective ambiguity" of any situated act in relation to the larger set of nested, intermingling, and overlapping acts in which it may be embedded.

Cole, 1989; Weisner, 1996; Whiting & Edwards, 1988), whereas an ecological realist approach sees members of the same species as detecting similar affordances in a physical layout (J. J. Gibson, 1979). Although people can perceive a similar layout by walking about, I mean to differentiate between *ecological optics* (the optics of perceiving) and *culturally directed perceiving*. (See Loveland, 1991, p. 105, for a related notion, *culturally preferred affordances*.) For instance, for a rural person who has recently arrived in Mexico City a toilet affords bathing feet; for urban dwellers toilets afford elimination. Although this example sharply contrasts the action potentials of familiar and unfamiliar artifacts, ethnomethodologists and linguistic anthropologists assume even the relentless ambiguity of everyday activities. They take the problematic and fleeting nature of reaching a working consensus as a central problem of daily life and as crucial to performing the most mundane daily activities with other people (C. Goodwin, 1994, 1995; Kendon, 1990; Macbeth, 1994; Moerman, 1988).

Ethnomethodologists and linguistic anthropologists acknowledge the importance of vision, but their analyses of adult members' methods for achieving a practical consensus or "intersubjectivity" do not explain how or why perceiving and acting are the key to knowing. Filling this gap, ecological realism demonstrates how individuals detect the perceptual structure that specifies what the world affords for action (J. J. Gibson, 1979). Combining these three approaches provides a means to address a social world that often demands a "consensus for all practical purposes" as events unfold. The following sections elaborate these themes further.

The Problem of Consensus

Ecological realism holds that organisms perceive the real world (Shaw & Bransford, 1977; Shaw & Turvey, 1981). Furthermore, what they perceive depends on their species as well as their perceptual history. An infrequently examined consequence of the latter is that no two creatures have the same perceptual history (J. J. Gibson, 1979), and their course of perceptual development differs as well (Turvey & Fitzpatrick, 1993). In addition, more than one creature cannot occupy the same point of observation at the same time (J. J. Gibson, 1979). These assumptions suggest that people rarely see "eye to eye." Their views are different, yet neither right nor wrong.

Perceiving is "neither true nor false" (Shaw & Bransford, 1977, p. 22) but adequate or inadequate for the task at hand. However, in order for people to get through the day, adequacy in cultural activities requires some degree of consensus for events to unfold. Ethnomethodologists suggest that, for the most part, a practical consensus suffices to get things done (Garfinkel, 1967; Schutz, 1962).[6] To reach a practical consensus, people negotiate what is happening as events emerge, building and repairing the coherence of events only out of what is at hand (C. Goodwin, 1995; Kendon, 1990; Mehan & Wood, 1975; Schegloff, 1972). That consensus, achieved and sustained by guiding each other's attention, also achieves a co-orientation to the perceptual flow in which all are immersed.

Prospects for the Study of Development

Aligning fields of view may be so ubiquitous among proficient members that the practice may "go without saying." However, when novice and expert meet "what everyone already knows" cannot be and is not taken for granted, but is often made explicit (Kendon, 1990; Zukow, 1986, 1989; Zukow-Goldring, 1997; Zukow-Goldring & Ferko, 1994). To shed light on that process, I suggest that the cycles of perceiving and acting proposed by J. J. Gibson (1979) provide a means to see how children come to participate in daily life as they learn "in the doing" to see and act with others (Weisner, 1987; Whiting & Edwards, 1988).

Perceptual Learning

E. J. Gibson and Rader (E. J. Gibson, 1982; E. J. Gibson & Rader, 1979) studied perceptual differentiation as children developed, noting that experience within various modalities refines perceiving and acting by educating attention. Studies of perceptual development documented changes in expertise over time, presupposing a process endogenous to children and their physical environment. Investigation of the effects of the social world on development, however, are conspicuously absent. This omission may derive from J. J. Gibson's position regarding the mediated nature of language use and

---

[6]In contrast, according to Garfinkel (1967), attempting to achieve a perfect intersubjective match would result in an endless search (infinite regress) for a definitive set of common presuppositions.

the problem of cultural relativism (Costall, 1995; J. J. Gibson, 1950, 1966; Still & Costall, 1991). Both follow from the dualisms attendant to theories of indirect perception: Language entails knowing mediated by representational systems, and relativism involves culture interceding between what can be known and what the world affords. Cultural relativism suggests that individuals from different cultures might perceive different affordances in the natural world, contrary to J. J. Gibson's view (1979, p. 139) that affordances exist independent of perceiver's ongoing, immediate actions.[7]

However, social interaction involving language need not entail knowing mediated by representational systems. Rather, language may guide perceiving (Dent, 1990; Millikan, 1984; Zukow, 1990). Furthermore, affordances for action would not seem to be different from culture to culture, but different perceptual histories, practices, and priorities in daily life may make different affordances prominent. Because neither of the Gibsons nor their early students conducted naturalistic or cross-cultural studies of perception, no one observed what humans do in ordinary settings outside the laboratory. Filling this void, observations in the home confirm that caregivers educate attention during cycles of perceiving and acting all day long, every day. The naturalistic investigations reported in this chapter document that caregivers from a range of cultures, language communities, socioeconomic and educational levels, and technological sites guide perceptual development. These studies suggest that gestures guide perceiving early on, with language joining somewhat later (Zukow, 1989, 1990; Zukow-Goldring & Ferko, 1994). Social ecological realism accounts for these practices more fully than perspectives based on language or culture mediated through mental mechanisms. In addition, perceiving different affordances from the same material object is not necessarily a contradiction for ecological realism. In fact, what the objects in Figure 1 afford children today is not the same as what they afforded the children of the culture that made them.

---

[7]This oft-cited passage in J. J. Gibson (1979) causes much controversy. Some would interpret these statements more strictly or literally at the species level (Reed, 1988), whereas others construe this section in terms of "an organism and its environment" (Loveland, personal communication, September 1995). As Costall (1989, p. 19) noted, "We are *in* culture; it *is* our world. Indeed, it is the only world we could ever directly perceive."

The Duality of Perceiving and Acting

Perceiving and acting do not develop separately but together as a unitary system (Turvey & Fitzpatrick, 1993). This inseparable reciprocity of perceiving–acting may inform cycles of perceiving and acting in others. During interaction infants and caregivers may form a nesting duality in which the perceiving and acting of one continuously and reflexively affects the perceiving and acting of the other. The numerous studies of perceiving and acting cycles by J. J. Gibson and those whose work he has informed (for edited collections and reviews, see Kubovy & Pomerantz, 1981; Reed, 1986; Shaw & Bransford, 1977; Turvey, Shaw, Reed, & Mace, 1981; Warren & Shaw, 1985) provide a well-articulated means to analyze the methods members use in assembling perceptual structure for themselves and, perhaps, for novice members as well. These methods may underlie achieving a practical consensus and becoming a proficient member.

Integrating Vygotsky and Gibson

A key assumption of my approach to a social ecological realism grounded in J. J. Gibson's theory of direct perception is that development depends on the dynamic structure of the social–interactive environment of caregiving (Dent, 1990; Zukow, 1989, 1990; see also E. C. Goldfield, 1983; Reed, 1993; Still & Costall, 1991). My contribution integrates aspects of the cultural–historical approach with that of J. J. Gibson. In particular, the Vygotskian perspective (1978) asserts that proficient members transmit cultural knowledge to those less practiced during social interaction. In this zone of proximal development, cultural knowledge, including linguistic knowledge, first arises for the child during social interaction and only later appears as an individual accomplishment.[8]

Empirical research of early development supports this supposition. When adult and older sibling caregivers guide an infant's play, the infant displays more advanced play than when the infant plays alone (Gaskins, 1990; O'Connell & Bretherton, 1984; Zukow, 1986, 1989; Zukow-Goldring, 1995). However, empirical evidence that caregivers' assistance facilitates

---

[8]Note that I depart from Vygotsky on the issue of mental mediation or indirect perception. See the section entitled *Perceptual Learning* and Dent-Read and Zukow-Goldring (this volume).

children engaging in culturally recognizable activities does not explain how caregivers accomplish this interactive work. How might adult caregivers assist infants when an evident disparity exists between the expressible effectivities and detectable affordances available to caregivers and those available to young children? Do others, such as siblings and peers, provide more accessible assistance because of fewer differences in effectivities and body scale? Supporting this speculation, much research reports that young children intently notice what siblings and peers do and subsequently emulate their actions appropriately in new situations (Eckerman, 1993; Martini, 1994; Zukow-Goldring, 1995).

However, the Vygotskian view does not articulate *how* one individual specifies what he or she knows to another nor how that other subsequently detects the knowing. According to J. J. Gibson (1979), the environment affords or offers particular benefits or dangers to particular creatures. For example, an insect might climb under or over the objects depicted in Figure 1 or might be crushed by them. Humans have other options. Social interaction itself becomes a field of affordances, of possibilities for selecting and detecting the structure in light, sound, odor, pressure, and so on that specifies what is going on.[9] Caregivers educate their infants' attention by making prominent the possibilities for perceiving and acting within everyday events (Zukow, 1990; Zukow-Goldring, 1997). For example, an infant might spontaneously roll or bang or stack the objects illustrated in Figure 1, whereas an older sibling might engage the infant in play using the disks as a token embedded in some culturally recognizable activity, such as pretending to use play money. The following section elaborates how caregivers make previously unnoticed affordances perceivable to infants.

---

[9]Note that some creatures who might not perceive the affordances of human artifacts on their own can do so with guidance. In the wild chimpanzees use and make tools (McGrew, 1993). Chimps perceive affordances for action and refine bodily actions with relatively little explicit tuition by observing conspecifics over several years, and patiently working out details by trial and error. Chimps use crushed leaves to sponge up water for drinking, sticks to fish for termites, and water to wash sweet potatoes before eating. They also fashion anvils for the crushing of nutshells with rock hammers. In contrast, human caregivers who have raised chimps and many other nonhuman primates in a variety of settings (from laboratory to human childlike environments modified for them) note that nonhuman primates learn to use comparable tools (sponges, joy sticks, hammers) quite rapidly with high degrees of skill, when explicitly taught (Savage-Rumbaugh, personal communication, July 1987).

Evidence That Detecting Affordances Is Culturally Directed

Caregivers not only guide children to notice important aspects of what is going on in their social worlds, but also the methods for noticing them. Perhaps caregivers afford practice that assists in attuning and differentiating the perceptual system. Whereas perceiving–acting cycles proceed reflexively, sometimes the "how" to notice seems to precede the "what" to do. That is, caregivers cannot assume children know how to perceive the dynamic configuration of elements that constitutes what everyone else knows how to do. The empirical research reported in this chapter begins by addressing just what coming to know, what adept cultural members take to be "nothing to speak of," looks like as it is done.

The elements participating in events, such as animate beings, fixed landmarks, and detachable objects, must be perceived in their spatial–temporal orientation to the self's body and to each other as these relations change dynamically as the organization of events unfold. Whether in rural Mexico or urban Los Angeles, a bucket of water, a doll, a set of containers provides opportunities for splashing, doll play, or stacking if the elements are strewn about on the ground at some distance from one another.[10] Left to their own devices, infants in the early half of the second year of life may simply slap a hand on the water's surface and bang dolls and containers on the ground (Zukow, 1981–1982). Arrayed differently, the same collection of elements invites bathing the doll when an older sibling demonstrates how to do so (Zukow, 1989). Similarly, objects separated in time–space from the culture that produced them invite present-day inhabitants to perceive different opportunities for action than the people who made and used them. For example, the items in Figure 1 often go unnoticed by the 20th-century residents of a semirural canyon near

---

[10]Loveland (1991) suggested that human artifacts, natural objects, animals, persons, and events have preferred affordances within a culture. Participation in cultural events predisposes people "to use objects, interpret events, and so on, in particular ways" (p. 101). Preference may predict overall frequency of occurrence, but I suspect that on any particular occasion of use the configuration of elements available, both animate, natural, and manufactured, will make what an object affords prominent and, thus, direct action. Screwdrivers frequently drive in or take out screws, but they can also pry open stuck windows, puncture a can, stave off an attacker, prop open a door, pound in a tack, even spread peanut butter. The things available at hand, the difficulty of finding the "preferred artifact," the urgency to do the job, and so on, inform what we do in particular lived settings. "Affordances do not *cause* behavior but constrain and control it" (J. J. Gibson, 1982, p. 411).

Los Arcos where they lay scattered in the dirt, although these disks might offer stacking, tossing, and rolling to anyone with a grasping hand and a rotatable wrist. While doing fieldwork with a family who made bricks by hand in this canyon, I asked what these objects afforded. No one knew or cared. Given the indifference of local residents, I tracked down a tiny museum several miles from this site. The curator told me that these were ear lobe plugs. These objects, then, had evident affordance for pre-Columbian, Tlaltilca children living more than 25 centuries earlier in the same secluded canyon (Zukow, 1981–1982). The pre-Columbian caregivers of Tlaltilco would have used those ear lobe plugs of various sizes to enlarge the holes in their children's ears so that they might be properly dressed on ceremonial occasions (see Figure 2).[11] Apparently these artifacts and, presumably, many natural objects, do not tell us what they afford. Someone else shows us (Costall, 1995; Zukow, 1990).

In sum, detecting (cultural) affordances appears to depend on caregivers educating attention. The empirical studies reported later in this chapter support the claim that caregivers assist infants to perceive animate and inanimate elements in their environments, their space–time configuration, and their relation to ongoing cultural events. Reciprocally, these accomplishments rely on consideration of whether and how infants' level of development or bodily effectivities affect the pickup of perceptual structure.

Duality of Effectivities and Affordances

In harmony with the inseparable nature of perceiving and acting (Turvey & Fitzpatrick, 1993), perhaps effectivities and affordances emerge in tandem. That is, as the body can do more, more affordances for action may

---

[11]Several scholars (Cole, 1989; Costall, 1995; Goodwin, 1995, in press) proposed that artifacts from tools to pathways offer a "material sedimentation of solutions" as members refine affordances over generations of users. But can these refinements be detected without guidance from competent members or without the relevant effectivities? Maybe not.

Despite the ear lobe plugs in Figure 1 having a rather sophisticated design, the concavity of the edge does not tell someone from another space–time what the function might be. The affordance is not dispreferred (cf. Loveland, 1991), but unavailable. Without the effectivity of openings of the proper size in the earlobes or having seen others who have them, this affordance is unavailable to notice. For those with piercings of a particular size, the indentation in the rim of the earplug permits the lobe to fit snugly around it, may enlarge the opening in the lobe somewhat, and, reflexively, the tight fit keeps the earplug from falling out.

213

Figure 2

Tlaltilco infant.

be perceived. In the same vein, acting on new affordances may provide new means for using the body effectively. The infant's limited range of effectivities will constrain the affordances for action he or she can explore. For example, children may be unable to pick up a tiny object and then examine it, if they cannot oppose thumb and forefinger in a pincer grip. Reciprocally, being unable to detect affordances for action precludes infants from realizing an action even if they have the effectivity. For instance, being able to push down does not help open up something if children do not detect that pushing a lever affords opening up a toy (Zukow-Goldring, 1997). A recent review of motor development supports some of these ideas. Bushnell and Boudreau's (1993) research suggests that the emergence of specific motor abilities may play a determining role in some aspects of perceptual and cognitive development. Their analysis of developmental subsequences constituting the course of haptic and depth perception shows that particular motor abilities precede and promote each step along the way to proficiency. For the most part, Bushnell and Boudreau described effective bodily movements as infants' autonomous achievements. However, they speculated that "someone else" may assist the infant. For instance, moving infants' fingers across a rough surface may provide an opportunity to detect texture.

Other suggestive findings come from linguistic anthropology and ethnomethodology. This work demonstrates that in a social setting people make evident and gradually bridge differences in perceiving and doing (C. Goodwin, 1994; Kendon, 1990; Mehan & Wood, 1975; Moerman, 1988; Schegloff, 1972). Furthermore, that caregiver–experts implicitly hold this view can be detected as they carefully, patiently, and persistently educate child–novices to notice what is happening (Zukow, 1989; Zukow-Goldring, 1997; Zukow-Goldring & Ferko, 1994). Caregivers make the prospects and possibilities of daily life prominent for their children, reducing ambiguity with the "tools at hand." In fact, in vignettes asking caregivers to assist particularly ineffective baby-sitters, adult European American caregivers often instruct a hypothetical baby-sitter to say-and-do so that communicative breakdowns can be overcome (Zukow, 1991a). In the same vein, siblings in Mexico show and tell ("You don't know how."/"Tu no sabes." or "*I'll* do it!"/"¡*Yo* lo hago!") infants what they do not know how to do (Zukow, 1989).

Caregivers have no lesson plan, no map for getting through the day. The meaning of events emerges ad hoc without a moment's notice (Garfinkel, 1967; M. H. Goodwin & Goodwin, 1986; Macbeth, 1994; Moerman, 1988) as caregivers find what to say and do "on demand." In the empirical section that follows, I explore how caregivers make mundane events meaningful to their infants. Caregivers educate infants' attention to notice their own bodys' effectivities and the environment's affordances for action. They afford their infants opportunities for practice so that their perceptual systems may differentiate in culturally preferred ways. Caregivers make action audio-visible by gathering the infants' attention to regularities (amodal invariant relations) in gesture and speech. As infants see and hear events as they emerge and unfold, caregivers unwittingly facilitate the emergence of the lexicon.

EDUCATING ATTENTION

Empirical Background

Early Attunements

Turning now from theory to practice, this section makes explicit some social and perceptual practices that may contribute to the emergence of the lexicon. Infants do not know "what everyone already knows," but they do not enter the world empty-handed. Infants arrive with a variety of preattunements for perceiving and acting. From their earliest days, newborns can detect amodal invariants (Bahrick & Pickens, 1994; Spelke, 1979, 1981); select hand-sized and mouth-sized graspables and suckables (El'konin, 1971; Kaye, 1982); avoid aversive, intense stimulation (Brazelton, 1973); and more. However, with a relatively simple set of preattunements, can infants educate their own attention to notice what the world affords for action and interaction without assistance? My answer is, probably not. First, to see and hear a message, infants must be monitoring their caregivers. Second, to pick up a relation between words and world, infants must perceive that these two different kinds of things share an "identity." The differentiation of early attunements may be the source of these crucial abilities.

Infants learn lexical items while participating in daily life. No theory suggests otherwise. Some suggest that life for the infant is much like a cafeteria with a full range of nutritious food; the infant actively explores, tests, and arrives at a "best" diet (Piaget, 1962). Perhaps, instead, life is more of a catered affair with live-in nutritionists continuously modulating the a la carte menu. Caregivers may adjust the range of perceiving–acting cycles available as infants display a growing proficiency as they enact new effectivities, noticing new affordances for action, and extending their cycles of attention. Support for this view comes from research documenting shifts from other-regulation of early attunements to more refined and differentiated abilities that gradually become self-regulated in sleep–wake cycles and in arousal–affect regulation.

Kaye (1982) and others have observed infants nursing from birth through the second month of life. During this period mothers encourage their young infants to remain awake for longer and longer intervals. After bursts of infant sucking, mothers jiggle their infants, promoting nursing cycles of increasing duration. Whether the mother assists with the harvest in a rural village in Mexico a few days after the birth of her child or teaches child development in a small upstate New York college town, pressures to regulate the sleep–wake cycles of infants exist for very pragmatic reasons across cultures. Sometime in the second month infants are alert beyond the nursing time, which demonstrates an ability to regulate this cycle autonomously.

At about this time, caregivers regulate the wake cycle, modulating and sustaining the infant's arousal or affect for longer and longer periods (Field & Fogel, 1982; Stern, 1977; Tronick, 1982). Too much stimulation results in an infant who cries or avoids interaction; too little in boredom or sleep. An enigma for infancy researchers has been how to relate these massively occurring experiences to later development. I suggest that these sequences not be interpreted narrowly as affect or arousal but in terms of their functional significance for later communication. That is, in these cycles of affect–arousal caregivers educate attention by gathering or drawing attention to themselves. By the end of the first year of life infants modulate their own attention to caregivers and carefully begin to monitor them and the fascinating things that they say and do (Zukow, 1991b).

Detecting Amodal Invariant Relations

Experimental studies in the laboratory suggest the perceptual means that caregivers may use to arouse and gather their infants' attention. Eleanor Gibson (1993, this volume), her intellectual descendants (Bahrick & Pickens, 1994; Spelke, 1979; Walker, 1982), and others (Lewkowicz, 1994) have documented shifts from infants' early attunements to later abilities that display optimization and economy in the selection and detection of amodal invariant relations. From 3 months on, these researchers have found that infants can detect amodal invariant relations uniting the auditory and visual flow that infants perceive in dynamic events. Some of the earliest studies investigated detection of temporal synchrony and tempo of action common to the impact of an object on a surface, such as a toy donkey hitting the top of a table (Spelke, 1979, 1981). Infants detect other redundancies across vision and audition, including rhythm, object substance and composition (Bahrick, 1983, 1994), faces and vowel sounds (Kuhl & Meltzoff, 1982), affective expression (Walker, 1982; Walker-Andrews, 1986), and changing distance (Walker-Andrews & Lennon, 1985). In all these investigations, the infant detects amodal invariant relations in events differentiating persistence (the something that something is happening to) and change (the something that is happening), such as, the auditory and visual regularities specifying the moving toy donkey hitting the fixed table top. Opportunities to practice detecting amodal invariants during early infant–caregiver interaction may promote educating the infant's attention not just to persistence and change in observed events but in noticing that the caregiver and infant may share perceiving similar regularities.

Stern (1993) elaborated how caregivers establish perceptually that the self is like another, what Trevarthen (1979) called *primary intersubjectivity*. Stern focused on how people evoke, share, and mutually regulate feelings. Accordingly, people directly observe the feelings of others. They detect invariant relations or regularities common to the feelings displayed by the other and co-occurring feeling qualities within the self. For instance, when someone smiles at an infant, the infant detects an amodal invariant relation between the smile she or he sees and the infant's own embodied action and internal affective expression. These patterns of affect "vitality" or accelerating–decelerating intensity may be simultaneous or adjacent in time. If the caregiver smiles back at an infant, the matching of the temporal contours of the caregiver's affect is "audio-visible" in the rising–falling intonation of the voice and in the facial contours as the caregiver's "yEAh" mimes the arc of the baby's smile. The mutual detecting of the form, intensity, and timing of affect in the expressive displays of different people constitutes a temporary sharing of feelings. That is, the detecting of amodal invariant relations specifies the similarity of two separate and different beings who are members of the same natural kind. Detecting shared affect may be a gateway to perceiving what one person wants another to notice.

When caregivers animate toys, such as jumping a toy dog across the distance between infants and themselves, the accelerating intensity in both sight and sound usually results in matching waves of positive affect (Stern, 1985). Extrapolating from Eleanor Gibson's view (1969) that perceptual learning proceeds in the order of increasing specificity or differentiation, perhaps caregivers and infants eventually detect "packages" of amodal invariants embedded or nested within one another. For instance, the accelerating affect of infant and caregiver may be the behavioral topology that testifies to joint perceiving as each notices that the other notices the amodal invariants that specify the jumping dog and the sharing of feelings. That is, detecting nested levels of repeating amodal invariants may momentarily link what caregiver and infant feel and may be pragmatically sufficient to show that both perceive the same thing for all practical purposes.

Yet another nested level would include detecting the routine relation among different kinds (word and world). The ubiquitous and continuous fluctuations in intensity during the most common activity may assist caregivers in gathering and directing attention so that infants pick up the relation between speech and ongoing events. Detecting amodal invariants that specify a higher order coalescing and dispersing of unities or self-organizing within, across, and between the nesting levels of events very well may be knowing, not schemas, innate ideals, or fixed patterns of neurons firing along some well-worn pathway.

Words do not relate arbitrarily to the world as children learn them. Children learn words as people routinely express themselves in similar contexts of use from day to day. The question then is how infants and others detect this relation. Researchers have demonstrated a relation between the emergence of the lexicon and joint or shared attention (Adamson, Bakeman, & Smith, 1988; Bruner, 1983; B. A. Goldfield, 1987; Tamis-LeMonda & Bornstein, 1989; Tomasello & Farrar, 1986) and the directing of attention (Zukow, 1989, 1990, 1991b) from about 9 to 21 months of age. In my work, during attention-directing interactions caregivers use gestures to mark the relation between the target of attention in messages and ongoing events. In this chapter, I argue that amodal invariants in gesture and speech foreground the routine relations between words and world as the stable patterns of daily life unfold and repeat.

Longitudinal Studies of Attention Gathering and Attention Directing

The work I report is based on data collected during monthly visits to the homes of six European American middle-class and six Latino low-income families from the time their infants were 6 months of age until they reached approximately 30 months (Zukow-Goldring, 1996; Zukow-Goldring & Ferko, 1994). The data are naturalistic videotapes, field notes of the caregiver interpreting the infant's speech and actions, and diary data. The collection of interactions I selected to investigate unequivocally display situations in which caregivers direct infants to notice one specific element, relation, or event over the myriad other possibilities available at any one time in any one place. The unit of interaction studied, attention-directing interactions, includes all instances of perceptual imperatives expressed by caregivers, such as *look, listen, and feel*, and their accompanying gestures, and the gestures alone.

Communication entails, in part, the ability to share what people know with others by getting others to monitor them and subsequently attend to their message. Because infants may not spontaneously monitor caregivers, they must do interactive work to make sure their infants do so. In the prelinguistic period from about 6 to 11 months, attention-directing interactions occurred nested within attention-gathering interactions, sequences in which caregivers modulated and sustained infants' attention–arousal.

Attention-Gathering Interactions

Familiar attention-gathering interactions occur so often that their importance may go unnoticed: banging and squeaking toys, looming in to the infant, and arousing him or her in repetitive sequences. In my data, this pattern appears repeatedly from 6 months through 10 or 11 as caregivers gather attention away from themselves, then to objects, back to themselves, and then to triadic interactions including infant, caregiver, and object (Zukow, 1991b).[12]

Attention-gathering interactions have common characteristics, described by Bahrick, Lewkowicz, Spelke, and Walker-Andrews in their research investigating the problem of intermodal perception. How do infants determine which patterns of stimulation belong together and originate from a single event and which are unrelated? Their work confirms that infants detect amodal invariant relations, such as tempo, rhythmicity, synchronous initiation, duration, and, I suggest, acceleration–deceleration of intensity. These amodal invariant relations co-occur across modalities during naturalistic events; that is, in sound, in action, in touch, in vision, in odor. For example, a caregiver shakes an open bottle of sweet smelling vitamins to gather her infant's attention before directing attention by showing the vitamins to her infant. When she says and does "*shakey* = *sha::key* = *SHA:::KEY!*,"[13] she coordinates in action, vision, odor, and sound the target of attention, cultivating perceptual pickup of amodal invariant relations through tempo, rhythmicity, synchronous initiation–termination, accelerating intensity, and so on. Similarly, when looming in to his infant with "*I'm gonna getcha* – *I'm Gonna Getcha* = *I'M GONNA GETCHA*," the caregiver gathers attention to her or himself as she or he steps up the face's increasing size, proximity, and detectable detail in synchrony with vocal volume.

Thus, we have a tangible way of seeing how infants detect invariance within a unitary whole and, I suggest, equivalence across dissimilars in action and speech, and, perhaps, particulars within a unitary whole.

Attention-Directing Gestures

In educating attention, I have called the first patterns of interaction *attention gathering* because attention must be drawn to caregivers before infants can direct attention to what the world affords for action, for survival.

---

[12]I speculate that future research will confirm that these caregiver–orchestrated interactions can account for infants' shift in attention about 5 to 6 months of age from a narrow focus within the dyad to a broader perspective including objects and events outside the dyad (Adamson & Bakeman, 1984; Snow, 1977; Trevarthen & Hubley, 1978; Zukow-Goldring & Ferko, 1994).

[13]Colons indicate syllable stretching (Zukow, 1982).

Once they have gathered attention, caregivers select, pick out, and make prominent detectable perceptual structure from the flow of events that links world and word for the infant to pick up. Caregivers direct attention with gestures that mark this relation. The relation of gesture to language learning has a long history. In the 4th century, St. Augustine (1961) ostensively remembered his own language learning. As others spoke around him, he described detecting the relation between the speaker turning toward something and saying its name. His description suggests bodily orientation and name pointing as means of connecting word and thing. Contrary to researchers who uncritically base their work on St. Augustine's remarks regarding ostension, a variety of gestures direct attention (Messer, 1978, 1981), not just pointing.

On the basis of an ethnography of attention directing (Zukow, 1989, 1990), the gestures vary on a continuum of other- to self-regulation of attention.[14] In *act-ons* caregivers put infants through the motions of some activity (caregivers pull infants up as they say *up*); in *shows* caregivers control the infants' line of sight with a translational movement in which they loom–magnify an object toward the infants (saying *ribbit* while looming a frog); in *demonstrations* infants who are monitoring their caregivers must detect or pick up in the perceptual flow the action to be repeated or completed (saying *hi* when catching gaze, smiling, and greeting), or infants may be invited to see–feel–say the texture of bristles in a broom while caregivers say *sticky*; finally in *points* infants must detect the intersection of a gesture's trajectory through space to the place where it intersects with some target of attention (caregivers pointing to and saying *over there*).

These gestures cultivate acting as well as perceiving. Caregivers assist infants to detect how both the infant's perceiving and acting relate to the routine expression of words. Caregivers embody messages by educating infants to perceive what the effectivities of their bodies can do and to detect affordances for action in the environment as they talk. During *act-ons* infants can perceive the shared effectivities–capabilities of their bodies and

---

[14]For source of terminology, see studies of caregiver–child problem solving (Wertsch, McNamee, McLane, & Budwig, 1980).

that of their caregivers as the caregivers put the infants through the motions of some activity or the infants shadow an activity as the caregivers move. (Our bodies complement action or do the same actions.) As caregivers *show*, infants can notice familiar effectivities of the caregivers' body and new affordances of the environment for perceiving–acting as the caregivers make perceptual structure prominent. (My body can do what your body can do.) When caregivers *demonstrate*, infants can monitor the caregivers enacting familiar effectivities of the body and affordances of the environment for perceiving–acting. In *supporting demonstrations*, caregivers provide a portion of the effectivity–affordance cycle (invitations to act). *Points* provide opportunities for following a trajectory through time–space to notice familiar effectivities of the body and affordances of the environment for perceiving–acting. As these infants develop, caregivers focus at first more on the effectivities of the infants' bodies and gradually on progressively more complex affordances of the environment.

Targets of Attention

Gestures are combined with various targets of attention expressed by caregivers throughout the prelinguistic and one-word periods (see Figure 3). The targets vary in semantic complexity. The first three degrees roughly parallel those of the three levels of semantic development described by Greenfield and Smith (1976; Zukow, Reilly, & Greenfield, 1982). The first degree includes occasions when caregivers might present nondynamic objects or animate beings in the child's line of sight, such as showing a toy or pointing to a person or animal while saying *Look at the duck/Grandpa*. Degree 2 consists of messages expressing an object or animate being undergoing some change in action (*Look, push them*) or in which a state or attribute is asserted about someone or something (*Look at the little doll*). For Degree 3 caregivers talk about more complex relations involving location (patch of dirt), instruments (eating utensils, crayons), part–whole relations (hair–head), or possession (my, your), such as saying *Look, put the bead in the pail*. Messages at Degree 4 express the relation between events (*Take your ball to your brother, so he can put it away*). These targets of attention embody structural and transformational invariants in the en-

a   Act-on

b   Show

c   Demonstration

d   Point

Figure 3

Attention-directing interactions: (a) Act-on, (b) show, (c) demonstration, (d) point.

vironment across space–time. That is, in messages caregivers express what persists and changes as events coalesce and disperse.

Infant's Expressive Level

The infants' levels of expressive development include Prelinguistic Level 1 in which infants do not attempt to get caregivers to fix or get things for them. At Prelinguistic Level 2, infants use caregivers instrumentally, constantly gesture for and catch gaze with caregivers to get objects or push objects into hands to be wound up, opened, and so on. At Lexical Level 1, the doing of the infant and the saying of the word are undifferentiated. That is, infants express "indicative objects" by pointing at and saying *nana* (banana), "volitionals" by reaching and whining while saying *eta* (galleta/cookie), or "performatives" by saying *down* while falling or throwing down. At Lexical Level 2, infants express agent–action–object–recipient by expressing this more complex relation partly through action and partly in speech. The infant may give a toy to daddy while saying *dada*. Often some temporal discontinuity separates action and speech. At Lexical Level 3, infants express location, possession, instrument, part–whole, and repetition of events, such as saying *bed* when getting up on one. (The lexical categories are based on Greenfield & Smith, 1976, and Zukow et al., 1982.) Infants express what they notice of their own effectivities and affordances of the environment nested in perceiving–acting cycles. At first the infant expresses what is attended to as an inseparable whole–unity. Next, infants express effectivities or actions of the body, who or what affords action, and who acts. Finally, the effectivities and affordances the infant expresses expand in space–time, such as tools as perceptual extensions of the self (Smitsman, this volume), possessions and parts–whole as relations between persons or person–object or parts of either to the whole through time–space, location as the relation between object or person and some surface(s) or medium over space–time, repetitions as successive perceivings of perceiving–acting cycles.

Figure 4 illustrates what caregivers express. Their messages increase in semantic complexity as their infants' expressive level gradually becomes more advanced. What caregivers communicate foreshadows what infants express several months later. Across levels of the infants' expressive development a significant shift occurs in the targets of attention that caregivers select for infants to detect from within a developing interactional context. What is done changes as well. The effectivities and affordances of infant, caregiver, and interactional context change over space–time. Infants' "level of expressive development" is depicted on the abscissa. As shown, the caregivers direct their infants to notice particular targets of attention well in

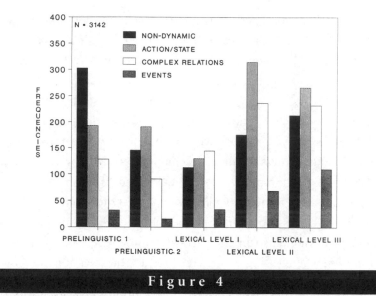

Figure 4

European American infants: The semantic complexity of caregiver messages foreshadows the infants' subsequent expressive level and increases as infants become more advanced.

advance of the infants' expressing those messages themselves. At first, caregivers make simple targets prominent almost exclusively (nondynamic objects–animate beings) and shift to more complicated (change–state, complex relations, relations between events) as the infant develops. As the figure illustrates, caregiver messages provide a range of affordances within each level of expressive development, but what new effectivities of the infant prompt caregivers to proffer more complex affordances for action and speech in their messages? If caregivers treat infants' subsequent actions or speech as adequate, the infants' level of message understanding provides a basis for the caregivers' shift to messages expressing more complex affordances for action and speech (Raver & Leadbeater, 1993; Zukow, 1991b).[15]

---

[15]Tomasello and his colleagues (Tomasello & Farrar, 1986; Tomasello & Todd, 1983) have argued that caregivers who control attention (by putting objects in the infant's line of sight as in SHOWing) rather than "follow in" to the infant's attention have a style that is correlated with infants with smaller vocabularies. My work suggests strongly that Tomasello's interpretation is an artifact of doing cross-sectional studies (see Pine & Lieven, 1991, for the problematic nature of taking age as a measure of developmental level). My longitudinal data confirm that caregivers of less advanced infants (not necessarily younger infants) engage in more *shows* and *act-ons*, shifting as the infant develops to more and more *demonstrating* and *pointing*.

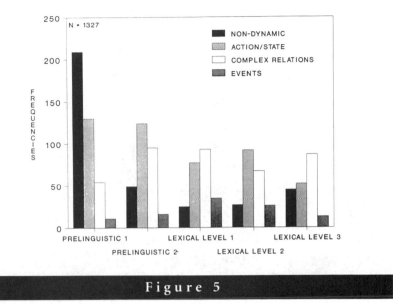

Figure 5

Latina infant: The semantic complexity of caregiver messages foreshadows the infant's subsequent expressive level and increases as the infant becomes more advanced.

These findings hold across race, culture, socioeconomic status, language community, and educational level of the caregiver, as Figure 5 confirms on a small portion of the Latino longitudinal data (Zukow, 1989, 1990; Zukow-Goldring, 1996; Zukow-Goldring & Ferko, 1994). The most robust relation in this work, however, is between gesture and target of attention.

Attention-Directing Interactions Embedded in Attention-Gathering Interactions

Amodal invariants detectable in gesture and speech may make the routine relation between word and world perceivable by providing an equivalence across dissimilar kinds. Attention-directing interactions embedded in attention-gathering interactions occur far more during the prelinguistic period. During this period caregiver messages are usually about nondynamic objects–animate beings and actions (see Figure 6). Usually *shows* occur with nondynamic objects or animate beings displaying structural invariants, whereas *demonstrations* and *act-ons* displaying transformational in-

227

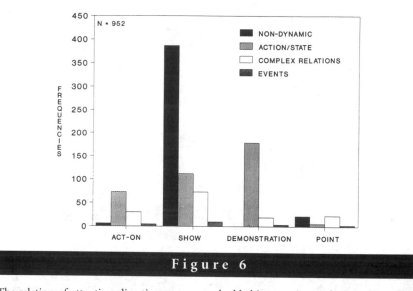

Figure 6

The relation of attention-directing gestures embedded in attention-gathering interactions to target of attention during the prelinguistic period: Shows occur most frequently with nondynamic objects or animate beings as targets of attention; act-ons and demonstrations co-occur with action or state.

variants co-occur with action. *Shows* may assist the infant in relating structural invariants to the names of "whole" objects–animate beings, whereas the transformational invariants displayed in *demonstrations* and *act-ons* may facilitate relating words to *affordances for action*. When attention-directing interactions are embedded in attention-gathering interactions, amodal invariants may make the relation between word and world "there to be seen," making prominent the regularities that specify the relation between unlike kinds of things.

Vignettes

Note that invariants across modalities relating gesture and speech are present in each of the following examples: tempo, rhythm, timing, and intensity. A "thicker" description or analysis of caregivers providing intermodal invariant relations in the perceptual flow to infants is seen in the following examples. In these segments of interaction, caregivers afford their children opportunities for detecting the routine relation between world and word including actions (*up*, *hi*), state (*sticky*), whole–part relations (*head–hair*), and a name (*ribbit*).

Example 1: act-on, action of pulling up and saying, "up." In Frame 1 of Figure 7, Lisa grasps the hands of Karen, aged 11 months, as she lies face-up on her mother's extended legs. Lisa smiles as she begins to pull Karen's arms and hands. In this *act-on*, as mother and infant catch gaze in Frame 2, Lisa's guttural, stretched "u:::" accompanies an effortful stretch of pulling on Karen's dead weight (Frames 2–4). The emphatic "pʰ::" co-occurs with rotating the nearly upright and quite delighted Karen forward to a seated position (Frames 4–5). Karen can see "upness" by picking up the angular shearing or deleting of the flow of background texture at the side of her head and the increasing of textural detail flowing toward her as her mother pulls her forward. Being put through the motions of *up* provides Karen with practice that may assist her in differentiating which effectivities of the body embody *up*. The amodal invariant that nests the doing and saying of *up* may let Karen see, hear, and embody whatever *up* may be.

Example 2: demonstration, action of greeting and saying, "hi!" A few seconds later in the midst of doing the "same" action, Lisa varies her placing of what she says and does in time–space (Figure 8) and clearly differentiates the two bouts from one another. She initiates pulling Karen up in Frame 1, takes an inbreathe in Frame 2 as she continues pulling. When Karen is nearly upright and the two start smiling face-to-face, Lisa begins with "H" in Frame 3. In Frames 4–6, as Lisa stretches the "i::::" and concomitantly widens her smile, she magnifies her face in Karen's line of sight by bringing their faces more rapidly together. Note that whereas Lisa's legs remained flat on the floor in Example 1, in this interaction her knees come up bringing Karen's face much closer to her mother's. In this ostensibly similar action, the timing, tempo, rhythm, and intensity of the amodal invariant common to gesture and speech clearly mark this saying-and-doing of *Hi* as quite distinct from that of *Up*.

Example 3: "demonstration, state of stickiness and saying, "sticky." Zeke, aged 12 months, and his mother are playing in the backyard. Zeke is

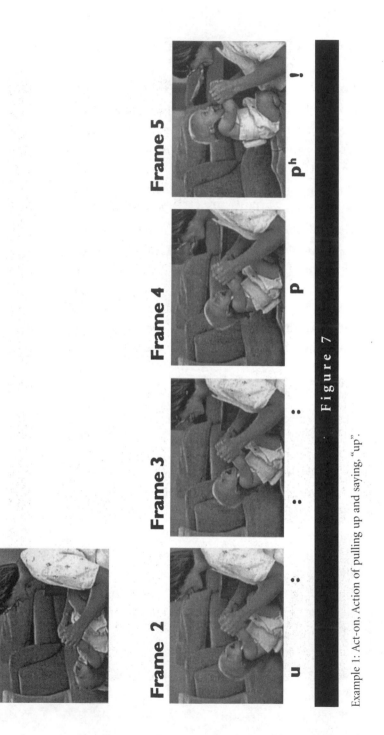

Figure 7

Example 1: Act-on, Action of pulling up and saying, "up".

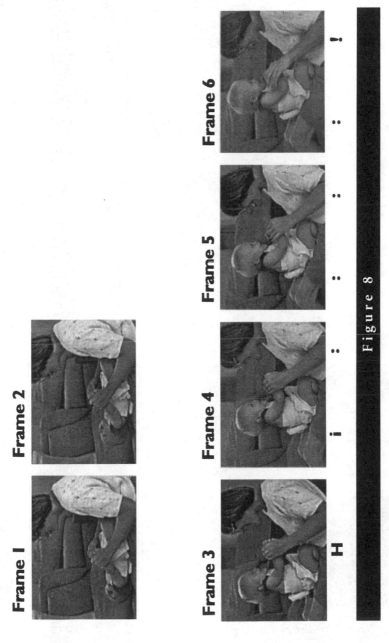

Figure 8

Example 2: Demonstration, Action of greeting and saying, "Hi!"

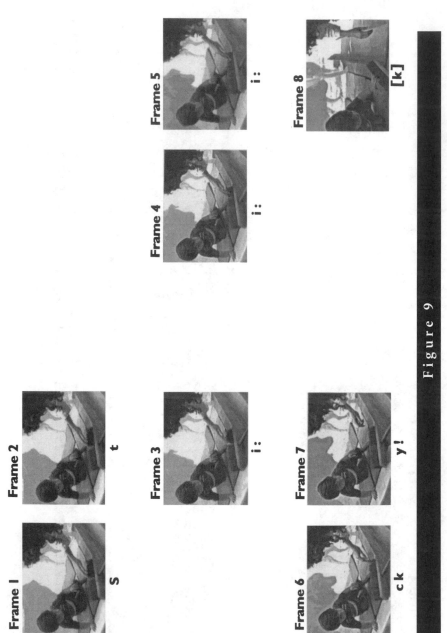

Figure 9

Example 3: Demonstration, State of stickiness and saying, "Sticky."

crouching at the top of a few steps, while Ann is standing at the bottom. Ann holds a broom directly in Zeke's line of sight and says, *"Wanna play with the broom, Zeke?"* Ann sets the broom down in front of Zeke with the bristles of the broom positioned upward and within his reach. As Ann moves her fingertips across the bristles, she says, *"Sti::cky!"* describing the prickly sensation of the bristles on her fingertips (Figure 9). Zeke carefully watches his mother, reaches out toward the broom, and strokes the bristles with his fingertips while saying, "[k]."

In this example, Ann invites her son to feel the sticky, prickly surface of the upturned broom as she demonstrates *sticky*. First, Ann makes a quick, irregular, and bouncing movement of translation as her hand travels over the bristles. She specifies the trajectory of her gesture by occluding background surface texture as her fingertips first cover the bristles and then reciprocally uncover them on the trailing edge. The repetitive, wave-like pattern that specifies the uneven surface below emerges from the shallow, rapid, bumpy path made by her fingers, superimposed on the complementary swiftly changing background flow (Zukow-Goldring & Ferko, 1994). The saying of "st" accompanies Ann's fingers as they rather smoothly traverse some of the bristles in Frames 1 and 2. Her voice quality changes to a more raspy, vibrating "i:::" in synchrony with her fingers repetitively touching and interrupting the flow of her hand across the broom bristles (Frames 3–5). With a slight pause on the "ck" as her hand ends its horizontal movement (Frame 6), Ann lifts away as she says, "y:" in Frame 7. Then, in Frame 8 Zeke touches the bristles, saying "[k]". The delicate timing of this caregiver coordinating the audio–visibility of saying-and-doing "stickiness" gives Zeke an opportunity to detect amodal invariants specifying a particular routine relation between word and world.

Example 4: act-on, part–whole relation of hair–head and saying, "cabeza"/"head" and "pelo"/"hair" In this segment of interaction, the mother, Ana, and her children, Alicia and Jorge, play in the living room. Ana reaches towards Alicia's head with her index finger extended as she says, "tu"/"your" (Frame 1 of Figure 10). Tapping Alicia's head, she continues with "cabeza"/"head". At the same time Jorge places and leaves his hand on his sister's head during the ensuing sequence. Ana extends the

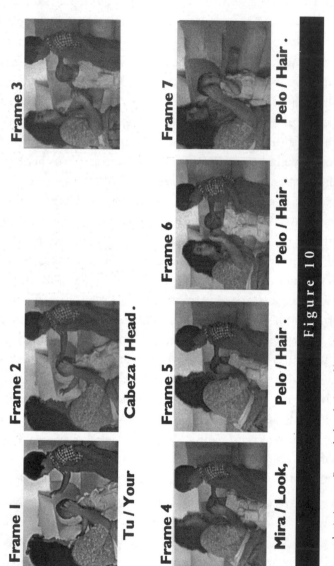

Example 4: Act-on, Part–whole relation of hair–head and saying, "Cabeza"/"Head" and "Pelo"/"Hair."

hand she has retracted toward her daughter again in Frame 3. As she grasps some of Alicia's wispy hair she says, "mira"/"look" in Frame 4. Ana completes her utterance and gesture by saying, "pelo"/"hair" as she pulls Alicia's hair at the back of her head in Frame 5. In Frames 6 and 7 Ana repeats "pelo"/"hair" while pulling next on the left side of Alicia's head and then on the right.

In this sequence of *act-ons*, the mother differentiates head (whole) and hair (part) both in the saying and the doing. The reverberating of firm taps on her head while Ana says, "cabeza" surely feels very different to Alicia than the gentle tugging of her hair accompanied by her mother saying, "pelo." The tingling of her scalp in three different locations most likely conveys more about hair than head.

This head tapping and hair pulling example has been selected to dispel some misunderstandings of Quine (1960) regarding the hypothesized ambiguity of reference that may occur when pointing (Zukow, 1990). Clearly the reverberations of tapping the skull as opposed to pulling hair leaves little room to claim that differentiation from whole and part cannot be accomplished through gesture. Caregivers do this constantly with body parts and objects. For instance, caregivers display a cup in its entirety by rotating it around a vertical axis one way and then the other, while saying, "cu::" and then "u::p". In contrast, when they display handles, rims, and contents caregivers usually run a finger over the former and plunge it in the latter. When communication does break down as a caregiver points, and it does, caregivers almost invariably revise subsequent messages by providing more perceptual structure to achieve understanding (Zukow-Goldring, 1997).

Example 5: show, nondynamic object and saying, "frog," then "ribbit" In this tape segment 17-month-old Karen learns an unconventional name to her mother's consternation. Karen bends over to pick up a hand puppet and gives it to her mother, Lisa. In Figure 11, her mother says, ".h[16] *hi, frog!*" as Karen approaches slowly. On the inbreathe (.h) Lisa finishes changing the tadpole into a frog (Frame 1). As she says, "hi," the white

---

[16]The transcription convention of .h indicates an inbreathe (Zukow, 1982).

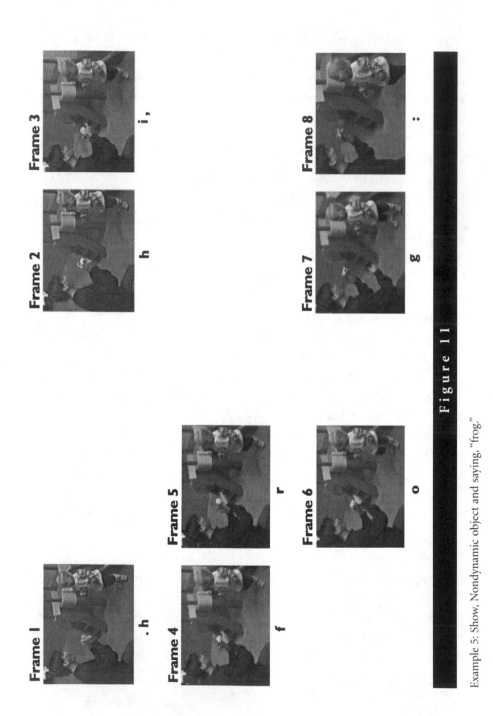

Figure 11

Example 5: Show, Nondynamic object and saying, "frog."

frog's face is directed to her (Frames 2–3). In Frame 4 the frog faces a bit beyond Lisa's right arm as her lips form "f." On the "r" in Frame 5 Lisa continues rotating the frog toward Karen. As Lisa says, "o" in Frame 6 the frog is turned facing away from both of them. In Frame 7 the frog faces Karen as Lisa says, "g." As she stretches the sound, Lisa brings the frog up into a more closely shared line of sight (Frame 8).

In Figure 12, Lisa quickly rotates forward on her knees as she says, "a:::," jumping the frog to within 8 inches of her daughter's face (Frame 9). Lisa says, "r:i::b" as the looming toy lands most closely to Karen's face (Frames 10–12). As she says, "bi," she sweeps through Karen's line of sight (Frame 13) and finishes retracting swiftly on the "t" (Frame 14). As the child slowly steps back, the frog gives chase leaping and "ribbiting" again. Karen pauses and points to the frog saying, "ribbit!" in Frames 15–16. Her mother says rather quizzically, "It's a frog." This exception may not prove a rule but may confirm a natural law.

In this sequence, the caregiver, Lisa, pairs the "true" name, *frog*, with the rotating of the toy's face from herself to Karen during Frames 1–6. In these frames she monitors the frog, not her daughter. The delayed and asynchronous showing of the toy co-occurs as Lisa says, "g:" and looks over the frog to Karen. Whereas the caregiver's eye gaze presumably could guide the infant to connect the toy and the word as some argue from laboratory experiments (Baldwin, 1991), the temporal discontinuity with showing appears disruptive. The speech does not match the action in tempo, rhythm, or initiation. In contrast, during the second, more synchronous presentation of the toy the caregiver embeds the attention directing, showing of the frog and saying, "ribbit," within attention gathering. Lisa repeatedly looms the toy at Karen, upping the affective and perceptual ante. The frog's face magnifies and sweeps through Karen's line of sight each time before it retreats quickly. Lisa's gesture and affect match the initiation, tempo, rhythm, and accelerating intensity of her saying of "r:i::bbit." This sequence illustrates how the detecting of amodal invariants in affect–arousal, gesture, and speech may make picking out the relation between dissimilar kinds, the routine relation of word and world, very vivid for the child. Perhaps this observation also helps to resolve the

Figure 12

Example 5: Show, Nondynamic object and saying, "ribbit."

enigma regarding why children across cultures tend to use onomatopoeia (the sound the animal makes) to express animal names and pick up many idiosyncratic early words (Bowerman, 1976).

This segment illustrates the speculation that natural laws manifested through perceptual structure (amodal invariant relations of tempo, rhythmicity, intensity, and timing) detected across modalities may underlie the emergence of the early lexicon. Researchers who discount the importance of gesture for word learning (Baldwin, 1991, 1993; Tomasello & Barton, 1994) base their arguments on theories that assume more elaborated innate mechanisms or assume that cognitive mechanisms mediate learning, rather than exploring the power of amodal invariant relations detected in naturalistic settings where word learning takes place. Furthermore, their experiments investigated word learning in toddlers 18 and 24 months of age who are far beyond the early levels of lexical development and may use other methods for adding to their vocabularies.

The picking out by the caregiver and the *picking up* by the infant of the same set of amodal invariant relations displayed simultaneously in very different events, one in speech and one in action, may be the processes that support the emergence of the lexicon. Finding this common ground may make perceivable that unlike things, such as word and world, can share a higher order identity. Words do not stand for things but may stand in for them, eventually directing attention so that participants can begin to negotiate a practical consensus. This work has implications for any situation in which expert and novice are communicating about some new abilities, in which something new is learned, especially with tools or implements of any kind at home, at school (Zukow-Goldring, Romo, & Duncan, 1994), or on the job.

CONCLUSIONS

A keystone of the social ecological realist approach holds that the emergence of cultural practices, including the emergence of the lexicon, depends on the dynamic structure of the social–interactive environment in which the child develops rather than on concepts or genetic plans. Within this interactive matrix individuals keep each other in touch with perceptual structure, continuously educating each other's attention to ongoing events, so that a practical consensus can be achieved. This nexus or mutuality is what is developing.

Other ecological theories do not address how knowing emerges continuously as individuals guide each other's perceiving of prospects for action. From the social ecological realist perspective, people afford each other new possibilities for selecting and detecting the structure in light, sound, odor, pressure, and so on that specifies the configuration and organization of cultural activities. Thus, caregivers provide infants with practice that promotes perceiving, acting, and knowing in culturally appropriate ways. While engaging in the most mundane daily activities, caregivers keep a step or two ahead of infants as they invite them gradually to enhance bodily effectivities or capabilities and to notice what the world affords for action.

My work focuses on what caregivers do to propagate infants' perceptual differentiation, specifically the "educating of attention" that contributes significantly to the emergence of the lexicon. I explore whether detecting amodal invariant relations constitutes perceiving identity at a general level, assisting infants in noticing the routine relation between world and word. The findings from this research document that caregivers make amodal invariant relations (timing, tempo, intensity, and rhythmicity) prominent as they gather and direct attention to animate beings, objects, and actions. Infants pick up these regularities in their caregivers' speech and action.

This series of studies conducted among Latino and European American caregivers and their infants in the United States and others carried out in Central Mexico documents how the perceptual structure provided by caregivers narrows the possible interpretations of situated speech and relates significantly to the emergence of the lexicon. These results suggest that detecting amodal invariants may underlie the emergence of the lexicon by picking out the regularities that specify the relation between unlike kinds of things: world and word. Other studies of communicative breakdowns at home and in Latino classrooms confirm the hypothesis that providing additional perceptual structure through gesture resolves message ambiguity and promotes shared meaning, whereas linguistic information alone is not as effective (Zukow et al., 1994; Zukow-Goldring, 1997).

The methods stemming from social ecological realism stress naturalistic, ecologically valid, longitudinal data collection methods. An ethnography can clear away cobwebs from received ideas, so that scholars can see what people actually do. The ethnography of attention directing that informed this research revealed that ostension has many forms, not just pointing as many since St. Augustine have assumed. The misunderstanding of Quine (1960) by child language researchers was clarified as well. He was not referring to first language learning at all, but to a translation or mapping problem from one language or meaning system to another. The confusion deriving from these misreadings resulted in scholars concluding that gestures inherently promote an ambiguity of reference. This purported ambiguity melts away when anyone observes the "lived orderliness" (Garfinkel, 1967) of what caregivers do in "normal environments" (Moerman, 1988), such as directing attention to a whole doll or to its parts. Furthermore, direct perception shows how detecting amodal invariant relations in the structure of the perceptual array assists communication and achieving a practical understanding. Finally, results from longitudinal studies point out the erroneous interpretations that can arise when age in cross-sectional studies is taken to be a measure of developmental level.

The power of social ecological realism combining direct perception, eco–cultural, and ethnomethodological approaches remains largely unexplored. These studies are a beginning and an impetus to go beyond these findings. Examining how cycles of perceiving and acting with the infant reciprocally educates the caregiver's attention remains implicit in my work and will inform future analyses. This approach does not yet provide the grounds for acting prospectively or retrospectively over time–space (but see, Rader, this volume). In the larger view, however, detecting amodal invariance from one situation to the next over the course of the lifetime may constitute continuously expanding knowing.

REFERENCES

Adamson, L., & Bakeman, R. (1984). Mothers' communicative acts: Changes during infancy. *Infant Behavior and Development, 7,* 467–478.

Adamson, L., Bakeman, R., & Smith, C. B. (1988). Gestures, words, and early object sharing. In V. Volterra & C. Erting (Eds.), *From gesture to language in hearing and deaf children* (pp. 31–41). New York: Springer-Verlag.

Bahrick, L. E. (1983). Infants' perception of substance and temporal synchrony in multimodal events. *Infant Behavior and Development, 6,* 429–451.

Bahrick, L. E. (1994). The development of infants' sensitivity to arbitrary intermodal relations. *Ecological Psychology, 6,* 111–123.

Bahrick, L. E., & Pickens, J. N. (1994). Amodal relations: The basis for intermodal perception and learning in infancy. In D. J. Lewkowicz & R. Lickliter (Eds.), *The development of intersensory perception: Comparative perspectives* (pp. 205–233). Hillsdale, NJ: Erlbaum.

Baldwin, D. A. (1991). Infants' contribution to the achievement of joint reference. *Child Development, 62,* 875–890.

Baldwin, D. A. (1993). Early referential understanding: Infants' ability to recognize referential acts for what they are. *Development Psychology 29,* 832–843.

Bowerman, M. (1976). Semantic factors in the acquisition of rules for word use and sentence construction. In D. M. Moorehead & A. E. Moorehead (Eds.), *Normal and deficient child language* (pp. 99–179). Baltimore: University Park Press.

Brazelton, T. B. (1973). *Neonatal behavioral assessment scales.* London: Spastics International Medical Publications.

Bronfenbrenner, U. (1979). *The ecology of human development: Experiments by nature and design.* Cambridge, MA: Harvard University Press.

Bruner, J. (1983). *Children's talk: Learning to use language.* New York: Norton.

Bushnell, E. W., & Boudreau, J. P. (1993). Motor development and the mind: The potential role of motor abilities as a determinant of aspects of perceptual development. *Child Development, 64,* 1005–1021.

Carey, S., & Gelman, R. (Eds.). (1991). *The epigenesis of the mind: Essays on biology and cognition.* Hillsdale, NJ: Erlbaum.

Cole, M. (1989). Cultural psychology: A once and future discipline? In J. J. Berman (Ed.), *Cross-cultural psychology: Current theory and research: Nebraska Symposium on Motivation* (Vol. 37, pp. 279–335). Lincoln: University of Nebraska Press.

Cole, M., Hood, L., & McDermott, R. P. (1978). Concepts of ecological validity: Their differing implications for comparative cognitive research. *The Quarterly Newsletter of the Laboratory of Comparative Human Cognition, 2,* 34–37.

Costall, A. (1989). A closer look at "direct perception." In A. Gellatly, D. Rogers, & J. A. Sloboda (Eds.), *Cognition and social worlds* (pp. 10–21). Oxford, England: Clarendon Press.

Costall, A. (1995). Socializing affordances. *Theory and Psychology, 5,* 1–27.

Dent, C. (1990). An ecological approach to language development: An alternative functionalism. [Special issue]. *Developmental Psychobiology, 23,* 679–704.

Eckerman, C. O. (1993). Toddlers' achievement of coordinated action with conspecifics: A dynamic systems perspective. In L. B. Lamb & E. Thelen (Eds.), *A dynamic systems approach to development* (pp. 333–357). Cambridge, MA: MIT Press.

El'konin, D. (1971). Symbolics and its function in the play of children. In R.E. Herron & B. Sutton-Smith (Eds.), *Child's play* (pp. 221–230). New York: Wiley.

Field, T., & Fogel, A. (Eds.). (1982). *Emotion and early interaction.* Hillsdale, NJ: Erlbaum.

Garfinkel, H. (1967). *Studies in ethnomethodology.* Englewood Cliffs, NJ: Prentice-Hall.

Gaskins, S. (1990). *Exploratory play and development in Maya infants.* Unpublished doctoral dissertation, University of Chicago.

Gibson, E. J. (1969). *Principles of perceptual learning and development.* New York: Appleton-Century-Crofts.

Gibson, E. J. (1994). Has psychology a future? *Psychological Science, 5,* 69–76.

Gibson, E. J., & Rader, N. (1979). Attention: The perceiver as performer. In G. A. Hale & M. Lewis (Eds.), *Attention and cognitive development* (pp. 1–21). New York: Plenum Press.

Gibson, J. J. (1950). *The perception of the visual world.* Boston: Houghton Mifflin.

Gibson, J. J. (1966). *The senses considered as perceptual systems.* Boston: Houghton Mifflin.

Gibson, J. J. (1979). *The ecological approach to visual perception.* Boston: Houghton Mifflin.

Gibson, J. J. (1982). Affordances and behavior. In E. S. Reed & R. K. Jones (Eds.), *Reasons for realism: Selected papers of J. J. Gibson* (pp. 410–411). Hillsdale, NJ: Erlbaum.

Ginsburg, G. P., & Harrington, M. E. (1993, August). Conceptual concerns about basic constructs: Context, action, affordance, intention, and emotion. In J. Good

& S. Valenti (Chairs), *Intersubjectivity*. Symposium conducted at the Conference on Event Perception and Action, Vancouver, British Columbia, Canada.

Goldfield, B. A. (1987). The contributions of child and caregiver to referential and expressive language. *Applied Psycholinguistics, 8*, 267–280.

Goldfield, E. C. (1983). The ecological approach to perceiving as a foundation for understanding the development of knowing in infancy. *Developmental Review, 3*, 371–404.

Good, J. J., & Still, A. (1989). Ecological psychology as a theory of social cognition. In A. Gellatly, D. Rogers, & J. A. Sloboda (Eds.), *Cognition and social worlds* (pp. 216–229). Oxford, England: Clarendon Press.

Goodwin, C. (1994). Professional vision. *American Anthropologist, 96*, 606–633.

Goodwin, C. (1995). Seeing in depth. *Social Studies of Science, 25*, 237–274.

Goodwin, C. (in press). Transparent vision. In E. Ochs, E. A. Schegloff, & S. Thompson (Eds.), *Interaction and grammar*. Cambridge, MA: Cambridge University Press.

Goodwin, M. H., & Goodwin, C. (1986). Gesture and coparticipation in the activity of searching for a word. *Semiotica, 62*, 51–75.

Gottlieb, G. (1991a). Epigenetic systems view of human development. *Developmental Psychology, 27*, 33–34.

Gottlieb, G. (1991b). Experiential canalization of behavioral development: Theory. *Developmental Psychology, 27*, 4–12.

Greenfield, P. M., & Smith, J. S. (1976). *The structure of communication in early language development*. New York: Academic Press.

Heft, H. (1989). Affordances and the body: An intentional analysis of Gibson's ecological approach to visual perception. *Journal for the Theory of Social Behavior, 19*, 1–30.

Ingold, T. (1991a). Becoming persons: Consciousness and sociality in human evolution. *Cultural Dynamics, 4*, 355–378.

Ingold, T. (1991b). Evolutionary models in the social sciences: Introduction. *Cultural Dynamics, 4*, 239–250.

Itard, J. M. G. (1982). *The wild boy of Aveyron* (G. Humphrey & M. Humphrey, Trans.). New York: Appleton-Century-Crofts. (Original work published 1801)

Johnston, T. D., & Gottlieb, G. (1990). Neophenogenesis: A developmental theory of phenotypic evolution. *Journal of Theoretical Biology, 147*, 471–495.

Kaye, K. (1982). *The mental and social life of babies: How parents create persons*. Chicago: University of Chicago Press.

Kendon, A. (1990). *Conducting interaction: Patterns of behavior in focused encounters*. London: Cambridge University Press.

Kubovy, M., & Pomerantz, J. R. (Eds.). (1981). *Perceptual organization*. Hillsdale, NJ: Erlbaum.

Kuhl, P. K., & Meltzoff, A. N. (1982). The bimodal perception of speech in infancy. *Science, 218*, 1138–1141.

Lave, J., & Wenger, E. (1991). *Situated learning: Legitimate peripheral participation*. New York: Cambridge University Press.

Lee, D. N. (1980). Visuomotor coordination in space–time. In G. E. Stelmach & J. Requin (Eds.), *Tutorials in motor behavior* (pp. 281–295). Amsterdam, The Netherlands: North-Holland.

Lewkowicz, D. J. (1994). Intersensory interactions in human development. In D. J. Lewkowicz & R. Lickliter (Eds.), *The development of intersensory perception: Comparative perspectives* (pp. 165–203). Hillsdale, NJ: Erlbaum.

Locke, J. (1938). *Some thoughts concerning education*. London: Churchill. (Original work published 1699)

Lombardo, T. J. (1987). *The reciprocity of perceiver and environment: The evolution of James J. Gibson's ecological psychology*. Hillsdale, NJ: Erlbaum.

Loveland, K. A. (1991). Social affordances and interaction II: Autism and the affordances of the human environment. *Ecological Psychology, 3*, 99–119.

Loveland, K. A. (1993). Autism, affordances, and the self. In U. Neisser (Ed.), *The perceived self: Ecological and interpersonal sources of self-knowledge* (pp. 237–253). Cambridge, MA: Cambridge University Press.

Macbeth, D. (1994). Classroom encounters with the unspeakable: "Do you see, Danelle?". *Discourse Processes, 17*, 311–335.

Mace, W. (1977). Ask not what's in your head, but what your head's inside of. R. E. Shaw & J. Bransford (Eds.), *Perceiving, acting, and knowing* (pp. 43–65). Hillsdale, NJ: Erlbaum.

MacLean, C. (1977). *The wolf children*. New York: Penguin Books.

Malpass, R. S. (1977). Theory and method in cross-cultural research. *American Psychologist, 32*, 1069–1079.

Markman, E. (1989). *Categorization and naming in children: Problems of induction*. Cambridge, MA: MIT Press.

Martini, M. (1994). Peer interactions in Polynesia: A view from the Marquesas. In J. P. Roopnarine, J. E. Johnson, & F. H. Hooper (Eds.), *Children's play in diverse cultures* (pp. 73–103). Albany: State University of New York Press.

McArthur, L. Z., & Baron, R. M. (1983). Toward an ecological psychology of social perception. *Psychological Review, 90,* 215–238.

McGrew, W. C. (1993). The intelligent use of tools: Twenty propositions. In K. R. Gibson & T. Ingold (Eds.), *Tools, language, and cognition in human evolution* (pp. 151–170). Cambridge, England: Cambridge University Press.

Mehan, H., & Wood, H. (1975). *The reality of ethnomethodology.* New York: Wiley.

Messer, D. J. (1978). The integration of mothers' referential speech with joint play. *Child Development, 49,* 781–787.

Messer, D. J. (1981). Nonlinguistic information which could assist the young child's interpretation of adults' speech. In W. P. Robinson (Ed.), *Communication and development* (pp. 39–62). London: Academic Press.

Michaels, C. F., & Carello, C. (1981). *Direct perception.* Englewood Cliffs, NJ: Prentice-Hall.

Millikan, R. G. (1984). *Language, thought, and other biological categories: New foundations for realism.* Cambridge, MA: MIT Press.

Moerman, M. (1988). *Talking culture: Ethnography and conversation analysis.* Philadelphia: University of Pennsylvania Press.

O'Connell, B., & Bretherton, I. (1984). Toddlers' play, alone and with mother: The role of maternal guidance. In I. Bretherton (Ed.), *Symbolic play: The development of social understanding* (pp. 337–368). Orlando, FL: Academic Press.

Oyama, S. (1985). *The ontogeny of information: Developmental systems and evolution.* Cambridge, England: Cambridge University Press.

Piaget, J. (1962). *Play, dreams, and imitation in childhood.* New York: Norton.

Pine, J. M., & Lieven, E. M. (1990). Referential style at thirteen months: Why age-defined cross-sectional measures are inappropriate for the study of strategy differences in early language development. *Journal of Child Language, 17,* 625–631.

Quine, W. V. O. (1960). *Word and object.* New York: Wiley.

Raver, C. C., & Leadbeater, B. J. (1993, March). Shared focus of attention between socially disadvantaged children at 12 and 20 months and their adolescent mothers. In C. Moore (Chair), *Joint attention: Its origins and role in development.* Symposium conducted at the meetings of the Society for Research in Child Development, New Orleans, LA.

Reed, E. S. (1986). Why do things look as they do? The implications of J. J. Gibson's *The ecological approach to visual perception.* In A. Costall & A. Still (Eds.), *Cognitive psychology in question* (pp. 90–113). New York: St. Martin's Press.

Reed, E. S. (1988). *James J. Gibson and the psychology of perception*. New Haven, CT: Yale University Press.

Reed, E. S. (1993). The intention to use a specific affordance: A conceptual framework for psychology. In R. H. Wozniak & K. Fisher (Eds.), *Development in context: Acting and thinking in specific environments* (pp. 45–76). Hillsdale, NJ: Erlbaum.

Schegloff, E. (1972). Notes on a conversational practice: Formulating place. In D. Sudnow (Ed.), *Studies in social interaction* (pp. 75–119). New York: Free Press.

Schutz, A. (1962). *Collected papers: The problem of social reality* (Vol. 1). Dordrecht, The Netherlands: Martinus Nijhoff.

Shaw, R., & Bransford, J. (1977). Introduction: Psychological approaches to the problem of knowledge. In R. Shaw & J. Bransford (Eds.), *Perceiving, acting, and knowing: Toward an ecological psychology* (pp. 1–39). Hillsdale, NJ: Erlbaum.

Shaw, R., & Turvey, M. T. (1981). Coalitions as models for ecosystems: A realist perspective on perceptual organization. In M. Kubovy & J. R. Pomerantz (Eds.), *Perceptual organization* (pp. 343–415). Hillsdale, NJ: Erlbaum.

Skinner, B. F. (1953). *Science and human behavior*. New York: Appleton-Century-Crofts.

Smith, D. L., & Ginsburg, G. P. (1989). The social perception process: Reconsidering the role of social stimulation. *Journal for the Theory of Social Behavior, 19,* 32–45.

Snow, C. E. (1977). The development of conversation between mothers and babies. *Journal of Child Language, 4,* 1–11.

Spelke, E. S. (1979). Perceiving bimodally specified events in infancy. *Developmental Psychology, 15,* 626–636.

Spelke, E. S. (1981). The infants' acquisition of bimodally specified events. *Journal of Experimental Child Psychology, 31,* 279–299.

St. Augustine. (1961). *Confessions*. Baltimore, MD: Penguine Books.

Stern, D. (1977). *The first relationship: Infant and mother*. Cambridge, MA: Harvard University Press.

Stern, D. (1985). *The interpersonal world of the infant: A view from psychoanalysis and developmental psychology*. New York: Basic Books.

Stern, D. N. (1993). The role of feelings for an interpersonal self. In U. Neisser (Ed.), *The perceived self: Ecological and interpersonal sources of self-knowledge* (pp. 205–215). New York: Cambridge University Press.

Still, A., & Costall, A. (1991). The mutual elimination of dualism in Vygotsky and Gibson. In A. Still & A. Costall (Eds.), *Against cognitivism: Alternative founda-*

tions for cognitive psychology (pp. 225–235). Hemel-Hempstead, England: Harvester-Wheatsheaf.

Tamis-LeMonda, C. S., & Bornstein, M. H. (1989). Habituation and maternal encouragement of attention in infancy as predictors of toddler language, play, and representational competence. *Child Development, 60,* 738–751.

Thelen, E., & Smith, L. B. (1994). *A dynamic systems approach to the development of cognition and action.* Cambridge, MA: MIT Press.

Tomasello, M., & Barton, M. (1994). Learning words in nonostensive contexts. *Developmental Psychology, 30,* 639–650.

Tomasello, M., & Farrar, M. J. (1986). Joint attention and early language. *Child Development, 57,* 1454–1463.

Tomasello, M., & Todd, J. (1983). Joint attention and lexical acquisition style. *First Language, 4,* 197–212.

Trevarthen, C. (1979). Communication and cooperation in early infancy: A description of primary intersubjectivity. In M. Bullowa (Ed.), *Before speech: The beginning of interpersonal communication* (pp. 321–347). London: Cambridge University Press.

Trevarthen, C., & Hubley, P. (1978). Secondary intersubjectivity: Confidence, confiding and acts of meaning in the first year. In A. Lock (Ed.), *Action, gesture and symbol* (pp. 183–239). New York: Academic Press.

Tronick, E. Z. (Ed.). (1982). *Social interchange in infancy: Affect, cognition, and communication.* Baltimore: University Park Press.

Turvey, M. T., & Fitzpatrick, P. (1993). Commentary: Development of perception–action systems and general principles of pattern formation. *Child Development, 64,* 1175–1190.

Turvey, M. T., Shaw, R. E., Reed, E. S., & Mace, W. M. (1981). Ecological laws of perceiving and acting: In reply to Fodor and Pylyshyn (1980). *Cognition, 9,* 237–304.

Valenti, S. S., & Good, J. M. M. (1991). Social affordances and interaction I: Introduction. *Ecological Psychology, 3,* 77–98.

Vygotsky, L. S. (1978). Interaction between learning and development. In M. Cole, V. John-Stiener, S. Scribner, & E. Souberman (Eds.), *Mind in society* (pp. 79–91). Cambridge, MA: Harvard University Press.

Wachs, T. (1992). *The nature of nurture.* Newbury Park, CA: Sage.

Walker, A. S. (1982). Intermodal perception of expressive behaviors by human infants. *Journal of Experimental Child Psychology, 33,* 514–535.

Walker-Andrews, A. S. (1986). Intermodal perception of expressive behaviors: Relation of eye and voice? *Developmental Psychology, 22*, 373–377.

Walker-Andrews, A. S., & Lennon, E. (1985). Auditory–visual perception of changing distance by human infants. *Child Development, 22*, 373–377.

Warren, Jr., W. H., & Shaw, R. E. (1985). *Persistence and change.* Hillsdale, NJ: Erlbaum.

Watson, J. B. (1930). *Behaviorism.* Chicago: Chicago University Press.

Weisner, T. S. (1987). Socialization for parenthood in sibling caretaking societies. In J. B. Lancaster, J. Altmann, A. S. Rossi, & L. R. Sherrod (Eds.), *Parenting across the life span: Biosocial dimensions* (pp. 237–270). New York: Aldine de Gruyter.

Weisner, T. S. (1996). The five to seven transition as an ecocultural project. In A. Sameroff & M. Haith (Eds.), *The five to seven transition: Reason and responsibility* (pp. 295–326). Chicago: University of Chicago Press.

Wertsch, J. V., McNamee, G. D., McLane, J. B., & Budwig, N. (1980). The adult–child dyad as a problem-solving system. *Child Development, 51*, 1215–1221.

Wexler, K. (1990). A reply to Susan Oyama's commentary. *Developmental Psychobiology, 23*, 753–755.

Whiting, B. B., & Edwards, C. P. (1988). *Children of different worlds: The formation of social behavior.* Cambridge, MA: Harvard University Press.

Zukow, P. G. (1981–1982). [Fieldnotes: Los Arcos and Museo Tlatilco, Estado de Mexico, Mexico; Ejido de Sta. Ana y Lobos, Guanajuato, Mexico.] Unpublished raw data.

Zukow, P. G. (1982). Transcription systems for videotaped interactions: Some advantages and limitations of manual and computer rendering techniques. *Applied Psycholinguistics, 3*, 61–79.

Zukow, P. G. (1986). The relationship between interaction with the caregiver and the emergence of play activities during the one-word period. *British Journal of Developmental Psychology, 4*, 223–234.

Zukow, P. G. (1989). Siblings as effective socializing agents: Evidence from Central Mexico. In P. G. Zukow (Ed.), *Sibling interactions across cultures: Theoretical and methodological issues* (pp. 79–105). New York: Springer-Verlag.

Zukow, P. G. (1990). Socio-perceptual bases for the emergence of language: An alternative to innatist approaches [Special Issue]. *Developmental Psychobiology, 23*, 705–726.

Zukow, P. G. (1991a). A socio-perceptual/ecological approach to language development: Affordances of the communicative context [Special issue]. *Anales de Psicologia, 7*, 151–163.

Zukow, P. G. (1991b, April). *Socio-perceptual/ecological approach to the emergence of the lexicon.* Poster presented at the meeting of the Society for Research in Child Development, Seattle, WA.

Zukow, P. G., Reilly, J., & Greenfield, P. M. (1982). Making the absent present: Facilitating the transition from sensorimotor to linguistic communication. In K. E. Nelson (Ed.), *Children's language* (Vol. 3, pp. 1–90). Hillsdale, NJ: Gardner.

Zukow-Goldring, P. (1995). Sibling caregiving. In M. Bornstein (Ed.), *Handbook of parenting: Vol. 3. Status and social conditions of parenting* (pp. 177–208). Hillsdale, NJ: Erlbaum.

Zukow-Goldring, P. (1996). *The relation between educating attention and the emergence of linguistic representation: Intra-ethnic studies in Central Mexico.* Manuscript submitted for publication.

Zukow-Goldring, P. (in press). Sensitive caregivers foster the comprehension of speech: When gestures speak louder than words. [Special Issue]. *Early Development & Parenting.*

Zukow-Goldring, P., & Ferko, K. R. (1994). An ecological approach to the emergence of the lexicon: Socializing attention. In V. John-Steiner, C. Panofsky, & L. Smith (Eds.), *Sociocultural approaches to language and literacy: Interactionist perspective* (pp. 170–190). New York: Cambridge University Press.

Zukow-Goldring, P., Romo, L., & Duncan, K. R. (1994). Gestures speak louder than words: Achieving consensus in Latino classrooms. In A. Alvarez & P. del Rio (Eds.), *Education as cultural construction* (pp. 227–238). Madrid: Fundacion Infancia & Aprendizaje.

Comment on Zukow-Goldring

Timothy D. Johnston

Zukow-Goldring's research illustrates the significance of cross-cultural differences in the search for general principles of development. The differences among cultures can be approached in a couple of ways. One way is to look just at the behaviors that people demonstrate in different cultures, and their development, and see whether any transcultural patterns can be determined that might reveal underlying constancies in development. This approach has been used by ethologists who study human behavior, such as Eibl-Eibesfelt (1979), and not infrequently leads to claims that there are "universals" (generally supposed to be innate) of human behavior.

Another approach to the study of differences draws more usefully on the comparative method in biology that gave rise to ethology and that is also more compatible with the principles of ecological psychology. In comparative analysis, one looks not just at variation in a behavior or structure, but also at variation in the context in which that behavior or structure functions. Thus, a comparative study of beak structure in birds would

Johnston comments on Zukow-Goldring from an ecological realist perspective.

not only ask "How do the beaks of different species of birds vary?" but also "What is the relationship between variation in beak structure and variation in (let's say) food type?" This *comparative ecological* approach to the study of variation reveals interesting regularities in the *relationships* between beak structure and food characteristics that are not revealed by looking at beak structure alone. A similar approach to cultural variation in ecological psychology would look not just at variation in behavior, but also at variation in the cultural context in which that behavior functions. Suppose one found that in different cultures the spatial relationship between mothers and their infants is regulated differently, mothers staying close to their infants in some cultures but not in others. This cultural variation, taken alone, might be hard to explain. But suppose the cultures also vary in their expectations about the extent to which 2-year-olds should act independently of their parents. One might find correlations between the two sets of variation that would be obscured by focusing on cultural variation in mother–infant relationships alone. As has been argued repeatedly during this conference, the ecological approach expects regularities to emerge from studying organisms in relation to their environments (whether physical or cultural), not from studying organisms alone.

As ecological psychologists look more closely at cultural variation, they must be careful of the distinction that is sometimes drawn between culture and nature. Zukow-Goldring used this distinction a couple of times in her talk, and I want to warn against it. The culture–nature distinction in the social sciences is precisely the same as the learning–instinct distinction in the study of behavior. Culture is variable, passed on by experience, readily modifiable, and so forth; nature is stereotyped, inherited, biological, fixed, and so on. All of the criticisms that have been aimed at the second of these distinctions applies to the first. One of the ways in which the distinction surfaces is in the notion of "arbitrary relations." Culturally established relations (e.g., between the forms of words and their meanings) are supposed to be arbitrary, whereas natural relations are not. I am not comfortable with the notion of arbitrariness in this context. A more useful approach is to think in terms of the different constraints that apply to relationships and linkages and to recognize that there is a nested hierarchy of such constraints. At the highest level are constraints imposed by logical necessity—all links and relationships must respect the demands of logic. Nested within those constraints are constraints imposed by natural law—the relationships described by ecological optics are determined by laws of physics, but one could imagine other physical laws that would still be logically possible and that would produce different optical relationships. Nested within natural-law constraints are a set of constraints imposed by historical contingencies, including evolutionary contingencies, cultural contingencies, and the contingencies of individual development. Mammals might have evolved six limbs, but they did not, and this fact imposes certain constraints on the way we, as mammals, interact with our environments. Each of us grew up in a culture that exposed us to certain regularities; we might have grown up in cultures with different regularities, but we did not, and the ones we actually encountered constrain our behavior in certain ways. None of these constraints is any more or less arbitrary than the others, but some apply widely, others more narrowly. For a given individual, however, they are all equally real and behaviorally effective components of the environment.

How, then, do infants learn about these constraints so that they can behave adaptively with respect to them? In her chapter, Zukow-Goldring described a variety of social processes by which caregivers guide, structure, and facilitate infants' learning of these constraints in culturally specific ways. It seems to me that some of these processes can be interpreted quite readily from the standpoint of Gibsonian ecological principles. Consider the learning of lexical items—words and their meanings. Children's use of words differs from that of adults in several well-known ways. I suggest that the differences between children's and adults' word usage might be understood in terms of the differences in the affordance structures of children's and adults' environments. If children learning language are mapping words on to affordances (as seems at least plausible) then "overextension of reference" may reflect differences between children's and adults' perceptions of the environment rather than children's errors. Thus the application of the word *dog* to any of a wide range of furry, four-footed animals may indicate the existence of a childish affordance not readily apparent to adults, not a labeling error. This might also explain why children learn basic category words (like *table* and *chair*) before either superordinate category words (like *furniture*) or subordinate category words (like *end table* or *armchair*). Basic categories are, I think simply the categories that map most directly on to the affordance structure of children's environments.

As Zukow-Goldring pointed out, children's learning of language and other social conventions is often actively facilitated by adults who point out, demonstrate, and instruct in a variety of ways. Demonstration, in particular, may serve to reveal the affordances of the environment by virtue of shared effectivities between the child and the adult. If a child learns, through interactions with his or her mother, that they share the ability to act on the world in certain ways, then watching the mother engage in one of these activities may be sufficient to reveal an affordance to the child directly. If, for example, the child has learned, perhaps through play, that they both can *grasp and pull on* certain objects, then observing the mother *grasp and pull on* an object X may reveal to the child that X affords the action *grasp and pull on.* In this way, actions of the caregiver, and indeed of any person with whom the child has learned that he or she shares effectivities, provide a kind of exploration by proxy. Direct exploration allows children to learn about the functional properties of things in their environments. Observation of others' exploratory behavior may operate in some of the same ways. So one question to ask is how children gain an understanding of the effectivities they share with others in their social group as part of an ecological account of how social interactions facilitate learning by children.

Zukow-Goldring's research provides a very nice set of observations, in different cultural contexts, of some of the variety of ways in which caregivers guide children's learning about their environment. I have suggested some further ways in which those observations might be analyzed and understood within the theoretical framework of ecological psychology.

REFERENCE

Eibl-Eibesfeldt, I. (1979). Human ethology: Concepts and limitations for the sciences of man. *Behavioral and Brain Sciences, 2*, 1–57.

8

A Naturalistic Study of Metaphor Development: Seeing and Seeing As

Cathy Dent-Read

Cady, at 18 months of age, first used a metaphor when she said, "wawa," her word for water, while pointing at a large skylight showing a blue sky. Previously, she had used "wawa" as adults use the word *water*. In the next two days she showed correct comprehension of the words *sky* (both as seen outdoors and as seen through windows and skylights) and *water*. When Cady was 3 years, 10 months old, she had been looking around at the trees and then up at the sky with small binoculars when she said, "The sky looks like the sea when I look through the 'myroscope'." The changes in the metaphor include verbal specification of the topic, the sky, and an elaboration of the vehicle or figurative term *water* to *sea* bringing in the vast extent of the water that corresponds metaphorically to the extent of the sky. How can one explain such elaborations and differentiations in the course of development?

The research reported herein was funded by a Research Foundation Grant from the University of Connecticut. I thank Richard Carter for collaboration on all phases of the diary study; Agnes Szokolszky for discussions of theoretical interpretations of the data on English and coordination of data collection in Hungary; and Joshua Boggis, Agnes Jadamec, Tamara O'Day, Ryan Rutledge, and Sheryl Sink for work on data reduction. I have benefited in writing this chapter from comments by Richard Carter, Agnes Szokolszky, John Pittenger, Patricia Zukow-Goldring, Katherine Loveland, David Miller, Claudia Carello, Esther Thelen, Catherine Best, Edward Reed, and an anonymous reader.

Most traditional work on metaphor development has focused on symbolic thought or actions based on mental representation to explain metaphor abilities (Ortony, 1979). These studies have suggested that metaphor grows out of pretend actions (e.g., Winner, 1979). The only study of early metaphor use in natural situations to date (Winner, 1979) has been interpreted using this approach. If, however, one takes perceiving as the starting point of knowing, rather than symbolic representations, then definitions of cognitive activities and expectations about the development of such abilities differ radically from those of the symbolic approach. This chapter outlines a direct-perceiving or ecological realist approach to metaphor, describes the early results of an on-going naturalistic study of metaphor development, and proposes some answers to general questions about development from an ecological realist point of view.

DEFINING METAPHOR

The phenomenon of metaphor may be analyzed into its components, processes, and pragmatics. (Sharratt in her 1993 article on metaphor and pretend used these categories but made quite different points under each, as she used a different approach to metaphor.)

Components

Metaphors typically have a *topic*, what the metaphor is about; a *vehicle*, the term that is used to refer simultaneously to the topic and to an object or event; and a *ground*, the actual resemblance between topic and vehicle. Segments of active DNA, introns, for example, have been called *islands* because they are surrounded by long segments of inactive DNA, exons (Weinberg, 1987). The ecological view (Dent, 1990; Dent-Read & Szokolszky, 1993; Verbrugge, 1980, 1985) defines metaphor as a species of perceptually guided action that may or may not be expressed verbally. Metaphor is distinguished from other forms of action, perception, or cognition in that (a) it involves the detection and use of structural or dynamic properties that remain invariant across kinds, and (b) one kind (the topic term, for example, active segments of DNA) is perceived in terms of another kind (the vehicle term, in this case *islands*). The basis of the metaphor (the ground) is some metaphoric resemblance; introns were referred to as islands because they are small and surrounded by long segments of inactive DNA.

Processes

The comprehension and production of metaphors, however, is not reducible to the metaphoric ground, as metaphors involve an active partial transformation of the topic under the guidance of the vehicle. In the previous example, certain relational properties are invariant across islands and introns, which is the basis of the metaphor; the metaphor is, however, constituted by the active perception of introns in terms of islands, which results in a transformed understanding of introns. Most researchers in psychology subscribe to some variant of this interaction view of metaphor, as opposed to the substitution view (the metaphoric term is a substitute name for the topic) or the comparison view (that the topic and metaphoric term are compared; see Winner, 1988, for a review). Theories differ, however, in characterizing the interaction process. Some describe the process as "seeing one object as if it were another" (Sharratt, 1993; Winner, 1988), some as "seeing one object as transformed into another" (Verbrugge, 1985). These definitions do not distinguish metaphor and pretend, which the ecological approach defines as different kinds of perceptual–cognitive acts. In my approach, metaphor is the kind of "seeing as" that glosses (i.e., inteprets) metaphoric utterances as saying, "notice the vehicleness of the topic" (*e.g.*, "notice the islandlike nature of introns" in the "introns are islands" metaphor). On the other hand, pretend utterances are glossed, "Let *x* stand in for *y*", as when a child says, "I'm riding a horse," while running on a broomstick.

The consequences of this theoretical distinction between pretend and metaphor are that the two activities can be analyzed according to the two main types of perceptual activity that have been detailed in work on ecological approaches to perception, that is, performatory and exploratory perception (E. Gibson, 1988; J. Gibson, 1966). In performatory action, perception supports action, and action has a specific purpose. Applied to pretend, the purpose is to create a world or scene, the main activity is imagining, and the process is taking one thing to stand for another. In exploratory action, action supports perception, and the purpose is to explore. Applied to metaphor, the main activity underlying a metaphor is observing or noticing, and the metaphor functions to communicate this insight to others.

Pragmatics

The pragmatics of metaphor have been investigated in terms of the difference between what a speaker says and what he or she means (Searle, 1979; Winner, 1988), but not in terms of the communicative function or social interaction context of metaphor use. An analysis of the social acts performed with metaphors again leads to a distinction between pretend and metaphor. Metaphors are almost always used to comment—to point out to the listener, in a certain way—something that the speaker has noticed. Pretend utterances, as they are in the context of imagining a scene or narrative, can function to comment, command, question, and so forth within the scene that is being created. Therefore, metaphors call for assent reactions, such as "oh yes, I see," whereas pretend utterances call for cooperation in imagining and utterances that sustain or elaborate the scene.

PREVIOUS RESEARCH ON EARLY METAPHOR

In a pioneering study of very early metaphor Winner (1979) analyzed previously collected diary data for the use of metaphor by one child from age 2.3 to 4.10 (years.months). The data were biweekly 2-hr sessions with investigators, parent, and child interacting. Contextual notes were taken by the investigators. For the study on metaphor, transcripts were scored for the use of language as literal, overextended, metaphoric, or anomalous. Metaphors were divided into pretend action (*e.g.*, pretending to eat, holding a pencil as if it were corn on the cob and calling it "corn"), nonpretend action (*e.g.*, putting the paper cover on a crayon while saying, "I'm putting on your clothes, crayon"), and nonaction (*e.g.*, red balloon on a green tube called "de apple on de tree"). Pretend action metaphors were most frequent at age 2 and decreased steadily to be least frequent at age 4. Nonaction metaphors showed the reverse pattern, increasing with age, whereas nonpretend action metaphors were infrequent at all ages.

This early diary investigation of metaphor used the criteria that an utterance could be scored as metaphoric only if evidence in the transcripts showed that the child knew the literal meaning of the metaphoric term or if the child showed in action that he understood the literal meaning. Given the limited time sampled for the diary and the fact that interaction may not have been typical of the child's daily activities, this criterion probably underestimated the frequency of metaphor in the early period of language acquisition. At the same time, the study conflated pretend naming and metaphor, possibly leading to the opposite effect of overestimating the occurrences of certain types of metaphor. Metaphor is a comment about a topic that communicates to self or others that the vehicleness of the topic has been noticed, for example, that the "appleness" of a red balloon has been noticed. Metaphor is not pretend in which one thing is taken to stand for another. In pretend action or naming the identity of the absent object is not commented on. By conflating pretend and metaphor, the incidence of early metaphors may have been overestimated.

Previous work, both theoretical (Sharratt, 1993) and empirical (Billow, 1981; Hudson & Nelson, 1984; Sharratt, 1993; Winner, 1979, 1988) has taken the position that young children's utterances during pretend play are true metaphors and that pretend play is the precursor of metaphor because the child shows that she or he can see one object as if it were another (Winner, McCarthy, & Gardner, 1980, p. 357). This identity between pretend and metaphor has been questioned, however (Marjanovic-Shane, 1989; Vosniadou, 1987). My approach, which takes perception as the basis of metaphor and metaphor as an insight that can be expressed in action as well as language, comes to the same conclusion: Metaphor and pretend are entirely distinct activities. Metaphor is always directed toward the reality at hand; one makes a comment (with words or action) about the real nature of an object, action, or situation. In pretend play, by contrast, a child does not say anything about the objects involved but uses them as prop, and the utterances about them are fictive. Children's utterances that link real objects to a fictional world (the so called renaming, for example, calling a pillow a spaceship) are not metaphors about the objects but simple introductions for the purpose of play (Marjanovic-Shane, 1989, pp. 227–229; see also Vosniadou, 1987, p. 873). Pretend play may be like opportunistic toolmaking in which people use found objects (*e.g.,* animal horns) for a new purpose (pounding food or bark) (Zukow-Goldring, personal communication, September 1994).

Thus, what has been taken for overextension in previous studies can sometimes be metaphor, as when a child uses a cup as a hat, knowing the literal use of both and only on one occasion (Rescorla, 1980, p. 326). (If the term is used repeatedly, it is likely to be an overextension.) Conversely, what has been taken as metaphor may be pretend renaming or pretend play (as when a child uses a horn as an eggbeater and says "mixer" in the context of playing at cooking and needing a mixer (Winner, 1988, p 93). Likewise, verbal metaphor is distinguished from pretend renaming in that the latter does not involve the perception of one structured object in terms of a different kind of structured object. For example, the utterance is a metaphor and not a renaming when a child says "pee" about water running out the bottom of a cup in the course of pouring water from the cup to another container, says it only once, uses *pee* literally before and after that, and accepts simple acknowledgment as a response. In general, in play in which one object is substituted for another, one can gloss either utterances or actions as, "Let this object stand for the other because I don't have that one" (*e.g.,* using a shoe in a back and forth motion on a board means "let this shoe stand for a saw"). In metaphor, in which one object is seen as another, one can gloss either utterances or actions as "notice the vehicleness of the topic" (*e.g.,* "don't saw with your voice" depends on noticing the rough grating qualities of a voice that make it sound like sawing).

SIGNIFICANCE OF AN ECOLOGICAL APPROACH TO PRETEND AND METAPHOR

The theoretical distinctions outlined herein constitute more than a simple redefinition of symbolic play using new terms. The approach I describe leads to a new understanding of the qualities of pretend play versus metaphor and, therefore, to a new understanding of the role these activities play in cognitive development. In the traditional approach to cognitive development based on Piagetian theory combined with information processing (or, more recently, with connectionism; Karmiloff-Smith, 1992), cognitive development consists of constructing mental models or schemas that are increasingly abstract and "removed" from the world, and manipulated in the mind. Pretend play is important to this enterprise because it is seen as the beginning of substituting one thing for another, which culminates in substituting word or logical symbols for things in the world. Metaphor, according to this approach, is seen as a species of pretend play because in both one object is seen as if it were another (Winner, 1988).

The basic problem with any mental representation theory is a logical one: All such theories posit that in the process of constructing mental representations an object must be categorized or classified in order to be perceived and known (Lakoff, 1987); but if the object is not known, how can it be classified (Dent, 1990; J. Gibson, 1979)? This logical problem with mental representation theories has been delineated elsewhere (Dent, 1990; Malcolm, 1977; Reed, 1987; Turvey, 1992; Wilcox & Katz, 1981) and is not detailed here. The consequences of positing knowledge of the world as existing only through mental models and as consisting of stored representations include (a) that accurate perception of natural objects and events is not studied, (b) perception is not seen as a means of knowing the world, and (c) cognitive development consists of building representations that are more and more adultlike (whether this progress is seen as taking place in stages or linearly).

In the ecological approach, cognitive development consists of changes in knowing, as opposed to stored knowledge (J. Gibson, 1979; Michaels & Carello, 1981; Turvey, 1992). Perception is seen as basically veridical and direct, although not complete (J. Gibson, 1979), and perceiving is seen as the basic way of knowing. Thus, the relation of the organism and environment through reciprocal perceiving and acting is studied. Specifically, research focuses on how organisms perceive what the environment affords

(J. Gibson, 1979) and how the perception of affordances becomes richer and more detailed with development (E. Gibson, 1982; E. Gibson & Spelke, 1983).

I have argued that the starting point of linguistic metaphor is a basic process of seeing or understanding one kind of thing as if it were a different kind of thing and that this process is fundamentally perceptual. Metaphors come from perceiving not only in the sense that they can be nonlinguistic (visual, or even acoustic) but also because language and knowing are intrinsically perceptual phenomena (Dent-Read & Szokolszky, 1993). If perceiving is a process of resonating to structure in the world, "perceiving as" is also a process of resonating; but there are at least two different types of perceiving as.

The first type kind of perceiving as takes place in pretend activities. The direct realist analysis of pretend defines it as perceiving that one thing can be used to *stand in* for another. The two things can be of the same kind (scissors used as a wrench), can be of a different kind (blanket used as blood pressure cuff), may exhibit minimal resemblance (toy car used as comb), and can even take place with no object standing in, as when a child pretends to pour from a cup with no object in hand. The verbal and action frame is "Let x stand in for y."

The second kind of perceiving as is metaphor in which the speaker or hearer perceives the vehicleness of the topic, for example, the "skatingness" of sliding on wood. The verbal and action frame is "Notice the $y$ness of x." Thus, the perceptual process is one of resonating to certain aspects of an object or event because of having resonated to the object's or event's resemblance to a different kind of object or event.

Pretend actions are seen as the opportunistic use of suitable objects for the purpose of engaging in imaginative acts or sequences; metaphor is seen as an epistemic act of gaining knowledge about an object or process involving an understanding of one thing in terms of another, already known thing. Imagining is the process basic to pretend play; observation of the physical and social world is the process basic to metaphor. This focus on the relationship of child to environment, specifically, on affordances, and the idea that what develops is the child–environment relationship (and not something mental or internal) would not be arrived at using a mental representation theory of cognition. The study described herein adds to ecological theory by investigating topics that are implicated by the theory but not yet detailed, such as imagining, noticing resemblances across kinds, and communicating about these processes with either actions or utterances.

By providing clear criteria for the abovementioned distinctions the current study systematically distinguishes abilities related to metaphor and play that have previously been conflated. To the extent that the study is successful, more accurate criteria will be made available to judge whether children's metaphors are true metaphors, along with a more accurate picture of the early emergence of metaphor abilities.

SIGNIFICANCE OF THE ECOLOGICAL APPROACH TO METAPHOR IN LANGUAGE

The ecological approach outlined earlier is beginning to be applied to language development (Dent, 1990; Dent-Read, 1993; Reed, 1995; Verbrugge, 1985; Zukow, 1990; Zukow-Goldring & Ferko, 1994; Zukow-Goldring, 1997, this volume) and to metaphor in particular (Dent & Rosenberg, 1990; Dent-Read, Klein, & Eggleston, 1994; Dent-Read & Szokolszky, 1993; Verbrugge, 1980, 1985). In the ecological approach, cognitive development consists of changes in knowing, as opposed to stored knowledge (J. Gibson, 1979; Michaels & Carello, 1981; Turvey, 1992). Perceiving is veridical and direct, although not complete (J. Gibson, 1979), and perceiving is the basic way of knowing. Research focuses on how organisms perceive the affordances of the environment (J. Gibson, 1979) and how the perception of affordances becomes richer and more detailed with development (E. Gibson, 1982; E. Gibson & Spelke, 1983). Affordances are what the environment provides or offers an organism. Affordances are neither subjective nor objective, but relational: An aspect of the environment has an affordance with respect to an animal (or group of animals), and an animal (or group of animals) has abilities with respect to the affordances around it (e.g., Turvey, Shaw, Reed, & Mace, 1981; Zukow-Goldring, 1997, this volume). Researchers have extended this view (E. Gibson, 1997, this volume; Pick & Heinrichs, 1989; Pick, 1997, this volume; Smitsman, 1997, this volume; Smitsman, van Loosbroek, & Pick, 1987) to include topics traditionally studied under the rubric of cognitive development. In this chapter, I report on a study of how children develop abilities to perceive affordances that guide metaphor in action and language. Metaphor, because it requires the apprehension of sameness in the midst of difference, may be a critical process in the differentiating of kinds or types of things in the physical, as well as in the emotional and social, world.

Previously my colleagues and I investigated the effect of perceptual information on the form and frequency of verbal metaphors used by children ages 5 to 10 and by adults (Dent, 1984; Dent & Ledbetter, 1986) and children's abilities to use pictures to show their comprehension of verbal metaphors (Dent, 1987). The first study involved showing children films of events, that is, moving objects or stationary objects in triads so that within each triad there was a metaphoric pair (e.g., wrinkled face, wrinkled apple; deer leaping, dancer leaping), a literal pair (wrinkled apple, smooth apple; dancer turning, dancer leaping), and a control pair (smooth apple, wrinkled face; deer leaping, dancer turning). We asked children and adults to indicate which two objects went together and then to think of the two things at the same time and say what they were thinking. Event triads elicited more metaphoric pairings than object triads, and metaphoric pairings for event triads were equivalent to literal pairings at age 7 as opposed to age 10 for object triads. Metaphoric language increased from ages 5 to 10, and action vehicles were more frequent for event than object pairs. A related study investigated the effect of perceptual experience on the comprehension of metaphors in text (Dent & Ledbetter, 1986). Six, 7-, and 10-year-old children were shown triads of filmed scenes and instructed to describe them. Two weeks later they were tested for recall of stories that included central metaphors, half of which were those depicted in the metaphoric pairs of scenes. The recall of metaphors in stories increased with age and was higher when the metaphor was based on previously perceived resemblance. In addition, the number of propositions recalled was higher in stories that contained figures with action vehicles, such as "the deer is dancing."

If children can detect metaphoric resemblance across pictured objects and events and indicate this apprehension with metaphoric language, can they also construct nonverbal, pictorial, expressions of metaphoric understanding? To answer this question I (Dent, 1987) showed 4- and 5-year-old children pictures of objects and events that resembled each other metaphorically. I then told a simple story about the two objects that ended in either a literal statement of likeness or a metaphor. After which, I asked the children to use the pictures, which had been cut into four sections, to show what the story meant. The compound pictures they produced were scored for completeness, coherence, and complexity. For example, for the story about a tree that was "king of the hill," children produced compound pictures that showed the crown of the tree at the top, surrounded by kneeling subjects at the bottom. These compound pictures were visual metaphors. In contrast to metaphors, literal sentences very rarely resulted in compound constructions.

Given that the children formed compound pictures, visual metaphors, to indicate their comprehension of verbal metaphors, would they comprehend visual metaphors and indicate this comprehension by using a verbal metaphor as a description? We (Dent & Rosenberg, 1990) thus presented children with visual metaphors in the form of three-dimensional miniature objects constructed to be one object with qualities of another, (e.g., a wrinkled apple with hair and a hat). Participants were children ages 5, 7, 10, and adults (college students); adults were included to provide an indication of mature performance. Half saw standard objects (a wrinkled apple and a wrinkled face) in metaphoric pairs, and the other half saw compound objects (a wrinkled apple with a hat and a wrinkled face with stem and leaves at the top). In describing compound objects, children as young as 7 used metaphor as often as adults; in describing standard objects children increased in their use of metaphor from age 5 to 10 and to adult. For all but the youngest children, moving objects were more likely to be described using action vehicles.

More recent work has concentrated on the fact that metaphors require objects different in kind for the topic and vehicle. Children do not make metaphors about objects they have indicated as different in kind, which confirms that their metaphors are truly metaphoric (Dent-Read & Szokolszky, 1996b). (This result is consistent with findings reported by Pick, 1997, this volume, showing that preschool children sort metaphoric objects by either topic or vehicle when asked to. Such objects included a flashlight that looks like a pen or a tea infuser in the shape of an egg.)

Finally, we studied (Dent-Read & Szokolszky, 1996a) the relation of metaphoric action and verbal metaphor at the preschool age. When allowed to handle objects that display metaphoric resemblance 4- and 5-year-old children sometimes treated one object as if it were another (e.g., making a wrinkled apple talk after playing with a stuffed toy wrinkled face). More important, when these children subsequently used verbal metaphors about the objects in the context of telling a story, they almost always treated the objects metaphorically in action. When this action was not shown, verbal metaphors were not used in the stories. The latter finding points to the process of seeing one object *as if* it were another as a central aspect of metaphor.

The purpose of the present chapter is to analyze this process in more detail and to illustrate the development of the seeing-as ability, or more generally the perceiving-as ability, using naturalistic diary data. Understanding one thing in terms of a different kind of thing takes place through perceiving invariants that exist in any of the modes detectable by humans (i.e., in visual, aural, tactual modes). For the sake of brevity, I refer to this process hereinafter as seeing as.

The direct realist approach leads to new research questions and methods with respect to metaphor. Specifically, if perceiving–acting organisms are naturally geared toward cross-kind invariants as well as within-kind invariants, then metaphoric ability must be an early phenomenon. Because the extraction of informational invariants is the assumed basis of acting, perceiving, and knowing as well (cf. Mace, 1977), it is expected that given proper information and attunement it is a natural activity even for young children to detect metaphoric resemblances in the world, which is the first step in perceiving metaphorically. Finally, if seeing as is an essential aspect of metaphor, there must be an analysis of its real-world informational basis, as well as of the perceiving, knowing, and acting processes that are involved in detecting and using this information to comprehend and express metaphors, whether verbal or nonverbal. The expression of metaphor in action could then be termed *acting as* and in language *speaking as* (this term was suggested by Smitsman, personal communication, October 1994). Thus, one is led to ask questions regarding the early ontogenesis of metaphor, both in action and language, and in natural settings. This early ontogenesis can be investigated using only ethological methods, thereby establishing a natural history of metaphor use by, at first, a small number of toddlers and children. In addition, one is led to focus on situations in which events, rather than stationary objects, form the matrix of the metaphor as perception is usually of dynamic events and not of stationary structures (J. Gibson, 1979).

NATURALISTIC STUDY OF EARLY METAPHOR

Systematic Diary Study of Metaphor in English and Hungarian

Using an event sampling technique (Altman, 1974; Mervis, Mervis, Johnson, & Bertrand, 1992) we (Dent-Read, Carter, Szokolszky, & Orban) are presently collecting longitudinal data on two English-speaking and two Hungarian-speaking children. The children have been given pseudonyms to provide anonymity. Cady and Adrienne (children of the author) are participants in the in-depth diary study of metaphor and pretend in English. Two Hungarian children residing in Budapest, Eva and Martsi (a boy), are being observed from 2.8 and 1.0 years, respectively, to the age of 5, for the occurrence of metaphors only. This chapter includes a preliminary analysis of one child in the in-depth diary study of metaphor and pretend. Thus, the first 16 months of data from Cady are presented, although examples from older ages are used to illustrate certain theoretical points.

Certain patterns should appear in the data on the emergence of metaphor on the basis of previous experimental work and ecological theory. First, if metaphor is more easily expressed in action than in language, action metaphors (such as turning a key in someone's mouth, smiling, until they open the mouth) will precede verbal metaphors. The Piagetian position that knowing is, at first, action makes the same prediction (see Winner, 1979). For example, in another early metaphor study pretend metaphors involving action predominated at the youngest ages (starting at 2.3: 2 years, 3 months). Second, if resemblances are easier to detect when they consist of action or movement (Dent, 1984), then metaphors based on action should precede those based on stationary configuration resemblances. For example, calling a stream of water coming from a hole in a cup "peeing" should precede such metaphors as calling a piece of green curly lettuce "buggy." Third, if similes with explicit comparison terms are less metaphoric than metaphors because they are based on comparison of the topic and vehicle rather than on interaction of the two (Kennedy, 1982), then similes should appear first; thus, metaphoric statements would not occur before the use of the word *like*.

The expectations regarding the different developmental curves for pretend and metaphor were that (a) metaphor will emerge before pretend because metaphor is a comment on the "object at hand" (Marjanovic-Shane, 1989), which is simpler than talking about an imaginary object, and (b) metaphor should occur in exploratory contexts, whereas pretend should occur in performatory contexts. In other words, the function of metaphor is to comment; the function of pretend is to substitute one object for another for the purpose of creating an imaginary scene or narrative.

I began keeping the diary on Cady at 10 months, when she spoke her first word, which was a phonetically consistent form (Dore, Franklin, Miller, & Ramer, 1976; Sachs, 1993). Data collection continued through her fourth year, to age 5, to overlap with the youngest ages included in experimental studies of metaphor. During the period of diary data covered in this chapter, Cady was with a baby-sitter outside of her home approximately 12–16 hours per week (11 waking hours).

In-Depth Study of Metaphor and Pretend

The diary study on metaphor and pretend in English has several components. First, narrative diary entries on word use, metaphor use in words or action, and comprehension displayed in reaction to probes are entered into a word processing computer file. Words are recorded the first time they are used, or when used for a new type of referent. Narrative diary entries are also kept on the metaphors in words or action that others use in interacting with the child or within the child's hearing. Second, when necessary, lexical items are tested with probes to determine literal understanding of topic and vehicle in the child's metaphors. Sample entries and metaphors are reported in Table 1.

Categories Scored

One of the main concerns of the in-depth study is systematically to distinguish metaphor in action and language from other nonliteral forms. Such a distinction requires defining categories specifically to make a clear distinction among literal action, pretend action, and metaphoric action in the action domain, and among overextension, pretend renaming, and metaphor in the language domain. The ecological view demands that one pay attention to affordance characteristics of objects and consider metaphor in the context of the agent–object–action system. Thus, the fit between object and agent must play a role in making the abovementioned distinctions.

In *literal action* an object is used in a manner that fits with its identity; the performed action fits with the affordance structure of the object so the action can be completed, and if completed, it will have real consequences (e.g., drinking water decreases thirst). In nonliteral action there is a partial nonfit between the action and the object; therefore, the action is fragmentary, and it does not have real consequences (e.g., drinking imaginary tea from a cup).

Pretend action and metaphoric action are two varieties of nonliteral action. *Pretend action* may or may not involve actual objects; however, the object is specified by the action even if not actually present (e.g., the presence of a cup is specified by the body movements involved in drinking).

Table 1

Sample Entries and Metaphors

Sample narrative entry

7/18/92 Sat., Age 1.8.2. (years, months, days) C lying on M's stomach, M's stomach gurgled. C sat up smiling, looking at stomach and said "ditty" (her pronunciation of "kitty"). M said "where's the ditty?," C turned and pointed out the door of the room (there were no cats in the room, the family has two cats). M said, "where's my tummy?" C put her finger on M's stomach.

Sample early metaphors in action

Age[a]	Action	Interpretation
1.7.3	Put key in M's mouth, turning it and laughing after 2 weeks of exploring how keys go in locks	Treating mouth as lock
1.8.7	"Aimed" toy wireless telephone at the TV, saying "zzz" after repeatedly using the toy as a telephone	Treating toy phone as remote control

Sample early verbal metaphors[b]

Age	Utterance	Interpretation
1.6.18	"Wawa" (water) while pointing to and looking at a skylight in the ceiling showing blue sky	Sky called water Ground: extent, blue color, uniformity of surface
1.8.1	"Ditty" (kitty) said about stomach rumbling, smiling	"Growling" called kitty Ground: guttural and high-pitched sounds
1.8.10	"Booboo" said about the red mouth on a stuffed doll	Mouth called scratch Ground: horizontal line, color
1.8.24	"Pee" about a stream of water coming from the bottom of a cup	Water draining called peeing Ground: substance, action

NOTE: M = mother; F = father; C = child. [a]Age is presented in years.months.days. [b]Appropriate literal use or comprehension documented for early verbal metaphors.

Pretend object use is the imaginative, loosely constrained substitution of one object for another object that does not involve the perception of a specific resemblance over kinds but has, instead, a pragmatic focus on substitution. It involves (a) blank objects that have low structural complexity and many degrees of freedom for action or facsimile objects, (b) the use of the blank object as a substitute in various contexts, and (c) the use of the object embedded in a sequence of pretend play. Facsimile objects are replicas of natural objects with high degrees of structural complexity, and this well-specified identity prevents their use as substitutes (a doll is not used as a horse or a sword). Their role in pretend play is guided and constrained by the role of objects or agents they replicate in real interactions.

Metaphoric action involves the transfer of action adapted to one kind of object to another kind of object. Such an action involves structurally complex objects; occurs in the specific context of the two objects, on the basis of a specific resemblance or group of resemblances; and occurs in a broader context than pretend play. Metaphoric action may also occur without the actual presence of an object, as when a standing child stretches his or her arms upward and says, "I am a tree." In this action the child specifics a structural resemblance and directs attention to the tree-like qualities of his or her body with a given posture.

In the language domain *overextension* represents a literal form of language. It is defined as the habitual nonconventional use of a word for a wide group of referents based on some shared nondifferentiated invariant (with sensible resemblance) within or across kinds. Its criteria include (a) the lack of literal names for the overextended referents; (b) habitual use, then dropping out; and (c) an overly broad range of referents (cf. Rescorla, 1980; Winner, 1988). When a child, for example, uses the word *ball* for peas, grapes, and marbles, the child is using the word in a way that adults would not, although adults could use the word that way because it is based on a sensible resemblance. If the overextended word is accompanied by action, the action is literal (peas and grapes are eaten, marbles rolled). Overextended words are used for any pragmatic function because they are literal; that is, the words can be used to request, to state, to question. Such usages elicit the appropriate complementary responses from adults when the basis of the overextension is clear.

Pretend renaming involves the pragmatic substitution of one conventional word for another conventional word in the context of pretending. The criteria for this usage include (a) availability of literal names for the referents, in either production or comprehension; (b) embedding in pretend action; and (c) nonhabitual use. *Metaphoric utterances* are those that meet the following criteria: (a) The utterance links different kind objects or events by calling one thing another or likening one thing to another; (b) a sensible and specific ground (i.e., resemblance) is clear; (c) the utterance is used once or twice, that is, is a novel metaphor (i.e., it does not become a new lexical item); (d) literal names for the referents or other evidence of literal knowledge of the topic and the vehicle in action is available; and (e) the speaker has not used the term in an overextended way previously to refer to the topic object. Metaphors are used to draw attention to something about the topic using its resemblance to a different kind of object or event, that is, the vehicle. Thus, the only pragmatic function is to comment—to call attention to the "vehicleness" of the topic (e.g., the "dancingness" of a leaping deer). A metaphor, for this reason, tends to elicit a response of shared insight, a "yes, indeed" reaction.

Metaphor differs from pretend in that a metaphor tells something about the topic, and pretend substitutes one object for another. In metaphor the topic is usually present, whereas the vehicle used to comment on it is not. In pretend, the topic is absent and the object used to substitute for it is present. When a 2-year-old sits on her or his step stool and rocks back and forth saying, "I riding," the child is not pointing out anything about the step stool but is using it to pretend. The child accepts responses that enter into that pretend, for example, "yes, you're riding," but not those that talk about the step stool. When a 2-year-old uses a metaphor such as "wheels" about the action of a tape recorder playing, having previously and subsequently used the word only for cars, trucks, and so forth, the child is commenting on the event she or he is seeing, not substituting that event for another one in an imaginary scene. In this analysis, pretend and metaphor are always distinct processes and may show various developmental patterns; that is, they may be independent of each other in development. Table 2 gives a concise statement of the differences between metaphor and pretend.

Although pretend and metaphor are conceptually distinct, identifying them in empirical studies may not always be simple, as is discussed later in relation to the present data. To aid in this effort, we used the following procedure based on discourse studies aimed at identifying the topic of an utterance (Keenan & Schieffelin, 1976). To identify the topic of an utterance, that is, what it is about, the listener tacitly asks, "what is the speaker trying to inform me of, what question is the speaker answering?" The proposition that the question presupposes is the topic of the discourse utterance. We asked, thus, about an utterance recorded in the diary, with verbal and nonverbal context described in addition, "what question is the utterance answering?" For example, when Cady at age (1.9) said about a cup with water draining out of a hole in the bottom, "peein" (peeing), one finds the she is asking "what is the water doing?" The primary presupposition of this question is that the water is doing something and what it is doing is like peeing. This is the topic of the utterance "peein," which allows it to be identified as a metaphor because the topic is present and the purpose of the utterance is to comment on that event.

In contrast, using the same procedure with the utterance "I riding" about rocking on a step stool results in the following analysis. The question being answered is "what am I doing?," and the main presupposition is that I am doing something, specifically, pretending to ride (we know from previous experience that the child knows the literal action of riding on a horse and the literal action of stepping on the step stool). Therefore, we can identify this utterance as expressing pretend because the topic is absent and the purpose of the utterance is to engage the listener in an imaginary scene.

In addition to the abovementioned categories, the data include examples of the following: Underextension appeared when the child excluded instances that were part of adult usage, mistakes, in which the child was mistaken in what she saw or heard, and other types of utterances that could not be interpreted. This category system has been applied to 176 di-

Table 2

Distinguishing Features of Pretend and Metaphor

Examples of pretend	Examples of metaphor
Biting block and calling it a "yummy cookie."	Putting a wooden shoe on water and calling it a "boat."
Oriented toward reality not "at hand"; focus is on the target object not on the substitute object (Marjanovic-Shane, 1989).	Oriented toward reality "at hand"; comment on reality reflecting new understanding (Marjanovic-Shane, 1989).
Purpose is to change the identity of the substitute object (Vosniadou, 1987).	Purpose is to communicate something about the topic object (Vosniadou, 1987).
Meaningless outside of the specific context of pretend (Vosniadou, 1987).	Meaningful in nonpretend context (Vosniadou, 1987).
Pretense = "*in place of*"; the identity of the substitute object is only broadly relevant.	Metaphor = "*in terms of*"; the identity of the vehicle object is critical.
The ground is a vague resemblance or a nonspecific general affordance.	The ground is a specific resemblance or affordance shared by the topic and the vehicle objects.
The pretend context brings out a gap between the target and the substitute; pretend action tends to have a "compromise" character.	The metaphoric context brings out a fitness between the vehicle and the topic that was not perceived before; metaphoric action has an "integrated character."
Pretend is an imaginative suggestion that elicits a reaction expressing consent (e.g., "OK").	Metaphor is an insight based on acute observation that elicits agreement (e.g., "Yes, indeed").

Definition of pretend	Definition of metaphor
Pretend action is the temporary, consensual extension of reality; it involves the performance of a familiar action with a substitute object whose affordances only minimally support the action.	*Metaphoric action* is action based on a changed understanding of reality; it involves the performance of a familiar action with a novel object (topic) whose affordances strongly support the action.
Pretend renaming is a verbal confirmation or suggestion consensually to extend reality.	*Verbal metaphor* is a comment reflecting the changed understanding of the topic in terms of the vehicle.

NOTE: From *Using An Object as if it Were Another: The Perception and Use of Affordances in Pretend Object Play*, by A. Szokolszky, 1995. Unpublished doctoral dissertation. Adapted with permission of the author.

ary entries from the diary on Cady describing events between the ages of 21 and 23 months; overall agreement between the author and a second trained observer was 88%.

Results and Discussion

I present an analysis of the early entries in the diary for Cady, that is, from the first word at age 10 months through 25 months. The entries were scored according to the system previously described, yielding frequencies of new literal terms (first uses), action and verbal metaphors, and first uses of overextensions. In addition, examples of types of pretend were scored. Underextensions, mistakes, and uninterpretable utterances were extremely rare, totaling six instances. I first present data on frequency of literal usage, frequency of metaphor, and frequency of overextension. I then discuss some examples of pretend and point out some timing relations between the development of metaphor and pretend.

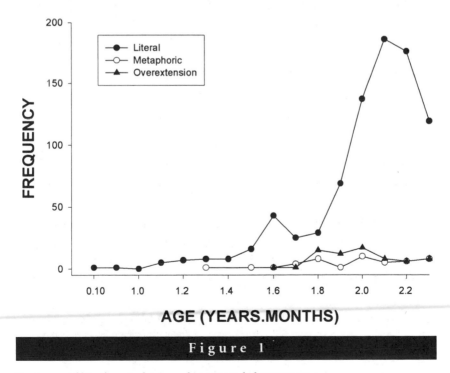

Figure 1

Frequency of literal, metaphoric, and overextended utterances.

Cady used new words at first rarely, and then from age 1.5 to 1.8 many new words were added; at age 1.9 the frequency curve shows a growth spurt that lasted to the end of the period covered in the present analysis (see Figures 1 and 2 for frequency and cumulative frequency curves, respectively). In the first 8 months of word use the range was 1–16 new words, in the next four months the range was 43–69 new words, and in the next four months the range was 119–186. These entries are important in that they can be checked for evidence of Cady's literal use of words she later used in metaphors. Although these data do not constitute a study of the lexicon (i.e., how word meaning differentiates with development) they show a similar growth pattern to other diary studies of early language acquisition (e.g., Nelson, 1973).

The frequencies of all types of metaphor in monthly intervals are displayed in Figures 3 and 4 (raw frequencies and cumulative frequencies, re-

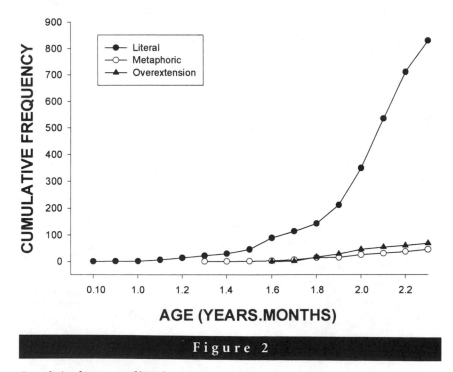

Figure 2

Cumulative frequency of literal, metaphoric, and overextended utterances.

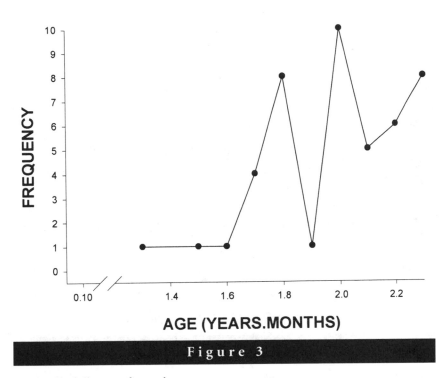

Figure 3

Frequency of all types of metaphor.

spectively). These data provide evidence of metaphor use a year earlier in development than any previous investigations. The monthly frequency of metaphor ranged between 0 and 4 until age 1.7 and then increased to 8 to 10. The total for this time period was 45. For all of these metaphors, the child had either used the metaphoric (vehicle) word literally before or shown literal knowledge of the object referred to in the phrase used metaphorically. For example, Cady watched a frantic horse pacing rhythmically back and forth in its stall and said, smiling, "dancing" (age 2.0) when she previously (and subsequently) used that word only as adults would.

Metaphors were further broken down into action versus verbal metaphors; verbal metaphors with and without supporting action, and verbal metaphors about objects versus events. Action metaphors occurred only five times, at ages 1.7, 1.8, and 1.10. For example, Cady (age 1.7) af-

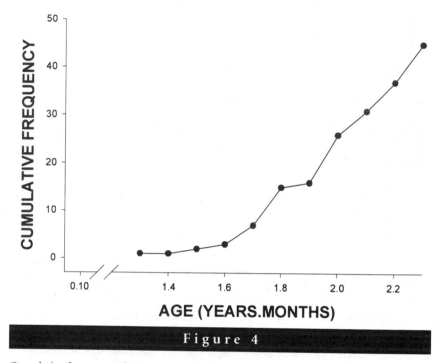

Figure 4

Cumulative frequency of all types of metaphor.

ter exploring how keys fit into locks for 2 weeks, took a key and tried to put it in her mother's mouth with a turning motion, smiling. This action was treating the mouth as a lock, when she clearly knew the difference between the two objects. In another example, Cady used a wooden toy car as a massager on a doll's back. In both cases the smooth and integrated character of the action, along with the observer's knowledge of her previous literal interaction with the topic and vehicle objects, provide evidence that the action was metaphoric. Criteria for distinguishing metaphoric and pretend action have been developed in an experimental study of these topics (see earlier definitions; Szokolszky, 1995) and are applied to the diary data in the present analysis.

Metaphoric action has not been studied previously and has not been distinguished from pretend. In the current analysis based on the perceptual activity posited as the basis of metaphor (i.e., that is seeing as), such activities are not pretend. Such activities are about the object at hand, they comment on something about the object (e.g., the "lockness" of a mouth or the "massagerness" of the toy car) rather than take an object to stand in for another in an imaginary scene. The response they elicit, and that the child accepts, is one of acknowledgment. In the first case, the adult first resisted the key in the mouth and then accepted it, laughing. In the second case, Cady was not looking at the adults present and seemed to be engaged in solitary play, they talked about her massaging the doll, and she continued with the action.

Verbal metaphors with supporting action are those in which an action performed at the time of the utterance elaborates on the meaning of the utterance. For example, when Cady put her underpants on her head and said, "hat" (age 2.1), the action of putting on the garment adds to the meaning of the metaphor because that is what people do with hats, but not with underpants. This type of metaphor occurred between 0 and 4 times per month from ages 1.6 to 2.1. Metaphors with supporting action constituted 25% of the verbal metaphors. This category roughly corresponds to that labeled *nonpretend action* metaphors in the diary study by Winner (1979), who found them to be infrequent at all ages from 2.3 to 4.10 in the record of one child's play sessions recorded at home. The difference in these findings could be due to several causes. Perhaps such metaphors are used more frequently at the younger ages examined in the present study, or individual children may vary in their use of types of metaphor. Finally, the notable difference in sampling method could lead to detecting different types of metaphors at different rates. Event sampling across all contexts the child naturally encounters would more likely detect relatively infrequent types of metaphor than time sampling in one play context (as in Winner, 1979).

The verbal metaphors were categorized on the basis of event or stationary object resemblance with the expectation that event metaphors would be early and predominate in frequency. The frequencies of the two verbal types are reported in Figure 5 and the cumulative frequencies, in Figure 6. Surprisingly, event metaphors, such as calling floating dust motes "buggie" (when Cady knew they were dust; age 1.10) did not predominate

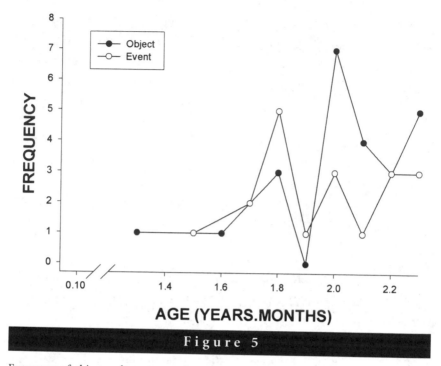

AGE (YEARS.MONTHS)

Figure 5

Frequency of object and event metaphors.

either in timing of occurrence or frequency. The earliest metaphors used reference to stationary objects as vehicles; event metaphors constituted 45% of the verbal metaphors. Event metaphors were more frequent than object metaphors only at ages 20 and 21 months.

Quite remarkably, the findings on action and event metaphors are not consistent either with expectations based on previous experimental results and theory based on direct perception (Dent, 1984; Dent & Rosenberg, 1990), nor with previous diary work based on Piagetian approaches to the development of symbolization (Winner, 1979). Experimental work with children ages 4–10 showed that they detected metaphoric resemblance more frequently when action was the resemblance (e.g., ballerina spinning, top spinning) and that they used more metaphors, and metaphors with action vehicles, when the ground of the metaphor was action. Also, young children were more likely to comprehend visual metaphors by talking about them, using verbal metaphors when action was the ground (i.e., the resemblance between topic and vehicle objects). Even the youngest children participating in these experimental studies were between 3 and 4 years older than the child in the diary study; results from that age group do not seem to carry back to the very early phases of metaphor development, at least for this child. This is the case even though action should be even more important for children just beginning to use language than for those more developed in their thinking and language use.

The other diary study found a predominance of pretend-action metaphors starting at age 2.3 and declining to age 4.10 (Winner, 1979). The definition of this type of metaphor was the renaming of substitute objects in play. Whereas action was always involved, according to the distinctions developed in the present study, many of these verbalizations were not metaphors. Thus, the results of the two studies are difficult to com-

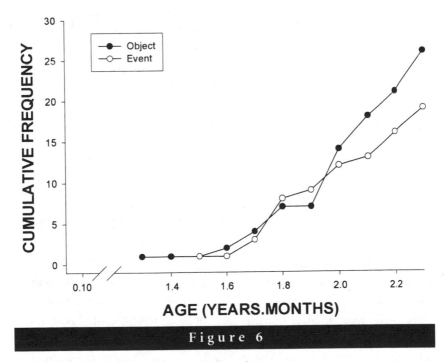

Figure 6

Cumulative frequency of object and event metaphors.

pare. Using the definition of renaming during pretend play for metaphor would result in a higher count than the more restricted definition used in the present study, in which the topic is commented on metaphorically rather than renamed for the purposes of pretend. Most likely the subset of utterances in the time-sampled record that might be metaphoric by our definition would have predicted a lower rate of action and event metaphors than would the data based on pretend.

The form of the verbal metaphors in these data was always a single word, the vehicle. Compound names, such as *moondeedas* (moonSanta Claus; age 2.0) for a Christmas ornament showing a profile of Santa Claus in a moon-sliver shape, are novel in English (although used in Icelandic and Old Norse poetry) but are linguistically simple. Compound names, however, did not predominate and did not occur at the earliest ages. They occurred four times between ages 2.0 and 2.1; for example, a picture of a girl with flowers in her hair elicited "flowerhat" (age 2.0), and a puffy red heart ornament elicited "appleheart" (age 2.1). Action metaphors most often consisted of nouns as vehicles and sometimes as action words. Four of the 18 event metaphors used action vehicles (e.g., the cup leaking called "peein" and the horse pacing called "dancing"). All the metaphors in this sample occurred before the child used the word *like* to mean similar, thus all preceded the use of similes.

The frequency of overextension shows a similar curve to that of metaphor (see Figure 1). Cady overextended words 3 months later than she first used metaphor, and she used overextensions slightly more frequently than metaphor at ages 1.8–1.10. For example, at age 2.1 she said, "open it," wanting to get a flat magnet off the refrigerator. Both metaphors and overextensions were, of course, much less frequent than literal language.

Analysis of the entries identified as pretend showed that the first instance of pretend occurred at age 1.1; Cady pretended to eat a wooden apple, not following through with the bite as she would for a real apple. Other early instances are blowing on a whistle, playing with a stuffed frog and then putting the whistle to the frog's mouth, and saying "ress" (rest) when pretending to sleep. Other examples that include utterances that might appear metaphoric actually involve extended sets of actions that create a scene or narrative, and within the scene the utterances are used to rename the objects used. For example, at age 2.1 Cady was playing with some coins and blankets on the bed. She said, "moneys . . . money sleep." Mother looked at her and said, "what are they doing?" and Cady said, "sleeping." Mother went over to see, picked up a corner of the blanket, and whispered, "sleeping, sleeping." Note that the reaction of the listener was to play along and that this was accepted and elaborated on by the child. In addition, there is no ground or resemblance between coins and animate beings that sleep. The coins are small objects that afford covering with blankets and therefore substituting for dolls, or real beings, in this pretend play scene.

Conclusions

The present study documents metaphor use 1 year earlier in development than in any previous study. Indeed, metaphors occurred not long after the beginning of language production (5 months after the first word). This early use of metaphor could be because the child we studied is precocious in her language use. When mean length of utterance (MLU) measures and examples of syntax used at various ages are analyzed, her development can be compared with others to determine her similarity to children in general on this variable. Another possible explanation is that the child's mother, the prinicple investigator, may use metaphor more frequently than most parents. This explanation is difficult to disprove. The diary data on metaphors used around the child have not yet been tabulated and scored. If results show a close association between types of metaphor the child heard and types she used, the role of specific language experience in the early ontogenesis of metaphor will be clearer. If, on the other hand, Cady's younger sibling shows less use of metaphor, even though she will likely have heard more from three family members than Cady did from two, this will suggest that the frequency of metaphors in the environment cannot account completely for Cady's early use of metaphor.

At least for this child, the types of metaphor produced did not correspond to expectations for early metaphors; the earliest metaphors did not tend to be action only or event based. Verbal metaphors with supporting action, previously termed *enactive* metaphors (Winner, 1979), also did not predominate in frequency or in proportion. Thus, neither the ecological approach nor the traditional Piagetian approach predicted what this child did with early metaphors. Longitudinal and naturalistic evidence from several more children is needed to understand the implications of these results for a general account of metaphor. Perhaps children who are more focused on objects than people at an early age come to understand objects metaphorically, whereas others may be more focused on actions and events. These two different foci have been the topic of a great deal of research in language and are also found in studies of social interaction (Fogel, 1997, this volume). Future reports of the diary study (Dent-Read & Szokolszky, 1997) will include data across children and across languages; perhaps a more complete picture of the role of events in metaphor development will emerge.

Finally, pretend actions and utterances, which Cady was developing at the same time as metaphor, do not seem to fit the frame "notice the *y*ness of *x*," that is, the metaphoric frame. For example, when Cady pretended to take a bite out of a wooden apple, the action was not metaphoric because the necessary condition of metaphoric resemblance across kinds was not met. In this situation there is only one kind of object, an apple (although the one being acted on is a *pretend* apple). The pretend wooden apple affords pretend biting. The imaginal perception of real apples may have been involved in this pretend action in that biting was the action used in pretense as opposed to mouthing. A small wooden object would most likely afford mouthing or actual biting, whereas the wooden *apple* guided pretend biting. These data support the conclusion that the seeing-as process is different for pretend than metaphor and that these two abilities develop in parallel.

The data on early metaphor use indicate that metaphor is a basic aspect of language that at least some children use almost as early as they use words. The use of words in a metaphoric way to guide one's own or another's attention in such a way that one thing is seen as another seems to be a primary use of language that even toddlers find important or interesting. The fact that the results on verbal rather than action, and object rather than event metaphors were the opposite of what was predicted points out the importance of these unique data on the earliest use of metaphor in natural settings recorded by a participant observer. Thus, this method newly applied to the topic of metaphor yields surprising results that may change the theory developed to account for them.

MAJOR QUESTIONS ABOUT DEVELOPMENT

What Develops and How?

A central question in developmental research is what develops and how. In ontogeny metaphors come from the increasingly differentiated perception of kinds and the resemblances across kinds, coupled with abilities to use language to draw the listener's attention to those resemblances (Dent-Read & Szokolszky, 1993). The perceptual ability to detect invariants specifying kinds and cross-kind resemblances develops first. That is, with increased experience, the child is able to attune to more subtle and higher order types of metaphoric resemblances. Using and understanding metaphor, however, goes beyond noticing resemblances. Thus, with regard to metaphor, what develops is the perceptual ability to detect resemblances across kinds, for example, snakes and winding roads, and the added perceptual ability to see one thing as another, to notice the vehicleness of the topic, for example, the snakiness of curvy roads. In relation to verbal metaphor, what develops is the ability to detect correspondences between words and their referents, and to use words to comment metaphorically. The data presented herein indicate that the understanding or use of the comparison term *like* is not necessary for the use of verbal metaphor. These abilities develop through experience with the world that continuously differentiates and elaborates, bringing the perceiver in contact with more of the world and with more general (usually termed *abstract*) aspects of the world.

To make these statements more concrete, I discuss three specific metaphors in terms of differentiation or elaboration, and in terms of the idea of organism–environment mutuality, which are ideas central to an ecological realist theory of perceiving and knowing. First, some metaphors are expressed at a simple level by young children, and the same metaphors are used by adults in a richer, more elaborated way. For example, Cady at the age of 3 years, 3 months, held a piece of broccoli vertically on the table and said "like a tree." A corresponding adult version of this metaphor is the title of a cook book and a particular dish, namely, *The Enchanted Broccoli Forest* (Katzen, 1982). The broccoli has become a complex, multipart main course dish, and the tree has become a forest.

Another example again comes from Cady, who at age 1 year, 8 months, said, "booboo," (scratch or minor wound) while pointing to the embroidered red mouth on a stuffed doll. Previous usage showed that she knew the meaning of "mouth" and "booboo" literally. An adult usage comes from a poem by Adrienne Rich entitled "Meditations for a Savage Child" (Rich, 1973, p. 59) which includes the lines

> When I try to speak
> my throat is cut
>
> . . .
>
> Yet always the tissue
> grows over, white as silk
>
> hardly a blemish,
> maybe a hieroglyph for a scream
>
> . . .

Here the metaphor is of the mouth as wound (the scar tissue is a "hieroglyph for a scream"). Although the differences between the one-word utterance "booboo" about a mouth and an extended poem are the focus here, it is interesting to note that in both cases, the topic, mouth, is only pointed to. In the first case the 18-month-old pointed with her finger; in the poem by a very accomplished poet, the line "hieroglyph for a scream" points to the mouth because it entails a mouth. The word *hieroglyph* also highlights the connection of perceiving and language: Written words are traces of experience in much the way a scar is a trace of a wound. In any case, the poem is an extremely differentiated, elaborated, and socially sophisticated version of the simple, primitive metaphor of the mouth as wound.

A final example shows the elaboration of a metaphor by an individual with development. I refer here to Cady's first metaphor, which was described at the beginning of the chapter. Recall that she said "wawa" (water) while pointing at a large skylight showing a blue sky, and then, 2 years later, "the sky looks like the sea when I look through the myroscope." The sky as water metaphor has developed from one word, the vehicle, to a full sentence with topic and vehicle verbalized. In addition, the vehicle or metaphoric term has become more precise—*sea* expresses the vast openness in a way *water* does not necessarily. This development may be a case of a change in the physical environment resulting in a change in the organism–environment system and, thus, development of the system. That is, the second metaphor was used shortly after moving from Connecticut to southern California, from a place of thick forest to a place of wide open skies. The vistas available had changed and this new environment may have led to the change in Cady's understanding of her environment and the utterance of a metaphor to comment on the sky.

Issues Confronted by the Direct Realist Ecological Approach

The direct realist ecological approach to development, as applied to metaphor, confronts the issue of how speakers and listeners are in contact with the world, either by perceiving the ambient array (E. Gibson, 1997, this volume; J. Gibson, 1979) or the structured correspondences of utterances and the world (Dent, 1990; Dent-Read, 1993; Zukow-Goldring, 1997, this volume). The only other ecologically related approaches to language that can serve as a contrast are the experiential theory of metaphor (Johnson, 1987) and some work on a dynamic systems approach to the lexicon (e.g., McCune, 1992) and to language in general (Tucker & Hirsch-Pasek, 1993). These approaches are ecological in a general sense because they focus on bodily experience (Johnson, 1987) and on the organism–environment system (McCune, 1992; Tucker & Hirsch-Pasek, 1993). Both of these approaches, however, maintain that the organism is not directly in contact with the environment, contra direct perception theory. Rather, experience must be constructed, or knowledge of the world must be obtained by means of a symbolic mental model. Thus, the direct realist approach answers questions about how organisms are actually in contact with the environment and, therefore, can exist in a mutuality with it. Because the organism and environment are in contact, changes in one automatically result in organized changes in the other—the definition of mutuality.

The experiential theory of metaphor takes as basic the human organism's experience in the world and what is general or shared in that experience. But the theory maintains that experience must be structured to make sense of the world. The process of metaphor is one of constructing a mental schema and then projecting it onto other domains. The role of experience in all knowing is central to both the direct realist approach and the phenomenological one; however, the definition of experience differs radically between the two theories.

The dynamic systems approach to language has been applied to the development of the early lexicon in order to analyze what subsystems are involved in learning to use language and how the use of language differs depending on which subsystem is not yet functioning fully (McCune, 1992). The ideas from dynamic systems theory may be valuable for solving some classic problems in language acquisition. For example, the idea of phase shift (a probabilistic discontinuity) may be helpful in deciding when a child is verbal, and the idea of subsystems that interact in different ways may aid in explaining individual differences in learning to use language. Dynamic systems ideas of developmental changes consisting of phase shifts from one steady state to another, and of change engendered by changing variables in the context, have also been applied to the traditional categories of phonology, semantics, and syntax in language with some guidelines about future research (Tucker & Hirsch-Pasek, 1993). However, some assumptions usually made in dynamic systems work are problematic. Specifically, most work in dynamic systems assumes that actions are assembled out of dynamics that already exist, and this is done by matching the body's dynamics to the information available through perception. Thus, the basic idea is that perception provides some information that is then acted on or used by some other process, rather than the direct perception idea that perceiving is contact with the world that continually guides action and is guided by action. As a consequence of this assumption, some dynamic systems work does not confront the problems with a mental representation approach to knowing. That is, the assumption that knowledge consists of mental representation is not questioned. In the case of the dynamic explanation of the lexicon, Piaget's idea of schemes constitutes the mental model; in the work on language in general innate knowledge of grammatical rules is the mental model. Problems with mental representation explanations are confronted in the direct realist approach to knowing, providing us with a way to begin to extend the theory from traditional topics in perception to other areas of knowing, such as language.

Limitations of the Direct Realist Approach

I assert that most developmental work, and probably most adult work, on direct perception has focused on the organism rather than the organism–environment mutuality. This is certainly true of my experimental work with metaphor. Development has been seen as consisting of changes that take place in the organism, due to experience, but still within the organism. Even in the naturalistic study reported herein, hypotheses specifically about mutuality and, in the case of metaphor, its relation to seeing as are lacking, and interpretation of results in terms of mutualities is just beginning. The challenge is to define development of a mutuality, a system, and place that definition within the context of learning and maturation, the traditional triumvirate in developmental psychology. My current approach is to propose that perceiving and knowing are relations of organisms to their environment and that development consists of the relations differentiating and elaborating. Because learning (J. Gibson & E. Gibson, 1955) and maturation are both processes of differentiation and elaboration (Oyama, 1985), they reduce to development.

Applied to the development of metaphor this approach leads to analyzing the process of seeing as, not only in relation to seeing but also in relation to the idea that organisms exist only as part of a system. That is, seeing as is a change in a system that results in a more elaborated relation between organism and environment and an organism more specifically attuned to the environment.

Questions: Irrelevant, Revised, and New

In the direct realist approach to the development of knowing, questions of how the child constructs a mental world—or knows the world by means of a mental model or theory of mind—are irrelevant. Questions of how action is internalized to allow accurate perception and thinking are irrelevant. Action is not internalized, but performed; knowing and thinking are types of action. Questions of how brain states or functions determine abilities or development are irrelevant. Brain states or processes do not determine perceiving, acting, or knowing, although the brain as part of the perception–action system supports perceiving, acting, and knowing. One cannot know or act without a brain, but it does not follow that the brain causes or determines acting and knowing. From a dynamic systems point of view, brain states or functions are part of the functioning of the system and can be important to understanding the system, for example, of coordinated limb movement. From a direct perception mutuality point of view, brain functioning is part of the functioning of the perception system, but not a privileged part. For example, the head, hand, and eye are as much a part of that perceptual system as is the brain, and as crucial to adaptive functioning; no part is both necessary and sufficient. The actions of the organism as it explores or performs in its natural environment is the topic of study, and brain functioning is a correlate of such overt action but does not explain it.

Questions about how the organism changes (or changes in response to the environment) or responds to aspects of the environment are revised to take into account the idea that organism and environment are complements. The idea of mutuality (J. Gibson, 1979) is entirely different from any ideas of interaction, reciprocal influence, or feedback because it focuses on the complementarity of organism and environment and the fact that the two do not exist without each other, not just that they are two separate elements that somehow interact or influence each other. For example, "the words *animal* and *environment* make an inseparable pair. Each term implies the other. No animal could exist without an environment surrounding it. Equally, although not so obvious, an environment implies an animal (or at least an organism) to be surrounded." (J. Gibson, 1979, p. 8).

Clearly, even J. Gibson (1979) used some of these terms, such as *complementary* and *reciprocal*, interchangeably, but that should be clarified. The dictionary meaning of *mutual* is an interchange of some kind between persons or things; *reciprocal* indicates a relation in which one act is given in return for another; and a *complement* is something that completes. Direct perceiving is what allows the organism to be in contact with the environment and, therefore, what allows the organism and environment to complement or complete each other forming the system that they do. Thus, researchers must revise questions of how children, or even social or cultural groups, develop to ask how child–environment systems develop, using both the social and nonsocial meanings of *environment.*

The new questions that emerge given the mutuality, direct realist approach include the following: If perceiving and knowing consist in coordinating one's self to one's environment, how does this coordination develop? Effective actions change with growth and experience, but how does one describe the orderliness of this change? What helps or hinders an organism's ability to coordinate with its environment—that is, what supports or sustains development as well as what constrains it? If the genes and innate ideas are not the source of form and organization in behavior and knowing, what is?

The point of this chapter is not only to ask these new questions but also to suggest ways in which answers may be found. The answers will come from researching the consequences for knowing in general, and for using language in particular, if perceiving is direct and reciprocal with acting. Metaphor in action and language, as it emerges out of ongoing coordination with the physical environment and with other people, offers a unique opportunity to understand how seeing becomes seeing as.

REFERENCES

Altman, J. (1974). Observational study of behavior: Sampling methods. *Behaviour*, *49*, 227–267.

Billow, R. M. (1981). Observing spontaneous metaphor in children. *Journal of Experimental Child Psychology*, *31*, 430–445.

Dent, C. (1984). The developmental importance of motion information in perceiving and describing metaphoric similarity. *Child Development*, *55*, 1607–1613.

Dent, C. (1987). Comprehending concrete metaphors: Developing an understand of topic–vehicle interaction. In K. Nelson & A. van Kleeck (Eds.), *Children's language* (Vol. 6, pp. 213–228). Hillsdale, NJ: Erlbaum.

Dent, C., & Ledbetter, P. (1986). Facilitating children's recall of metaphor in text using films of natural objects and events. *Human Development*, *29*, 231–235.

Dent, C., & Rosenberg, L. (1990). Visual and verbal metaphor: Developmental interactions. *Child Development*, *61*, 983–994.

Dent, C., & Zukow, P. (Guest eds.). (1990). An ecological approach to language development: An alternative functionalism. [Special issue]. *Developmental Psychobiology*, *23*, 679–703.

Dent-Read, C. (1993, August). A realist theory of language development. Paper presented at the International Society for Ecological Psychology, Vancouver, BC.

Dent-Read, C., Klein, G., & Eggleston, R. (1994). Metaphor in visual displays designed to guide action. *Metaphor and Symbolic Activity*, *9*, 211–232.

Dent-Read, C., & Szokolszky, A. (1993). Where do metaphors come from? *Metaphor and Symbolic Activity*, *8*, 227–242.

Dent-Read, C., & Szokolszky, A (1995a). The affordances of metaphoric resemblance and visual metaphors: Metaphor in action and language. Manuscript in preparation.

Dent-Read, C., & Szokolszky, A. (1995b). The development of metaphor: Kinds, resemblances, and contexts. Manuscript in preparation.

Dent-Read, C., & Szokolszky, A. (1997). *The natural history of metaphor: A cross-linguistic diary study*. Manuscript submitted for publication.

Dore, J., Franklin, M. B., Miller, R. T., & Ramer, A. L. H. (1976). Transitional phenomena in early language acquisition. *Journal of Child Language*, *3*, 343–350.

Gibson, E. (1982). The concept of affordances in development: The renascence of functionalism. In W. A. Collins (Ed.), *Minnesota Symposia on Child Psychology: Vol. 15. The concept of development* (pp. 55–81). Hillsdale, NJ: Lawrence Erlbaum.

Gibson, E., (1988). Exploratory behavior in the development of perceiving, acting, and the acquiring of knowledge. *Annual Review of Psychology, 39*, 1–41.

Gibson, E., & Spelke, E. (1983). Development of perception. In P. H. Mussen (Series ed.), *Handbook of child psychology*: Vol. 3. New York: Wiley.

Gibson, J. (1966). *The senses considered as perceptual systems.* Boston: Houghton Mifflin.

Gibson, J. (1979). *The ecological approach to visual perception.* Boston: Houghton Mifflin.

Gibson, J., & Gibson, E. (1955). Perceptual learning: Differentiation or enrichment? *Psychological Review, 62*, 32–41.

Hudson, J., & Nelson, K. (1984). Play with language: Overextensions as analogies. *Journal of Child Language, 11*, 337–346.

Johnson, M. (1987). *The body in the mind: The bodily basis of meaning, imagination, and reason.* Chicago: University of Chicago Press.

Karmiloff-Smith, A. (1992). *Beyond modularity: A developmental perspective on cognitive science.* Cambridge, MA: The MIT Press.

Katzen, M. (1982). *The enchanted broccoli forest.* Berkeley, CA: Ten Speed Press.

Keenan, E., & Schieffelin, B. (1976). Topic as a discourse notion: A study of topic in the conversations of children and adults. In C. Li (Ed.), *Subject and topic* (pp. 335–384). New York: Academic Press.

Kennedy, J. (1982). Metaphor in pictures. *Perception, 11*, 589–605.

Lakoff, G. (1987). *Women, fire, and dangerous things.* Chicago: University of Chicago Press.

Mace, W. (1977). James Gibson's strategy for perceiving: Ask not what's inside your head but what your head is inside of. In R. Shaw & J. Bransford (Eds.), *Perceiving, acting and knowing: Toward an ecological psychology* (pp. 43–66). Hillsdale, NJ: Lawrence Erlbaum.

Malcolm, N. (1977). *Memory and mind.* Ithaca, NY: Cornell University Press.

Marjanovic-Shane, A. (1989). "You are a pig": For real or just pretend? Different orientations in play and metaphor. *Play and Culture, 2*, 225–234.

McCune, L. (1992). First words: A dynamic systems view. In C. Ferguson, L. Menn, & C. Stoel-Gammon (Eds.), Phonological development: Models, research, implications (pp. 313–336). Baltimore, MD: York Press.

Mervis, C. B., Mervis, C. A., Johnson, K. E., & Bertrand, J. (1992). Studying early lexical development: The value of the systematic diary method. In C. Rovee-Collier & L. Lipsitt (Eds.), *Advances in infancy research* (Vol. 7, pp. 291–378). Norwood, NJ: Ablex Publishing.

Michaels, C., & Carello, C. (1981). *Direct perception.* New York: Prentice-Hall.

Nelson, K. (1973). Structure and strategy in learning to talk. *Monographs of the Society for Research in Child Development, 38*(1–2, Serial No. 149).

Ortony, A. (Ed.). (1979). *Metaphor and thought.* New York: Cambridge University Press.

Oyama, S. (1985). *The ontogeny of information: Developmental systems and evolution.* Cambridge, England: Cambridge University Press.

Pick, A., & Heinrichs, M. (1989, July). Perceptual learning in conceptual development. Paper presented at the Fifth International Conference on Event Perception and Action, Miami University, Oxford, OH.

Reed, E. (1987). Why ideas are not in the mind: An introduction to ecological epistemology. In A. Shimony & D. Nails (Eds.), *Naturalistic epistemology* (pp. 215–229).

Reed, E. (1995). The ecological approach to language development: A radical solution to Chomsky's and Quine's problem. *Language and Communication, 15,* 1–29.

Rescorla, L. (1980). Overextension in early language development. *Journal of Child Language, 7,* 321–335.

Rich, A. (1973). *Diving into the wreck.* New York: W. W. Norton and Company.

Sachs, J. (1993). The emergence of intentional communication. In Gleason, B. (Ed.), *The development of language* (3rd. ed, pp. 37–60). Columbus, OH: Charles E. Merrill.

Searle, J. (1979). Metaphor. In A. Ortony (Ed.), *Metaphor and thought* (pp. 83–111). New York: Cambridge University Press.

Sharratt, P. (1993). *A theoretical view of the relationship between metaphor production and pretend play in early child development.* Unpublished manuscript.

Smitsman, A., van Loosbroek, E., & Pick, A. (1987). The primacy of affordances in categorization by children. *British Journal of Developmental Psychology, 5,* 265–273.

Szokolszky, A. (1995). *Using one object as if it were another: The perception and use of affordances in pretend object play.* Unpublished doctoral dissertation, University of Connecticut, Storrs.

Tucker, M., & Hirsch-Pasek, K. (1993). Systems and language: Implications for acquisition. In L. Smith & E. Thelen (Eds.), *A dynamic systems approach to development: Applications* (pp. 359–384). Cambridge, MA: MIT press.

Turvey, M. (1992). The ecological approach to cognition: Invariants of perception and action. In H. Pick, P. Van den Broek, & D. Knill (Eds.), *Cognitive psychology: Conceptual and methodological issues* (pp. 85–117). Washington, DC: American Psychological Association Books.

Turvey, M., Shaw, R., Reed, E., & Mace, W. (1981). Ecological laws of perceiving and acting: In reply to Fodor and Pylyshyn (1981). *Cognition, 9,* 237–304.

Verbrugge, R. (1980). Transformation in knowing: A realist view of metaphor. In R. Honeck & R. Hoffman (Eds.), *Cognition and figurative language* (pp. 87–126). Hillsdale, NJ: Lawrence Erlbaum.

Verbrugge, R. R. (1985). Language and event perception: Steps toward a synthesis. In W.W. Warren, Jr., & R. E. Shaw (Eds.), *Persistance and change* (pp. 157–194). Hillsdale, NJ: Lawrence Erlbaum.

Vosniadou, S. (1987). Children and metaphors. *Child Development, 58,* 870–885.

Weinberg, R. (1987). The case against gene sequencing. *The Scientist, 1,* 11.

Wilcox, S., & Katz, S. (1981). The ecological approach to development: An alternative to cognitivism. *Journal of Experimental Child Psychology, 32,* 247–263.

Winner, E. (1979). New names for old things: The emergence of metaphoric language. *Journal of Child Language, 6,* 469–491.

Winner, E. (1988). *The point of words.* Cambridge, MA: Harvard University Press.

Winner, E., McCarthy, M., & Gardner, H. (1980). The ontogenesis of metaphor. In R. Honeck & R. Hoffman (Eds.), *Cognition and figurative language.* Hillsdale, NJ: Erlbaum.

Zukow, P. (1990). Socio-perceptual basis for the emergence of language: An alternative to innatist approaches. *Developmental Psychobiology, 23,* 705–726.

Zukow-Goldring, P., & Ferko, K. (1997). An ecological approach to the emergence of the lexicon: Socializing attention. In V. John-Steiner, C. Panofsky, & L. Smith (Eds.), *Sociocultural approaches to language and literacy: Interactionist perspectives* (pp. 170–190). New York: Cambridge University Press.

Comment on Dent-Read

Katherine A. Loveland

Cathy Dent-Read's chapter on the development of metaphor in young children embraces a variety of thorny topics with which ecological psychology is currently struggling. She argues that a direct realist approach can be used to describe language, that language is a directly perceivable event that exists in relation to the mutuality of organism and environment (Dent, 1990). This view has the implication that language can be studied in much the same way as other events, as a dynamic part of the perception–action cycle. The advantage to this view, from the direct realist perspective, is that it removes the need to make reference to mental structures of any kind when explaining language. Dent-Read's discussion of the direct realist view of language and its application to the study of metaphor raises a number of important issues.

Dent-Read's choice of metaphor as a topic of study is significant, because metaphor stands at one of the clearest intersections between language and perception. In the development of metaphor, one can see the child's growing ability to use language to capture and make available to

---

Loveland comments on Dent-Read from an ecological realist perspective.

someone else her or his perception that two things or actions share invariance. Dent-Read's approach to distinguishing metaphor from pretend is particularly welcome because of the tendency of those working within a cognitivist approach to conflate metaphor with pretend and to interpret any nonliteral activity by young children as pretend play based on symbolic mental activity.

The distinction between metaphor and pretend is conceptually elegant, but may, as Dent-Read notes, be difficult to apply empirically. In the example of the 2-year-old who sits on her step stool and rocks back and forth and says "I riding," Dent-Read classifies this activity as pretend, because it is not designed to point out anything about the stool, which merely stands in for the horse. However, the child's choice of the stool is not accidental. The stool shares *affordances* with the horse in that it is "sit-on-able" by the child, and it affords a ridinglike motion. Thus, although one may infer that the child's intent is not exploratory but performatory in nature (i.e., she is not doing this to tell something about the stool but to enact her imaginary play about the horse), her activity nonetheless entails the perception and communication of something shared between the stool and the horse. Similarly, the example (Dent-Read, this volume, Table 2) in which a block is called a "yummy cookie" by a child who pretends to eat it shows that the child has chosen the block for its ability to be acted on in some of the ways that one might act on a cookie. Thus, despite their differences, metaphor and pretend share a basis in the perception of real, and meaningful, commonalities between things or actions. Dent-Read alludes to this sharing of affordances in pretend play in her discussion of the "sleeping" coins, wherein the ability of the coins to be covered up with blankets allows them to be substituted for dolls or people.

Another question concerns how the concept of affordances fits within the larger framework of a direct realist account of language. What do language events afford us? Real communicative events are usually embedded in social interaction that embraces much more than simply *language*. When two people converse, for example, there is a complex and dynamic relation between the two that involves mutuality on many levels. Those aspects of communication traditionally called *metalinguistic* (e.g., intonation, rhythm, and rate of speech; gesture) co-occur with language events and are not really separable from them, much as the workings of the eye are not separable from the orienting of the head in the visual perception system. Nor are dyad-specific behaviors, such as postural accommodations, or culturally significant objects, events, and relationships (e.g., a job interview situation) separable from the language events with which they occur. Thus, we should broaden our approach to thinking about the affordances of language events and begin to think about the affordances of *communicative events* that occur on several levels and across more than one modality. In general these afford information not only about a topic of discussion (semantic content) but also about the speaker (or writer) performing the act, the listener (or reader), their relationship, and the sociocultural context in which they are embedded. Communicative events function to help us to perceive what the world, particularly other people, affords us.

Dent-Read's finding that metaphor can be present very early in life is intruiging. Although her results do not permit conclusions about the developmental sequence of acquiring various types of metaphorical skills, they do suggest that even very young children are interested in pointing out or commenting on shared invariance between things or actions and that with development the use of metaphor becomes increasingly differentiated and elaborated. The finding that it is not necessary first to have mastered the term *like* to carry out metaphor helps underscore the point that metaphor is not only a symbolic–representational process but may also be a basic and early-developing way of knowing. Research on joint attention between parent and child has shown the importance of directing and being directed to the important features of the human environment. Without the ability to share in joint attention with others, the child lacks a key means of access to adult perceptions of what is important, interesting, connected, and so forth. In the case of children with autism, just this sort of failure of joint attention is thought to occur (Loveland, 1991). Interestingly, although children with autism can sometimes use joint attention strategies to request, they are particularly unlikely to point out things in the environment to others, to simply comment on them. Thus, one would predict that metaphor—as a way of pointing out shared invariance between things—might be rare in verbal children with autism. The failure to engage in this way of knowing may in turn contribute to the difficulty children with autism have in coming to know the human world in ways that are shared with others and the tendency they have to be poorly acculturated. Because the study of metaphor offers a window on the child's developing understanding of the human environment, it has great potential to illuminate the study of both normal and abnormal development.

REFERENCES

Dent, C. (1990). An ecological approach to language development: An alternative functionalism [Special issue]. *Developmental Psychobiology, 23*, 679–703.

Loveland, K. (1991). Social affordances and interaction: Autism and the affordances of the human environment. *Ecological Psychology, 3*, 99–119.

9

The Development of Tool Use: Changing Boundaries Between Organism and Environment

A. W. Smitsman

Tool use has evolved in humans at a scale that surpasses that of any other species. It has reshaped and continues to reshape the environment in which children grow up, but it also alters the action potential of the human body. The potential of humans for perceiving and acting evolves with the evolution of implements for perceiving and acting. Both processes influence one another. This evolution concerns individuals and society as a whole, including the children who grow up in a particular society. In Western society implements are available for nearly every activity. These implements form an essential component of the skills and knowledge children obtain and should obtain with age. Tool use is the road for transmitting insights from older to younger generations and from experts to novices.

The significant role tool use plays in the transmission of skills and knowledge among individuals makes the study of tool use highly relevant to anyone interested in development. Questions about how development takes place and what causes it warrant careful investigation of the fundamental role tool use plays in and among individuals. It is therefore remarkable that tool use was rarely studied by developmentalists. A major interest in the study of tool use concerned not the activity itself; it stemmed from the hope of unraveling cognitive mechanisms that would differentiate human or primate intelligence from that of lower species (see, e.g., van Leeuwen, Smitsman, & van Leeuwen, 1994). Scientists were mainly interested in hypothetical higher order problem-solving functions of the brain that might explain differences in tool use among species. Although the architecture of the human prehensile system is far more advanced and consequently more adapted for tool use than that of any other species including primates (Jouffroy, 1993), study of this system has received very little attention, with few exceptions (Conally & Dalgleish, 1989; Newell, Scully, McDonald, & Baillargeon, 1989). Tool use remains beyond the scope of most research. Consequently, there has been little basic thinking about what happens to a person's body and its possibilities for perceiving and acting when an implement is added to that body. The ecological view on perception and action enables us to address such questions.

ECOLOGICAL VIEW OF TOOL USE

The ecological view that stems from the writings of J. J. Gibson and others (see, e.g., Michaels & Beek, 1995; Michaels & Carello, 1981) rests on a few core ideas. When the problem of tool use is approached from the ecological perspective, these ideas must be considered. The first idea is that with respect to an organism's behavior the organism and the environment form a unified system and not two separate entities. The unification of organism and environment entails more than just acknowledging that behavior is related to the environment or that the organism's behavior and the environment form interacting systems, as argued by Bronfenbrenner's ecological approach (see, e.g., Wachs, 1992). Many students of behavior acknowledge the existence of a relation between what an animal does and the environment within which the animal does it. The very notions of adaptation and context underscore the significance of a relation between the two. However, the idea of a unified system makes clear not just that a relation exists but that the environment itself forms part of the behavioral organization. The environment enables an organism to do things, just as feet enable a person to keep the body upright and to locomote.

J. J. Gibson (1979) used the example of tool use to clarify this fundamental notion of a unified system. The term *tool* expresses the fundamental notion that environmental entities may become temporarily part of the behavioral organization of an organism. However, the contribution of the environment to an organism's behavior is not confined to tool use. For instance, the resistance and rigidity of the ground on which a pedestrian walks is exploited by the movement organization of the limbs. In a manner of speaking, properties of the ground are used as a means to an end. They are not tools, however.

The second core idea is that perception and action form a unified system. One cannot act without perceiving, and one must act in order to perceive. Action exploits environmental properties, but perception enables an organism to become aware of the properties that have to be and are exploited. This union of perception and action forms the basis for the third core idea. The coupling of perception and action made J. J. Gibson (1977, 1979) realize that the environmental properties actors are aware of must have meaning to behavior in the first place. They are what the environment affords a person to do. Therefore, Gibson called the properties that are perceived under action *affordances*.

The concept of *affordance* is important to our understanding of tool use. J. J. Gibson (1979) used tool use as an example to clarify what he meant by affordances. In this way, both the concept of affordance and a fundamental property of tools were highlighted. One generally thinks about tools as objects and especially as a particular category of objects. The reason for this may be that in daily life some objects have that label. However, objects are not tools because they are conceived and labeled as tools. In J. J. Gibson's view (1979, pp. 40–41), tools are objects that can be attached to the body to fulfill specific functions. Attached to the body, tools extend the capacity of perceiving and acting, and they change the boundary between body and environment. A tool refers to the possibility for environmental entities to become temporarily part of the behavioral organization of an organism and to support behavior. It may be questioned whether this possibility confines itself to objects as Gibson suggested. According to Gibson, tools are graspable, transportable, and manipulable objects. Indeed, these affordances allow an object to be easily implemented into the arm–hand system. In my view, the use of implements is not confined to graspable objects; other forms of implementation include the use of symbolic media or the use of another person's actions and gestures to perform a task.

Tool use entails the implementation of environmental entities to the bodies of humans and animals. However, implementation by itself is insufficient for an object to become a tool. An object can be graspable and transportable but nevertheless useless as a tool. What else is needed to acknowledge a form of behavior as tool use? Psychologists, anthropologists, biologists, and palaeontologists have struggled with this question for years and still struggle with it (Berthelet & Chavaillon, 1993; Greenfield, 1991). However, their focus on internal cognitive mechanisms rather than the activity of tool use itself has led to answers that are more confusing than enlightening.

The focus on cognitive mechanisms has led to the view that tool use concerns not so much what a person does as the way a person conceives what he or she does. It has been proposed that a person must conceive an entity as a means to an end. For example, by the end of their first year of life, children love to drop objects on the ground. Some researchers (Bard, 1993) saw this activity as an example of tool use. Their idea was that children have discovered gravity and intentionally exploit this property as a means to get the object downwards. The child's intention would determine gravity to be used as a tool to let the object drop. The problem with this argument is that gravity concerns a property that cannot be manipulated by a child. Gravity cannot be varied.

Nevertheless, tossing reveals essential properties of tool use. Irrespective of whether a child tosses an object deliberately or not, a relation between the object and the ground is involved. Force is exerted on the ground at a distance, and this fact is revealed by the sound or hole that is created. Sound making, hole making, and tossing are coordinated. Because they are coupled, the child may discover how the ground can be acted on and eventually be changed at a distance. In tool use, the manipulation is directed at the relation between implement and environment. In grasping, the hand is the end–effector; in tool use, the end–effector is displaced from the hand to the implement. Major questions that should be addressed in the study of tool use and the way it develops are what happens to a child's action systems when an implement becomes part of a system and which affordances arise as a result of this change. Other questions concern the perceptual variables that enable persons to manipulate the relation between implement and environment and to discover and exploit new affordances.

It is often tacitly assumed that an implement that is added to a system continues to exist as an independent component with respect to the system. The complementary assumption is that an action system to which an implement is added does not change dynamically, and consequently that it also continues to exist the way it was before. That is, the dynamic effects of holding an object for the prehensile system are completely overlooked. Finally, it is assumed that implement and environment constitute separate components for which relations must be inferred. The widely shared idea that tool use involves a cognitive means–ends problem for the organism rests on these assumptions. These assumptions turn tool use into a mainly cognitive problem, namely, the problem of integrating information from three separate sources: tool–object, target–object, and body (Bates, Carlson-Luden, & Bretherton, 1980; Brown, 1990; Conally & Dalgleish, 1989; van Leeuwen et al., 1994; Parker & Gibson, 1977; Piaget, 1954).

In the next sections of this chapter, I examine the above assumptions in greater detail by presenting research conducted during the past years in collaboration with my students. This research addresses three related questions. The first question concerns young children's ability to perceive the instantaneous change that occurs in the relation or, more specifically, the fit between their bodies and the environment, when an object is attached to the body. Manipulation of the relation between an implement as the end–effector and an environmental object, the goal of tool use, requires attention to the spatial layout of objects, the functional relations that are supported by this layout, and the motion of the objects in space and time. Tools are implements, but they are also objects of a particular spatial layout and substance.

The second question concerns the ability of infants to perceive functional relations between objects given the spatial layout and motion of those objects and the perceptual variables that guide infant's perception of the functional relations that emerge in space over time. The third question concerns the relation to which young children's attention is directed when an object is attached to their prehensile system. Will their attention indeed concern the relation between implement and environmental objects or between implement and their own body? In other words, is the end–effector indeed displaced from the hand that holds the implement to the implement being held?

A final issue that I discuss concerns the consequences of the ecological view of tool use to theorizing on development. I argue that the study of tool use can lead to a new look on development. Instead of confining development to changes within the child, tool use shows that development involves changes with respect to both the child and the environment. Both are modified and as a consequence the relation between child and environment is modified as well. In closing, I argue that tool use and the evolution of tools within culture largely contribute to the modification of both the child and the environment.

TOOLS AS IMPLEMENTS

The hypothesis that implement and action system remain (or initially constitute) unrelated components that must be integrated is untenable from the perspective offered by the dynamic systems approach to movement coordination (Beek & Bingham, 1991; Kugler, Kelso, & Turvey, 1982; Michaels & Beek, 1995; Smith & Thelen, 1994; Thelen & Ulrich, 1991). According to this approach, task specific actions are assembled from the dynamical resources available to the action system. For the prehensile system, the resources concern metric and dynamical properties of the arm and shoulder (e.g., its length and inertial properties). A hand-held implement changes the underlying dynamics of the prehensile system instanta-neously as soon as it is grasped. The change concerns the system as a whole and forms the basis for the emergence of new action possibilities and the loss of existing ones. For example, an implement such as a hand-held rod of a certain length and mass changes the length of the arm as well as the inertial forces at the different linkages, such as the wrist, elbow, and shoul-der. The arm and hand feel differently and move differently when an ob-ject is held. When a stick of some length is held, the arm requires more space to move freely and moves more slowly. More muscle force is required to start and stop a movement, depending on the mass and length by which the implement has changed the arm. Solomon and Turvey's (Solomon & Turvey, 1988; Solomon, Turvey, & Burton, 1989) research on wielding shows that individuals feel how far the arm reaches in space when a rod is held and wielded. Reaching distance was felt on the basis of inertial forces that were caused by arm and rod. The hand-held rod formed an in-tegral part of the system, not because the rod was conceived that way, but just because it was held.

Thelen and Ulrich's (1991) research in infants also showed that young infants experience an instantaneous change caused by an implement. Moreover, their research indicated that such a change may involve the emergence of action possibilities that ordinarily occur later in develop-ment. Their research did not involve the prehensile system and grasping but the locomotory system and walking. They investigated infants' step-ping behavior on a treadmill. Infants were placed in an upright position on a rotating belt. The treadmill became functionally part of the infant's body as soon as the infant stood on this belt. Stepping behavior occurred in young infants who ordinarily show this behavior months later.

In Solomon and Turvey's (1988) research on wielding, the implement did not function as a tool, that is, the changed action system did not ex-ploit other environmental properties. Their research explains how imple-ments may affect the system, but not which affordances are perceived given that the system has been changed. Such would be the case if individuals were asked to use their rod-lengthened arm to displace other objects. Re-searchers who study the measurement of affordances have shown that affordances such as the sit-on-ableness of a chair (Mark, 1987), the pass-through-ableness of doors (Warren & Whang, 1987), and the step-on-ableness of stairs (Warren, 1984) can be expressed in terms of dimensionless variables. Body dimensions such as shoulder width and leg length provide a yardstick for the scientist to measure what environmental properties, such as door width and riser height, mean to behavior.

A conclusion that may be drawn from the above-mentioned affordance studies is that if, for example, shoulder width is instantaneously increased by a constant factor because of an implement, the pass-through-ableness of doors that individuals perceive is also increased by the same factor. In a study to investigate this hypothesis, we (Smitsman & Reinders, 1996) asked two groups of children (2–3 years and 3–4 years of age) to displace a plastic toy duck on a table in front of them (see Figure 1). The table on which the duck stood had a hole to the side of the duck. Below this gap was a water basin. When the duck was displaced toward the gap, it fell through the gap into the basin. To perform the task, children were

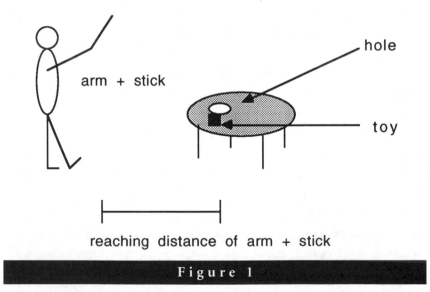

Figure 1

In walking toward the table, a person will stop at a certain distance from the table to push the toy into the hole by a hand-held stick. This distance is the reaching distance the person perceives for the arm plus the length of the stick.

asked to walk toward the table until they perceived the duck was within reach. They walked across a 2.00 × 0.75-meter-long path marked on both sides by ropes and with a grid structure on the floor. On their way toward the table, children were expected to stop as soon as the toy duck was at a comfortable reaching distance of their arm. Then they were expected to (further) extend their arm to touch the duck with the end of the stick and to displace it toward the gap. In walking toward the table, children were asked to hold the stick such that it extended upward from their waist. They were allowed to extend the stick in front of them toward the object as soon as they stopped. To perform the task, children were given a series of seven very light, easily graspable plastic sticks that varied in length from 10 centimeters to 70 centimeters in 10-centimeter increments. On one end of the stick, a place was marked for holding. Each child performed the task four times with each of the sticks and four times without a stick. We measured the place at the ground where each child stopped to extend the arm and the arm and body postures during performance of the task.

Distances from the place where a child stopped toward the place of the toy duck measured horizontally were regressed against stick length. These analyses on the scores of each of the children separately as well as the combined scores for each of the two age groups showed that perceived reaching distance increased linearly with stick length. Linear regressions of mean distances stopped and stick length were significant for both age groups ($\beta = .66$, $r = .85$, $p < .001$ for 2-year-olds, and $\beta = .81$, $r = .87$, $p < .001$ for 3-year-olds). Differences in slopes between the older and younger children were nonsignificant. Intercepts of the linear regressions ($y = .66\ x + 6.67$ for 2-year-olds, and $y = .81\ x + 6.48$ for 3-year-olds) reveal the reaching distance of a child's arm without a stick. Although older children were generally slightly taller than younger children, this difference was not revealed in a different intercept. The distance across which older children stretched their arm without a stick was comparable to the distance younger children stretched their arms. With a stick, perceived arm length increased linearly with stick length.

For both age groups, the mean stopping distance corresponded reasonably well with the actual increased arm length. Nevertheless, children

generally underestimated the increase for the longer sticks, as demonstrated by the slopes of the regressions equations. The reason for the underestimated arm length is unclear. It might be that children really mis-
perceived the available arm length in the case of longer sticks. It might
also mean that arm posture as well as arm length were taken into account.
Controlled displacement of the object on the table by arm movement may
require a less fully extended arm when the arm increases in length. Observation of arm postures indicated that children indeed extended their
arms less fully when the sticks were longer. However, further investigation
of whether, for example, dynamical length instead of metrical length was
perceived required that mass and moment of inertia be varied in addition
to stick length.

PERCEPTION OF FUNCTIONAL
RELATIONS BETWEEN OBJECTS

Guided by Newtonian physics and Cartesian thinking, we easily assume
that objects form the basic units of perception and action but that functional relations must be inferred from object properties and motion properties (see, e.g., Baillargeon, 1993; Spelke, 1994; Spelke, Breinlinger,
Macomber, & Jacobson, 1992). A function is often conceived as something
that is superimposed on objects. Indeed, a function is not a property that
an object owns, such as its outline and size. However, functions are not
superimposed on objects; they concern properties that objects share with
other objects. Functions are relations between objects that occur in space
over time. For example, "cutting" involves a cutting edge, a surface that
may be cut by this edge and a force that pushes the cutting edge through
the surface. A function involves a dynamic relation between the surfaces
and substances of objects.

The reason that people conceive of functions as superimposed entities is perhaps the striking unity and boundedness of objects. This unity
leads easily to the assumption that the outline of the object is all there is.
However, as J. J. Gibson (1979) clearly argued years ago, an object is not
just an outline but a relation of surfaces. When people perceive the unity

and boundedness of an object they perceive in fact a relation of surfaces. However, that is not the only relation that exists. Objects do not populate an empty space. They stay in front of, to the side of, or behind surfaces and are supported from below by surfaces. The interface between an object's outline and surrounding surfaces forms another arrangement, another relation. This relation concerns the spatial arrangement of an object's edges and surfaces with other objects, in front of, behind, or to the side of the object. The arrangement an object forms with surrounding objects and surfaces also has a shape just as the arrangement that forms the outline of the object (see J. J. Gibson, 1979, chapter 6). The difference between both is that the arrangement that forms the interface changes, whereas the arrangement that forms the outline stays the same as an object is displaced. The shape of the interface specifies the momentary function of an object. However, it also provides information about the outline of the object, as any artist knows. One may picture an object by only picturing its interface. When an object is displaced, the changing shape of the interface specifies the annihilation of existing functions and the emergence of new ones. The shape of the outline specifies only an object's identity. Thus, *shape* is a rather ambiguous term to describe objects. *Identity* and *function* would perhaps be better terms.

Research that Margriet Sitskoorn and I have conducted (Sitskoorn & Smitsman, 1995, 1994, in press) on infants' perception of objects indicates that perceiving an object's identity and perceiving its function are not necessarily different things: The one implies the other. We investigated infants' ability to perceive whether a block that descended toward the opening of a box would pass through the opening or would be obstructed and supported by the rims of this opening (see Figure 2). In different studies, we varied the size and path of approach of the descending object. Variation altered conditions that allowed for passing through into support and vice versa.

To perceive whether a descending object would pass through, the infant must see whether the opening provided sufficient room for the object. For a rigid opening and object, passing-through-able room depends both on the object's size and shape in relation to the opening's size and

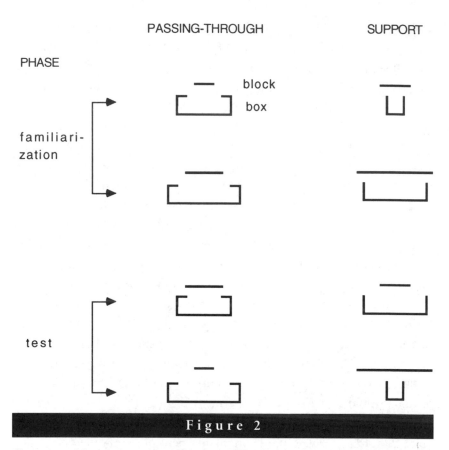

PASSING-THROUGH   SUPPORT

PHASE

familiari-
zation

block
box

test

Figure 2

Illustration of the relative width of a block and box opening on familiarization and test tri-als. On familiarization trials, passing through and support agreed with the widths of the block and the box opening. On test trials, passing through and support took place, irre-spective of the widths of the block and the opening. From "Infants' Perception of Dynamic Relations Between Objects: Passing Through or Support?," by M. M. Sitskoorn and A. W. Smitsman, 1995, *Developmental Psychology, 31.* Copyright 1995 by the American Psycho-logical Association.

shape and on the object's path of approach. The Cartesian view on ob-jects would predict that infants attend to object and motion variables sep-arately instead of attending to a collective variable that concerns the in-terface and that includes both the relevant object and motion variables. However, that is not what our results revealed. In one study, Sitskoorn and Smitsman (1995) found that from 6 months of age on, infants perceive whether the width of an opening to the width of a descending block allows the block to pass through this opening or to be supported by the rims of this opening. Using a preferential looking method, 6- to 12-month-old infants were familiarized to blocks that descended toward an open box placed below. In one experiment, a block passed through this opening and was subsequently lifted to its original position. In another experiment, motion of a block was obstructed by the rims leading to support by these rims. After that the block was lifted to its original position. On different familiarization trials two different combinations of block and opening width were shown: a relatively wide block in combination with a relatively wide opening and a small block in combination with a relatively small opening (see Figure 1). In the passing-through experiment, the wide block could not possibly pass through the small opening. In the support experiment the small block could not be supported by the rims of the wide opening.

On test trials the block–box combination was altered during familiarization. A wide block was combined with a small opening, and a small block was combined with a wide opening. However, in the passing-through experiment, passing-through was shown for both combinations. In the support experiment support was shown for both combinations. Results showed longer looking times on test trials where a wider block passed through the smaller opening or the motion of the smaller block was obstructed in midair at the level of the wider opening than on test trials where the outcome agreed with the relative width of block and opening. These results were obtained for 6-, 8-, and 12-month-old infants and were comparable to results of other studies such as those of Spelke et al. (1992).

In the study just described, a descending object always headed to the center of the opening. However, whether an object passes through an opening or becomes supported on the rims of this opening depends also on the object's precise heading toward an opening. Heading is a motion variable, of interest to the perception of functional relations. In a subsequent series of experiments, Sitskoorn and Smitsman (in press) varied the trajectory of the descending object (see Figure 3). Instead of aiming the descending object toward the center of the opening, trajectories were dis-

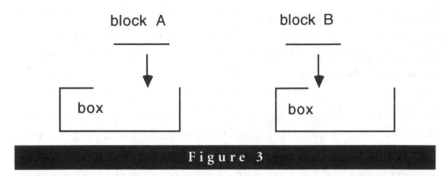

Figure 3

Particular headings of a block toward the opening of a box may generate ambiguous situations for infants to visually perceive what will happen. On descent, block A will occlude just the inside of the box, indicating that it can enter the opening. Block B will also generate this optical variable for "passing through," but only on its right side. On its left side, it continues to occlude a rim, indicating that it cannot unobstructedly pass through.

placed away from the center to the side of the opening. Nevertheless, displacement of trajectory affected neither the pass-through-ability of the object for infants who were familiarized with passing-through nor the possibility of becoming supported on rims for infants who were made familiar with support. On test trials, similarly displaced trajectories were shown. On some test trials, however, the block headed toward one side rim, instead of toward neither or both, and collided with this rim. On other test trials, the block headed as it did on familiarization trials. On both test trials the object entered the opening or became supported on the rim toward which it headed and with which it collided, depending on the event with which infants were made familiar. When colliding with a rim, it nevertheless miraculously passed through this rim or was supported by this rim. Contrary to the earlier obtained results, 6- and 9-month-old infants were not able to anticipate the event that would happen for the descending object. Only infants from 12 months of age were able to anticipate passing-through or support adequately.

What made infants believe that the event they were familiarized with would still happen although the direction of heading of the object could not possibly lead to this event? It is highly unlikely that their inability to discriminate differences in heading was the cause of their belief. Other studies have shown that even infants younger than 6 months of age are able to discriminate whether an object heads toward another object and will collide with it or not (Baillargeon, 1993). A more likely reason turned out to be the kind of optical variable infants attended to (see Figure 3). Generally, objects are put into openings of boxes or cups from above and the opening is below eye level. Occlusion of the rims and inside then take place before the object enters the opening. Occlusion is a higher order perceptual variable for the arrangement of surfaces that emerges for a descending object and an opening when an observer looks from above to the object. The optic variable includes object properties as well as motion properties. The occlusion pattern covaries precisely according to the size and shape of a descending object, its path of approach, and the size and shape of the opening. For example, any object that passes through an opening finally occludes only the inside of an opening. An object that collides with rims continues to occlude those rims. The changing occlusion pattern specifies whether entrance or collision with the rims of an opening will occur. In the heading experiment, variation in heading on test trials generated the optical variable for passing-through and the optical variable for collision with a rim at the same time, but at different places (see Figure 3). On one side the descending object headed toward the inside of the box and occluded only this inside. On the other side the object headed toward a rim and continued to occlude this rim on descent.

To investigate whether the optic variable infants used to perceive passing-through or support involved occlusion, the first study was replicated (Sitskoorn & Smitsman, 1994). Infants of 6, 8, 12, and 18 months of age were familiarized with events that concerned passing-through and support as in the earlier study. Familiarization and test trials involved variation in relative width of object and opening as in the earlier study. However, the test trials were presented on two different conditions. One group of infants of each age group perceived the test events, while a small screen on top of the front side of the box concealed how the bottom of descending block occluded the opening just before and during entrance. When the block passed behind this screen, it remained only partly visible because it was larger than the screen. The other group of infants perceived the events as in the earlier study, without a screen that concealed occlusion of the opening by the object. The results showed that the screen clearly affected infants' perception. None of the younger age groups were able to perceive whether the relative width of object and opening allowed for passing-through or support when a screen prevented infants from perceiving occlusion. Only 18-month-old children could still perceive which outcome would take place when the widths of object and opening varied, when a screen was placed on the top of the box.

The results of our studies on infants' perception of passing-through and support indicate that attention to higher order perceptual variables enables infants to anticipate functional relations that emerge when an object is displaced toward another object. The variables that specify functions and to which infants attend concern the shape of the interface of an object and its surroundings and the changing shape of this interface on displacement of an object, for instance, occlusion. Occlusion is certainly not the only higher order variable of relevance to the perception of functional relations. However, the finding that infants attend to this variable indicates that the interface of an object and its surroundings and changes that may occur with respect to this interface form an important source of information to them.

TOOL USE: THE MANIPULATION OF FUNCTIONAL RELATIONS

Establishment of functional relations involves activity that exploits the spatial layout of interacting objects in space and over time. Functional relations arise and are annihilated in the course of events, including events that are caused by human action. Action is needed to establish a relation. To get an object into a container, the object must be displaced toward the container or the container toward the object. No further action is required to keep the object in the container. Action is often also required to maintain a relation. In the peeling of a potato, a cutting edge must be kept and pushed forcefully at a proper angle under the skin of the potato. An event is generated and the outcome of this event is a changed object.

Establishment and maintenance of functional relations form the core of tool use. Neither target nor tool are the units of perception and action in tool use but functional relations between environmental entities, such as objects. To establish such a relation between objects, one or both of the objects must be implemented to the actor. For instance, when peeling a potato both peeler and potato are manipulated by the prehensile system. Manipulation may generate new action possibilities, but it may lead also to a considerable loss of possibilities. It is therefore not surprising that young children's activities begin to be directed at functional relations after their manipulatory skill has sufficiently been developed. Establishment of a relation is possible as long as a hand-held object preserves the necessary action potential of the prehensile system.

When an object is grasped so as to establish a relation to another object, the meaning of grasping changes. Grasping has a different meaning for behavior when a functional relation forms the goal of action than when the object forms the goal. In grasping an object, the relation of the object to the prehensile system is important. The hand and fingers have to be adapted to the shape and size of the object. When grasping involves establishing a functional relation to another object, the "fit" of the grasped object to the prehensile system and the fit of this object to the other object are of concern. In other words, a child must perceive what the functional relation affords to his prehensile system; the possibility of establishing a proper arrangement of surfaces between objects or a properly shaped interface has to be discovered.

The difference between the different goals of grasping may be highlighted by a simple example. Ordinarily the different parts of an object need not be held together when the object is grasped. To a certain extent, the arrangement of surfaces of which an object is composed forms a stable structure. This structure will not change because of grasping and certainly is not made by grasping. However, a tower composed of piled up blocks is less stable. When the tower is grasped and carried its structure must be maintained. Something like this happens when actions are aimed at functional relations between objects. The arrangement of surfaces that forms the functional relation is then of concern and must be made and maintained. The making of the shape of the interface of objects forms the goal of action.

To study the relation at which a child's manipulation of an object was directed, we asked (partially reported in van der Kamp, Steenbergen, & Smitsman, 1993) young children of 21–47 months of age to scoop rice with different spoons. To investigate whether the grasping of a spoon was aimed at the relation of spoon and prehensile system, we made different spoons. In ordinary spoons, both relations concern differently shaped places at the object. Graspability is afforded by the handle and holding and transportation of food by the scoop. Handle and scoop are connected to one another in such a way that graspability supports the possibility to transport food for most users. To investigate whether young children's grasping and manipulation of a spoon was aimed at the relation of spoon and food rather than at the relation of the spoon and arm, we perturbed the relation between scoop and handle (see Figure 4). For some spoons a fit to the prehensile system was incompatible to a fit between food and

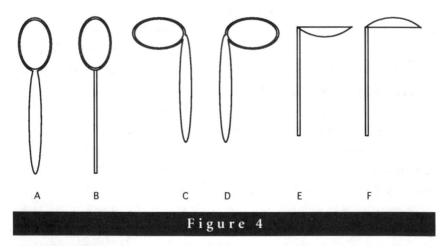

Figure 4

Illustration of an ordinary spoon (A) and five transformations of this spoon. Transformations involve 90° rotations of the scoop with respect to the handle over: a longitudinal axis to the handle (spoon B), a vertical axis to the handle (spoons C, D), and a horizontal axis perpendicular to the handle (spoons E, F). From *Studies in Perception and Action*, by J. van der Kamp, B. Steenbergen, and A. W. Smitsman, 1993, Hillsdale, NJ: Erlbaum. Copyright 1993 by Erlbaum. Adapted with permission.

scoop and vice versa. That is, a comfortable grip would be at the cost of control on scooping, and control on scooping would be at the cost of comfortable hand and arm postures. The relation between scoop and handle was perturbed by rotating the scoop of ordinary spoons with respect to the handle on three different axes. It was rotated by 90° on a horizontal axis perpendicular to the handle in two directions (spoons E, F). In one direction the concave side of the scoop formed an angle of 90° with the handle (spoon F); in the other direction the convex side formed an angle of 90° with the handle (spoon E). The other axes were a vertical axis to the handle and a longitudinal axis to the handle. On the vertical axis, rotation was also performed by 90° in two directions, namely to the left and the right (spoons C, D). On the longitudinal axis the scoop was rotated by 90° in only one direction (spoon B). Rotation in the opposite direction would yield a similar spoon. This procedure provided five different new spoons. The children were asked to scoop rice several times with each of these spoons and with an ordinary spoon. On each occasion we observed the grip a child used, the place where a spoon was held (at the end of the handle, in the middle of the handle, or near the scoop) and the orientation of the scoop (concave side upward or convex side upward). When a child intended to control the relation between scoop and rice, variation in grip was expected. Moreover, in order to scoop the concave side should be maintained upward even at the cost of a comfortable arm and body posture.

The results showed that all children without exception adapted grip and arm and body posture such that the concave side of the scoop was kept upward. No child scooped with the convex side of the scoop upward. Figure 5 shows the grip variation across spoons for both age groups. Grips concerned mainly ulnar grips and varied from clenched palmar to digital grips (see, e.g., Conally & Dalgleish, 1989). Older as well as younger children varied their grip across spoons. Grip variation involved mainly an increase in power grips for the more difficult spoons. When scooping could less easily be performed because of the way the relation between scoop and handle had been transformed, digital grips were submitted for palmar grips. Figure 5 shows that this change in grips mainly involved spoon

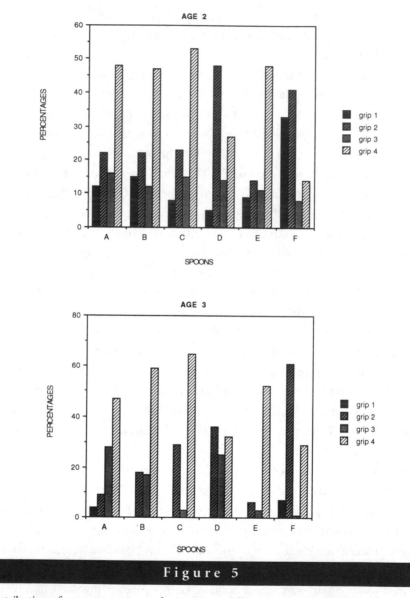

Figure 5

Distribution of mean percentages of grips over 6 different spoons in children of 2 and 3 years of age. Grips are all ulnar (see Conally & Dalgleish, 1989) and involve a clenched transverse digital grip (grip 1), a transverse palmar grip (grip 2), and transverse digital grips (grips 3 and 4). The fingers are most active in grip 4.

D and spoon F. To maintain control over the relation between scoop and food, children reduced the number of degrees of freedom of their hand provided by the fingers.

Functional relations between objects have a particular shape. This shape specifies how the surfaces of objects should be arranged with respect to one another and what the objects are. However, transformations of the state of objects, such as displacements, are needed to make this shape. Sometimes those displacements open up vistas to proceed. Attention to the changing shape of the interface of objects on displacement may guide a child's activities to produce the appropriate transformations and shape. Van Leeuwen and colleagues (1993) asked young children to grasp and displace a hook toward an object such that the object could be displaced by means of the hook, for instance, toward the child. The hook was placed on a table together with the object in front of the child in different positions to the side of the object. The hook was formed by a stick that was bent into a semicircle at one end. To displace an object by such a hook or a stick, surfaces of hook and object must be arranged in particular ways. Hooking involves a particularly shaped interface of hook and target. For instance, to displace an object with a hook the concave side of the hook must point to the direction of displacement of the object and the convex side in the opposite direction. In some conditions, the concave side of the hook pointed already into the direction of displacement of the object (see Figure 6). In such a position, rectilinear displacement of the hook toward the object generates the appropriately shaped interface. In other conditions, the concave side pointed away from this direction. In that case displacement would generate an inappropriately shaped interface of hook and object unless the hook was rotated with respect to the object. The results indicated that young children discovered the possibility to move the target object nearby more easily when the hook needed only to be displaced without rotation. Children attended to the interface of hook and target that was afforded by the position of the hook with respect to the target to perceive the hook as a tool.

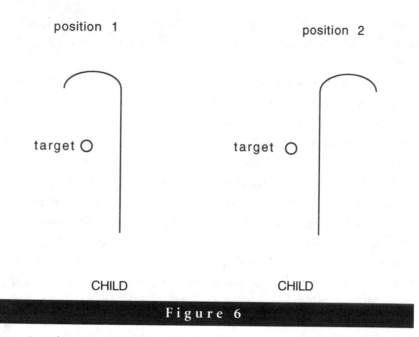

Figure 6

Illustration of two spatial positions of hook to target of the sort used by van Leeuwen, Smitsman, and van Leeuwen (1994). Pulling the hook by the child generates a functional relation between hook and target to move the target nearby in position 1, but a dysfunctional relation in position 2.

TOOL USE AND DEVELOPMENT: CHANGING BOUNDARIES BETWEEN ORGANISM AND ENVIRONMENT

The study of tool use may highlight developmental mechanisms that are easily overlooked. According to ecological views, the developing child and the environment form a unified organism–environment system. As a consequence, development should concern the whole organism–environment system rather than only one part of it (the child). Nevertheless, developmentalists easily conceive the child as only changing within an environment that remains relatively unaltered rather than changing complementary to the child's growing skills. In this view, improved effectivities of the child may lead to the discovery of new affordances but not to the creation of affordances by modifying the environment. Education of attention and growth of the child's body and skill are suggested to facilitate the discovery of existing affordances (E. J. Gibson, 1988; Zukow-Goldring & Ferko, 1994).

Tool use reveals a different developmental process that concerns the child as well as the environment of the child. Tool use shows how evolving effectivities do lead to the modification of the environment and as a consequence the emergence of new affordances. The world today differs greatly from that of yesterday. Many affordances that form a normal part of our daily life were not available to our ancestors. At best they may have dreamt of affordances for travelling, communication, and living that are common today. The ability to modify the environment provided new affordances and thus enabled us to exploit their dreams. Improved "effectivities," for instance, for travelling, such as cars, created the need for highways that afford travelling by car and vice versa.

Development does concern both parts of the organism–environment system. Both the child and the environment are evolving complementary to one another. Culture and social life reveal such an evolutionary process. For instance, the affordances available in parental actions and the perceptual variables to perceive those affordances evolve in relation to children's activities as Alan Fogel has pointed out (Fogel, 1993). The same happens to culture. From the moment an infant is born, culture constrains the infant's activities. However, culture also evolves at the very same time because of coregulated activities of caretaker and infant (Fogel, this volume). This evolutionary process is not confined to particular domains of the organism–environment system, such as the social domain, but is fundamental to the system itself.

Tool use highlights how exploitation of affordances that are provided by functional relations between environmental entities leads to modification of both effectivities and the environment. Exploitation of functional relations requires that entities involved in a relation are implemented to a child's action system. Instantaneous and momentary changes of the child's effectivities are the result of the implementation. These changes also involve the child's attention. Children may discover new meanings for behavior when their effectivities change. Caretakers may take advantage of this flexible boundary between child and environment to educate the child's attention (Zukow-Goldring, this volume). The material culture of toys, tools, and many other products of industrial design that are available provides important sources for the education of attention and the discovery of affordances. These products are often looked at as entities by themselves. However, in most cases their meaning arises first, after they are implemented, because the affordances they offer exist only for actions systems that contain those products as implements. For instance, "comfortable sitting" does not explain the variety of chairs. When we sit down we change our body posture and consequently our ability to do things. The way our surroundings look and what these afford to us varies depending on how a chair changes our body posture when we sit down. Discovery of the affordances provided by conversation with another person requires another way of comfortable sitting than discovery of the affordances of the keyboard of a piano for making music.

New affordances are not only discovered. They are also created when the environment is modified by exploitation of functional relations. Young children's play with objects show numerous examples of the creation of new affordances. An activity young children love to perform consists of putting objects and substances into containers. Substances such as a fluid afford carrying and transporting to another place after they have been put into an object that can be grasped and held. Transportation of a fluid in a cup without spilling requires a specific grip that controls the often unstable relation between cup and fluid. Transportation of materials contained by other objects is not merely the result of human action but occurs everywhere in nature. A similar situation exists for products of human technology. For instance, products such as hydraulic systems and wings were already formed by nature before they were invented by humans. As adults may mimic nature with their technology, children may also mimic nature in their play with objects.

A container is made when a child pushes an object through an opening into the enclosure of another object. Often the particular arrangement of surfaces to perform the action has to be made first by rearranging the objects' surfaces in relation to one another. Arrangements that arise convey information about future actions. By (purposely or haphazardly) reshaping the interface of objects, the child generates not only the possibility for future actions but also the information that may guide those actions (Smitsman, 1994). In this sense rearranging objects to one another is comparable to finding one's way to hidden places. Going from one place to another "involves the opening up of the vista ahead and closing in of the vista behind" (J. J. Gibson, 1979, p. 198).

In making containers, young children often show persistent efforts in pushing large objects into small openings. Are these children "misperceivers," or do their efforts reveal a fundamental trust in the own capacity to make the environment and to generate the information for how to proceed? Our research on infants' perception of passing-through and support showed that the higher order optical variable young children attend to concerns the changing shape of the interface of an object when it moves toward an opening. The way an approaching object occludes an opening before passing-through allows the child to perceive whether the object can pass through. However, emergence of this optical variable depends not only on the objects but also on the child's manipulation of these objects. For flexible objects, the relevant optical variable emerges easily by pushing one object into the other one. For rigid objects, emergence of the optical variable may require careful manipulation of the objects' positions in space to one another. However, when an appropriate position cannot be found, alteration of the shape or size of the objects (or both) may solve the problem. In any of these cases, the appropriately shaped interface and the optical variables that specify this interface are produced. Perception and action form two sides of the very same process that generates environmental entities as well as the perceptual variables to perceive the entities that are made.

The heretofore presented view on tool use offers new perspectives on development and its causes. Development involves age-related changes with respect to a child's effectivities for perceiving and acting. Dynamical perspectives on development as offered by Thelen and Ulrich (1991) and others indicate that causes of development may be diverse and involve the child's environment as well as growth of the child's body. Moreover, it shows that no single cause may be responsible for development to occur. Development is a creative process (Fogel, 1993, this volume). Perceptual differentiation theory (E. J. Gibson 1969, 1988) attributes development to perceptual learning, which implies changes in attention and efficiency of search for information.

The study of tool use may shed new light on possible causes of such changes. It shows that changes may arise instantaneously because of implements. Moreover, it suggests that such changes may concern children's effectivities for perceiving and acting, but also their environment. Tool use opens up vistas to children that would otherwise remain hidden and provides them effectivities to modulate environmental events and to produce new entities. Implements that afford tool use are discovered and made by children but are to a large extent also offered by culture. They include artefacts, symbolic media, methods, and even theories. The cognitive skills children obtain with age largely emerge because of their ability to learn how to handle these tools. Physics, mathematics, and artificial intelligence provide rich examples of how symbolic media and instruments provide tools even to perceive and act with respect to worlds that exist only as virtual realities (see, e.g., Smets, 1995).

Scientists who embrace the ecological view of perception and action address often rather simple tasks, such as locomotion, ball catching, and grasping. Extension of the ecological approach to more complex domains that traditionally form the focus of attention of cognitive psychology such as tool use may provide insight into mechanisms of cognitive development without an a priori drawback on explanations in terms of representations and schemas. The mechanism of tool use may provide an alternative for those schemas.

REFERENCES

Baillargeon, R. (1993). The object concept revisited: New directions in the investigation of infants' physical knowledge. In C. E. Granrud (Ed.), *Visual perception and cognition in infancy* (pp. 265–313). Carnegie Mellon Symposia on Cognition. Hillsdale, NJ: Erlbaum.

Bard, K. A. (1993). Cognitive competence underlying tool use in free-ranging orangutans. In A. Berthelet & J. Chavaillon (Eds.), *The use of tools by human and non-human primates* (pp. 103–113). Oxford, England: Oxford University Press.

Bates, E., Carlson-Luden, E., & Bretherton, I. (1980). Perceptual aspects of tool using in infancy. *Infant Behaviour and Development, 3,* 127–140.

Beek, P. J., & Bingham, G. P. (1991). Task-specific dynamics and the study of perception and action: A reaction to von Hofsten (1989). *Ecological Psychology, 3,* 35–54.

Berthelet, A., & Chavaillon, J. (1993). *The use of tools by human and non-human primates.* Oxford, England: Oxford University Press.

Brown, A. L. (1990). Domain-specific principles affect learning and transfer in children. *Cognitive Science, 14,* 107–133.

Conally, K., & Dalgleish, M. (1989). The emergence of a tool-using skill in infancy. *Developmental Psychology, 6,* 894–912.

Fogel, A. (1993). *Developing through relationships. Origins of communication, self, and culture.* New York: Harvester Wheatsheaf.

Gibson, E. J. (1969). *Principles of perceptual learning and development.* New York: Appleton-Century-Crofts.

Gibson, E. J. (1988). Exploratory behavior in the development of perceiving, acting, and the acquiring of knowledge. *Annual Review of Psychology, 39,* 1–41.

Gibson, J. J. (1966). *The senses considered as perceptual systems.* Boston: Houghton Mifflin.

Gibson, J. J. (1977). The theory of affordances. In R. Show & J. Bransford (Eds.), Perceiving, acting, and knowing (pp. 67–82). Hillsdale, NJ: Erlbaum.

Gibson, J. J. (1979). *The ecological approach to visual perception.* Boston: Houghton Mifflin.

Greenfield, P. M. (1991). Language, tools and brain: The ontogeny and phylogeny of hierarchically organized sequential behavior. *Behavioral and Brain Sciences, 14,* 531–595.

Jouffroy, F. K. (1993). Primate hands and the human hand: The tool of hands. In A. Berthelet & J. Chavaillon (Eds.), *The use of tools by human and non-human primates* (pp. 6–33). Oxford, England: Oxford University Press.

Kugler, P. N., Kelso, J. A. S., & Turvey, M. T. (1982). On the control and coordination of naturally developing systems. In J. A. S. Kelso & J. E. Clark (Eds.), *The development of movement control and coordination* (pp. 5–87). New York: Wiley.

Mark, L. S. (1987). Eyeheight-scaled information about affordances: A study of sitting and stair climbing. *Journal of Experimental Psychology: Human Perception and Performance, 13,* 361–370.

Michaels, C. F., & Beek, P. J. (1995). The state of ecological psychology. *Ecological Psychology, 7,* 259–278.

Michaels, C. F., & Carello, C. (1981). *Direct perception.* Englewood Cliffs, NJ: Prentice Hall.

Newell, K. M., Scully, D. M., McDonald, P. V., & Baillargeon, R. (1989). Task constraints and infant grip configurations. *Developmental Psychobiology, 22,* 817–831.

Parker, S., & Gibson, K. R. (1977). Object manipulation, tool use and sensorimotor intelligence as feeding adaptations in cebus monkeys and great apes. *Journal of Human Evolution, 6,* 623–641.

Piaget, J. (1954). *The construction of reality in the child.* New York: Basic Books.

Sitskoorn, M. M., & Smitsman, A. W. (1994). *Infant's attentiveness to visible arrangements of surfaces specifying interactions between objects: Perception of width relation.* Unpublished manuscript.

Sitskoorn, M. M., & Smitsman, A. W. (1995). Infants' perception of dynamic relations between objects: Passing through or support? *Developmental Psychology, 31,* 437–447.

Sitskoorn, M., & Smitsman, A. W. (in press). Infants' perception of object interactions: Perception of constraints of directions of approach. *Infant Behavior & Development.*

Smets, G. J. F. (1995). Industrial design engineering and the theory of direct perception and action. *Ecological Psychology, 7,* 329–374.

Smith, L. B., & Thelen, E. (Eds.). (1994). *A dynamic systems approach to development.* Cambridge, MA: MIT Press.

Smitsman, A. W., & Reinders, A. (1996). *Perceiving reachability of objects for an instantaneously changed prehensile system in young children.* Unpublished manuscript.

Smitsman, M. M., & Smitsman, A. W. (in press). Infants' perception of object interactions: Perception of constraints of directions of approach. *Infant Behavior and Development.*

Solomon, H. Y., & Turvey, M. T. (1988). Haptically perceiving the distances reachable with hand-held objects. *Journal of Experimental Psychology: Human Perception and Performance, 14,* 404–427.

Solomon, H. Y., Turvey, M. T., & Burton, G. (1989). Perceiving rod extents by wielding: Haptic diagonalization and decomposition of the inertia tensor. *Journal of Experimental Psychology: Human Perception and Performance, 15,* 58–68.

Spelke, E. S. (1994). Initial knowledge: Six suggestions. *Cognition, 50,* 431–445.

Spelke, E. S., Breinlinger, K., Macomber, J., & Jacobson, K. (1992). Origins of knowledge. *Psychological Review, 99,* 605–632.

Thelen, E., & Ulrich, B. D. (1991). Hidden skills. *Monographs of the Society for Research in Child Development, 56,* 1–106.

van der Kamp, J., Steenbergen, B., & Smitsman, A. W. (1993). In S. Stavros & J. B. Pittenger (Eds.), *Studies in perception and action* (Vol. 2, pp. 329–332). Hillsdale, NJ: Erlbaum.

van Leeuwen, L., Smitsman, A. W., & van Leeuwen, C. (1994). Affordances, perceptual complexity, and the development of tool use. *Journal of Experimental Psychology: Human Perception and Performance, 20,* 174–191.

Wachs, T. D. (1992). *The nature of nurture.* Newbury Park, CA: Sage.

Warren, W. H. (1984). Perceiving affordances: Visual guidance of stair climbing. *Journal of Experimental Psychology: Human Perception and Performance, 10,* 683–703.

Warren, W. H., & Whang, S. (1987). Visual guidance of walking through apertures: Body scaled information for affordances. *Journal of Experimental Psychology: Human Perception and Performance, 13,* 371–383.

Zukow-Goldring, P., & Ferko, K. R. (1994). An ecological approach to the emergence of the lexicon: Socializing attention. In V. John-Steiner, C. P. Panofsky, & L. W. Smith (Eds.), *Sociocultural approaches to language and literacy* (pp. 170–190). Cambridge, England: Cambridge University Press.

Comment on Smitsman

Edward S. Reed

The most important aspect of Smitsman's chapter is his elegant and powerful new experimental method for studying the perception and use of affordances. In this comment I would like to highlight why this novel experimental paradigm is so important.

The affordances of the environment are what it offers an animal. Affordances can be simple features of the environment that make possible a course of action, or they can be clusters of such features—even complex, interrelated clusters. In all cases, however, what makes them affordances is that they make it possible for an animal to engage in some specific action (Gibson, 1979; Reed, 1996).

Animals can discover existing affordances in their surroundings, or they can invent new affordances by combining and rearranging features of their environment. This is true even with tools: The sea otter *finds* rocks that are small enough for it to carry but hard enough to enable the otter to crack shellfish open against. In contrast, some chimpanzees in the wild have been observed to make an anvil out of a stone or stones and against

Reed comments on Smitsman from an ecological realist perspective.

which they crack nuts (see McGrew, 1993). Making an anvil involves not only finding a big enough and flat enough rock, but also setting it up in such a way that it remains stable despite receiving repeated blows.

Children live in an environment full of ready-made special affordances: not only tools, but also clothes, toys, houses, vehicles, and more are found in the human environment. Children need not invent all this technology; nevertheless, they must discover its meaning and utility. As Smitsman notes, this means that children always grow up in a populated environment that encourages them to experience a variety of ways of altering their environment. Children not only poke, pound, and transport objects with their hands, but they also learn how to use tools and toys to poke, pound, and transfer.

However, mainstream psychology has been very skeptical that such things as affordances exist, except as mental states, or "concepts." "A function," Smitsman notes, "is often conceived of as something that is superimposed on objects" (p. 310). The Gibsons and other ecological psychologists have argued that this is incorrect, that functions are as much properties of things as color or shape. However, Smitsman's experimental paradigm in this chapter is more likely to convince a skeptic than any argument.

In one of the experiments he reports, Smitsman was interested in spoons but not in their shapes or size; rather, he was interested in what *affords spooning* and whether young children perceive the affordances of spoons. What in fact affords spooning is an object with a handle that is easily grasped and transported unimanually; attached to the handle there must be a concavity (bowl) capable of holding some noticeable amount of a substance throughout the act of transporting the whole tool from substance to a container. To embody this affordance, spoons must be made out of a relatively rigid material, the handle must be at least as long as the bowl (preferably twice or thrice as long), and it is desirable to have the axes of the handle continued into the bowl.

Smitsman noticed that this last feature, although desirable, is not necessary. He therefore constructed a series of spoons where the long axis of the bowl was orthogonal to the long axis of the handle (see his Figure 4). To be used for spooning, such tools require a very unusual grip. Moreover, because of their unfamiliarity, children would not have had any prior experience with either these unusual objects or the relevant grips. Hence, if young children can spontaneously use these novel tools as spoons, this is strong evidence that they perceive the object in terms of its functional properties, its affordances. Smitsman found that children as young as 21 months of age, given these novel spoons, spontaneously vary their grip in such a way as to preserve the functional act of spooning.

Smitsman's method is one that can be generalized to great effect: Experimentally vary relevant but noncrucial features of affordances and see whether individuals functionally modify their actions so as to preserve the functional characteristics of the affordances in question. Given that such modified objects and actions tend to be completely novel, this is strong evidence that perception itself provides information about both the meaning and use of affordances.

REFERENCES

Gibson, J. J. (1979). *The ecological approach to visual perception.* Boston: Houghton Mifflin

McGrew, W. (1993). *Chimpanzee material culture.* Cambridge, England: Cambridge University Press.

Reed, E. S. (1996). *Encountering the world: Toward an ecological psychology.* New York: Oxford University Press.

10

Perceptual Learning, Categorizing, and Cognitive Development

Anne D. Pick

O ur perceptual systems enable us to detect many differences among similar objects and events. How do people cope with such diversity in a world in which no two entities are exactly alike? It would surely be maladaptive to act differently toward every distingishable leaf on a tree, blade of grass, or book on a bookshelf. On the other hand, we want to be able to use our sensitivity to distinguish among entities when it is to our advantage to do so. *Categorizing* is the process of acting on or thinking about distinguishable entities as though they are equivalent. Historically, categorizing has been thought to be particularly problematic for young children. What possible bases might they have for coping with diversity by categorizing?

In any collection of objects, many similarities or relations can be specified. Are the different relations discernible in such a collection of equal

The research discussed herein was partially supported by the Center for Research in Learning, Perception and Cognition at the University of Minnesota. This research was conducted in collaboration with Diane Bales, Gedeon Deak, and Patricia Melendez. I am grateful to them and also to Doug Gentile, Marian Heinrichs, Louise Hertsgaard, Kathleen Kremer, and Nelson Soken for many fruitful discussions of the issues considered in this chapter. Finally, I thank Herbert L. Pick, Jr., for provocative and constructive reflections on the ideas considered here.

significance to children? Clearly not. How children categorize objects may reflect what they know about them. Currently, there is dispute about the bases for children's early categorization. Underlying this dispute are some fundamental and contradictory assumptions about perceptual and cognitive development. In this chapter I consider two contemporary views of the relation of perceptual and cognitive development. One view pervades current research on cognitive development. I argue that it may lead us to misunderstand what young children know about objects. The other view is an ecological perspective. I illustrate its usefulness by discussing research my colleagues and I have carried out on preschool children's categorization. The first view shares a critical assumption with a historical, traditional account of perception and cognition, and I begin with that account.

THE HISTORICAL VIEW OF
PERCEPTION AND COGNITION

Early in the history of the study of perception, perception and cognition were thought to be closely bound together. Perception was taken to be a cognitive process (associative, computational, or inferential) because the information available about the world was assumed to be impoverished and insubstantial. Helmholtz wrote about the unconscious inferences he presumed people engage in as they perceive (Boring, 1950, pp. 308–311). Much earlier in this tradition, Bishop Berkeley implied that size constancy was achieved by registering image size on the retina and correcting for distance (Boring, 1950, pp. 182–184).

Kaufman and Rock's (Kaufman, 1974, pp. 362–366; Rock & Kaufman, 1962) more recent account of the moon illusion exemplifies this philosophical and historical legacy: When the moon is seen on the horizon, it is usually viewed over a textured surface such as terrain. We register this distance as far compared with the distance of the moon viewed overhead across empty space. Unconsciously then, we infer that if two equal size images are registered as being at different distances, the farther one must be larger, and this is the way we perceive the moon on the horizon. (In the case of the moon illusion, the inferential story is even more complicated because if people are explicitly asked to judge the distance of the moon, they judge the moon on the horizon as closer. According to Rock and Kaufman, this judgment is based on a second inference. Because we know the moon is the same size at horizon and zenith, if it looks bigger on the horizon, it must be closer.) Contemporary information-processing and computational (e.g., Ullman, 1980) accounts of perception are rooted firmly in this same tradition, although now it is the computers in our heads that carry out the computations to achieve perception rather than our unconscious making inferences.

A radically different account of perceiving, based on Darwinian selectionism, has recently been proposed by the neuroscientist Edelman (1987, 1988, 1989, 1992), who has offered a sweeping neurobiological theory of the brain and mind. Although he vigorously rejected information processing, his account of perceiving is consistent with the earlier tradition because, in his account, perceiving *is* categorizing (Edelman, 1987, pp. 26–32, 209–256; Edelman, 1992, pp. 87–94). A fundamental assumption of all accounts of perception as cognition is that the information available for perceiving is impoverished and insufficient to support veridical perception.

CONTEMPORARY DEVELOPMENTAL APPROACH TO PERCEPTION AND COGNITION

A predominant contemporary developmental perspective frames the relation of perception and cognition differently from the historical view but shares with that view the critical assumption that information is ambiguous and impoverished. According to this developmental perspective, perceiving and conceiving are assumed (implicitly by some, explicitly by others) to be discontinuous. In the course of development, perceiving becomes over-ridden by knowledge acquired cognitively. This assumption of discontinuity has influenced at least two decades of research, both in terms of how cognitive development has been characterized and in the kinds of tasks children have been asked to do in experiments on cognitive development.

One effect of assuming discontinuity (at least implicitly) of perceiving and conceiving has been to characterize cognitive development in terms of dichotomies. For example, Keil (1989; Keil & Batterman, 1984) has argued that young children progress from a reliance on characteristic features of objects when labeling them or making judgments about them to a reliance on defining features. This shift occurs at different ages for different domains, but nonetheless it is thought to be a shift from using one kind of feature to using another. Distinctions similar to Keil's that are the focus of current research programs include that between nonobvious and obvious properties of objects (Baldwin, Markman, & Melartin, 1993) and the distinction of Gelman and Wellman (1991) between insides, essences, and nonobvious properties on the one hand and external appearances on the other hand. Merriman, Scott, and Marazita (1993) have argued that there is a shift, during early childhood, from object naming that is based on appearances to object naming that is based on function. Flavell and colleagues (Flavell, Flavell, & Green, 1983; Flavell, Green, & Flavell, 1986) following Piaget, have argued that understanding a distinction between appearance and reality is an important developmental conceptual achievement. Prior to acquiring this understanding, young children are thought to make the mistake of assuming that appearance and reality coincide. During the preschool or early school years, they learn this is not necessarily so.

Perhaps the most common general dichotomy presumed in discussions of cognitive development is that drawn between perceptual similarity on one hand and conceptual similarity or knowledge on the other (e.g., Gelman & Medin, 1993; Mandler, 1993). A recent issue of the journal *Cognitive Development* featured a special section containing a lead article by S. Jones and Smith (1993) titled "The Place of Perception in Children's Concepts." They challenged the commonly held view that what they call *nonperceptual knowledge* (e.g., insides, essences, nonobvious properties, defining features, functions) is at the core of concepts and that *perceptual knowledge* (e.g., outsides, appearances, characteristic properties, surface properties) is peripheral and, at best, provides cues or clues to category membership. Instead they argued that "conceptual knowledge encompasses both perceptual and nonperceptual knowledge as equal and inter-acting partners" (p. 113). The four commentaries on the lead article represented views ranging from general agreement (e.g., Mervis, Johnson, & Scott, 1993) to vigorous disagreement (Mandler, 1993) about the relevance of perceiving for conceiving. Mandler (1993) asserted that "from early in infancy, perceptual information is continually being transformed into a form of knowledge that is more properly called conceptual," that "perceptual categories are patterns that by themselves do not have meaning," and that "what turns a pattern into a concept is a process I call *perceptual analysis* (which) redescribes perceptual information into a conceptual format" (pp. 145–146). She distinguished what she termed *primitive concepts*, those of young infants, from perceptual categories—the latter having to do with "what things look like rather than what they are" (Mandler, 1993, p. 146).

From my reading of these and other articles on these topics, it seems to me that despite disagreements about some of the issues concerning the development of perceiving and conceiving, there is a fundamental idea about which there is wide consensus: Both those who argue that knowledge acquired by perceiving is relevant or even important in conceiving and those who argue the converse share an assumption that is at least implicit and frequently explicit in their writing, namely, that perceiving and conceiving are discontinuous. The idea seems to be that perceiving yields knowledge that is more or less useful for understanding the world (depending on your point of view) but that, in the course of development, perceiving gives way to or is superseded by knowledge acquired by "higher" cognitive processes. Perceiving can be deceptive, illusory, as in Flavell's (Flavell et al., 1983; Flavell et al., 1986) description of young children's belief that appearance and reality coincide. Eventually, knowledge acquired by other processes yields information about the way things really are.

The assumption that perceiving and conceiving are discontinuous is reflected in the kinds of tasks constructed to assess young children's knowledge about objects. These tasks require children to make dichotomous choices about objects without opportunity to explore them so as to discover their properties and how they function. Flavell et al. (1983) asked children whether a stone painted to look like an egg was really an egg or really a stone, and they were not invited to reply that it was a stone painted to look like an egg. Gelman and colleagues (Gelman & Markman, 1987; Gelman & Medin, 1993, p. 163) sought to investigate whether children make inferences on the basis of appearances (i.e., the shape or orientation of line drawings of objects) or knowledge (i.e., category names), and they distinguished between "perception or appearance" and "conceptual knowledge." For the task of one such study, children were shown sets of line drawings (see Figure 1 for examples of Gelman and Markman's line drawings). The drawings included a target (the cat in a particular posture) about which the children were taught a "fact." The children were then asked whether the fact was true of each of the other drawings of objects. The other objects were construed as varying in whether they shared category membership with the target and in whether they shared perceptual appearances with the target. From the examples in Figure 1, it can be seen that *category membership* is species membership, and *perceptual appearances* are shading (black or white), presence or absence of white stripe, and orientation from a static observer's perspective. (The object, of course, is static as well.) Category membership and perceptual appearances are treated as independent variables, manipulable in a factorial design.

In a similar vein, Gelman and Wellman (1991) showed children pictures of three objects (e.g., a pig, a piggy bank, and a cow; a glass of milk, a glass of orange juice, and a carton of milk). The children were asked which pictures looked most alike and which had the same kinds of insides. The correct answer to the first question was the pig and the piggy bank, and the glasses of milk and orange juice. The correct answer to the second question was the pig and cow, and the glass and carton of milk. From their studies demonstrating that children have considerable knowledge about insides, Gelman and Wellman suggested that children may have a cognitive predisposition for believing essentialism to be a basis for identity, a predisposition they believe is useful for accounting for observations "that even young children construct considerable knowledge about the non-obvious" (p. 243).

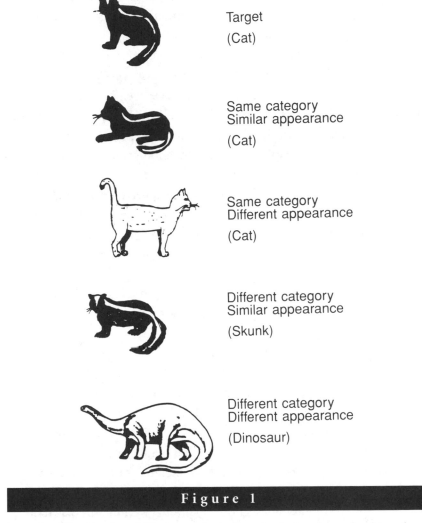

Target
(Cat)

Same category
Similar appearance
(Cat)

Same category
Different appearance
(Cat)

Different category
Similar appearance
(Skunk)

Different category
Different appearance
(Dinosaur)

Figure 1

Examples of line drawings children were shown in study of category membership and perceptual appearances from "Young Children's Inductions From Natural Kinds: The Role of Categories and Appearances," by S. Gelman and E. Markman, 1987, *Child Development*, *58*, p. 1535. Copyright 1987 by the Society for Research in Child Development. Reprinted with permission.

Finally, S. Jones, Smith, and Landau (1991) argued that there is a "synergistic relation between immediate perceptual properies and knowledge in categorization. Perceptual properties activate knowledge; then that knowledge may guide attention to other relevant properties" (p. 514). They further proposed that different "kinds of knowledge—perceptual, nonperceptual, linguistic, and perhaps social" are weighted differently by children performing different experimental tasks, and experimenters should manipulate "both the perceptual knowledge and the nonperceptual knowledge [made] available" to understand how different weightings emerge (S. Jones & Smith, 1993, p. 137).

In all of these formulations, knowledge acquired by perceiving is implicitly segregated from knowledge acquired by other cognitive activities. Furthermore, perceiving is static, snapshot-like, and passive. In experimental tasks, the opportunity to perceive object properties is frequently provided only by making available outline drawings, pictures, or plastic toy representations of objects. Children's judgments about artificial or represented objects is assumed to reflect how they perceive the objects that furnish their world. Exploration and discovery seem to have no role in these views of perceiving. Thus, Baldwin et al. (1993) wrote that "nonapparent underlying properties cannot be directly experienced; they must be inferred from the presence of surface features" (p. 713). They further commented that children might "accidentally" discover properties of objects during "miscellaneous handling" of them (pp. 714–715). In the general view that these comments reflect, perceiving frequently, and developmentally is corrected by knowledge otherwise acquired (e.g., by inferring).

Another point about the contemporary view of perceiving and conceiving as discontinuous and segregated should be emphasized again. This view shares the assumption of the historical perspective about the nature of information that is the basis for perceiving. Specifically, the information available to support perception is insufficient and inadequate, necessitating processes of supplementation, construction, computation, interpretation, and the like. Thus, Mandler (1988), in an article titled "How to Build a Baby" wrote of a perceptual system that "provides the information that gets interpreted conceptually" (p. 132) and, furthermore, that "when we just see we are unconscious—it is only when we analyze or compare that we become fully aware human beings" (p. 133).

AN ECOLOGICAL APPROACH TO PERCEPTION AND COGNITION

An account of cognitive development during infancy and childhood based on the ecological approach differs from the prevailing view in important ways. The idea that perceiving and other cognitive processes are segregated, discontinuous, or bounded is explicitly rejected. James Gibson (e.g., 1967, 1979, pp. 253–255, 258) hypothesized the continuity of perception with memory and thought. This hypothesis is, in turn, based on the important concept of information and the theory that perceiving is based on stimulus information and not on sensations.

Twenty-five years ago, Kaplan (1969) conducted his famous study about the occluding edge. He presented observers with filmed displays of random texture in which texture elements were deleted on one side of a contour and retained on the other side. The observers perceived one surface going behind another and continuing to exist. More recent research by Baillargeon and colleagues (Baillargeon, 1987; Baillargeon, Spelke, & Wasserman, 1985) demonstrated that young human infants also appear to apprehend the continued existence of an object seen being occluded by a screen. In these experiments, infants watched a solid screen rotating back and forth through an arc of 180 degrees. After they attained a criterion of habituation, they saw a box placed behind the screen. Next, they watched two events: a "possible" event in which the screen rotated back and forth to the location of the hidden box and an "impossible" event in which the screen rotated back and forth through an arc of 180 degrees and thus through the location of the solid object. In both events, as the screen rotated, it progressively revealed and concealed the solid object, but in the case of the impossible event, the screen moved through the area occupied by the solid object after it had been completely concealed. Infants as young as 4 1/2 months, and even some 3 1/2-month-olds, looked longer at the impossible events than at the possible ones. Thus, in the context of the massive literature on infants' habituation and dishabituation, the infants behaved as though the impossible event was novel or surprising or a violation of their expectations. Baillargeon and colleagues discussed these findings in terms of infants' "realization," "understanding" (e.g., Baillargeon, 1993; Needham & Baillargeon, 1993), and assumptions "that objects continue to exist when occluded and that objects cannot move through the space occupied by other objects" (Baillargeon, 1987, p. 663). The burden of explanation rests on the infants' "intuitions" and "reasoning" about objects (e.g., Baillargeon, 1993; Needham & Baillargeon, 1993).

A different but plausible interpretation might attribute these findings not to infants' reasoning but to their perceiving the continuing existence of the object as it gradually goes out of sight. As Kaplan's (1969) experiment revealed, observers see a surface continue to persist as it is being concealed at an occluding edge. More recently, Granrud et al. (1984) presented 5- and 7-month-old infants with moving random dot dislays in which the only information for two surfaces was texture accretion and deletion at an edge. Infants at both ages reached for the apparently nearer surface, indicating they perceived the occlusion event from the kinetic accretion and deletion information specifying it.

Perhaps the infants in Baillargeon's experiments perceived the persistence of the solid object as the occlusion event unfolded. Perhaps also their surprise at the impossible event was not based on their reasoning about objects but on their perception of what the eventual screen motion specified. The motion of the screen in the impossible situation began as an occlusion event, but its continued motion specified not the covering up but the disappearance of the object as it passed through the location of the object. The motion information initially specified the going out of sight of the object, but then it specified its going out of existence—a radically different kind of disappearance (J. Gibson, 1979, pp. 79–80; Reed, 1988, pp. 277–288).

A fundamental idea of the ecological approach to perceiving is that information for perceiving is specific to its sources in the environment. If this is so, then opportunities for exploring those sources is unlimited. From an ecological perspective, a distinction between what something *looks like* and what *it is*—the distinction explicitly made by Mandler, among others—is inconsistent because of the central concept of affordance. The most important things we perceive about objects and events are their affordances, the possibilities they provide for our behavior—what we can do with them. What one can do with an object, in an important sense, defines its identity, specifies what it is. Different objects may afford a common action, and if the affordance is specified in the optic array, it is available to be discovered through exploration. Children do explore objects to discover what they can do with them, and as I discuss next, children's explorations of the functions of objects have consequences for the similarities they perceive among objects and how they categorize them.

I now discuss my research. In a first set of studies, we investigated preschoolers' categorization of objects and representations of objects. In a second set of studies, we investigated preschoolers' categorization of objects according to varying criteria. In both sets of studies, we deliberately asked children to consider properties that some investigators have argued are apprehended by different cognitive processes. Our purpose was to assess the usefulness of the distinction between perceiving and conceiving and the dichotomies that distinction has led to.

CATEGORIZING OBJECTS AND OBJECT REPRESENTATIONS

In the first studies, conducted with Melendez and Bales (Melendez, Bales, & Pick, 1993; Melendez, Bales, Ruffing, & Pick, 1995), we investigated how 4-year-old children use their knowledge about objects in circumstances allowing direct and indirect perception. This distinction between direct and indirect perception was first made by James Gibson (1979, p. 147, pp. 166–168, 238–262, 270–291; Reed, 1987; Sedgwick, 1980), and it concerns the information available as a basis for perceiving. Direct perception is hypothesized to be based on information that uniquely specifies its sources in the environment. An object structures light in the optic array, providing information for an active explorer. An active explorer is essential for direct perception. It is through action that affordances, or possibilities for action, are perceived. Information specifying functional properties of objects, what one can do with them, can be detected through active exploration.

Information specifying objects can also be displayed in photographs or drawings, and James Gibson (1979, p. 283) referred to perception of such represented objects as indirect. A picture, he wrote, "is a surface that specifies something other than what it is" (p. 273). It is a display of information for something else. When information about an object is presented in a static array, such as a picture, it is not possible to actively explore the object. The picture as a surface can be explored, but the object represented in the picture can only be explored in a limited way (e.g., by looking at details of parts). The information available about the object is only that which the picture maker has selected. A picture "works" because it is information from the array specifying the object that has been selected. But it is only a sample, frozen in time (J. Gibson, 1979, pp. 267–274).

As I noted earlier, much of the empirical knowledge of how children categorize things rests on the assumption that objects and their representations are equivalent, that how children categorize line drawings or photographs or miniature plastic toy objects informs us how they would categorize the represented objects. From an ecological perspective, the assumption that objects and their representations are equivalent is questionable because they do not provide equivalent information. Our first studies (Melendez et al., 1993; Melendez et al., 1995) are about how preschoolers classify objects under conditions allowing direct and indirect perception, that is, when the children have opportunity to actively explore objects compared with when they have static pictorial representations of them. Specifically, we hypothesized that whether children's classifications were based on function, color, or size would depend on their opportunities for exploration.

For the first study, we (Melendez et al., 1993; Melendez et al., 1995) collected 64 toys and assembled eight function sets. Our selection was guided by a general goal of providing toys that would likely engage young children. The collection included toys with wheels, books, puzzles, toy musical instruments, toys to be blown, cuddly toys, bat-and-ball toys, and toys to be looked through. The toys of each function set were also selected to be different rather than similar in contour or appearance, although of course contour or shape and function are inextricably bound—the function of something being a consequence of its substance and surface layout.

The sets were constructed to promote sorting them as similar to a "target" toy in either of two ways: according to function or according to color or size. One set, depicted in Figure 2, included three types of puzzles, all blue in color (one made of sponge, a flat hard type, and a 3-D puzzle), one white puzzle, three white toys with wheels (a truck, a tricycle, and a baby buggy), and a blue motorcycle. Another set, depicted in Figure 3, included four red instruments (a piano, a tambourine, a trumpet, and a flute), a silver saxophone, two silver "look-through" toys (a kalaidoscope

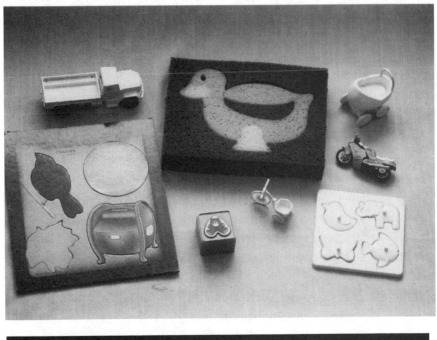

Figure 2

Puzzle and wheel toys.

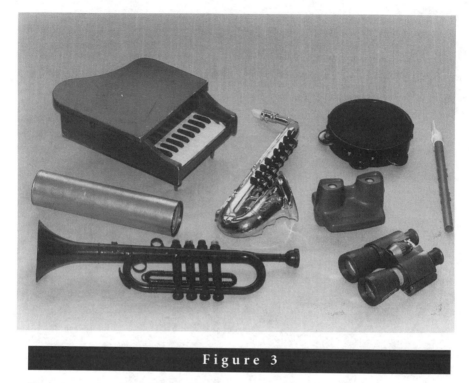

Figure 3

Toy instruments and "look-through" toys.

and binoculars), and a red viewmaster. A third set, depicted in Figure 4, included three small stuffed animals, one large stuffed animal, three large instruments (a drum, a guitar, and a saxophone), and a small harmonica. Thus, a set included two function groups and either two colors or two sizes. The target items in each set (the white puzzle and blue motorcycle in the first set, the silver saxophone and red viewmaster in the second set, and the large stuffed animal and small harmonica in the third set) were similar in function to the toys in one group but similar in color or size to toys in the second group.

Representations of the toys were constructed by first photographing them against a white, nearly textureless background (white objects were photographed against a dark background). Then line drawings were constructed by tracing the photographs with colored pencils and filling them

Figure 4

Stuffed animals and toy instruments.

in to be the same color as the objects they depicted. Pictures or line draw-ings vary in terms of how well they make available information for the identity of a represented object. In her dissertation, Rebecca Jones (1982) established that pictures in which edges specify hidden surfaces are espe-cially effective in providing information for the solid shapes of represented objects. We (Melendez et al., 1993; Melendez et al., 1995) tried to use this guide in selecting perspectives from which to photograph our toys. Thus, our line drawings were quite informative about the objects represented. Frequently, when line drawings are used to study children's classification, they are intentionally drawn to highlight noninvariant features over in-variant ones (cf. Figure 1).

Each colored line drawing was presented on a 4 in. × 6 in. laminated card, and they were assembled into sets identical to the sets of real toys.

The absolute size of an object photographed against a textureless background is indeterminate. Hence, for the function/size sets, the toys were photographed and drawn such that the representations of the large and small toys could be distinguished by the approximate amount of surface they occupied on the cards. Figures 5 and 6 depict line drawings of the sets of objects shown in Figures 2 and 4 (the puzzles and wheel toys and the stuffed animals and toy instruments).

Four-year-old children participated either in a real object condition or in a line-drawing condition. The children in the real object condition were first presented the toys of one set in an unsystematic heap and invited to play with them (which they did eagerly). After the children had explored all the toys in a set, the experimenter picked up the target toys (e.g., blue motorcycle and white puzzle, silver saxophone and red view-

Figure 5

Line drawings of puzzle and wheel toys.

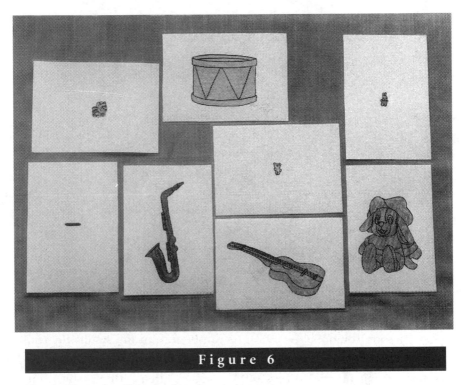

Figure 6

Line drawings of stuffed animals and toy instruments.

master, or large stuffed animal and small harmonica) and placed each on a separate table. The children were then asked to place the remaining toys with the (target) items with which they belonged. The relevant question was whether the children would sort the toys systematically, either according to their function or according to their color or size. When the children completed their sorting of one set of toys, the toys were removed, and the children were invited to play with the toys in a second set. The procedure continued until the children had played with and sorted all eight sets of toys. The procedure was identical for the children presented with line drawings, except that these children looked through all the drawings rather than explored the toys themselves.

The results are shown in Table 1. A criterion for consistent sorting for a child was established as sorting 30 or more of the 48 toys by one or the

	Table 1
Condition	Result
Real toys	11 children sorted consistently by function ($p < .001$)
	2 children sorted consistently by size/color
Line drawings	4 children sorted consistently by function ($p < .05$)
	7 children sorted consistently by size/color ($p < .001$)
Photographs	5 children sorted consistently by function ($p < .01$)
	1 child sorted consistently by size/color
Explore toys; Sort line drawings	4 children sorted consistently by function ($p < .05$)
	8 children sorted consistently by size/color ($p < .001$)
Real toys; No exploration	7 children sorted consistently by function ($p < .001$)
	No children sorted consistently by size/color

NOTE: $n = 16$ in each condition. Consistent sorting was established as sorting 30 or more of 48 toys (binomial $p < .05$).

other criterion (binomial $p < .05$). As can be seen in the results for real toys, most of the children who had played with the toys sorted them according to their functions ($p < .001$). These children sorted by function in spite of the variation in contour or shape and the specific manner in which the different functions could be acted on. Furthermore, they sorted by function in spite of the seemingly salient but superficial similarity in color (or size) for toys with different functions. The two children in this condition who sorted toys by size or color both sorted the toys consistently according to size; none of the children sorted consistently by color.

By contrast, 7 children in the line drawings condition consistently sorted the drawings by color or by size ($p < .001$). Especially when the property contrasting with function was color, children were likely to sort the drawings according to their color. When the contrasting property was size, 4 children did sort the drawings according to their functions, but significantly fewer than the 11 children who had sorted the toys by their functions ($p < .02$).

The importance of functional properties of objects (their affordances) for how young children classify them is revealed in these results. Exploring objects is an important means for learning what one can do with them. When 4-year-old children had the opportunity to actively explore objects, to discover the common and varied actions they afforded, they categorized them by different criteria than when they could only see the objects represented in pictures or line drawings.

The role of an affordance in categorization by young children was the focus of earlier research I conducted with Smitsman and Loosbroek (Smitsman, Loosbroek, & Pick, 1987; Smitsman & Pick, 1983) on children's understanding of class inclusion relations in collections of toys. Specifically, we found that children more accurately answered questions about class inclusion relations when the affordance of "cuddliness" was the superordinate property and a species (such as duck) was the subordinate than when the relation of these properties was reversed (i.e., when species was the superordinate and subordinate classes were distinguished by being cuddly or not). We interpreted these findings as reflecting the importance of affordances for categorization, especially by young children. Cuddliness as a property is complicated for the psychologist to describe precisely, much more difficult than applying the species labels of *duck*, *dog*, and so forth. However, cuddliness is acted on early in life, and the species represented by infants' toys are quite irrelevant to infants' behavior with the toys.

In considering the contrast in the present study in how the children sorted the line drawings and the toys themselves, a question can be raised about the nature of the representations themselves. Specifically, was it important for how the children categorized that the representations were line drawings or that they were, more generally, representations? One cannot explore an object represented in a photograph any more than one can explore an object represented in a line drawing. On the other hand, a good photograph makes it possible to see what one can do with some toys, even though it is still a static display. Another group of 4-year-olds was recruited to carry out the procedure as before, but with our original high quality photographs of the toys. The photographs, like the line drawings, were presented on 4 in. × 6 in. laminated cards. Figures 7 and 8 depict the photographs of the sets of objects shown in Figures 2 and 4.

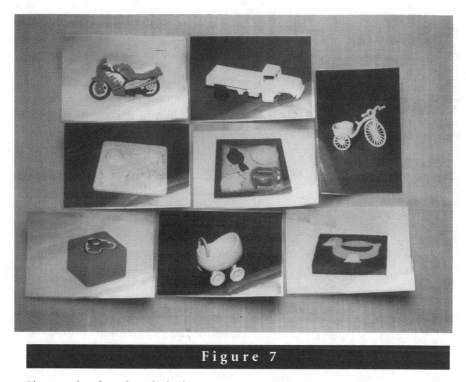

Figure 7

Photographs of puzzle and wheel toys.

As can be seen in the results for photographs in Table 1, several children (5) consistently sorted the photographs according to the functions of the represented objects. The number of children who did this was about the same number as had done so with the line drawings and was significantly fewer than the number of children who had sorted the real toys according to their functions ($p < .05$). Unlike the line drawings, however, the photographs did not elicit sorting by color or size. More children who had sorted photographs were inconsistent than children who had sorted line drawings. The greater complexity and detail in the photographs apparently diminished the prominence of the color or size distinctions among the represented objects, but it did not promote more sorting by the functions of the objects.

Would learning acquired by exploring and playing with the toys gen-

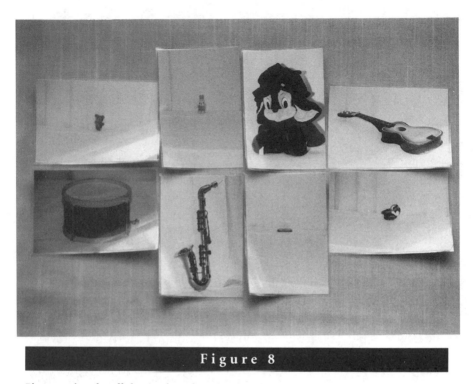

Figure 8

Photographs of stuffed animals and toy instruments.

eralize to subsequent sorting of representations of them? In other words, if children played with the toys, learning what actions they afforded, and subsequently sorted line drawings of them, might the children's exploratory experience promote more frequent classification of the drawings according to the represented objects' affordances? A new group of 4-year-olds participated in this explore toys/sort line drawings condition. There was no evidence of generalization from the children's exploration of the toys to their classification of the representations. The results (presented in Table 1) were nearly identical to those for the children who had looked through and then classified the line drawings. Most of the children sorted the drawings consistently (unlike the children sorting photographs) and according to color or size. A few children (four) did sort the drawings consistently according to the functions of the represented objects. However, we found no reason to think their consistency was related to their exploratory activity with the objects themselves because the same number of children had initially sorted line drawings according to function.

Finally, we sought to document more specifically the importance of the children's exploratory activity for learning about the toys' affordances and for subsequently classifying the toys according to their affordances. A new group of 4-year-olds was asked only to sort the toys but not to explore them. The results for this real toys/no exploration condition are presented in Table 1. In these circumstances, although some children consistently sorted the toys by "what one can do with them" ($p < .001$), many more children were inconsistent, either sorting some sets but not others systematically or placing toys in two collections according to no apparent criterion. Thus, exploring the toys and discovering what one could do with them promoted using their functions as a basis for categorizing them.

Young children do not categorize objects and line drawings in the same way if they have explored the objects. Through exploratory activities, including play, children learn about and act on common affordances provided by different objects, and they can categorize objects according to their affordances. Assuming that objects and representations of objects are equivalent, an assumption characterizing hundreds of studies of children's categorizations, may have provided many misleading findings. Our findings provide no support for the coherence or usefulness of a distinction between how different properties are apprehended, that is, that some objective properties (e.g., color, shape) are perceived, whereas others are conceived. A distinction that is relevant for these studies, however, is that discussed earlier between direct and indirect perceiving: the importance of exploratory activity in enhancing what can be learned when there is opportunity for perceiving directly and the constraints on opportunities for exploration when only representations of objects are available to be manipulated.

CATEGORIZING OBJECTS BY FUNCTION AND BY SHAPE (CONTOUR)

The research I have just described concerns young children's categorization in circumstances in which the children are relatively unconstrained as to how they categorize—according to one of the two criteria available for sorting systematically or simply sorting unsystematically. In the second set of studies, all conducted with Gedeon Deak (Deak & Pick, 1994), we investigated preschoolers' flexibility in using different criteria for systematically sorting interesting objects. Following the assumption of segregated perceiving and conceiving, a number of investigators have argued that young children categorize objects primarily according to "physical appearance" (e.g., shape and color), and that such properties are salient and perceived, in contrast to properties such as function, which are said to be abstract and conceived and therefore difficult for preschoolers to use (e.g., Fenson, Cameron, & Kennedy, 1988; Gentner, 1978, 1989; Tomikawa & Dodd, 1980; Tversky, 1985). (Perhaps because most investigators of children's categorization treat representations as equivalent to objects, they use the term "shape" when the object property being referred to is its contour.) Even when it has been demonstrated that preschoolers can categorize objects according to their function as well as to their shape, the latter is presumed to be "salient" and a "perceptual attribute," whereas objects' functions are presumed to be apprehended by some other way (Corrigan & Schommer, 1984; Kemler-Nelson, 1991).

The general procedure in our second studies was to invite 4-year-old children to explore each of a set of three objects and subsequently to categorize a target object with one of the remaining two. Figure 9 depicts one set that included an egg-shaped tea infuser, an egg-shaped kitchen timer, and a tea infuser with a handle. The egg-shaped tea infuser had a contour similar to the timer, and it had the same function as the tea infuser with a handle. Figure 10 depicts a set that included a penlight (a flashlight with the same contour as a writing pen), a writing pen, and a flashlight. Another set included a small football, a telephone, and a telephone having the contour of a football.

It was quite difficult to assemble several sets of these objects for the obvious reason that, as noted earlier, what one can do with objects is a consequence of what they are made of and their surface layout. It is rather unusual to discover objects having similar surface layout and different mechanical functions. Of course, it is also true that the objects of these sets

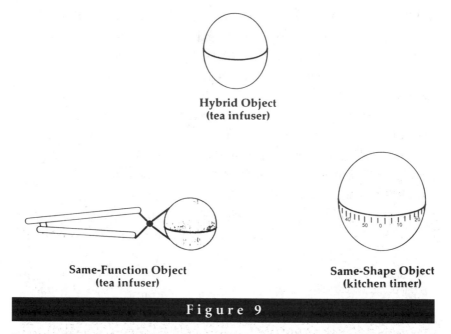

Figure 9

Egg-shaped tea infuser, egg-shaped timer, and tea infuser with handle.

having similar contours also had many of the same affordances: They could be grasped in similar ways, they could impact surfaces in similar ways, and so on. The critical feature for our research was that in these sets an interesting or complex function was shared by two objects having different shapes or surface layouts.

After the children explored the three objects of a set, had been shown their functions, and had produced the effects themselves, the two nontarget objects were each placed in a separate box, and the children were asked to put the target object in a box with one of the other objects. In a baseline (control) condition, the children were given no particular training or instructions; they were simply asked to put the target object in a box with the "one it goes with." The children explored and sorted eight sets in all.

A second group of children, in a shape-training condition, explored and sorted two "training" sets of objects for which they were told to put the target object in the box with the one that "is the same shape." For these

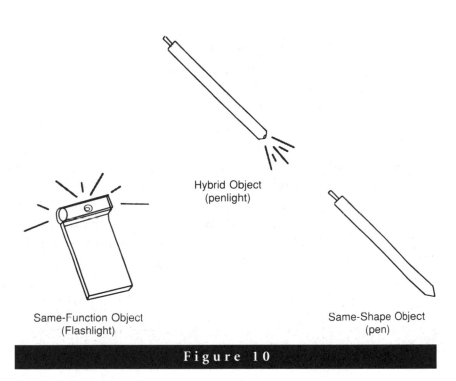

Hybrid Object
(penlight)

Same-Function Object
(Flashlight)

Same-Shape Object
(pen)

Figure 10

Pen, flashlight, and penlight.

two training sets, the children were reminded of the criterion if they did not sort according to shape. However, they then proceeded through the same eight sets with no further reference to object shape; the children were simply asked to put target objects in the boxes with the one it goes with.

A third group of children, in a function-training condition, explored and sorted two training sets for which they were told to put the target object in the box with the one that "does the same thing." They too then proceeded to explore and sort the eight other sets with no further reference to the objects' function. At the end of the procedure, all three groups of children were asked to label all of the objects. For this task, the objects were presented one at a time, out of the context of their sets, and the question, "What is this called?" was asked about each. Thus, for the children in all three groups, the procedure of exploring, sorting, and subsequently naming the eight sets of objects was identical. The only difference among the groups was the pretraining provided two groups to sort the target objects either with the same-shaped objects or with the same-function objects.

The children were very engaged in the task, as the objects were interesting and were presented with appropriate props. For example, the tea infusers were presented with tea and water that changed color as the infusers were swished in it.

The results for the three groups are depicted in the first three bars (left to right) in Figure 11. The children in the function-training group sorted most of the sets by function, whereas the children in the shape-training group sorted most of the sets by shape. The baseline (control) group children also sorted many of the sets by shape. The scores for all of the groups were significantly ($p < .01$) different from each other and from chance. A criterion for consistent sorting for a child was established as sorting six or more of the eight sets in the same way (binomial $p < .15$). The children were highly consistent in how they sorted the objects, as can be seen in Figure 12.

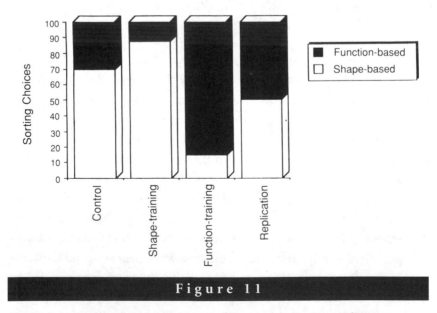

Figure 11

Children's sorting choices in initial three conditions and replication condition.

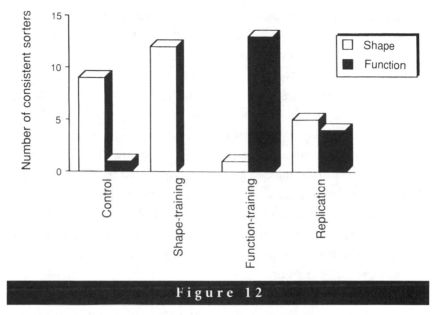

Figure 12

Number of children who sorted consistently in initial three conditions and replication condition. $n = 15$ in each condition.

Most children in the function-training group consistently sorted the objects according to their functions ($p < .001$), and most children in the shape-training group consistently sorted the objects according to their shapes ($p < .001$). Thus, simply telling the children, in the context of two pretraining object sets, to categorize according to one or another criterion had a dramatic effect on their subsequent sorting choices. When given clear directions, and interesting objects to investigate, these preschool children easily and systematically categorized according to either of the criteria of interest in this study.

More children in the baseline group sorted according to shape than according to function. This finding is consistent with the assertion of many investigators (e.g., Baldwin, 1989; Gentner, 1978; Landau, Smith, & Jones, 1988; Tomikawa & Dodd, 1980) that preschoolers are predisposed or even constrained to categorize objects according to shape or contour. However, there are some circumstances of the task itself that could have promoted the use of contour as a basis for categorization in the ambiguous baseline condition. Specifically, when the children were asked to make a sorting decision, they were no longer engaged in exploring the objects. Instead, the objects were in what might be termed a static state. The football-shaped telephone was closed; the tea infuser had been removed from the water and was resting on the table as was the penlight, which had been turned off. In such circumstances, the mechanical functions of the target objects may have been less obvious or apparent and their contours relatively more obvious.

We recruited another group of children for whom the procedure was exactly the same as for the first baseline group except that when we asked the children to make a decision about how to categorize the target objects, we displayed them in circumstances that enhanced their mechanical functions. The tea infuser was swished in water; the receiver of the football-shaped telephone was separated from it, revealing the dial and cord; and the penlight was turned on.

The results for this replication group are depicted in Figure 11. As is evident there, the children showed no predisposition to make sorting decisions according to contour; they sorted half of the sets according to contour and half according to function. Furthermore, as can be seen in Figure 12, nine children ($p < .001$) were consistent in how they sorted the objects, and they were approximately equally divided between those who sorted by shape and those who sorted by function in this still ambiguous situation. Thus, any proclivity to use a particular property as a basis for categorizing objects may reside not in the children but, as Smitsman argues (chapter 9, this volume), in the variable boundary or interaction of the children's actions on objects in their context. That some children used one property and other children used another simply reflects that both were available and perceived.

In the last phase of the procedure, the children had been asked to name each of the 24 objects. We tabulated the children's names for the target objects according to whether they referred in some way to the same-shape objects or to the same-function objects. For example, one set included an unusually shaped harmonica, a disk-shaped harmonica (pitch pipes), and a disk-shaped tape measure. If both harmonicas were called "whistles" and the tape measure was called a "measuring thing," the label "*whistle*" for the target object (the disk-shaped harmonica) was designated as a function label because it was the same name given to the same-function object. For the tea infuser/timer set, if a child called the handled tea infuser a "teaspoon," and called the target egg-shaped tea infuser an "egg," that label was designated as a shape label because it referred to its contour and that of the egg-shaped timer. A few labels (8%) were not clearly codable. For example, when a child labeled the target object with a conventional label but did not also use the same name for one of the other objects, that label was not coded, as it was not clear what aspect of the object the label reflected for the child. An example would be if a child called the penlight a "flashlight" but did not refer to the other flashlight as a "flashlight."

We were most interested in how the children labeled the eight target objects and whether their names for these objects would reflect the experimental condition in which they had participated (baseline, shape training, or function training). The results are depicted in Figure 13.

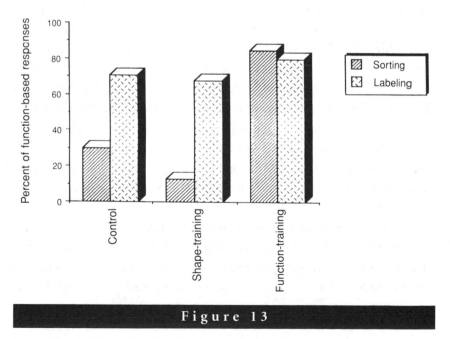

Figure 13

Percentages of children's function-based sorting and labeling responses.

Most of the children's object names referred to the object functions. This was true for the children in all three experimental conditions. Thus, although how the children categorized the target objects varied dramatically depending on the group in which they participated, their names for those objects were unaffected by their prior categorization choices. That the children's labels did not mirror their systematic categorization of the objects is a demonstration of the children's facility for considering various object properties in different contexts or tasks.

Young children are both flexible and systematic in how they sort and refer to objects they have explored. Are there limits to the consistency or systematicity with which young children can categorize interesting, complicated objects? Specifically, if children are engaged in categorizing objects systematically by one criterion, can they change their basis for categorizing them? A fifth group of 4-year-olds participated in a condition which, in effect, combined sequentially the shape-training and function-training conditions. We asked these children to change criteria midtask. The children first explored and sorted two training sets with explicit directions to categorize the target objects according to one criterion. They then explored and sorted four sets without any explicit directions, after which they were told that the game would be played a "different way," and they explored and sorted two training sets with directions to categorize the target objects according to the other criterion. Finally, they explored and sorted the final four sets, again without explicit directions.

The results were clear. Nearly all (89%) of the children's sorting decisions were consistent with their immediately prior training experiences. They were easily able to change their criteria for categorizing from function to shape, or vice versa, when they were asked to do so and to continue to use the new criteria even in the absence of explicit requests to do so.

PERCEPTUAL LEARNING AS THE FOUNDATION OF KNOWING

I have described two sets of studies about how young children categorize objects they have played with and explored. The results provide a clear demonstration that preschoolers are not bound to categorize objects in particular ways. Rather, such children can systematically categorize objects in multiple ways, reflecting opportunities provided by tasks and contexts.

The results of these studies also demonstrate that preschoolers attend to the functions of objects for which perceptual information is available. The facility with which children use different criteria for categorizing objects does not lend support to a view that some objective properties are perceived whereas others are conceived, nor does it support the underlying assumption that perceiving and conceiving are discontinuous. When the children were shown what they could do with the objects—when they manipulated them and discovered common affordances—they could spontaneously and consistently categorize them on the basis of those affordances. Exploration is an important means of learning about the properties of things (E. Gibson, 1988), but exploration is only possible when there is sufficient information to be explored. Line drawings and other representations do not permit exploration of the represented object. Perhaps earlier ideas about the development of categorization skills, and particularly about the relative ease with which young children can use shape and function as a basis for categorization, are partly a consequence of the items children have been asked to categorize.

An alternative to the idea that perceiving and conceiving are segregated is the idea, based in the ecological perspective, that there is variation in the accessibility of properties to being perceived directly. An important goal of much perceptual activity and exploration is to obtain information. As soon as they are able, infants bring objects closer than arm's length to scrutinize them and they crawl around objects to explore them from all sides. Many adults have learned how to manipulate microscopes to examine miniscule objects and surfaces, and it was little more than 25 years ago when humans were first able to observe directly the back side of the moon. To perceive the underlying structure of a flower stem, it is necessary to take it apart. However different these exploratory activities are, their purpose is similar: to reveal information for perceiving objective properties. The cognitive models referred to by Neisser (1987) and others are, after all, attempts to make sense of our observations and to enable us to predict possible new observations. In other words, our knowledge of "underlying structure" summarizes and makes explicit what someone has observed even if we have not.

From the perspective of ecological theory, one can hypothesize that an important outcome of perceptual learning in cognitive development is to make possible the perception of increasingly subtle and complex properties of objects and events in the world. Perceptual learning promotes cognitive development. Thus, learning to distinguish appearance on the one hand from function (or reality, or insides, or essences) on the other; characteristic or obvious features from defining or nonobvious features and the like; may be a matter of engaging in further exploration and scrutiny rather than a matter of learning to let cognition prevail over perception. Accounts of development based on mental representations of important properties of the world still leave the question, If representations *underlie* development, how are they acquired in the first place? Frequently, such representations are inferred from the very phenomena for which they are intended to account.

A hypothesis from ecological theory is that conceptual development is grounded in perceptual learning rather than that people think and perceive in different ways. From this ecological perspective, perception is not to be contrasted with cognition; it is the most basic kind of cognition. Perception is cognitive, not in the sense taught by Helmholtz and his successors but because it yields knowledge (E. Gibson, 1988). Tacit knowledge acquired through perceiving makes possible remembering, conceptualizing, thinking, representing, and the like (J. Gibson, 1979, pp. 260–261; Reed, 1987).

I suggest that properties used by young children to categorize objects are perceived and do not have to be constructed. Children's concepts are based in and refined by their discovery, through exploring and perceiving, of the objective properties of the world. Such discoveries as the actions different objects afford are made possible by the existence of information specifying these properties. The discoveries are achieved, and conceptual change occurs through perceptual learning, by differentiating affordances and abstracting similarities across objects.

REFERENCES

Baillargeon, R. (1987). Object permanence in 3 1/2- and 4 1/2-month-old infants. *Developmental Psychology, 23,* 655–664.

Baillargeon, R. (1993). The object concept revisited: New directions in the investigation of infants' physical knowledge. In C. Granrud (Ed.), *Visual perception and cognition in infancy* (pp. 265–315). Hillsdale, NJ: Erlbaum.

Baillargeon, R., Spelke, E., & Wasserman, S. (1985). Object permanence in five-month-old infants. *Cognition, 20,* 191–208.

Baldwin, D. (1989). Priorities in children's expectations about object label reference: Form over color. *Child Development, 60,* 1291–1306.

Baldwin, D., Markman, E., & Melartin, R. (1993). Infants' ability to draw inferences about nonobvious object properties: Evidence from exploratory play. *Child Development, 64,* 711–728.

Boring, E. G. (1950). *A history of experimental psychology* (2nd ed.). New York: Appleton-Century-Crofts.

Corrigan, R., & Schommer, M. (1984). Form versus function revisited: The role of social input and memory factors. *Child Development, 55,* 1721–1726.

Deak, G., & Pick, A. (1994). *What is a "football-telephone?" Preschoolers use shape and function to categorize objects.* Manuscript submitted for publication.

Edelman, G. (1987). *Neural Darwinism.* New York: Basic Books.

Edelman, G. (1988). *Topobiology: An introduction to molecular embryology.* New York: Basic Books.

Edelman, G. (1989). *The remembered present: A biological theory of consciousness.* New York: Basic Books.

Edelman, G. (1992). *Bright air, brilliant fire.* New York: Basic Books.

Fenson, L., Cameron, M., & Kennedy, M. (1988). Role of perceptual and conceptual similarity in category matching at two years. *Child Development, 59,* 897–907.

Flavell, J., Flavell, E., & Green, F. (1983). Development of the appearance–reality distinction. *Cognitive Psychology, 15,* 95–120.

Flavell, J., Green, F., & Flavell, E. (1986). Development of knowledge about the appearance–reality distinction. *Monographs of the Society for Research in Child Development, 51* (1, Serial No. 212).

Gelman, S., & Markman, E. (1987). Young children's inductions from natural kinds: The role of categories and appearances. *Child Development, 58,* 1532–1541.

Gelman, S., & Medin, D. (1993). What's so essential about essentialism? A different perspective on the interaction of perception, language, and conceptual knowledge. *Cognitive Development, 8*, 157–167.

Gelman, S., & Wellman, H. (1991). Insides and essences: Early understandings of the non-obvious. *Cognition, 38*, 213–244.

Gentner, D. (1978). A study of early word meaning using artificial objects: What looks like a jiggy but acts like a zimbo? *Papers and Reports on Child Language Development, 15*, 1–6.

Gentner, D. (1989). The mechanisms of analogical learning. In S. Vosniadou & A. Ortony (Eds.), *Similarity and analogical reasoning* (pp. 199–241). Cambridge, England: Cambridge University Press.

Gibson, E. (1988). Exploratory behavior in the development of perceiving, acting, and the acquiring of knowledge. *Annual Review of Psychology, 39*, 1–41.

Gibson, J. (1967). New reasons for realism. *Synthese, 17*, 162–172.

Gibson, J. (1979). *The ecological approach to visual perception.* Boston: Houghton Mifflin.

Granrud, C., Yonas, A., Smith, I., Arterberry, M., Glicksman, M., & Sorkness, A. (1984). Infants' sensitivity to accretion and deletion of texture as information for depth at an edge. *Child Development, 55*, 1630–1636.

Jones, R. (1982). *An ecological approach to the development of picture perception.* Unpublished doctoral dissertation, University of Minnesota, Minneapolis.

Jones, R., & Pick, A. (1981). Categorization and affordances. *The Behavioral and Brain Sciences, 4*, 292–293.

Jones, S., & Smith, L. (1993). The place of perception in children's concepts. *Cognitive Development, 8*, 113–139.

Jones, S., Smith, L., & Landau, B. (1991). Object properties and knowledge in early lexical learning. *Child Development, 62*, 499–516.

Kaplan, G. (1969). Kinetic disruption of optical texture: The perception of depth at an edge. *Perception and Psychophysics, 6*, 193–198.

Kaufman, L. (1974). *Sight and mind: An introduction to visual perception.* New York: Oxford University Press.

Keil, F. (1989). *Concepts, kinds, and cognitive development.* Cambridge, MA: MIT Press.

Keil, F., & Batterman, N. (1984). A characteristic-to-defining shift in the development of word meaning. *Journal of Verbal Learning and Verbal Behavior, 23*, 221–236.

Kemler-Nelson, D. (1991, March). *Principle-based inferences in preschoolers' catego-*

rization of novel artifacts. Poster presented at the Biennial Convention of the Society for Research in Child Development, Seattle, WA.

Landau, B., Smith, L., & Jones, S. (1988). The importance of shape in early lexical learning. *Cognitive Development, 3,* 299–321.

Mandler, J. (1988). How to build a baby: On the development of an accessible representational system. *Cognitive Development, 3,* 113–136.

Mandler, J. (1993). On concepts. *Cognitive Development, 8,* 141–148.

Melendez, P., Bales, D., & Pick, A. (1993). *Direct and indirect perception: Four-year-olds' grouping of toys.* Poster presented at the Society for Research in Child Development, New Orleans, LA.

Melendez, P., Bales, D., Ruffing, M., & Pick, A. (1995). *Preschoolers' categorization of objects and representations.* Poster presented at the Society for Research in Child Development, Indianapolis, IN.

Merriman, W., Scott, P., & Marazita, J. (1993). An appearance–function shift in children's object naming. *Journal of Child Language, 20,* 101–118.

Mervis, C., Johnson, K., & Scott, P. (1993). Perceptual knowledge, conceptual knowledge, and expertise: Comment on Jones and Smith. *Cognitive Development, 8,* 149–155.

Needham, A., & Baillargeon, R. (1993). Intuitions about support in 4.5-month-old infants. *Cognition, 47,* 121–148.

Neisser, U. (1987). From direct perception to conceptual structure. In U. Neisser (Ed.), *Concepts and conceptual development* (pp. 11–24). Cambridge, England: Cambridge University Press.

Reed, E. (1987). James Gibson's ecological approach to cognition. In A. Costall & A. Still (Eds.), *Alternatives to cognitivism* (pp. 142–173). Brighton: Harvester.

Reed, E. (1988). *James J. Gibson and the psychology of perception.* New Haven, CT: Yale University Press.

Rock, I. & Kaufman, L. (1962). The moon illusion, II. *Science, 136,* 1023–1031.

Sedgwick, H.A. (1980). The geometry to spatial layout in pictorial representations. In M.A. Hagen (Ed.), The perception of pictures (pp. 33–90). San Diego, CA: Academic Press.

Smitsman, A., Loosbroek, E.v., & Pick, A. (1987). The primacy of affordances in categorization by children. *British Journal of Developmental Psychology, 5,* 265–273.

Smitsman, A., & Pick, A. (1983). Perception of inclusion in collections of objects. In D. Rogers & J. Sloboda (Eds.), *Acquisition of symbolic skills* (pp. 335–342). New York: Plenum.

Tomikawa, S., & Dodd, D. (1980). Early word meanings: Perceptually or functionally based? *Child Development, 51,* 1103–1109.

Tversky, B. (1985). Development of taxonomic organization of named and pictured categories. *Developmental Psychology, 21,* 1111–1119.

Ullman, S. (1980). Against direct perception. *The Behavioral and Brain Sciences, 3,* 373–381.

Comment on Pick

Karl M. Newell

A nne Pick examines the role of affordances in the ecological approach
to perception and action within the context of children's perceptual
learning and cognitive development. The experimental work clearly reveals that under different task constraints than is the norm for extant developmental perceptual learning studies one obtains different outcomes
and, as a consequence, support for different theoretical inferences. In discussing Pick's chapter I have organized my comments around three
themes: the concept of task, the concept of exploration, and the old developmental chestnut of continuity and discontinuity in the change of behavior over time.

TASK CONSTRAINTS

The basic experimental finding Pick presents is that the task change from
drawings and pictures to actual objects produces a dramatic difference in
young children's perceptual categorization of objects. The functional as-

Newell comments on Pick from an ecological realist perspective.

pects of the objects seem to be more readily incorporated into the categorization when the objects may be physically explored. In short, the change from a two- to a three-dimensional representation of the object produces qualitatively significant differences in children's perceptual categorization.

This finding is an example of the notion that small changes in the task constraints (in this case from pictures to objects) can alter the domain outcome quite significantly and often promote different theories or models for the behavior under consideration. This task and theory specificity has long been evident in the movement domain wherein the examination of so-called simple movement tasks has also led to the formation of relatively complex theories and vice versa. It appears that if one minimizes the dynamical structure in the task interaction, as in the keypress or single joint positioning tasks that have dominated the movement field for a hundred years, one tends to generate rather complex accounts of those movement phenomena. On the other hand, when a rich dynamical structure is inherent in the interaction with the environment in pursuit of the task outcome, the learner can take advantage of that structure, and, furthermore, less complexity is required of the theorizer. *Complexity* is used here to mean the degree of detail in the representational theories that are generated to account for the behavior.

Pick's perceptual studies are consistent with this relation between the relative structures of tasks and theories. If one examines the invariant and variant properties between the line drawings of objects, photographs of those same objects, and the objects themselves in a playful, interactive setting for the child, one notices that certain properties are preserved across these situations. Furthermore, in the playful interaction setting there is a richer presentation, not only of the properties of the objects but also of the dynamical properties that are available in the interaction with those objects. This seems to be a nice example of the problems of doing theoretical work on so-called simple tasks wherein we tend to simplify the situation for ourselves as experimenters but then we have made it more complicated for the individual and, ultimately, for our own theorizing.

Task constraints are a significant source to the confluence of constraints that are present in action and interact with organismic and environmental constraints in channeling the dynamics of behavior in perceiving and acting. Task constraints may be viewed as action goals and rules that specify or constrain particular coordination solutions. Small changes in task constraints can lead to large-scale, qualitative changes in the emerging movement dynamics and the perception of what the environment affords.

Affordances and tasks are linked in that task goals can arise from the affordance in the circumstance. In Pick's experiments a good number of these task constraints are provided implicitly. It is important to note that some of the previous examinations of the affordance concept have had the task goal provided explicitly, whereas in other cases they are merely implicit. A number of the body-scaling tests of the affordance concept have been compromised by the explicit presentation of a task goal by the experimenter. One of the advantages of doing work with infants (though it is usually seen as a disadvantage) is that infants often do not understand an oral transmission of an extrinsically determined action goal. There are clearly important links between tasks and affordances, and these offer interesting areas for future theoretical and empirical work.

EXPLORATION

Pick promotes rather strongly the idea that exploration is a significant factor in organizing the functional categorization of the objects. It appears, however, that there is more going on in the children's interaction with the objects than mere exploration. It could well be that the children are actually engaged in other cognitive activities while interacting with the object, and one could ask whether the functional categorizations made were in any way linked to the activities that the children were engaged in while playing with the objects. There needs to be a distinction between exploration and actual engagement in other actions, and an investigation of the degree to which other cognitive activities may influence perceptual categorization. In other words I am suggesting that exploration is only part of the story in these perceptual studies, and it is being used by Pick in a broader sense than may ultimately be useful.

Exploratory behavior has some systematic components to it. The systematic components may be revealed in the search strategies adopted by the individual in the task situation. In Pick's experiments it would be revealing to determine whether there is structure to the children's exploration of the objects and how the search behavior varies with the nature of the object and the individual. There are a number of domains in which the concept of search strategies have been examined, and object categorization is another area in which it could be fruitfully applied. The concept of exploration clearly plays a strong role in the effects that Pick has shown, but my sense is that it needs to be unpacked a little bit more from the experimental findings to determine the nature and influence of this functional activity in the development of perceptual categorization. Theoretically, task constraints contribute to channeling the search of the perceptual–motor workspace in the ecological approach to perception and action.

CONTINUITY–DISCONTINUITY

Pick interprets her findings as consistent with a continuous account of the development of different cognitive activities such as perceiving and knowing, and this is articulated as consistent with E. J. and J. J. Gibson's position. However, one needs to be clear in distinguishing what is being compared when one infers continuity or discontinuity from changes in behavior over time. One may observe parallel trajectories over time between the development of different cognitive activities, but the function of those trajectories themselves could be discontinuous. One can also observe continuity or discontinuity in terms of the change within a particular cognitive activity over time. Thus, the general issue of continuity–discontinuity in development can be looked at in different frames of reference, and the frame of reference being used to interpret the particular change in behavior must be clear. Pick is suggesting continuity between the development of particular activities over time rather than emphasizing the continuity of the development of a particular cognitive event over time.

One of the major issues arising is the operational problem of measuring continuity and discontinuity. When is a change in behavior continuous, and when is it discontinuous? Furthermore, discontinuities in development can occur at one level of analysis, whereas continuities may exist at another level of analysis. These contrasts represent examples of the importance of determining the appropriate frame of reference to characterize change in behavioral development. Thus, although Pick's data are consistent in suggesting a continuous account of perceptual learning, they do not provide a direct test of this issue. Change in behavior can be, or is often, discontinuous, but to demonstrate that development is anything other than continuous is operationally a very difficult task.

Dynamic Systems

Dynamic Systems

Cathy Dent-Read and Patricia Zukow-Goldring

The second part of this book includes chapters from researchers using dynamic systems theory. Work from the dynamic systems approach explicates in detail how organism and environment function as a system, using models of dynamic self-organizing systems in physics (e.g., Butterworth, 1993; Thelen & Smith, 1994). Development is not the specification of some preordained outcome, but the process of becoming. In a dynamic system, elements assemble for functional ends in a fluid, task-specific manner. All elements have equal causal potential, properties of the system emerge over time, and changes can be linear or nonlinear. Variability indicates reorganization rather than error to be explained away. As new options open up, a stable state is lost, chaos ensues, new stabilities emerge, and the cycle continues.

Because dynamic systems theory has the capacity to integrate micro- (neural excitation) and macro-levels (limb movement) of functioning, more powerful and comprehensive explanations of the emergence of complex behaviors result from this approach than from reductionist traditional theories (Aslin, 1993). Although it explains how changes in state emerge, dynamic systems theory does not predict when or how long it will take to reach a new stability (von Hofsten, 1989).

Within a dynamic systems approach to development, the performance of a task depends on assembling aspects of the system that have the potential for continuously affecting each other. For example, maturational status, experience, and the current context of action continuously coordinate and modify each other as an activity emerges. The dynamic systems approach states that as organisms develop, their response modes (called *attractor states*, the states the system wants to be in) become increasingly stable and well-defined. The same processes underlie development and learning; only the time scale differs.

Researchers have used dynamic systems models primarily to study motor development (Thelen & Ulrich, 1991) and speech (Saltzman, 1989). Others have extended this method to the development of conventionalized behavior, such as language and communication, including the lexicon (McCune, 1992; Smith, 1995) and social interaction (Fogel & Thelen, 1987). This approach leads to studying not only obvious vocalizations and gestures but also other relevant systems such as respiration, locomotion, and visual orienting (Fogel & Thelen, 1987; Goldfield, 1993; McCune, 1992).

The two chapters in this section represent a classic motor development topic and a newer topic of research from the dynamic systems perspective, namely, social interaction. Jane Clark delineates the development of skill, because becoming skilled emerges from the reciprocal control of organism and environment. Clark uses locomotion as a window on behavioral development as she follows infants on their paths from nonlocomoting to easily locomoting in a cluttered world. Weaving together the seeming complexity of muscles, receptors, and neurons, Clark's application of the dynamical systems approach reveals a variable that accounts for walking and the change from an unskilled to a skilled walker: shank motion.

Alan Fogel describes development as a co-creative process between the individual and the environment, including other people, that results in the emergence of dynamically stable frames that constrain future co-action. Illustrating these ideas with studies of prereaching, enabled reaching, and postreaching, he and his colleagues observed changes in infant–mother interaction in the course of laboratory observations. Fogel suggests that the culture of toys and methods of infant care coregulate patterns of action within the infant–mother relationship system.

From a dynamic systems perspective, the dynamic relation of organism characteristics and environmental variables relevant for a task changes with development. Such a system becomes more complex and less perturbable with development through the action of contextual variables that move the system from one steady state to another. Clark shows that postural support moves the systems of the locomoting child into a new organization, walking, when shank motion stabilizes around an attractor. Fogel shows that the infant–mother–toy system changes as infants gain the ability to reach and when mothers show affect along with using toys.

Several questions emerge when one considers dynamic systems work on development. How does an organism affect its environment, not just coordinate with an unresponsive environment? How is the organism in contact with the environment? To what degree do dynamic systems approaches draw on assumptions and theory from the indirect perception/mental mediation point of view? Do the same principles apply to dynamic systems within animate beings as in animate–inanimate systems? In other words, whose goals enter into accepting or assigning a task? Self-organization belies the need for *a priori* internal plans as causes of behavior, but what is the self in such a system? Do all dynamic systems investigations require the use of certain mathematical models or analyses in order to qualify as dynamic systems?

REFERENCES

Aslin, R. (1993). Commentary: The strange attractiveness of dynamic systems to development. In L. Smith & E. Thelen (Eds.), *A dynamic systems approach to development: Applications* (pp. 385–399). Cambridge, MA: MIT Press.

Butterworth, G. (1993). Dynamic approaches to infant perception and action: Old and new theories about the origins of knowledge. In L. Smith & E. Thelen (Eds.), *A dynamic systems approach to development: Applications* (pp. 171–187). Cambridge, MA: MIT Press.

Fogel, A., & Thelen, E. (1987). Development of early expressive and communicative action: Reinterpreting the evidence from a dynamic systems perspective. *Developmental Psychology, 23,* 747–761.

Goldfield, E. (1993). Dynamic systems in development: Action systems. In L. Smith & E. Thelen (Eds.), *A dynamic systems approach to development: Applications* (pp. 51–70). Cambridge, MA: MIT Press.

McCune, L. (1992). First words: A dynamic systems view. In C. Ferguson, L. Menn, & C. Stoel-Gammon (Eds.), *Phonological development: Models, research, implications* (pp. 313–336). Baltimore: York Press.

Saltzman, E. (1989). A dynamical approach to gestural patterning in speech production. *Ecological Psychology, 1,* 333–382.

Smith, L. (1995). Self-organizing processes in learning to learn words: Development is not induction. In C. Nelson (Ed.), *The Minnesota Symposium on Child Development: Vol. 28. Basic and applied perspectives on learning, cognition, and development* (pp. 1–32). Hillsdale, NJ: Erlbaum.

Thelen, E., & Smith, L. (1994). *A dynamic systems approach to the development of cognition and action.* Cambridge, MA: MIT Press.

Thelen, E., & Ulrich, B. D. (1991). Hidden skills. *Monograph of the Society for Research in Child Development, 56*(1, Serial No. 223).

von Hofsten, C. (1989). Motor development as the development of systems: Comments on the special section. *Developmental Psychology, 25,* 950–953.

11

A Dynamical Systems Perspective on the Development of Complex Adaptive Skill

Jane E. Clark

The study of human behavioral development is the study of life span behavioral change and the processes that underlie that change. Whatever the domain of behavior, two questions are central to the developmentalist's study: (a) What changes? and (b) How does change occur, that is, what is the nature of the processes underlying change? In this chapter, I outline how a developmentalist might use the dynamical systems perspective to pursue these questions. The chapter is not intended as an exhaustive discussion of the dynamical systems perspective, in general, or its application to development, in specific. The literature contains many excellent reviews on the subject, and the interested reader is referred to these for a more detailed presentation than is possible in the present chapter (cf. Levine & Fitzgerald, 1992; Smith & Thelen, 1993; Thelen & Smith, 1994; Thelen & Ulrich, 1991). Here I focus on what I believe are the major concepts essential to understanding dynamical systems. I follow this with an account of how these concepts have been applied to the problem of understanding developing systems. The chapter ends with a discussion of the limitations and challenges of a dynamical systems perspective for the understanding of behavioral development. To anchor the discussion, my examples are drawn from the behavioral domain of *skill* development. Whereas my own research has a much narrower focus, namely, the development of *motor* skill, in this chapter I expand the window to the broader issues of skill to include all domains of skilled or competent behavior.

SKILL: THE DEVELOPMENT OF ORGANISM–ENVIRONMENT MUTUALITIES

Skill is a good exemplar for a discussion of ecological approaches to development. Although there are many definitions of skill, all include a concept of skill that embodies the mutuality of the organism and environment. Children have a skill for swimming, a skill for communicating with others, a skill for feeding themselves, a skill for mathematical operations. In each case, the child's skill is in a context, in an environment (Fischer, Bullock, Rotenberg, & Raya, 1993).

Indeed, the three often mentioned characteristics of skill include an implied if not explicit reference to defining skill in context. For example, skill is often characterized as efficient. The individual has accomplished the task with some minimal effort. A flailing swimmer or child struggling for a long time to work through a math problem would not be considered skilled. So how does one know when one is skillful? If the criterion is efficiency, one would look to the context, the environment to define what might be considered efficient.

Skill also connotes an organism that behaves adaptively. If the environment changes, the skilled individual adjusts. To a skilled mathematician, solving new problems presents little difficulty. Skilled readers can adapt to handwritten texts that are nearly illegible, whereas the young reader just learning cursive script may have considerable difficulty with the same text. Again, the characteristic of skill is defined by what the individual can do in an environment. Finally, definitions of skill include the notion that the goal is achieved with maximal certainty (Guthrie, 1952). For example, a skilled golfer is one whose shot travels to its intended target with a high probability. Similarly, the child skilled at arithmetic is one who with reasonable certainty arrives at the correct answer to a math problem.

Implied in all these characteristics of skill is the organism–environment mutuality. Efficient for what? Adapted to what? Maximal certainty at what? The environment provides the context within which skill is defined. Change the context and the individual's level of performance may change. When a tennis player competes against an individual of the same or lower level of skill, the player may exhibit all the characteristics of skillfulness. However, if that same tennis player competes against someone at a much higher ranking, he or she may look like a struggling novice. Similarly, an infant may demonstrate skilled cup usage that can disappear when larger cups are involved or when the cup is filled to the brim. Skill, it is argued, can only be understood as an organism–environment transaction.

Thus, the development of skill provides a window through which one can examine how the organism changes in its interactions with the environment. Moreover, it defines an end state, namely skillfulness, from which to view the course of the developmental path.

ESSENTIAL CONCEPTS OF A DYNAMICAL SYSTEMS APPROACH

Three broadly defined concepts are essential to an understanding of a dynamical systems approach. The first is a definition and description of what a dynamical system is. The second and third include concepts about the origins and behaviors of dynamical systems.

A Dynamical System

A *dynamical system* is a system that changes over time (Crutchfield, Farmer, Packard, & Shaw, 1987; Rosen, 1970). The system is one of many interacting elements. In mathematical terms, the dynamical system is a system of differential equations that describe the way the system changes over time. These equations, however, are not easily understood when taken together. Separately they can be tracked, but if one wants to understand the *system* of equations, then the problem is intractable. The mathematician Smale is given credit for reviving the notion originally proposed by Poincaré in the late 1800s that a dynamical system can be understood globally by examining its geometry (Gleick, 1987; Stewart, 1989). At any instant in time, the state of a system can be represented by a point on a geometric shape. As the system changes in time, the point changes and an orbit or trajectory emerges, giving the system its characteristic shape. This shape is described in the system's *state space*, that is, the geometric space in which all the states of the system can be found (Abraham, Abraham, & Shaw, 1992). The geometric shape is defined by state variables that capture the system's behavior. The trajectories of dynamical systems are attracted to certain points, areas, or orbits. Three fundamental shapes or attractors of dynamical systems have been identified: point, periodic, and chaotic.

The dynamical system reveals itself if one finds the appropriate state variables to capture the behavior of the system. This is no trivial matter. In physical systems such as a swinging pendulum, the state variables that capture the system's behavior are straightforward. For example, Rosen (1970) has suggested that a variable and its first derivative would be sufficient in many cases to completely describe a system. Indeed this is the case for the simple pendulum where mapping the pendulum's position and velocity fully captures the pendulum's behavior. However, when biological systems are considered, behaviors such as skill become a challenge for the dynamicist. What variables does one choose that will "capture" skill? No variables have privilege. If one is to succeed, however, one must find the minimum set of variables that capture the system's behavior.

For purposes of illustration, the development of skill using the standard performance curve (Figure 1, Panel a) may be examined. The changing performance on some skill over a period of time might represent the number of words a child has in his or her vocabulary, the distance a ball can be thrown, or the number of items remembered. The top curve is based on the logistic equation—that is, a curve derived as a function of the individual's present performance versus the rate of growth of that performance. In Figure 1a, the y-axis represents the performance scores for three individuals who have different rates of change in performance. To represent the system in state space, one must find a set of variables that captures the dynamical system. Using Rosen's suggestion (1970), one may

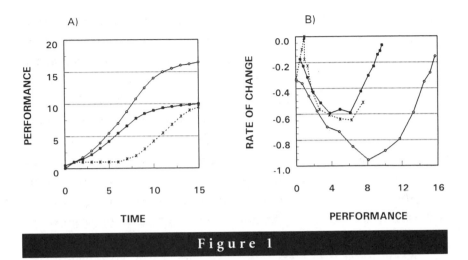

Figure 1

Panel A: The performance scores of three individuals plotted across time. Panel B: The same three subjects' performance is plotted on the x-axis while the rate of change of this performance is plotted on the y-axis.

plot the dependent variable (i.e., the performance score) against its first derivative (i.e., the rate of change of performance). Figure 1b then represents a plot of the performance score (x) and its rate of change $(\dot{x})$. This plot is a state space description of a skill's development in three individuals. First note that each has a different trajectory. Although the three learners begin at about the same point and actually seem to travel together at the start of learning, they clearly end in different places. These three data sets have no typical or average path to the end state. All three trajectories, however, result from the same set of dynamical equations. What causes the differences seen in Figure 1b are differences in the rate of skill acquisition.

As a starting point, this state space representation of skill acquisition could serve as a model for dynamical system theorizing. Of course, one could explore other models as well. For example, one could plot a child's performance against parental expectation or a child's performance against the child's own expectancies. One model that I found very compelling was one described by Boysson-Bardies (1990) in which infants' vowel production was modeled by two speech variables (F1 and F2), as presented in Figure 2. She and her colleagues measured infants from several language groups (French, English, Cantonese, Algerian). Figure 2 represents the state space for the infants' vocalizations. Notice the separate basins of attraction formed by the four language groups. One might imagine that if these infants had been followed across the development of their speech from the onset of babbling to first word production, their state space representation may well have revealed the emergence of separate basins of attraction arising from a global, shared basin. That is, at the onset of babbling all of the infants would be attracted to one region of the state space, but with increased exposure to their native language, separate basins of attraction would appear—in a process reminiscent of Werner's orthogenetic principle in which development proceeds from a state of relative globality to one of increasing differentiation (Werner, 1957).

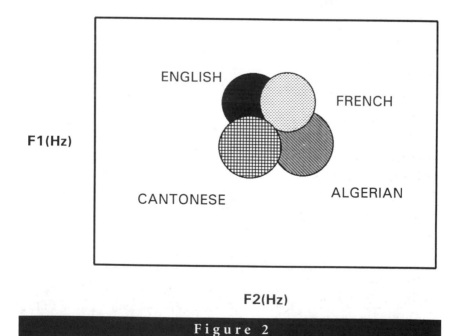

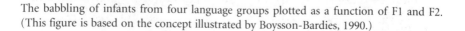

Figure 2

The babbling of infants from four language groups plotted as a function of F1 and F2. (This figure is based on the concept illustrated by Boysson-Bardies, 1990.)

To understand where this dynamical model or any other dynamical model might fit in development in general and skill development specifically, we require two additional concepts, constraints and self-organization.

Behavior Emerges From a Multitude of Constraints

It is important to recognize that the dynamical system's behavior is an emergent property. Therefore, the attractors that might be revealed in dynamical modeling are emergent phenomena. Behavior is not prescribed by some all-knowing executive that resides in the brain, but emerges from external and internal constraints. These constraints are information to the system that set the boundaries or limits for behavior.

Constraints arise from three sources: the organism itself, the environment, and the task (Newell, 1986). The *organism constraints* are those constraints embodied in the individual. These include the many subsystems of the individual, both physical (e.g., muscular, skeletal, endocrine) and psychological (e.g., memory, attention). *Environmental constraints* refer to the physical as well as sociocultural environment surrounding the individual. The physical environmental constraints might include gravity, ambient light, or the support surface. The sociocultural milieu also offers constraints. Reed's (1993; Reed & Bril, 1996) concept of a *field of promoted action*—namely, those actions and affordances emphasized by a culture— is an example of how the environment constrains an infant's behavior. The third source of constraint arises from the task at hand. What is to be done? What behavior is required? This latter source of constraints marshals the system for the observed action.

A Self-Organizing System

Constraints are necessary for the emergence of behavior, but they are not sufficient. One more ingredient must be added, namely, the concept of self-organization (Prigogine & Stengers, 1984). This is the key to understanding how ordered behavior emerges out of high degree-of-freedom open systems. Complex, biological systems are composed of many subsystems (i.e., constraints). These subsystems are in constant fluctuation.

Interactions between subsystems are often nonlinear and far from equilibrium. As a result of these instabilities, behavioral patterns emerge that are not specified or apparent by examination of any one subsystem. Similarly, changes in other constraints, namely environmental or task, can push the system to re-organize itself.

Self-organizing systems have several properties that have consequences for developing behavioral systems. First, self-organizing systems exhibit multiple stable states. Second, these states change when a constraint or subsystem (referred to as a *control parameter* in this instance) is scaled to some critical level. Third, as the control parameter is being scaled, the system passes through a region of instability. At that time, the system is particularly sensitive to perturbations or changes in constraints.

A DYNAMICAL SYSTEM PERSPECTIVE ON DEVELOPING BEHAVIORAL SYSTEMS

The general aim of all scientists is to find order in disorder. Theories of course are intended to help accomplish that aim. They provide sets of explicit propositions intended to bring order and explanation to a domain. Although the term *theory* is often juxtaposed with dynamical systems, *perspective* or *approach* is a more appropriate term to describe scientific efforts to date. However the literature includes a number of hypotheses and propositions that suggest that scientists are getting closer to an explicit dynamical systems theory of behavioral development. Certainly those who have adopted the perspective have a different approach to the developmentalist's two questions posed at the beginning of this chapter than those coming from other perspectives. A dynamical systems perspective, like any viewpoint, gives a developmentalist a particular angle on the phenomenon of interest that is quite different from other perspectives. Moreover, the perspective filters out some phenomena and zooms in on others. As I stated at this chapter's onset, the study of human behavioral development is the study of life span behavioral change and the processes that underlie that change. This definition is not unique to a dynamical systems approach. What is unique, however, is how a dynamical systems approach answers the two fundamental questions of the developmentalist: What changes, and how does change occur?

What Changes?

Since the time of Tiedemann (1787, as cited by Borstelmann, 1983), scientists have been detailing the remarkable changes that occur in the first years of life. The field of human development is rich with descriptions of changing behavior. But what are we trying to understand? What should we be looking at? What should we be describing, measuring, and analyzing? These are not trivial questions, and the answers we give surely differ with our perspective.

Patterns

From a dynamical systems perspective, behavioral *patterns* are the phenomena of interest (cf. Kelso, DelColle, & Schöner, 1990; Thelen & Ulrich, 1991; Turvey & Fitzpatrick, 1993). Patterns, it is argued, compress the incredible number of degrees of freedom from which the behaviors arise. Using the strategies of synergetics (Haken, 1977), a collective variable (or order parameter) is identified for a behavioral pattern. The collective variable is then mapped in state space and its attractor dynamics determined. As mentioned earlier, finding the variables to map in state space is a challenge made more difficult for the developmentalist because often variables are sought that track over a long time scale. For example, in analyzing skill development, what measure or measures would capture the performance of a 2-, 10-, 40-, and 80-year-old?

Constraints

The dynamical systems approach also draws attention to the constraints that are within and surround the developing system. If behavioral patterns emerge from constraints, then it follows that changes in those constraints are critical to an understanding of the developing behavioral patterns. One must examine multiple constraints simultaneously, and the examination should include constraints arising from the organism, the environment, and the task itself. Constraints change at different rates. Some are fast growers, others are slow and steady, and still others grow in spurts. Although behavior emerges from the interaction of all the surrounding constraints, only a few may be developmentally relevant. Thelen (1986), for example, proposed eight potential constraints that might limit the rate of development for the attainment of upright locomotion. In later work (Thelen & Ulrich, 1991), this approach yielded a picture of how these developing subsystems coalesce when infants are placed on a treadmill. This work also suggested the possibility that several constraints acted as *control parameters* in the development of treadmill walking.

Control Parameters

A control parameter is a constraint that when scaled to a critical level changes the state of the dynamic system. Thelen and Ulrich (1991), for example, found evidence that would suggest that particular neurological and musculoskeletal properties of the legs may act as control parameters to push the infant toward a more mature pattern of alternating steps. Similarly, posture and strength may well be the control parameters that operate in the transition from crawling to upright independent walking (Clark & Phillips, 1993). From a dynamical systems perspective, control parameters are critical to understanding developing systems. Careful description of potential control parameters is an important first step in a dynamical analysis of a developing system.

Periods of Transition

In deciding what phenomena to examine, one also must decide *when* to examine the phenomena. The general idea behind dynamical systems analysis is to characterize and understand stable patterns of behavior. However, it is clear that if systems are to develop, well-established patterns must give way to new patterns. As systems pass from one stable regime to another, they go through a period of *instability*. This is a transition period and an important window of opportunity for a dynamical analysis. Manipulating constraints during this period should reveal which is acting as a control parameter for the emergence of the new behavior. Thus, for example, if one suspects that a particular change in a constraint brings about the new behavior, manipulating that constraint through this transition period should move the system into the new behavior or conversely back to the previous behavior. Indeed, the organism seems particularly sensitive during this period to changes in the control parameter.

The Individual

The emphasis in traditional theories of development is on group data. Theoretical hypotheses are framed such that the average performance of one age group is contrasted with the average performance of another age group. Differences in group means are taken as differences in hypothetical underlying mechanisms. In a dynamical systems approach to understanding the developmental process, the emphasis is shifted from aggregate data to the examination of the individual. The principles of development are revealed not in studying group performance, but in studying individuals in great detail. Dense longitudinal data from multiple measures hold the most promise for revealing the transitional periods and the control parameters that operate during these periods. The focus on the individual, however, should not be misunderstood. The dynamical systems approach seeks to understand global principles of development but differs from other approaches by suggesting that global principles of development should be sought in the local details of the interactions of many processes (Smith & Thelen, 1993). The emphasis is on understanding the process or processes by which an individual acquires a skill.

How Does Change Occur?

It should be obvious from the foregoing section that the dynamical systems approach presents a way to understand not only what is changing, but also the processes that underlie developmental change. Thus, this approach has a strong emphasis on *how* change occurs. Unlike many theoretical perspectives, the dynamical systems approach does not posit "structures" or "ghosts in the machine" that direct behavior; rather, behavior is an emergent phenomenon. Therefore, how behavior arises is an important issue for the dynamical systems approach.

An Open, Nonlinear, Dissipative System

To understand the processes of any system one must understand the type of system under study. Systems may be identified as isolated, closed, or open (Çambel, 1993). Humans are open systems, that is, systems that exchange matter, energy, and information over their boundaries. Open systems can be in equilibrium with their environment or they can be in a nonequilibrium state. Systems that are far from equilibrium seek equilibrium. Under certain constrained conditions, however, nonequilibrium can be sustained (Nicolis & Prigogine, 1989). Systems can be conservative or dissipative. In conservative systems, global properties such as energy are maintained over time. Dissipative systems, on the other hand, are systems that lose energy. Open, dissipative systems are nonlinear systems. Linear systems are those systems in which the output is proportional to the input. Nonlinear systems, however, may have a disproportionate change to a small input in critical regions. Humans can be described as open, nonlinear, dissipative dynamical systems.

Constraints as Information

Boundary conditions or constraints act as parameters on dynamical systems. They are the force that shapes the emerging behavior. For the dynamical system, constraints are information. If the system changes, one can say that a constraint changed. Information has flowed into the system. This is a property of dynamical systems that pertains to physical systems as well as human ones. Although it might have psychological meaning, information flow is nonetheless a property of all dynamical systems. Information from the organism, the environment, and the task converge to produce a dynamical system. Constraints (i.e., information) are essential ingredients of change in a dynamical system.

Scaling a Control Parameter

To have behavioral change, a stable pattern of behavior must give way to a new pattern. If behavioral patterns are emergent from constraints, then it follows that if constraints change, the pattern may well change. However, the behavioral pattern changes only if one or more constraints are *scaled* to some critical system-sensitive value. Operationally, constraints that change the system's behavior are termed *control parameters*. As a control parameter is scaled in value, it may cause the system to go through a *bifurcation*—that is, the point where the system spontaneously changes to a new behavioral pattern. This bifurcation is a qualitative change in the system's underlying dynamics. Obviously, bifurcations are important to developmentalists because they signify new behavioral patterns. The challenge, of course, is to find the collective variable that describes the stable patterns and the control parameter or parameters that has pushed the system into the new pattern.

Feedback

Classically, information about the difference between a desired end state and the present state is referred to as *feedback*. If a child reaches for a toy and misses, there is information in this miss. However, information is only available if the system recognizes the information. That is, *information* is operationally defined as something that affects the system. Feedback can act linearly or it can have nonlinear effects. Imagine the effect of visual information that is scaled up slowly having small incremental and proportional effects on a behavior, but in some region of the system's behavioral regime, that small incremental change has a dramatic effect on the system's behavior. This might happen in driving a car, where the slowing of the car in front of one leads to an easing off the accelerator. However, at some point, easing off the accelerator abruptly ends and slamming on the brake results. Feedback is an important component of how change occurs in a dynamical system, particularly for change toward some desired end state.

Self-Regulation

Unlike physical systems, humans are capable of self-regulation. They are capable of controlling constraints and of setting end-state goals, such as reaching for a cup. They have intention. In a dynamical systems perspective intentions act to set constraints. If individuals intend an action, they must constrain their system. Learning which constraints to use and the level at which to set the constraint is critical to many behavioral patterns. Indeed, some skilled behaviors are so far from equilibrium that maintaining them is a difficult balancing act (Kelso, DeGuzman, & Holroyd, 1991).

Task Dynamics

It is often the case that no one constraint (i.e., control parameter) forces the system to a new behavior or that the same constraint has the same ef-

fect each time in changing a behavior. Indeed, looking for a singular control parameter as the cause of behavioral change is often a fruitless effort.
Kelso and his colleagues (Schöner & Kelso, 1988a, 1988b; Zanone & Kelso,
1992, 1994; Zanone, Kelso, & Jeka, 1993) suggest that as we attempt to
change behavior or learn a skill, the requirements of the task (of which
there are often many) act as behavioral information that itself has a dynamic. Learning a new skill reflects the cooperative or competitive interplay between the organism's intrinsic dynamics and the task dynamics.[1]
Task dynamics, like behavioral patterns, arise not from a single constraint
but from a collection of constraints that surround the required action.
They act as a perturbation to the stable behavioral pattern. Zanone and
Kelso (1994) hypothesized that learning a skill is dependent on the distance between the to-be-learned pattern and the nearest existing pattern
of the organism. Abrupt changes occur, they argued, when the to-be-
learned pattern is far from the intrinsic pattern, and smooth change occurs when the two dynamics are close.

AN EXAMPLE OF LOCOMOTOR
SKILLS DEVELOPMENT

To help explain what a dynamical systems perspective means for the study
of development and the study of skill in specific, I examine the development of locomotor skills, that is, those skills that propel individuals about
in their environments. The human infant arrives in the world unable to
move from one place to another without the actions of a caregiver. About
a year later, that same infant is capable of rising to a two-footed position
and independently traversing a living room. Much attention has been given
to the attainment of this dramatic feat, however, the development of locomotor skills is far from over. From those first walking steps follow a

---

[1] *Task dynamics* is used here to refer to the dynamics surrounding the task requirement (i.e., the behavioral information that specifies the task at hand). This differs from the way the term was originally used
by Saltzman and Kelso (1987). The concept is closer to the term *environmentally specified dynamics*, used
by Schoner and Kelso (1988a). However, I agree with Newell (1986) that the distinction between *environmental* and *task* constraints is an important one and therefore distinguish here between the environmental and task dynamics.

repertoire of locomotor skills—including such recognizable forms as a skip or a polka step to such undistinctive acts as moving along a crowded sidewalk. Across the life span, skillfulness in locomotion continues to change. How might this development be viewed from a dynamical systems perspective?

WHAT CHANGES?

Developmentalists have extensively catalogued the motor milestones preceding the attainment of upright independent locomotion (e.g., McGraw, 1940; Shirley, 1931). It is well-established when infants sit, crawl, stand, and walk. How then might one see the origins and transformations of these behaviors in a dynamical systems fashion? Zanone, Kelso, and Jeka (1993) and Muchishky, Gershkoff-Stowe, Cole, and Thelen (1996) offer a similar approach. For both, the developmental course of locomotion is represented as a *landscape* in the tradition of Waddington's epigenetic landscape proposed almost 40 years ago (Waddington, 1957). In Muchishky et al.'s representation (see Figure 3), the locomotor milestone behaviors are plotted along the x-axis. The z-axis depicts time and the y-axis reflects the frequency or attractiveness of these behaviors. One difference that emerges from this topological representation is that development can be characterized as a changing landscape of behavioral states represented as "wells" on the landscape. At any one time in the life of the infant, multiple behavioral states co-exist. As behaviors become preferred states as well as more skillful, the depth of the wells increases. The authors argued that variations in the frequency of a behavior are due to changes in the stability of the underlying attractive states. Another way to visualize this landscape is to recall the original Waddington landscape in which guy wires were attached to the surface and anchored on pegs below. The surface changed as the length of the guy wires shortened or lengthened. In a dynamical systems perspective, these guy wires might be envisioned as constraints. As these constraints change, so too will the behaviors exhibited. For example, in a culture that promotes motor behaviors such as sitting and standing as is done in some tribes of Africa (i.e., a field of pro-

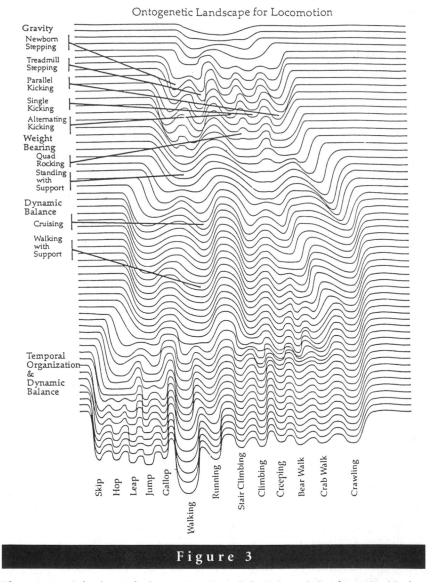

Figure 3

The ontogenetic landscape for locomotion. From "The Epigenetic Landscape Revisited: A Dynamic Interpretation," by M. Muchishky, L. Gershkoff-Stowe, and E. Thelen, 1996, in C. Rovee-Collier, *Advances in Infancy Research*. Norwood, NJ: Albex. Copyright 1996 by Albex Publishing. Reprinted with permission.

moted action for locomotion), one might expect to see a different landscape from that of an infant raised in a culture where no such behaviors are promoted.

Another way of looking at *what changes* is to look at the movement itself. To walk upright, humans use their two legs to propel and balance their torsos, heads, and arms. The two legs must work together in an organized fashion as must the segments of each leg (viz., the thigh, shank, and foot). In adult walking, the thigh and shank swing forward and back in much the same way as a pendulum would. However, this pendulum is actually two pendula (one for each segment) coupled together. Furthermore, pendulumlike legs do not swing freely; they cyclically hit the ground. To capture the *pattern* that changes, the leg's movement can be mapped in a state space defined by the position and velocity of the segments. Figure 4 is an exemplar phase portrait for the shank motion of an adult walking over four walking cycles. Note that the cycles tend toward the same region of state space, except for the first portion of the first cycle (i.e., initiation). These cycles were taken from a standing start where initiation represents the first step in the series. As the adult begins to walk, there is a *transient* period before the leg motion stabilizes into its "attractive" behavioral regime. The phase portrait of the adult's shank motion is typical of a limit cycle attractor. This type of attractor is one that forms a closed periodic orbit.

In contrast to the adult's stable limit cycle behavior, the newly walking infant demonstrates a much less stable behavioral state (Figure 5, Panel a). Clearly the trajectories are far less attracted to the same region of state space. One month later (Figure 5, Panel b), this same infant finds the attractive state for the shank's motion, and after 2 months of walking (Figure 5, Panel c) that infant displays a pattern very similar to that seen in the adult. This instability and subsequent stability of the shank's behavior as well as the thigh's has been documented for other newly walking infants (Clark & Phillips, 1993). We (Clark, Whitall, & Phillips, 1988) found similar instability at the onset of walking when we examined the interlimb coordination (i.e., the phasing relationship between the two legs at footfalls).

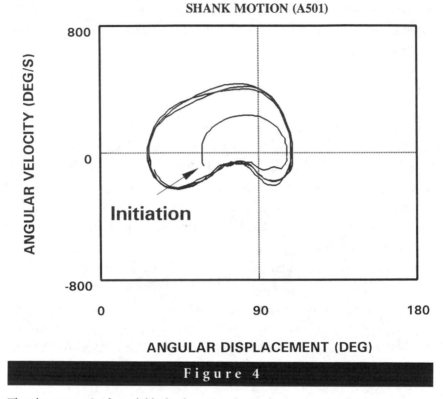

Figure 4

The phase portrait of an adult's shank motion during four cycles of walking.

Whether examining the topological landscape of attractive behaviors or the continuous mapping of the action itself, the dynamical systems approach places the behavioral *pattern* into focus. From the incredible complexity of the muscles, receptors, and neurons, the tools of this approach present a picture of a baby walking that compresses these multiple variables into a single picture that captures the system's behavior *and* its developmental change.

How Does Change Occur?

The other important question for the developmentalist is how does change occur? From a dynamical systems perspective, the behavioral pattern emerges from constraints. Thus, examination of the constraints that sur-

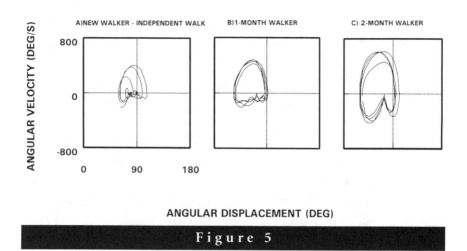

ANGULAR DISPLACEMENT (DEG)

Figure 5

Panel A: Phase portrait of a new walker's shank motion. Panel B: Phase portrait of the same infant after one month of walking experience. Panel C: Phase portrait of the same infant after two months of walking experience.

round the infant as these locomotor skills emerge and change is a first step to understanding how skill development occurs. Are the constraints changing? What are the relevant constraints to study? What constraint(s) acts as control parameter(s) to move the system to the new behavior? In 1986, Thelen proposed seven candidate components for control parameters in locomotor development: articular differentiation, posture, visual flow sensitivity, extensor strength, motivation, body proportions, and tonus control. Although some of these constraints are multidimensional and inter-related, they offer a starting point for investigation. For example, in our study of interlimb coordination (Clark et al., 1988), we found that supporting the newly walking infant (i.e., changing the postural constraint) increased the stability of the phasing relationship between the legs. We also found that segmental phase portraits stabilized at about the same time that gait measures reflecting increased balance control attained adultlike values (Clark & Phillips, 1993).

Walking is not the only locomotor skill, nor am I suggesting that it is skillfully executed after a few months of walking. Indeed, measures of bio-mechanical efficiency indicate that children's walking does not achieve adultlike levels until 3 years and possibly as late as 7 years of age (Bernstein, 1967; Okamoto & Kumamoto, 1972; Sutherland, Olshen, Cooper, & Woo, 1980). Other later emerging locomotor skills include (in order of appearance) running, galloping, hopping, and skipping (Clark & Whitall, 1989). Running and walking share the same interlimb phasing relationship, but how does the toddler change from the 180° phase relationship of walking and running to the asymmetrical phasing of a gallop? When do these locomotor behaviors become skillful? Similarly, what other aspects of locomotor skillfulness develop? For those who seek to achieve skill in dance or sports, understanding the process by which these motor skills develop is clearly important. Like any window on the development of complex adaptive skills, locomotor behavior offers a unique vantage point for an inquiry into developmental processes from a dynamical systems perspective. However, the approach is by no means limited to this domain.

LIMITATIONS AND CHALLENGES TO THE DYNAMICAL SYSTEMS APPROACH

For those who seek to understand human development, the dynamical systems perspective holds considerable promise. The fundamental premise that human behavior can best be understood not by reducing it, but by embracing its complexity, would seem compatible with the approach of many developmentalists. The approach embraces the mutuality of the organism and its environment. Behavioral development is a dynamic process arising from a mosaic of intrinsic and extrinsic subsystems. The tools and concepts of nonlinear dynamics provide the means with which to study complex human behaviors. However enthusiastic one might be about the prospects for a dynamical systems perspective, one must also acknowledge its limitations and challenges.

The most daunting drawback to those contemplating adopting this perspective would have to be the physics and mathematical tools and concepts that must be understood. For those trained in psychology, the terminology is confusing at best and off-putting at its worst. One might feel a bit like one of my colleagues who was interested in the dynamical systems perspective , but as he told me, he felt as though he were standing at the edge of an abyss deciding whether or not to take the plunge. Like all paradigms, the unique concepts, language, and tools of the field offer its greatest promise and its greatest barriers to adoption. To see the world in a new and different way is the excitement and also the challenge of science.

A second challenge for the field is one of moving beyond the metaphor to empirical work that tests specific, theoretically derived hypotheses. In a recent commentary on a special issue of *Child Development* in which the dynamical systems paradigm was featured, Turvey and Fitzpatrick (1993) detailed an inventory of developmental hypotheses they saw as emerging from the articles in that volume. Future work must proceed to examining these and other specific hypotheses if the field is to go beyond the metaphor and beyond the descriptive.

Yet another challenge for those seeking to approach development from a dynamical systems perspective is mastering new analytical tools and experimental designs that provide the scientific evidence required to test theoretical hypotheses. Time series analyses, multidimensional designs, and mathematical modeling and simulations are just some of the techniques that must be used in this paradigm. New ways of presenting and validating scientific evidence push the limits. However, if the concepts outlined in this chapter are to be the theoretical bases for research, then nothing less suffices.

The ultimate challenge, of course, is to offer a compelling theory of development that persuades other researchers, theorists, and practitioners of its scientific worth. A new approach is only sustained if it replaces previously held views, and that occurs only if the approach can explain more. For those who have embraced the approach, the challenge is assumed.

REFERENCES

Abraham, F. D., Abraham, R. H., & Shaw, C. D. (1992). Basic principles of dynamical systems. In R. L. Levine & H. E. Fitzgerald (Eds.), *Analysis of dynamic psychological systems: Vol. 1. Basic approaches to general systems, dynamic systems and cybernetics* (pp. 35–143). New York: Plenum Press.

Bernstein, N. A. (1967). *The coordination and regulation of movements.* Elmsford, NY: Pergamon Press.

Borstelmann, L. J. (1983). Children before psychology. In W. Kessen (Ed.), *Handbook of child psychology: Vol. 1. History, theory, and methods* (4th ed., pp. 1–140). New York: Wiley.

de Boysson-Bardies, B. (1990). Some reflexions (sic) on sensory–motor organization of speech during the first year of life. In H. Bloch & B.I. Bertenthal (Eds.), *Sensory–motor organizations and development in infancy and early childhood* (pp. 457–466). Boston: Kluwer Academic.

Çambel, A. B. (1993). *Applied chaos theory. A paradigm for complexity.* New York: Academic Press.

Clark, J. E., & Phillips, S.J. (1993). A longitudinal study of intralimb coordination in the first year of independent walking: A dynamical systems analysis. *Child Development, 64,* 1143–1157.

Clark, J. E., & Whitall, J. (1989). Changing patterns of locomotion: From walking to skipping. In M. Woollacott & A. Shumway-Cook (Eds.), *Development of posture and locomotion across the lifespan* (pp. 128–151). Columbia: University of South Carolina Press.

Clark, J. E., Whitall, J., & Phillips, S. J. (1988). Human interlimb coordination: The first 6 months of independent walking. *Developmental Psychobiology, 21,* 445–456.

Crutchfield, J. P., Farmer, J. D., Packard, N. H., & Shaw, R. S. (1987). Chaos. *Scientific American, 254(12),* 46–57.

Fischer, K. W., Bullock, D. H., Rotenberg, E. J., & Raya, P. (1993). The dynamics of competence: How context contributes directly to skill. In R.H. Wozniak & K.W. Fischer (Eds.), *Development in context: Acting and thinking in specific environments* (pp. 93–117). Hillsdale, NJ: Erlbaum.

Gleick, J. (1987). *Chaos. Making a new science.* New York: Viking.

Guthrie, E. R. (1952). *The psychology of learning.* New York: Harper & Row.

Haken, H. (1977). *Synergetics: An introduction.* Heidelberg, Germany: Springer.

Kelso, J. A. S., DeGuzman, G. C., & Holroyd, T. (1991). The self-organized phase attractive dynamics of coordination. In A. Babloyantz (Ed.), *Self-organization, emerging properties, and learning* (pp. 41–62). New York: Plenum Press.

Kelso, J. A. S., DelColle, J. D., & Schöner, G. (1990). Action–perception as a pattern formation process. In M. Jeannerod (Ed.), *Attention and performance: Vol. 13. Motor representation and control* (pp. 139–169). Hillsdale, NJ: Erlbaum.

Levine, R. L. & Fitzgerald, H. E. (Eds.). (1992). *Analysis of dynamic psychological systems: Vol. 1. Basic approaches to general systems, dynamic systems and cybernetics.* New York: Plenum Press.

McGraw, M. B. (1940). Neuromuscular development of the human infant as exemplified in the achievement of erect locomotion. *Journal of Pediatrics, 17,* 747–771.

Muchishky, M., Gershkoff-Stowe, L., Cole, E., & Thelen, E. (1996). The epigenetic landscape revisited: A dynamic interpretation. In C. Rovee-Collier (Ed.), *Advances in infancy research* (Vol. 10, pp. 121–159). Norwood, NJ: Albex.

Newell, K. M. (1986). Constraints on the development of coordination. In M. G. Wade & H. T. A. Whiting (Eds.), *Motor development in children: Aspects of coordination and control* (pp. 341–360). Boston: Martinus Nijhoff.

Nicolis, G., & Prigogine, I. (1989). *Exploring complexity: An introduction.* New York: W. H. Freeman.

Okamoto, T., & Kumamoto, M. (1972). Electromyographic study of the learning process of walking in infants. *Electromyography, 12,* 149–158.

Prigogine, I., & Stengers, I. (1984). *Order out of chaos: Man's new dialogue with nature.* New York: Bantam.

Reed, E. S. (1993). The intention to use a specific affordance: A conceptual framework for psychology. In R. H. Wozniak & K. W. Fischer (Eds.), *Development in context: Acting and thinking in specific environments* (pp. 45–76). Hillsdale, NJ: Erlbaum.

Reed, E. S., & Bril, B. (1996). The primacy of action in development. In M. L. Latash & M. T. Turvey (Ed.), *Dexterity and its development* (pp. 431–451). Hillsdale, NJ: Erlbaum.

Rosen, R. (1970). *Dynamical system theory in biology: Vol. 1. Stability theory and its application.* New York: Wiley.

Saltzman, E., & Kelso, J. A. S. (1987). Skilled actions: A task-dynamic approach. *Psychological Review, 94,* 84–106.

Schöner, G., & Kelso, J. A. S. (1988a). A dynamic pattern theory of behavioral change. *Journal of Theoretical Biology, 135,* 501–524.

Schöner, G., & Kelso, J. A. S. (1988b). Dynamic patterns of biological coordination: Theoretical strategy and new results. In J. A. S. Kelso, A. J. Mandell, & M. F. Shlesinger (Eds.), *Dynamical patterns in complex systems* (pp. 77–102). Singapore: World Scientific.

Shirley, M. M. (1931). *The first two years: A study of twenty-five babies* (Vol. 1). Minneapolis: University of Minnesota Press.

405

Smith, L. B., & Thelen, E. (Eds.). (1993). *A dynamic systems approach to development: Applications.* Cambridge, MA: MIT Press.

Stewart, I. (1989). *Does God play dice? The mathematics of chaos.* Cambridge, MA: Basil Blackwell.

Sutherland, D. H., Olshen, R. A., Cooper, L., & Woo, S. (1980). The development of mature gait. *Journal of Bone and Joint Surgery, 62-A,* 336–353.

Thelen, E. (1986). Development of coordinated movement: Implications for early human development. In M. G. Wade & H. T. A. Whiting (Eds.), *Motor development in children: Aspects of coordination and control* (pp. 107–124). Dordrecht, The Netherlands: Martinus Nijhoff.

Thelen, E., & Smith, L. B. (1994). *A dynamic systems approach to the development of cognition and action.* Cambridge, MA: MIT Press.

Thelen, E., & Ulrich, B. D. (1991). Hidden skills: A dynamic systems analysis of treadmill stepping during the first year. *Monographs of the Society for Research in Child Development, 56* (1, Serial No. 223).

Turvey, M. T., & Fitzpatrick, P. (1993). Commentary: Development of perception–action systems and general principles of pattern formation. *Child Development, 64,* 1175–1190.

Waddington, C. H. (1957). *The strategy of the genes.* London: Allen & Unwin.

Werner, H. (1957). The concept of development from a comparative and organismic point of view. In D. B. Harris (Ed.), *The concept of development* (pp. 125–148). Minneapolis: University of Minnesota Press.

Zanone, P.-G., & Kelso, J. A. S. (1992). The evolution of behavioral attractors with learning: Nonequilibrium phase transitions. *Journal of Experimental Psychology: Human Perception and Performance, 18,* 403–421.

Zanone, P.-G., & Kelso, J. A. S. (1994). The coordination dynamics of learning: Theoretical structure and experimental agenda. In S. P. Swinnen, J. Massion, H. Heuer, & P. Casaer (Eds.), *Interlimb coordination: Neural, dynamical, and cognitive constraints* (pp. 461–490). New York: Academic Press.

Zanone, P.-G., Kelso, J. A. S., & Jeka, J. (1993). Concepts and methods for a dynamical approach to behavioral coordination and change. In G. J. P. Savelsbergh (Ed.), *The development of coordination in infancy* (pp. 89–135). New York: North-Holland.

Comment on Clark

Karl M. Newell

The revival of interest in motor development over the past 15 years in part is due to the embracing of dynamical systems approaches to the study of movement. This trend is reflected in an increasing number of articles being published in this emerging framework, a recent book by Thelen and Smith (1994), and a special section of *Child Development* (Thelen & Lockman, 1993). The dynamical systems approach to motor development is now firmly established and is, perhaps, the dominant theoretical position in relation to the development of movement coordination and control.

One intuitive reason for this theoretical development is that the study of motor development is very much concerned with the emergence of *new* structural and functional properties of the infant and young child. It has always been a mystery as to where these new body and movement forms come from, and the dynamical systems framework offers at first pass a very intuitively appealing and tangible theoretical approach to examine these problems. In addition, of course, it also provides us with the formal

---

Newell comments on Clark from an ecological realist perspective.

tools of nonlinear dynamics, stability theory, and so on to investigate the emergence of new forms. I suspect that Arnold Gesell would have liked to have known about these methodological tools back in the 1930s and 1940s. One might not want to embrace Gesell's (1929) maturational theory of development, but he was clearly interested in characterizing a dynamic geometry of the emergence of movement in infant action and used dynamically relevant terms, such as *stability, gradient, potential*, and so on.

Another point to mention about the metaphor of dynamical systems in development is that there seems to be some confusion about the relation of the variety of approaches in which dynamical systems is being invoked in theoretical perspectives in psychology and biology. It is clear that dynamical systems is part of the ecological approach to perception and action, but it is not synonymous with it (E. J. Gibson, 1969; 1979). One could examine motor development from a dynamical systems viewpoint and not be doing work necessarily consistent with the ecological approach to perception and action. Thus, the application of dynamical systems to motor development or other domains in psychology does not *necessarily* reveal the theoretical persuasion of the work at hand.

A particular concern for some is whether the dynamical systems approach gives sufficient recognition to the concept of information in action. Many current applications have a straight physical description of the development of movement in action without reference to information and other traditional concepts of psychology. In the ecological approach to perception and action, a very direct formal basis links information and movement dynamics. To some degree this may be one of the distinguishing and important features of the ecological approach to perception and action.

I would like to pick up on three particular points from Jane Clark's chapter: the concept of skill, the issue of preferred coordination modes and stability, and the topic of walking dynamics.

SKILL

It is interesting that Clark has the word *skill* in the title of her chapter because, typically, the word *skill* is rarely used in the study of the development of the fundamental movement sequences. In fact, some would argue, as Bernstein (1967) did, that the word *skill* is not appropriate for the phylogenetic activities of walking, crawling, running, and so on. Some prefer *skill* to be reserved for ontogenetic activities where the emphasis on learning has been given center place. Part of the problem also comes from the slipperiness of the term. *Skill* is used both as a noun and as an adjective. As a noun it is used like the word *task*, and as an adjective it is used to characterize action beyond mere performance outcome. Adaptation is part of skill, and recent approaches to complex adaptive systems would seem ripe for application in the motor development domain.

In most theoretical perspectives to action, skill is typically more than performance outcome. *Skill* is an emergent property used to describe the characteristics of the performance. One can think of skill on an intrinsic individual specific basis or an extrinsic more absolute basis. Skill could be construed as the potential that is available in the interaction of the individual with the environment in the pursuit of a particular goal, rather than some absolute extrinsic set of standards that might be interpreted with respect to the population. In the intrinsic approach, an individual may have a poorer performance than another person but actually be more skilled than that person. One of the polemics in the issue of skills is to rationalize an intrinsic perspective versus an extrinsic framework for skill in action.

PREFERRED COORDINATION MODES

A phrase (or some analogy) that is used in the dynamical systems approach to movement control is "preferred modes of coordination," and this notion is often linked to the concept of stability. I now pick up on an image that Clark used from a recent article by Zanone, Kelso, and Jeko (1993). In this schematic there is a characterization of the frequency of occurrence of particular activities as a function of the age in days of an individual child. One notices that the frequency of occurrence of particular activities (crawling, standing, walking, and so on) changes over time. The probability of a particular mode of coordination is linked to the relative stability of these modes of coordination. The figure from Zanone and colleagues is, however, simply a plot of the frequency occurrence of an activity as a function of age.

A more central approach to the problem of relative stability is that it should be considered in the context of the same task goal. In this view one would determine the function of preferred coordination modes at different ages while attempting to engage in the same task goal. In the original Zanone figure one observes, for example, that the probability of lying down is much lower than walking in the older child. Even though stability is a slippery concept, probably no one would think that lying down is less stable in a relative sense than walking. The concept of stability in the development of coordination must also be examined with respect to the goal of the possible action.

A variety of criteria can be involved in the formation of a coordination mode in relation to a particular task goal. This list might include energy expenditure and concerns for the pick-up of some particular aspect of information. The point is that stability may not be the only concept to consider in examining the dynamical properties of preferred modes or the patterns in the changes over time of those coordination modes. One might be able to change the probability of emergence of a particular coordination mode by changing the cost–benefit ratios associated with the action. Stability in some ways might seem the antithesis of adaptability. The concept of adaptability is particulary important to consider in respect to changing coordination modes, both in the short- and more long-term time cycles of development.

•

WALKING DYNAMICS

Finally, I would like to raise a point about the dynamics of walking. Extant attempts to characterize the dynamics of walking have given strong emphasis to the knee–hip complex. A question not approached in Clark's analysis is, why should that joint complex be the focus of analysis? This biokinematic linkage is obviously an important element of the walking coordinative structure, but why should this particular joint complex be the focus of analysis in this task? One of the major challenges in this approach is to characterize the order parameter or parameters of the coordination mode.

It would be interesting to know what particular properties in the movement pattern specify the acts of walking and running. This is a basic question in the perception of biological motion problem, but despite the interest generated some 30 years ago by Johansson (1964) and J. J. Gibson (1966), we do not seem to have answers to these kinds of questions, even in the basic phylogenetic activities. A study by Hoenkamp (1978) suggested that the knee–hip complex does not provide the critical information that defines running and walking. Locomotory activities are very much concerned with traveling between locations in an environment. It would seem that some measure in this locomotory collective is required that reflects the organization of the motion of the body with respect to that environment.

REFERENCES

Bernstein, N. (1967). *The co-ordination and regulation of movements.* Oxford: Pergamon Press.

Gesell, A. (1929). Maturation and infant behavior pattern. *Psychological Review, 36,* 307–319.

Gibson, E. J. (1969). *Principles of perceptual learning and development.* New York: Appleton-Century-Crofts.

Gibson, J. J. (1966). *The senses considered as perceptual systems.* Boston, MA: Houghton Mifflin.

Gibson, J. J. (1979). *The ecological approach to visual perception.* Boston, MA: Houghton Mifflin.

Hoenkamp, E. (1978). Perceptual cues that determine the labeling of human gait. *Journal of Human Movement Studies, 4,* 59–69.

Johansson, G. (1964). Perception of motion and changing form. *Scandanavian Journal of Psychology, 5,* 181–208.

Thelen, E., & Lockman, J. (1993). Dynamical biodynamics: Brain, body, behavior connections [Special section]. *Child Development, 64,* 953–1190.

Thelen, E., & Smith, L. B. (1994). *A dynamic systems approach to the development of cognition and action.* Cambridge, MA: MIT.

Zanone, P. G., Kelso, J. A. S., & Jeka, J. J. (1993). Concepts and methods for a dynamical approach to behavioral coordination and change. In G. J. P. Savelsbergh (Ed.), *The development of coordination in infancy* (pp. 89–136). Amsterdam: North-Holland.

12

Information, Creativity, and Culture

Alan Fogel

In this chapter, I expand on J. J. Gibson's (1966, 1979) theory of direct perception and action as a starting point for a theory of development. Gibson's notions of direct perception and ecological realism suggest that information emerges in the dynamic relationship between individuals and environments. A theory of relationship development based upon a dynamic systems perspective is coupled with Gibson's approach to perception and action. In the theoretical issues section of this chapter, I suggest how a theory of action dynamics that is not only relational, but is creative and cultural, contributes to making the ecological approach into a theory of development. The theoretical issues section is divided into the following subsections that focus on the central features of an ecological developmental theory: (a) Real or relational? (b) Detection or creation? and (c) Natural or cultural? In the research section of the chapter, I illustrate the implications of my perspective with research on the development of

This work was supported by grants from the National Institute of Health (R01 HD21036), the National Science Foundation (BNS9006756), and the National Institute of Mental Health (R01 MH). The author wishes to thank the following individuals for their thoughtful commentaries on prior drafts of this paper: Cathy Dent-Read, Alyson Fearnley, Gerry Ginsburg, Hui-chin Hsu, Maria Lyra, Melissa McDonald, Christy Nelson, Ed Reed, Lisa Taylor, Esther Thelen, Ted Wachs, and Pat Zukow-Goldring.

mother–infant–object interactions. Finally, I conclude with a summary of an ecological approach to development.

THEORETICAL ISSUES

Real or Relational?

In this section, I suggest that there is no inherent contradiction between ecological realism and the relational perspective of ecological psychology. In ecological *realism*, information is not to be found in the physical features of the environment (the low-level features of wave-length, intensity, or timing) but in the invariant patterns found in the dynamic changes of the environment with respect to the individual's actions over time (the high-level invariants; J. Gibson, 1979). Information is specific to the individual–environment system in the way in which the individual moves with respect to the environment and in the scaling of the dimensions of the system (Kugler, Kelso, & Turvey, 1982; Michaels & Carello, 1981). Ecological realism is the view that the environment can be perceived without the mediation of ideas or concepts: that perception is directly available in the relationship between the individual and the environment. Because the individual perceives the high level relational invariants, realism is a psychological construct rather than a physical one (J. Gibson, 1966, 1979; Michaels & Carello, 1981; Reed, 1987).

From the *relational* perspective in ecological psychology, there is a mutual relationship between individual and environment (J. Gibson, 1966, 1979). According to proponents of the relational perspective, individual and environment are "mutually constraining components of a single system" (Kugler et al., 1982, p. 46). One cannot describe the individuals without reference to the environment, and one cannot describe the environment without reference to the individuals.

The meaning of these general principles of ecological psychology for a theory of action has been the subject of some controversy. So long as information is defined with respect to invariants in the individual–environment system, there is no contradiction between the realist and relational views. Gibson, however, asserts that the existence of the environment does not depend on it being perceived and that the environment can afford action to one but not to another individual (J. Gibson, 1979). According to Reed (1987), information in the environment is real, so long as that environment is defined with respect to some universal set of perception and action abilities and a universal set of affordances. If different individuals were to enter into a relationship with the environment, each in the same manner and each having the same abilities and similar needs, then they could all detect the same set of invariants in that environment. Information, therefore, can be both real and relational (Reed, 1987).

The relational nature of ecological psychology sets the stage for an examination of the developmental implications of Gibson's theory. Gibson did not elaborate on a theory of development. Implications for a developmental theory have been elaborated by others (E. Gibson, 1988; Kugler et al., 1982; Reed, 1982). In these views, the task of developing individuals is to "tune" their action systems to detect a wider range of the universal set of affordances. This *education of attention* (J. Gibson, 1966) requires that individuals explore their relationship to the environment in systematic ways. Attention can be tutored, as it is in directing novices' attention to an affordance or constraining their action to educators' broader views of the possible relations between individual and environment. These exploratory activities can also occur solo because the detection of invariants leads naturally to the discovery of dynamically stable modes of action with respect to the environment (Kugler et al., 1982; Newell & McDonald, 1993; Thelen, 1989).

The Limits of Relationship in Ecological Realism

If the premise that ecological realism is a relational theory of action is accepted, then what model of a relationship should be incorporated in the theory? Gibson said this:

> The information for perception is not transmitted, does not consist
> of signals, and does not entail a sender and a receiver. The environ-
> ment does not communicate with observers who inhabit it. Why

should the world speak to us? The world is *specified* in the structure of the light that reaches us, but it is entirely up to us to perceive it . . . Perceiving is an achievement of the individual. (J. Gibson, 1979, pp. 63, 239)

What kind of a relationship is implied in these statements? Any particular individual must make an effort to perceive the relational affordances. The world, on the other hand, makes no effort to perceive or otherwise communicate with the observer. The environment is not passive: It is clearly dynamic because it must be perceived through action. However, from the point of view of the observer, the only "achievement" entailed in his or her relationship with the environment is the detection of information leading to functional activity.

As I think about the various forms of relationship in which I engage, this is a rather impoverished type of relationship. I venture to say that it is not the kind of relationship that an individual would consider to be warm and friendly. It lacks some of the basic characteristics of an interpersonal relationship: for example, feelings of accomplishment, commitment, a sense of shared history, and a sense of belonging. The Gibsonian observer is adapted to the world, can "tune into" it, but doesn't ever settle down in it, doesn't ever make it a home.

One could counter that it is not exactly fair to compare one's personal relationships to one's relationships to the natural environment. One could also dismiss what I am about to say as misplaced passion better reserved for the study of love and friendship than for the serious business of perceiving the world as it is. Perhaps. But I am going to suggest that people's relationships with the natural world share more with our personal relationships than we might at first think. Although it is clear that relationships with people have a very different quality than relationships with objects (J. Gibson, 1966), in the following section, I propose that a more vital model of the relationship between individual and environment can contribute to the developmental implications of the theory of ecological realism. To do so requires a closer look at the concept of relational information.

Detection or Creation?

Information is partly abstract and amodal—detected at a higher level than the physical features of the environment. However, there is more to the story of information than the detection of invariants. This is because information is realized through action and action is registered within an embodied individual that strains or flows, gets frustrated or elated, or feels lazy or energetic. These embodied features of action, the phenomenology of action, need not be conceptualized as mediators of action. They are directly perceived as part of the information in the individual–environment system.

Compared with indirect mentalistic approaches to knowing the environment, the body's ways of sensing and feeling are directly part of the phenomenology of action and perception (Hermans & Kempen, 1993; Johnson, 1987; Shotter, 1983). Participants are more likely to recognize and remember lists of words, for example, if the lists are presented in similar colors, sizes, and locations on the page in both the familiarization and test phases of an experiment (Kolers & Roediger, 1984). Infants in the first months of life can remember how to make a mobile move by repeating a pattern of kicking that they been taught weeks earlier (Rovee-Collier, Enright, Lucas, Fagan, & Gekoski, 1981). However, if they are crying when the initial training takes place, they fail to remember the kicking pattern on later occasions when they are not crying. They also fail to remember the procedure if the experimenter changes the crib decorations between training and testing (Butler & Rovee-Collier, 1989; Fagen, Ohr, Singer, & Klein, 1989; Rovee-Collier et al., 1981). These findings are consistent with ecological realism—that information is directly perceived—but they add something else. The embodied process of perceiving and acting is not simply a means of detecting higher order invariants in the dynamic flow, but it becomes part of the information that is available.

Information in the individual–environment system has a unique character that depends on how the actions are performed, on where they are performed, on when they occur vis-a-vis other actions and events, and on the neuromotor and sensory systems used. This does not mean that one perceives the physical features of mass, force, or wave length of the body. It means that action and perception are situated activities that derive their informative character from the total individual–environment system, which includes the body (Bruner, 1990; Ginsburg, 1985; Heft, 1989; Hermans & Kempen, 1993; Sarbin, 1986).

The concept of *situated action* is consistent with the dynamic systems perspective on development (Fogel & Thelen, 1987; Thelen, 1989; Thelen & Fogel, 1989). In a dynamic system, individual and environment are components of one system. In addition, the form of an act is an emergent stable attractor resulting from the cooperativity among all the elements in the system, including muscle movements, neural processes, and higher level coordinations between them and the environment. Situated action also suggests that "the affordances of the environment refer to the body in a much more fundamental manner than mere body scaling *per se*" (Heft, 1989, p. 11). If perception were mere detection, the body and the environment would melt into the background as invariant structure was revealed. Gibson described the perception of animate objects in terms of such invariants: "Light, sound, odor, and a mechanical encounter ('touch') may all thus carry the same *information*, in a sense, inasmuch as they are all specific to the same living thing" (J. Gibson, 1966, p. 23). This may indeed happen when action is ritualized or automatic. At other times, however, the body or the environment become foregrounded. This is more likely to occur when novelty or indeterminacy enters the system.

Seen from the outside, novelty creates instability in attractor configurations that may lead to transitions or bifurcations into new state regimes (Prigogine, 1973). Experienced phenomenologically, novelty leads to a self-awareness that is directly perceived. It may be that direct perception of our feelings, thoughts, or movements is a phenomenological cue that something has changed in the system. If one is driving on a smooth dry road and it begins to rain or snow, one becomes suddenly focused on the environment outside the car. One may also become aware of the body: the tightening grip on the steering wheel or the stiffness of the neck starting to feel painful. One directly perceives anxiety or fear.

As part of the self-organization of novelty into the system, the individual has the direct perception of being a creator of information. In the driving example, one perceives directly that one's safety arises from a creative negotiation of the self–environment system; one perceives the self as having responsibility (ownership, belonging) for the safety of self and others. The individual is not merely detecting, but creatively taking charge, experiencing agency. It is the distinction between the self as "finder" or "user" and the self as "maker" (Sheets-Johnstone, 1990; Shotter, 1983; Smitsman, this volume). The world, to the individual, is not simply a set of conditions and structures that facilitate action. The world is something to be discovered through one's creative efforts regardless of the fact that what one discovers may have the same form as what many others have discovered in the same environment. The world is directly perceived as having meaning and value: not a simple push–pull valence, but one with a real value of morality, aesthetics, and passion (Dewey, 1896; Fogel, 1993; Merleau-Ponty, 1962; Piaget, 1954).

Schachtel captured this creative quality of action in the following way:

> A painter may spend many days, weeks or months, or even years, in looking at the same mountain, as Cezanne did . . . without tiring of it and without ceasing to discover something new in it. The same is true . . . of the naturalist's perception of the plant or animal with which he has to live for long periods of time in order to acquire that intimate knowledge from which eventually new meaning and understanding will be born. (Schachtel, 1959, p. 239)

Schachtel's metaphor of the birth of new meaning emphasizes the creative aspects of information for the actor–perceiver, and the image of the individual returning to the "same mountain," although the perceived mountain is never the same, reflects the sense of commitment to and aesthetic feeling for the individual's relationship with this aspect of the environment. The image of the birth of new meaning also suggests how a theory of creative action can also be a theory of development, by making the creation of novelty a fundamental feature of everyday action.

Consider the experience of walking through an open field with contours. Depending on where you begin and the route you take across the field, you will discover different information about your relationship to the field. In one direction you may go uphill, in another downhill. You may see it from the north at a particular time of day in specific weather conditions.

A focus on *detected information* would assume that with enough walks through the field, one could specify its invariant structure regardless of changing conditions, or one could use the field appropriately with respect to its affordances. The pathways one takes through the field are relatively unimportant. What matters is that the field gets plowed, mapped, or walked across in the most energy efficient manner.

A focus on *created information* would emphasize the conditions under which the field is explored and on the process of discovery. One's emotions at the time or the smell or look of the field will become part of his or her direct perception of it. If one is plowing the field, there is likely to be an aesthetic sense of the "best" way to proceed around its contours that is a fundamental part of the information of the person–field relationship. One on a pleasure walk may have a favorite path or stopping place and a real attachment to the field as a source of escape or inspiration. Caring, obligation, and beauty are part of the direct perception of the field and one's actions in it. If information is taken with reference to the individual, then created information must be taken with reference to the whole individual as an emotional and aesthetic being-in-the-world.

When information is created, there is an element of indeterminacy that arises out of the change exigencies of the process of its formation. Indeterministic processes are irreversible in the sense that they can't be repeated. Initial conditions are important, but so are changing conditions that occur during the evolution of the process. From a dynamic systems perspective, indeterminism arises spontaneously during self-organization such that perfect predictability of the next state of the system is impossible (Gleick, 1988; Pattee, 1987; Prigogine, 1973).

Shotter (1983) refers to the perception of indeterminacy in action as the *reality of vagueness*. According to Shotter (1983), "prior to the performance of some further activity . . . the only clear and accurate description of an environment which can be given, is one in terms of the actions so far taken within it. What further action it may afford must remain to a degree uncertain" (p. 27). This uncertainty is real in the sense that the action a person did perform could always have been some other action, and because part of the direct perception about her- or himself and the environment is related to the specific process of forming those actions, the individual can directly detect the incompleteness, no matter how slight.

The reality of vagueness does not deny the fact that action can be planned, and is prospective and intentional (E. Gibson, this volume; Hofsten, this volume). Rather, it suggests that plans and intentions are themselves dynamic components of action allowing the individual to make a creative, unplanned response to changing conditions in the individual–environment system. Not only does the individual need to have the ability to create information and action, one also has to be able to perceive uncertainty at any point in time.

I developed the concept of *co-regulation* to describe action that is perceived as indeterminate, embodied, and creative (Fogel, 1992, 1993). Action is co-regulated to the extent that it is susceptible to being continuously modified by the continuously changing set of conditions in the self-environment system. Co-regulated action has the characteristic of a stable attractor because lines of action are formed and repeat under similar conditions. Nevertheless, stability is dynamic in the sense that action is assembled continuously as an emergent process and can be altered creatively according to changing conditions. Action is not just performed, it is created out of embodied experience at the juncture between the known and the unknown.

The environment "out there" may not be trying to communicate with the individual, but the dynamic aspect of perceiving and acting assures that the environment in reference to the individual has an active, vital presence. The artist and the scientist, as Schachtel (1959) described, experience a dialogue with their subjects. The mountain as physical object does not have a dialogue with Cezanne: It is the perceived mountain that engages him and hooks him into continuously evolving processes of information creation. In this sense, the vitality of the environment derives from one's imaginary dialogue with it. By analogy to interpersonal relationships, people attribute to the environment a living presence that derives from our mutuality with it. The artist may also become self-aware through this process—as the maker of the work, as connected to the mountain, as inadequate or brilliant, or as lauded or ignored by the public.

Some environments feel cold and distant, but so do some people. Some environments feel distinctly warm. Examples of potentially warm environments include one's home, place of work, a valued possession, a favorite pair of shoes, a musical instrument, or a snowy mountain to a skier. Although infants appear to distinguish between animate and inanimate objects, people, and things, preschool children attribute animacy to a host of nonliving objects and events (Legerstee, 1991; Piaget, 1954). This chapter is not the place to discuss a taxonomy of social versus nonsocial forms of information. I merely point out that the issue is not nearly as simple as it may seem at first. There is a phenomenological borderland in which inanimacy shades into the perception of animacy, in which things come alive, in which people can belong to places, and in which things belong to people (Ihde, 1979).

The creative process that ensues from the co-regulation of self and environment is one source of inspiration that propels action from one to the next moment. That same creative process, constituted as a real part of everyday action, is one source of developmental change. There is also a phenomenological continuum from detection to creativity, or from automaticity to the generation of novel forms of action. To understand development, therefore, the conditions under which action is or is not creative must be studied. A developmental psychology of the education of attention as detection is not sufficient. A developmental psychology must include a phenomenology of the creative process and the way in which meaning, attachment, and responsibility change within the self–environment relationship.

Natural or Cultural?

Thus far, I have discussed the relational and creative features of action that are required for an ecological theory of development. In this section, I turn to a consideration of the cultural features of action. Much of the research in ecological psychology has been done with respect to the natural environment. The concept of created information in an ecosystem is analogous, in social relationship research, to the concept of meaning in the dialogical perspective. The *dialogical perspective* presents social relationships as inherently dynamic and as constituted by a continuous process forming temporary stabilities in the midst of countervailing tendencies and tensions. A three-step dialogical process is the minimal unit of analysis in the following way: A acts and B responds. However, as B is composing the response, A is already changing and perhaps the observed changes in A alter the response of B as it is unfolding in time. The result is that both A and B are changing at the same time and in relation to each other (Bakhtin, 1988; Markova, 1990).

Co-regulated action is spontaneous and creative because these dynamics of coactivity cannot be predicted in advance (Fogel, 1993). Using co-regulation, the difference between social and nonsocial relationships can be more clearly specified. Co-regulation with the social environment, compared to the natural environment, involves a relationship in which the environment—the other individual—is also a center of situated activity that is directed toward the self at the same time that the self is directed toward the other (cf. J. Gibson's [1966] concept of a *behavioral loop* between two individuals). Because the other is trying to communicate with the self, the possibility to create information is opened more efficiently than if all the effort of forming the relationship was up to the individual alone or the individual in relation to his or her imaginary dialogue with the nonsocial environment. In addition, moral obligations, aesthetic attractiveness, emotional attachments, and lasting commitments are directly perceived as part of the creativity of forming and maintaining a social relationship (Fogel, 1993).

In social relationships, there are invariant patterns of co-regulated action called *frames* (Bateson, 1955; Fogel, 1993; Goffman, 1974; Kendon, 1985). Frames are regular and repeatable routines such as conversational forms, arguments, games, and rituals. Frames can be conceptualized as dynamically stable attractors in the landscape of a developing communication system. The developmental trajectory of the relationship system depends crucially on the history of attractors in the landscape to the extent that frames constrain the activity of the participants who return time and again to similar rituals and similar communicative patterns.

At times in all social relationships, one partner is a more explicit guide for the other. Relating to such a partner gives the individual an inside track toward the discovery of information that may not have been discovered alone (Rogoff, 1990; Vygotsky, 1978). Generally speaking, all cultural tools do the same: They guide the user toward particular types of information because the tools were designed, built, and made available by other people. Tools facilitate the detection of information about their uses and they change how people create information about themselves in relation to the environment (Smitsman, this volume).

In a study of the prehistorical origins of thinking, Sheets-Johnstone (1990) suggests that the human mind was formed, well before the advent of language and symbols, by the perceptual embodiment of tactile–kinesthetic relationships. The body is "not simply *implicated* in meanings through its very acts," argues Sheets-Johnstone, "but is the very source or standard upon which those meanings are forged in the first place" (p. 361). A particular stone that is selected as a tool affords certain kinds of action, but the body is part of the evaluation of the tool. Not all tools are transparent to the user (Ihde, 1979). A metal rod that is too heavy will still allow one to poke at a fire, but the weight of the rod imposes itself on the tactile experience. This embodied information is not mediated by the tool, it is a direct part of the phenomenology of using the tool.

Tools and technology extend the body into the environment, rather than just bringing the body to the environment in order to detect its structure (Dewey, 1896). In that field I mentioned earlier, I will probably walk on paths made by others as the most direct or energy-efficient routes. I will wear shoes I purchased that facilitate such a walk. I will interpret what I see and hear according to the cultural ethos of my time and place that tells me the field contains either wildflowers or weeds. I will buy a map or a guidebook that connects my perception of the field to the history of cultural knowledge about all such fields. Each of these tools becomes part of the direct experience of the field.

The recognition of the role of the body and creativity in perception and action does not deny the reality of the environment. According to Arnheim (1966),

> The creative individual has no desire to get away from what is normal and ordinary . . . He is not striving to relinquish the object but to penetrate it according to his own criterion of what looks true.
>
> (p. x)

Culture, although partially arbitrary, also has its own reality from the perspective of information perception (Costall, 1985).

For humans, there are no acultural environments. The only example I can think of is to be lost in a wilderness as a result of an accident that destroys all possessions, including clothing, and leaves one all alone with total amnesia. People's actions are virtually always co-regulated by cultural systems rather than being due to our own efforts to communicate with an impassive natural environment (Shweder, 1993; Vygotsky, 1978; Wertsch, 1991). Culture pre-disposes people to recreate for ourselves information that was discovered by someone else and communicated as part of our relationship to and through cultural tools and practices (cf. Rader, this volume). According to Lock (1980), cultural systems such as language are generative because they contain affordances that guide their own reinvention by individual users.

A theory of action must incorporate both creativity and culture in order to serve as a theory of development. Without the guidance of other individuals and tools made by other individuals, people would be cast adrift in a natural environment that is slow to reveal its secrets. Few could survive for long in an acultural environment and if some people did, they would be creatively detecting those aspects of the natural environment that match their already acquired cultural patterns of perception and action. Without culture, each individual would have to begin again to discover the natural affordances of materials and nutrients.

The issue of culture becomes salient with respect to development in early infancy. The immaturity of human infants requires not just an adult caregiver, but an elaborate cultural system of infant-care practices. Patterns of behavior, beliefs, and infant-care tools make up this cultural system. In the remainder of this chapter, I illustrate the role of relationships, creativity, and culture in early infant development by examining infants' first introduction to toy objects in the context of the mother–infant relationship.

RESEARCH ON MOTHERS, INFANTS, AND OBJECTS

Methods

In this section, I illustrate the manner in which a research methodology can be constructed to study the development of perception and action in a social context; it is a methodology guided by a concept of information as relational, created, and cultural. I describe research in progress on the development of infants' relationship to toy objects during mother–infant play.

A dialogical perspective on the study of social process requires a research design in which the self–environment relationship can be investigated as a system of action through time: a within-dyad, historical approach. This approach has two central features: (a) Dyads are observed on repeated occasions for a long enough time to capture three periods before, during, and after a behavioral or developmental change. (b) Dyads are observed at time intervals that are considerably shorter than the time intervals required for the behavioral or developmental change (Fogel, 1990a; Fogel & Thelen, 1987). In the study presented here, at the level of behavior change, observation sessions last between 5 and 10 minutes, which allowed sufficient time for a variety of actions on objects to unfold. At the developmental level, there was one observation on each dyad per week between 1 and 8 months of age to encompass the period before, during, and after the acquisition of visually guided reaching.

In this case-study approach, 13 mother–infant dyads were videotaped playing with a standard set of 8 age-appropriate toys. The toys were chosen with regard to the kinds of action affordances typically seen in this age group, such as reaching, grasping, fingering, mouthing, shaking, and squeezing. Size and shape differences between the objects afforded different kinds of actions (Bushnell & Boudreau, 1991; Piaget, 1954; Rochat, 1989; von Hofsten & Ronnqvist, 1988). Mothers were asked to play spontaneously with their babies and were told only that the researchers were studying the development of mother–infant play. Thus, mothers were free to choose any of the objects and their own style of play.

Results: Culture and Object Information

Because toy objects and mothers' actions are determined in part by the culture of infant care, any description of the social communication process involving mothers, infants, and toys is the first step in understanding the role of culture in development. Our research began with a sequential analysis of developmental changes in the timing relationships between mother and infant action, gaze direction, and facial expression. Results of this analysis showed that patterns of mother–infant interaction with objects changed dramatically before and after the infant acquired visually-directed reaching. Mothers demonstrated object affordances to infants and used objects to touch infants' hands and bodies before reaching was acquired. They also scaffolded initial attempts at reaching, and therefore may have contributed to the development of reaching. After reaching was acquired, mothers played more of a partnership role, helping infants acquire and manipulate the objects of their choice and introducing play routines with objects (Fogel, 1990b; West & Fogel, 1990).

Implications

One implication of these findings is that, for infants at this age, the object is not a tool. Objects are presented as part of the cultural environment. In some sense, however, the mother is a cultural tool for obtaining and exploring objects. Without her, the infant's contact with objects would be limited. In the mother-as-tool metaphor, she does not mediate the infant's experience with objects. The infant experiences the objects directly through perception and action. The mother presents the objects in ways that highlight their affordances for the infant and make it easier for the infant to act on those objects. It is not objects per se that infants perceive, but objects as offered by the mother-as-tool in the context of the mother–infant relationship. It is the temporal, auditory, tactile, and visual patterning of action, objects, clothing, posture, and nonverbal expressiveness that forms the living cultural context of infancy. These cultural patterns become fundamental constituents of the information perceived by the infant about self and object.

Objects for young infants are also cultural because they are replicas of toys that have been used with small infants for centuries. Their design has been worked out in the partnership among infants, parents, and manufacturers over many generations. Their colors, sounds, and shapes fit with what infants can do (Fogel, 1993). It is possible that maternal action is as much co-regulated by these cultural features of toys as the infant's action. In this manner, the culture of toys and infant-care practices establishes the patterning of action in the mother–infant relationship system, and not just in one or the other alone. In the next section, I explore further the importance of the mother–infant relationship in the development of information related to objects.

Relationship History and Object Information

The study of relationships as creative and cultural requires a multimethod research approach. I refer here not only to social relationships, but to any individual–environment relationship in which creativity and culture play a role. In addition to the more standard sequential analysis of the cooccurrences and contingencies between mother and infant action, one can approach the relationship from the perspective of an ethnographer. This more qualitative approach to research takes the insights of ecological psychology, with respect to the individual–environment relationship system, and applies them to the scientist–subject relationship system. This approach has some distinguishing features:

1. Scientist observers become part of the system under study in the sense of relying on empathic and phenomenological methods. In

other words, observers use their own bodies to create hypotheses about the embodied meaning of the experience for the participants in the system (Belenky, Clinchy, Goldberger & Tarule, 1986; Ihde, 1979; Sheets-Johnstone, 1990). I believe that anyone doing research on perception–action systems uses their own experience as a basis for generating hypotheses. A scientific methodology based on created, embodied information accounts explicitly for the complicity of the observer in the process of creating information about the subjects.

2. Scientist observers must recognize the inherent limitations of the information they create about their subjects. Because there is an indeterminacy to action—Shotter's reality of vagueness—the scientist should accept that inferences made from their observations are only temporary positions in a continuing dialogue between themselves and their subjects, and between themselves and their colleagues (Belenky et al., 1986; Reinharz, 1984).

The ethnographic approach to the exploration of the mother–infant–object system in the present study confirmed that information created in relation to objects depends crucially on the history of the manner in which the infant has related to that object in the company of others (Lyra, Pantoja, Cabral, & Fogel, 1994; Pantoja, Cabral, Lyra, & Fogel, 1994). Typically, in the early weeks of life, infants and mothers share a frame of face-to-face interaction in which objects are not a part. Mothers introduce objects into this face-to-face frame. Some mothers find their infants relatively receptive to visual demonstrations of an object that they bring between their face and the infants'. Other mothers find that they must touch the infant with the object to introduce the object as an innovation into the face-to-face frame.

Once the mother establishes the new frame of infant attention to the object in the context of face-to-face play, she may introduce another innovation. This is typically the demonstration of the object's properties while the infant watches or touches the object. From this frame as a foundation, mothers may introduce additional innovations such as bringing the object close to the infant's hand or putting the object in the infant's hand. Once these routines are firmly established, the mother will hold the object within the infant's reach and encourage reaching for the object.

A communication frame at any point in time exerts a powerful influence on the subsequent transformations within the dyadic relationship system (Fogel, 1993). Dynamic systems are extremely sensitive to initial conditions. This finding lends support to the hypothesis that the means by which information is created—in this case the way in which objects are integrated into the communication frame—is preserved as part of the perception–action system in the dyad. The objects are brought into the frame and the frame provides part of the meaning of the object. Through this historical process, each dyad develops a different set of frames in which objects are explored as lines of situated action (Ginsburg, 1985; Lyra et al., 1994).

In the present study, our examination of all the dyads in the sample suggests that two general relationship patterns emerged: an object-focused relationship and a more social-focused relationship (Reimers & Fogel, 1992). In the object-focused pattern, infants easily made the transition from face-to-face play frames into frames for attending to objects. The mother alternated between demonstrating the object's properties to the infant (shaking a rattle) and moving the object gently into the infant's reach space for visual and tactile inspection. Later, she highlighted the object's affordances, maintained attention on the object, and vocally marked different types of actions that the infant performed with her help. The infant remains alert and attentive to the object and the mother waits until the infant loses attention to one object before presenting another. After they acquire reaching, these infants develop exploratory routines that combine different actions and sensory modalities, such as combining looking and touching (see Figure 1).

In the social-focused pattern, the mother's attempts to introduce objects into the face-to-face frame were short-lived, and the communication quickly reverted to bouts of face-to-face play in which the object served merely as the route into more social activity. Later, the mother's demonstrations of the object's properties were not sequentially related to infant attention and she may have demonstrated one object while the infant was

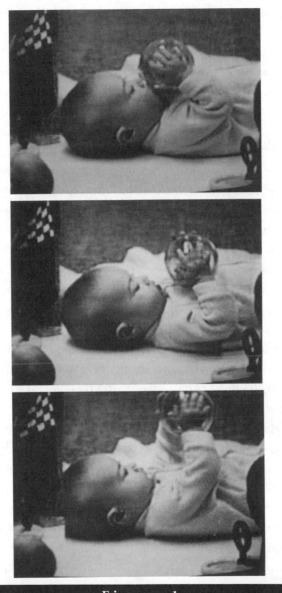

Figure 1

Infant examines ball toy by mouthing followed by looking, thus making a systematic comparison between touch and vision in the creation of information between infant and object.

holding onto or attending to another. When these infants began to reach for objects on their own, they tended to put the objects directly into their mouths, keeping their attention on the mother (Figure 2).

It seems that different information was created about the same set of objects by each of these groups of infants. The object-focused infants were discovering the affordances of objects: They were shaking rattles and squeezing soft objects. They were also systematically relating information between different sensory and action modalities. The social-focused infants had a smaller repertoire of exploratory actions, which was confined mainly to reaching, grasping, and mouthing, and the integrating of these with mother-directed actions. Statistical tests using standard coding categories confirm these patterns in the sample (Fogel, West, Hsu, & Pantoja, work in progress). These findings were supported by other research showing individual differences in sustained attention to objects that emerge in the first half year and are relatively stable over the first year (Ruff, Lawson, Parinello, & Weissberg, 1990). Infants with high levels of sustained attention to objects had mothers who displayed objects one at a time for extended periods and who did not insert bids for social play into object-play routines (Gray, 1978; Parinello & Ruff, 1988). In a related finding, infants who were more emotional in a social situation at 3 months had lower scores on object-related sensorimotor tasks at 5 and 6 months (Lewis, 1993).

Each infant creates information about objects with respect to the historical social process in which the object was embedded. There are individual differences in what the infants detect about the affordances of objects. These differences arise in a relationship that has emotional meaning and in which infant and mother have a historical investment. Infants perceive themselves as belonging to this relationship and as playing a part in its transformation over time. Thus, it is likely that information about objects is a creative achievement imbued with relational meanings that go beyond mere detection.

Embodied Perception and Object Information

Thus far, culture and relationship history have been studied as possible aspects of the quality of information created with respect to objects. In this

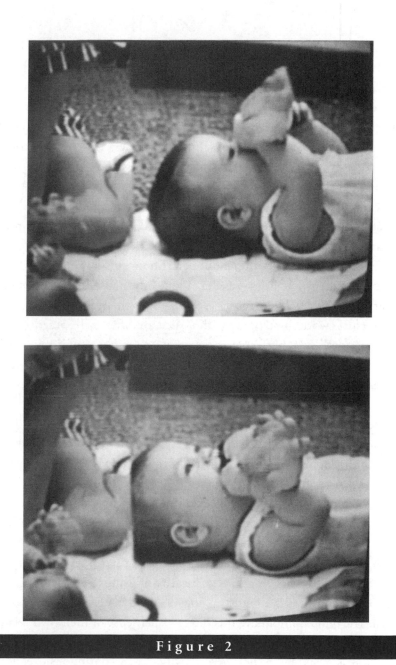

Figure 2

Infant mouths toy for long periods while looking elsewhere or at mother. The information about the toy is created in the context of the infant's relationships to mother and other objects.

section, I explore the way that individual differences in preferences for the sensory systems used to perceive objects may also play a role in the creation of information. My colleagues and I have found that the social-focused infants, for example, show a tendency to prefer tactile and auditory modalities. They are responsive to mother's touches, the sounds she makes, and the sounds of the toys, but they are less responsive in the visual modality. Object-focused infants prefer to gaze intently and quietly for long periods at the toy the mother holds. These infants are more visually oriented. They are more likely to turn toward and attend to some object in the near environment. Once they do, they are relatively immobile and tend to become visually captured by the object for long periods.

Can the specific embodiment of perception—visual compared to tactile and auditory modalities—create unique information? In the *Dioptrics*, Decartes (as quoted by Gregory, 1966, p. 191) noted how a blind person discovers the world by tapping with a stick and that, with practice, "they feel things with such perfect exactness that one might almost say they see with their hands." An argument can be made for cross-modal equivalences between touch and vision by invoking the notion of structural invariance (Stern, 1985; E. Gibson, 1993). Similar invariances may be detected in a textured surface by touch and vision, for example. On the other hand, Descartes used the word *almost* to suggest that vision and touch may also produce distinctive and unique forms of information that are associated with the process of perceiving by means of those modalities.

The importance of Descartes' description of cane tapping is that information about surfaces must be acquired through the cane via a series of connected actions. There is no analogy in touch of a visual glance in which one takes in an entire field of spatial relations, including the relation of the self to other things. The linearity of using language to describe a set of relationships is a better analogy to the dynamics of touch than is vision. The blind do not have this direct visual sense of their own relation to space. Thus, "without such assurance, the blind woman's walk through the world is an intensely *narrative* activity . . . , a continuous exercise of memory and prediction" (Swan, 1992, p. 327). Helen Keller, who was both deaf and blind wrote, "my fingers cannot, of course, get the impression of a large whole at a glance, but I feel the parts, and my mind puts them together" (Keller, 1908, p. 12). Similar observations have been made about blind infants (Fraiberg, 1977; Gibson, 1993).

These reflections are not meant to equate infants who prefer tactile exploration with blind adults. Rather, the analogy may serve to highlight that different sensory modalities are not merely neutral pathways or channels for the transmission of detected information about a world of invariant forms. These sensorimotor systems are fundamental in the creation of information in relation to the environment: They endow that environment with particular meaning that informs future actions and perceptions. The sensorimotor systems can also interact to produce unique phenomenological patterns. Because vision is such a powerful modality— owing to its depth and simultaneity—it can easily dominate and therefore alter perceptual experiences in other modalities.

From Aristotle to Descartes to the present day phenomenologists (Ihde, 1979), the dominance of vision has been recognized and examined. Perception has been described as *polymorphic* to the extent that a preferred sensory system, or a cultural bias toward vision compared to touch, can orient the perceptual system. Even within a single sensory system such as vision, people can see in different ways, such as in the change in artistic vision with the introduction of perspective drawing during the Renaissance (Ihde, 1979; Merleau-Ponty, 1962).

Research on human infants shows that cross-modal equivalence does not occur uniformly. Visual patterns can dominate and alter auditory perception and sensory specialization develops with respect to sensory-specific experiences (Lewkowicz, 1988, 1992). Infant preferences for sensorimotor pathways may become amplified and stabilized by the historical processes in the mother–infant–object social system. A mother may use more visual demonstrations with infants who do more looking, and more sounds and touches with less visual infants. These early patterns affect the means by which infants act on objects and, therefore, affect the meaning of objects for the infants.

CONCLUSION

Because relationships create frames that serve as the basis for future action and innovation while preserving the history of the relationship, very small early differences in environmental opportunities, individual propensities, or social processes may become amplified into emergent frames that regulate the system for an indefinite period. The preservation of early conditions as frames for the later development of a system is one of the major features of a dynamic systems perspective on development. Early frames, the later effects of differential timing of sensory and motor developmental pathways, and their mutual influences are the constraints for uniquely emergent developmental pathways (Fogel & Thelen, 1987; Thelen & Fogel, 1989).

From the perspective of ecological psychology, individual differences in development must be understood with respect to information, and not to the mere physical features (e.g., masses, forces, wave lengths) of the environment or of the body (Fogel, 1993; E. Gibson, 1979; Oyama, 1985). I have proposed that if one focuses on detected information only, however, there is still more psychology to be done. My contribution to an ecological theory of development is to suggest ways to understand how information is created, and that requires the study of the embodied information by which individuals relate to their environment. Because most of the objects and most of the means people use are historical products of cultural systems, it is important to understand how culture is involved in the creation of information via perception and action.

Ecological psychology can advance to a developmental theory by embracing the study of relationships through time, creativity, and culture. There is a great deal to learn. The study of relationships through time has only begun for the field of social relationships, and it is almost nonexistent with respect to repeated encounters with the nonsocial environment. How does action and information change over time through commerce with the same environment? The study of creativity is given little attention with the mainstream of psychology. Researchers need to understand how creative engagement with the environment engenders aesthetic, moral, and emotional information and how that influences action. The systemic conditions under which creativity is enhanced or suppressed must be examined.

Finally, the role of culture in both highlighting affordances and in creating novel affordances must be understood. People do not know what any particular material affords for action until someone acts upon it, makes it available to others, and finds a way to communicate about it to others. What ecological psychologists refer to as natural affordances are the set of actions inherited from culture, the history of uses to which an object has been put. In other species, culture could be replaced theoretically by the historical set of organism–environment connections in a niche that—along with the genes—is part of what each individual inherits (Oyama, 1985). Examples of historical connections are migratory pathways, trails, nests, and locally communicated actions such as bird song variants. In this sense, development occurs not only within the individual–environment system, but within the system of co-regulating individuals through historical time (Fogel, 1993). Developmental theory needs to encompass change at both the individual and group levels; at real-time, developmental-time, and historical-time scales; and study the interface between them.

At this point, I can summarize my answers to the four questions posed by the organizers of the conference from which this chapter originated:

What is development? Development in dynamic systems of communicating individuals entails the co-regulated creation and self-organization of novel information within relationship frames. Relationship frames are dynamically stable attractors in real time, developmental time, and historical time.

What is unique about this perspective? The guiding features of this view are the focus on relationships as the primary unit of analysis; the inclusion of relationships with social and nonsocial worlds; a recognition that information is both detected and created, and historical and cultural. The study of variability in opportunities for creative action and cultural variations can serve to highlight the process of developmental change.

What are the limitations of the perspective? It is difficult to study whole systems and their natural histories from both the observers' and subjects' points of view. Methods need to be articulated within the scientific culture by which the researcher can make systematic choices in the process of their own information creation about the system being studied. To study created and cultural information requires the researcher to move readily between quantitative and qualitative approaches to understand the world from the perspective of particular subjects in the context of the entire developmental system.

<u>What new questions are raised, and what old ones discarded?</u> This view raises questions about how best to define and to study relationships and their changes over time, and how to focus inquiry at the level of information. If ecological psychologists are to be receptive to information as created and cultural—in both ourselves and in our subjects—then we have to recognize that every developmental psychologist will take a different path over the field of developmental research. As observers, we are often unaware of our own complicity in the creation of scientific knowledge. We believe ourselves to be discovering the invariant structural laws of development, when in fact we are creating those laws with respect to our own intellectual history, and through the lens of our scientific culture (Gergen, 1994; Hermans & Kempen, 1993; Jahoda, 1992). When we frame our theories and methods in relational terms—relationships to colleagues, our scientific culture, and our research participants—we enhance the probability of creatively perceiving the transformational process of developmental change.

REFERENCES

Arnheim, R. (1966). *Toward a psychology of art.* Berkeley: University of California Press.

Bakhtin, M. M. (1988). Discourse in the novel. In N. Mercer (Ed.), *Language and literacy from an educational perspective* (Vol. 1, pp. 47–58). Philadelphia: Open University Press.

Bateson, G. (1955). The message: "This is play." In B. Schaffner (Ed.), *Group processes* (Vol. 2). Madison, NJ: Madison Printing Co.

Belenky, M. F., Clinchy, B. M., Goldberger, N. R., & Tarule, J. M. (1986). *Women's way of knowing: The development of self, voice, and mind.* New York: Basic Books.

438

Bruner, J. (1990). *Acts of meaning.* Cambridge, MA: Harvard University Press.

Bushnell, E. W., & Boudreau, J. P. (1991). The development of haptic perception during infancy. In M. A. Heller & W. Schiff (Eds.), *The psychology of touch* (pp. 139–166). Hillsdale, NJ: Erlbaum.

Butler, J., & Rovee-Collier, C. (1989). Contextual gating of memory retrieval. *Developmental Psychology, 22,* 533–552.

Costall, A. (1985). How meaning covers the traces. In N. H. Freeman & M. V. Cox (Eds.), *Visual order: The nature and development of pictorial representation* (pp. 17–31). New York: Cambridge University Press.

Dewey, J. (1986). The concept of the reflex arc in psychology. *Psychology Review, 3,* 13–32. Reprinted in W. Dennis (Ed.), *Readings in the history of psychology.* New York: Appleton-Century-Crofts.

Fagen, J. W., Ohr, P. S., Singer, J. M., & Klein, S. J. (1989). Crying and retrograde amnesia in young infants. *Infant Behavior and Development, 12,* 13–24.

Fogel, A. (1990a). The process of developmental change in infant communicative action: Using dynamic systems theory to study individual ontogenies. In J. Colombo & J. Fagen (Eds.), *Individual differences in infancy: Reliability, stability and prediction,* (pp. 341–358). Hillsdale, NJ: Erlbaum.

Fogel, A. (1990b). Sensorimotor factors in communicative development. In H. Bloch & B. Bertenthal (Eds.), *Sensorimotor organization and development in infancy and early childhood* (NATO ASI Series pp. 75–88). Amsterdam, The Netherlands: Kluwer.

Fogel, A. (1992). Co-regulation, perception and action. *Human Movement Science, 11,* 505–523.

Fogel, A. (1993). *Developing through relationships.* Chicago: University of Chicago Press.

Fogel, A., & Thelen, E. (1987). Development of early expressive and communicative action: Reinterpreting the evidence from a dynamic systems perspective. *Developmental Psychology, 23,* 747–761.

Fogel, A., West, L., Hsu, H., & Pantoja, A. (1996). *Mothers, infants, and objects: A relational–historical approach.* Manuscript submitted for publication.

Fraiberg, S. (1977). *Insights from the blind.* New York: Basic Books.

Gergen, K. J. (1994). Exploring the postmodern: Perils or potentials? *American Psychologist, 49,* 412–416.

Gibson, E. J. (1988). Exploratory behavior in the development of perceiving, acting, and the acquiring of knowledge. In M. R. Rosenzweig & L. W. Porter (Eds.), *Annual review of psychology,* (pp. 1–41). Palo Alto, CA: Annual Review, Inc.

Gibson, E. J. (1993). Ontogenesis of the perceived self. In U. Neisser (Ed.), *The perceived self* (pp. 25–42). New York: Cambridge University Press.

Gibson, J. J. (1966). *The senses considered as perceptual systems.* Boston: Houghton Mifflin.

Gibson, J. J. (1979). *The ecological approach to visual perception.* Boston: Houghton Mifflin.

Ginsburg, G. P. (1985). The analysis of human action: Current status and future potential. In G. P. Ginsburg, M. L. Brenner, & M. von Cranach (Eds.), *Discovery strategies in the psychology of action* (pp. 255–279). London: Academic Press.

Gleick, J. (1988). *Chaos: The making of a new science.* New York: Viking.

Goffman, E. (1974). *Frame analysis: An essay on the organization of experience.* Cambridge, MA: Harvard University Press.

Gray, H. (1978). Learning to take an object from the mother. In A. Lock (Ed.), *Action, gesture and symbol: The emergence of language* (pp. 159–182). New York, NY: Academic Press.

Gregory, R. L. (1966). *Eye and brain: The psychology of seeing.* New York: World University Library.

Ihde, D. (1979). *Technics and praxis.* Boston: D. Reidel Publishing.

Heft, H. (1989). Affordances and the body: An intentional analysis of Gibson's ecological approach to visual perception. *Journal for the Theory of Social Behavior, 19,* 1–30.

Hermans, H. J. M., & Kempen, H. J. G. (1993). *The dialogical self: Meaning as movement.* San Diego, CA: Academic Press.

Hofsten, C., von, & Ronnqvist, L. (1988). Preparation for grasping an object: A developmental study. *Journal of Experimental Psychology: Human Perception and Performance, 14,* 610–621.

Jahoda, G. (1992). *Crossroads between culture and mind: Continuities and change in theories of human nature.* Cambridge, MA: Harvard University Press.

Johnson, M. (1987). *The body in the mind: The bodily basis of meaning, imagination, and reason.* Chicago: University of Chicago Press.

Keller, H. (1908). *The world I live in.* New York: The Century Company.

Kendon, A. (1985). Behavioral foundations for the process of frame attunement in face-to-face interaction. In G. P. Ginsburg, M. Brenner, & M. von Cranach (Eds.), *Discovery strategies in the psychology of action.* London: Academic Press.

Kolers, P. A., & Roediger, H. L. (1984). Procedures of mind. *Journal of Verbal Learning and Verbal Behavior, 23,* 425–449.

Kugler, P. N., Kelso, J. A. S., & Turvey, M. T. (1982). On coordination and control in naturally developing systems. In J. A. S. Kelso & J. E. Clark (Eds), *The development of movement coordination and control* (pp. 5–78). New York: Wiley.

Legerstee, M. (1991). Changes in the quality of infant sounds as a function of social and nonsocial stimulation. *First Language, 11,* 327–343.

Lewis, M. D. (1993). Emotion-cognition interactions in early development. *Cognition and Emotion, 7,* 145–170.

Lewkowicz, D. J. (1988). Sensory dominance in infants: 1. Six-month-old infants' response to auditory–visual compounds. *Developmental Psychology, 24,* 155–171.

Lewkowicz, D. J. (1992). Infants' responsiveness to the auditory and visual attributes of a sounding/moving stimulus. *Perception and Psychophysics, 52,* 519–528.

Lock, A. (1980). *The guided re-invention of language.* New York: Academic Press.

Lyra, M., Pantoja, A., Cabral, E., & Fogel, A. (1994, June). *Plasticity in the construction of mother-object-infant interactions.* Poster session presented at the International Society for the Study of Behavioral Development, Amsterdam.

Markova, I. (1990). Why the dynamics of dialogue? In I. Markova & K. Foppa (Eds.), *The Dynamics of Dialogue* (pp. 1–22). New York: Springer-Verlag.

Merleau-Ponty, M. (1962). *Phenomenology of perception* (C. Smith, Trans.). London: Routledge and Kegan Paul.

Michaels, C. F., & Carello, C. (1981). *Direct perception.* Englewood Cliffs, NJ: Prentice-Hall.

Newell, K. M., & McDonald, P. V. (1993). The evolving perceptual-motor workspace in infancy. In G. J. P. Savelsbergh (Ed.), *The development of coordination in infancy,* (pp. 175–199). New York: North-Holland.

Oyama, S. (1985). *The ontogeny of information: Developmental systems and evolution.* Cambridge, England: Cambridge University Press.

Pantoja, A., Cabral, E., Lyra, M., & Fogel, A. (1994, November). *A construcao das interacoes "Mae-objeto-bebe": Caracteristicas da relacao produto/processo* [The construction of mother–object–infant interactions: Characteristics of the relationship product and process]. Paper presented at Brazilian Psychological Society, University of Sao Paulo.

Parinello, R. M., & Ruff, H. A. (1988). The influence of adult intervention on infants' level of attention. *Child Development, 59,* 1125–1135.

Pattee, H. H. (1987). Instabilities and information in biological self-organization. In F. E. Yates (Ed.), *Self-organizing systems: The emergence of order* (pp. 325–338). New York: Plenum.

Piaget, J. (1954). *The construction of reality in the child.* New York: Ballantine Books.

Prigogine, I. (1973). Irreversibility as a symmetry-breaking process. *Nature, 246,* 67–71.

Reed, E. S. (1982). An outline of a theory of action systems. *Journal of Motor Behavior, 14,* 98–134.

Reed, E. S. (1987). Why do things look as they do? The implications of J. J. Gibson's "The ecological approach to visual perception." In A. Costall & A. Still (Eds.), *Cognitive psychology in question* (pp. 90–114). New York: St. Martin's Press.

Reimers, M., & Fogel, A. (1992). The evolution of joint attention to objects between infants and their mothers: Diversity and convergence. *Analise Psicologia, 1,* 81–89.

Reinharz, A. (1984). *On becoming a social scientist.* New Brunswick, NJ: Transaction.

Rochat, P. (1989). Object manipulation and exploration in 2- to 5-month-old infants. *Developmental Psychology, 25,* 871–884.

Rogoff, B. (1990). *Apprenticeship in thinking.* New York: Oxford University Press.

Rovee-Collier, C. K., Enright, M., Lucas, D., Fagan, J., & Gekoski, M. J. (1981). The forgetting of newly acquired and reactivated memories of 3-month-old infants. *Infant Behavior and Development, 4,* 317–331.

Ruff, H. A., Lawson, K. R., Parrinello, R., & Weissberg, R. (1990). Long-term stability of individual differences in sustained attention in the early years. *Child Development, 61,* 60–75.

Sarbin, T. R. (1986). *Narrative psychology: The storied nature of human conduct.* New York: Praeger.

Schachtel, E. G. (1959). *Metamorphosis: On the development of affect, perception, attention, and memory.* New York: Basic Books.

Sheets-Johnstone, M. (1990). *The roots of thinking.* Philadelphia: Temple University Press.

Shotter, J. (1983). "Duality of structure" and "intentionality" in an ecological psychology. *Journal for the Theory of Social Behavior, 13,* 19–43.

Shweder, R. A. (1993). The cultural psychology of the emotions. In M. Lewis & J. M. Haviland (Eds.), *Handbook of emotions* (pp. 417–431). New York: Guilford.

Stern, D. N. (1985). *The interpersonal world of the infant.* New York: Basic Books.

Swan, J. (1992). Touching words: Helen Keller, plagiarism, authorship. *Cardozo Arts & Entertainment Law Journal, 10,* 321–364.

Thelen, E. (1989). Self-organization in developmental processes. Can systems approaches work? In M. Gunnar (Ed.), *Systems in development* (pp. 77–118). Hillsdale, NJ: Erlbaum.

Thelen, E., & Fogel, A. (1989). Toward an action-based theory of infant development. In J. Lockman & N. Hazen (Eds.), *Action in social context: Perspectives on early development* (pp. 23–64). New York: Plenum.

Vygotsky, L. S. (1978). *Mind in society.* Cambridge, MA: Harvard University Press.

West, L., & Fogel, A. (1990, April). Maternal guidance of object interaction. Paper presented at International Conference on Infant Studies, Montreal, Quebec, Canada.

Wertsch, J. V. (1991). *Voices of the mind.* Cambridge, MA: Harvard University Press.

Comment on Fogel

Reuben M. Baron and Endre Kadar

Fogel's chapter "Information, Creativity, and Culture" is a daring and ambitious attempt to apply a "revisionist" version of the theory of direct perception (Gibson, 1979), and attempts to use a perception–action approach to social development. Furthermore, it attempts to combine the ecological perspective with aspects of the nonlinear, dynamical systems approach. We contend that the aspects of the chapter that deal with theory, as opposed to those grounded in research, are a mixed bag. The theoretical points are, by turns, creative and needlessly polemical, and provide criticisms both needed and misguided.

REVISING DIRECT PERCEPTION THEORY

The Problem of Creativity

A good deal of Fogel's critique is a plea for ecological psychologists who use direct perception theory (Gibson, 1979) to allow a more generative role for the perceiver–actor in the creation as opposed to the discovery or

---

Baron and Kadar comment on Fogel from an ecological realist perspective.

detection of affordances. Whereas we are sympathetic to this direction of change, we wonder why linking affordances to dynamical systems concepts such as emergence and self-organization does not already accomplish this in a way that avoids the subjectivity that Fogel imparts in regard to making creating affordances sound so experiential as to become mystical in its richness. The best example in the published literature is Warren's (1984) doctoral research on stair climbing in which he ties in the phase transition from 2- to 4-limb involvement to strains in person–environment fit, which, in turn, create shifts in perceived climbability of stairs when riser height exceeds a certain level. In this case, there is a perceiving–acting system in which shifts in action mode and affordances are emergent outcomes of shifts in fit. In the social domain, one can interpret a recent article in *Behavior and Brain Sciences* by Dunbar (1993) in a similar way in the sense that as group size increases (the control parameter), social affordances regarding social-cohesion building shift from hands-on, direct perception–action modes to categorical treatment of others as types in the context of the evolution of language as an interaction mode. That is, we believe that it is unnecessary to highlight the dynamic nature of information pickup by coining the notion of information creation, especially if it is contrasted with detection of information. We believe that in direct perception theory, information detection is an exploratory dynamic process. By introducing the notion of information creation, one could get the impression that information detection is a snapshot-like phenomenon, which clearly contradicts core ideas of direct perception theory.

Unique Properties of Social Affordances

On the topic of social affordances, Fogel is, again, essentially correct that the physical affordance model is not sufficiently complex relationally to capture a social situation in which there is reciprocal, dynamical interaction. However, such a critique does not imply that the direct perception approach is inadequate if it fails to capture the phenomenology of social relations, for example., a sense of belonging or rapture, and so forth. Rather, the complexity of social interaction calls for interpreting direct perception in terms of dynamical systems models as a way of better capturing social affordances in the context of reciprocal coordination. For example, Newtson (1994) looks at how waves of information and action are coordinated at the nonverbal level.

PHILOSOPHICAL GROUNDING OF DIRECT PERCEPTION THEORY

Direct perception theory can be related to many philosophical movements (e.g., pragmatics, functionalism, new realism, hermeneutics). Fogel mentioned only two of them in the context of philosophical grounding of the direct perception approach. Direct realism was explicitly discussed in analyzing the real-versus-relational dichotomy. This is probably one of the least controversial aspects of direct realism. Nevertheless, there are scientists who have different opinions on direct realism, ranging from *naive realism* (see Ullman, 1980) to a unique *"relational" direct realism* (see Shaw & Turvey, 1981). Fogel also discusses another philosophical school, *phenomenology* (see Ihde, 1977; Merleau-Ponty, 1962). Although we accept that direct perception theory can be viewed as a type of phenomenology, this claim is questionable and requires clarification. To emphasize this point, Gibson (1979) often expressed his appreciation of Merleau-Ponty's (1962) phenomenological theory of perception (Heft, 1989; Kadar & Effken, 1994; Sanders, 1993), but was very critical about transcendental phenomenologies of the Husserlian type. The work of phenomenological sociologists (e.g., Luckmann, 1973, 1978; Schutz, 1972; Schutz & Luckmann, 1973, 1989) is helpful in clarifying this issue. Specifically, when Fogel emphasized the role of ethnography in addressing the cultural aspects, he might have used phenomenological ethnomethodology (see works of Harold Garfinkel, 1967, and Aaron Cicourel, 1967) as a potential resource to exploit.

Beyond such omissions, the more serious problem in Fogel's treatment of phenomenology is that direct perception theory does not treat sensory experience as experience per se. Rather, direct perception theory treats sensory experience as a window on the world that is to be acted in. Thus, the directness of phenomenology is different from psychological direct perception; in the latter, the invariants that look toward the world are at issue rather than the richness of the experience regarding self-knowledge. Perhaps this confusion occurs because Fogel sometimes seems to forget that in direct perception theory perceiving is for doing (or interacting), not for reflecting.

METHODOLOGICAL–EPISTEMOLOGICAL ISSUES

Extending direct perception theory to developmental phenomena raises a host of difficulties, especially in regard to social interaction. Even in the most mathematically developed sciences such as, for example, physics, inanimate objects provide a difficult problem when their interactive behaviors are modeled (e.g., the three-body problem, particles in a field). Nevertheless, as a first step, the problem of social interaction could be clarified by being more specific on formalization. Using a relational approach in modeling direct perception theory is too generic. Relational approaches became popular at the turn of the century (e.g., Russell, 1914, Simmel, 1950, the new realists) and provided a basis for a renewal of debates on old philosophical issues (e.g., internal vs. external relations), which indicates that the use of relationships has its philosophical pitfalls. With a dynamical systems perspective, theorists can focus on contemporary formalism and characterize interpersonal relations as coupled systems. For example, Buder (1991) has used the logistic equation to model social interaction.

In addition to a lack of reference to dynamical systems models, which is a strange critique given Fogel's strong track record in this area, when he does use such models, he does so in an idiosyncratic way. For example, are frames really attractors? What are the control parameters, the order parameters? When is hysteresis occurring? Thelen's work on motor development (e.g., Thelen & Ulrich, 1991; Thelen & Smith, 1994) answers these questions to a much greater extent than Fogel does in his treatment of social development.

What concerns us in Fogel's chapter is that, for all its virtues, it will confuse the audience not familiar with direct perception theory, that is, the work of James J. Gibson and others who have followed. Specifically, Fogel's proposal is prematurely mentalistic and dualistic. Whether this is too high a price to pay for broadening direct perception theory in order to better encompass the social–cultural dimensions of development, we leave to the reader to decide.

RESEARCH ON SOCIAL INTERACTION

The chapter, however, also contains a necessarily limited, but nevertheless exciting, description of Fogel's recent mother–child interaction research that finds intriguing differences among infants in whether they are more focused on objects or people. Indeed, the section describing Fogel's research more than any other lives up to the title "Information, Creativity, and Culture."

REFERENCES

Buder, E. H. (1991). A non-linear dynamic model of social interaction. *Communication Research, 18,* 174–198.

Cicourel, A. V. (1967). *Method and measurement in sociology.* Free Press: New York.

Dunbar, R. I. M. (1993). Coevolution of neocortical size, group size, and language in humans. *Behavioral and Brain Sciences, 16,* 681–735.

Garfinkel, H. (1967). *Studies in ethnomethodology.* Englewood Cliffs, NJ: Prentice Hall.

Gibson, J. J. (1979). *The ecological approach to visual perception.* Boston: Houghton-Mifflin.

Heft, H. (1989). Affordances and the body: An intentional analysis of Gibson's ecological approach to visual perception. *Journal for the Theory of Social Behavior, 19,* 1–30.

Ihde, D. (1977). *Experimental phenomenology.* New York: Capricorn Books.

Kadar, O., & Effken, J. (1994). Heideggesian meditations on an alternative ontology for ecological psychology: A response to Turvey's 1992 proposal. *Ecological Personality, 6,* 297–341.

Luckmann T. (1973). Philosophy, sciences and everyday life. In M. Natanson (Ed.), *Phenomenology and the social sciences.* Evanston, IL: Northwestern University Press.

Luckmann, T. (Ed.). (1978). *Phenomenology and sociology.* New York: Penquin Books.

Merleau-Ponty, M. (1962). *Phenomenology of perception* (C. Smith, Trans.). London: Rutledge.

Newtson, D. (1994). The perception and coupling of behavior waves. In R. R. Vallacher & A. Nowak (Eds.), *Dynamical systems in social psychology* (pp. 139–168). San Diego, CA: Academic Press.

Russell, B. C. (1914). *Our knowledge of the external world.* London: Open Court.

Sanders, J. T. (1993). Merleau-Ponty, Gibson, and the materiality of meaning. *Man and World, 26,* 287–302.

Schutz, A. (1972). *The phenomenology of the social world.* London: Rutledge.

Schutz, A., & Luckmann, T. (1973). *The structures of the life-world* (Vol. 1). Evanston, IL: Northwestern University Press.

Schutz, A., & Luckmann, T. (1989). *The structures of the life-world* (Vol. 2). Evanston, IL: Northwestern University Press.

Shaw, R. E., & Turvey, M. T. (1981). Coalitions as ecosystems: A realist perspective. In M. Kubovy & J. R. Pomerantz (Eds.), *Perceptual organization* (pp. 343–425). Hillsdale, NJ: Erlbaum.

Simmel, G. (1950). *The sociology of Geog Simmel* (Wolff, Trans.). Glencoe, IL: Free Press.

Thelen, E., & Smith, L. B. (1994). *A dynamic systems approach to the development of cognition and action.* Cambridge, MA: MIT Press.

Thelen, E., Ulrich, B. D. (1991). Hidden skills. *Monographs of the Society for Research in Child Development, 56*(1, Serial No. 223).

Ullman, S. (1980). Against direct perception. *Behavioral and Brain Sciences, 3,* 373–415.

Warren, W. H. Jr. (1984). Perceiving affordances: Visual guidance in stair climbing. *Journal of Experimental Psychology: Human Perception and Performance, 10,* 683–703.

Epigenetic Systems

PART THREE

Epigenetic Systems

Cathy Dent-Read and Patricia Zukow-Goldring

Epigenesis has been defined as the emergence of new physical structures and of new behaviors during the course of individual development (Gottlieb, 1991a, 1991b). According to Johnston (1987) developmental regularities emerge from genetic and environmental contributions,
but neither alone accounts for any aspect of the process. Instead, the organism and its internal and external environment continuously inform
one another. Changes occur throughout the entire system, rather than to
separate parts (Johnston, 1988; Miller, 1988).

The epigenetic systems view defines a system as having levels of organization with two-way causal effects across each level (see Bertenthal,
1991). These levels exist both within organisms and between organism and
environment. For example, the system is sometimes analyzed into levels
such as environment, behavior, neural activity, and genetic activity (Gottlieb, 1991b). This view includes work on development such as ecological–social (Bronfenbrenner, 1979), contextual (Lerner & Kaufman, 1985),
interactive (Johnston, 1987), and probabilistic epigenetic (Gottlieb, 1991b)
studies, as well as serves as a basis to critique reductionism in psychology
(Oyama, 1985, 1989). Epigenetic systems theory, far more than ecological

realism or dynamic systems, examines the assertion that changes in behavior may affect experience of the environment, which in turn canalizes or shapes behavior (Gottlieb, 1991b). For example, neonates' and infants' preference for head position leads to asymmetries in reactions to sound, and in visual experience with infants' hands. This preference has been studied in relation to hemispheric specialization of the brain and effects on cognition (Turkewitz, 1993).

In this view, the process of canalization determines developmental pathways for all members of a species. Canalization applies to all levels of a developing system (environment, behavior, neural activity, and genetic activity), including species-typical experiences. For example, most children first crawl and then move to walking. This change in locomotion leads to changes in the child's social environment in that adults more often interact with babies after they can walk than before (Gustafson, 1984). This change in the environment leads to changes in the infant due to the effects of social interaction (Gustafson, 1984; Green & Gustafson, 1997, this volume). Experience, the dynamic relation between organism and environment, causes development at the organismic level. In this view, experience maintains, facilitates, or induces not only behavior but also anatomy and physiology. An example from the early development of the nervous system illustrates this principle. Neural activity (which is correlated with acting and perceiving) regulates the amount of protein synthesis carried out by the DNA in the nucleus of the cell in particular neurons (Born & Rubel, 1988), illustrating that higher level influences affect the genes.

The epigenetic systems view is represented in this book by Miller's work on ducklings' responses to maternal alarm calls and Green and Gustafson's investigation of adults' responses to infants' cries. Miller studied ducklings in the wild and in the laboratory to look for experiences that might cause the development of the ability to respond adaptively to the maternal alarm call, on the basis of the idea that what develops is the transaction between the organism and its environment. By taking a transactional approach that explores the significance of self-stimulation and other nonobvious forms of experience, his research demonstrates compellingly the role of experience in the development of a behavior commonly assumed to be "innate," that is, controlled by the genes.

In humans, certain patterns of social interaction may be species typical. Green and Gustafson report on research designed to delineate age-related changes in social interactions in everyday environments. Observing infants at ages 6, 8, and 12 months, they found that social interactions became more frequent, but shorter, across this age span; they also found that crying and fussing as directed social behaviors increased in frequency between ages 6 and 12 months. Mothers incorporated different infant actions into social interactions depending on the age of the infant. As with development in birds, human development is revealed as consisting of changes in the infant–environment system by means of the experience the infant has of the environment, and effects the infant has on its social environment.

Several questions emerge from this work based on a epigenetic systems perspective. What role does development play in evolution? How does experience affect the environment, making the transaction between organism and environment? Are some levels of analysis more different than others—do molecular genes and inanimate environments constitute different kinds of phenomena than living organ systems and individuals? How do organisms form a system with their environment; specifically, how do organisms perceive and know and act in their surround? The intriguing chapters in this section lead us to ask these difficult questions and, thus, to begin to answer them.

REFERENCES

Bertenthal, B. I. (1991). Special section: Canalization of behavioral development. *Developmental Psychology, 27*, 3–39.

Born, E., & Rubel, E. (1988). Afferent influences on brain stem auditory nuclei of the chicken: Presynaptic action potentials regulate protein synthesis in nucleus magnocellularis neurons. *Journal of Neuroscience, 8*, 901–919.

Bronfenbrenner, U. (1979). *The ecology of human development.* Cambridge, MA: Harvard University Press.

Gottlieb, G. (1991a). Epigenetic systems view of human development. *Developmental Psychology, 27,* 33–34.

Gottlieb, G. (1991b). Experiential canalization of behavioral development: Theory. *Developmental Psychology, 27,* 4–13.

Gustafson, G. (1984). Effects of the ability to locomote on infants' social and exploratory behaviors: An experimental study. *Developmental Psychology, 20,* 397–405.

Johnston, T. (1987). The persistence of dichotomies in the study of behavioral development. *Developmental Review, 7,* 149–182.

Johnston, T. (1988). Developmental explanation and the ontogeny of bird song: Nature/nurture redux. *Behavioral and Brain Sciences, 11,* 629–641.

Lerner, R., & Kaufman, M. (1985). The concept of development in contextualism. *Developmental Review, 5,* 309–333.

Miller, D. (1988). Beyond interactionism: A transactional approach to behavioral development. *Behavioral and Brain Sciences, 11,* 653–654.

Oyama, S. (1985). *The ontogeny of information: Developmental systems and evolution.* Cambridge, England: Cambridge University Press.

Oyama, S. (1989). Ontogeny and the central dogma: Do we need the concept of genetic programming in order to have an evolutionary perspective. In M. Gunnar & E. Thelen (Eds.), *Minnesota Symposium on Child Development, Vol. 22. Systems and development.* (pp. 1–34). Hillsdale, NJ: Erlbaum.

Turkewitz, G. (1993). The influence of timing on the nature of cognition. In G. Turkewitz & D. Devenny (Eds.), *Developmental time and training* (pp. 125–142). Hillsdale, NJ: Erlbaum.

13

The Effects of Nonobvious Forms of Experience on the Development of Instinctive Behavior

David B. Miller

"The *development* of *instinctive* behavior." Years ago, some individuals might have considered this statement an oxymoron. After all, aren't instincts preprogrammed by genes? Do instincts not simply lie dormant awaiting expression at a particular time of life, much like alarm clocks set to go off at different times? And, if this is so, isn't the environment either unimportant or only important to the extent that it plays a supportive

The research on the mallard maternal assembly call was supported by a grant from the National Institute of Child Health and Human Development to Gilbert Gottlieb. Much of the research on alarm call responsivity was supported by grants to David B. Miller from the National Science Foundation and the University of Connecticut Research Foundation.

I am grateful to Gilbert Gottlieb, Jay S. Rosenblatt, and the editors of this volume who read earlier drafts of this chapter and provided many helpful suggestions. I take full responsibility for any shortcomings that remain.

Throughout the 20 or so years of my investigation of alarm call responsivity, many individuals have played key roles in influencing the developmental trajectory of this endeavor. Foremost among these individuals are Charles F. Blaich and Gilbert Gottlieb. I also extend special appreciation to Gloria Hicinbothom. Others who have made important contributions to this research program include Lynn Elmore, Jay T. Hirsch, Janice L. Johnson, Martin Krugman, William Lexton, Linda L. Miller, Kathryn L. Muller, Gail Richmond, Michael K. Russell, and William C. West.

This chapter was originally inspired by my esteemed colleague, Sergei N. Khayutin, who suggested I write such a piece for what was to be the first Russian-language volume on developmental psychobiology. Professor Khayutin was the director of the Laboratory of the Ontogenesis of Behavior, Institute of Higher Nervous Activity, USSR Academy of Sciences in Moscow, and is known worldwide for his behavioral and neurophysiological studies on the development of defensive behaviors in a variety of avian species. The project was abandoned on his untimely death in 1992. I dedicate this chapter to his memory.

(rather than constructive) role, like the table upon which the alarm clock sits? Instinctive behavior is species-typical, is highly stereotyped, develops without obvious forms of practice, and is well-developed on its initial occurrence. If the expression of instinctive behavior is inevitable when the organism encounters the environmental stimulus required to elicit it, then why worry about its development?

Some have challenged the inevitability of instinctive behavior by advocating that both genes and environment are important (without really specifying how such an interaction might take place). Interactionism has not offered any real solutions and, indeed, has been clouded by a literature laden with misunderstood questions that are appropriate in the domain of population genetics but inappropriate in explaining individual development (e.g., the heritability quotient). Interactionists have also been accused of being extreme environmentalists who deny any significant role of genetic factors. The confused questions that have emerged from this interactionist approach have elevated development to some level of importance, but often have done little more than pose dichotomies that remain impotent with respect to advancing our understanding of developmental mechanisms (see review by Johnston, 1987).

In this chapter, I discuss an ecological view of instinctive behavior that is not entirely new but that still has not been well incorporated into mainstream psychological and biological thinking. This *transactional* (rather than interactional) approach concerns how an organism–environment system changes over time as a function of the ongoing activity occurring among levels of organization that compose the system. After discussing some general concepts related to the development of instinctive behavior, I present a line of research on perinatal ducklings that exemplifies this view, both methodologically and conceptually. I then present a brief overview of ecological theory as informed by these empirical investigations. The label *instinct* has been associated with both human as well as nonhuman behavior—from verbal to nonverbal communication, from aggression to sexual behavior, and so on. Thus, the study of instinctive behavior is relevant to both human and nonhuman organisms.

THE DEVELOPMENT OF INSTINCTIVE BEHAVIOR

If, as Schneirla (1966) proclaimed, "behavioral ontogenesis is the backbone of comparative psychology" (p. 284), then the heart of the discipline (and certainly the most challenging endeavor) is the search for actual developmental mechanisms underlying the expression of species-typical phenotypes. Yet, the complexity of this search can be intimidating because of the multidimensional nature of possible experiential factors. Developmental mechanisms are not only behavioral but also neurobiological, anatomical, physiological (e.g., hormonal), genetic, and ecological. These can be reduced further to include underlying physical laws (e.g., kinetic, kinematic), biochemical structure (e.g., DNA), and so on. Kuo (1970) was sagacious, therefore, in advising that the only way to gain a firm grasp of development is by adopting a multidisciplinary approach. This strategy, according to Kuo, is the most effective way to understand how development proceeds across these levels of organization, which compose both the internal and external environment of the organism and thereby are part and parcel of the organism–environment system.

Such an approach, then, is consistent with the transactional view of development, according to which (a) the proper unit of analysis is the organism–environment system, (b) this system is in a continuous state of flux, such that (c) at every point in time (t), and across all levels of organization, the system is somehow different at $t + 1$ than it had been at t or $t - 1$ (Miller, 1988a). This latter point renders the transactional view of development highly dynamic compared with the more static interactional approach—a distinction first made by Dewey and Bentley (1949). Interactionist approaches typically imply the coaction of dichotomous entities, usually genes and experience. How such entities coact remains obscure; moreover, the static characterization of the interactionist view is due to its failure to capture the emergent nature of a changing system over time. Accordingly, and as Dewey and Bentley (1949) also noted, the transactional view renders development a process that is in a continuous state of emergence.

The continuous emergence nature of transactionism should not be confused with the continuity–discontinuity issue in development. Whereas

I would argue that everything that happens in this emergent process depends on everything that has already happened, I would not necessarily argue that everything that happens will necessarily have an effect on that which is yet to happen; in other words, I acknowledge discontinuities in development, or what Oppenheim (1981) referred to as "ontogenetic adaptations." Some things happen without necessarily directly influencing the emergence of subsequent developmental events, except, perhaps, at the most global level of analysis (i.e., the organism might not be alive were it not for the emergence of such ontogenetic adaptations).

The dynamic transaction occurring across the levels of organization composing the organism–environment system renders developmental analyses rather complex. However, this view need not necessarily change the way experiments are conducted, although it certainly can and might very well affect the kinds of experiments that are conducted and the nature of the stimuli and experiential variables chosen to manipulate, as I exemplify in this chapter. In any event, this view ought to affect the way we as researchers interpret the outcomes of our experiments and, accordingly, our view of the developmental process.

If we are to understand developmental processes, we must move beyond mere (but necessary) description of developmental milestones and attempt to account for such events in terms of the aforementioned mechanisms. Because of the multiplicity of mechanistic factors composing a developmental system, true explanation necessitates a thorough analysis of many underlying mechanistic processes rather than merely attributing causality to any single mechanism. Metaphorically, understanding the mechanism underlying the functioning of a light bulb is certainly a necessary but highly insufficient explanation for understanding how a table lamp works. One also needs to know something about the lamp's switch, the cord, the wall outlet, fuses, and so forth for a thorough understanding of how the lamp functions.[1] The same is true of organismic behavior. In other words, claiming that a behavior is caused by genes (as is so often

---

[1] This lamp metaphor was devised by Charles F. Blaich. I have found it very useful in explaining mechanistic causality and the nature–nurture issue to students over the years.

done when attempting to describe species-typical behavior) does not bring us any closer to explaining the behavior's development than to claim that it is caused by ecology, neurobiology, anatomy, and so forth. Such a superficial analysis merely provides convenient labels rather than true explanation. This "nominal fallacy," or pseudoexplanation by way of labeling or naming, does little to advance our understanding of the development of instinctive behavior. Rather, it provides a convenient way to avoid the complex task of accounting for the ontogenetic origin and developmental trajectory of highly stereotyped behavior patterns—a most challenging task given that behavioral stereotypy is sometimes taken to mean experientially buffered or genetically "canalized" (e.g., Waddington, 1975).

Some scientists have realized that seemingly fixed or innate developmental trajectories and outcomes may involve experiential influences that are not altogether obvious (e.g., Gottlieb, 1976), but this is a relatively modern view. There are, I believe, certain historical factors that hampered the emergence of this view. The domineering influence of behaviorism in American psychology during the growth of ethology in Europe from the 1940s through 1960s may have contributed to the polarity of positions regarding the influence of experience on behavioral development. Behaviorism fostered an interest in phenomena associated with learning, which, of course, is a very overt form of behavioral development involving rather obvious kinds of experiential influences. Learning theorists were not interested in subtleties but rather in how very obvious forms of experience (e.g., food deprivation, stimulus presentation, schedules of reinforcement, etc.) result in changes in behavior directly related to those forms of experience. Developmentalists, as well, were primarily interested in the effects of early experience on behavioral development, focusing mostly on how individual manipulations of straightforward forms of experience affect change in the organism's corresponding behavior (e.g., the effect of restricted movement on motor development, the effect of restricted vision on the development of visually guided behavior, etc.).

Ethologists, on the other hand, were interested in highly stereotyped, species-typical behavior patterns—behaviors that appear to develop in the

absence of obvious experiential input. The mind-set that dominated ethological thinking is typified by an early experiment by Spalding (1875). He
reared hatchling swallows in small cages in which they could neither extend their wings nor "practice" flying. They were released when fully
fledged, and Spalding reported that they were able to fly, albeit with some
degree of awkwardness at first. In some respects they were indistinguish-
able from wild swallows, such as in their ability to avoid flying into objects. Thus, it seemed straightforward to conclude that "birds do not *learn*
to fly" (p. 507) in the sense that flying occurs in the absence of practicing
obvious forms of flight movements. There was little reason to entertain
the possibility that subtle wing movements occurring throughout development inside the small cages play any kind of constructive role in the development of full-blown flying behavior. And so, fueled by the emphasis
placed on learning and unitary manipulations of obvious forms of experience by developmentalists, the tradition continued among ethologists to
search only for obvious experiential factors in the development of behavior. In the absence of such apparent influences, it seemed plausible to conclude that experience simply was not involved—an unfortunate view that
still pervades modern literature despite occasional attempts to clarify the
issue (e.g., Dawkins, 1986, pp. 45–82; Lehrman, 1970).

Given the inadequacy of explaining developmental processes by
merely labeling them (i.e., the nominal fallacy referred to earlier), as well
as the inadequacy of traditional forms of learning in explaining the development of species-typical behavior (Gottlieb, 1976), it might be pru-
dent to adopt a different metatheoretical view of development by shifting
attention toward the influence of seemingly subtle events in ontogeny. By
subtle or *nonobvious*, I mean influences that would not appear to have a
direct relationship with a particular developmental outcome because of
their dissimilarity from the outcome (e.g., auditory experience affecting
visual capability, social rearing affecting auditory discrimination), or that
might only be taken to have a supportive rather than a constructive influence on development (e.g., temperature, humidity, gravity, etc.). Stated
similarly, Gottlieb (1992; from whom I borrow the term *nonobvious*) recently referred to the emergent nature of developmental systems as often

being the result of "nonlinear causality," as did Thelen (1989), who stated that "the process of development itself is nonlinear, and as the systems regroup and coalesce, these nonlinearities serve as a continuing wellspring for new forms" (p. 92). Specifically, Gottlieb (1992) stated, "In developmental systems the coaction of X and Y often produces W rather than more of X or Y, or some variant of X or Y" (p. 169). This concept is strikingly similar to a hypothesis posited recently by Turvey and Fitzpatrick (1993), who argued for a dynamics approach to understanding the development of perception–action systems as an alternative to conventional approaches. Specifically, they suggested that "the properties, features, dimensions, and so on, whose changes lead to new perception-action patterns, are unspecific to the new patterns, neither resembling them nor prescribing their details" (p. 1187).

Accordingly, I posit that when attempting to search for developmental mechanisms underlying highly stereotyped, instinctive behavior, one is much more likely to encounter nonobvious influences than when explaining the ontogeny of more variable behavioral outcomes. Thus, I suggest that there is oftentimes an inverse relationship (portrayed in Figure 1) between the obviousness of experience and the extent of species typicality of behavior. The greater the stereotypy of the behavioral outcome, the less obvious are the experiences that influence its development. For example, birds that sing dialects must be exposed to the dialect they will eventually sing. This is a very obvious form of experience; to sing the dialect, the bird must hear the dialect. The behavioral outcome is variable in the sense that virtually any dialect within the species-typical song range could be learned, and there is a one-to-one correspondence between the nature of experience and the nature of behavioral development. For behavior that is more stereotyped, however (i.e., behavior that appears to be more "hardwired," with a much tighter or narrower range of developmental outcomes), the correspondence between experience and the outcome might not be so obvious. This is where the search for ontogenetic mechanisms becomes rather difficult. For example, Wallman (1979) found that preventing chicks from seeing their own feet affects their feeding responses to mealworms. Rather than focusing on early feeding experiences

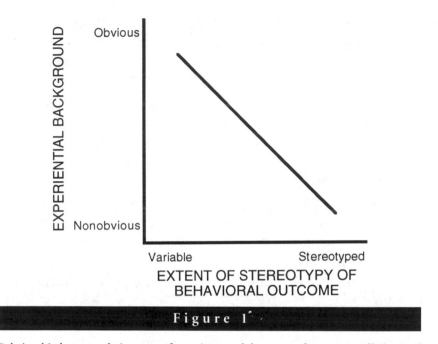

Figure 1

Relationship between obviousness of experience and the extent of stereotypy of behavioral outcome.

per se, Wallman found a nonobvious experiential factor (seeing one's own feet) that contributes to the highly stereotyped manner in which young chicks handle mealworms. More recently, and equally intriguing, Masataka (1994) found that laboratory-born squirrel monkeys (*Saimiri sciureus*) developed a strong species-typical fear of snakes only if live insects had been part of their diet. Laboratory-born monkeys fed with only fruits and monkey chow did not develop the characteristic fear response exhibited by wild monkeys.

Next, I describe in some detail another situation involving subtle, nonobvious forms of experience: alarm call responsivity of mallard ducklings (*Anas platyrhynchos*). To place this work in its proper context, however, I first briefly describe how mallard ducklings come to identify the maternal assembly call of their own species, as the two lines of research, to some extent, run parallel.

NATURALISTIC OBSERVATIONS OF PARENT–OFFSPRING INTERACTIONS IN MALLARD DUCKS

Like most waterfowl species, mallards are ground-nesting birds and build their nests in shallow crevices lined with feathers and vegetation, often in secluded sites. The hen lays about 6 to 15 eggs (average = 10) and incubates them for around 25 days. Several days before they hatch, the embryos penetrate the inner shell membrane and move into the air space of the egg, at which time they begin to vocalize. About a day later, they pip the outer shell and begin to make the circular cut that will eventually liberate them from the egg in yet another day. During this late prenatal period, the hen begins to vocalize frequently, uttering what has come to be known as an "attraction call" (Gottlieb, 1971), "pre-exodus call" (Miller & Gottlieb, 1978), "maternal call" (Abraham, 1974; Bjärvall, 1968) or "assembly call" (Gottlieb, 1975; Miller, 1980). A day or so after the ducklings have hatched, the hen uses a slight variant of this vocalization (Miller & Gottlieb, 1978) to call her young off the nest: an event known as the nest exodus. (This call is sometimes referred to as the "exodus call"; however, for ease of exposition, I hereafter refer to this maternal vocalization, whether it be of the pre-exodus or exodus variety, as the assembly call.)

Mallard hens sometimes utter another type of maternal vocalization while brooding their ducklings on the nest. This "reconnaissance" or "alarm call" (Abraham, 1974; Miller, 1980; Miller & Gottlieb, 1978) is uttered when there are disturbances in the vicinity of the nest, such as potential predators. While uttering this very low-amplitude call, the hen adopts a seemingly wary posture, stretching her neck and extending her head upward. The alarm call causes ducklings to cease all vocal and locomotor activity (Miller, 1980).

Mallard assembly and alarm calls are quite distinct from each other in a variety of acoustic features (Miller, 1980). Sound spectrograms of the two types of calls are shown in Figure 2, and Table 1 summarizes the main acoustic differences. Of particular importance is the striking dif-

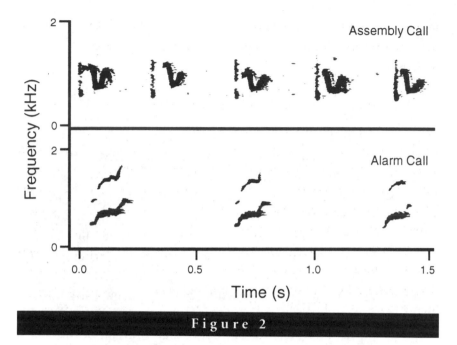

Figure 2

Narrow-band sound spectrograms of mallard maternal assembly and alarm calls.

Table 1

Acoustic Features of Mallard Maternal Assembly and Alarm Calls

	Maternal call	
Acoustic feature	Assembly	Alarm
Frequency modulation	Descending	Ascending
Dominant frequency	970 ± 337 Hz	676 ± 77 Hz
Note duration	112 ± 27 ms	161 ± 39 ms
Repetition rate	3.7 ± 1.1 notes/s	1.1 ± 0.4 notes/s
Notes per burst	3.5 ± 1.7	2.1 ± 1.2
Notes having impulsive sound	85%	9%

NOTE: notes/s indicates the repetition rate of the notes of the call.

ference in the repetition rate of the notes of the calls (notes/s), for, as discussed next, this acoustic feature has particular perceptual salience for ducklings.

Responsiveness of Ducklings to the Assembly Call

Gottlieb (1971) has demonstrated that maternally naïve (i.e., incubator-hatched) ducklings exhibit a preference for the mallard assembly call when given a choice between that call and the assembly call of other species (e.g., chicken, wood duck, pintail). The primary acoustic feature of the assembly call to which mallard ducklings (and embryos) are sensitive is the characteristic fast repetition rate of the notes (around 3.7 notes/s). Gottlieb (1979, 1980) found that domestic mallard (Peking breed) embryos and hatchlings that have been denied normally occurring auditory experience (i.e., self- and sibling-produced vocalizations) fail to show a preference for their species' assembly call. In other words, Gottlieb documented an interesting link between exposure of the ducklings to their own vocalizations and their subsequent responsiveness to the hen's maternal assembly call. Gottlieb's studies typify the sort of subtle, nonobvious experiential effect previously discussed, and they provided a basis for my own investigations on alarm call responsivity of mallard ducklings.

I begin the description of my investigations with a structural (acoustic) analysis of the alarm call, followed by an assessment of the acoustic features to which ducklings are particularly attuned. I then describe developmental changes in alarm call responsivity and the relationship of these changes to the nesting ecology of mallards and the possible role that arousal might play in affecting the developmental trajectory of the freezing response. Next, I focus on two developmental mechanisms underlying alarm call responsivity: auditory experience and social context. The experiments on auditory experience include an assessment of how the concept of critical periods may or may not apply in the development of the freezing response. The experiments on social context show how multiple pathways can affect the development of a behavioral outcome and how such experience can actually broaden behavioral specificity.

Responsiveness of Ducklings to the Maternal Alarm Call

As is the case with responsiveness to the assembly call, incubator-hatched ducklings respond to the initial presentation of the maternal alarm call in a species-typical fashion. But, unlike the excitatory approach response (including increased vocal activity) generated by the assembly call, the alarm call causes ducklings to cease all vocal and locomotor activity, or what is referred to as "freezing." The contrasting responses to assembly and alarm calls are shown in Figure 3. The basic plan of my research was to (a) identify the particular acoustic features of the alarm call to which ducklings are responsive and (b) use that information as a basis for examining various ontogenetic influences and patterns associated with the freezing response. In this manner, I have striven to address the broader question of how instinctive (i.e., species-typical) behavior develops—not by labeling it the product of some hypothetical genetic code, program, or blueprint (which we do not believe exists, as genes produce proteins, not behaviors), but, rather, by identifying ontogenetic mechanisms, particularly those at the behavioral and ecological levels. (One of the most elegant essays I have read debunking the misguided concept of genetic codes or blueprints is by Bonner, 1987, p. 717.)

Unless noted otherwise, all of the experiments I discuss herein involve domestic mallard ducklings of the Peking breed. Peking ducklings are available year round from game farms and, barring only a few quantitative exceptions, do not differ behaviorally from their wild counterparts (Miller, 1977b; Miller & Gottlieb, 1981). All of the ducklings in these experiments were hatched and brooded in the laboratory under very stringent sound controls; that is, aside from constant, low-frequency motor and fan noises generated by incubators and ventilation systems, the only patterned sounds to which they were exposed prior to testing were their own perinatal vocalizations and those of broodmates. Ducklings in the devocalization experiments were not exposed to such perinatal vocalizations (except for those devocalized ducklings that received "replacement" auditory stimulation through loudspeakers prior to testing). We based each data point on either 30 individually tested ducklings or, for social tests, 20 groups of 8 to 12 ducklings per group. In our experiments ducklings are

Figure 3

Peking duckling's approach response to the assembly call (top) and freezing response to the alarm call (bottom).

tested only once; thus, all data points are independent of one another. I recorded the maternal alarm calls used in the tests from wild mallard hens on nests in the field. A duckling's behavior was scored as a freeze only if it exhibited total vocal and locomotor inhibition within 10 s of the broadcast of the alarm call and remained in that state for at least the duration of the broadcast of the alarm call (2 min in most tests). For tests involving groups of ducklings, the same criteria for freezing applied for all members of the group; thus, if only one duckling failed to meet the criteria, the entire group was scored as a nonfreeze. Such stringent criteria were used because of their ecological validity; that is, on a natural nest, a single utterance by a single duckling in a brood might be sufficient to reveal the location of the nest to a predator. (Our observations indicate that hens only utter alarm calls when there are potential predators near the nest.) Additional details regarding housing and testing conditions can be found in the articles cited in each of the following sections.

The Role of Repetition Rate in Alarm Call Responsivity

Knowing that Peking ducklings are particularly sensitive to the moderately fast repetition rate of the notes of the assembly call (Gottlieb, 1979, 1980), and that the modal repetition rate of assembly call notes (3.7 notes/s) is considerably different from the modal rate of alarm calls (1.1 notes/s; Table 1), we began our investigation by assessing the extent to which the slow repetition rate of alarm notes affects the freezing response of ducklings. To do this, we assessed the responsiveness of maternally naïve ducklings to one of four calls: (a) an unaltered alarm call pulsed at 1.4 notes/s; (b) an unaltered assembly call pulsed at 3.7 notes/s; (c) the alarm call used in Condition a but altered such that it was quickened to a rate of 3.7 notes/s; or (d) the assembly call used in Condition b but altered to a rate of 1.4 notes/s. The assembly and alarm calls were recorded from the same hen on a nest in the field. This procedure allowed us to vary only repetition rate, keeping all of the other acoustic features (e.g., dominant frequency, frequency modulation, note duration) constant.

As shown in Table 2, the alarm call and assembly call pulsed at 1.4 notes/s yielded a very high incidence of freezing, whereas ducklings did not freeze on exposure to either call pulsed at 3.7 notes/s. In fact, ducklings typically responded to the faster rate calls by approaching the loudspeaker and increasing their incidence of uttering contentment calls. Thus, repetition rate is clearly a very important acoustic feature that differentially affects freezing (i.e., inhibition) and approach (i.e., excitation): Slow rates cause ducklings to freeze, and fast rates cause them to approach (Miller, 1980).

Table 2

Incidence of Freezing to Assembly and Alarm Calls With Normal and Altered Repetition Rates

Call and notes/s	No. freezing ($n = 30$)
Alarm 1.4	25
Assembly 1.4	26
Assembly 3.7	0
Alarm 3.7	0

NOTE: notes/s indicates the repetition rate of the notes of the call.

But, just how slow must repetition rate be to promote freezing, or how fast must it be before the duckling will exhibit an excitatory response? To assess the range of slow repetition rates affecting behavioral inhibition and the boundary at which ducklings begin to exhibit excitation, we altered the rate of an alarm call by decrements and increments of 0.2 s. Some ducklings were given tests in which the alarm call began at a rate of 0.2 notes/s and increased in rate every minute by increments of 0.2 notes/s up to a maximum of 3.7 notes/s (the final increment was from 3.4 to 3.7 notes/s—a 0.3 notes/s increment). Another group of ducklings was tested with an alarm call that began at 3.7 notes/s and decreased every minute by 0.2 notes/s (except for the initial decrement of 0.3 notes/s, from 3.7 to 3.4 notes/s) down to 0.2 notes/s. We measured the particular repetition rate at which ducklings froze and unfroze.

These experiments revealed that there is an acoustical boundary along the repetition rate continuum that demarcates those rates affecting inhibition and those affecting excitation at around 2.6 to 2.8 notes/s. Rates below this boundary reliably cause ducklings to freeze, whereas rates above this boundary are typically associated with excitation. Moreover, the optimal range of slow repetition rates affecting behavioral inhibition is between 0.8 and 1.8 notes/s, with 1.6 notes/s being particularly salient (Miller, 1983a, 1983b).

Experiments that we conducted involving alterations of other acoustic features (i.e., note duration, frequency modulation, and dominant frequency) indicated little or no effect on alarm call responsivity (Miller & Blaich, 1986). Thus, repetition rate is an important acoustic feature for mallard ducklings not only in species identification as evinced by their responsiveness to the assembly call but also in the context of predator avoidance vis-à-vis their responsiveness to the alarm call.

The communicative significance of temporal properties of acoustic signals (such as repetition rate) occurs across a wide range of taxa, including many avian (as well as non-avian) species (e.g., Beletsky, 1989; Brush & Narins, 1989; Clarkson, Clifton, Swain, & Perris, 1989; Emlen, 1972; Myrberg, Spanier, & Ha, 1978; Popp, 1989). However, generalizing across species too readily can be risky, even among waterfowl. For example, wood ducklings (*Aix sponsa*) identify the maternal assembly call of their species not by repetition rate but, rather, by frequency modulation (Gottlieb, 1974). Wood ducks, of course, are hole nesters, whereas mallards are ground nesters. It would be of considerable interest to assess the extent to which such potential mechanisms as nesting ecology affect cues used in auditory communication. Although such an ambitious endeavor has not been undertaken, preliminary data from our laboratory reveal certain physical (ecological) factors associated with sound degradation that may, at least in part, explain the importance of frequency modulation by wood ducklings but not by mallards (Blaich & Miller, 1984). Specifically, we found that nest cavities degrade the frequency modulation of notes that have an amplitude modulation with a rapid rise time, such as mallard notes. The frequency modulation of notes having an amplitude modulation with a slow rise time, such as wood duck notes, is not greatly affected by the resonance properties of nest cavities. Thus, nest cavities preserve, rather than degrade, the acoustic feature of the wood duck hen's assembly call (frequency modulation) to which wood ducklings are responsive. Further investigations in this area could render exciting information linking ecological and developmental mechanisms.

Age-Related Changes in Alarm Call Responsivity

Incidence of freezing in the neonatal period Each of the abovementioned experiments involved ducklings that were tested for their responsiveness to the alarm call at 24 hr ($\pm$6 hr) after hatching. Having found that slow and fast repetition rates of alarm notes differentially affect behavioral inhibition and excitation, respectively, it was of conceptual importance to assess alarm call responsivity at different neonatal ages because of Gottlieb's (1979) discovery of differential responsiveness to slow- and fast-rate calls well before hatching. For example, might the postnatal freezing response to the alarm call be some sort of developmental vestige of an inhibitory process that begins prenatally, or does it arise de novo in the postnatal period?

Gottlieb's (1979) measure of prenatal inhibition differed from our postnatal measure of freezing; yet, the two measures are probably analogous in that they involve reduction in behavioral activity. Specifically, Gottlieb's measure was a decrease (from baseline) in the rate of bill clapping by the embryo, whereas our measure was total cessation of vocal and locomotor activity. The prenatal emergence of behavioral inhibition to slow-rate calls and excitation (increase in bill clapping relative to baseline) to fast-rate calls is shown in Table 3. Peking ducks hatch on Day 27; yet, there is evidence of behavioral inhibition to slow-rate auditory stimuli as early as Day 22. (As demonstrated by Konishi, 1973, neurons in the cochlear nuclei of Peking duck embryos are sensitive to the low frequencies characteristic of mallard maternal alarm calls as early as Day 22.)

Table 3

Prenatal Ages at Which Significant Levels of Behavioral Inhibition (I) and Excitation (E) of Bill Clapping Occur at Different Repetition Rates

	Repetition rates (notes/s)			
Age	1.0	2.3	3.7	6.0
Day 22	—	—	I	—
Day 24	—	I	E	—
Day 26	I	I	Ė	E

NOTE: Dashes indicate that no data were collected for those repetition rates for those days.

We tested different groups of 30 ducklings to the modal alarm call (pulsed at 1.6 notes/s) at six different postnatal ages: 12 hr, 24 hr, 36 hr, 48 hr, 60 hr, and 72 hr. As shown in Table 4, the incidence of freezing was very high in younger birds (especially at 12 hr) but dropped precipitously at older ages (48 hr, 60 hr, and 72 hr).

Given the high level of freezing at 12 hr, there appears to be continuity between the prenatal inhibitory response as measured by bill clapping and the postnatal freezing response. But why should embryos exhibit behavioral inhibition to slow-rate calls? There appears to be no link between nesting ecology and the latter stages of incubation that would account for this form of prenatal inhibition (see the next section). The prenatal emergence of behavioral inhibition is characteristic of the anticipatory nature of development, meaning that the capacity to exhibit species-typical behavior develops prior to the time that an organism actually needs to exhibit such behavior in adapting to its ecological niche (cf. Anokhin, 1964). This ensures that the organism is ready to behave in an adaptive manner when it has reached the point in its "developmental niche" that necessitates the performance of such a behavior.

Relationship of alarm call responsivity and nesting ecology My field observations indicate that nesting mallard hens do not begin to utter the alarm call in response to disturbances in the vicinity of the nest until the

Table 4

Age-Related Changes in Alarm Call Responsivity

Age (hr)	No. freezing ($n = 30$)
12	29
24	26
36	22
48	16
60	15
72	10

eggs have begun to hatch. It also appears likely that they do not utter the alarm call after the nest exodus (around 24 hr after the ducklings have hatched), although we have not attempted to make recordings by telemetry after the nest exodus. Two pieces of evidence strongly suggest that the alarm call is used only or primarily during the pre-exodus brooding period. First, the alarm call is a very low-amplitude call, almost imperceptible (by humans and sensitive microphones) beyond 2 m from the hen. Second, we have observed that when hens are faced with potential danger after the nest exodus, they call their ducklings to water using the assembly call rather than freeze them on land with the alarm call.

It is of considerable interest, then, that the age at which the alarm call is most effective (i.e., 12 hr) corresponds to the time that ducklings are most likely to encounter this call in nature (i.e., posthatch, prenest exodus). This is a good example of what Oppenheim (1981) referred to as an "ontogenetic adaptation"—a behavior that occurs only at a particular period in the life cycle enabling the organism to adapt to a particular situation (in this case, predator avoidance while still on the nest).

It is noteworthy that a study of older (1-week-old) Peking ducklings indicates a persistent physiological (albeit, not behavioral) response to slow-rate calls (Evans & Gaioni, 1990). On exposure to an alarm call, these older ducklings exhibit a brief phasic acceleration in heart rate followed by prolonged, tonic deceleration. For comparison, the assembly call provokes a brief phasic acceleration as well as a tonic increase in heart rate. Thus, although the behavioral freezing response to the alarm call decreases with age, the underlying physiological response remains.

Possible role of arousal As previously stated, it appears that the gradual decline in freezing between 24 hr and 72 hr is an ontogenetic adaptation associated with the timing of the nest exodus. There is, however, an alternate explanation having to do with our rearing procedures. Our ducklings have always been reared without food and water due to sanitation and other practical considerations, and, moreover, it is well documented that ducklings remain in good condition for several days without food or water (Kear, 1965) and that many Anatidae delay eating edible substances for 2 to 3 days posthatch in the wild (Weller, 1964). The question remains whether the lack of food and water in our experiments resulted in an increased level of arousal that might have interfered in some way with the freezing response in older ducklings.

To test this hypothesis, we reared one group of 30 ducklings with food and water from hatching to the time of testing at 72 hr and another group of 30 ducklings without food and water. At 72 hr, the ducklings were tested to the maternal alarm call and were subsequently weighed. *Arousal* is a multidimensional concept (Andrew, 1974)—one for which there is little definitional agreement. We use the term in a descriptive, behavioral manner to denote heightened activity as evinced by increased vocal behavior (see also Kaufman & Hinde, 1961). Accordingly, Miller and Hicinbothom (1991) measured arousal by counting the number of distress calls uttered by each duckling during a 2-min pretest period in which the duckling was placed in the testing arena prior to the 2-min broadcast of the alarm call.

As shown in Table 5, ducklings that were fed and watered weighed significantly more than those that were not, and they uttered significantly more distress calls during the 2-min pretest period, indicating that they were more aroused. This result counters the hypothesis that food and water deprivation would increase arousal. In any event, there was no difference between the ducklings that were fed and watered and those that were not in terms of the incidence of freezing or in the duration of freezing. Thus, in accord with our original conclusions, the decline of

Table 5

Effect of Food and Water on Age-Related Changes in Alarm Call Responsivity

Duckling data	Food and water	No food or water	$p <$
Weight (gm)	65 ± 9	42 ± 6	.0001
No. of distress calls in pretest	214 ± 9	175 ± 14	.02
No. freezing ($n = 30$)	13	15	.80
Duration of freezing (s)	205 ± 13	199 ± 11	.71

freezing in 72-hr-old ducklings seems to be an ontogenetic adaptation associated with the timing of the nest exodus rather than an artifact of experientially induced arousal. In this regard, the persistence of the cardiac response to the alarm call in older birds (Evans & Gaioni, 1990) is intriguing. It is theoretically possible that the physiological response to danger is a fairly continuous process throughout development but that the behavioral responses vary in accord with the age of the animal (Miller & Hicinbothom, 1991). Thus, there may be a decoupling of the behavioral and physiological responses to alarm calls such that different forms of behavioral inhibition develop at certain ages and then disappear. For example, as noted previously, the prenatal behavioral response to the alarm call is a deceleration in the rate of bill clapping. The early postnatal response is freezing, which decreases after several days and is probably replaced by another form of adaptive defensive behavior, such as tonic immobility, which is a form of freezing that occurs once an organism has actually been captured by a predator. Along these lines, it may be noteworthy that tonic immobility is difficult to demonstrate experimentally in neonatal birds and develops only after about 1 week of age (Gallup, 1974).

Summary

Our experiments on age-related changes in freezing indicate that postnatal alarm call responsivity is probably a manifestation of some general inhibitory response system that develops prenatally. The freezing response is at its peak at 12 hr, remains fairly high at 24 hr, and starts to drop at 36 hr. Between 48 hr and 72 hr, there is a marked reduction in the incidence of freezing, and this does not appear to be associated with potentially interfering levels of arousal. There is a close fit between the nesting ecology of mallards and these age-related effects; specifically, ducklings are most responsive to the alarm call around the age that they are most likely to encounter this call in nature—prior to the nest exodus. Although the physiological response to the alarm call persists in ducklings as old as 1 week, the behavioral response does not.

DEVELOPMENTAL MECHANISMS: I. NORMALLY OCCURRING AUDITORY EXPERIENCE

The search for developmental mechanisms necessitates somehow interfering with the course of normal development and assessing the result of the perturbation. As discussed by Gottlieb (1977) and Miller (1981), experience can either be *attenuated* (i.e., a reduction in normally occurring events), *enhanced* (i.e., exposing an organism to more than it would normally encounter), *substituted* (i.e., attenuating or removing one form of experience but replacing it with another), *transposed* (i.e., spatially rearranging experiential elements without attenuating any of them), or *displaced* (i.e., temporally rearranging experiential events, as in attempting to ascertain sensitive periods). Our first group of studies on developmental mechanisms underlying alarm call responsivity involved three of these modes of developmental analysis—experiential attenuation, substitution, and displacement.

Experiential Attenuation

Because Gottlieb (1971) had previously demonstrated that attenuating perinatal auditory experience greatly affects species identification vis-á-vis preferential responsiveness to the maternal assembly call, we decided to ascertain the effects of this manipulation on alarm call responsivity.

Elimination of Sibling Auditory Experience

Our first experiment simply involved hatching eggs in individual incubator compartments, thereby denying embryos and hatchlings the opportunity to hear the perinatal vocalizations of siblings prior to testing (Blaich & Miller, 1988). As shown in Table 6, significantly fewer ($p < .05$) of these *vocal, isolated* ducklings froze upon being tested to the maternal alarm call, as compared with *vocal, communal* ducklings (i.e., ducklings hatched in a communal incubator and placed in individual plastic boxes arranged in a common brooder, thereby providing ample sibling auditory stimulation prior to testing). Thus, auditory experience provided by siblings affects alarm call responsivity. (Further experiments on the importance of sibling auditory experience are described in the Experiential Substitution section.)

Table 6

Effect of Normally Occurring Auditory Experience on Alarm Call Responsivity

Group	Age (hr)	No. freezing ($n = 30$)
Vocal, communal	12	27
Vocal, isolated	12	20
Devocal, isolated	12	12
Devocal, isolated	24	6
Devocal, stimulated	12	24

Attenuation of Self-Produced Auditory Experience and Elimination of Sibling Auditory Experience

This set of experiments was designed to deny embryos and hatchlings not only the opportunity of hearing sibling vocalizations but their own, self-produced sounds as well (Blaich & Miller, 1988).

Starting around Day 24 to 25 of incubation, Peking duck embryos move into the air space of the egg by penetrating the chorioallantoic membrane. As soon as they breathe the air in the air space, they begin to vocalize (two to three days prior to hatching). We used a devocalization technique (Gottlieb & Vandenbergh, 1968) that denies the embryo the opportunity to vocalize.

As shown in Table 6, there was a further, significant reduction in the incidence of freezing in these *devocal, isolated* birds when compared with both vocal, communal ducklings ($p < .001$) and to vocal, isolated ducklings ($p < .05$). To assess whether this reduction in freezing was a transient developmental phenomenon, we (Miller & Blaich, 1984) tested a different group of devocalized, isolated ducklings at 24 hr of age (i.e., 12 hr later than the first group) and found yet a further (albeit nonsignificant, $p < .10$) reduction in the incidence of freezing (Table 6). Taken together, these experiments indicate that both sibling and self-produced auditory experience is important in the development of alarm call responsivity.

Experiential Substitution

The importance of normally occurring auditory experience can be assessed further by a combination of attenuation and replacement (i.e., experiential substitution). Accordingly, we (Miller & Blaich, 1988) devocalized a group of ducklings and stimulated them with a tape recording of embryonic "long–slow" notes (so named by Scoville & Gottlieb, 1980, because of the relatively long duration and slow repetition rate of the notes). Stimulation began 1.5 days after the devocalization operation and continued until testing at 12 hr of age at a rate of 1 min every 2 hr. (The rate and starting date of stimulation were derived from unpublished experiments by Blaich and Miller in which the perinatal vocal activity of ducklings was monitored.)

As indicated in Table 6, substituting a tape recording of normally occurring sounds for actual auditory social interactions significantly increased alarm call responsivity. The incidence of freezing by these *devocal, stimulated* ducklings was significantly greater than that for 12-hr-old devocal, isolated ducklings ($p < .005$) and comparable with that of vocal, communal and vocal, isolated ducklings ($p < .30$). Thus, providing social auditory experience reinstated the freezing response, indicating that sibling auditory stimulation alone is sufficient for maintaining alarm call responsivity.

Experiential Displacement

Experiments on experiential displacement assess when, in the course of normal development, particular forms of experience might be either necessary or sufficient for the development of behavior patterns. The search for such critical, or sensitive, periods typically is fraught with methodological difficulties that few investigators have addressed empirically. For example, as noted by Bateson and Hinde (1987), most critical period experiments fail to acknowledge a confound in the critical period-to-test interval. As depicted in Figure 4 (Panel A), the usual way to go about searching for critical periods is to administer a particular form of experience at different stages of development (as indicated by the thick, horizontal, black rectangles along the three time lines) and then assess the effect of such exposure when the organism reaches a specified age (the triangle at the end of each time line, designated Test Z). By doing this, however, notice that the three different critical period-to-test intervals (designated A, B, and C) have different durations. Any differences observed in behavior could be attributed not only to the three different exposure periods but also to the different postexposure intervals (see also Gottlieb, 1981, 1982, 1985).

Attempting to resolve this confound only introduces a new confound, as indicated in Figure 4 (Panel B). By equalizing durations of the three different critical period-to-test intervals (designated on each time line as CP-to-Test Interval A), the organisms now must be tested at different ages

A. Different Critical Period-to-Test Intervals; Test at Same Age

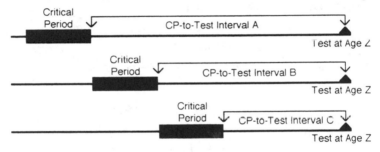

B. Same Critical Period-toTest Intervals; Test at Different Ages

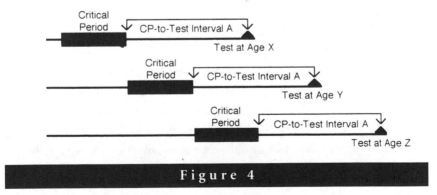

Figure 4

Methodological confounds in the study of critical periods (CP). Panel A shows different CP-to-test intervals for tests conducted when ducks were at the same age; Panel B shows CP-to-test intervals with tests conducted when ducks were of different ages.

(designated by the triangles along the time lines as Age X, Age Y, and Age Z). Thus, differences in behavior might not only be due to the different ages at which exposure to a particular experience occurred but also to different maturational factors, extra-critical period experiential factors associated with different ages at the time of testing, or both.

One particular factor that interested us was the potential role that extra-critical period experience might play on behavioral development. One of the four roles that experience can play in the development of behavior and the nervous system (Bateson, 1983; Gottlieb, 1976) is *maintenance;* that is, experience might be necessary to maintain a previously developed state or to preserve a developmental trajectory or ongoing pathway. (The other three roles are *facilitation,* in which experience hastens development; *induction,* in which experience channels or sharpens development; and *predisposition,* in which one experience primes the organism to be sensitive to another form of experience.) As noted previously, because behavioral inhibition to sounds with slow repetition rates occurs as early as Day 22 of incubation in Peking duck embryos, we do not yet know what forms of experience influence the development of that behavior prior to Day 22. However, alarm call responsivity appears to be the postnatal manifestation of this prenatally developed capability. The question remains whether experience between the prenatal and early postnatal period maintains responsiveness to slow-rate calls (i.e., freezing on exposure to the maternal alarm call).

We addressed this question by using a typical critical period methodology, but carrying it a step further (Miller & Blaich, 1988). As in our experiential substitution experiments described earlier, we exposed different devocalized ducklings at different stages of development to a repetitive tape recording of a call composed of embryonic long–slow notes for 1 min every 2 hr. Some ducklings were stimulated perinatally (Day 25.5 to 12 hr posthatch), others were stimulated only prenatally (Day 25.5 to hatching), and others only postnatally (hatching to 12 hr). All ducklings were tested to the maternal alarm call at 12 hr.

As shown in Table 7, devocalized ducklings that received auditory stimulation only during the prenatal period exhibited significantly less

Table 7		

Effect of Auditory Experience at Different Stages of Development on Alarm Call Responsivity

Auditory experience	Age at test (hr)	No. freezing ($n = 30$)
Perinatal: Day 25.5 to 12 hr	12	24
Prenatal only: Day 25.5 to hatch	12	16
Postnatal only: Hatch to 12 hr	12	20
Postnatal only: Hatch to 12 hr	24	10

freezing than those stimulated throughout the perinatal period ($p < .05$), whereas those stimulated only postnatally behaved comparably with those stimulated perinatally ($p < .70$). However, it would be premature to conclude that there is a prenatal critical period, even though denying normally occurring auditory stimulation during this period resulted in a significant decrement in behavior. The reason for this is that the two groups that behaved comparably (perinatally and postnatally stimulated groups) shared something in common that was not shared by the prenatally stimulated group; namely, the birds in the former two groups received auditory stimulation right up to the time of testing. Thus, it might be the case that auditory experience maintains alarm call responsivity.

To test this hypothesis, we gave another group of devocalized birds auditory stimulation during the postnatal period only (from hatching to 12 hr), but instead of testing them at 12 hr, we tested them at 24 hr. As shown in Table 7, these birds exhibited a significant decrement in freezing as compared with the postnatally stimulated birds that were tested at 12 hr ($p < .01$). This decrement in responding at 24 hr was not due to maturational changes, because normal 24-hr-old ducklings have a high incidence of freezing (26 out of 30, as discussed earlier in the Incidence of Freezing in the Neonatal Period section).

Thus, whenever a temporal gap is introduced between auditory stimulation and testing, alarm call responsivity drops significantly. It would appear, therefore, that normally occurring auditory experience maintains freezing during the postnatal period and that there is no prenatal critical period for this form of experience, at least within the methodological constraints of our experiments. (However, using a different form of auditory stimulation involving calls with variable repetition rates, Gottlieb, 1982, found a prenatal critical period for auditory experience vis-à-vis species identification of the assembly call; we have not as yet tried other forms of auditory stimulation with respect to alarm call responsivity.) In any event, what occurs after an alleged critical period (in this case, maintenance) can be just as important for development as what occurs within the period. Our data attest to the importance of examining the possible roles of experience at all points along the developmental trajectory rather than only within a suspected critical period.

Summary

The experiments previously cited were conducted to demonstrate the importance of normally occurring auditory experience on the development of alarm call responsivity. Paralleling Gottlieb's (1971, 1980, 1981) studies on species identification, we found that there appears to be a subtle, nonobvious, developmental link between auditory experience and instinctive behavior: namely, the adaptive freezing response exhibited by ducklings to the maternal alarm call is affected by experience of their own perinatal vocalizations. Sibling auditory experience is sufficient to foster normal development, and such experience appears to maintain the developmental trajectory postnatally.

DEVELOPMENTAL MECHANISMS: II. SOCIAL CONTEXTS

These experiments attest to the importance of normally occurring auditory experience in the development of alarm call responsivity. In fact, we believed that this form of experience was so important that we once concluded, "Our data clearly demonstrate that perinatal auditory experience is *necessary* to maintain alarm call responsiveness" (Miller & Blaich, 1984,

p. 424, emphasis added). We now know that this was an overstatement. Our most recent research has revealed that auditory experience is not necessary; rather, it is sufficient. There are some contexts in which it appears necessary, but, as is discussed next, there are other contexts in which other factors can compensate for the lack of auditory experience.

Effects of Social Experience

I have often argued for the importance of adopting an ecological approach to experimental manipulation—an approach that incorporates as many natural history variables as possible (e.g., naturalistic stimuli, species-typical response measures, etc.; Miller, 1977a, 1981, 1985, 1988b). Yet, our own research on alarm call responsivity failed to incorporate the physical, social, interactive character of real nests. Our reasons, however, were well justified. First, we needed to keep track of ducklings individually so that they could be tested individually at specified ages from the time of hatching; thus, they had to be physically segregated. Housing each duckling in its own individual plastic box accomplished this, and arranging the boxes in groups provided auditory interaction, even though visual and tactile interaction was prevented. Second, and of particular importance, this housing arrangement did not seem to interfere with the freezing response. Broadcasting the alarm call at its optimal repetition rate usually rendered between 90% and 100% responsiveness in 12- to 24-hr-old ducklings; thus, we did not seem to be doing anything "wrong" in the sense of maintaining ecological validity. However, it was not until we removed our experimental "blinders" that we realized that we had been leading ourselves (and perhaps others) astray due to a very tidy, convenient methodology.

Because natural nests are highly social settings, providing a great deal of physical interaction among ducklings (and, of course, between ducklings and the hen), we decided to rear ducklings socially in groups of 8 to 12 (comparable with a natural mallard clutch size) from hatching to the time of testing, around 24 hr after hatching (Blaich & Miller, 1986). To our astonishment, only 8 out of 30 socially reared ducklings froze (compared with 24 out of 30 that had been reared individually; see Table 8). (Lickliter, 1989, obtained a similar result in a different species and with

Table 8

Effect of Social Rearing on Alarm Call Responsivity

Rearing condition	No. freezing ($n = 30$)
Individual boxes	24
Social	8
Social; stimulated with duckling distress notes	22
Social; stimulated with duckling contentment notes	18
Social; stimulated with maternal assembly call	20

respect to a different type of behavior. Socially reared bobwhite quail chicks [*Colinus virginianus*] failed to exhibit their usual preference for the bobwhite maternal assembly call—a call that individually reared chicks find highly attractive, as demonstrated by Heaton, Miller, and Goodwin, 1978. Similarly, Dyer and Gottlieb, 1990, and Lickliter and Gottlieb, 1986, found that social rearing disrupts visual imprinting in Peking ducklings.) Why would rearing birds in a seemingly more natural fashion (social) obliterate a species-typical behavior that occurs reliably when rearing is seemingly less natural (nonsocial)?

As in our previous experiments, the answer to this question involved auditory stimulation. After obtaining what seemed to be a most unusual result, we monitored the vocal activity of socially reared and individually reared birds during the posthatch brooding period and found that the socially-reared birds were significantly less vocal than the birds housed individually (but in auditory contact). Because our data on devocalized ducklings already suggested that auditory experience is important (even necessary) for the development of alarm call responsivity, we stimulated three groups of socially reared birds with three different kinds of sounds that they typically encounter on natural nests: One group was stimulated with duckling "distress notes" (or long–slow notes; Scoville & Gottlieb, 1980), another group with duckling contentment notes (or short–fast notes), and the third group with the maternal pre-exodus assembly call. When tested to the alarm call at 24 hr, each of these groups exhibited significantly greater levels of freezing than the unstimulated, socially reared birds and were comparable with that of the individually reared birds (Table 8).

These data further attest to the importance of auditory stimulation, but, at the same time, they raise an interesting question. Because birds on natural nests are reared socially, why does alarm call responsivity occur reliably in the field? (Applying criteria similar to that used in our laboratory tests, I found that ducklings on natural nests exhibit an incidence of freezing at 79%; Miller, 1980.) One highly plausible answer to this question is that on natural nests, ducklings receive much more auditory stimulation than do birds that are socially reared in the laboratory. Although we have not been able to reliably ascertain the extent of vocal behavior by ducklings on natural nests (because, in part, of our inability to reliably hear low-amplitude calls over background noise), we do know that they receive considerable exposure to the maternal pre-exodus assembly call.

But this is not the only answer, for another important ecological factor had been missing from our testing paradigm. Ducklings are not only reared socially on natural nests, but they are still in a social group when they encounter the maternal alarm call; in other words, they are "tested" socially in the wild. All of our experiments described herein (even those in which ducklings were socially reared) involved testing birds individually in the laboratory.

Interaction of Developmental and Testing Contexts

To assess the effect of exposing ducklings to the alarm call in the context of a social brood (thereby simulating a nest situation) necessitated applying the same stringent criteria for freezing that we had been using for individual ducklings to the entire brood as a unit (i.e., each of the 12 ducklings in the brood had to exhibit total vocal and locomotor inhibition within 10 s of the broadcast of the alarm call and remain in that state for the duration of the 2-min broadcast period).

In these experiments, we retained our usual sample size of 30 ducklings per group for non-social (i.e., individually reared, individually tested, or both) conditions, but decreased the sample size to 20 groups (each group composed of 12 ducklings) for social conditions. Thus, although some comparisons involved 30 (nonsocial) ducklings versus 20 (social) groups of ducklings, those 20 data points, in reality, represent the behavior of 240 ducklings (i.e., 20 groups of 12 ducklings). All ducklings were tested around 24 hr of age. Further details can be found in Blaich, Miller, and Hicinbothom (1989).

As shown in Table 9 and as discussed previously in the Effects of Social Experience section, when socially reared ducklings were tested individually (nonsocially), the incidence of freezing was quite low, compared with ducklings reared nonsocially in plastic boxes and tested nonsocially. However, ducklings provided with the most ecologically meaningful set of contexts (i.e., social development and social testing), exhibited a very high incidence of freezing. The question remained whether social testing alone is sufficient for the manifestation of freezing. To assess the hypothesis that social testing is sufficient in promoting freezing, we reared a group of ducklings nonsocially (i.e., in individual plastic boxes in a communal brooder) but tested them socially (by forming social groups 30 min prior to testing). The incidence of freezing by these ducklings was low (Table 9).

Thus, neither social rearing nor social testing alone is sufficient for the development and manifestation of alarm call responsivity. Rather, there is an interaction between the developmental and testing contexts that greatly effects the expression of the freezing response. When there is a dis-

Table 9

Interaction Between Developmental and Testing Contexts

Context		
Developmental	Testing	Percentage freezing
Social	Nonsocial	37
Nonsocial	Nonsocial	87
Social	Social	80
Nonsocial	Social	35

crepancy between contexts, ducklings exhibit a low rate of freezing. Only when the contexts are similar (socially reared and socially tested or nonsocially reared and nonsocially tested) do ducklings exhibit the high rate of freezing found on natural nests. Because the matching social contexts mimic a natural situation, this result is perhaps not altogether surprising. And, it also helps to explain why social rearing alone is not sufficient to promote freezing (see previous Effects of Social Experience section). However, we are unable to explain why the matching nonsocial contexts resulted in such a high rate of freezing, because such contexts bear little resemblance to the nesting ecology of this species. Perhaps the unusually high level of auditory experience associated with nonsocial rearing compensates for this species-atypical developmental context, which would be consistent with the notion of multiple pathways in development as discussed next. At the very least, however, these data attest to the importance of considering the combined effects of developmental mechanisms, ecological mechanisms, and contextual mechanisms in studying the ontogeny and expression of species-typical behavior (cf. Kuo, 1967).

Multiple Pathways of Normal Development in Devocal Birds

The experiments on social rearing and social testing cast doubt on the necessity of auditory experience for the development of the freezing response in socially reared birds. As indicated in the experiments described in the Effects of Social Experience section, auditory experience is important only in certain contexts, such as when testing socially reared birds in a nonsocial situation. The experiments in the Interaction of Developmental and Testing Contexts section indicate that testing socially reared birds in a social situation can override the effects of attenuated auditory experience occurring during social rearing. This suggests that there are multiple pathways in the development of alarm call responsivity. Metaphorically, just as a person can travel from one city to another by means of different routes, so are there multiple developmental trajectories connecting experiential events and behavioral outcomes. A block in one path can be circumvented if development is allowed to detour to another path.

It is noteworthy that the notion of multiple experiential pathways converging on a common endpoint is quite contrary to certain modern conceptions of behavioral development. For example, Waddington's (1975) epigenetic landscape metaphor illustrates the self-righting tendency of a developing organism as it passes along the base of a genetically prescribed developmental "valley," which, in essence, is a single developmental pathway. The deeper the valley, the more rigidly canalized is the course of development. In this metaphor, if the organism deflects to a different valley (due to a lesser degree of genetically determined canalization), its developmental endpoint will be different from that which it would have reached had it remained on its original path. This model has influenced a number of developmental theorists (e.g., Fishbein, 1976; Harper, 1989; Oyama, 1985; Scarr & McCartney, 1983). Yet, the view of development that it portrays is rather rigid in the sense that it does not allow for multiple developmental pathways converging on a single outcome.

If the concept of multiple pathways is correct, then one might expect to find an alternate route to normal behavioral development available to devocalized ducklings, for, as was described in the section titled Attenuation of Self-Produced Auditory Experience and Elimination of Sibling Auditory Experience, devocalization places a major obstacle in the course of normal development. The obstacle can be circumvented by providing auditory experience to muted ducklings, which represents one pathway; but, are there other pathways that will foster normal development for these birds?

To answer this question, we assessed the role of social rearing and social testing on the freezing response of devocalized ducklings that have not had any auditory experience (Miller, Hicinbothom, & Blaich, 1990). Following the devocalization operation, birds were allowed to hatch in individual incubator compartments. After hatching, they were placed into social groups containing other devocalized ducklings. The groups were tested socially to the alarm call at 24 hr of age—an age associated with very little freezing (20%) in devocal, isolated birds tested individually (Table 6). All birds were fully muted, and the same stringent criteria applied for freezing in these groups as for those in the previous section, Interaction of Developmental and Testing Contexts.

As shown in Table 10, alarm call responsivity was reinstated in devocalized ducklings that were reared and tested socially. These ducklings exhibited significantly greater levels of freezing than devocal, isolated ducklings ($p < .001$) and behaved comparably with vocal ducklings that had been reared and tested socially and comparably with normal ducklings on nests in the field. They also behaved comparably with devocalized ducklings that had received auditory stimulation and were tested (at 12 hr) nonsocially.

Thus, in the absence of normally occurring auditory experience, social experience is sufficient to promote alarm call responsivity. Likewise, in the absence of normal social interactions, auditory experience proves to be sufficient. If both auditory and social experiential factors are absent (as in devocal, isolated ducklings), development proceeds along a species-atypical trajectory.

Social Experience Broadens Repetition Rate Specificity

The data reported in the preceding section indicate the overwhelming influence that social rearing and testing can have on the development and expression of instinctive behavior. This is by no means unique to alarm call responsivity in mallard ducklings. Social context has been found to influence kin recognition in certain anuran species (Blaustein & Waldman 1992), vocal behavior in a variety of bird species (Byers & Kroodsma 1992; Karakashian, Gyger, & Marler, 1988; King & West, 1989), and social pref-

Table 10	
Effect of Socially Rearing and Socially Testing Devocalized Duckings	
Condition	Percentage freezing
Devocal, isolated, nonsocially tested	20
Devocal, socially reared and tested	70
Devocal, auditory stimulated, nonsocially tested	80
Vocal, socially reared and tested	80
Vocal, on nests in the field	79

erences in golden lion tamarins, *Leontopithecus rosalia* (Inglett, French, & Dethlefs, 1990); ducklings (Gottlieb, 1991); and bobwhite quail, *Colinus virginianus* (Lickliter & Hellewell, 1992), just to cite a few examples. Given that, for social species, social rearing and testing represent the most ecologically valid set of contexts for the experimental analysis of behavioral development, I applied this strategy to attempt to account for a seemingly anomalous finding arising from our research program.

As noted in the section The Role of Repetition Rate in Alarm Call Responsivity, there is an optimal range of repetition rates of the notes composing the maternal alarm call. Specifically, the highest levels of freezing occurred when the alarm notes were pulsed between 0.8 and 1.8 notes/s. However, on natural nests, mallard hens sometimes utter single alarm notes rather than bursts of notes. These so-called singlet notes have either no or extremely slow repetition rates. Moreover, on natural nests, ducklings were observed to freeze 60% of the time when hens uttered singlets (Miller, 1980). However, this observation was discordant with laboratory tests (Miller & Blaich, 1987) that revealed a freezing incidence of only 7% when ducklings were tested to an extremely slow repetition rate of 0.2 notes/s—a rate that mimics that of singlets. These experiments on repetition rate specificity were conducted several years before our work on social context. In other words, these ducklings were reared and tested individually. Thus, I decided to assess the extent to which this anomalous finding might be a function of an ecologically questionable experimental paradigm.

In this study (Miller, 1994), 17 groups of ducklings (eight ducklings per group) were tested to a maternal alarm pulsed at 0.2 notes/s. To assess whether any hypothesized effects of social rearing were specific or general, another set of 17 groups of ducklings were tested to the alarm notes pulsed at 2.6 notes/s. This faster rate is above the optimal range of 0.8 to 1.8 notes/s and is not very effective in promoting freezing (as discussed in the section on The Role of Repetition Rate in Alarm Call Responsivity); that is, only 30% of the individually reared and tested ducklings froze to this repetition rate. (This was not considered an anomaly, however, because of the typical excitatory effect that faster rate calls have on ducklings, as is characteristic of assembly calls.)

As shown in Table 11, social rearing and testing significantly increased the incidence of freezing to the 0.2 notes/s alarm call ($p < .004$) but not to the 2.6 notes/s alarm call ($p = .63$). Moreover, the incidence of freezing between socially reared and tested ducklings was comparable with that observed on natural nests in the field when hens uttered singlets ($p = .13$). Thus, social rearing and testing broadened repetition rate specificity but in a highly specific rather than a general fashion. These contextual data also reconcile the discrepancy between our field observations and our earlier experiments in which individually reared and tested ducklings exhibited unusually low levels of freezing to the 0.2 notes/s alarm call.

Summary

In an attempt to render our experimental methodology more ecologically valid (i.e., attuned to the nesting ecology of the species), we reared birds in social groups to simulate real nests, which provide birds with considerable tactile, visual, and auditory stimulation. These experiments rendered some unexpected but exciting data on the interrelationship between auditory experience and social context. This relationship further revealed that there can be multiple pathways in development, such that different developmental trajectories lead to similar behavioral outcomes (see also

Table 11

Effect of Social Rearing and Social Testing on Repetition Rate Specificity

Rearing and testing contexts	Repetition rate (notes/s)	Percentage freezing
Nests in the field (social)	Singlet	60
Social	0.2	41
Individual	0.2	7
Social	2.6	24
Individual	2.6	30

NOTE: notes/s indicates the repetition rate of the notes of the call.

Caro & Bateson, 1986; Thelen & Fogel, 1989). Moreover, social rearing and testing broadens behavioral specificity in a manner that is specific to a form of stimulation that ducklings normally encounter on natural nests. Taken together, these data illustrate that context can be an overwhelmingly important, although often neglected, variable in behavioral research.

I now shift my emphasis away from empirical description toward areas of broader conceptual interest. Specifically, I conclude this chapter by relating the previous empirical data to recent advances in developmental theory, including the relationship of development and evolution, and an ecological approach to developmental analysis.

CONCLUSION

Genetic Explanations of Instinctive Behavior in Development and Evolution

Nesting mallard hens utter vocalizations to which the young are highly responsive. It is unlikely that anyone would question the instinctive character of this communicative system—instinctive in the sense that the components are species-typical and highly stereotyped, develop without obvious forms of practice, and seem to be fully developed on initial occurrence. It is also unlikely that anyone (even staunch anti-hyperselectionists) would question the presumed adaptive significance of these behaviors—an acoustic basis of species identification by which the hen calls her young off the nest (assembly call) and predator avoidance (alarm call). How straightforward it would seem, then, to simply explain these instinctive, adaptive behaviors as the behavioral manifestations of "closed" genetic programs (e.g., Mayr, 1974), highly buffered from experiential influences.

Such reasoning, in fact, provides a perfect example of the tangled web between evolutionary and developmental mechanisms (see Cairns, Gariépy, & Hood, 1990, for an elegant attempt to disentangle this web with regard to social development and, especially, aggressive interactions in mice). Development and evolution are processes that entail change over time; in the case of development, changes occur within a generation, and in the case of evolution, changes are cross-generational. Moreover, the two processes are intimately related to one another. Changes occurring in development can affect evolutionary change (i.e., heterochrony; de Beer, 1958); likewise, the kinds of evolutionary changes that take place will affect or constrain the kinds of events that occur in development. Although these processes each involve temporal change and are interrelated, a conceptual problem (and source of much confusion) arises in assuming that they share isomorphic underlying mechanisms (see also Cairns, et al., 1990). In evolution, phenotypic variation is associated with genotypic variation. The underlying mechanism of evolution, natural selection, works by increasing the incidence of adaptive phenotypes (and, therefore, corresponding genotypes) across generations, as long as such phenotypes continue to be adaptive (or, at least, are not counteradaptive). Thus, the focus of evolutionary change is on an entire population rather than on any particular individual. Development, however, focuses on changes occurring within the individual organism–environment system. But that does not yet solve the question of explaining how all individuals of a population develop the same behavior (or strikingly similar behaviors). The key lies in what is being selected during evolution. Selection acts not only on the developmental outcome but also on the entire developmental process leading up to that outcome (Gottlieb, 1971, p. 156), including the context or contexts in which development takes place and those in which the outcomes are expressed—the so-called ontogenetic niche (West & King, 1987). Freezing on hearing the alarm call might be considered the adaptive phenotypic outcome on which natural selection will take place; those ducklings that freeze will avoid predation and those that fail to freeze will perish (along with their close relatives who happen to share significant amounts of genetic material). Whatever genes are associated with developing the ability to freeze will certainly get passed along to the next generation, giving those individuals the genetic *potential* of developing similarly to their ancestors. However, not only is freezing selected for, but so are all of the events that our experiments indicate might be important for the development of that behavior (i.e., sensitivity to certain acoustic features that occur reliably in maternal alarm calls; the ability to be affected by self- and sibling auditory stimulation; the ability to express behavior in certain contexts but not in others; and so forth. Genes produce proteins, not the array of environmental possibilities that affect alarm call responsivity. Genes are important; they provide certain developmental constraints. But they do not dictate the developmental process. If they did, then one would expect to find little variability in the events leading up to the developmental outcome. Otherwise, the concept of genetic determinism would have to be carried to yet a further extreme by allowing genes to have multiple "codes" for multiple pathways leading to a common outcome. This would certainly render the concepts of determinism and code meaningless. (They are meaningless anyway, at least when applied to behavioral development, but for different reasons!)

Metaphorically, the action of flour during the cooking process will depend on the nature of the ingredients with which it is mixed as well as whether the combined ingredients are fried or baked (Miller, 1988c). When flour is combined with salt and water in a frying context, the endpoint is a flour tortilla; when combined with the same ingredients but placed in a baking context, the endpoint is a matzo (unleavened bread). When yeast is added to the latter context, there is yet a different developmental endpoint—bread. Flour does not code for tortillas and for matzos and for bread. Rather, the developmental outcome of which it is a part varies in accord with different events that occur in development (i.e., different cooking ingredients) and the different contexts in which development occurs (i.e., different cooking processes). Similarly, we have shown how different developmental events (auditory experience; social experience) can lead to the same outcome (freezing).

Thus, although genes are involved in both evolution and development, they neither determine nor control these processes. Genes are, in a sense, the excess baggage of evolution, because evolution selects directly for phenotypes and the entire process involved in phenotypic expression. In terms of development within an individual, they are no more (nor no less) important than any other factor influencing the developmental process. A building cannot exist without bricks, nor can an organism become a physical structure without genes; but bricks do not dictate the nature of the building, nor do genes determine the nature of the beast, although bricks and genes do place certain constraints on the range of possibilities of both the building and the beast, respectively. Genes are, then, inadequate explanations for developmental (and, for that matter, evolutionary) processes.

Ecological Approach

The research program described in this chapter was directed at finding alternative mechanisms to unrealistic genetic explanations underlying the seemingly simple phenomenon of freezing. Every attempt at understanding drew us further from simplicity and, at the same time, illustrated the inadequacy of genetic deterministic explanation. Instead, we learned about the overwhelming significance of nonobvious forms of experience, the interaction of contextual variables during development and assessment of developmental outcomes, an alternative explanation for critical periods, and the necessity of thoroughly understanding ecological variables and incorporating such factors into the experimental assessment of behavioral development. We also discovered multiple pathways toward developmental outcomes, supplanting the notion of experiential necessity with experiential sufficiency.

These concepts are hardly novel, nor are they unique to the behavioral phenomena described in this chapter, but they seem to have remained on the outskirts of mainstream developmental science. Behavioral ecologists tend to be well steeped in evolutionary and functional explanations and often assume that the only important developmental mechanisms are genetically based. On the other hand, the search for "mechanisms" in developmental psychobiology has directed attention toward neuroanatomy/physiology and away from natural history with the corresponding failure to acknowledge the mechanistic character of ecological and contextual variables. The problem becomes evident merely by observing how some investigators view and interact with their animals in laboratories. On the one hand, some neuroscientists tend to view their animals as "preparations"—a mere means by which cells or other internal entities can be readily accessed. On the other hand, many behavioral scientists tend to house and test animals solely in accord with animal care guidelines that may obscure the very factors that influence species-typical behavioral development. In a most pessimistic sense, one might view the result as a science based on the study of species-atypical behaviors emitted in species-atypical contexts by species-atypical creatures (i.e., highly inbred strains of domestic rodents) in the presence of species-atypical stimuli.

A resolution to this problem, and one that has guided the research described in this chapter, is to adopt an ecological approach that involves three essential components (Johnston, 1981; Miller, 1985): (a) naturalistic observation and description of species-typical behavior, (b) "task description" (i.e., identifying the kinds of problems animals are faced with as they adapt to environmental pressures rather than focusing on contrived laboratory tasks), and (c) experimental manipulation aimed at elucidating the mechanisms underlying these tasks. This approach can be applied not only at the behavioral level but at all levels of investigation. The research programs by Khayutin (1985) and Nottebohm (1989) provide excellent examples of how this approach has been applied in neuroscience.

The transactional view of development, combined with the ecological approach discussed herein renders simplistic interactionist questions attendant to the nature–nurture issue untenable and irrelevant in understanding behavioral development. The only remaining spark that may continue to fuel what have already been seemingly endless debates surrounded by misunderstanding concerning nature versus nurture is the important distinction between the role of genes in population genetics and their role in individual development (see Dawkins, 1986). Population geneticists quite correctly talk about genes "for" certain traits in the sense of assessing genetic variability among individuals of a population and then using the heritability quotient (the outcome of which is totally dependent on environmental variability!) to discuss the inheritance of such traits. This is not at all isomorphic with genes, traits, and inheritance as these terms relate to development in individual organisms. Genes produce proteins— not structures and certainly not behaviors. Even at the level of proteins (which is many steps away from the emergence of tissues and structures), there is considerable opportunity for environmental interactions that affect the subsequent developmental trajectory, including protein–protein interactions (e.g., Raff, 1994). Thus, to speak about a gene for a behavior in the developmental sense is overly simplistic, entirely misleading, and fails to capture the essence of the transactional, emergent nature of development. Although the problem of why one can speak about genes for behavior in one discipline but not in another is more than a semantic one, certainly the use of a common vocabulary between the two disciplines is of little help in remedying conceptual confusion.

The new and revised questions that emerge from viewing development as an emergent transactional process across levels of organization include an appreciation for the constructive (rather than merely supportive) effects of nonobvious forms of stimulation, the teasing apart of experiential factors from contextual ones, the nature of developmental constraints, and the ever-fascinating relationship between ontogenetic and phylogenetic mechanisms. Although the approach that I have described attempts to confront these issues, technological and other problems often hinder progress. For example, although the prenatal period is potentially wealthy in terms of nonobvious experiential influences, there are technological limitations in studying embryos at all but the later stages of prenatal development. This, in turn, renders the study of developmental constraints rather difficult, at least for those constraints that exert an effect very early in development. (Research in experimental embryology has been advancing in overcoming many technological limitations; however, problems persist at the behavioral level.) As for the relationship between development and evolution, much of the research in that area in recent years has been at the molecular and anatomical levels, as these areas are somewhat less speculative than behavior that does not directly fossilize. Finally, one of the frequent criticisms I have heard directed toward the transactional approach in terms of recognizing the importance of research on nonobvious experiential influences is that once a relationship between a nonobvious experience and a developmental outcome has been experimentally established, the experience is no longer nonobvious! It is, perhaps, the seemingly mischievous, tongue-in-cheek nature with which that criticism has been levied that keeps me from gasping in despair.

Perhaps one of the reasons why the study of development has been fraught with persistent, emotionally laden controversies (e.g., nature vs. nurture, continuity vs. discontinuity, phase specificity vs. nonspecificity, etc.) is that investigators have often striven to obtain simple answers to seemingly straightforward questions. Development, however, is not a simple process. It has a multidimensional, almost mischievous character that seems to wallow in the delight of evading any attempt to extract simplicity from complexity. And, the moment one senses the illusion of being on the path toward understanding, one gap in our knowledge narrows only as another widens. Yet, we persist, hoping to elucidate the mechanisms underlying behavioral development; after all, that is what makes this quest both challenging and exciting.

REFERENCES

Abraham, R. L. (1974). Vocalizations of the mallard (*Anas platyrhynchos*). *Condor, 76*, 401–420.

Andrew, R. J. (1974). Arousal and the causation of behaviour. *Behaviour, 51,* 135–165.

Anokhin, P. K. (1964). Systemogenesis as a general regulator of brain development. In W. A. Himwich & H. E. Himwich (Eds.), *The developing brain* (pp. 54–86). New York: American Elsevier.

Bateson, P. (1983). Genes, environment and the development of behaviour. In T. R. Halliday & P. J. B. Slater (Eds.), *Animal behaviour 3: Genes, development and learning* (pp. 52–81). New York: W. H. Freeman.

Bateson, P., & Hinde, R. A. (1987). Developmental changes in sensitivity to experience. In M. H. Bornstein (Ed.), *Sensitive periods in development* (pp. 19–34). Hillsdale, NJ: Erlbaum.

Beletsky, L. D. (1989). Communication and the cadence of birdsong. *American Midland Naturalist, 122,* 298–306.

Bjärvall, A. (1968). The hatching and nest-exodus behaviour of mallard. *Wildfowl, 19,* 70–80.

Blaich, C. F., & Miller, D. B. (1984, August). *Nest cavities preserve the critical acoustic feature of wood duck (Aix sponsa) maternal calls.* Paper presented at the meeting of the Animal Behavior Society, Cheney, WA.

Blaich, C. F., & Miller, D. B. (1986). Alarm call responsivity of mallard ducklings (*Anas platyrhynchos*): IV. Effects of social experience. *Journal of Comparative Psychology, 100,* 401–405.

Blaich, C. F., & Miller, D. B. (1988). Alarm call responsivity of mallard ducklings (*Anas platyrhynchos*): VI. Effects of sibling and self-produced auditory stimulation. *Journal of Comparative Psychology, 102,* 56–60.

Blaich, C. F., Miller, D. B., & Hicinbothom, G. (1989). Alarm call responsivity of mallard ducklings: VIII. Interaction between developmental history and behavioral context. *Developmental Psychobiology, 22,* 203–210.

Blaustein, A. R., & Waldman, B. (1992). Kin recognition in anuran amphibians. *Animal Behaviour, 44,* 207–221.

Bonner, J. T. (1987). The next big problem in developmental biology. *American Zoologist, 27,* 715–723.

Brush, J. S., & Narins, P. M. (1989). Chorus dynamics of a neotropical amphibian assemblage: Comparison of computer simulation and natural behaviour. *Animal Behaviour, 37,* 33–44.

Byers, B. E., & Kroodsma, D. E. (1992). Development of two song categories by chestnut-sided warblers. *Animal Behaviour, 44,* 799–810.

Cairns, R. B., Gariépy, J.-L., & Hood, K. E. (1990). Development, microevolution, and social behavior. *Psychological Review, 97,* 49–65.

Caro, T. M., & Bateson, P. (1986). Organization and ontogeny of alternative tactics. *Animal Behaviour, 34,* 1483–1499.

Clarkson, M. G., Clifton, R. K., Swain, I. U., & Perris, E. E. (1989). Stimulus duration and repetition rate influence newborn's head orientation toward sound. *Developmental Psychobiology, 22,* 683–705.

Dawkins, M. S. (1986). *Unravelling animal behaviour.* Essex: Longman.

de Beer, G. (1958). *Embryos and ancestors.* London: Oxford University Press.

Dewey, J., & Bentley, A. F. (1949). *Knowing and the known.* Boston: The Beacon Press.

Dyer, A. B., & Gottlieb, G. (1990). Auditory basis of maternal attachment in ducklings (*Anas platyrhynchos*) under simulated naturalistic imprinting conditions. *Journal of Comparative Psychology, 104,* 190–194.

Emlen, S. T. (1972). An experimental analysis of the parameters of bird song eliciting species recognition. *Behaviour, 41,* 130–171.

Evans, C. S., & Gaioni, S. J. (1990). Conspecific calls evoke characteristic cardiac responses in mallard ducklings. *Animal Behaviour, 39,* 785–796.

Fishbein, H. D. (1976). *Evolution, development, and children's learning.* Pacific Palisades, CA: Goodyear.

Gallup, G. G., Jr. (1974). Animal hypnosis: Factual status of a fictional concept. *Psychological Bulletin, 81,* 836–853.

Gottlieb, G. (1971). *Development of species identification in birds.* Chicago: University of Chicago Press.

Gottlieb, G. (1974). On the acoustic basis of species identification in wood ducklings (*Aix sponsa*). *Journal of Comparative and Physiological Psychology, 87,* 1038–1048.

Gottlieb, G. (1975). Development of species identification in ducklings: I. Nature of perceptual deficit caused by embryonic auditory deprivation. *Journal of Comparative and Physiological Psychology, 89,* 387–399.

Gottlieb, G. (1976). Conceptions of prenatal development: Behavioral embryology. *Psychological Review, 83,* 215–234.

Gottlieb, G. (1977). The development of behavior. In K. Immelmann (Ed.), *Grzimek's Encyclopedia of Ethology* (pp. 579–606). New York: Van Nostrand Reinhold.

Gottlieb, G. (1979). Development of species identification in ducklings: V. Perceptual differentiation in the embryo. *Journal of Comparative and Physiological Psychology, 93,* 831–854.

Gottlieb, G. (1980). Development of species identification in ducklings: VI. Specific embryonic experience required to maintain species-typical perception in Peking ducklings. *Journal of Comparative and Physiological Psychology, 94,* 579–587.

Gottlieb, G. (1981). Development of species identification in ducklings: VIII. Embryonic versus postnatal critical period for the maintenance of species-typical perception. *Journal of Comparative and Physiological Psychology 95,* 540–547.

Gottlieb, G. (1982). Development of species identification in ducklings: IX. The necessity of experiencing normal variations in embryonic auditory stimulation. *Developmental Psychobiology, 15,* 507–517.

Gottlieb, G. (1985). Development of species identification in ducklings: XI. Embryonic critical period for species-typical perception in the hatchling. *Animal Behaviour, 33,* 225–233.

Gottlieb, G. (1991). Social induction of malleability in ducklings. *Animal Behaviour, 41,* 953–962.

Gottlieb, G. (1992). *Individual development & evolution: The genesis of novel behavior.* New York: Oxford University Press.

Gottlieb, G., & Vandenbergh, J. G. (1968). Ontogeny of vocalization in duck and chick embryos. *Journal of Experimental Zoology, 168,* 307–326.

Harper, L. V. (1989). *The nurture of human behavior.* Norwood, NJ: Ablex.

Heaton, M. B., Miller, D. B., & Goodwin, D. G. (1978). Species-specific auditory discrimination in bobwhite quail neonates. *Developmental Psychobiology, 11,* 13–22.

Inglett, B. J., French, J. A., & Dethlefs, T. M. (1990). Patterns of social preference across different social contexts in golden lion tamarins (*Leontopithecus rosalia*). *Journal of Comparative Psychology, 104,* 131–139.

Johnston, T. D. (1981). Contrasting approaches to a theory of learning. *Behavioral and Brain Sciences, 4,* 125–173.

Johnston, T. D. (1987). The persistence of dichotomies in the study of behavioral development. *Developmental Review, 7,* 149–182.

Karakashian, S. J., Gyger, M., & Marler, P. (1988). Audience effects on alarm calling in chickens (*Gallus gallus*). *Journal of Comparative Psychology, 102,* 129–135.

Kaufman, I. C., & Hinde, R. A. (1961). Factors influencing distress calling in chicks, with special reference to temperature changes and social isolation. *Animal Behaviour, 9,* 197–204.

Kear, J. (1965). The internal food reserves of mallard ducklings. *Journal of Wildlife Management, 29,* 523–528.

Khayutin, S. N. (1985). Sensory factors in the behavioral ontogeny of altricial birds. *Advances in the Study of Behavior, 15,* 105–152.

King, A. P., & West, M. J. (1989). Presence of female cowbirds (*Molothrus ater ater*) affects vocal imitation and improvisation in males. *Journal of Comparative Psychology, 103,* 39–44.

Konishi, M. (1973). Development of auditory neuronal responses in avian embryos. *Proceedings of the National Academy of Sciences, 70,* 1795–1798.

Kuo, Z.-Y. (1967). *The dynamics of behavior development: An epigenetic view.* New York: Random House.

Kuo, Z.-Y. (1970). The need for coordinated efforts in developmental studies. In L. R. Aronson, E. Tobach, D. S. Lehrman, & J. S. Rosenblatt (Eds.), *Development and evolution of behavior: Essays in memory of T. C. Schneirla* (pp. 181–193). San Francisco: W. H. Freeman.

Lehrman, D. S. (1970). Semantic and conceptual issues in the nature-nurture problem. In L. R. Aronson, E. Tobach, D. S. Lehrman, & J. S. Rosenblatt (Eds.), *Development and evolution of behavior: Essays in memory of T. C. Schneirla* (pp. 17–52). San Francisco: W. H. Freeman.

Lickliter, R. (1989). Species-specific auditory preference of bobwhite quail chicks (*Colinus virginianus*) is altered by social interaction with siblings. *Journal of Comparative Psychology, 103,* 221–226.

Lickliter, R., & Gottlieb, G. (1986). Training ducklings in broods interferes with maternal imprinting. *Developmental Psychobiology, 19,* 555–566.

Lickliter, R., & Hellewell, T. B. (1992). Contextual determinants of auditory learning in bobwhite quail embryos and hatchlings. *Developmental Psychobiology, 25,* 17–31.

Masataka, N. (1994). Effects of experience with live insects on the development of fear of snakes in squirrel monkeys, *Saimiri sciureus. Animal Behaviour, 46,* 741–746.

Mayr, E. (1974). Behavior programs and evolutionary strategies. *American Scientist, 62,* 650–659.

Miller, D. B. (1977a). Roles of naturalistic observation in comparative psychology. *American Psychologist, 32,* 211–219.

Miller, D. B. (1977b). Social displays of mallard ducks (*Anas platyrhynchos*): Effects of domestication. *Journal of Comparative and Physiological Psychology, 91,* 221–232.

Miller, D. B. (1980). Maternal vocal control of behavioral inhibition in mallard ducklings (*Anas platyrhynchos*). *Journal of Comparative and Physiological Psychology, 94,* 606–623.

Miller, D. B. (1981). Conceptual strategies in behavioral development: Normal development and plasticity. In K. Immelmann, G. W. Barlow, L. Petrinovich, & M. Main (Eds.), *Behavioral development: The Bielefeld interdisciplinary project* (pp. 58–82). New York: Cambridge University Press.

Miller, D. B. (1983a). Alarm call responsivity of mallard ducklings: I. The acoustical boundary between behavioral inhibition and excitation. *Developmental Psychobiology, 16,* 185–194.

Miller, D. B. (1983b). Alarm call responsivity of mallard ducklings: II. Perceptual specificity along an acoustical dimension affecting behavioral inhibition. *Developmental Psychobiology, 16,* 195–205.

Miller, D. B. (1985). Methodological issues in the ecological study of learning. In

T. D. Johnston & A. T. Pietrewicz (Eds.), *Issues in the ecological study of learning* (pp. 73–95). Hillsdale, NJ: Erlbaum.

Miller, D. B. (1988a). Beyond interactionism: A transactional approach to behavioral development. *Behavioral and Brain Sciences, 11,* 641–642.

Miller, D. B. (1988b). Development of instinctive behavior: An epigenetic and ecological approach. In E. M. Blass (Ed.), *Handbook of behavioral neurobiology, Vol. 9: Developmental psychobiology and behavioral ecology* (pp. 415–444). New York: Plenum.

Miller, D. B. (1988c). The nature–nurture issue: Lessons from the Pillsbury Doughboy. *Teaching of Psychology, 15,* 147–149.

Miller, D. B. (1994). Social context affects the ontogeny of instinctive behaviour. *Animal Behaviour, 48,* 627–634.

Miller, D. B., & Blaich, C. F. (1984). Alarm call responsivity of mallard ducklings: The inadequacy of learning and genetic explanations of instinctive behavior. *Learning and Motivation, 15,* 417–427.

Miller, D. B., & Blaich, C. F. (1986). Alarm call responsivity of mallard ducklings: III. Acoustic features affecting behavioral inhibition. *Developmental Psychobiology, 19,* 291–301.

Miller, D. B., & Blaich, C. F. (1987). Alarm call responsivity of mallard ducklings: V. Age-related changes in repetition rate specificity and behavioral inhibition. *Developmental Psychobiology, 20,* 571–586.

Miller, D. B., & Blaich, C. F. (1988). Alarm call responsivity of mallard ducklings: VII. Auditory experience maintains freezing. *Developmental Psychobiology, 21,* 523–533.

Miller, D. B., & Gottlieb, G. (1978). Maternal vocalizations of mallard ducks (*Anas platyrhynchos*). *Animal Behaviour, 26,* 1178–1194.

Miller, D. B., & Gottlieb, G. (1981). Effects of domestication on production and perception of mallard maternal alarm calls: Developmental lag in behavioral arousal. *Journal of Comparative and Physiological Psychology, 95,* 205–219.

Miller, D. B., & Hicinbothom, G. (1991). Alarm call responsivity of mallard ducklings: X. Ontogenetic adaptation or artifact of arousal? *Bird Behaviour, 9,* 114–120.

Miller, D. B., Hicinbothom, G., & Blaich, C. F. (1990). Alarm call responsivity of mallard ducklings: Multiple pathways in behavioural development. *Animal Behaviour, 39,* 1207–1212.

Myrberg, A. A., Jr., Spanier, E., & Ha, S. J. (1978). Temporal patterning in acoustical communication. In E. S. Reese & F. J. Lighter (Eds.), *Contrasts in behavior* (pp. 137–179). New York: Wiley.

Nottebohm, F. (1989). From bird song to neurogenesis. *Scientific American, 260,* 74–79.

Oppenheim, R. W. (1981). Ontogenetic adaptations and retrogressive processes in the development of the nervous system and behaviour: A neuroembryological perspective. In K. J. Connolly & H. F. R. Prechtl (Eds.), *Maturation and development: Biological and psychological perspectives* (pp. 73–109). Philadelphia: J. P. Lippincott.

Oyama, S. (1985). *The ontogeny of information.* New York: Cambridge University Press.

Popp, J. W. (1989). Temporal aspects of singing interactions among territorial ovenbirds (*Seiurus aurocapillus*). *Ethology, 82,* 127–133.

Raff, M. C. (1994). Cell death genes: *Drosophila* enters the field. *Science, 264,* 668–669.

Scarr, S., & McCartney, K. (1983). How people make their own environments: A theory of genotype → environment effects. *Child Development, 54,* 424–435.

Schneirla, T. C. (1966). Behavioral development and comparative psychology. *Quarterly Review of Biology, 41,* 283–302.

Scoville, R., & Gottlieb, G. (1980). Development of vocal behaviour in Peking ducklings. *Animal Behaviour, 28,* 1095–1109.

Spalding, D. A. (1875). Instinct and acquisition. *Nature, 12,* 507–508.

Thelen, E. (1989). Self-organization in developmental processes: Can systems approaches work? In M. R. Gunnar & E. Thelen (Eds.), *Systems and development. The Minnesota Symposia on Child Psychology, Vol. 22* (pp. 77–117). Hillsdale, NJ: Erlbaum.

Thelen, E., & Fogel, A. (1989). Toward an action-based theory of infant development. In J. Lockman & N. Hazen (Eds.), *Action in a social context: Perspective on early development* (pp. 23–62). New York: Plenum.

Turvey, M. T. T., & Fitzpatrick, P. (1993). Commentary: Development of perception–action systems and general principles of pattern formation. *Child Development, 64,* 1175–1190.

Waddington, C. H. (1975). *The evolution of an evolutionist.* Ithaca, NY: Cornell University Press.

Wallman, J. (1979). A minimal visual restriction experiment: Preventing chicks from seeing their feet affects later responses to mealworms. *Developmental Psychobiology, 12,* 391–397.

Weller, M. (1964). The reproductive cycle. In J. Delacour (Ed.), *The waterfowl of the world, Vol. 4* (pp. 35–79). London: Country Life.

West, M. J., & King, A. P. (1987). Settling nature and nurture into an ontogenetic niche. *Developmental Psychobiology, 20,* 549–562.

Comment on Miller

Timothy D. Johnston

David Miller's research provides a very nice illustration of the way in which ecological principles can be used in the study of behavioral development. He has demonstrated the importance of examining the development of behavior in relation to the natural environment in which both the behavior and its development occur, and his work shows how a knowledge of natural contexts can help make sense of results gathered in the laboratory. Before proceeding to the meat of my discussion of his chapter, I make two brief points. First, I think researchers still need to be very careful about using the term *instinctive* in talking about development. Miller has defined this term carefully to avoid any connotations of innateness or genetic determinism, but I am afraid that the term carries those connotations so strongly that not even the most careful definition can eliminate them. Listeners (especially students) will inevitably read ideas of innateness into its use, making our task, which is already a difficult one, even harder. Second, let me emphasize a point that Miller also makes in his chapter. Even though those of us working on development from an

---

Johnston comments on Miller from an ecological realist perspective.

ecological perspective have tended to focus on the roles of experience in the develpment of behavior, we all recognize the great importance of genetic influences. Genes contribute essentially to development, and it is a substantial current challenge to explicate what those contributions are and how they should be theoretically characterized. I now move on to more substantive issues.

Miller described the way in which some aspects of a duckling's experience (hearing its own embryonic calls and associating with broodmates) contribute to the development of its response to the maternal alarm call. Following Gilbert Gottlieb, he called these kinds of experience "nonobvious" because they do not seem to bear any straightforward relation to the behavior whose development they support. In my discussion, I focus primarily on this notion of nonobvious experience because I think it captures some theoretically salient features of the ecological analysis of development.

The modern study of behavioral development draws on two very old historical traditions. The first is what I call the *natural history tradition*, which is concerned with describing and explaining the various natural phenomena of the world. In modern times, this tradition provided the foundation for Darwin's writings, from which are derived the 20th-century sciences of ethology, sociobiology, behavioral genetics, and the rest of the biological disciplines that study animal behavior and its development. The second tradition I call the *epistemological tradition.* This is a philosophical tradition, dating back to Plato and Aristotle, that inquires into the origins and reliability of our knowledge of the world. In modern times, this tradition led to scientific inquiry into the origins of knowledge and behavior, culminating in 20th-century psychological theories of perception, learning, memory, and other cognitive processes.

Both of these traditions influence the contemporary study of behavioral development, but they do not fit together very comfortably. The natural history tradition is thoroughly empirical—it aims to describe the brute facts of natural phenomena and then tries to explain them. The episteological tradition, by contrast, has been far more rationalist—it has relied for most of its history on *a priori* logical analysis, supplemented by thought experiments (of which Descartes's is the most famous but by no means the only example). Both traditions have influenced modern thinking about development, but in different and not entirely compatible ways.

Ideas about development that grow out of the epistemological tradition tend to focus on precursors that are *rationally related* to the behaviors for which they are supposedly responsible. That is, the tendency has been to assume that if some precursor *P* is the developmental cause of a behavior *B*, it should be apparent *a priori* that *P* could indeed (at least in principle) rationally determine *B*. So it is acceptable within this tradition that (for example) a duckling might have to hear the alarm call of its species, perhaps associated with the sight of a predator, before showing an adaptive response to the call—one can mount a fairly coherent rational argument for why that should be the case, even though it turns out that it is in fact not the case. There is no coherent rational argument that might lead one to suppose that the duckling has to hear its own embryonic call before showing an adaptive response to the alarm call. Another way of putting this point is to say that certain kinds of relationships between precursors and behavior evince a sort of intelligent design that makes them rationally transparent, whereas others seem just odd and *prima facie* implausible.

I think this accounts, in part, for why certain kinds of relationships between experience and behavior met with ridicule when they were first proposed. For example, John Garcia (1981) has described the great difficulty he experienced in publishing his first studies of taste-aversion learning in the 1960s, because the curious relationships he reported seemed to lack any rational basis. (One reviewer remarked that Garcia's results were no more likely than finding birdshit in a cuckoo clock.) Zing-Yang Kuo (1932) suggested that the up-and-down movements of a chick embryo's head caused by the beating of its heart might be important for the development of pecking movements after hatching. Konrad Lorenz (1965) ridiculed this suggestion (which has never been empirically investigated) by asking rhetorically what on earth the chick could learn about pecking from these embryonic movements. In both these cases, no rational relationship seemed to exist between the precursor and the behavior and so the proposed developmental influence appeared to be *prima facie* unlikely.

To the extent that our understanding of behavioral development subscribes to the rationalist tradition, nonobvious precursors like these have had a hard time making much theoretical headway. Not, I suggest, simply because they are not obvious but because they are not rationally related to their outcomes; that is, one cannot readily give reasons why things should work the way they do. One consequence of the rationalist stance on this issue is that any precursor that is not rationally related to its outcome gets referred to a different set of processes, specifically those loosely termed *biological,* and specifically *genetic.* Look at language development—rationalists like Jerry Fodor (1981) claim to have shown that there is no rationally explainable way in which one can learn the semantic categories of a language, so therefore those cateogires must be innate, specified by the genes. Processes of learning that are rationally transparent seem to require no special explanation, but those that are not require biological (i.e., genetic) predispositions or constraints. Nonobvious precursors of the kind Miller has described seem to be somehow more biological, to require more in the way of supporting explanations, than do those that involve a more rationally accessible relationship between precursor and outcome.

Precursors that are rationally related to their outcomes seem to suggest a kind of "transparency" of the organism to the experience, so that experience can be easily viewed as directly influencing behavior, without the need for lots of complicated intervening machinery. Of course, that's not really so, and there is a large literature on the biological basis of learning that tries to explicate that intervening machinery even for the most clearly rationally related cases. Yet somehow one gets the feeling that this explication is optional, whereas in the case of nonobvious relationships, explaining the machinery seems almost necessary to get the whole thing to make sense. Systems in which there are lots of nonobvious relationships seem to require a lot more biological analysis than those in which the relationships are those of rational relatedness.

I do not believe that there are in fact two kinds of precursors, obvious and nonobvious. Rather, I believe that rationalist traditions have led researchers to privilege certain kinds of relationships as relatively transparent and to treat others as needing special and rather *ad hoc* accounts, involving appeal to biological predispositions and the like. I think that the tendency to accept these two kinds of explanations as fundamentally different in some way is one of the things that makes the nature–nurture dichotomy so persistent. When a rationalist like Fodor (1981) says that semantic categories are "innate," he means (I think) that the relationship between precursor and outcome is not transparent to the kind of rational explication favored by the rationalist tradition. However, because the term *innate* is also used to mean something like "caused by the genes" he also seems to be offering an empirical explanation for the origin of the categories. If one rebuts the *empirical* content of such explanations, by showing that genes simply do not work in the way this kind of explanation requires, the result is likely to be a demand that one provide some account of a different precursor–outcome relationships that has the same kind of rational transparency as the one being criticized. If that cannot be done (as it almost certainly cannot) then the audience is likely to feel dissatisfied and go home believing that one has not really explained the origin of the behavior in question.

As Miller has suggested, the development of behavior undoubtedly involves numerous nonobvious relationships of the kind he has been investigating. I suspect that incorporating these relationships into a satisfying theory of development will be harder than one might imagine, in part because they fail to fit comfortably into the rationalist tradition that implicitly informs so much of modern thinking about the origins of behavior.

REFERENCES

Fodor, J. A. (1981). The present status of the innateness controversy. In J. A. Fodor (Ed.), *Representations: Philosophical essays on the foundations of cognitive science* (pp. 257–316). Cambridge, MA: MIT Press.

Garcia, J. (1981). Tilting at the paper mills of academe. *American Psychologist, 36,* 149–158.

Kuo, Z. Y. (1932). Ontogeny of embryonic behavior in Aves: IV. The influence of embryonic movements upon behavior after hatching. *Journal of Comparative Psychology, 14,* 109–122.

Lorenz, K. Z. (1965). *Evolution and modification of behavior.* Chicago: University of Chicago Press.

14

Perspectives on an Ecological Approach to Social Communicative Development in Infancy

James A. Green and Gwen E. Gustafson

In the context of everyday activities at home, mothers and infants repeatedly engage one another in social interaction, and they do so for different reasons and via different behaviors.

(Green, Gustafson, & West, 1980, p. 199)

Fifteen years ago, when this statement helped us to introduce a study of mother–infant interactions, we were graduate students with an agenda, and the issues seemed clear. Social interactions were becoming the focus of much research in social development, yet there was far too little observational and normative research on the changing character of social interactions during infancy. Our goals, then, were to describe developmental changes in social interactions between infants and mothers and to relate them to developmental changes in the capabilities of infants.

Because of this early research, and because of subsequent research on parent–infant communication, we represent the epigenetic ecological ap-

Much of this research was supported by National Institutes of Health Grant HD22871 to G. E. Gustafson.

proach in this volume on ecological approaches to development. As we suggest later, the term *ecological psychology* has varied, but related, meanings. For example, at the University of Connecticut, we have close spatial relations with an ecological psychology of perception and action in the tradition of James and Eleanor Gibson. Indeed, we feel a genuine attraction for that position. However, this ecological psychology is not our own; in fact, we think we have never used the word *ecological* in our writings!

However, the work we describe herein does have strong roots in psychobiological and social–transactional models of behavioral development (Cairns, 1979; Gottlieb, 1983, 1991; Schneirla, 1957). One of its primary purposes has been to examine how the development of species-typical behaviors in infants affects the social environment and, thereby, has the potential to provide feedback and affect further development of the infant. Although the social environment plays an active role in this process (as subsequent data show), our focus has been on changes in infant social behavior and how they affect the social environment. This relatively narrow focus is a necessary step in beginning to understand the much larger epigenetic developmental process in which behavioral development is the result of coactions among genetic, neural, behavioral, and environmental levels of causation (Gottlieb, 1991).

Our strategy in this chapter, then, is to consider the senses in which this epigenetic approach is ecological and consider what ecological psychology can bring to the study of social development. In reflecting on these issues, we have detected a gradual change in theorizing about development. The notion of a paradigm shift is certainly overused, but an emergence of sorts does seem to be taking place in developmental psychology. From many different perspectives, a consensus is forming that development is a complex, multilayered process wherein behavior is organized, at least in part, as a consequence of behaving in the world (i.e., the organism acting in particular contexts) rather than as a consequence of genetic activity or tutelage from the environment. The different ecological approaches illustrated in this volume have much in common with, and much to offer, this new perspective.

Our aims for this review were spurred by the editors' charge, namely, to define our approach to the major issues in social development, to describe our research in relation to those issues, and to discuss the strengths and weaknesses ecological approaches bring to the study of social development. To fulfill these aims, we discuss our theoretical roots and then illustrate, with data from our laboratories, what we believe to be some of the major issues in the study of social development. Finally, we comment more generally on the study of social development and the linkages between it and the various approaches called "ecological."

DEVELOPMENT OF SOCIAL INTERACTIONS IN INFANCY: THE AGENDA

We define *social interactions* as behavioral exchanges between social partners; others refer to *interchanges* (Cairns, 1979) or *transactions*. During a social interaction, each participant's behavior influences the other's behavior in a focused or direct manner. For example, an infant playing alone on the floor cries and looks at a parent, who walks over and picks up the infant. The infant behaves (in this case, actually directing behavior toward the parent by visual regard), and the adult responds in a reciprocal or interwoven fashion.

Defined in this way, social interactions can be agreed on by observers; further, they have content as well as structure (i.e., features such as "turn-taking"). Social interactions are influenced by the current states of both participants as well as by the participants' past history with each other and with other partners. Social interactions offer a look at ongoing processes of development and at the same time serve as an arena in which current level of social skill and organization can be assessed. That is, participation in interactions affects the developing organism in ways that carry over into future interactions. However, social interactions also offer a chance to assess the current level of organization of social behavior and to evaluate the skills and capabilities of the developing organism. Social interactions may be the social analogue of the "tasks" or "functional units" E. J. Gibson (1994) described in her prolegomena for an ecological psychology of perceptual development.

The theoretical orientation behind our early studies of social interactions was eclectic: From comparative psychology came a focus on mutuality of organism and environment during development and a systems orientation; from ethology came an emphasis on observation and description in naturalistic environments; and from social learning came attention to changes in behavior as a result of experience, particularly experience in social interactions. These matters are still important, and they are part and parcel of some of the new trends in developmental psychology (see, for example, Ford & Lerner, 1992; Gunnar & Thelen, 1989; Turkewitz & Devenny, 1993; Wozniak & Fisher, 1993). The value of observational studies in naturalistic contexts has been recognized for a long time (see review by Wright, 1960); thus we do not repeat those arguments here. The need for a reconceptualization of the effects of experience remains critical; we discuss this problem briefly at the end of this chapter. For the moment, however, we comment on some different meanings of the term *organism–environment mutuality*.

It has long been recognized that there is mutual influence in social development, perhaps because of the very nature of social phenomena—the developing organism affects the social environment, and vice versa. This mutual influence occurs at different scales of time, however. Three of these time scales, in particular, stand out (although the distinctions blur somewhat with closer inspection). One of these time scales is relatively long-term, involving effects measured in years in the case of humans. In the late 1960s, classic articles by Bell (1968) and Rheingold (1969) brought widespread attention to the effects that children might have on parents. These studies were meant, at least in part, to shift the theoretical focus away from the effects parents have on infants, a focus that had not led to a coherent empirical base on social–personality development (Yarrow, Campbell, & Burton, 1968). It is no longer permissible to study child rearing as a unidirectional process whereby individual differences in parental attitudes and behaviors produce children with various personalities and behaviors. (It is probably no coincidence that studies of temperamental differences among infants began to flourish in the 1970s; for example, see Thomas & Chess, 1977.)

A second time scale of mutual influence is shorter, involving day-to-day and week-to-week changes during ontogeny. This type of mutual influence between developing organism and environment was the focus of comparative psychologists (e.g., Roth & Rosenblatt, 1967; Schneirla, Rosenblatt, & Tobach, 1963). This work examined changes in the way young organisms stimulate the parent, the role these changes play in altering the hormonal and behavioral status of the parent, and the feedback to the young organism from these changes. For example, Schneirla et al. (1963) examined the influence of changing locomotor abilities in kittens on the initiation of feeding sequences and, eventually, to weaning.

Indeed, for these comparative psychologists, development was defined as the changing organization of systems:

> In *development* the emphasis is on progressive changes in the organization of an individual considered as a functional, adaptive system throughout its life history. . . . Typical patterns of successive self-stimulative effects, as well as of other feedback effects and of inevitable experiences, offer key factors for the progression of stages characteristic of species ontogeny. (Schneirla, 1957, p. 79)

This definition is surprisingly current. For example, in a recent review of the role of experience in behavioral development, Gottlieb (1991) suggested that a "systems view" of development has been "slowly catching on. . . . The systems view sees individual development as hierarchically organized into multiple levels (e.g., genes, cytoplasm, cell, organ, organ system, organism, behavior, environment) *that can mutually influence each other*" (p. 5, emphasis added). It is this mutual, reciprocal influence among the levels of organization that helps define the epigenetic point of view.

The emphasis on feedback and integration of systems was important in this comparative work, but also important was a focus on species-typical developmental processes. Individual differences in parent or infant characteristics were not the focus, but rather changes that all members of the species usually undergo during development. Note that the previous definition of *development* refers to "typical patterns" of self-stimulation and to "inevitable experiences"; we believe these factors to be key mechanisms of developmental change.

The notion of mutuality has been used in yet a third sense, with an even shorter time frame. A great deal of work was undertaken in the 1970s and 1980s to show that turns in social interactions depended on previous turns. Perhaps the best known example of this work is the article by Conden and Sander (1974), in which it was argued that even newborn infants' movements are synchronized to the speech of their mothers. Although some early claims about infants' competence in turn-taking have been challenged, a substantial body of data and methodology resulted from this "microanalytic" approach to the study of social interaction process.

Of the three time scales of mutuality,[1] we have been most engaged with the moment-to-moment dynamics of social interactions (Green et al., 1980; Gustafson, 1984; Gustafson, Green, & West, 1979). The three time scales are nested, however, as the moment-to-moment exchanges influence the day-to-day and week-to-week developments, which in turn influence the long-term effects. The hierarchical nature of these time scales is critically important, and additional effort is required to conceptualize these relations in a coherent theoretical framework. Novel methods may also be required to study these relations.

The studies we describe herein have as a major focus, then, the study of mutuality of organism and environment, defined as reciprocal influences along these three time scales. This emphasis is in keeping with the epigenetic notion that development proceeds through interactions among several levels of behavioral causation (e.g., Gottlieb, 1991). It is clear, however, that the term *mutuality* has different meanings in other ecological approaches (see, for example, J. J. Gibson, 1979). We return to these issues after we present relevant data.

---

[1] The editors remind us that the word *mutual* has many meanings, as do the words *reciprocal, complementary,* and *interactive.* In particular, J. J. Gibson's (1979) ecological psychology uses *mutuality* to refer to the inseparability of organism and environment, such that neither is defined without reference to the other.

DESCRIPTIONS OF SOCIAL
INTERACTIONS IN INFANCY

Consistent with the comparative and ethological approaches, one of the first goals of our research was to describe age-related changes in social interactions in everyday environments. We hoped to show that developmental changes in infants' social behaviors were related to changes in mothers' behaviors during social interactions (Green et al., 1980). We observed 14 pairs of mothers and infants in their homes for 80 min at each of three ages—6, 8, and 12 months, using a longitudinal design. (The sample size for this study was very small, but these results have been replicated in later studies, described next.) The ages were chosen to span the time when most infants begin to locomote and to use first words. Data were collected in a seminarrative shorthand format with a stopwatch for timing.

In this study, the social interaction, or bout, was considered the fundamental unit of behavior. That is, our focus was on those periods of time when infant and mother appeared to be engaged with one another. A 10-s period with no behavioral exchanges was taken as the operational definition of the end of a social interaction. We sought to describe basic characteristics of social interactions, that is, their frequency, their duration, how they were initiated, what they were about, and how all of this changed during the second half year of the infant's life.

From some conventional views about the development of social skills in the first year, one might predict longer bouts of social engagement at the end of the first year, but we found the opposite. Social interactions between infants and mother became more frequent, but shorter, between 6 and 12 months of age (see Figure 1).

To help explain these global changes, we examined who initiated interactions, and whether the first behavior was specifically directed at the partner (i.e., coupled with visual regard or physical approach) or whether the first behavior was nondirected but "picked up" by the partner to begin the interaction. Infants initiated interactions more frequently both in directed and nondirected fashions at later ages, probably accounting for

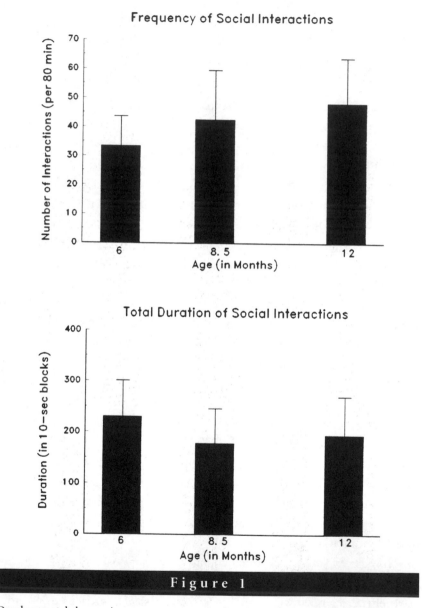

Figure 1

Developmental changes in summary measures of mother–infant interactions in the second half year of life. Data from "Effects of Infant Development on Mother–Infant Interaction," by J. A. Green, G. E. Gustafson, & M. J. West, 1980, *Child Development, 51*, p. 202. Copyright 1980 by the Society for Research in Child Development. Adapted with permission.

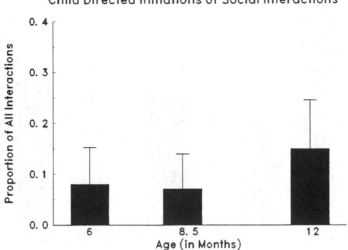

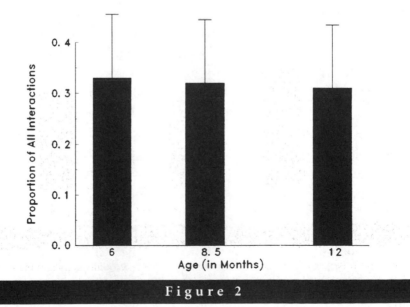

Figure 2

Developmental changes in directed initiations of mother–infant interactions in the second half year of life. Data from "Effects of Infant Development on Mother–Infant Interactions," by J. A. Green, G. E. Gustafson, & M. J. West, 1980, *Child Development, 51*, p. 203. Copyright 1980 by the Society for Research in Child Development. Adapted with permission.

the rise in frequency over age. In fact, mothers directly initiated interactions less frequently at 12 months, whereas infants directly initiated interactions more frequently (see Figure 2).

This change in the balance of directed initiations of interactions reflected, apparently, emergent properties in infants' social–communicative repertoire. Infants more often directed mothers' attention to themselves or to objects by offering, giving, showing, pointing, and waving, and they more often fussed at mothers at 8 and 12 months than at 6 months.

Infants also engaged more frequently in nondirected initiations of social interactions over time. Reliable changes were found in the proportion of interactions initiated when infants contacted objects or simply rolled, crept, or walked. These initiations of interactions, of course, reflect more general changes in perceptual–motor skills, skills that would not traditionally be labeled *social* or *communicative*. Importantly, these new skills affected social interactions through mothers' ability to incorporate the new behavior into the initial turns of interactions. For example, mothers named the objects infants contacted, initiated games of peek-a-boo with infants, crawled behind curtains, and so on.

In the midst of these changes in initiations of social interactions, there was remarkable rank order stability of global interactional measures over time. Correlations between pairs of ages for measures of frequency and duration of interactions ranged between .26 and .77, with a median of .64 (see Table 1). These cross-age correlations were remarkably high for measures obtained in infancy, a period during which rapid change generally means very little predictability from one age to another (e.g., McCall, 1979). Thus, despite significant changes in the structure of interactions (e.g., how they are initiated and by whom), and in their content (see Green et al., 1980), global measures of social interactions showed consistent differences between dyads over time.

The ability of the social environment to provide structure in the face of emergent infant characteristics is remarkable and, we think, potentially important in understanding some unique aspects of social development. The social environment appears to be active in the way it structures experiences for the infant, active in a way that the physical environment is

Table 1			

Cross-Age Stability of Social Interactions Between Infants and Mothers

	Age (in months)		
Social interaction	6	8	12
Frequency			
6	—	.69	.71
8		—	.26
12			—
Duration			
6	—	.59	.77
8		—	.38
12			—

NOTE: Data from "Effects of Infant Development on Mother–Infant Interactions," by J. A. Green, G. E. Gustafson, & M. J. West, 1980, *Child Development, 51*, p. 203. Copyright 1980 from the Society for Research in Child Development. Adapted with permission.

not in perceptual development, for example. Standard ecological approaches (especially the Gibsonian approach) may need modification to accommodate notions of an environment that actively participates in development (see, for example, Zukow, 1990).

These analyses also seem to show that summary measures, like the frequency and duration of social interactions, have characteristics different from measures of individuals' behaviors in those interactions (which did not show cross-age stability). When the focus shifts from individuals to dyads, multiple levels of organization become apparent in the data.

EFFECTS OF CHANGE IN LOCOMOTOR STATUS ON SOCIAL INTERACTIONS

One of the explicit goals of our approach to social development was to look at feedback effects, or what we have called "mutuality of organism and environment." When the infant changes, how does the social environment respond? (These effects, then, are of the sort taking place in the second of the three time scales mentioned earlier.)

The observational data just described provided the opportunity to explore the effects of locomotor ability on the social environment. Locomotion is perhaps unique in its potential as a model for how an emergent ability enters into dynamic relations with the social environment. It is universal, its onset is relatively clear-cut, and it occurs with great temporal regularity across infants. Furthermore, it is a dramatic change, obvious to all who interact with the infant.

The 14 infants in the abovementioned study began to locomote at different points between 6 and 12 months of age, so we classified infants not just by their age but by their locomotor status as well (see Green et al., 1980). It was possible, then, to demonstrate that changes at the group level in certain types of interactions were primarily the responsibility of the subset of infants who changed in locomotor status. Specifically, one of the "themes" of the interactions was labeled *unpermitted activity*, which was coded whenever mothers attempted to interrupt or redirect the ongoing activities of infants. For the group of 14 infants, the frequency of unpermitted activity interactions increased from 6 to 12 months. However, additional analyses showed that the infants who changed in locomotor status between adjacent ages were responsible for the change in group means and that infants who did not change in locomotor status showed no change in unpermitted activity interactions (see Table 2).

As has been noted often in the past (e.g., Wright, 1960), age is sometimes not a very good proxy variable for development. Even in studies of social development, locomotor status should be considered an organizing variable.

A second way in which the effects of locomotion were assessed in the previously described study was by a natural experiment. Mothers sometimes placed their nonlocomoting infants in walkers during the observation intervals, which temporarily gave infants the ability to locomote. Changes in social interactions when infants were compared in and out of walkers showed a number of similarities to age-related changes in social interactions. Interactions were shorter when infants were in versus out of

Table 2

Unpermitted Activities: Mean Changes Related to Locomotor Status

	Mean changes in frequency	
Group	6 to 8 mos	8 to 12 mos
All infants ($N = 14$)	2.4	3.9
Infants who changed locomotor status ($n = 4$)	4.5	5.2
Infants who did not change ($n = 10$)	0.4	1.0

NOTE: Data from "Effects of Infant Development on Mother–Infant Interactions," by J. A. Green, G. E. Gustafson, & M. J. West, 1980, *Child Development, 51*, p. 204. Copyright 1980 by the Society for Research in Child Development. Adapted with permission.

walkers, and infants more often initiated with nondirected behaviors when in walkers. This natural experiment, then, substantiated the conclusion that changes in locomotor status contributed significantly to many of the longitudinal changes in social interactions (see Green et al., 1980, for more details).

To follow up this natural experiment, we devised a controlled test of the effects of locomotion on social behavior, on the premise that "species-typical developments in infancy lead to new species-typical experiences, which in turn contribute to further development" (Gustafson, 1984, p. 398). Of course, social interactions were seen as playing a major role in this chain of events. Accordingly, we assessed the effects of locomotor ability on social and exploratory behaviors.

Twenty infants who could not yet locomote were observed in a standardized laboratory environment for 10 min while in a walker and for 10 min out of the walker. As one might expect, while in the walker, infants traveled more, and more frequently approached adults and toys in the room.

The ability to locomote permitted more subtle changes in social and exploratory behavior, as well. Infants more frequently looked at adults while in the walker, and they looked more frequently at a toy hung in the room as well as at fixtures in the room. They also smiled and vocalized at adults more frequently. None of these behavioral changes was an obvious consequence of locomotor ability per se; yet the behavioral changes attest to potentially powerful reorganizing effects of changes in locomotor status. These data may provide an illustration of the motivating aspect of new actions for the infant, a phenomenon that requires further study.

To restate, here, behaviors traditionally labeled *nonsocial* (e.g., locomoting, contacting objects) contributed to changes in the structure and content of social interactions in the first year. In an organismic or dynamic model, every aspect of the system is potentially important (see, for example, arguments by Fogel & Thelen, 1987), and the control parameters for a system may not be obvious (Miller, 1997, this volume; Thelen, 1989).

DEVELOPMENT OF FUSSING AND CRYING AS COMMUNICATIVE ACTS

Changes Across Age

We have investigated social interactions for the effects of another dramatic achievement of infancy, the development of communicative abilities. In particular, we examined several aspects of communication through infant fussing and crying, including the acoustic attributes of cries that carry information about individual identity of the infant (Green & Gustafson, 1983; Gustafson, Green, & Tomic, 1984), the acoustic basis of perceived distress (Gustafson & Green, 1989), the multidimensional character of perception by parents and nonparents (Green, Jones, & Gustafson, 1987), the role of experience in perception and caregiving behavior (Gustafson & DeConti, 1990; Gustafson & Harris, 1990), and the emergence of fussing and crying as communicative acts (Gustafson & Green, 1991).

Of most relevance to an ecological perspective is our work on developmental changes in fussing and crying as communicative acts. One often reads that crying changes from a reflex to an operant in the first year of life, yet there is little data tracing the natural history of this phenomenon. More important, there has been no systematic attempt to investigate how species-typical experiences might contribute to species-typical changes in infants' use of fuss and cry sounds to initiate interactions or communicate needs and wishes.

In the study of social interactions described previously (Green et al., 1980), we noted that there was a significant increase from 6 to 12 months in the number of social interactions that were initiated by infants' fussing at their mothers. "Fussing at" was a category of *directed social behavior*, operationally defined as behavior accompanied by looking at or approaching the social partner. Thus defined, directed social behaviors are examples of what language researchers have called "speech acts" (e.g., Lock, 1976; or proto-imperatives, Bates, O'Connell, & Shore, 1987), and thus should be considered a part of prelinguistic communication. Indeed, Bates et al. (1987) and others specifically mentioned fussing in discussions of intentional communication before words.

One of our goals, as we mentioned earlier, has been description. In this study, then, our focus was the developmental course of cry sounds and their linkage to visual regard and to gestures. We identified four kinds of couplings of visual regard and gesture with cry sounds and sought to chart their occurrence in infants' social interactions from 3 to 12 months of age (Gustafson & Green, 1991). Definitions of the four patterns of initiations of social interactions by cry sounds follow: (a) *simple cry*, crying in the absence of looking at or gesturing; (b) *uncoordinated cry and look*, crying accompanied by looking, but the two behaviors are separated by at least 10 s; (c) *coordinated cry and look*, crying and looking occurring within 10 s; and (d) *elaborated cry*, onset of cry accompanied by gesture or gesture and looking.

The data for this study consisted in part of the narrative records described previously, namely, 80 min of time-marked, sequenced, shorthand codes for behaviors of mothers and infants at 6, 8, and 12 months of age. However, a second cohort of 12 mother–infant pairs was added. Pairs were observed for 60 min when infants were 3, 4 and 6 months of age. (The two cohorts did not differ at 6 months on any of the measures, so data were pooled to obtain statistics for that age.)

We then analyzed the proportion of infants who exhibited each of the four patterns of fussing and crying just described. The proportion of infants who showed the elaborated pattern increased significantly from 3 months (when no infant elaborated a fuss/cry sound) to 12 months (when the majority of infants elaborated). In complementary manner, the proportion of infants who exhibited the uncoordinated pattern decreased from 3 to 12 months. There were no significant changes in the proportion of infants who exhibited the coordinated or simple patterns.

At the time, we suggested that there might be a hierarchical relation over development among the patterns, such that a relatively loose coupling of the behavior with visual regard occurs first, followed by a closer temporal relation, followed by coordination with other emerging communicative skills such as gesturing. For each of the 26 infants in the study, the highest pattern in the hierarchy achieved at the earliest age was compared with the highest pattern achieved at the latest age. Only one infant violated the hierarchy, suggesting that there may indeed be a regular progression across age in the sophistication with which infants use fuss and cry sounds in ongoing social interactions.

Processes Affecting Development

After charting this progression, we began to wonder what process brings about these developments? A number of authors have suggested that "social dialogues" surrounding cry interactions may be important to the development of infants' prelinguistic communication skills (Bruner, 1977; Lamb, 1981; Schaffer, 1984). Infants fuss and cry frequently throughout the day, and parents usually respond. This sequence is repeated many times a day, from the day of birth throughout infancy (and beyond). This sequence of behavior between parent and infant may be optimal for fostering the development of intentionality and conventionality (see, for example, Bates et al., 1987) in that a primitive sort of meaning on the part of the infant (his or her own distress) is connected both with sound production and with an effect from the environment.

Interestingly, the presumed *evolutionary function* of crying (ensuring survival through signaling of distress) may create a social situation that predisposes certain aspects of communicative development. Along these lines, Gekoski, Rovee-Collier, and Carulli-Rabinowitz (1983) showed that infants develop expectations over the first 6 months of life for a response to their crying. Lamb and Malkin (1986) provided similar data and argued for a similar process.

To further support this hypothesized process, we undertook three lines of inquiry. First, we initiated additional studies of the linkage between cry sounds and other communicative behaviors, which are ongoing. Second, observational and laboratory work has provided evidence that the social environment regularly responds to fussing and crying and that the response is regular both within and across caregivers. Third, we have initiated a comparison of cry sounds with noncry vocalizations to determine whether the developmental progressions are similar.

Linkage Between Cry Sounds and Other Communicative Behaviors

A recent study replicated and extended the earlier results on visual regard, gestures, and crying (see Figure 3). A new database was generated on a larger sample using more sophisticated methods. Using a cross-sectional design, we videotaped 15 dyads of infants at home at ages 3, 6, 8, and 12 months. Approximately 4 hr of videotape were collected for each dyad.

Each bout of fussing or crying was logged from the videotape using computer-generated time code recorded onto an unused audio channel. Bouts were then viewed repeatedly to score communicative pattern of the fuss or cry, mothers' responses to the sound, proximity of mother and infant, and function of the sound. The findings presented next are the preliminary results from this labor-intensive data collection.

In all, we worked with a database of 5,190 bouts of fussing and crying from about 240 hr of videotape. As in the previous study (Gustafson & Green, 1991), the frequency of these bouts did not change significantly from 3 to 12 months, although the total amount of time spent fussing and crying decreased (see Figure 4). The average number of bouts of fussing and crying per hour in the 3- to 12-month-period was about 26, and the average length of a single bout was about 11.5 s.

Despite the differences in precision of data collection, then, these data

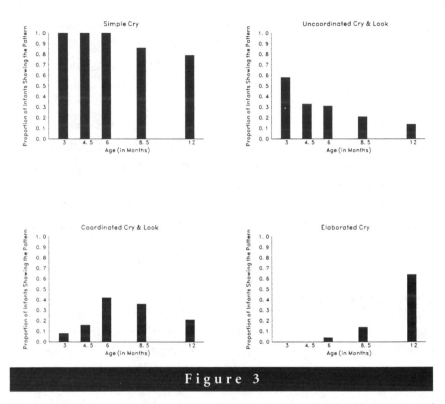

Figure 3

Developmental changes in the proportion of infants who showed each of four patterns of coordination of cry sounds with visual regard and gestures.

support those presented earlier. Bouts of fussing and crying were relatively frequent but relatively short. (Although intensity of the cry sound was not coded, most of these bouts quite obviously were not full-blown, intense crying.) In addition, the frequency of these bouts was relatively constant across the first year, although the average length of the bouts decreased over age. Other investigators, using a variety of methodologies, have generally supported these findings on developmental changes in frequency and duration of fussing and crying (see review by Barr, 1990, and data by St. James-Roberts & Halil, 1991).

We used the newer, larger database to explore further the notion that coupling of fussing and crying with other communicative behaviors changes in a regular progression across the first year (see Figure 3). Using

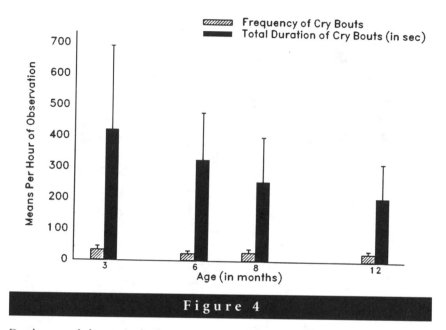

Figure 4

Developmental changes in the frequency and duration of bouts of crying in the first year of life.

definitions of initiations by cry sounds similar to those presented earlier,[2] we reviewed each bout of fussing and crying to determine which kind of communicative pattern was present. Figure 5 shows the proportion of bouts in which the four patterns were found.

Although the measuring system was more precise, and the definitions were changed slightly, the major trends from the earlier study were replicated in the newer cohort. In particular, the proportion of fuss/cry bouts elaborated with gestures or words increased from 3 to 12 months, replicating previous findings. The proportion of coordinated cry and look bouts also increased over time, whereas the proportion of simple cry bouts decreased significantly from 3 to 12 months.

---

[2] Because of the greater precision afforded by videotape, the temporal criteria for the uncoordinated and coordinated categories changed. If looking occurred within 2 s of the onset of fussing, the bout was coded as coordinated cry and look. If the looking occurred between 2 and 5 s of the onset of fussing, the bout was coded as uncoordinated cry and look. Also, elaborated bouts were expanded to include bouts in which a gesture or word was used to "disambiguate" the meaning of the fuss/cry sound.

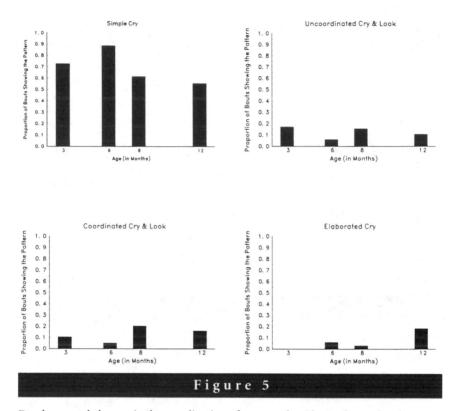

Figure 5

Developmental changes in the coordination of cry sounds with visual regard and gestures at the onset of bouts of cry sounds (see Footnote 2).

Consistency of Caregivers' Responses to Fuss/Cry Sounds

Is there evidence to support the notion that caregivers' responses to fussing and crying play a role in the emergence of these more sophisticated communicative forms late in the first year? On the basis of preliminary analyses of the videotaped interactions described earlier, we can provide two kinds of evidence to support this hypothesis. First, mothers usually responded to fussing and crying. Across all ages, only 15% of fuss/cry bouts were ignored by the mother. Second, most of the time, the first and only response to bouts of fussing and crying was social (i.e., mother and infant interacted). Generally, mothers do not simply give care in response to cry sounds, rather they talk to, touch, pat, rock, and hold their infants. Most of the time, infants quiet after these social responses, and feeding, diapering, putting to bed, or other caregiving responses are not necessary. In fact, cry sounds initiate social dialogues.

The patterning of response to cry sounds, that is, social behavior followed by caregiving behavior, has been replicated in a laboratory simulation study as well (Gustafson & Harris, 1990). In addition, this patterning turned out to be a measure sensitive to amount of caregiving experience. Women who had not yet had children were more likely to try caregiving (e.g., feeding or diapering) early in the sequence of responses to crying.

Comparison of Cry Sounds and Other Vocalizations

The question could be raised whether negative sounds (fusses and cries) are special. Do they function during social interactions in a manner similar to other vocalizations? Do the processes we have illustrated simply reflect more general ones that apply to all infant sound making?

Again, although preliminary, the more recent data can shed light on whether cry sounds are special because all noncry vocalizations were logged from the videotapes and coded in an identical manner as the cry sounds. Initial analyses showed that, although the proportions of vocalizations and cry sounds that were elaborated increased from 3 to 12 months, there was an interaction between age and sound type (Figure 6). The increase over age was steeper for cry sounds than for other vocalizations, $F(3, 56) = 12.83$, $p < .001$. At perhaps a more basic level, mothers simply did not respond as consistently to vocalizations as to cry sounds. Across all ages, mothers ignored 35% of the infants' vocalizations compared with 15% of their cry sounds.

Summary

These studies demonstrate that cry sounds have properties that set them apart from other infant sounds and that may facilitate the development of early communicative competence. Furthermore, although crying is not the only infant behavior that elicits social interactions, it is unique in that it is linked (at least in young infants) to physiological states that should be of particular salience to the infant, states that continue and may even

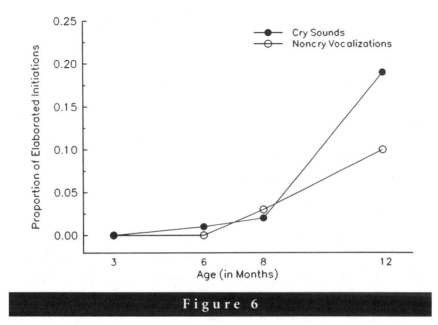

Figure 6

Developmental changes in the coordination of two types of infant sounds with gestures and words.

intensify until a caregiver intervenes. In fact, as soon as infants begin to make noncry sounds (in the first or second month of life), there is a primitive, differentiated sound-meaning system in place. It is probably this system that should be the focus of future research, rather than cry or noncry sounds alone.

As with locomotion, the emphasis of this research was not on crying per se, but on crying as it functions in the process of social development. Most research on crying has focused on differentiating "normal" from atypical infants (see reviews in Lester & Boukydis, 1985) or on the prediction of individual differences in outcome measures (see Lester, 1987). Yet the research on individual differences has omitted a consideration of developmental processes that lead from neonatal crying to poor performance on the outcome measure. As Wolff (1985) noted,

> There seems to be a significant lack of systematic observational or
> experimental data concerning the development of crying after early

infancy. . . . Cry production should from an evolutionary and developmental perspective contain many of the components that will contribute essentially to differentiated forms of social communication. (pp. 353–354)

THE DEVELOPMENT OF SOCIAL INTERACTIONS IN INFANCY

The original agenda for this research included describing the social environment in a manner that reflected its important characteristics for infants and demonstrating mutual adjustments between infants and parents. Our assumption has been, and continues to be, that participation in social interactions contributes to social development (and probably to all other kinds of development, as well). On the basis of this assumption, we have taken social interactions themselves as the behaviors to be studied and have addressed basic questions about their structure and function. Perhaps most significantly, these questions have been addressed in a developmental framework, meaning that change over time is a primary focus, along with bidirectional effects of organism and environment.

The approach we have taken to social development focuses on experiences and behaviors common to most infants and mothers. We have, on occasion, even referred to these as species-typical experiences and species-typical behaviors. Although the data are extremely limited, observations of other cultures support this claim (e.g., Barr, Konner, Bakeman, & Adamson, 1991).

The focus on species-typical processes is somewhat unique in that, as noted earlier, a great deal of research on social development is concerned with individual differences. How are individual differences in outcomes predicted (e.g., attachment classifications), what are the origins of individual differences (e.g., in temperament), and how are different individuals treated differently? Of course, there is a long tradition of concern with individual differences in psychology (see Cronbach, 1957), and the study of individual differences can be a crucial part of truly developmental investigations (see Wohlwill, 1973). However, the points of view are distinct.

We expect that all infants use emerging skills in social interactions and that participation in those interactions, with more skilled partners, might facilitate social development (see, for example, Rogoff, 1993).

Some aspects of this work can be seen as compatible with a new approach to development, namely the dynamic systems perspective (e.g., Ford & Lerner, 1992; Thelen & Smith, 1994). In particular, our efforts to trace the development of cry sounds that are directed at caregivers seems to us, on the surface at least, to resemble the emergence of a novel form of behavior, assembled from existing behaviors under the constraints of the task (see Thelen & Smith, 1994). After all, looking and crying are behaviors that are present from birth onward, and they appear to become integrated gradually into conventionalized communicative acts.

To be extended to social development, however, the notion of a self-organizing, dynamic system must encompass not just the child but also the other relationships in which the child participates. We have included one parent (the mother) to define a dyadic system, and have shown that it develops and has measurable properties not inherent in either the child or mother alone. But clearly, there are a host of other systems in which the child develops.

The complexity of these systems and their interrelations seems, at times, to defy analysis, despite an increasing willingness to call for a multilevel approach to development. In addition, we have yet to even mention genetic, neurochemical, cultural, or physical–environmental levels of analysis (see, e.g., Gottlieb, 1991). From the beginning, however, developmental psychologists have recognized the need for multidisciplinary approaches (for a history of ideas and controversies in developmental psychology, see Cairns, 1983). The time now seems to be right to make more concerted efforts in this direction.

RELATIONS AMONG THEORETICAL APPROACHES CALLED *ECOLOGICAL*

Other chapters in this volume are written by experts in various approaches termed *ecological*. We do not fall into this category, but we take the opportunity here to offer some of our own thoughts about these ecological approaches and their relevance to social development in infancy.

When our observational work on social interactions got started, ecological psychology meant observing organisms in everyday environments, using molar descriptions of behavior, and analyzing the environment as well as the organism's behaviors in the environment. That is, ecological psychology was closely identified with the work of Barker and Wright and their colleagues (see also a retrospective by Schoggen, 1991).[3] The rationale for this kind of ecological psychology is summarized in Barker's (as cited in Schoggen, 1991) application to the National Institute of Mental Health in the 1940s:

> Although we know a great deal about how children behave under relatively controlled, standardized conditions, such as intelligence- and personality-testing situations, we know little about how they react to them. Preoccupation by investigators with behavior under controlled conditions has crowded out concerns with naturally-occurring situations and with the interrelations between them and behavior. (p. 284)

The richness of Barker and Wright's ecological descriptions of daily behavior was truly unique; unfortunately, that same richness may have also contributed to the failure of this method to take hold. The data were difficult to collect, hard to analyze, and not in keeping with psychology's perceived need for standardization and control. To some extent, however, Barker's emphasis on molar description of behavior and of the environment has been taken up again in recent years, particularly with the increase in interest in Vygotsky and the "activity" school and with Bronfenbrenner's (1979) focus on context. Descriptive ecological work is sure to continue in the coming decade, if only to establish the important problems to be studied.

For the study of social behavior in particular, Bronfenbrenner's (1979) approach soon became identified as the "ecological" approach. Most undergraduate courses in child development today cover the hierarchy of

---

[3] The emphasis on describing and cataloging behavior, and on observational methods, has much in common with the ethological approach to behavior. Of course, ethology's focus on "innate" behaviors is not compatible with a developmental approach.

contexts Bronfenbrenner labeled *micro-, meso-, exo-,* and *macrosystems.* The notion that development is influenced by the broader contexts in which it occurs, and that developmental level may vary according to the specific context in which it is assessed, is attractive and has spread rapidly. Two recent volumes, titled *Context and Development* (Cohen & Siegel, 1991) and *Development in Context: Acting and Thinking in Specific Environments* (Wozniak & Fisher, 1993), attest to the current interest in the approach and to its success in guiding empirical work.

Of course, yet a third ecological psychology is flourishing, a center for which has been created at the University of Connecticut. Here, ecological psychology is an integrated approach to the study of perception and action, and it is based on the writings of J. J. Gibson (for more detailed explications of this approach, see E. J. Gibson, 1994, and Reed, 1987).

What of the relations among these three approaches, namely, Barker's, Bronfenbrenner's, and Gibson's? All share a historical link to Kurt Lewin (see, for example, Lewin, 1938), although this link is most direct for Barker and Bronfenbrenner. The common ancestor means that there is an emphasis in each approach on a theory of the environment and of the relation of organisms to environment. This common link also means a common interest in real behavior of real persons in the real world. It is no longer acceptable to study perception only in the context of snapshots or to study aggression only in the context of a laboratory and Bobo doll.

However, what does an emphasis on contextual determinants of behavior mean? Wozniak and Fisher (1993) offered a few basic propositions of an emerging "contextualized" view of cognitive development. Among these are the key notions that "psychological events are transactions that take place between individuals and their specific environments" and that "the environment, both social and physical, participates directly in behavior" (p. xii). It is no longer defensible to conceptualize individuals as collections of cognitive capacities or competencies that are immutable across different situations (or worse, across time).

> How we perceive the world, act on objects, interact with people, and
> generate symbols to represent events must be understood as the joint

product of the physical and social situations that individuals find
themselves in and the personal characteristics that individuals bring
with them to these situations. (Wozniak & Fisher, 1993, p. xii)

This theoretical reorientation requires different methods, and Wozniak and Fisher (1993) suggested a need for studying development in natural contexts as well as enriched laboratory situations. Furthermore, they
suggested a need for focus on process as well as outcome, which requires
different research designs and analyses. Kessen (1993) argued for similar
emphases in his article on the new, contextualized, developmental psychology, including the study of everyday behavior and of variations in behavior across contexts.

The three ecological approaches we have discussed are related in several important ways, then, although their subject matter and methods may
differ. The importance of studying the environment, and the individual in
the environment are key, as is an emphasis on interactions between individuals and environments.

All three ecological approaches thus are compatible with the *social* aspect of social development research by virtue of their concern with environments. It should be possible to extend these approaches to cover apparently unique properties of the social environment, including its
responsiveness, its activity, and its plans for the developing child.

However, we would suggest that each approach has some difficulty
with the *development* aspect of social development. The study of
development is the study of change, emergence, and novelty. None
of the three ecological approaches has as its central concern the study of
change.[4] Indeed, it may be necessary to add considerable complexity to
the theoretical formulations in order to address notions of change and

---

[4] In fact, most theories of development have the same problem, including those in developmental biology.
Gottlieb (1991) noted that, although the original meaning of *epigenetic* had to do with the emergence of
novel structures during embryological development, there is as yet no adequate theory of *morphogenesis* or tissue differentiation. The difficulty in addressing emergence and change within a coherent theoretical framework is thus a general problem, rather than one specific to ecological theories of behavior
(see Turvey & Fitzpatrick, 1993, for a thoughtful discussion of the complexities of biological systems and
of the attempts to account for emergent properties and for patterning by analogy to physical systems).

emergence—whether that be change that occurs during development in the affordances of objects, in the relation between organism and context, or, indeed, change in mechanisms that produce these changes.

Even if the none of the ecological approaches have yet offered a full explanation of emergence in development, each approach can offer important methodological guidelines for the study of social development in infancy. From Barker's ecological approach, social developmentalists can adopt an emphasis on typical children in typical environments, a focus on molar aspects of behavior, and a judicious use of observational techniques. The recognition that social development is affected by variables beyond the child, and immediate family, is a crucial message from Bronfenbrenner, a message already heard by many.

Finally, social developmentalists might borrow from those interested in direct perception (e.g., E. J. and J. J. Gibson) a focus on the structure provided by the social environment and the processes by which developing organisms perceive that structure. Such an emphasis might help redefine how experience influences the developing organism by forcing researchers to look at the critical moments when structure or the detection of structure changes in crucial ways. Social developmentalists certainly have moved beyond characterizing social environments in terms of the number of smiles per hour, as was done in the 1960s and 1970s, but more can be done.

From the epigenetic perspective, development is considered a fundamentally biological phenomenon, and multiple levels of analysis (e.g., genetic, neurochemical) should be considered to help explain social development, as should multiple processes. Clearly, more data of an ecological variety are required. Yet, just as clearly, also required are new accounts of social development that emphasize emergence and change as well as tasks and traits, that emphasize species-typical phenomena as well as individual differences, and that focus on processes of change as well as prediction of outcomes. Such new, synthetic accounts of social development will no doubt emerge from a theoretical base that includes these various approaches called ecological.

REFERENCES

Barr, R. G. (1990). The normal crying curve: What do we really know? *Developmental Medicine and Child Neurology, 32,* 356–362.

Barr, R. G., Konner, M., Bakeman, R., & Adamson, L. (1991). !Kung San infants: A test of the cultural specificity hypothesis. *Developmental Medicine and Child Neurology, 33,* 601–610.

Bates, E., O'Connell, B., & Shore, C. (1987). Language and communication in infancy. In J. D. Osofsky (Ed.), *Handbook of infant development* (2nd ed., pp. 149–203). New York: Wiley.

Bell, R. Q. (1968). A reinterpretation of the direction of effects in studies of socialization. *Psychological Review, 75,* 81–95.

Bronfenbrenner, U. (1979). *The ecology of human development.* Cambridge, MA: Harvard University Press.

Bruner, J. S. (1977). Early social interaction and language acquisition. In H. R. Schaffer (Ed.), *Studies in mother–infant interaction* (pp. 271–289). New York: Academic Press.

Cairns, R. B. (1979). *Social development.* San Francisco: Freeman.

Cairns, R. B. (1983). The emergence of developmental psychology. In P. H. Mussen (Series Ed.) & W. Kessen (Vol. Ed.), *Handbook of child psychology: Vol. 1. History, theory, and methods* (4th ed., pp. 41–102). New York: Wiley.

Cohen, R., & Siegel, A. W. (1991). (Eds.). *Context and development.* Hillsdale, NJ: Erlbaum.

Conden, W. S., & Sander, L. B. (1974). Neonate movement is synchronized with adult speech. *Science, 183,* 99–101.

Cronbach, L. J. (1957). The two disciplines of scientific psychology. *American Psychologist, 12,* 671–684.

Fogel, A., & Thelen, E. (1987). The development of expressive and communicative action in the first year: Reinterpreting the evidence from a dynamic systems perspective. *Developmental Psychology, 23,* 747–761.

Ford, D. H., & Lerner, R. M. (1992). *Developmental systems theory: An integrative approach.* Newbury Park, CA: Sage.

Gekoski, M. J., Rovee-Collier, C., & Carulli-Rabinowitz, V. (1983). A longitudinal analysis of inhibition of infant distress: The origins of social expectations? *Infant Behavior and Development, 6,* 339–351.

Gibson, E. J. (1994, September). *Prolegomena for an ecological approach to perceptual development.* Invited presentation at the American Psychological Association Conference on Changing Ecological Approaches to Development: Organism–Environment Mutualities, Storrs, CT.

Gibson, J. J. (1979). *The ecological approach to visual perception.* Boston: Houghton Mifflin.

Gottlieb, G. (1983). The psychobiological approach to developmental issues. In P. H. Mussen (Series Ed.) & W. Kessen (Vol. Ed.), *Handbook of child psychology: Vol. 1. History, theory, and methods* (pp. 1–26). New York: Wiley.

Gottlieb, G. (1991). Experiential canalization of behavioral development: Theory. *Developmental Psychology, 27,* 4–13.

Green, J. A., & Gustafson, G. E. (1983). Individual recognition of human infants on the basis of cries alone. *Developmental Psychobiology, 16,* 485–493.

Green, J. A., Gustafson, G. E., & West, M. J. (1980). Effects of infant development on mother–infant interactions. *Child Development, 51,* 199–207.

Green, J. A., Jones, L. E., & Gustafson, G. E. (1987). Perception of cries by parents and nonparents: Relations to cry acoustics. *Developmental Psychology, 23,* 370–382.

Gunnar, M. R., & Thelen, E. (1989). (Eds.). *Systems and development.* Hillsdale, NJ: Erlbaum.

Gustafson, G. E. (1984). Effects of locomotion on infants' social and exploratory behavior: An experimental investigation. *Developmental Psychology, 20,* 397–405.

Gustafson, G. E., & DeConti, K. A. (1990). Infants' cries in the process of normal development. *Early Child Development and Care, 65,* 45–56.

Gustafson, G. E., & Green, J. A. (1989). On the importance of fundamental frequency and other acoustic features in cry perception and infant development. *Child Development, 60,* 772–780.

Gustafson, G. E., & Green, J. A. (1991). Developmental coordination of cry sounds with visual regard and gestures. *Infant Behavior and Development, 14,* 51–57.

Gustafson, G. E., Green, J. A., & Tomic, T. (1984). Acoustic correlates of individuality in the cries of human infants. *Developmental Psychobiology, 17,* 311–324.

Gustafson, G. E., Green, J. A., & West, M. J. (1979). The infant's changing role in mother–infant games: The growth of social skills. *Infant Behavior and Development, 2,* 301–308.

Gustafson, G. E., & Harris, K. L. (1990). Women's responses to young infants' cries. *Developmental Psychology, 26,* 144–152.

Kessen, W. (1993). Rumble or revolution: A commentary. In R. H. Wozniak & K. W. Fisher (Eds.), *Development in context: Acting and thinking in specific environments* (pp. 269–279). Hillsdale, NJ: Erlbaum.

Lamb, M. E. (1981). Developing trust and perceived effectance in infancy. In L. Lipsitt & C. Rovee-Collier (Eds.), *Advances in infancy research* (Vol. 1, pp. 101–127). Norwood, NJ: Ablex.

Lamb, M. E., & Malkin, C. M. (1986). The development of social expectations in distress–relief sequences: A longitudinal study. *International Journal of Behavioral Development, 9*, 235–249.

Lester, B. M. (1987). Developmental outcome prediction from acoustic cry analysis in term and preterm infants. *Pediatrics, 80*, 529–534.

Lester, B. M., & Boukydis, C. F. Z. (Eds.). (1985). *Infant crying: Theoretical and research perspectives.* New York: Plenum Press.

Lewin, K. (1938). *The conceptual representation and the measurement of psychological forces.* Durham, NC: Duke University Press.

Lock, A. (1976). 'Acts' instead of 'sentences.' In W. von Raffler-Engel & Y. Lebrun (Eds.), *Baby talk and infant speech* (pp. 148–161). Amsterdam: Swets & Aeitlinger.

McCall, R. B. (1979). Qualitative transitions in behavioral development in the first two years of life. In M. Bornstein & W. Kessen (Eds.), *Psychological development from infancy* (pp. 183–224). Hillsdale, NJ: Erlbaum.

Rheingold, H. L. (1969). The social and socializing infant. In D. A. Goslin (Ed.), *Handbook of socialization theory and research* (pp. 779–790). Chicago: Rand-McNally.

Rogoff, B. (1993). Children's guided participation and participatory appropriation in sociocultural activity. In R. H. Wozniak & K. W. Fisher (Eds.), *Development in context: An introduction* (pp. 121–153). Hillsdale, NJ: Erlbaum.

Roth, L. L., & Rosenblatt, J. S. (1967). Changes in self-licking during pregnancy in the rat. *Journal of Comparative and Physiological Psychology, 63*, 397–400.

Schaffer, H. R. (1984). *The child's entry into a social world.* New York: Academic Press.

Schneirla, T. C. (1957). The concept of development in comparative psychology. In D. B. Harris (Ed.), *The concept of development* (pp. 78–108). Minneapolis: University of Minnesota Press.

Schneirla, T. C., Rosenblatt, J. S., & Tobach, E. (1963). Maternal behavior in the cat. In H. L. Rheingold (Ed.), *Maternal behaviour in mammals* (pp. 122–168). New York: Wiley.

Schoggen, P. (1991). Ecological psychology: One approach to development in context. In R. Cohen & A. W. Siegel (Eds.), *Context and development* (pp. 281–301). Hillsdale, NJ: Erlbaum.

St. James-Roberts, I., & Halil, T. (1991). Infant crying patterns in the first year: Normal community and clinical findings. *Journal of Child Psychology and Psychiatry, 32,* 951–968.

Thelen, E. (1989). Self-organization in developmental processes: Can systems approaches work? In M. R. Gunnar & E. Thelen (Eds.), *Systems and development* (pp. 77–117). Hillsdale, NJ: Erlbaum.

Thelen, E., & Smith, L. B. (1994). *A dynamic systems approach to the development of cognition and action.* Cambridge, MA: MIT.

Thomas, A., & Chess, S. (1977). *Temperament and development.* New York: Bruner/Mazel.

Turkewitz, G., & Devenny, D. A. (Eds.). (1993). *Developmental time and timing.* Hillsdale, NJ: Erlbaum.

Turvey, M. T., & Fitzpatrick, P. (1993). Commentary: Development of perception–action systems and general principles of pattern formation. *Child Development, 64,* 1175–1190.

Wohlwill, J. F. (1973). *The study of behavioral development.* New York: Academic Press.

Wolff, P. H. (1985). Epilogue. In B. M. Lester & C. F. Z. Boukydis (Eds.), *Infant crying: Theoretical and research perspectives* (pp. 349–354). New York: Plenum.

Wozniak, R. H., & Fisher, K. W. (Eds.). (1993). *Development in context: Acting and thinking in specific environments.* Hillsdale, NJ: Erlbaum.

Wright, H. F. (1960). Observational child study. In P. H. Mussen (Ed.), *Handbook of research methods in child development* (pp. 71–139). New York: Wiley.

Yarrow, M. R., Campbell, J. D., & Burton, R. V. (1968). *Child rearing: An inquiry in research and methods.* San Francisco: Jossey-Bass.

Zukow, P. G. (1990). Socio-perceptual bases for the emergence of language: An alternative to innatist approaches. *Developmental Psychobiology, 23,* 705–726.

Comment on Green and Gustafson

Timothy D. Johnston

The chapter by James Green and Gwen Gustafson emphasizes the complexity of interactions between the developing infant and the environment that are responsible for the emergence of mature patterns of social interaction. That complexity is manifest in a number of ways in the data they present and issues they highlight. For example, they report a developmental link between locomotion and social interaction, two domains of competence that would seem to have little to do with one another. Here one sees an example of the kind of nonobvious developmental relationship on which David Miller (this volume) focused in his chapter. Their finding reinforces the point that it is important for researchers to attend to the possible existence of developmental links among domains that seem *prima facie* to be quite separate from one another.

The chapter also highlights the importance of individual differences in developmental research. In their discussion of the effects of locomotor activity on social interactions, Green and Gustafson note that some of the group-level changes they observed were primarily due to the behavior of

---

Johnston comments on Green and Gustafson from an ecological realist perspective.

a subset of infants in their sample. All behavioral research, of course, recognizes that there are differences in individual response; that is why we select appropriate sample sizes, perform statistical tests, and try to identify main effects. Sometimes, however, this focus on group effects and group differences can obscure the emergence of order at the level of individuals, and this seems to be especially true in the analysis of developmental processes. The dynamic systems approach to development, pioneered especially by Esther Thelen (Thelen & Smith, 1994) in the study of locomotor development, shows very clearly the need for individual longitudinal analysis and also highlights the tremendous practical difficulties that are involved. One empirical strategy in the dynamic systems approach is to identify control variables that shift the developing system, sometimes quite abruptly, from one stable state to another. Green and Gustafson suggest that locomotion may be a control variable that shifts the system in this way in regard to social interactions. It probably is not possible to detect such changes unless one proceeds individual by individual, something that runs counter to the group-level analysis of most experimental psychology.

As I noted earlier, one prediction from dynamic systems theory is that many developmental changes occur quite abruptly as a result of system reorganization. If this is correct, it becomes particularly important to devise techniques for the fine-grain analysis of individual developmental trajectories. The point at which a control variable produces the shift from one state to another is likely to vary among individuals, increasing the likelihood that group means will obscure the very developmental phenomena we are trying to explain, especially if groups are defined by a proxy variable like age. If much developmental change takes place during the relatively brief periods of transition between states, researchers will need to be able both to identify the relevant periods and to analyze the dynamics of the rapid change taking place within them. Once this is accomplished, it may turn out that the kinds of explanations needed to account for that change will look quite different from those that have been constructed to explain patterns of change derived from analyses of group data. Something rather similar to this has happened in the study of biological evoution over the last 20 years, as a growing body of evidence has come to suggest that evolution may also occur more by intermittent spurts than by slow, gradual modification. This is the theory of punctuated equilibrium. Some theorists have proposed that the traditional evolutionary mechanisms—gradual accumulation of genetic change by natural selection—cannot adequately account for the rapid punctuational change envisioned by this theory.

The emphasis on group-level analysis in much of psychology reflects, I think, a kind of essentialism in psychological theory that is reflected in our methodology. If the goal of scientific psychology is to account for a set of essential properties of human behavior and cognition, then deviations from any putative essential properties are seen as confusing and distracting, and we have devised methods (group comparison, calculations of central tendencies, analyses of variance) to separate the essential properties from the deviations. On this account, individual variation is noise, whereas from the dynamic systems point of view, variation is important data. Such a shift in emphasis should be especially congenial to students of social psychology, whose area of the discipline is more directly concerned than most with the reality of individual differences and with the dynamic nature of the systems they study.

REFERENCE

Thelen, E., & Smith, L. B. (1994). *A dynamic systems approach to the development of cognition and action.* Cambridge, MA: MIT Press.

Epilogue: Where Does the Animal End and the Environment Begin . . . and End?

Patricia Zukow-Goldring and Cathy Dent-Read

The proper unit for study is an organism in the environment in which it evolved, functioning in a reciprocal relationship. The environment affords opportunities for an animal to act by way of its evolved perception and action systems. These opportunities include events, objects, and places of all kinds, both physical and social.

E. Gibson

This volume provides three overlapping perspectives for assessing evolving explanations of development. We encourage integrating these views as a first step on the path to a more comprehensive theory of development. Ecological realism and dynamic and epigenetic systems each make a unique contribution to this daunting enterprise. E. Gibson's chapter provides guidelines for reviewing the similarities among this research, for perceiving the accomplishments of this work, and, most important, for

Special thanks are extended to John Pittenger for his cogent suggestions on an earlier version of the manuscript.

detecting a path to the future. E. Gibson provides the field with three sets of propositions, along a continuum of applicability. The most fundamental set explicates ecological realist theory, including approaches to organism–environment reciprocity, perception–action coupling, behavior as functional tasks composed of nested units, the embeddedness of tasks in ongoing events, and the three hallmarks of behavior: control/agency, prospectivity, and flexibility. In the second set she elaborates these fundamentals of ecological realism to explain learning and change in the course of perceptual development. Finally, E. Gibson extends her approach to support her assertion that cognition is grounded in perception and develops along similar functional routes. She has drawn a map rich with possibilities and potential for furthering the study of (perceptual) development. Although her words are clear, succinct, and direct, the task she foresees is far from simple. The contributors to this volume adhere to many of these propositions and explore their path-breaking potential, focusing especially on an active organism exploring and performing in its functionally coupled environment. However, defining what we mean by *environment* and "finding" it by developing the appropriate ethnographic and experimental methods for psychology appears more demanding. The first section examines how various authors address the topics in E. Gibson's chapter, emphasizing the developing organism in its environment. The second section sketches the variety of theoretical and empirical "environments" encountered, some of the complexity and ambiguity underlying various interpretations, and prospects for finding a common ground. Chapters most central to the discussion illustrate each topic, but others explore these issues as well.

ORGANISM–ENVIRONMENT MUTUALITY: ORGANISMS ACTING IN THEIR ENVIRONMENTS

Each of the participants in this volume has made innovative and substantial strides in explicitly theorizing about and empirically investigating subsets of E. Gibson's propositions. This wide range of studies encompasses and integrates motor, perceptual, emotional, social, or cognitive development. Despite some differences in disciplinary roots and variations in trajectories of view, with few exceptions, in each chapter authors relate organism–environment reciprocity or mutuality explicitly to their focus of research. Many of them delineate how cycles of perceiving and acting inform their approach. For example, Cooper's (Chapter 3) studies of infant speech perception clearly show the empirical and theoretical value of explaining development in terms of the fit between the infant and detectable acoustic structure in the infant's environment. Specifically, development occurs in the changing dynamic between the perceptual experience of infants and their social context. Infants initially prefer to attend to speech that is highly contrastive in its acoustic properties and gradually detect the difference between intonation patterns. Eventually they relate particular intonational regularities to the contexts in which caregivers consistently express specific intentions (comfort, attention, prohibition). Rochat discusses of another early example of the coupling of organism and environment, that of the most primordial relationship of infant nursing. He proposes that a functional reciprocity or mutuality exists a priori between bodily capabilities of the organism (the infant's oral activity) and action potentials in the environment (the maternal breast). The functionality of fit between organism and its surround contributes to survival in other species as well. As illustrated by Miller, multiple pathways, both acoustic and social, assure that newly hatched ducklings respond to maternal alarm calls by freezing. In work further up the phylogenetic tree, Green and Gustafson demonstrate that infants' upright locomotion introduces a cascade of reciprocal changes in infants' and caregivers' flow. These alterations flow back and forth as infants invite and initiate interaction in an ever-widening range of events and settings. Fogel describes development as a co-creative process between the individual and the environment, including other people. This interacting leads to the emergence of dynamically stable frames that constrain future coaction. He seeks to construct a purely relational theoretical model of development. By coupling a dynamic systems perspective and the theory of direct perceiving–acting, Fogel proposes an approach that would more explicitly integrate physiological and affective subsystems.

Perceiving–Acting Cycles

Cycles of perceiving and acting play a prominent part in many of the chapters. In disparate situations, detecting perceptual structure informs what a creature will do next by making affordances prominent. Concomitantly, acting on affordances makes more perceptual structure available for emerging action (see especially von Hofsten's and Zukow-Goldring's chapters). Perceiving differentiates as the infant continuously stays in contact with the environment, including the picking out of regularity and change from the flow of ongoing activities. Studies of perceptual structure specifying invariance and change suggest that the detection of amodal invariants (regularities) in self-produced movement forms the basis of early self-knowledge. Rochat's very discerning speculations regarding "double touch" suggest how self-touching may exclusively identify the self distributed within the skin and no other. Other researchers extend the detecting of regularities across modalities and kinds of things to reveal more about the world. Zukow-Goldring suggests that the caregiver-assisted detecting of amodal invariants in caregivers' gesture and speech supports infants' early lexical development. She speculates that detecting amodal invariance across different kinds and settings expands knowing throughout life. Dent-Read conceptualizes metaphor as a way of seeing one thing in terms of a different kind of thing it resembles. This "seeing as" (detecting invariance through time space) promotes knowing something new about the object or action. This type of knowing is a unique source of insight about the world and differentiates continually with experience. Rader extends the frontiers of perceptual development into less conventional areas by examining past perceptual experience as motivation for present action. She also studies maturation and ontogenetic variation as shown in the behavior of children with Down syndrome and normally developing children.

Nesting Units and Levels of Behavior

Smitsman and Pick most clearly study the relation of task subsegments to one another and to the problem-solving situation. Smitsman's studies of tool use, with von Leeuwen in particular, illustrate how the developing child gradually coordinates the triadic relation of agent–tool, tool–object, and agent–object (van Leeuwen, Smitsman, & van Leeuwen, 1994). Tools actually extend the self. The use of implements simultaneously enlarges a person's capacity for perceiving and acting as well as embodies new effectivities, as the child reaches beyond ordinary levels of behavior. Pick's elegant studies of categorization in young children demonstrate conclusively that directly exploring objects affects categorizing. Passively investigating or indirectly inspecting photographs and line drawings of these objects leads to very different behavior. In addition, this research forcefully foregrounds the power of instructions as framing devices. Laboratory procedures informed by theory, unwittingly or wittingly, bias performance. (For other discussions of nesting and embedding, see Fogel, Green and Gustafson, von Hofsten, and Zukow-Goldring.)

The Hallmarks of Behavior

Several chapters highlight one or several of the three hallmarks of behavior (agency/control, prospectivity, flexibility), whereas many others treat them directly but less centrally. Clearly, Rochat's proposal of an "ecological self," Smitsman's explanations of the far-reaching potential of tool use, and Rader's studies of motivation and brain maturation address issues of agency and control (von Hofsten addresses control during reaching; Zukow-Goldring addresses emerging effectivities). Reasoning that all actions are necessarily geared to the future, von Hofsten argues that guiding action requires prediction of the future. Children learn to guide action by moving and thereby perceive variants and invariants as they accomplish tasks. He concludes that this information allows children to guide their action prospectively. Finally, Clark's discussion of skilled performance makes prominent that flexibility plays an essential role in adept behavior of any kind. She presents the multiple, nonlinear, and interacting constraints or subsystems that inform the stability of behavioral form in the face of variable conditions. That is, the development of skilled walking entails the meshing of many dynamic components that ensure locomoting with efficiency under less than optimal bodily and environmental circumstances.

What the organism is with respect to organism–environment mutuality and how to carry out our investigations seem unproblematic in the preceding summary of the propositions covered in the chapters. We agree on many levels and have a common language regarding the organism, but what of the environment?

ORGANISM–ENVIRONMENT MUTUALITY: ENVIRONMENTS SUPPORTING ORGANISMS' ACTION

Learning must be studied in the species-typical environment, in the context of development.

E. Gibson

E. Gibson's legacy emphasizes a basic tenet of ecological realism: The organism must be studied in its environment, as behavior has no meaning otherwise. The organism and the econiche mutually implicate each other. This quote from E. Gibson admonishes us even more strongly than the earlier one to study the organism in its species-typical environment. If we understand the second part, "in the context of development," as referring to what we know through the literature on normal development, we can find some comfort. Each of us knows the literature on development and has grounded our studies therein. However, can and does *context* have other meanings in this regard? If it does, and it can as a detailed history of individual ontogeny, what of *environment*? In the same vein, most assume that the organism is what is changing and learning, but others suggest that the organism–environment itself changes and grows. Explaining what we mean by *environment* may prove complicated, perplexing, and puzzling. How do these positions relate to our definitions, theorizing, and method? Do many of us actually study organisms in species-typical environments? If we do, why? If we work in controlled laboratory settings, why? What is gained or lost? What does a transition from one to the other or a coupling of the two look or feel like? Perhaps, our methodology has entered the period of destabilization that comes before reorganization as described in chaos theory. With so many points of view can we reach a common viewing point?

The history of science offers some guidance. Ludwig Fleck (1935/1979) wrote a book titled *Genesis and Development of a Scientific Fact*. He analyzed the history of ideas out of which arose the research on syphilis and the eventual discovery of the Wassermann reaction used to diagnose this disease. According to Fleck, knowing is a social practice. He argued that discoveries emerge from a melange of many failures and detours based on false assumptions. Most critically, Fleck elaborated the continuous modulating of the current collective approach among people working on similar issues in the same and related fields. As a community of scholars exchanges understandings, the members polish, adjust, support, and attenuate emerging findings in continuous, reflexive cycles. Eventually "one particular way of seeing and acting and no other" (p. 64) will come to the fore in "a kind of harmony of illusions" (p. 28). The old ways of knowing often become incomprehensible to the new. In fact, according to Fleck results from Wassermann's early experiments probably could not be replicated because the practices or methods once considered absolute, immutable, and reproducible have become inscrutable. Now as then, despite the difficulty in communicating across intra- and interdisciplinary collectives and the relative impermanence of "facts," new ways of knowing manifest themselves through a process of chaos, constraint, and direct perceiving. That is, a period of instability leads to emergent forms or facts that constrain what the collective can and does notice (cf. Kuhn's, 1971, 1979, collective agreement within a paradigm; Latour's, 1987, characterization of scientific literature as "immutable mobiles").

As Fleck noted, misunderstandings belong to no one person, and, significantly, do not lack meaning. However, researchers can find answers and can understand one another (Kessen, 1993). Eventually, collective knowing is more coherent than that of a single individual (Fleck, 1935/1979). In designing experiments, puzzling out the meaning of laboratory results or analyzing behavior in natural contexts, researchers implicitly or explicitly concur that behavior is not in the organism, but instead depends on the environment to manifest (Johnston, 1985). Conversely, what the environment might be depends on what the organism is (Johnston, 1985).

How do we as developmentalists define environment? Which environment are we talking about? How far does it extend in time–space? The one available to an entire species, the one potentially accessible to an individual organism throughout its entire lifetime, the one an organism is inside of or contained in, or the one that manifests as the organism perceives and acts? Do scholars' theoretical statements and methodological choices correspond? To ascertain the source of researchers' definitions of environment we might compare cross-sectional laboratory studies of changes in behavior to naturalistic longitudinal ones of behavior changing. In the former, researchers document the behavior of experimental subjects taking a point of view at one moment in time–space. This method is designed to determine what children can do and why under certain controlled conditions (agency/control). In contrast, in the everyday settings investigators document the conduct of individuals moving along a trajectory, embodying an evolving viewing point as they perceive and act. This method of inquiry delineates how children come to do what they do under the most mundane circumstances of daily life (flexibility, learning). We might compare one with the other, assess the advantages and disadvantages, and make an informed choice. Not so easy. Messy, in fact. Finding consistency by analysis on the basis of theoretical approach proves no more satisfactory. Little agreement can be found. Alternatively, does the task or problem to be solved affect how the researcher envisions and operationalizes environment? Perhaps.

All of the authors in this volume have addressed some topics that foreground the environment in broad terms as part of their literature reviews or discussions of theory. Three more specific issues link various chapters: species-typical environments, the line between organism and environment, and the conditions that reveal affordances for action. Some explicitly collect data in species-typical environments. One subset integrates naturalistic data or methods for promoting species-typical behavior into its laboratory studies, whereas the other conducts research more thoroughly informed by ethnographic or ethological field methods. A second issue emerges when explaining results from investigations. Often the authors invoke the environment, defining it with precision as the immediate circumstances or context arising from their procedures. To elucidate challenging findings, the authors examine the fluctuating border between organism and environment as a function of tool and task. Finally, the embedding of tasks in particular social, cultural, and ontogenetic contexts reveals specific affordances relating to behavior and motivation.

Species-Typical Environments

Not surprisingly, those of us who work in the field of child language or comparative psychology have most frequently collected naturalistic data or used ethnographic methods, as these are standard procedures in our subfields. These methods have provided a unique lens through which to refine our views of the process of development. Cooper's contribution to the field of infant speech perception entails the importance of using naturalistic data—speech from the mother of the infant. In so doing, she integrates initially contradictory and confusing findings to explain how the infant's perceptual differentiation of acoustic patterns may relate to later communication during social interaction. Zukow-Goldring studied the emerging lexicon longitudinally at home in the sociocultural context in which children learn language. She views social interaction as a field of affordances, confirming that (lexical) learning is both "direct and culturally directed." She concludes that effectivities of the body and affordances of the environment gradually emerge from the lived relation of persons, place, and culture. Dent-Read's participatory method of sampling the child's emerging speech provides a record not only in time but in all contexts that the child encountered. The breadth of this interactional history provides a means to interpret meanings through time, not just in present circumstances. She proposes that naturalistic data will drive theory reformulation.

Green and Gustafson's naturalistic, longitudinal studies attest to the advantages of looking at motor and social development, not separately but as systems continuously affecting each other. Nonsocial behaviors, such as crying and walking, have social effects that encourage changes in both the infant and his or her caregivers. They stress that events are a joint product of physical and social settings as well as of personal characteristics.

Miller uses ethnographic observation to refine his carefully crafted laboratory studies of the development of species-typical perception of calls in ducklings. He demonstrates that development of this "perceptual" ability consists of changes in the system. These changes are not always obvious but are caused by activity at different levels of organization. In this case, the nonobvious social level of sibling coaction fosters perceiving and acting that enhance survival. Clearly, naturalistic data, ethnographic and ethological methods, or longitudinal studies of development show that previously hidden or nonobvious social and cultural fields of action couple (inform and perform) with perceptual, motor, and affective behaviors day in and day out to bring about subtle and pervasive changes (cf. H. Pick, 1989).

Where to Draw the Line Between Organism and Environment

Another subset of authors has focused on the flexibility of the boundary between organism and environment. Others have explored the curious effect of embedding the same task in different settings or engaging a different set of organisms in the same task setting. Smitsman asserts that the boundary between organism and environment changes from moment to moment, challenging unexamined assumptions regarding the fixedness of that boundary. For example, any hand-held tool changes the prehensile system as a whole and "becomes" part of the organism. (For a classic article discussing a blind man and his cane, see Bateson, 1972; cf. Cole, 1995.) Tools temporarily alter the capabilities of the body and reciprocally the action potential of the environment. New action patterns may ensue, not because of the growth of the system nor because of increased skill but because the boundary between environment and organism fluctuates, promoting change or development. (Dent-Read, Fogel, Green and Gustafson, and Zukow-Goldring agree with Smitsman that what changes or develops is the organism–environment mutuality.) Pick demonstrates the power of context by exploring the sequencing of task subsegments embedded in various instructions to act. She concludes that the ease of directly perceiving the properties of objects varies with their situation of use. Pick suggests that the proclivity to act (sort) on the basis of any particular object property resides not in the child but emerges in and through the child's actions on objects in context. For Clark, changes in context entail a reorganizing of the subsystems supporting a skill that may result in changes in skill level. A barefooted novice walker may traverse a walkway with little difficulty, while heavy, inflexible shoes may lead to a wider stance, slower stepping, and more than a bit of wobbling. Von Hofsten's task space is the context. Using a geographical metaphor, he explains how mastery of that hypothetical landscape relates to mastery of the body. The topography of this experimental environment may not correspond closely to the real world events in which the infant participates. These tasks, however, carefully delineate the boundaries of what infants can do in uncommon or unusual situations. Finally, Rader's work illustrates rather starkly that the environment of one is not the environment of all. Children with Down syndrome respond quite differently to an opportunity for social interaction, their mothers' approach after a brief separation, than do children who do not have Down syndrome, pushing them further along an already separate path of ontogenetic specialization. Each of these studies suggest that definitions of *environment* and *context* depend intimately on task and organism. The role of the social and cultural environments remains relatively unexplored among these researchers but offers future opportunities to understand the evolving skills of the developing child.

Theories of practice and other approaches that examine how people unceasingly organize and structure their social and cultural lives may provide a resource. Despite disparate disciplinary or theoretical backgrounds, developmental psychologists in recent years have addressed the relation of context to learning and knowing (Dell, 1985; Moes, Elder, & Lüscher, 1995; Resnick, Levine, & Teasley, 1991; Wozniak & Fischer, 1993), as have anthropologists and sociologists concerned with its relation to development, social practice, and communication (Bourdieu, 1980/1990; Chaiklin & Lave, 1993; Giddens, 1979; Goodwin & Duranti, 1992; Hanks, 1990; Lave & Wenger, 1991). Many of the themes covered reflect common issues or harmonious points of view regarding how and what people know. However, differences in terminology and difficult problems regarding basic assumptions must be set aside to appreciate these parallels. Many of these scholars investigate the emergent nature of affordances for action, as people perceive and act when engaged in particular tasks in particular settings; assume the centrality of detecting regularities and change for development and learning; define knowing as a sort of embodied history; note the contradiction in terms of decontextualized knowing; examine the ways the "same" act manifests differently on each occurrence depending on the particulars of persons, place, and activity; and stress that organism and environment continuously alter or perturb each other, but do not "cause" each other to act (Bourdieu, 1980/1990; Giddens, 1979; Hanks, 1990; Keller & Keller, 1993; Lave, 1993; Maturana & Varela, 1987; Varela, Thompson, & Rosch, 1991). Related and recurrent themes include the notion that knowing is reflexive (changes as people act), rather than merely the recursive, repetitive enacting of plans. Some of these approaches contend that diverse daily activities from the most ordinary to the most esoteric scientific practices involve the contributions of several individuals. Many agree that knowing is distributed. When engaged in various mundane daily activities, knowing is not to be found in any single individual, activity, or tool but in the relations among them.

These approaches have articulated the fluctuating, multiple nestings of behavior within the social and cultural context in ways that afford opportunities for expanding points of view in the future. Eventually, lines must be drawn, theoretical issues and technical terms clarified, but a period of opening borders to cross-fertilizing could lead to enriching the understanding of organism–environment systems.

Revealing Affordances for Action

How might physiological state and motivation affect opportunities for action? Several authors discuss motivation or effectivities of bodily state on behavior both in terms of what the environment offers the organism under such circumstances and whether another person might detect the other's bodily state as an affordance. Fogel reminds us that the affective states of organisms inform what an individual notices and, hence, how he or she acts. If these states are perceivable as some assert (Thelen, 1996; Turvey, 1992), Fogel's work with caregiver–infant dyads suggests that personality dispositions or effectivities may be perceived as affordances for action (whether person or object oriented). His longitudinal studies of caregiver–infant while interacting in a lab setting describe the emergence of at least these two very different co-regulated patterns of dynamic style. Rader's experiments of "hidden affordances" demonstrate in another setting that a seemingly identical visual environment offers different affordances to infants with different histories of interaction. Apparently, "an environment is an environment is an environment" does not hold. An environment is never the environment without an organism. Sometimes, however, the most informative environment is the body itself. Rochat argues persuasively that contact with the environment continuously provides the infant with perceptual structure for knowing the self as well as the environment. This self-referential system perceives the self as an agent situated in her or his environment with a body that has permanence as do other objects, providing the basis for the "ecological self" from birth.

J. Gibson (1979) asserted that rather than endowing the organism with a priori knowledge, researchers should investigate how the environment supports its behavior. Each of the contributors to this volume has taken steps toward making the information or perceptual structure that sustains perceiving and acting in species-typical environments in the context of development easier to perceive. Whereas calls for research in situ increase (Kessen, 1993; Pick, 1989), a complimentary move, Johnston (1985) stressed, is the importance of taking findings from normal environments back to the laboratory. What is learned during the course of an organism's everyday life may benefit from being precisely clarified under artificially altered conditions to determine how various systems contribute to ongoing development. However, Miller (this volume) and Johnston (1985) warn that demonstrating that an organism can learn something under nonnatural settings does not mean that is how or what organisms usually learn.

THE PATH AHEAD

We envision animal and environment as inseparably linked, self-organizing systems in and through which development occurs. Animal–environment mutualities or systems perturb and reverberate. Living creatures detect perceptual structure from the continuous environmental flux that informs and re-forms acting and precipitates differentiation and resulting changes in behavior. Simultaneously and reflexively, creatures affect each other and their environments, propagating waves of further potential change. Whereas theoretical advances and a robust body of empirical research attest to the fecundity and achievements of these approaches, opportunities to enlarge the approach beckon, and limitations await resolution. We do not have the answers, but seek them and invite others to join us in this pursuit. These perceptive words from the past hold promise for the future. It is for today's researchers to harvest their wisdom.

> *"This world is the nurse of all we know,*
> *This world is the mother of all we feel."*

(Percy Bysshe Shelley, 1816/1909)

REFERENCES

Bateson, G. (1972). Form, substance, and difference. In G. Bateson (Ed.), *Steps to an ecology of mind* (pp. 448–468). San Francisco: Chandler.

Bourdieu, P. (1990). *The logic of practice.* Cambridge, England: Polity Press. (Original work published 1980)

Chaiklin, S., & Lave, J. (Eds.). (1993). *Understanding practice: Perspectives on activity and context.* Cambridge, England: Cambridge University Press.

Cole, M. (1995). The supra-individual envelope of development: Activity and practice, situation and context. In J. J. Goodnow, P. J. Miller, & F. Kessel (Eds.), *Cultural practices as contexts for development* (pp. 105–118). San Francisco: Jossey-Bass.

Dell, J. P. (1985). Understanding Bateson and Maturana: Toward a biological foundation for the social sciences. *Journal of Marital and Family Therapy, 7,* 1–20.

Fleck, L. (1979). *Genesis and development of a scientific fact.* Chicago: University of Chicago Press. (Original work published 1935)

Gibson, J. J. (1979). *The ecological approach to visual perception.* Boston: Houghton-Mifflin.

Giddens, A. (1979). *Central problems in social theory: Action, structure and contradiction in social analysis.* Berkeley: University of California Press.

Goodwin, C., & Duranti, A. (1992). Rethinking context: An introduction. In A. Duranti & C. Goodwin (Eds.), *Rethinking context: Language as an interactive phenomenon* (pp. 1–42). Cambridge, England: Cambridge University Press.

Hanks, W. F. (1990). *Referential practice: Language and lived space among the Maya.* Chicago: University of Chicago Press.

Johnston, T. D. (1985). Introduction: Conceptual issues in the ecological study of learning. In T. D. Johnston & A. T. Pietrewicz (Eds.), *Issues in the ecological study of learning* (pp. 1–24). Hillsdale, NJ: Erlbaum.

Keller, C., & Keller, J. D. (1993). Thinking and acting with iron. In S. Chaiklin & J. Lave (Eds.), *Understanding practice: Perspectives on activity and context* (pp. 125–143). Cambridge, England: Cambridge University Press.

Kessen, W. (1993). Rumble or revolution?: A commentary. In R. H. Wozniak & K. W. Fischer (Eds.), *Development in context: Acting and thinking in specific environments* (pp. 269–270). Hillsdale, NJ: Erlbaum.

Kuhn, T. (1971). *The structure of scientific revolutions.* Chicago: University of Chicago Press.

Kuhn, T. (1979). *Genesis and development of a scientific fact* [foreword]. Chicago: University of Chicago Press.

Latour, B. (1987). *Science in action: How to follow scientists and engineers through society.* Milton Keynes, England: Open University Press.

Lave, J. (1993). Introduction: The practice of learning. In S. Chaiklin & J. Lave (Eds.), *Understanding practice: Perspectives on activity and context* (pp. 3–32). Cambridge, England: Cambridge University Press.

Lave, J., & Wenger, E. (1991). *Situated learning: Legitimate peripheral participation.* Cambridge, England: Cambridge University Press.

Maturana, H. R., & Varela, F. J. (1987). *The tree of knowledge: The biological roots of human understanding.* Boston, MA: New Science Library.

Moen, P., Elder, G., & Lüscher, K. (1995). *Examining lives in context: Perspectives on the ecology of human development.* Washington, DC: American Psychological Association.

Pick, H. L., Jr. (1989). Motor development: The control of action. *Developmental Psychology, 25,* 867–870.

Resnick, L. B., Levine, J. M., & Teasley, S. D. (Eds.). (1991). *Perspectives on socially shared cognition.* Washington, DC: American Psychological Association.

Shelley, P. B. (1909). On death. In T. Hutchinson (Ed.), *The complete poetical works of Percy Bysshe Shelley.* London: Oxford University Press. (Original work published 1816)

Thelen, L. (1996). *Affordances and effectivities as a functional link among personality psychology, social psychology, and environmental psychology.* Unpublished manuscript, University of California, Irvine.

Turvey, M. (1992). Affordances and prospective control: An outline of the ontology. *Ecological Psychology, 4,* 173–187.

Varela, F. J., Thompson, E., & Rosch, E. (1991). *The embodied mind: Cognitive science and human experience.* Cambridge, MA: MIT Press.

van Leeuwen, L., Smitsman, A., & van Leeuwen, C. (1994). Affordances, perceptual complexity, and the development of tool use. *Journal of Experimental Psychology: Human Perception and Performance, 20,* 174–191.

Wozniak, R., & Fischer, K. (1993). *Development in context: Acting and thinking in specific environments.* Hillsdale, NJ: Erlbaum.

Author Index

Numbers in italics refer to listings in the reference sections.

Subject Index

About the Editors

Cathy Dent-Read, PhD, is Research Scholar at the Center for the Study of Women, University of California, Los Angeles. While editing this book she was at the Center for the Ecological Study of Perception and Action in the Psychology Department, University of Connecticut, Storrs. Dr. Dent-Read is on the editorial board of *Metaphor and Symbol* and was guest editor of a special issue of *Developmental Psychobiology.* Her research for the past 16 years has focused on the role of perceiving in processes of knowing and in using language as children develop from infancy into childhood. Specifically, she has studied how direct perceiving forms the basis of metaphor in both language and action and how metaphors develop in complexity both in terms of content and of structure. Such a realist approach to knowing and to language builds on ecological theories of perception and provides an alternative to traditional approaches to knowledge and language.

Patricia Zukow-Goldring, PhD, is Research Scholar at the Center for the Study of Women, University of California, Los Angeles. During the preparation of this volume, Dr. Zukow-Goldring was in the Psychology and Social Behavior Department, School of Social Ecology, University of California, Irvine. Dr. Zukow-Goldring has edited *Sibling Interaction Across Cultures: Methodological and Theoretical Issues* and has served as guest editor of *Developmental Psychobiology.* Her research explores how children come to notice, participate in, and communicate within daily activities at home and at school. She proposes a social ecological realist approach that documents how a range of caregivers, including family members and teachers, propagate perceiving, acting, and knowing by educating children's attention. Dr. Zukow-Goldring has conducted her studies among rural and urban families in central Mexico, and among Latino working-class and European American middle-class families in the western United States.